LATIN MANUSCRIPT BOOKS BEFORE 1600

LATIN MANUSCRIPT BOOKS BEFORE 1600

A List of the Printed Catalogues
and Unpublished Inventories
of Extant Collections

by

Paul Oskar Kristeller

THIRD EDITION

FORDHAM   UNIVERSITY   PRESS
NEW   YORK

First published in TRADITIO, Studies in Ancient
and Medieval History, Thought and Religion, 6 (1948)
227-317 and 9 (1953) 393-418.

New Edition, Revised, 1960
© Fordham University Press, 1960, 1965

Library of Congress Catalogue Card Number : 60-7726

TABLE OF CONTENTS

PREFACE TO THE THIRD EDITION

When the revised edition of this bibliography, published as a separate book in 1960, nearly went out of print Father E. A. Quain, S. J. invited me to gather further material that would be added as a Supplement to a reprint of the former edition. In this supplement, I shall attempt to correct some of the more important misprints and errors of the 1960 edition, and to give a number of additional entries that have either been newly published, or that have come to my attention but recently. I shall give both corrections and additions in the order of the 1960 edition, referring to its pages throughout. The entries contained among the Addenda of the 1960 edition (p. 233-234) will also be included in this supplement, in their proper places.

The new material in this volume will be found beginning at p. 233, divided into Sections A, B and C, each entry under the page number where it would fit in the body of the book. We regret that this will be of some slight inconvenience to scholars using the book since for full information on a particular item, he will have to look in two places. However, our desire to make this additional material available had to be confronted with the very substantial cost of resetting the whole book and we trust that we will be accorded the reader's indulgent understanding.

The edition of 1960 has had on the whole a friendly reception from colleagues and librarians, and even from reviewers. Its shortcomings have been pointed out, including a few of which I had been aware from the beginning. Yet I shall not be able to remove some of the worst of these deficiencies. It is not feasible to analyze completely all titles in section B for the libraries they cover, or even to make cross references in all cases where they have been analyzed. The cross references in section C must be limited to those general titles which contain substantial information on the respective collections. Exceptions have been made only for small collections, and for collections, or parts of collections, that have no complete printed catalogues. Moreover, it would have been much preferable to give cross references for each library, rather than for the cities only, but it would have been very complicated to carry out this principle. Hence I must warn the user once more that in some instances very substantial catalogues are described in section B and covered only by cross references under the city in which the respective library is located.

There is no such thing as a complete bibliography, and the inclusion or exclusion of specific titles is evidently often a matter of subjective judgment or arbitrary decision. Since some reviewers have criticized me for not listing certain titles which I had considered and intentionally excluded as not relevant, I should like to explain that I have followed only two criteria in choosing a given entry for inclusion: it may either help a scholar to locate a manuscript containing a text in which he is interested, or it may help him to find a catalogue description of a manuscript which he knows already. Everything else I have intentionally omitted, especially studies that deal exclusively with the history of libraries or with palaeography, with illuminations or bindings, with copyists or former owners. Among the studies of this kind, I have included only those that contain specific information on the content and location of extant manuscripts. For this reason, I have omitted most studies and editions of old library inventories, that is, all those that fail to indicate the present location and identity of the manuscripts listed. I have included only a few exhibition catalogues on account of the mss. they describe, and even fewer sales catalogues. The latter often do describe interesting mss., but they are as a rule hard to trace, and the catalogues are hence of less immediate use than those of more or less permanent collections. In view of the scope of this bibliography that is expressed in its title, I have omitted most descriptions of archival material, except for the collections of manuscript books, or of literary documents, that are preserved in archives rather than in libraries. I have omitted studies of individual mss. since they are too numerous, and lists of mss. of a single author because they can be easily found through bibliographies. In doubtful cases, I have tended to decide for inclusion, as in the case of cross references, when small or relatively unknown collections are involved. I have also excluded catalogues of manuscripts in languages other than Latin although Greek and vernacular manuscripts often do contain Latin texts. There was no need to list catalogues of Greek manuscripts since they have been adequately described by Marcel Richard (*Répertoire des Bibliothèques et des Catalogues de Manuscrits Grecs*, 2nd ed., Paris 1958). Since there is no comparable bibliography for vernacular manuscripts, I have occasionally included catalogues of French, German or Spanish, and especially of Italian manuscripts when they seemed to be of potential interest for the study of Latin texts or authors.

Also the division between sections A and B seems to have puzzled some users and reviewers, and hence to call for another explanation. I admit that the division is arbitrary in some instances. Yet I should like to explain that I put Borchling or Priebsch into section A because they do not describe a single manuscript relevant to this bibliography, but do give information on the existence or strength of certain collections that may contain mss. of the type concerning us. On the other hand, Byvanck is in Section B because he does describe some mss. relevant to our task.

I have followed the practice of affixing an asterisk to those cities whose libraries I do not know at first hand, and to those libraries which I have not visited. Since this fact concerns the degree of responsability I can assume for the accuracy of the information supplied, I should like to list the cities and libraries which I have visited since 1960, and which should therefore have their asterisk removed (including a few that I had visited before 1960 and that had received an asterisk by mistake): Admont, Ancona, Aschaffenburg, Athens, Belluno, Berlin (Kunstbibliothek), Bonn, Budapest, Chantilly, Chapel Hill, Chicago, Donaueschingen, Eugene, Fiesole, Fischbach, Freiburg (Stadtarchiv and Augustinermuseum), Fribourg (Cordeliers), Fritzlar, Fulda (Priesterseminar), Hannover (Kestner-Museum), Innsbruck (Staatsarchiv, Servitenkloster, Ferdinandeum, Stift Wilten), Isny, Istanbul, Ithaca, Konstanz, Lambach, Lausanne, London (College of Arms, Guildhall Library, Inner Temple, Lincoln's Inn, Sir John Soane's Museum), Louvain, Lugano, Mantova (Archivio di Stato), Mariemont, Modena (Accademia delle Scienze, Archivio del Comune, Biblioteca Capitolare, Raccolta Molza-Viti), Monza, Munich (Nationalmuseum), Naples (Oratoriana), Oxford (Pembroke College), Parma (Archivio di Stato), Pienza, Recanati, Rome (S. Maria sopra Minerva, S. Sabina), Rottenburg, San Daniele, Sankt Gallen, Sankt Paul, Sarnen, Schwaz, Sion, Toronto, Tübingen (Wilhelmsstift), Urbana, Vigevano, Wien (Dominikanerkonvent, Staatsarchiv), Würzburg, Zürich (Staatsarchiv).

Through an oversight, I have used in the 1960 edition and not explained the following abbreviation: AB stands for *Accademie e Biblioteche* and refers to the list of catalogues published in that periodical and described on p. 3 of the 1960 edition.

In conclusion, I should like to thank all those scholars and librarians, some of them known to me and others unknown, who reviewed my bibliography or who wrote to me, and to whom I am indebted for numerous corrections and additions that went into the present supplement: Zofia Ameisenowa (Cracow), Lilian Anderson (Boston), Rev. Rudolf Arbesmann O. S. A., (Fordham University), Luisa Banti (Florence), Ludwig Bieler (Dublin), Giuseppe Billanovich (Milan), Emilie Boer (Berlin), P. Bohigas (Barcelona), W. H. Bond (Harvard University Library), Leicester Bradner (Brown University), Geoffrey Bullough (London), W. Bulst (Heidelberg), Rolf Burmeister (Hamburg), F. de A. Carreras (Valencia), Cecil Clough (Birmingham), Rev. M. Coens (Brussels), F. Edward Cranz (Connecticut College), A. Daneu Lattanzi, (Palermo), H. Deckert (Dresden), R. G. Dennis (Harvard University Library), Sheila Edmunds (Smith College), Rev. Francis Firth (St. Michael's College, Toronto), Hugo Friedrich (Freiburg), Rev. A. García y García (Salamanca), H. Gerson (The Hague), Felix Gilbert (Institute for Advanced Study), H. M. Goldbrunner (Rome), M. A. Goukovsky (Leningrad), Helga Hajdu Juhasz (Budapest), Lewis Hanke (Columbia University), Richard Harrier (New York University), John Harris (London), R. Hayes (Dublin), Elisabeth Feist Hirsch (Trenton State College), Rudolf Hirsch (University of Pennsylvania Library), Fritz Hoffmann (Erfurt), W. Hörmann (Munich), R. W. Hunt (Oxford), James J. John (Cornell University), Neil Ker (Oxford), Edwin Knowles (Pratt Institute), Josef Koch (Cologne), Imrich Kotvan (Bratislava), Stephan Kuttner (Yale University), Dom Jean Leclercq (Clervaux), the late Paul Lehmann (Munich), Edward R. Lerner (Queens College), Robert E. Lewis Jr. (Indiana University), Maria Teresa Liaci (Lecce), Karl Manitius (Dresden), F. De Marco (Rome), Herbert Matsen (Converse College), Otto Mazal (Vienna), Rev. Vittorino Meneghin (Venice), Anne Marie Meyer (London), Kathleen Morand (Institute for Advanced Study), Helen Northup (University of Wisconsin Library), Kåre Olsen (Copenhagen), G. N. Orsini (University of Wisconsin), B. Paradisi (Naples), George Parks (Queens College), Bernard M. Peebles (Catholic University of America), Emma Pirani (Milan), Alessandro Pratesi (Bari), Serafino Prete (Bologna), Sesto Prete (Fordham University), Rev. Tarcisius Rattler (Augustinian Institute, New York), Robert Raymo (New York University), Pier Giorgio Ricci (Florence), March. Roberto Ridolfi (Florence), Bernard M. Rosenthal (New York), Braxton Ross (Institute for Advanced Study), L. Rossetti (Padua), Rev. Francis Roth O. S. A. (Augustinian Institute, New York), J. Rott (Strasbourg), Arthur Schiller (Columbia University), Peter L. Schmidt (Kiel), Charles Schmitt (Fordham University), R. J. Schoeck (University of Toronto), Mrs. Joan Selby (University of British Columbia Library), Eugene Sheehy (Columbia University Library), Keith Sinclair (Sydney), Josef Soudek (Queens College), Jaroslav Šůla (Jasenná, Czechoslovakia), R. D. Sweeney (Detroit), R. Sylvester (Yale University), Charles De Tolnay (Princeton), T. Tomasic (Paris), Rev. Damasus Trapp (Augustinian Institute), K. Van Acker (Ghent), Giuseppe Velli (Smith College), Mlle. Jeanne Vielliard (Paris), John Waddell (Columbia University Library), Luitpold Wallach (Marquette University), Sister Agnes Clare Way (Our Lady of the Lake College, San Antonio), Bernard Weinberg (University of Chicago), Paul Wilpert (Cologne), C. E. Wright (London). I may be permitted to add a general, but no less heartfelt expression of gratitude to the numerous librarians in many countries who answered my queries and gave or sent me information on the printed or unpublished catalogues of their own libraries.

New York, Columbia University.
November 1964

PREFACE TO THE REVISED EDITION

The first edition of this bibliography appeared in *Traditio* 6 (1948 and 9 (1953) in two separate parts covering printed catalogues and unpublished inventories, respectively. When the available copies of the first part went out of print, I was invited by Fordham University Press to prepare a revised edition of both parts, and it was decided to publish them together as a separate book.

Since I explained the purpose of this bibliography, and the method followed in compiling it, in the prefaces to the first edition, I shall here only indicate the changes made in preparing this new edition. I did not merely try to bring the bibliography up to date by adding the new catalogues which have appeared since the publication of part I twelve years ago. I have also made an effort to fill the gaps, and to correct the errors, concerning older published catalogues as well as handwritten inventories. In this effort, I was greatly helped by extensive information sent to me, upon request and even unsolicited, by many librarians and other scholars who had the patience to go through the bibliography with an experienced and critical eye. I also was able to undertake four extensive trips to Europe since the war, and I wish to thank again the foundations and other agencies which, through grants and fellowships, made these trips possible: the American Philosophical Society, the Columbia University Council for Research in the Social Sciences, the Fulbright Committee for Italy, the Guggenheim Foundation, and the Ford Foundation. Thus I could not only examine in Europe many printed catalogues not available to me in the United States, and thus remove from my list most of the double asterisks (and often the titles themselves when the opportunity to examine the books also enabled me to eliminate them as unimportant or irrelevant). Above all, I thus could revisit, with a new purpose, the Italian libraries known to me from pre-war times, and also visit for the first time many libraries previously unfamiliar to me. I visited more than once the more important libraries in Switzerland, France, Belgium, Holland and Great Britain. I visited Spain, Portugal and Sweden in 1952, Yugoslavia, Austria, West Germany and again Spain in 1955, and in 1958 I could also visit Czechoslovakia, Poland, East Germany and Russia. Thus I obtained first-hand information on some of the more interesting collections in various countries, ascertained on the spot their resources in printed and unpublished catalogues, and was initiated into the mysteries concerning shelf marks and 'fondi' that seem to characterize every self-respecting library,—

at least into the lesser mysteries that can be revealed even to a hasty visitor. A knowledge of the greater mysteries I can claim only for the Italian libraries with which I have been acquainted for a longer period, and even there, I suspect there is room for further initiation if I may judge from the additional *arcana* to which I was introduced last year. All these secrets, or at least most of them, I shall disclose to the attentive reader of this rather bony compilation, provided he peruses it with the right spirit that should contain the appropriate doses both of knowledge and of curiosity.

The most important change made in this revised edition is due to the decision to merge the two parts that had been kept separate in the first edition, or to be more precise, to merge the second part with section C of the first part. In other words, I have attempted to list together, for each city, and wherever possible, for each library and collection, both the printed catalogues and the unpublished inventories in which their content is described. This involved, on the other hand, an equally important change, at least for what formerly was the first part of the bibliography, namely an attempt to divide the material concerning each city, as far as possible, according to the various libraries located in the city, and even to the distinct collections found in each library. This division had been carried out in the second, but not in the first part of the former edition. It is hoped that this new arrangement will make the distinction between the various libraries and collections apparent even to those readers who have no personal familiarity with the cities and libraries concerned. For each library and collection, the printed catalogues, usually in chronological order, will be listed before the unpublished inventories, indicating as far as possible how the latter supplement the former. Both groups will be preceded by works of a more general nature, but limited in scope to the city or library concerned (works concerning more than one city will appear, as in the first edition of part I, in sections A and B): that is, works supplying bibliographical or statistical information concerning the respective city or library, and catalogues describing more than one collection in a library, or even more than one library in the city. The name of the city will again be followed by cross references to the general works listed in Section B (or more rarely, in Section A). It has not been possible to apply the division of libraries and collections consistently to these cross-references. An attempt to do so threatened to lead to unnecessary complications. However, the libraries covered by each cross reference entry will usually appear in Section B where the corresponding general work is analyzed. If no library is specifically indicated for some towns, it means that there is only one library which has manuscripts, most commonly, the city library.

I hope the practice of combining printed and unpublished catalogues for each library will not cause confusion. The unpublished catalogues are usually recognizable by the absence of some standard bibliographical data such as place and date of publication and number of pages. I shall again use asterisks to indicate that I have not visited a library, or not seen a catalogue. In the case of printed catalogues, I have indicated the library in the United States or in Europe where I saw it, or where it is available, using for American libraries the standard abbreviations of the *Union List of Serials*.[1] If no such library location is indicated, it means that I have seen the book in the Columbia University Library, or that I own it myself. In the case of unpublished inventories, it is always understood that I saw it in the respective library. If I did not see it, I use an asterisk and indicate my source of information. If a microfilm of an unpublished inventory is available in the United States, I indicate this fact when it is known to me.

Concerning the criteria of selection followed in this bibliography, I should like to refer once more to the prefaces of the first edition. The chief criterion is relevance, and I resisted the temptation to include courtesy references, or to list unimportant titles because I examined them. I excluded catalogues describing only archival or modern material, or dealing with material in languages other than Latin. I made an exception for Italian manuscripts. Since most libraries are not divided according to languages, the number of titles thus added to the bibliography was not very large. I have again excluded, as a rule, studies dealing with a single manuscript or with the manuscripts of a single author; catalogues of exhibitions; lists of collections of microfilms or photostats; studies dealing with the history or organization of libraries, or with the provenance or external appearance of certain manuscripts; finally, old inventories of extant or dispersed collections unless they identify the present locations and shelf marks of the manuscripts. The reason for these exclusions, as well as for the exceptions occasionally made, lies in the basic purpose of this bibliography: it is intended as a working tool for those who want to find certain texts contained in the manuscripts described. This time I have included the catalogues of some famous collections scattered in fairly recent times, such as Ashburnham or Phillipps, because we easily en-

---

[1] Here are a few additional abbreviations used in this bibliography that did not appear in the first edition:

CoDB: Denver Public Library. DDO: Dumbarton Oaks Research Library, Washington. DHN: Holy Name College, Washington. DSI-M: U. S. National Museum, Washington. MoSU: St. Louis University. NNF: Fordham University, New York. NNJ: Jewish Theological Seminary, New York. NStC: St. Bonaventure College, St. Bonaventure, N. Y. ODW: Ohio Wesleyan University, Delaware, Ohio; OO: Oberlin College, Oberlin, Ohio. WU: University of Wisconsin, Madison, Wisconsin.

counter manuscripts from these collections in libraries that have no printed catalogues, and the printed catalogue of the former collection thus gives us the best available description of the manuscript. I have also been more inclined than in the first edition to include smaller collections, provided they contain at least one early manuscript, both in my listings and in the cross references. As a matter of fact, the cross references to the French *Catalogue Général* and to Mazzatinti are now intended to be complete.

Another change has been to bring the political geography of this list up to date. The first edition largely followed the situation as it prevailed between the wars. This time, I have distinguished between West and East Germany, and have placed the main entries for former German towns under their present Polish or Russian names, giving merely a cross reference under the German name. Where a place has merely changed its name, I use the formula 'See'. However, when a collection has been transferred to another place, I use the formula 'See under.' For example, to indicate that Breslau is now called Wroclaw, I say : 'Breslau, see Wroclaw'. To indicate that the Ossolineum formerly in Lwow is now located in Wroclaw, I say : 'Lwow, see under Wroclaw'. A number of libraries are omitted even though I visited them or corresponded with them, since there is no evidence that they have Latin manuscript books before 1600, or since there is evidence that they have none. When I say : 'no information,' this means that I have reason to believe that the library has relevant manuscripts, but that my enquiries were not favored with a reply.

Again it is a pleasant duty to express my thanks and appreciation to the numerous scholars who helped me with advice or information. First of all I should like to thank the librarians and archivists who have patiently answered my questions and letters over the years, often volunteered additional information, supplied me with microfilms and, sometimes, with rare catalogues. A special word of thanks is due to Miss Constance Winchell, Mr. John N. Waddell, Mr. Eugene Sheehy and to the other staff members of the Reference Department of the Columbia University Library who helped me on many a knotty bibliographical problem. I wish to thank Rev. Edwin A. Quain, S.J., of Fordham University Press for the encouragement and support he has given to this undertaking, as well as to the technical help he and his assistants have given to it. To Prof. William Harkins of Columbia University I am indebted for his help in transcribing and transliterating the titles in the Slavic languages with which I am not familiar. For various suggestions and data I am indebted to the following scholars : Mlle Marie-Thérèse d'Alverny (Bibliothèque Nationale), Josip Badalic (Zagreb), Luisa Banti (Florence), Josephine Bennett (Hunter College), Ludwig Bieler (Dublin), Giuseppe

Billanovich (Fribourg), Bernhard Bischoff (Munich), Mme. Denise Bloch (Bibliothèque Nationale), Herbert Bloch (Harvard University), Morton Bloomfield (Ohio State University), the late Rev. Philotheus Boehner, O.F.M.. (St. Bonaventure University), Dr. Emilie Boer (Berlin), John Bowden (St. John's University, Brooklyn), Vittore Branca (Fondazione Cini, Venice), Giles Constable (Harvard University), Walther Bulst (Heidelberg), Augusto Campana (Vatican Library), Mario E. Cosenza (Dean Emeritus, Brooklyn College), Karl H. Dannenfeldt (Arizona State University), Ruth Dean (Mount Holyoke College), Rev. E. Dekkers (Steenbrugge), Rev. Victorin Doucet O.F.M. (Quaracchi), R. Elze (Bonn), Vittorio Fanelli (Rome), George B. Fowler (University of Pittsburgh), Ezio Franceschini (Università Cattolica, Milan), A. L. Gabriel (Medieval Institute, University of Notre Dame), Prof. M. A. Goukovsky (Leningrad), Dr. Haas (Heidelberg), Dr. Helga Hajdu (Budapest), Elisabeth Feist Hirsch (Trenton), Sir R. W. Hunt (Bodleian Library), William Jackson (Harvard University Library), James John (Institute for Advanced Study, Princeton), Neil R. Ker (Oxford), Guido Kisch (Basel and New York), Ludmilla Krestan (Akademie der Wissenschaften, Vienna), Stephan Kuttner (Catholic University of America), the late M. L. W. Laistner (Cornell University), Dom J. Leclercq, O.S.B. (Clervaux), Paul Lehmann (Munich), Dean P. Lockwood (Haverford), F. Masai (Bibliothèque Royale, Brussels), Dr. Martin McGuire (Catholic University of America), the late A. P. McKinlay (University of California, Los Angeles), Loren MacKinney (University of North Carolina), Dr. Dana Martinkova (Prague), R. A. B. Mynors (Oxford), Dott. Angelo Paredi (Biblioteca Ambrosiana), Bernard M. Peebles (Catholic University of America), the late Mons. Auguste Pelzer (Vatican Library), Rev. C. Piana O.F.M. (Quaracchi), Robert Pratt (University of Illinois), Reinhold Regensburger (Cambridge), Erla Rodakiewicz (New York), Teresa Rogledi Manni (Milan), Edward Rosen (City College, New York), Dorothy Schullian (National Library of Medicine, Cleveland), Mr. Niels H. Sonne (New York), Josef Soudek (Queens College), Friedrich Stegmueller (Freiburg), Dom Anselm Strittmatter O.S.B. (Washington), Lynn Thorndike (Columbia University), B. L. Ullman (University of North Carolina), Mlle Jeanne Vielliard (Institut de Recherches et d'Histoire des Textes, Paris), A. Weinberger (Harvard University Library), C. E. Wright (British Museum), Joseph Zambelli (New York), Jerzy Zathey (Cracow).

This bibliography has developed in close connection with two projects in which I have been involved for some years and which are now at last approaching publication : the *Catalogus Translationum et Commentariorum*, a cooperative project sponsored by the Union Académique Internationale and other learned societies of which the first volume is in the press ; and the *Iter*

Italicum, a list of uncatalogued Renaissance manuscripts, of which the first volume will go to the press in the near future. I also hope that it may continue to spur the efforts that have been made in recent years to collect the microfilms of unpublished inventories of manuscripts in the Library of Congress and in various European depositories. [2]

New York, Columbia University
July 29, 1959.

---

[2] Cf. Lester K. Born, 'Universal Guide to Catalogs of Manuscripts and Inventories of Archival Collections: A Proposal for Cooperative Listing,' *College and Research Libraries* XVII (1956) 322-329. See also the papers by G. B. Fowler and B. L. Ullman listed below in Section A.

PREFACE TO THE FIRST EDITION

PART I

The study of Latin manuscripts has been of vital importance not only to the student of classical and patristic literature but also to every serious scholar interested in the literature, theology, philosophy and science of the Middle Ages and of the Renaissance. In this field, the manuscripts contain not merely new variants of well-known texts but an often unsuspected amount of new textual material that never got into print but often had as wide a circulation and importance as some of the printed works. This material is by no means easily accessible. If a collection of manuscripts has no printed catalogue, there is no way of investigating its content except by working on the spot. On the other hand, printed catalogues, when available, permit the location of pertinent material from a distance, and hence are a definite scholarly aid and desideratum. Since even the printed catalogues are often inadequate and sometimes rare, it has seemed useful to compile an annotated bibliography of these catalogues, which would serve as a guide to medievalists and Renaissance scholars in general, and in particular to the contributors to the project of 'Medieval and Renaissance Latin Translations and Commentaries,' which has been undertaken by a group of scholars under the auspices of several learned societies. The present bibliography was originally compiled for the purposes of that project, and it has been decided to print it, since previous bibliographies of a similar nature were either conceived along narrower lines, like Weinberger's, or were inaccurate, like Richardson's.

The geographical distribution of the collections of Latin manuscript books significantly coincides with the boundaries of the medieval Latin Church, important exceptions being the United States, Canada, New Zealand, Leningrad, Istanbul, Athens, and Tokyo. Many of these collections have no printed catalogues, or their printed catalogues are incomplete. Information concerning such undescribed or partially described collections may be found in the works listed under Section A. On the whole, cataloguing of the manuscript collections has been completed in France, and carried very far in Great Britain, Belgium, and a few other countries. Large gaps still exist not only for Spain but also for Italy and Germany. The ultimate goal, of course, is to describe in print all extant collections. Meanwhile, all handwritten catalogues available on the spot in the various libraries should be microfilmed as soon as possible. This task has become imperative in the light of recent losses and possible dangers. Whereas in the century preceding 1939 only three major catastrophes occurred, Strasbourg (1871), Turin (1904), and Louvain (1914), the losses due to World War II cannot yet be estimated but must have been considerable, especially in France (Chartres, Tours), Poland (Warsaw), and Germany. Nobody knows what the future may bring, and it is the responsibility of scholars, librarians, and government officials alike to provide in advance for the protection and preservation of this irreplaceable material. Otherwise, medieval and Renaissance civilization may suffer the same fate as ancient civilization did, through the destruction of the library in Alexandria.

This bibliography, in the main, takes for its basis the manuscript collections as they existed in the period between the two world wars, and also follows the political geography and place names of that period. Its emphasis is definitely upon public collections extant during that period, and upon the content rather than the external characteristics or provenance of the manuscripts. Although the list doubtless contains gaps and errors due to oversight, many categories were consciously omitted as irrelevant to our purpose, i.e. : general works on manuscripts or on paleography ; travel books containing occasional mention of libraries ; books dealing with the history or condition of particular libraries ; old inventories of collections no longer extant, except when those collections survive as parts of larger collections, or when the present locations and content of their scattered manuscripts have been indicated;[1] catalogues of manuscripts in Greek, Oriental, or modern vernacular languages; studies dealing with individual manuscripts, or with the manuscripts of individual authors; catalogues of archives, unless they include manuscript books ; sales catalogues, and other catalogues of private collections ; catalogues that are either antiquated or unverifiable ; studies dealing with scribes, miniatures, or bindings without reference to content; and catalogues of printed books. I have tended to be more inclusive in the case of collections for which no systematic catalogues are available, and hence borderline studies must serve as substitutes. Unless indicated otherwise, I have inspected the books described, and this is more important than it may seem, since the titles are often wrongly listed in previous bibliographies and in library catalogues, and bibliographical ghosts are not infrequent in this type of literature. I have included lists compiled for very special scholarly purposes, such as catalogues of illuminated, classical, patristic, juristic, theolo-

---

[1] A bibliography of the old inventories of Medieval and Renaissance libraries would be an important task all by itself but is beyond the scope of this bibliography, which is intended to serve as a guide to extant manuscripts according to their content.

gical, philosophical, hagiographic, liturgical, historical, or scientific manuscripts, but the reader should remember that such lists are rarely complete for the libraries they cover.

The bibliography comprises three sections. Section A contains general works giving primarily bibliographical or statistical information about manuscript collections but containing, as a rule, no catalogues of manuscripts. Section B contains manuscript catalogues that cover libraries in more than one city; a number of these works have been fully analyzed, especially the French *Catalogue Général* and Mazzatinti, in order to identify the numerous reprints made of their component sections. Section C contains the catalogues of individual libraries, arranged alphabetically by cities.

The arrangement of Section A and of Section B is alphabetical, by author or title. The arrangement of Section C, on the other hand, is by the name of the city in which the library is located. If the name of a city is followed by an alternative name of that same place in another language, the main entry for that city will be found in Section C under the latter name. The main entry for every city will be recognized by the fact that it is immediately followed by the name of the country to which it belonged during the interval 1918-1938. In the main entry, before the special catalogues pertaining to that city are enumerated, cross-references are given to the more general works listed in Sections A and B. When the cross-reference is to a work in Section A, it is always specifically so designated, but the cross-references to works listed in Section B, being much more numerous, are not so specifically designated. Cross-references in Section C to Sections A and B are given only in those cases where the volume referred to provides essential information or concerns at least fifty manuscripts.

In Section C, the name of the author is given in parentheses when it does not appear on the title page. As a rule, libraries list such catalogues either under the author, or under the title, or under the place. I have given the customary bibliographical data, including the title of a periodical or series in which a catalogue may appear in order to facilitate identification. I regularly give the number of pages, and in most cases also the number of manuscripts described. These data, in conjunction with the title, will often indicate the relative importance of the item described. Sometimes I add a few critical comments which, however, had to be brief for reasons of space. If there is no indication to the contrary, an index of authors appears at the end of the volume described, in the cases where I have personally examined the book. If there is no index, or the index is inadequate, or is found in an unexpected place, I call attention to it. For items concerning the same library, I usually follow the chronological order of publication. Catalogues that have been superseded by later and better ones are either omitted or given in parentheses. Each item, unless stated otherwise, has been located in some American library. I have not attempted to give multiple locations but merely indicated the library whose copy I have seen, using for that purpose, wherever possible, the abbreviations of the Union List of Serials.[2] Where I give no library location, I have seen the book at the Columbia University Library. I place one star on those items which I have not seen myself, and two stars on items that I have not been able to locate in this country. I have checked most of the major libraries in the East from Washington to Boston, including the Union Catalog in the Library of Congress.

I wish to acknowledge the generous help and assistance which I have received from numerous persons and institutions. Without this help, I should not have been able to complete my work. I should like to mention especially the libraries which gave me access to their stacks or sent me their books through interlibrary loan or written information concerning their books; Miss Jean Macalister and her colleagues of the Reference Department of the Columbia University Library; Professor B. L. Ullman of the University of North Carolina, who put at my disposal his typewritten list of Catalogues of Latin Manuscripts in the University of Chicago Libraries; Professors Harry Caplan, James Hutton, M. L. W. Laistner and Dr. Henry King of Cornell University, who allowed me to use Dr. King's typewritten list of Catalogues of Collections of Latin manuscripts containing works of the Church Fathers at the Cornell University Library, as well as his extensive file of additional titles; Professor Archer Taylor of the University of California, who sent me his as yet unpublished article on the history of manuscript cataloguing; the University of Pennsylvania Library, for its typewritten Bibliography of Manuscript Catalogues not in the University of Pennsylvania Library, com-

---

[2] *CSmH*: Huntington Library, San Marino, Cal. *CtY*: Yale University. *DCU*: Catholic University, Washington. *DLC*: Library of Congress. *DSG*: Army Medical Library, Washington. *ICJ*: John Crerar Library, Chicago. *ICN*: Newberry Library, Chicago. *ICU*: University of Chicago. *I U*: University of Illinois, Urbana. *MB*: Boston Public Library. *MH*: Harvard University. *MiU*: University of Michigan. *MnU*: University of Minnesota. *NIC*: Cornell University. *NN*: New York Public Library. *NNC*: Columbia University. *NNFr*: Frick Art Reference Library, New York. *NNG*: General Theological Seminary, New York. *NNGr*: Grolier Club, New York. *NNM*: American Museum of Natural History, New York. *NNMM*: Metropolitan Museum of Art, New York. *NNN*: New York Academy of Medicine. *NNU*: New York University. *NNUT*: Union Theological Seminary, New York. *NjP*: Princeton University. *NjPT*: Princeton Theological Seminary. *OCl*: Cleveland Public Library. *OCU*: University of Cincinnati. *PP*: Free Library, Philadelphia. *PPAP*: American Philosophical Society, Philadelphia. *PU*: University of Pennsylvania. *RPB*: Brown University.

piled by A. K. Borden; Professors E. A. Lowe of the Institute for Advanced Study in Princeton and Lynn Thorndike of Columbia University, who allowed me to use their valuable private collections of catalogues; Professor Eva M. Sanford of Sweet Briar College and Messrs. William Jackson and Arnold Weinberger of Harvard University, who did extensive checking for me at the Harvard University Library; finally Deans Mario E. Cosenza of Brooklyn College and Martin McGuire of the Catholic University of America, and Professors Hans Baron of the Institute for Advanced Study, George Fowler of the University of Pittsburgh, Otis Green of the University of Pennsylvania, Werner Jaeger of Harvard University, Sears R. Jayne of the University of California, Henry and Renée Kahane of the University of Illinois, Stephan Kuttner of the Catholic University of America, Berthe Marti of Bryn Mawr College, Franz Rosenthal of Hebrew Union College, Edmund Silk of Yale University, and S. Harrison Thomson of the University of Colorado; Mr. Samuel Ives of the Yale University Library, Miss Brita Stina Nordin-Pettersson of the Library of The Academy of Sciences in Stockholm, Mlle. J. Vielliard, Mlle. Brayer and M. Richard of the Institut de Recherche et d'Histoire des Textes in Paris, who all helped by giving me additional references or by examining books that were not directly accessible to me. I also wish to thank Dr. Mark Jupiter of Columbia University Library, who helped me with the proofreading of titles in several languages with which I am unfamiliar.

I trust that this bibliography will be useful to scholars and librarians. A work of this nature, it is almost needless to say, cannot hope to be free from blemishes. Additions and corrections will be gratefully received by the author.

Columbia University.
1948

PART II

The following list is a logical sequel to the bibliography of printed catalogues published some years ago (*Traditio* 6 [1948] 227-317), and it serves the same purpose, namely to facilitate the study of Latin manuscript books, which is important to classical and patristic scholars as well as to historians of the Middle Ages and of the Renaissance. A continuing exploration of the extant collections still leads to the discovery of unpublished writings, brings to light copies of known texts that are of special interest, or at least gives statistical evidence for the diffusion of certain well known works at the time when the manuscript book was the predecessor or rival of the printed book. Information on the general importance and content of the various manuscript collections proved essential both for the project of 'Medieval and Renaissance Latin Translations and Commentaries,' which has been undertaken by a group of scholars under the auspices of several learned societies, and for a summary list of philosophical and literary manuscripts of the Renaissance which I am preparing for the Warburg Institute in London. The present list is an outgrowth of these two undertakings, and it was first compiled in a less elaborate fashion for the former project and issued in mimeographed form under its auspices in 1951.

The manuscript collections which have no printed catalogues and are hence briefly called 'uncatalogued' are no less important for the scholar than the catalogued ones. Under normal circumstances, their content cannot be ascertained without an actual visit, but on the other hand, and for that very reason, they are likely to contain greater surprises in the way of unpublished texts. Now, contrary to a widespread belief, the case where such collections have no lists whatsoever and must be explored by actually handling every single manuscript is comparatively rare. In most instances, the 'uncatalogued' collection has a handwritten list which may be used on the spot and fulfills there the function of a 'catalogue.' These unpublished catalogues vary greatly in their quality and usefulness, but they are the only and indispensable keys to the respective collections. It is now possible to have them reproduced in photostat or microfilm, if the originating library permits it, and thus to study the general content of a collection before or without actually visiting the library. The usefulness of this procedure for scholars is. obvious.

The handwritten catalogues are arranged in different ways. They may be on index cards or in continuously written volumes. The card system is useful for checking individual entries, but when it is necessary to glance through a whole collection, a volume is preferable. The handwritten catalogues in volumes appear in two main types of arrangement: either they are shelf lists describing the manuscripts one after another in the order of their shelf marks, or they are alphabetical indices of names or subjects. The former type is commonly known as a 'topographical inventory,' and this term will be used in some of our descriptions. Some collections have only a shelf list (although this is rare), others only an index (which is more frequent). In the many cases where there is both a shelf list and an index, I have usually found the shelf list more useful than the index because it gives a more direct picture of the collection as a whole. Consequently, in my list I have placed greater emphasis on topographical inventories than on indices except in the cases where the index was definitely better, or where there was nothing but an index.

There are many sources of reference for printed catalogues, but published information on handwritten inventories is surprisingly scanty. Such well known and reliable reference works as *Minerva*, or the *Minerva-Handbücher* dedicated to libraries, or Beer's 'Handschriftenschätze Spaniens' say nothing or nearly nothing on the handwritten inventories of uncatalogued collections. While information is available for a few famous libraries such as the British Museum, the Bodleian, and the Vatican, I have come across only few publications which give this information on more than one library. One is the series of reports on Italian libraries published in the periodical *Accademie e Biblioteche*. This publication is quite valuable for Italian libraries, but it varies in quality and completeness. Its major inconvenience is the fact that the data which interest us are scattered in six bulky volumes of a periodical and that the handwritten inventories are mentioned along with printed catalogues, lists of printed books, and many other pieces of information. A few additional data are found in the work of Apolloni and Arcamone, which covers the libraries of Northern Italy. The other publication is a booklet by L. K. Born, recently issued by the Library of Congress, which covers many Western European countries, but omits Italy, Spain, Portugal, and the Scandinavian countries. From our point of view, it has two main shortcomings: first, it puts a heavy emphasis on archives and lists comparatively few library collections of manuscript books, and secondly, it fails to give the original titles of the inventories listed, thus making their identification sometimes difficult. I have utilized these publications (see below for bibliographical details) and shall refer to them for every single inventory which they mention. I venture to add the sign *Cf.* to the reference whenever I give information not supplied by them.

If analyzed by countries, the list reflects some peculiar facts and difficulties. Obviously, the number of handwritten inventories will be in inverse proportion to the number of available printed catalogues since in most cases the former are superseded by the latter. Among the countries which have important collections in our field, cataloguing has been nearly completed in France and the United States, and is fairly well advanced in Great Britain, Belgium, Holland, and Switzerland. The gaps are greater in Spain, Sweden, Austria, and Italy, and, unfortunately, in Germany, where so many collections were destroyed or dislocated during the last war. The list which I am able to present is necessarily incomplete, since it depends on the opportunities I had to visit the various libraries, and on the additional information I was able to gather by correspondence from librarians or other scholars. This may account for the fact that the list is more complete for Italy than for any of the other countries, and very scanty indeed for all libraries behind the Iron Curtain. Collections in Eastern Germany, Czechoslovakia, Poland, and Hungary as well as the public library in Leningrad are or were rich in Latin manuscript books, but under the present political circumstances it has been impossible to visit them or to obtain much information about them.

The inventories included in the hand list have been selected according to the following criteria: I included only inventories of extant collections, and excluded those of collections which no longer exist, except when they survive as separate units within an extant larger collection. The emphasis is on public rather than on private collections, although a few of the latter are included. Since we are concerned with manuscript books (*codices*) and not with charters or other documents, inventories of archives have been excluded, except in those cases where an archive possesses a separate collection of manuscript books. I excluded collections which contain only modern MSS. Finally, we are primarily concerned with Latin MSS rather than with those in other languages. However, most of the collections are not divided according to languages, and thus I mentioned in a few cases, where an important un-catalogued collection is subdivided by languages, also its inventories of Greek and Italian manuscripts.

The style of my arrangement follows on the whole the model of the Bibliography of Printed Catalogues. The list is arranged alphabetically by cities, using the native name of each city and following the political geography of the period between the two world wars. The present list has been improved over the Bibliography by making a clear distinction between the various libraries in the same city, and also between the various collections (*Fondi*) within each library. I place an asterisk both before libraries which I did not visit, and before inventories which I did not see. The two cases do not always coincide, since I have used copies or microfilms of inventories which describe libraries I never visited, and on the other hand, I visited many libraries, especially some years ago, without taking down precise data on their inventories. Most of the inventories included in this list without an asterisk were seen by me in 1949 and 1952, and I assume the responsibility for the errors which may have occurred in describing them. In the case of inventories listed with an asterisk, I give my source of information.

In the description proper, I treat the handwritten inventories like real books, giving their original titles wherever possible, and the number of volumes though not the number of pages or folios. Each inventory is in one handwritten volume unless stated otherwise. As often as possible, I give the number of manuscripts or the shelf marks of the first and last manuscript described in each volume. Since shelf marks present their peculiar problems and are almost a matter of luck in certain places, I shall sometimes explain their system, and call attention to cases where shelf marks have been changed or do not correspond to printed catalogues. If an inventory has been partly superseded by a printed catalogue, I shall try to make clear to what extent the inventory is still needed, (and refer to *Traditio* 6 for the printed catalogues listed in that volume.) I shall indicate the cases in which an inventory is particularly superficial, or fails to give important data such as centuries or actual shelf marks.

I wish to express my gratitude for the valuable help which I have received from many persons and institutions and which has made the compilation of the list possible: the Fulbright Committee, which granted me a fellowship in 1952; the American Philosophical Society and the Columbia University Council for Research in the Social Sciences, which awarded travel grants to me in 1949 and in 1952, and the Scuola Normale Superiore in Pisa, whose hospitality I enjoyed on both occasions; Mr. D. A. Bullard of the Fulbright Committee in Rome and Mr. Frederick Cromwell of the American Embassy in Madrid; Prof. G. Arcamone, Direttore Generale delle Accademie e Biblioteche in Rome; Sr. Francisco Sintes, Director General de Archivos y Bibliotecas, Sr. Amadeo Tortajada of the Consejo Superior de Investigaciones Cientificas, and Sr. Miguel Bordonau, Inspector General de Archivos in Madrid; Sr. J. Gomes Branco of the Instituto para a Alta Cultura in Lisbon. I owe a special debt of gratitude to the library directors and librarians in the various places who shared their information with me or replied to my queries, and especially to the Very Rev. A. M. Albareda and Msgr. A. Pelzer of the Vatican Library. Mlle M. Th. d'Alverny of the Bibliothèque Nationale, Dott. Giorgio E. Ferrari of the Biblioteca Marciana, Sig.[rina] Teresa Lodi of the Biblioteca Laurenziana, the Rev. P. Longas and Sr. R. Paz of the Biblioteca Nacional in Madrid, Sig.[ra] Berta Maracchi of the Biblioteca Nazionale in Florence, Sig.[ra] Teresa Rogledi Manni of the Biblioteca Nazionale Braidense, and Mr. C. E. Wright of the British Museum. The following scholars also helped me through valuable advice or by suggesting additions to my mimeographed list: L. Bertalot (Friedrichsdorf), L. Bieler (Dublin), G. Billanovich (Fribourg), Rev. P. Boehner (Franciscan Institute), Dr. Emile Boer (Berlin), Dr. H. Boese (Berlin), A. Campana (Vatican Library), L. Delaissé (Brussels), C. Fahy (Manchester), E. Franceschini (Milan), J. Garcia Morales (Madrid), Otis H. Green (University of Pennsylvania), the late E. Kaufmann (Los Angeles), N. Ker (Oxford), Dr. Ludmilla Krestan (Vienna), S. Kuttner (Catholic University), Dom J. Leclercq (Clervaux), D. P. Lockwood (Haverford), E. Loenroth (Uppsala), A. Mancini (Pisa), Berthe Marti (Bryn Mawr), R. A. B. Mynors (Cambridge), Miss B. S. Nordin Pettersson (Stockholm), B. Peebles (Catholic University), A. Perosa (Pisa), Miss Virginia Rau (Lisbon), Miss Toni Schmid (Uppsala), Dorothy Schullian (Armed Services Medical Library), F.

Stegmüller (Freiburg), Dom Anselm Strittmatter (Rome), S. H. Thomson (University of Colorado), L. Thorndike (Columbia University), B. L. Ullman (University of North Carolina), Mlle Jeanne Vielliard (Paris), R. Weiss (London), and F. Wormald (London). I am especially indebted to G. B. Fowler (University of Pittsburgh) for ample information on Austrian collections, and wish to express my appreciation for the opportunity to use the microfilms of Austrian inventories, obtained by Prof. Fowler with the help of Frau Prof. E. Patzelt (Vienna) and under the auspices of the American Philosophical Society, and now deposited in the Library of Congress.

I hope that the hand list will be useful as far as it goes, and provide orientation for some of those uncatalogued collections which are important and relevant for our field of study. I am aware of the numerous gaps which I was obliged to leave, and shall be grateful for any additions or corrections which scholars or librarians in various places may care to send me.

Columbia University.
1952

SECTION A

BIBLIOGRAPHY AND STATISTICS OF LIBRARIES AND THEIR COLLECTIONS OF MANUSCRIPTS

K. Aland, *Die Handschriftenbestände der Polnischen Bibliotheken insbesondere an griechischen und lateinischen Handschriften.* Berlin 1956. 66 pp. Lists printed and unpublished catalogues of the libraries in Warszawa, Lublin, Kraków, Wrocław, Poznań, Gniezno, Kórnik, Gdańsk and Toruń. Describes some mss. in Warszawa (p. 19-25), Kraków (28-35), Wrocław (47-48), Poznań (49-53), Kórnik (56), Gdańsk (60-61), Toruń (62-64). Lists mss. lost or preserved in Warszawa (18-19; 24-25), Wrocław (37-46), Gdańsk (57-60).

Annuario delle biblioteche italiane, 1933-34. Florence (1933). 347 pp. Arranged alphabetically by cities.

Annuario delle Biblioteche Italiane. 3 vols. Rome (1949). Arranged alphabetically by cities.

—*Aggiornamento per il 1954.* (Rome) 1954. 159 pp.

—2nd ed., 2 vols. Rome (1956-58).

E. Apolloni and G. Arcamone, *Le Biblioteche d'Italia fuori di Roma: Storia, classificazione, funzionamento, contenuto, cataloghi, bibliografia.* 3 vols. Rome 1934-38. Arranged by provinces and cities. vol. 1: Piemonte, Lombardia. vol. 2: Veneto, Venezia Giulia, Venezia Tridentina. vol. 3: Emilia, Liguria. Not yet completed.

Gli Archivi di Stato Italiani, Bologna (1944) X, 606 pp.

R. Beer, 'Handschriftenschätze Spaniens: Bericht über eine im Auftrage der kaiserlichen Akademie der Wissenschaften in den Jahren 1886-1888 durchgeführte Forschungsreise,' *Sitzungsberichte der Kaiserlichen Akademie der Wissenschaften* [Vienna], *Philosophisch-Historische Classe*

CXXIV (1891) no. 6. 80 pp. Arranged alphabetically by cities. A—Barcelona.
—CXXV (1892) no. 3. 72 pp. Barcelona-Cordoba. Lists 72 mss. at Cordoba, Cabildo, from Heine, *Serapeum* VII (p. 58-61). no. 7. 72 pp. Escorial.
—CXXVI (1892) no. 2. 60 pp. Gerona-Madrid. Lists 10 mss. at Gerona from Borao, *Boletin bibliografico español* VII 1866 (p. 12).
—CXXVIII (1893) no. 8. 80 pp. Madrid-Murcia. Lists some mss. at Madrid, Biblioteca Nacional (p. 9-14; 19-20; 24-25) no. 12, 80 pp. Oviedo-Sevilla.
—CXXIX (1893) no. 4. 80 pp. Sigüenza-Valencia. Lists mss. of Seo de Urgel from ms. BN Paris lat. 18604. (p. 56-70, 157 mss.). No. 6. 70 pp. Valladolid-Zaragoza. Lists mss. at Vich, Cabildo, from Heine, *Serapeum* VIII (p. 23-28). Lists mss. of Zaragoza, Biblioteca Provincial y Universitaria, from *Anuario del Cuerpo de Archiveros* I-II (p. 37-42).
—CXXXI (1894) no. 7. 80 pp. Alphabetical index, A-Ruvialis. no. 11. 81 pp. Index concluded. List of dated mss.

Le Biblioteche della Campania e della Calabria: Elenco e Consistenza. (I quaderni della Biblioteca Nazionale di Napoli, ser. 3, no. 3). Naples (1950). (By G. Guerrieri). 96 pp. Alphabetical list, with statistics of mss.

Biblioteche Pubbliche Romagnole, Bologna, 1954. 131 pp.

Bibliothèque Nationale [Paris], Département des Manuscrits. *Catalogue alphabétique des Livres Imprimés mis à la disposition des lecteurs dans la Salle de Travail.* 4th ed. Paris 1933. 142 pp. p. 24-71: 'Catalogues des manuscrits.'

A. Blau, 'Verzeichniss der Handschriften-katalogue der deutschen Bibliotheken,' *Centralblatt für Bibliothekswesen* III (1886) 1-35; 49-108; 120; 160. Arranged alphabetically by cities.

F. Blume, *Iter Italicum.* 4 vols. Berlin and Halle 1824-36. Arranged by provinces. vol. 1: Austrian provinces and Kingdom of Sardinia. vol. 2: Parma, Modena, Massa, Lucca, Tuscany, Papal States and S. Marino. vol. 3: Rome (including the Vatican). vol. 4: Kingdom of Naples. Indices of places, subjects and names in vol. 4.

J. Bohatta and M. Holzmann, *Adressbuch der Bibliotheken der Österreichisch-Ungarischen Monarchie.* Vienna 1900. 573 pp. Two sections for Austria and Hungary, each arranged alphabetically by cities. The same, 'Nachtrag zum Adressbuch der Bibliotheken der österreichisch-ungarischen Monarchie,' *Mittheilungen des österreichischen Vereines für Bibliothekswesen* V (1901) 33-37; 79-83; VII (1903) 13-16; 126-29; VIII (1904) 39-41; XI (1907) 137-39 (NN).

E. Borao, 'Apéndice á la Biblioteconomía de Mr. Constantin,' *Boletin Bibliografico Español* VI (1865) 291-92; VII (1866) 9-12; 42-48; 53-60; 66-72; 79-84; 91-96; 104-08; 116-24; 131-36; 140-48; 152-160; 166-72; 176-82. (MH). Two sections on Spanish libraries (VII, 54ff.) and on non-Spanish libraries (VII, 119), each arranged alphabetically by cities. Mentions a few mss. at Gerona (66) and Zaragoza (116-19). (NjP.).

C. Borchling, 'Mittelniederdeutsche Handschriften in Norddeutschland und den Niederlanden, Erster Reisebericht,' *Nachrichten von der Königl. Gesellschaft der Wissenschaften zu Göttingen, Geschäftliche Mittheilungen aus dem Jahre 1898* (1899), 79-316. (NN)

—*Mittelniederdeutsche Handschriften in Skandinavien, Schleswig-Holstein, Mecklemburg und Vorpommern. Zweiter Reisebericht.* (Nachrichten von der Königl. Gesellschaft der Wissenschaften zu Göt-

tingen, Philologisch-Historische Klasse, Beiheft). 1900. 204 pp.

—*Mittelniederdeutsche Handschriften in Wolfenbüttel und einigen benachbarten Bibliotheken. Dritter Reisebericht.* (*Ibid.*). 1902. 263 pp.

—*Mittelniederdeutsche Handschriften in den Rheinlanden und in einigen anderen Sammlungen. Vierter Reisebericht.* (*Ibid.*). 1913. 256 pp.

L. K. Born, *Unpublished Bibliographical Tools in Certain Archives and Libraries of Europe: A Partial List.* Washington 1952. 25 pp. Covers mainly archival collections in Northwestern Europe.

B. Botfield, *Notes on the Cathedral Libraries of England.* London 1849. 527 pp. Arranged alphabetically by cities. No index.

C. Brunel, *Bibliographie des manuscrits littéraires en ancien provençal* (Société de publications romanes et françaises 13). Paris 1935. XVII, 146 pp. Arranged by countries and cities.

C. Bursian, ed., *Jahresbericht über die Fortschritte der classischen Alterthumswissenschaft.* IV (1877) 1-48: C. Bursian, 'Bericht über die in den Jahren 1874 und 1875 veröffentlichten auf die Geschichte der classischen Alterthumswissenschaft bezüglichen Arbeiten.' Covers catalogues of manuscripts.

—XCVIII (1899) 187-310: R. Beer and W. Weinberger, 'Bericht über die auf Paläographie und Handschriftenkunde bezügliche Litteratur der Jahre 1874-96.' Arranged by countries.

—CVI (1901) 168-233: W. Weinberger, 'Bericht über Paläographie und Handschriftenkunde (1897-1900).' Arranged by countries.

—CXXVII (1906), 214-56. Cont. (1901-02). Arranged by cities. CXXXV (1908), 15-53. Cont. (1903-06). CLVIII (1912), 96-131. Cont. (1907-10). CLXXII (1915), 1-30. Cont. (1911-15) CXCIII (1923), 79-105. Cont. (1916-21). CCIX (1926), 1-25. Cont. (1922-25). CCXXXVI (1932), 85-113. Cont. (1926-30).

'I cataloghi delle Biblioteche Italiane,' *Accademie e Biblioteche* I (1927-28) no. 2, 67-71; no. 3, 72-87; no. 4, 84-95; no. 5-6, 91-104; II (1928-29) no. 1, 62-78; no. 2, 46-66; no. 3, 51-67; no. 4-5, 83-94; no. 6, 99-109; III (1929-30) 59-66; 253-65; 359-70; 467-81; 550-60; IV (1930-31) 69-73; 171-82; 247-59; 404-19; 544-54; V (1931-32) 97-108; 283-91; 424-29; 509-17: VI (1932-33) 62-67; 174-81; 270-77; 484-88; 549-55. (NNC) There is a volume of reprints, having the same title and pages, Rome n.d., in which a table of contents and an index of cities are added at the beginning. (NjP)

G. Cecchini, *Le Biblioteche Pubbliche degli Enti Locali*. Rome 1957. 161 pp. Arranged by regions and provinces.

E. Chwalewik, *Zbiory polskie, archiva, biblioteki, galerje, muzea...* 2 vols. Warsaw-Cracow 1926-27. Arranged alphabetically by cities. (NN)

A. Collard, *Annuaire des Bibliothèques de Belgique*. Roulers 1912. VIII, 189 pp.

L. A. Constantin, *Essai d'une statistique des bibliothèques publiques des pays étrangers de l'Europe*. Paris 1841. 60 pp. Arranged by countries. (NN)

[Ch. P. Cooper, Appendices to a Report on Rymer's Foedera]. (No title page). 'This volume contains a portion of the Appendices to a Report on Rymer's Foedera intended to have been made, to the late Commissioners on Public Records, by Mr. Charles Purton Cooper, their Secretary. As these Appendices have been in store since the year 1837 . . . I have directed the Appendices . . . to be distributed . . . London, 1869.' vol. I: Appendix (A) and Supplement to Appendix (A). 259 and 116 pp. Contains a list of libraries, mostly in Central Europe, arranged alphabetically by cities, with notes and references. For many libraries, lists of manuscripts are given, though mostly from printed sources, and without shelfmarks, namely for Admont (pp. 1-2); Altdorf (2-4); Augsburg (7-13); Bamberg

(13-15); Basel (19-26); Bern (29-46); Breslau (49-52); Karlsruhe (58-60); Kassel (60-61); Köln (62-63); Corvey (66); Dresden (68-69); Eberach (70); Einsiedeln (70-71); Erfurt (72); Erlangen (73-74); Frankfurt a.M. (75-76); Freising and Freiburg (77); St. Gallen (78-95); Genève (97-103); Gotha (103-06); Göttweih (107); Halle (108); Hamburg (108-21); Heidelberg (122-23); Heiligenkreuz (123); Heilsbronn (124-26); Jena (128); Leipzig (142-48); Lilienfeld (149); Lübeck (149-57); Lüneburg (157-58); Marburg (159); Mainz (159-60); Melk (161-63); München (166-78); Münster (179); Muri (179-80); Nürnberg (180-84); Ochsenhausen (184); Leningrad (186-87); Polling (188); Praha (188-90); Quedlinburg (191); Rajhrad (192-96); Rebdorf (196); Regensburg (197-200); Rheinau (200-01); Salmansweiler (202); Salzburg (202-04); Schaffhausen (204); Seitenstetten (205); Stuttgart (207-08); Tegernsee (209); Ulm (210-11); Wien (212-39); Warszawa (240-41); Weingarten (242); Wettingen (243); Wolfenbüttel (245-53); Würzburg (253-54); Zürich (255-58); Zwiefalten (259); Annaberg (Suppl. 1); Kassel (10-11); Eichstätt (14); Frankfurt a.M. (16-17); St. Gallen (20-23); Melk (29); München (45-58); München, Universitätsbibliothek (59-62); Rebdorf (63); Verden (80); Wien (81-82); Windberg (83); Würzburg (84-86); No index. Information largely superseded or antiquated.

Dansk biblioteksfører, 3rd. ed. by H. Einersen and M. Iversen, Copenhagen 1955, 137 pp.

D. Djaparidzé, *Medieval Slavic Manuscripts*. (Mediaeval Academy Publications 64) Cambridge, Mass. 1957. 134 pp.

H. Dölzl-Rheinsberg, 'Handschriften-Kataloge,' *Zentralblatt für Bibliothekswesen* XXXII (1915) 373-94.

Elenco delle Biblioteche d'Italia. Milan 1926. 197 pp.

C. Erdmann, 'Papsturkunden in Portugal,' *Abhandlungen der Gesellschaft der Wissenschaften zu Göttingen, Philologisch-His-*

torische Klasse N.F. XX (1927) no. 3. 384 pp. Surveys archives and lists many documents in Portugal. Lists a few historical mss. at Lisbon (116-18).

A. Esdaile, *National Libraries of the World: Their History, Administration and Public Services.* London 1934. XII, 386 pp.

—2nd ed., rev. by F. J. Hill. London 1957. XV, 413 pp.

P. Faider, *Bibliographie des catalogues des manuscrits des Bibliothèques de Belgique.* Bruges 1933. 15 pp. (NN)

A. Ferrão, *Os Arquivos e as Bibliotecas em Portugal.* Coimbra 1920. 331 pp. (NN)

R. Foulché-Delbosc and L. Barrau-Dihigo, *Manuel de l'hispanisant.* New York 1920. vol. I, 183-376; 449-95: Bibliography of Spanish libraries.

G. B. Fowler, 'Intellectual History and Monastic Discipline in Mediaeval Austria,' *Year Book of the American Philosophical Society,* 1952, p. 221. Lists the microfilms of Austrian inventories obtained for the Library of Congress.

G. Gabrieli, *Notizie statistiche bibliografiche delle collezioni di manoscritti oggi conservati nelle biblioteche italiane.* Milan 1936. 227 pp. Arranged alphabetically by cities. Indispensable yet often inaccurate.

A. Goldmann, 'Verzeichniss der österreichisch-ungarischen Handschriftenkataloge,' *Centralblatt für Bibliothekswesen* V (1888) 1-37; 55-73.

J. Gomez Perez, 'Catálogos de manuscritos conservados en las bibliotecas de Italia,' *Revista de Archivos, Bibliotecas y Museos* LXIV (1958) 113-34.

L. Gougaud, 'Inventaires de manuscrits provenant d'anciennes bibliothèques monastiques de Grande-Bretagne,' *Revue d'histoire ecclésiastique* XXXIII (1937) 789-91. Bibliography on the subject, with emphasis on extant materials.

Guide-Manuel des Bibliothèques de Rome. (ed. by the Institut Historique Néerlandais). Revised ed. Rome 1932. 100 pp. Covers also the Vatican.

F. W. Hall, *Companion to Classical Texts.* Oxford 1913. 363 pp. p. 199-285: MS. authorities for the text of the chief classical writers. p. 286-357: The Nomenclature of MSS., with the names of former possessors.

Miss M. S. G. Hands, 'The Cathedral Libraries Catalogue,' *The Library,* Fifth Series, II (1947) 1-13. p. 11-13: Appendix. Margaret S. Smith, 'Printed Catalogues of Books and Manuscripts in Cathedral Libraries: England and Wales.'

R. Hoecker, *Das spanische Bibliothekswesen* (Archiv für Bibliographie, Buch- und Bibliothekswesen, Beiheft II). Linz, 1928. 62 pp.

W. Holtzmann, 'Papsturkunden in England. 1. Bibliotheken und Archive in London. I. Berichte und Handschriftenbeschreibungen,' *Abhandlungen der Gesellschaft der Wissenschaften zu Göttingen, Philologisch-Historische Klasse* N.F. XXV (1930-31) 1-210. 2. 'Die kirchlichen Archive und Bibliotheken. I. Berichte und Handschriftenbeschreibungen,' *Ibid.* Dritte Folge, no. 14-15 (1935-36) 1-128. Surveys archives and libraries and lists many documents in England. Lists some historical mss. in London (pt. 1); Winchester (pt. 2, p. 40-42), Salisbury (*ibid.* 46-47), Exeter (49-52), Hereford (57-59), Lincoln (73-75), York (107f.), Durham (120-23).

J. Van Hove, *Répertoire des Organismes de Documentation en Belgique.* Brussels 1947. 335 pp.

A. Hübl, 'Die österreichischen Klosterbibliotheken in den Jahren 1848-1908,' *Mittheilungen des österreichen Vereins für Bibliothekswesen* XII (1908) 201-16. (NN)

E. Hübner, *Bibliographie der Klassischen Altertumswissenschaft* . . . 2nd ed. Berlin 1889. p. 58-64: 'Die hauptsächlichsten gedruckten Verzeichnisse von Handschriften klassischer Schriftwerke.' Arranged by countries.

R. Istituto Storico Italiano per il Medio Evo. *Guida storica e bibliografica degli Archivi e delle Biblioteche d'Italia.* vol. I: *Provincia di Firenze.* pt. 1, Rome 1932: R. Piattoli, *Prato.* 177 pp.

—vol. II: *Provincia di Pistoia.* pt. 1, Rome. 1934: R. Piattoli, *Pistoia.* 229 pp.

—vol. III, 1937: Fernanda Ascarelli, *Biblioteche e Istituti Stranieri in Roma.* 156 pp.

—vol. IV, 1937; L. Mattei Cerasoli, *Badia della SS. Trinità di Cava.* 45 pp. Gives a brief list of 162 mss. (29-34). No index.

—vol. V, 1939: Tullia Gasparrini Leporace, *I manoscritti Capilupiani della Biblioteca Nazionale Centrale di Roma.* xxiv, 145 pp. Describes 73 mss. (Vittorio Emmanuele, 1008-80). Index (127ff.).

—vol. VI: *Provincia di Aquila.* pt. 1, Rome 1940: L. Cassese, *Città di Aquila.* xix, 104 pp. Surveys mss. (46-48).

(Italy) Consiglio Nazionale delle Ricerche. *Enti culturali italiani,* by G. Magrini. 2 vols. Bologna 1929. vol. II p. 173ff.: Libraries. (NN)

(Italy. Direzione generale della statistica). *Statistica del Regno d'Italia. Biblioteche.* Florence 1865. cxxviii, 47 pp. Lists some mss. in Cesena (p. xlvi-l) and Messina (lxxvi-lxxvii). (MH)

(Italy) Ministero di Agricoltura, Industria e Commercio. Direzione Generale della Statistica. *Statistica delle Biblioteche.* 3 vols. in 2, Rome 1894-96. Arranged by provinces.

(Italy) Ministero dell' Educazione Nazionale. Direzione Generale delle Accademie e Biblioteche. *Le Accademie e le Biblioteche d'Italia nel sessennio* 1926/27-1931/32. Rome 1933. 945 pp. Arranged by provinces.

(Italy) Ministero dell'Educazione Nazionale. Direzione generale delle Accademie e Biblioteche. *Le Biblioteche d'Italia dal 1932-X al 1940-XVIII.* Rome 1942. 1115 pp.

(Italy) Ministero della pubblica istruzione. *Le Biblioteche governative italiane nel 1898.* Rome 1900. 464 pp.

Jahrbuch der Deutschen Bibliotheken. Vol. 37 (Wiesbaden 1957). VIII, 466 pp.

Jahrbuch der Oesterreichischen Wissenschaft.

4. Jahrgang (Vienna 1957-58). 760 pp. p. 289-380: Bibliotheken.

P. Kehr, 'Papsturkunden in Spanien: Vorarbeiten zur Hispania Pontificia. I. Katalanien. I. Archivberichte,' *Abhandlungen der Gesellschaft der Wissenschaften zu Göttingen, Philologisch-Historische Klasse* N.F. XVIII, 2 (1926) 1-236. II. 'Navarra und Aragon. I. Archivberichte,' *Ibid.* XXII, 1 (1928) 1-252. Surveys the archives, and lists many documents, of the Spanish provinces of Catalunya, Navarra and Aragon. Lists a few historical mss. at Barcelona (I, 74-77), Gerona (134ff.), and Seo de Urgel (165ff.).

N. R. Ker, *Catalogue of Manuscripts containing Anglo-Saxon.* Oxford 1957. LXIV, 567 pp. and plates. Arranged alphabétically by cities.

E. Koschmieder, 'Bericht über eine Studienreise in Polen 1930,' *Zentralblatt für Bibliothekswesen* XLIX (1932) 130-46.

P. O. Kristeller, 'Latin Manuscript Books before 1600: A Bibliography of the Printed Catalogues of their Extant Collections,' *Traditio* VI (1948) 227-317.

—'Part II: A Tentative List of Unpublished Inventories of Imperfectly Catalogued Extant Collections,' *ibid.* IX (1953) 393-418.

Cf. *Aevum* XXIX (1955) 291; *Roczniki Biblioteczne* II (1958) 283-286, by Anna Jałbrzykowska.

—'Renaissance Manuscripts in Eastern Europe.' *Renaissance News* XII (1959), 83-90.

R. Kukula, 'Statistik der wichtigsten ausserdeutschen Bibliotheken der Erde,' *Centralblatt für Bibliothekswesen* XI (1894) 111-24; XII (1895) 311-26. Arranged alphabetically by countries and cities.

F. Lautenschlager, *Bibliographie der Badischen Geschichte.* 2 vols. Karlsruhe 1929-38. Vol. I, p. 10-12: Handschriftenverzeichnisse. Vol. II, pt. 2, p. 362-381: Bibliotheken.

H. von Lenz, 'Über schwedische Bibliotheken: Reiseerinnerungen,' *Mittheilun-*

*gen des österreichischen Vereins für Biblio-
thekswesen* XI (1907) 49-65; 119-25. (NN)

E. Lesne, *Histoire de la propriété ecclésiastique en France.* IV. *Les livres, 'scriptoria'
et bibliothèques du commencement du VIII*e
*à la fin du XI*e *siècle.* (Mémoires et
Travaux publiés par les professeurs des
Facultés Catholiques de Lille, fasc. 46).
Lille 1938. 849 pp.

'Liaison Committee on Microfilming Manuscript Catalogues' (by B. L. Ullman),
Renaissance News VII (1954) 156-160.
Lists some microfilms of Italian inventories obtained for the Library of Congress.

*The Libraries Museums and Art Galleries
Year Book.* London and New York 1955.
XXVIII, 648 pp. Many previous editions
since 1897.

*Il Libro e le Biblioteche. Atti del Primo
Congresso Bibliologico Francescano Internazionale.* (Bibliotheca Pontificii Athenaei
Antoniani 5-6). 2 vols. Rome 1950.
vol. I, p. 397-412: A. Pelzer, 'Osservazioni e riflessioni sui manoscritti e le
biblioteche.' vol. II, p. 127-182; L. Di
Stolfi, 'Le principali biblioteche francescane d'Italia di ieri e di oggi.' p. 347-359:
B. Pesci, 'I fondi religiosi nella Biblioteca
Nazionale di Roma.'

Manuscrits occidentaux conservés en Italie.
4 typed vols. Arranged alphabetically by
cities. Omits Rome. (Institut de Recherches et d'Histoire des Textes, Paris).

F. Mateu y Llopis, 'Los catálogos de las
bibliotecas y archivos eclesiásticos de
España,' *Hispania Sacra* I (1948) 207-
228. Arranged by cities.

G. Meier, 'Verzeichniss der Handschriften-
Kataloge der schweizerischen Bibliotheken,' *Centralblatt für Bibliothekswesen* IV
(1887), 1-19.

J. G. Meusel, *Teutsches Künstler-Lexicon.*
2nd ed. III (Lemgo 1814) 297-554: alphabetical list of libraries in Germany and
Switzerland, with some data and references. (DLC)

Minerva: Jahrbuch der Gelehrten Welt. Abteilung: *Forschungsinstitute, Observatorien,*
*Bibliotheken, Archive, Museen, Kommis-
sionen, Gesellschaften.* Leipzig 1937. 1765
pp. Alphabetically by cities.

Minerva-Handbücher. Section I: *Die Bibliotheken.* vol. I, 1929: H. Praesent, *Deutsches Reich.* 999 pp. vol. II, 1932: R.
Teichl, *Österreich.* 312 pp. vol. III, 1934:
F. Burckhardt, *Schweiz.* 240 pp.

—Section II: *Die Archive,* by P. Wentzke
and G. Lüdtke. Vol. I, Berlin-Leipzig,
1932. 658 pp. Covers Germany, Denmark, Estonia, Finland, Latvia, Lithuania,
Luxemburg, the Netherlands, Norway,
Austria, Sweden and Switzerland.

G. Moldenhauer, 'Bibliographischer Wegweiser zu den Handschriftenbeständen
in Portugal,' *Zentralblatt für Bibliothekswesen* XLII (1925) 25-31.

Nederlandse Bibliotheekgids. 4th ed., by
C. J. Nissink. Amsterdam 1949. X, 336
coll. Older editions since 1913.

L. Newcombe, *The University and College
Libraries of Great Britain and Ireland.*
London 1927. 220 pp. Alphabetical list
arranged by cities, with statistics.

S. Nicolini, *Bibliografia degli antichi cataloghi a stampa di biblioteche italiane (secoli XVII e XVIII).* Florence 1954.
132 pp.

'Notizie degli Archivi Toscani,' *Archivio
Storico Italiano* CXIV (1956) 320-692.
Alphabetical list with statistics and bib-
liography.

H. Oesterley, *Wegweiser durch die Literatur
der Urkundensammlungen.* 2 vols. Berlin,
1885-86. Arranged by historical subjects.
(NN)

G. Ottervik, *Libraries and Archives in Sweden.* Stockholm 1954. 216 pp.

G. Ottino and G. Fumagalli, *Bibliotheca
bibliographica italiana* ... Rome 1889,
and supplement of 1895. Has a section
on mss.

A. Pelzer, 'Répertoires d'incipit pour la
littérature latine philosophique et théologique du moyen âge,' *Revue d'Histoire
Ecclésiastique* XLIII (1948) 495-512.
(NNUT)

—Édition augmentée. Rome 1951. 33 pp.

J. Petzholdt, *Literatur der sächsischen Bibliotheken*. Dresden and Leipzig 1840. xviii, 53 pp. (NN)

Philobiblon Society. *Miscellanies*. I (1854): R. Curzon, 'A Short Account of the most celebrated libraries of Italy.' 59 pp. B. Botfield, 'Notes on Libraries.' 17 pp. III (1856-57): Botfield cont. VI (1860-61): Botfield, 'Notices of Libraries.' 96 pp.

J. von Pflugk-Hartung, *Iter Italicum*. Stuttgart 1883. 908 pp. p. 1-166 and 737-802: alphabetical list of archives and libraries.

J. Enoch Powell, 'A List of Printed Catalogues of Greek Manuscripts in Italy,' *The Library*, Fourth Ser. (Transactions of the Bibliographical Society, Second Ser.) XVII (1937) 200-13.

R. Priebsch, *Deutsche Handschriften in England*. 2 vols. Erlangen 1896-1901. (MH)

Vicente G. Quesada, *Las Bibliotecas Europeas y algunas de la America Latina*. Buenos Aires 1877. 651 pp.

Répertoire des Bibliothèques de France. 3 vols. Paris 1950-51. Vol. I, Paris. Vol. II: Départements.

Revista de Filologia Española I (1914)-XXX (1946). Has a bibliographical section that lists many catalogues of mss.

S. De Ricci. *English Collectors of Books and Manuscripts (1530-1930)*. Cambridge 1930. IX, 203 pp.

M. Richard, *Répertoire des Bibliothèques et des Catalogues de Manuscrits Grecs*. (Centre National de la Recherche Scientifique, Publications de l'Institut de Recherche et d'Histoire des Textes 1). Paris 1948, XV, 131 pp.

—2nd ed., Paris 1958. XIX, 277 pp.

E. C. Richardson, *A Union World Catalogue of Manuscript Books* (ed. by the American Library Association. Committee on Bibliography). Vol. I, New York 1933: *The World's Collections of Manuscript Books: A Preliminary Survey*. 40 pp.

—vol. II, 1933: Henry A. Grubbs, *The Manuscript Book Collections of Spain and Portu-*gal. 134 pp. p. 57-91: 'Eight Spanish Collections.' Lists mss. of Silos (from Whitewill), Pamplona (from Hunt), León (from Garcia Villada), Vich (from Gudiol), Tortosa (from Denifle), Valencia University (from Gutierrez del Caño), Valencia Cathedral (from Olmos Canalda) and Burgo de Osma (from Rojo Orcajo). p. 93-134: 'Cumulative index' (of authors in these collections).

—-vol. III, 1935: *A List of Printed Catalogs of Manuscript Books*. 386 pp. Alphabetically by cities. Indispensable but uncritical and full of errors.

—vol. IV, 1934: N. A. Faris, *A Demonstration Experiment with Oriental Manuscripts* 74 pp.

—vol. V. 1935: Henry A. Grubbs, *A Supplement to the Manuscript Book Collections of Spain and Portugal*. 302 pp. Lists mss. of the Escorial (from Antolín), Barcelona, Archivo de la Corona de Aragón (from García Villada), Barcelona, Biblioteca de Catalunya, Granada (from Caparros), León, Biblioteca Provincial (from Alvarez), León, San Isidoro (from Llamajares), Madrid, Academia de la Historia (from Perez Pastor), Madrid, Biblioteca Nacional (from Loewe and Hartel), Madrid, Archivo (from the same), Madrid, Museo Arqueologico (from the same), Madrid, Real Biblioteca (from the same), Monserrat (from Albareda), Zaragoza (from Sancho Izquierdo), Vich (from Gudiol). Index of authors (p. 147-302) covers this volume and vol. II together.

—vol. VI, 1937: E. C. Richardson, *Summary of Method*. 85 pp.

Cf. A. Pelzer, 'Un essai américain de catalogue sommaire de tous les manuscrits,' *Revue d'Histoire Ecclésiastique* XXXII (1936) 621-630. (NNUT)

Les Richesses des Bibliothèques Provinciales de France, by P. Neveux and E. Dacier. 2 vols. Paris 1932. Alphabetically by cities. (NN)

U. Robert, 'État des catalogues des manuscrits des bibliothèques de Belgique et de

Hollande,' *Le Cabinet Historique* XXIV, 2 (1878) 196-225.

The same, Etat des catalogues des manuscrits des bibliothèques de Danemark, d'Islande, de Norvège et de Suède,' *Ibid.* XXVI, 2 (1880) 119-38.

The same, 'État des catalogues des manuscrits des bibliothèques d'Espagne et de Portugal,' *Ibid.* XXVI 2 (1880) 294-99.

F. Rullmann, *Über die Herstellung eines gedruckten Generalkataloges der grossen Manuscriptenschätze im deutschen Reiche.* Freiburg i.B. 1875. 62 pp. (MH) Surveys collections by territories.

O. Schissel, *Kataloge Griechischer Handschriften.* (Bücherkunde in Einzeldarstellungen I). Graz 1924. xii, 84 pp. Useful also for Latin mss. Arranged by cities. Index of compilers.

Dorothy M. Schullian, 'The John Griswold White Collection,' *Classical Philology* XXXIV (1939) 253-54. Surveys the collection of catalogues of mss. at the Cleveland Public Library.

P. Schwenke, *Adressbuch der deutschen Bibliotheken* (Centralblatt für Bibliothekswesen, Beiheft 10). Leipzig 1893. 411 pp.

Scriptorium. This periodical contains rich information on manuscripts and their bibliography. Note especially: I (1946-47) 181-189; 329-354. L. Bieler, 'Latin Manuscripts, Facsimiles, Editions, Studies published in Great Britain, Ireland, Canada, and the United States since July 1939' (p. 185-186: Catalogues of Manuscripts and Records).

III (1949) 303-316: M. Cappuyns and H. Bascour, 'Les Catalogues de Manuscrits: Premier Supplément aux listes de Weinberger et de Richardson.'

IV (1950) 149-155: J. N. Garvin 'Publications in the United States and Canada relating to Manuscripts, 1946-1949' (p. 150-151: Catalogues of Manuscripts).

V (1951) 125-145: B. Bischoff, 'Deutsches Schrifttum zur lateinischen Palaeographie und Handschriftenforschung, 1939-1945' (p. 129-130: Kataloge und Verwandtes).

VII (1953) 139-152: A. Mundó, 'Les publications espagnoles relatives aux manuscrits, 1936-45' (p. 143-144: Inventaires et catalogues).

298-318: B. Bischoff, 'Deutsches Schrifttum zur lateinischen Paläographie und Handschriftenforschung' (p. 307-308: Moderne Bibliotheken).

319-323: J. N. Garvin, 'Publications in the United States and Canada relating to Manuscripts, 1950-52' (p. 320: Collections of Manuscripts).

VIII (1954) 323-328: T. J. Brown and G. R. C. Davis, 'Western Manuscripts: Publications in Great Britain, 1951-53' (p. 326: Catalogues).

IX (1955) 294-326: M.-Th. Vernet-Boucrel, 'Les publications françaises relatives aux manuscrits, 1939-45 et 1946-50' (p. 306: Catalogues).

X (1956) 123-127. J. N. Garvin, 'Publications in the United States and Canada relating to Manuscripts, 1953-1954' (p. 124-125: Collections or Lists of Manuscripts).

303-318: P. Spunar, 'Manuscript Studies in Czechoslovakia' (p. 306: The Catalogues of Manuscripts).

XI (1957) 292-317: J.-A. Lefèvre and A. Cockx, 'Publications Belges relatives aux manuscrits, 1948-1955' (p. 297: Collections actuelles).

XII (1958) 300-312: J. N. Garvin, 'Publications in the United States and Canada relating to Manuscripts, 1955-57' (p. 302: Collections).

Société des Nations, Institut International de Coopération Intellectuelle. *Guide International des Archives, Europe.* Paris-Rome (1934). VIII, 393 pp.

E. Sparn, *Las bibliotecas con Quinientos y más manuscritos del viejo mundo* (Republica Argentina. Academia Nacional de Ciencias. Miscelanea No. 21). Cordoba 1937. 174 pp.

B. G. Struve, *Bibliotheca historiae literariae selecta. . .* ed. J. F. Jugler. vol. I, Jena 1754, deals with libraries.

Tesori delle biblioteche d'Italia. vol. I: D. Fava, *Emilia e Romagna.* Milan 1932. 694 pp.

Utrecht, Universiteitsbibliotheek. *Catalogus der Handbibliotheek in de Handschriften-Leeszaal.* Utrecht 1910. 32 pp. (Leiden, Bibliotheek der Rijksuniversiteit).

G. Vajda, *Répertoire des Catalogues et Inventaires de Manuscrits Arabes.* Paris 1949. VI, 49 pp.

G. Valentinelli, 'Delle Biblioteche della Spagna,' *Sitzungsberichte der Kaiserlichen Akademie der Wissenschaften* [Vienna], *Philosophisch-Historische Classe* XXXIII (1860) 4-178.

The same, 'Delle Biblioteche e delle Società scientifico-letterarie della Neerlandia,' *Ibid.* XXXVIII (1861) 305-569.

**The same, 'Le Biblioteche italiane,' *Circolare della Libreria Italiana* II (Milan 1865) fasc. 4; 8; 10; 11; 17; 18; 20; 22.

The same, 'Dei cataloghi a stampa di codici manoscritti,' *Atti del Reale Istituto Veneto di Scienze, Lettere ed Arti,* Ser. IV, vol. I (1871-72) 93-142; 346-78; 505-64. Covers Italy only.

B. Varjas, *The Development of Librarianship in Hungary.* Budapest 1956. 59 pp. p. 16-58: Survey of the most important Hungarian libraries.

Verzeichnis Oesterreichischer Bibliotheken. (Biblos-Schriften 1). Vienna 1953. XV, 191 pp.

E. G. Vogel, *Literatur früherer und noch bestehender europäischer öffentlicher und Corporations-Bibliotheken.* Leipzig 1840. 548 pp.

A. Voisin, *Documents pour servir à l'histoire des bibliothèques en Belgique.* Ghent 1840. 350 pp.

W. Weinberger, 'Beiträge zur Handschriftenkunde,' *Sitzungsberichte der Kaiserlichen Akademie der Wissenschaften* [Vienna], *Philosophisch-Historische Classe* CLIX (1908), no. 6, 89 pp. CLXI (1909) no. 4, 150 pp. Gives survey (p. 25ff.) and bibliography (p. 79ff.) of important Western collections. Index of authors (146-50).

The same, *Catalogus catalogorum: Verzeichnis der Bibliotheken, die ältere Handschriften lateinischer Kirchenschriftsteller enthalten,* Vienna 1902. 56 pp. (NNUT)

The same, *Erstes Supplement zum Catalogus Catalogorum* (1901-1907). Privately printed. Vienna 1907. 8 pp. (NNUT)

The same, 'Wegweiser durch die Sammlungen altphilologischer Handschriften,' *Sitzungsberichte der Akademie der Wissenschaften in Wien, Philosophisch-Historische Classe* CCIX (1930), no. 4. 136 pp. Indispensable but limited in scope.

The same, see also above under Bursian.

W. J. Wilson, 'Manuscript Cataloging,' *Traditio* XII (1956) 457-555.

The World of Learning, 9th. ed. London 1958-59. 1139 pp. Lists for each country the more important libraries.

Yugoslav Libraries. Zagreb 1954. 61 pp.

SECTION B

Works Describing Manuscripts of More than One City

(Académie Royale des Sciences, des Lettres et des Beaux-Arts de Belgique, Brussels). Commission royale d'histoire, *Compte-rendu des séances . . . ou Recueil de ses Bulletins*. I (1837): Notes on mss. at Liége (25-26), Tournai (26ff.), Ghent (58). 'Inventaire de divers manuscrits existans dans quelques dépôts publics.' Covers Louvain (169-72, lists 19 mss.); Ghent (172-76); Malines (177-80); Mons (214-31); Bruges (231-35); Liége (271-76); Tournai (290-91); Namur (291-92); Hamburg (382, 5 mss.).

—II (1838): Malines (35-36).

—IV (1841): 'Notices sur les documents manuscrits concernant la Belgique . . .' Giessen (13-16); Trier (16-41); Koblenz (42-51).

—V (1842): E. Gachet, 'Notice d'un manuscrit de la Bibliothèque Royale' (130-67, Brussels ms. 10147-58).

—IX (1845): 'Rapport de M. Gachard sur ses recherches en Espagne' (234-318).

—Ser. II vol. II (1851) 6-78: Gachet, 'Rapport . . . sur les manuscrits relatifs à l'histoire de la Belgique, qu'il a examinés à la Bibliothèque de la Haye.'

—IV (1852) 285-352: 'Rapport de M. Émile Gachet sur ses recherches dans plusieurs dépôts littéraires de France.' V (1853), 5-196: cont.

—X (1858) 8-100: Borgnet, 'Voyage littéraire en Italie.'

—XI (1858) 123-62: 'Rapport de M. Ernest Van Bruyssel sur les archives et les bibliothèques d'Angleterre.' 419-82; Kervyn de Lettenhove, 'Notes sur quelques manuscrits de la Bibliothèque de Bourgogne.'

—XII (1859) 19-82: 'Deuxième rapport de M. Van Bruyssel sur ses recherches dans les archives et les bibliothèques d'Angleterre.'

—Ser. III vol. III (1862) 119-59: E. Van Bruyssel, 'La Bibliothèque de Sir Th. Phillipps, Baronet.'

—IV (1863) 187-90: The same, 'Manuscrits relatifs à l'histoire de la Belgique, conservés dans la bibliothèque Egerton, au Musée Britannique.'

—V (1863) 235-390: Gachard, 'Notices des manuscrits concernant l'histoire de la Belgique qui existent à la Bibliothèque Impériale, à Vienne.'

—VI (1864) 25-218: The same, 'Une visite aux Archives et à la Bibliothèque Royale de Munich.'

—IX (1867) 245-90: Ruelens, 'Notes sur les bibliothèques de Milan, Rome et Florence.'

—X (1869) 219-44: Gachard, 'La Bibliothèque des princes Chigi, à Rome.'

—XI (1870) 27-202: The same, 'La Bibliothèque des princes Corsini, à Rome.' 245-344: The same, 'Les Archives Farnésiennes, à Naples.'

—Ser. IV vol. I (1873) 11-70: The same, 'Notice des manuscrits concernant l'histoire de la Belgique qui existent à la Bibliothèque Royale, à Berlin.' 211-386: The same, 'Les Archives du Vatican.'

—X (1882) 263-76: E. Pasquet, 'Notice sur les documents manuscrits se rapportant à la Belgique, qui se trouvent dans les archives et bibliothèques du royaume scandinave.'

—XII (1885) 184-86: Ch. Piot, 'Note sur les manuscrits de l'abbaye d'Everbode.'

—Ser. V. vol. II (1892) 139-84: A. Cauchie, 'Notes sur quelques sources manuscrites de l'histoire belge à Rome.'

—VI (1896) 415-56: E. Poncelet, 'Rapport

sur les cartulaires et documents manuscrits se rapportant à la Belgique, qui se trouvent dans les archives communales et hospitalières et dans les bibliothèques publiques et autres des provinces de Hainaut, Liège, Limbourg, Luxembourg et Namur.'

—VIII (1898) 113-70: U. Berlière, 'Notes sur les manuscrits de l'abbé Hugo d'Étival conservés à Nancy.'

—IX (1899) 357-422: M. Huisman, 'Inventaire des nouveaux manuscrits concernant l'histoire de la Belgique, acquis par la Bibliothèque royale de Berlin.'

W. Allen Jr., 'The four Corvinus Manuscripts in the United States,' *Bulletin of the New York Public Library* XLII (1938) 315-23. Covers New Haven (1 ms.) and New York (3 mss.).

Analecta Bollandiana. I (1882) 485-530; 609-32: 'Catalogus codicum hagiographicorum Bibliothecae Publicae Civitatis Namurcensis' (Namur, 12 mss.). II (1883) 130-60; 279-354: The same cont. (appendix of texts).

—III (1884) 167-216: 'Catalogus codicum hagiographicorum Bibliothecae Publicae Civitatis et Academiae Gandavensis' (Ghent, 20 mss.). IV (1885) 157-206: The same cont. (appendix of texts).

—V (1886) 313-83: 'Catalogus codicum hagiographicorum Bibliothecae publicae Civitatis et Academiae Leodiensis' (Liège, 25 mss.).

—VI (1887) 161-208: 'Catalogus Codicum Hagiographicorum Bibliothecae Regiae Hagensis' ('s Gravenhage, 23 Latin mss.).

—VIII (1889) 86-208: 'Catalogus codicum hagiographicorum Bibliothecae Civitatis Carnotensis' (Chartres, 36 mss.).

—IX (1890) 263-77: 'Catalogus codicum hagiographicorum Bibliothecae Civitatis Montensis' (Mons. 11 mss.).

—X (1891) 453-66: 'Catalogus codicum hagiographicorum Bibliothecae Civitatis Brugensis' (Bruges, 15 mss.).

—XI (1892) 205-368: 'Catalogus codicum hagiographicorum latinorum Bibliothecae Ambrosianae Mediolanensis' (Milan, 72 mss.).

—XII (1893) 43-73: 'Catalogus codicum hagiographicorum latinorum Bibliothecae publicae Cenomanensis' (Le Mans, 8 mss.). 409-40: 'Catalogus codicum hagiographicorum Bibliothecae Cl. Viri Alphonsi Wins apud Praetorium Nivigellense iudicis' (Nivelles, 5 mss.).

—XIV (1895) 5-88: 'De codicibus hagiographicis Johannis Gielemans Canonici Regularis in Rubea Valle prope Bruxellas.' 231-83: 'Catalogus codicum hagiographicorum qui Vindobonae asservantur in bibliotheca privata serenissimi Caesaris Austriaci' (Wien, Kaiserliche Privatbibliothek, 31 mss.).

—XX (1901) 361-470: 'Catalogus codicum hagiographicorum latinorum Bibliothecae Publicae Duacensis' (Douai).

—XXIII (1904) 129-275: A. Poncelet, 'Catalogus codicum hagiographicorum latinorum Bibliothecae Publicae Rotomagensis' (Rouen).

—XXIV (1905) 425-72: H. Moretus, 'Catalogus codicum hagiographicorum latinorum Bibliothecae Bollandianae.'

—XXVIII (1909) 417-78: A. Poncelet, 'Catalogus codicum hagiographicorum latinorum Bibliothecae Nationalis Taurinensis' (Torino).

—XXX (1911) 137-251: The same, 'Catalogus codicum hagiographicorum latinorum bibliothecarum Neapolitanarum' (Naples).

—XXXI (1912) 45-48: The same, 'Catalogus codicum hagiographicorum latinorum musei Meermanno-Westreeniani' ('s Gravenhage).

—XXXII (1913) 408-38: The same, 'Catalogus codicum hagiographicorum latinorum bibliothecae Universitatis Wirziburgensis' (Würzburg).

—XXXIV-XXXV (1915-16) 228-305: H. Moretus, 'Catalogus codicum hagiographicorum latinorum bibliothecae scholae medicinae in Universitate Montepessulanensi' (Montpellier).

—XLI (1923) 326-56: A. Poncelet, 'Catalogus codicum hagiographicorum latinorum bibliothecae Capituli Ecclesiae cathedralis Eporediensis' (Ivrea).

—XLII (1924) 320-70: The same, 'Catalogus codicum hagiographicorum latinorum bibliothecae Universitatis Bononiensis' (Bologna).

—XLIII (1925) 330-76: The same, 'Catalogus codicum hagiographicorum latinorum Bibliothecae Capituli Novariensis' (Novara).

—XLVI (1928) 81-148: P. Grosjean, 'Catalogus codicum hagiographicorum latinorum Bibliothecarum Dubliniensium' (Dublin). Covers Trinity College (82-108), Marsh's Library (108-11), Franciscan Library (111-16, now in Killiney), St. Patrick's College, Maynooth (116-18).

—XLVII (1929) 31-38: The same, 'Catalogus codicum hagiographicorum latinorum bibliothecarum Edinburgensium' (Edinburgh, 4 mss.). 241-306: 'Catalogus codicum hagiographicorum latinorum, Bibliothecae Publicae Audomaropolitanae' (St. Omer).

—XLIX (1931) 102-16. cont. (appendix). 241-75: 'Catalogus codicum hagiographicorum latinorum seminarii et ecclesiae cathedralis Treverensis' (Trier).

—LI (1933) 337-77: 'Catalogus codicum hagiographicorum latinorum Bibliothecae Capituli Ecclesiae Cathedralis Beneventanae' (Benevento, 18 mss.).

—LII (1934) 157-285: M. Coens, 'Catalogus codicum hagiographicorum latinorum bibliothecae civitatis Treverensis' (Trier).

—LV (1937) 226-43: F. Halkin, 'Catalogus codicum hagiographicorum latinorum Paderbornensium et Osnabrugensium' (Paderborn and Osnabrück).

—LXI (1943) 140-201: M. Coens, 'Catalogus codicum hagiographicorum latinorum Archivi historici civitatis Coloniensis' (Köln). (NNUT; vol. XXXIV-XXXV: NN)

P. d'Ancona. *La miniatura fiorentina (secoli XI-XVI)*. 2 vols. Florence 1912. vol. II: describes 1717 mss. Indices of libraries and authors.

G. Andres, *Catalogo dei codici manoscritti della famiglia Capilupi in Mantova*. Mantua 1797. 364 pp. 129 mss. Some remain in Suzzara, many went to the Biblioteca Nazionale, Rome, the others are scattered. (MH)

(G. Andres) *Lettera dell' abate Giovanni Andres al sig. abate Giacomo Morelli sopra alcuni codici delle Biblioteche Capitolari di Novara e di Vercelli*. Parma 1802. 110 pp. No index. (NN)

M. Andrieu, *Les Ordines Romani du Haut Moyen Age*. I. *Les Manuscrits*. (Spicilegium Sacrum Lovaniense II). Louvain 1931. xxiii, 631 pp. p. 32-464: List of mss. by cities. Index of mss. (581-83). (Pierpont Morgan Library).

Annuario del Cuerpo facultativo de Archiveros, Bibliotecarios y Anticuarios. I (1881, published 1882). Lists some manuscripts at Madrid University (197-98), Valencia (240-41), Palma (252-53), Zaragoza (265-66), Oviedo (274-76), Huesca (286-88), Granada (299-300). No index. (NN)

—II (1882, published 1883). Lists some mss. at Salamanca (149-50), Sevilla University (163), Zaragoza (196-226), Orihuela (251), Burgos (276-78), Tarragona (283). No index. (Hispanic Soviety).

Archiv der Gesellschaft für ältere deutsche Geschichtskunde. I (1820) 111-14: Ebert, 'Verzeichniss der Handschriften von Historikern des Mittelalters auf der königl. Bibliothek zu Dresden.' 143-53; 226-79: Dümge and Mone, 'Literarische Reise, durch einen Theil des vordern Schwabens und der Schweiz.' 317-21: Delius, 'Auszug aus dem Verzeichniss der Handschriften der Profan-Schriftsteller der kaiserl. Bibliothek zu Wien.' 322-24: Matthiäs, 'Verzeichniss der auf der Stadtbibliothek zu Frankfurt am Main befindlichen Handschriften, die für die Sammlung etwa benutzt werden könnten.' 325-26: 'Nachricht des... Herrn Völkel in Cassel von den in dortiger churfürstl. Bibliothek vorhandenen Handschriften derjenigen Quellenschriftsteller, deren Titel in der

Ankündigung der Gesammtausgabe ange-geben sind.' 327-28: 'Verzeichniss der-jenigen in der herrschaftlichen Bibliothek zu Fulda sich befindenden Manuscripte historischer Schriftsteller des Mittelalters, welche der Gesellschaft für Deutschlands ältere Geschichtskunde etwa zum Ge-brauche dienen könnten.' 375-418: C. Dümge and F. Mone, 'Adnotationes de codicibus manuscriptis historicis et anec-dotis in itinere brevi Alemannico repertis.'. Covers Stuttgart, Einsiedeln, Muri, etc. 430-39: I. F. Mone, 'Über einige Hand-schriften deutscher Geschichtsquellen.' Covers Heidelberg. 466-74: Pertz, 'Hand-schriften der königl. Bibliothek zu Han-nover, zur Geschichte des deutschen Mit-telalters.'

—II (1820) 75-76: Wilken, 'Verzeichniss der für die Sammlung brauchbaren Hand-schriften in der königl. Bibliothek zu Berlin.' 197-212: Schlosser, 'Auszug aus dem Verzeichnisse der Handschriften der St. Bartholomäus-Stifts-Bibliothek zu Frankfurt a.M.'

—III (1821) 209-65: Dümge and Mone cont. 266-80: J. D. G. Compter, 'Ausführliche Beschreibung dreier, auf der Jenaischen Universitäts-Bibliothek befindlichen Ma-nuscripte.' 391-413: G. H. Pertz, 'Auszug aus dem neuern Handschriftenverzeich-niss der K. K. Hofbibliothek' (Vienna). 414-30: 'Verzeichniss verschiedener Hand-schriften deutscher Geschichts-Quellen in der Bibliothek des Vatikan.' Arranged alphabetically. 431-46: D. Färber, 'Ver-zeichniss von Handschriften deutscher Geschichtsquellen in den Bibliotheken zu Oxford und Cambridge.' Alphabetical. 447-50: Grautoff, 'Verzeichniss der auf der Stadtbibliothek zu Lübeck befindlichen Handschriften, die bei der Sammlung deutscher Geschichtsquellen vielleicht be-nutzt werden könnten.' 451-53: Stentzel, 'Verzeichniss einiger Handschriften deut-scher Geschichts-Quellen der Universitäts-Bibliothek in Breslau.'

—IV (1822) 93-120: Stenzel, 'Erstes Ver-zeichniss der auf der Central-Bibliothek in Breslau befindlichen, zur Geschichte Deutschlands im Mittelalter gehörigen Handschriften der Quellenschriftsteller ...' 139-67: Pertz, 'Verzeichniss der Hand-schriften der St. Marcus-Bibliothek zu Venedig, für deutsche und italienische Geschichte des Mittelalters.' 264-71: 'Manuscripta apographa im Besitz des Hrn. Gubernialsecretärs Cerroni in Brünn.' 285-336: Dümge and Mone, 'Adnota-tiones,' cont. 337-51: Wigand, 'Berich-te aus Westphalen über die daselbst vor-räthigen Quellen deutscher Geschichte. pt. 1, Corvey.' 515-20: Tross, 'Verzeich-niss derjenigen Handschriften auf der Pau-linischen Bibliothek zu Münster, die ent-weder ganz historischen Inhalts sind, oder doch zur Erläuterung einzelner Punkte in der Geschichte dienlich seyn können.' 528-35: G. H. Pertz, 'Auszug aus dem Handschriftenverzeichniss der Fürstlich Chigi'schen Bibliothek in Rom.' 535-42: The same, 'Auszug aus dem Handschrif-tenverzeichniss der Fürstlich Barberini-schen Bibliothek zu Rom.'

—V (1824) 1-514: G. H. Pertz, 'Italiänische Reise vom November 1821 bis August 1823.' 527-31: F. C. Levret, 'Nachträge zum Reisebericht der Herrn Dümge und Mone im vierten Bande des Archivs S. 286.' Covers Stuttgart. 575-92: Bluhme, 'Vermischte Nachrichten von italiänischen Bibliotheken und Archiven im Sommer 1822.' Covers Verona, Capitolare (575-80); Vatican, Fondo Ottoboniano (581-84, old shelf marks); Bologna, Collegio di Spagna (590-91); Perugia, Comunale (591-92). 593-630: The same, 'Bericht über die im Sommer 1823 in Oberitalien ausgeführten Arbeiten.' Covers Venice, Marciana.

—VI (1831) 1-34: Ebert, 'Handschriften der Herzoglichen Bibliothek zu Wolfen-büttel zur ältern deutschen Geschichte.' 35-39: Tross, 'Verzeichniss einiger histo-rischen Handschriften welche sich auf der gräfl. Plettenbergschen Bibliothek zu

Nordkirchen vorfinden.' 33 mss. 40-79: Jäck, 'Handschriften der Königl. Bibliothek zu Bamberg.' 80-92: Ukert, 'Handschriften der Herzogl. Bibliothek zu Gotha.' 93-94: Stenzel, 'Zweites Verzeichniss der auf der Central-Bibliothek in Breslau befindlichen, zur Geschichte Deutschlands im Mittelalter gehörigen Handschriften der Quellenschriftsteller.' 95-99: The same, 'Verzeichniss der zur Geschichte Deutschlands im Mittelalter gehörigen Handschriften, welche sich in der Bibliothek zu St. Elisabeth in Breslau befinden'. 27 mss. 100-31: G. H. Pertz, 'Auszug aus dem Verzeichniss der Handschriften des K. K. geheimen Haus-, Hof-, und Staatsarchivs zu Wien.' 132-39: 'Auszug aus Martin Georg und Jul. Niclas Kovachich von Schenkwitz, Repertorium expeditionis diplomatico literariae per archiva et bibliothecas Hungariae, Transylvaniae, Slavoniae et Croatiae, annis 1810 usque 1816. Covers, Zagreb, and Kalocsa. 140-61: Pertz, 'Verzeichniss von Handschriften zur Deutschen Geschichte im Museum des Herrn Niklas von Jankovich zu Pesth' (Budapest). 67 mss. 162-81: A. Muchar, 'Handschriften des Stiftes Admont in Steyermark.' 59 mss. 182-99: Pertz, 'Nachträgliche Bemerkungen über Handschriften Oesterreichischer Stifter.' Covers Heiligenkreuz (182-84), Lilienfeld (185-86), Klosterneuburg (186-90), Göttweih (190-92), Melk (192-94), Seitenstetten (194-96) and Kremsmünster (196-99). 200-02: The same, 'Handschriften der Königl. Universitäts-Bibliothek zu Göttingen.' 203-05: The same, 'Handschriften der Churfürstlichen Bibliothek zu Cassel.' 206-07: The same, 'Handschriften der Königl. Universitäts-Bibliothek zu Halle.' 5 mss. 207-14: The same, 'Handschriften der Raths-Bibliothek zu Leipzig.' 214-21: The same, 'Handschriften der Königl. Universitäts-Bibliothek zu Leipzig.' 222-28: 'Handschriften des Königl. Sächsischen Geheimen Archivs zu Dresden.' 21 mss. 229-48: Lappenberg, 'Verzeichniss der Handschriften der Hamburger Stadt-Bibliothek für die ältere deutsche Geschichte.' 249-50: 'Handschriften in der Sammlung des Kaiserl. Russischen Reichskanzlers Grafen Romanzow zu St. Petersburg.' 7 mss. (NNU)

—VII (1839) 1-19: G. H. Pertz, 'Reise nach den südlichen Niederlanden, Paris und England, vom 16. Oktober 1826 bis 3. November 1827.' 34-36: 'Brüsseler Handschriften.' 36-72: 'Handschriften der Königl. Bibliothek zu Paris.' 72-82: 'Handschriften des Britischen Museums.' 82-83: 'Handschriften der Bibliothek des Erzbischofs von Canterbury in Lambethhouse zu London.' 83-84: 'Handschriften der Universitätsbibliothek zu Cambridge. 84-87: 'Handschriften der Collegien zu Cambridge.' 87-93: 'Handschriften der Universitätsbibliothek zu Oxford.' 93-95: 'Handschriften der Collegien zu Oxford.' 95-101: 'Handschriften des Sir Thomas Phillipps zu Middlehill.' 102: 'Handschriften der bischöflichen Bibliothek zu Durham.' 102-04: 'Handschriften anderer Bibliotheken in England und Irland.' 105: 'Bibliotheca manuscripta Stowensis.' 105-08: Pertz, 'Reise nach Franken und Baiern vom 24. Juli bis 29 August 1833.' 108-11: 'Handschriften der Königl. Bibliothek zu Würzburg.' 111-12: Handschriften der Königl. Bibliothek zu Erlangen.' 112: 'Handschriften der Stadtbibliothek zu Nürnberg.' 112-13: 'Handschriften der Königl. Universitätsbibliothek zu München.' 113-28: 'Handschriften der Königl. Hofbibliothek zu München.' 128-30: Pertz, 'Reise nach den Niederlanden im August und September 1835.' 130-32: 'Handschriften der Königl. Bibliothek im Haag' ('s Gravenhage). 132-33: 'Handschriften der Universitäts-Bibliothek zu Uetrecht.' 133-38: 'Handschriften der Universitätsbibliothek zu Leyden.' 138-42: Böhmer, 'Handschriften der Stadtbibliothek zu Trier.' 142-45: Lappenberg, 'Reise nach England und Irland im Sommer 1836.' 146-50: Waitz, 'Untersuchung

der handschriftlichen Sammlungen zu Kopenhagen im Herbste 1836.' 150-65: 'Handschriften der Königl. Bibliothek.' 165-67: 'Handschriften der Universitätsbibliothek.' 168-73: Pertz, 'Reise nach der Schweiz und Savoyen im August und September 1837.' 174-76: 'Handschriften der Universitätsbibliothek zu Basel.' 176-77: 'Handschriften der Universitätsbibliothek zu Genf.' 178: 'Handschriften der Universitätsbibliothek zu Chambéry.' 178-80: 'Handschriften des Stifts Engelberg.' 180: 'Handschriften des Stifts Einsiedeln.' 181: 'Handschriften der Universitätsbibliothek zu Zürich.' 181-82: 'Handschriften des Stifts Rheinau.' 183-91: Waitz, 'Reise nach dem südlichen Frankreich vom August bis November 1837.' 191-206: 'Handschriften der Universitätsbibliothek zu Montpellier.' 206-07: 'Handschriften des Musée Fabre zu Montpellier.' 207-08: 'Handschriften der Bibliothek zu Carpentras.' 208-10: 'Handschriften des Musée Calvet zu Avignon.' 211-14: 'Handschriften der Bibliothek zu Lyon.' 214-17: 'Handschriften der Bibliothek zu Dijon.' 217-20: 'Handschriften der Bibliothek zu Troyes.' 220-21: 'Handschriften der Bibliothek zu Chalons.' 221-26: Pertz, 'Handschriften der Herzogl. Bibliothek zu Wolfenbüttel, ein Nachtrag zum Archiv VI 3ff.'
—VIII (1843) 1-3: Pertz, 'Reise nach Paris im October und November 1839.' 3-24: Waitz, 'Reise nach Lothringen, Paris, Luxemburg und Trier vom October 1839 bis August 1840.' 25-101: Bethmann, 'Reise durch die Niederlande, Belgien und Frankreich vom Juni 1839 bis September 1841.' 102-252: 'Heinrich Friedrich Knust's Reise nach Frankreich und Spanien in den Jahren 1839 bis 1841.' 253-59: Pertz, 'Reise nach dem Elsass vom 2. bis 19. September 1841.' 260-83: Waitz, 'Reise nach Thüringen und Sachsen vom September bis November 1841, nebst Bemerkungen von der Reise nach Berlin im Mai 1842.' 284-860: 'Handschriftenverzeichnisse.' Covers Paris (284-366); Meaux (366-67); Rouen (367-74); Le Havre (374-76); Évreux (376-78); Avranches (378-85); Chartres (385-91); Orléans (391-92); Laon (392-93); Reims (393-95); Amiens (395-401); Arras (401-04); Boulogne (404-07): St. Omer (408-21): Douai (421-31); Cambrai (431-35); Valenciennes (436-43); Verdun (443-48); St. Mihiel (448-49); Metz (450-58); collection Noel in Nancy (458-60); Strasbourg (461-66); Colmar (466-68); Mons (468-75); Namur (475-77); Liège (477-81); Louvain (481-86); Bruxelles (486-549); Ghent (549-56; 552-553: Cathedral); Bruges (556-58); Tournai (559-64); Anvers (564-66); 'sGravenhage (566-70); Leiden (570-78); Amsterdam (579-81); Haarlem (582); Utrecht (582-88); Groningen (588-91); Leeuwarden (591-92); Luxembourg (592-96); Trier (596-610); Cues (610-12); Koblenz (612-17); Darmstadt (617-22); Freiburg (622); Meersburg (623); Fulda (624-27); Corvey (627-29); Hannover (630-53); Halberstadt (653-59); Quedlinburg (660-62); Merseburg (662-71); Meiningen (671-74); Koburg (674-75); Gotha (675-76); Erfurt (676-85); Weimar (685-93); Jena (694-705); Zeitz (705-06); Altenburg (706-07); Zwickau (707-11); Freiberg (711-12); Wurzen (712-15); Dresden (715-23); Zwettl (724-29). 729-32: Böhmer, 'Kurze Nachrichten über einige im Jahre 1833 zu Wien gesehenen Handschriften.' Then lists for Schaffhausen (733-36); Einsiedeln (736-52; by Gallus Morel); British Museum (753-62); Middlehill (Cheltenham, 762-68); Madrid (768-809); Escorial (809-21); Sevilla (821); Toledo (822); Valencia (822); Berlin (823-60). Index for the whole volume (861-97).
—IX (1847) 463-85: G. H. Pertz, 'Reise nach Böhmen, Oestreich, Salzburg und Mähren im September 1843.' Covers Praha (469ff.), Salzburg (481ff.), Olomouc (484-85). 486-504: The same, 'Reise nach London und Middlehill, Juli bis September 1844.' Covers also Holkham Hall (503-04). 505-07: Lappenberg, 'Handschriften

der Hamburger Stadtbibliothek.' 513-658: Bethmann, 'Reise durch Deutschland und Italien in den Jahren 1844-1846.' Covers Pommersfelden (525ff.), Bamberg (548-49), Nürnberg (549ff.), Eichstätt (551-74), Giessen (574ff.), Heidelberg (579ff.), Augsburg (587), Lindau (587-88), St. Gallen (Stadtbibliothek, 588-93; Stiftsarchiv, 593-99); Torino (599-611; Biblioteca Reale, 599-601), Ivrea (611-27), Aosta (627-36), Milano (636-42; Brera: 636-637; S. Ambrogio, 638-40), Fermo (642-44), Valletta (644-45), Istanbul (645ff.). (NN)

—X (1851) 426-693: Wattenbach, 'Reise nach Österreich in den Jahren 1847, 1848, 1849.' Covers Wien (447-593), Klosterneuburg (593-94), Heiligenkreuz (594-600), Göttweih (600-01), Melk (601-07), Zwettl (608-11), Linz (611-13), Salzburg (614-19), Mattsee (619-20), Graz (621-25), Reun (625-26), Vorau (626-31), Admont (631-44), Praha (657-70), Hohenfurt (Vyšší Brod, 671), Olomouc (671-85), Brno (685-92), Milulov (692-93). (NNU)

—XI (1858) 248-514: 'Beschreibung einiger Handschriften welche in den Jahren 1839-42 näher untersucht worden sind.' 515-32: Bethmann, 'Handschriften-Verzeichnisse.' Covers Wiesbaden (515), Bruxelles (515ff.), Valenciennes (518ff.), Lille (526ff.) Winnocsberg (Bergues, 2 mss., p. 530), Alencon (530ff.). 688-756: 'Aus Preussischen Handschriften-Verzeichnissen.' Covers Berlin (688), Frankfurt a.O. (689), Stettin (689), Greifswald (689-90), Stralsund (690), Stargard (690), Köslin (691), Königsberg (691ff.), Danzig (693-94), Elbing (694-95), Frauenburg (695), Toruń (695), Poznań (696), Gniezno (696-97), Breslau (697ff.), Brieg (711-12), Diebau (712), Fürstenstein (712ff.), Görlitz (714ff.) Liegnitz (717-18), Lüben (718), Löwenberg (718), Oels (719), Magdeburg (719ff.), Erfurt (724ff.), Halberstadt (727), Halle (727ff.), Merseburg (729), Mühlhausen (729ff.), Nordhausen (731), Pforta (731-32), Quedlinburg (732), Sangerhausen (732), Zeitz (733), Münster (733ff.), Arnsberg

(735), Soest (735), Dortmund (735), Herford (735-36), Paderborn (736-37), Soest (737-38), Aachen (738), Bonn (738ff.), Kleve (740), Koblenz (741), Köln (741ff.), Cues (746), Düsseldorf (747ff.), Trier (756). 757-77: 'Handschriften des Geh. Staats- und Kabinets-Archives zu Berlin.' 778-79: Bethmann, 'Handschriften zu Lüneburg.' 782-85: O. Abel, 'Grossherzogl. Hofbibliothek zu Karlsruhe.' 791-804: v. Muralt, 'Handschriften der Kaiserlichen Bibliothek zu St. Petersburg' (Leningrad). (NN)

—XII (1872) 201-425: L. Bethmann, 'Nachrichten über die von ihm für die MGH benutzten Sammlungen von Handschriften und Urkunden Italiens, aus dem Jahre 1854.' Covers Vatican (210ff.), Rome (374ff.). 474-758: The same cont. Covers Subiaco (485ff.), Farfa (489ff.), Monte Cassino (498ff.), Napoli (514ff.), Salerno (529-30), Assisi (538-41), Gubbio (542-43), Perugia (546ff.), Todi (549-50), Fermo (557ff.), Bologna (573ff.), Ferrara (587), Cesena (587-88), Vercelli (605-06), Novara (607), Milano (609ff.), Monza (621-22), Pavia (623-24), Venezia (638ff.), Verona (658ff.), Padova (667ff.), Treviso (670-72), Parma (687ff.), Modena (696-700), Lucca (704ff.), Firenze (718ff.), Pisa (735ff.), Siena (744). This article contains also much on statistics and bibliography of Italian collections.

The lists of mss. in the *Archiv* are poorly indexed, in most cases narrowly selective of strictly historical material, and often superseded, yet they remain indispensable for a number of collections. For continuation see *Neues Archiv*.

Archives des missions scientifiques et littéraires. I (1850) 241-92: 'Mission en Italie confiée à MM. Daremberg et Renan. Premier rapport à M. le Ministre de l'instruction publique et des cultes. 365-409: 'Rapport adressé à M. le Ministre de l'instruction publique et des cultes par M. Ernest Renan, chargé d'une mission scientifique et littéraire en Italie, conjointement avec M. le docteur Daremberg.' 429-44: 'Premier rapport,' cont. 485-502: Dom Pitra, 'Premier rapport à M. le Ministre de l'instruction publique et des cultes, sur quelques recherches littéraires et historiques dans les principales bibliothèques de l'Angleterre.' 557-79: The same, 'Second Rapport.' 632-51: 'Premier (Deuxième, Troisième) rapport adressé à M. le Ministre de l'instruction publique, par M. F. Danjou, chargé, en 1847, d'une mission en Italie.' Covers medieval music and musical theory.

—II (1851) 113-68; 470-71; 484-89: Ch. Daremberg, 'Notices et extraits des manuscrits médicaux grecs et latins des principales bibliothèques d'Angleterre.' 549-59: 'Rapport adressé à M. le Ministre de l'instruction publique et des cultes, par M. Ernest Renan, sur quelques recherches faites en Angleterre.'

—III (1854) 1-76: Daremberg, 'Notices . . .' cont. Covers mostly Greek mss. 77-149: 'Rapport adressé à M. le Ministre de l'instruction publique et des cultes, par M. Geffroy . . . chargé d'une mission en Danemark et en Suède.'

—IV (1856) 93-113: 'Rapport présenté à M. le Ministre . . . par M. l'abbé Pitra, sur une mission littéraire accomplie en Angleterre pendant les mois d'août, septembre, octobre, novembre et décembre 1849, janvier et février 1850.' 153-84: The same, 'Deuxième rapport.' 185-401: M. Geffroy, 'Notices et extraits des manuscrits concernant l'histoire ou la littérature de la France qui sont conservés dans les bibliothèques ou archives de Suède, Danemark et Norvège.' Covers Stockholm (253ff.). 473-652: The same cont. Covers Stockholm and Skokloster.

—V (1856) 49-63: E. de Certain, 'Rapport à M. le Ministre de l'instruction publique sur une mission accomplie à Rome en 1854 et 1855.' 117-28: The same,' Deuxième rapport.' 365-480: Geffroy, cont. Covers Upsala and Oslo. This report was also published separately (Paris 1855, 512 pp.). No index.

—VI (1857) 241-74: 'Premier rapport adressé à Son Excellence Monsieur le Ministre de l'instruction publique et des cultes par M. Alphonse Dantier, sur la mission qu'il a été chargé de remplir en Suisse, en Allemagne et en Belgique, pendant les mois d'août et de septembre 1855.' Concerns the correspondence of Mabillon. 274-502: The same. 'Deuxième rapport.'

—X (Ser. II vol. II, 1865) 231-319: E. Boutaric, 'Rapport . . . sur une mission en Belgique à l'effet de rechercher les documents inédits relatifs à l'histoire de France au moyen âge.' 359-72: A. Demersay, 'Rapports sur les résultats d'une mission dans les archives d'Espagne et de Portugal.' 373-432: Le Comte Hector de la Ferrière, 'Rapport sur les recherches faites à la Bibliothèque Impériale de Saint-Petersbourg concernant les lettres originales et manuscrits français sortis de France.' 433-56: C. Hippeau, 'Rapport sur une mission en Italie.'

—XI (III, 1866) 1-53: De la Ferrière, 'Deuxième Rapport.' 247-328: Paul Meyer, 'Rapport sur une mission littéraire en Angleterre.'

—XII (IV, 1867) 1-114: De la Ferrière, 'Troisième Rapport.' 115-67: Meyer, 'Deuxième Rapport.'

—XIII (V, 1868) 139-272: The same, 'Troisième rapport.' 305-422: Le Comte H. de la Ferrière, 'Premier rapport sur les recherches faites au British Museum et au Record Office, concernant les documents relatifs à l'histoire de France au XVIe et au XVIIe siècle.'

—XVII (Ser. III vol. II, 1875) 1-146: The same, 'Deuxième rapport.' 315-56: A. Lecoy de la Marche, 'Rapport sur une mission en Italie et à Marseille.' 497-627: Ch. E. Ruelle, 'Rapports sur une mission littéraire et philologique en Espagne.' With index.

—XVIII (III, 1876) 607-732: De la Ferrière, 'Troisième Rapport.'

—XIX (IV, 1877) 99-133: E. Sayons, 'Mémoire sur une mission en Hongrie.'

—XX (V, 1879) 85-110: Ch. Fierville, 'Renseignements sur quelques manuscrits latins des bibliothèques d'Espagne et principalement sur les manuscrits de Quintilien.' No index. 111-36: Ch. Graux, 'Rapport sur une mission en Espagne.' Treats Greek mss. but adds general data on collections. 137-212: F. Molard, 'Rapport sur les bibliothèques de Gênes, Inventaire des manuscrits relatifs à la Corse.'

—XXVIII (XIII, 1887) 819-54: A. Berthelot, 'Rapport sur les manuscrits alchimiques de Rome.'

—XXIX (XIV, 1888) 133-336: Ch. Molinier, 'Rapport à M. le Ministre de l'instruction publique sur une mission exécutée en Italie de février à avril 1885.' Concerns inquisition and heresy.

—XXXI (XV bis, 1890): General index of the entire periodical.

Archivum Franciscanum Historicum. I (1908) 116-25; 433-42; II (1909) 123-30; 319-24; 480-84; III (1910) 333-40; 551-58; 739-48; IV (1911) 360-65; 748-54; V (1912) 352-59; VI (1913) 156-67; 328-37; 748-57: A. Lopez, 'Descriptio codicum Franciscanorum Bibliothecae Riccardianae Florentinae.'

—I (1908) 623-26: S. Gaddoni, 'Descriptio duorum codicum Bibliothecae S. Cataldi (Mutinae)' (Modena.).

—II (1909) 642-45: S. Gaddoni, 'Descriptio codicum Franciscanorum qui in Bibliotheca D.D. Matthaei Campori Marchionis Mutinensis exstant.'

—IV (1911) 354-59; 589-93; V (1912) 102-09; 737-51: H. Lippens, 'Descriptio codicum Franciscanorum Bibliothecae Academiae Leodiensis' (Liége).

—V (1912) 89-94: A. Corna, 'Codices olim franciscani in Bibliotheca Landiana Placentiae' (Piacenza). 95-101: S. Gaddoni, 'Codices Bibliothecae Estensis Mutinae' (Modena).

—VI (1913) 546-56: H. Lippens, 'Descriptio codicum Franciscanorum Bibliothecae Namurcensis' (Namur).

—VII (1914) 122-31; 341-46; 527-32; 739-48: The same, 'Descriptio codicum Franciscanorum bibliothecae maioris Seminarii Leodiensis.' 749-59: Th. A. O'Reilly, 'Franciscan Manuscripts in the Convent, Merchant's Quay, Dublin.' 6 mss. (NNUT)

—VIII (1915) 226-73; 618-57; IX (1916) 395-442; XIII (1920) 586-603; XIV (1921) 243-58; XV (1922) 155-70; 508-24; XVI (1923) 545-56: S. Tosti, 'Descriptio codicum Franciscanorum Bibliothecae Riccardianae Florentinae.'

—XXI (1928) 362-70; 591-600; XXII (1929) 391-400; 548-57; XXIII (1930) 383-89; XXIV (1931) 370-78; 523-34: H. Lippens, 'Descriptio codicum Belgo-franciscalium diversis in locis asservatorum.'

—XLIV (1951) 191-209. L. Meier, 'Aufzeichnungen aus vernichteten Handschriften des Würzburger Minoritenklosters.'

—XLV (1952) 171-92. G. Pagnani, 'Alcuni codici della libreria di S. Giacomo della Marca, scoperti recentemente.' Describes 12 mss. in the Archivio dei Frati Minori delle Marche, Falconara.

—XLVIII (1955) 131-46. The same, cont. mss. 13-32.

—XLIX (1956) 434-482. S. Clasen and J. Van Gurp, 'Nachbonaventurianische Franziskusquellen in niederländischen und deutschen Handschriften des Mittelalters.' Covers Anvers, Minderbroederklooster (p. 437, 2 mss.); Sint Agatha, Kruisherenklooster (p. 444, 1 ms.); Weert, Minderbroederklooster (2 mss); Wien, Franziskanerkonventualen (1 ms.); Wittem, Redemptoristenklooster (1 ms.).

Catalogue of the Manuscripts at Ashburnham Place. Part the First, comprising a collection formed by Professor Libri. London n.d. 1923 mss. *Part the Second, comprising a collection formed by Mons. J. Barrois.* London n.d. 702 mss. *Appendix.* London n.d. 251 mss. Index, separately printed under the title: *A Catalogue of the Manuscripts at Ashburnham Place.* London 1853. 173 unnumbered pages. The Libri collection went to Florence (except for a few items that went to Paris), the other collections were scattered. (Pierpont Morgan Library).

Catalogue of a Portion of the Collection of Manuscripts known as the 'Appendix,' made by the late Earl of Ashburnham. London 1899. 100 pp. 177 mss. (Pierpont Morgan Library).

The Ashburnham Library. Catalogue of the Portion of the famous Collection of Manuscripts the property of the Rt. Hon. the Earl of Ashburnham known as the Barrois Collection. London 1901. 229 pp. 628 mss. (Pierpont Morgan Library). Cf. below, Omont.

T. Ayuso Marazuela, 'Manuscritos bíblicos españoles del ciclo aragonés,' *Universidad* (Zaragoza) XVIII (1941) 529-50; XX (1943) 201-31; XXI (1944) 24-68; XXII (1945) 1-50; XXIII (1946) 161-210 (NN)

B. Balbinus, *Bohemia docta,* ed. R. Ungar. 3 vols. in 2, Prague 1776-80. Pt. III, 230 pp.: 'De Bibliothecis et manuscriptis codicibus in Bohemia.' Covers several public, monastic and private collections. Largely superseded. The same, ed. Candidus a S. Theresia, Prague 1777, vol. II, 116 pp. Contains the same material. (DLC)

E. Barwiński, L. Birkenmajer, and J. Łosc, *Sprawozdanie z Poszukiwań w Szwecyi.* Cracow 1914. XXVII, 364 pp. Describes 451 mss. concerning Poland in Linköping, Lund, Stockholm, Uppsala, and other Swedish libraries. (MH)

A. Beccaria, *I codici di medicina del periodo presalernitano.* Rome 1956. 500 pp. 145 mss.

Beiträge zur Geschichte und Literatur, vorzüglich aus den Archiven und Bibliotheken des Kantons Aargau I (1846-47). p. 107-26: H. Kurz, 'Die Aargauische Kantonsbibliothek.' Lists over 30 mss. p. 461-87: Streuber, 'Die Briefsammlung der Reformatoren aus der Stadtbibliothek zu Zofingen.' (NN)

V. Beltrán de Heredia, 'Los manuscritos de los teólogos de la Escuela Salmantina,' *Ciencia Tomista* XLII (1930) 327-49. Arranged by authors. Gives mss. in Spanish collections. No index.

M. Bernards, 'Zur Überlieferung mittelalterlicher theologischer Schriften, Neue Handschriften,' *Recherches de Théologie ancienne et mediévale* 19 (1952) 327-36. Arranged by authors. Covers Basel, Darmstadt, Düsseldorf, Frankfurt, Koblenz, Köln, Mainz, Milano (Ambrosiana), Salzburg (St. Peter), Vatican. (NNUT)

[E. Bernardus], *Catalogi librorum manuscriptorum Angliae et Hiberniae.* 2 vols. in 1, Oxford 1697. vol. I pt. I: Oxford, Bodleian Library. 8716 mss. Index.

—vol. I pt. II: Oxford Colleges. 2525 mss. Index.

—vol. I pt. III: Cambridge, University Library and Colleges. 2502 mss. Index.

—vol. II pt. I: York Minster Library (p. 3-4, 65 mss.); Durham Cathedral (p. 5-12, 678 mss.); Carlisle Cathedral (p. 13, 8 mss.); Worcester Cathedral (p. 16-22, 252 mss.); Salisbury Cathedral (p. 23-27, 164 mss.); Westminster (p. 27-29, 230 mss.); Winchester Cathedral (p. 30, 17 mss.); Winchester College (p. 31, 43 mss.); Lichfield Cathedral (p. 32, 65 mss.); Coventry College (p. 33-34, 17 mss.); Bristol City Library (p. 40, 15 mss.); Gray's Inn, London (p. 41-42, 25 mss.); Hereford Cathedral (p. 43-45, 206 mss.); Eton College (p. 46-48 ,115 mss.); Exeter Cathedral (p. 55-56, 46 mss.); Gresham College, London (p. 74-84, 562 mss.); Wells Cathedral (p. 104, 3 mss.); Sion College, London (p. 106-07, 68 mss.); Viscount of Longueville (p. 113-174, 187 Yelverton mss., now in the British Museum); College of Arms, London (p. 175-78, 150 mss.); Lincoln's Inn, London (p. 179-82, 192 mss.); Warwick Church (p. 203-06, 36 mss.); Samuel Pepys (p. 207-10, 129 mss., now in Cambridge, Magdalen College); Canterbury Cathedral (p. 223-26, 86 mss., and p. 389, 13 mss.); Royal collection, London (p. 239-48, 970 mss.); Hans Sloane (p. 251-55, 264 mss.); Gray's Inn, London (p. 255 bis, 12 mss.) Also many private collections together 10072 mss. Index.

—vol. II pt. II: Ireland. Covers Trinity

College, Dublin (p. 16-48, no. 141-849). Index. Still indispensable, especially for some of the Cathedral Libraries.

L. Bertalot, *Eine humanistische Anthologie.* Thesis, Berlin 1908. 93 pp. p. 89-90: Index of mss.

The same, *Humanistisches Studienheft eines Nürnberger Scholaren aus Pavia.* Berlin 1910. 110 pp. p. 104-07: Index of mss. (NN)

Bibliotheca Corvina: La Biblioteca di Mattia Corvino Re d'Ungheria, by G. Fraknói, G. Fógel, P. Gulyás and E. Hoffmann. Ital. tr. by L. Zambra. Budapest 1927. 186 pp. Describes 152 Latin mss., extant in many different libraries (p. 65-83). Index (175ff.)

L. Bieler, *Codices Patriciani Latini.* Dublin 1942. XVIII, 72 pp.

The same, 'Codices Patriciani Latini: Addenda et Corrigenda,' *Analecta Bollandiana* LXIII (1945) 242-256. (NNUT)

B. Bischoff, *Die südostdeutschen Schreibschulen und Bibliotheken der Karolingerzeit* (Sammlung bibliothekswissenschaftlicher Arbeiten, 49). Leipzig 1940. 280 pp. Discusses mss. in different libraries. No index of authors.

B. Bischoff and J. Hofmann, *Libri Sancti Kyliani: Die Würzburger Schreibschule und die Dombibliothek im VIII. und IX. Jahrhundert.* Würzburg 1952. XI, 200 pp. and plates. p. 188-91: Index of mss. Many of them remain in Würzburg.

F. Blume, *Bibliotheca librorum manuscriptorum Italica.* Göttingen 1834. 272 pp. Lists selected mss. at Genoa (p. 1ff.), Vercelli (5ff.), Milan (8ff.), Venice (12ff.), Verona (29ff.), Modena (35ff.), Florence (40ff.), Lucca (51ff.), Bologna (81ff.), Perugia (120ff.), Vatican City (125ff.), Rome (135ff.), Naples (191ff.), Monte Cassino (219ff.), Agrigento (225), Messina (225ff.), Palermo (230-31), Siracusa (231), San Daniele (232), Padua (233), Vicenza (234), Parma (234ff.), Cortona (236). Index covers also vols. I-III of his *Iter Italicum* (237ff.).

Catalogo di manoscritti ora posseduti da D. Baldassarre Boncompagni. By E. Nar-

ducci. Rome 1862. XXII, 219 pp. Collection scattered. (MH)

—2nd ed. Rome 1892. VIII, 520 pp. 614 mss. *Catalogue de la Bibliothèque de son Exc. M. le Comte D. Boutourlin.* Florence 1831. (Pt. 1). Manuscripts. 26 pp. 244 mss. Other parts separately paged. Collection scattered.

R. Bruck, *Die Malereien in den Handschriften des Königreichs Sachsen.* Dresden 1906. 469 pp. (Aus den Schriften der Kgl. Sächsischen Kommission für Geschichte, vol. XI). Describes 225 mss. Index (434ff.). Covers Dresden, Leipzig, Marienthal, Zittau and Zwickau.

A. Bruckner, *Scriptoria Medii Aevi Helvetica: Denkmäler Schweizerischer Schreibkunst des Mittelalters.* 8 vols. Geneva 1935-55. I (1935): Diocese of Chur. II (1936) and III (1938): St. Gall. IV (1940): Zurich. V (1943): Einsiedeln. VI (1952): Allerheiligen. VII (1955): Aargau. VIII (1950): Engelberg. Lists manuscripts written in those centers and now scattered. Covers mss. in St. Gallen (Stiftsarchiv, vol. I), and Sarnen (Bibliothek des Kollegiums, vol. VII).

A. Brückner, 'Bericht... über seine von der Königlichen Akademie subventionierte Reise 1889/90,' *Sitzungsberichte der Königlich Preussischen Akademie der Wissenschaften zu Berlin,'* 1890, pt. 2, 1335-40. Covers material on Polish literary history in Leningrad, Warsaw, Cracow, Lwow, and other libraries, but gives no specific references.

J. A. C. Buchon, *Quelques souvenirs de courses en Suisse et dans le pays de Baden, avec des notices sur plusieurs anciens manuscrits des Bibliothèques publiques ou particulières relatifs à l'histoire littéraire ou politique de la France.* Paris 1836. 488 pp. Gives selective lists for Karlsruhe, St. Gall, Zurich, Einsiedeln, Bern, Geneva, Constance and Heidelberg. No index. (RPB)

K. Burdach, 'Bericht über Forschungen zum Ursprung der neuhochdeutschen Schriftsprache und des deutschen Humanismus,' *Abhandlungen der Königl. Preussischen Akademie der Wissenschaften*, 1903. Philosophisch-Historische Classe, no. 1. 62 pp. Covers mss. in Olomouc, Brno, Třebon, Prague as well as some libraries in Austria, Italy, Sweden and France. No specific details.

G. de Bure, *Catalogue des livres de la bibliothèque de feu M. le duc de la Vallière. Première partie.* 3 vols. in 7. Paris 1783. Arranged by subjects. Mss. listed with editions. Index in vol. 3, pt. 2. Collection scattered. Many mss. went to the Biblioteca Durazzo in Genoa.

A. W. Byvanck, *La miniature dans les Pays-Bas Septentrionaux.* Paris 1937. 187 pp. and plates. p. 117-59: List of mss. No index of authors.

A. W. Byvanck and G. J. Hoogewerff, *La miniature hollandaise dans les manuscrits des 14e, 15e et 16e siècles.* Hague 1922-26. 3 vols. (of which 2 vols. of plates). Describes 182 mss. in different libraries. Index of mss. (75-78).

Le Cabinet Historique. XXIII (Ser. II vol. I, 1877) 1-15: L. Delisle, 'Notes sur quelques manuscrits de la bibliothèque d'Auxerre.'

—XXIV, 2 (1878) 1-35: B. Prost, 'Catalogue des manuscrits de la Bibliothèque de la Ville de Salins (Jura).' 174 mss. Index (34-35). 174-95: H. Omont, 'Catalogue des manuscrits de la Bibliothèque de Conches.' 9 Latin mss. Index.

—XXVIII (1882) 141-54: The same, 'Catalogue des manuscrits de la Bibliothèque de Louviers.' 36 mss. Index (152-54). 162-63: The same, 'Manuscrits de la Bibliothèque de Verneuil (Eure).' 10 mss. No index. 556-72: The same, 'Notes sur quelques manuscrits conservés au Grand Séminaire d'Autun.' No index.

—XXIX (1883) 134-36: H. Stein, 'Catalogue des manuscrits de la Bibliothèque Publique de Montargis (Loiret).' 22 mss. No index.

A. Calmet, *Diarium Helveticum.* Einsiedeln 1756. 149 pp. Describes mostly theological mss. in Swiss libraries. No index.

H. Caplan, *Mediaeval Artes Praedicandi: A Hand-List.* Ithaca 1934. 52 pp.

—*A Supplementary Hand-List.* Ithaca 1936. 36 pp.

I. Carini, *Gli archivi e le biblioteche di Spagna in rapporto alla storia d'Italia in generale e di Sicilia in particolare.* 2 vols. Palermo 1884-97. Lists some mss. at Barcelona (I, 29ff. and 41ff.), Madrid (105ff.), Valladolid (269ff.), Escorial (412ff.), Toledo (483ff.). Index of authors (p. i-xcix at the end.) Further lists for Madrid (II, 283ff.) and Escorial (509ff.).

G. Caselli, *Alcuni codici della Libreria di S. Giacomo della Marca esistenti nella Biblioteca Vaticana: Fondo Rossiano. Con appendice delle tre Tabulae librorum e Indice dei codici rimasti nel Municipio di Monteprandone.* Montalto Marche 1934. 73 pp. pp. 12-33: 10 mss. of Fondo Rossiano. 65-73: 65 mss. in Monteprandone. No index. (Vat. Library; micr. at NNC)

Catalogue général des manuscrits des bibliothèques de Belgique. I (Gembloux 1934). P. Faider and others, *Catalogue des manuscrits conservés à Namur.* 585 pp. Covers Bibliothèque du Musée Archéologique (including Fonds de la Ville and Fonds de la Société Archéologique, 196 and 79 and 145 mss.), Évêché (75 mss.), Grand Séminaire (122 mss.), Musée des Belles Lettres (26 mss.) and Collège de N. D. de la Paix (4 mss.). Index.

—II (1934). A. De Poorter, *Catalogue des manuscrits de la Bibliothèque de la Ville de Bruges.* 762 pp. 610 mss. Index. Cf. A. Pelzer, 'Le nouveau catalogue des manuscrits de la ville de Bruges,' *Revue néo-scolastique de philosophie* XXXVIII (1935) 344-351.

—III (1946). P. Faider, P.-P. Debbaudt and Mme. Faider-Feytmans, *Catalogue des manuscrits de la Bibliothèque Publique de la Ville de Courtrai.* 285 pp. 524 mss. Index. Cf. A. Teetaert a Zedelgem, 'Manuscripta franciscana in bibliothecis Belgicis,' Collectanea Franciscana X (1940) 239-55. (DCU)

—IV (1937). C. De Clercq, *Catalogue des manuscrits du Grand Séminaire de Malines.* 198 pp. 188 mss. Index.

—V (1939). A. Dermul, *Catalogue des manuscrits de la Ville d'Anvers.* 190 pp. 258 mss. Index.

—VI (1950). P. Faider and P. Van Sint Jan, *Catalogue des manuscrits conservés à Tournai.* VIII, 314 pp. Covers Bibliothèque de la Ville. (25 preserved mss., 10 recently acquired, and 130 out of 222 mss. lost during the last war) and Bibliothèque du Séminaire (141 mss.). Index.

Catalogus Codicum Hagiographicorum Latinorum in Bibliothecis publicis Namurci, Gandae, Leodii et Montibus asservatorum... (Subsidia Hagiographica 25). Brussels 1948. 156 and 204 pp. Reprinted from *Analecta Bollandiana* I-V and IX, with added indices. (OCl)

T. M. Charland, *Artes praedicandi.* Paris-Ottawa 1936. 421 pp. p. 414-420: List of mss.

*U. Chevalier, *Manuscrits et incunables liturgiques du Dauphiné* (Bibliothèque Liturgique 18, 2). Paris 1920. 24 pp. (NIC)

A. Chiappini, 'Reliquie letterarie Capestranesi: Storia, codici, carte, documenti,' *Bullettino della R. Deputazione Abruzzese di Storia Patria,* Ser. III, vol. IX-X (1918-19) 27-185; XI-XIII (1920-22) 7-71; XIV (1923) 55-140. Also separately, Aquila 1927 313 pp. Describes 65 mss. (p. 24-118 of the separate edition) and 557 documents (163-266) in Capestrano, and mss. in Naples from Capestrano (nos. 66-536, p. 118-61). The index (301-12) does not cover the mss.

K. Christ, *Die Bibliothek des Klosters Fulda im 16. Jahrhundert: Die Handschriften-Verzeichnisse* (Zentralblatt für Bibliothekswesen, Beiheft 64). Leipzig 1933. 343 pp. Table of mss. extant in different libraries (340-41).

'Cistercian Manuscripts in England,' *Collectanea Ordinis Cisterciensium Reformatorum* XIV 1952, 208-212; 265-277. Arranged by subjects. (MH; micr. at NNC)

Charles Upson Clark, 'Collectanea Hispanica,' *Transactions of the Connecticut Academy of Arts and Sciences* XXIV (1920). 243 pp. and plates. Lists 214 Visigothic mss. extant in different libraries (28-64). No index of authors.

J. M. Clark, *The Abbey of St. Gall as a Centre of Literature and Art.* Cambridge 1926. 322 pp. Lists St. Gall mss. in other libraries (304-05).

Clossius, 'Über die Handschriften auf Russischen Bibliotheken,' *Neues Archiv für Philologie und Pädagogik* III (1828), no. 2, p. 20-32. Covers Tartu (p. 21, 1 ms.), Leningrad (p. 21-31), Moscow (p. 31-32). (ICU)

G. Coggiola, 'Il ricupero a Vienna dei Cimeli bibliografici italiani,' *Emporium* XLIX (1919) 198-217. Discusses and reproduces some of the mss. returned to Naples.

Collection de documents inédits sur l'histoire de France. Documents historiques inédits tirés des collections manuscrits de la Bibliothèque Royale et des archives ou des bibliothèques des Départements. I (1841): 'Rapports, notices et inventaires.' Lists some mss. at Semur (92-95), Clairmarais (393).

—III (1847) 258-376: P. Lacroix, 'Notices et Extraits des manuscrits concernant l'histoire de France et la littérature française, conservés dans les bibliothèques d'Italie.' Lists some mss. at the Vatican (263ff.), Naples (290ff.), Bologna (297ff.), Padua (299ff.), Parma (301ff.), Modena (306-07), Florence (307ff.), Turin (321ff.), Milan (332ff.) and Venice (345ff.). No index.

I. Collijn, 'Franciskanernas Bibliotek på Gråmunkeholmen i Stockholm,' *Nordisk Tidskrift för Bok- och Biblioteksväsen* IV (1917) 101-71. Lists 23 mss. (p. 129-66) now in Stockholm and Uppsala.

Comune di Savona, Ente Provinciale Turismo Savona. *Mostra Codici, Pergamene, Incunabuli, Libri Antichi.* (Savona) 1950. 24 unnumbered pages. Lists mss. in Albenga, Savona and other neigboring institutions.

A. Cordoliani, 'Inventaire des manuscrits de comput ecclésiastique conservés dans les

Bibliothèques de Catalogne,' *Hispania Sacra* IV (1951) 359-84. Covers Gerona (366-76); Lerida (377-79); Montserrat (380-83). V (1952) 121-64. Covers Seo de Urgel (123-24); Solsona (124); Tarragona (125-33); Tortosa (133-50); Vallbona de las Monjas (150-52); Vich (152-63); Villanueva y Geltru (163-64).

J. Corminas, *Suplemento á las memorias para ayudar á formar un diccionario crítico de los escritores catalanes . . . que en 1836 publicó . . . F. Torres Amat . . .* Burgos 1849. 369 pp. The appendix (p. 285-331) indicates some mss. in many Spanish libraries. No index. (NN)

Catalogo della prima parte della Biblioteca appartenuta al Sig. March. Costabili di Ferrara (by G. Antonelli). Bologna 1858. XVI, 343 pp. p. 1-46: 375 mss. Collection scattered, but many mss. went to Ferrara, Biblioteca Comunale.

M. Curtze, 'Eine Studienreise,' *Centralblatt für Bibliothekswesen* XVI (1899) 257-306. Describes mss. of scientific authors in various German and Austrian libraries. No index.

Ch. Daremberg, *Notices et Extraits des manuscrits médicaux grecs, latins et français des principales bibliothèques de l'Europe.* pt. I: *Manuscrits grecs d'Angleterre.* Paris 1853. 243 pp. Reprinted, with additions, from *Archives des Missions* (see above). Covers a few Latin items. Index.

De La Fage. See La Fage.

L. Delisle, *Mélanges de paléographie et de bibliographie.* Paris 1880. 505 pp. 53-116: 'Manuscrits de l'abbaye de Silos acquis par la Bibliothèque Nationale.' 42 mss. 149-65: 'Manuscrits du Cabinet de M. Didot acquis pour la Bibliothèque Nationale.' 11 mss. 195-238: Notes sur différents manuscrits de Belgique et de Hollande.' Describes 23 mss. at the Hague, Brussels and Leyden. 359-499: 'Manuscrits divers acquis pour la Bibliothèque Nationale en 1876, 1877 et 1878.' Arranged alphabetically by authors and subjects. No index.

N. Denholm-Young. 'The Cursus in England,' *Oxford Essays in Mediaeval History Presented to H. E. Salter* (Oxford 1934) 68-103. p. 91-101: List of mss. of Artes dictaminis in England, by authors. p. 102-103: Index of Incipits. Reprinted in N. Denholm-Young, *Collected Papers on Mediaeval Subjects* (Oxford 1946) 26-55.

De Ricci, see under R.

J. Destrez, *La Pecia dans les manuscrits universitaires du XIIIᵉ et du XIVᵉ siècle.* Paris 1935. 104 pp. and plates. Describes 36 mss. in different libraries (p. 90-101). No index.

Th. F. Dibdin, *A Bibliographical, Antiquarian and Picturesque Tour in France and Germany.* 2nd ed. 3 vol. London 1829. Index of authors in vol. I.

W. Diekamp, 'Westfälische Handschriften in fremden Bibliotheken und Archiven,' *Zeitschrift für vaterländische Geschichte und Alterthumskunde,* ed. by the Verein für Geschichte und Alterthumskunde Westfalens, XLI (1883) 137-47; XLII (1884) 153-57; XLIV (1886) 48-97. Covers Trier, Dombibliothek (XLI), Vienna, Hofbibliothek and Staatsarchiv (XLII), Berlin and Hannover (XLIV). (NN)

H. Diels, 'Die Handschriften der antiken Ärzte,' *Abhandlungen der Kgl. Preussischen Akademie der Wissenschaften, Philosophisch-Historische Classe,* 1905, no. 3, 158 pp; 1906, no 1, xxiii and 115 pp. Arranged by Greek authors. Covers the Latin translations.

A. Diestelkamp, 'Geschichte der Halberstädter Dombibliothek im Mittelalter,' *Sachsen und Anhalt* III (1927) 177-225. Identifies mss. at Halberstadt, Domgymnasium, and in Halle. No index (NjP)

Bibliothek Alexander Fürst Dietrichstein. 2 vols. Lucerne 1933-34. Mss. are listed in vol. I, p. 69-86 (nos. 364-421) and II, p. 32-37 (nos. 270-300). Collection scattered. The part that remained in Mikulov and then went to Brno is not listed in this catalogue.

I. Dobrowsky, *Litterarische Nachrichten von einer auf Veranlassung der böhm. Gesell-*

schaft der Wissenschaften im Jahre 1792 unternommenen Reise nach Schweden und Russland. Prague 1796. 272 pp. Mentions a few Latin mss. No index. (CtY)

J. Domínguez Bordona, *Manuscritos con pinturas: Notas para un inventário de los conservados en colecciones públicas y particulares de España.* 2 vols. Madrid 1933. Arranged by libraries. I: Avila-Madrid. II: Escorial-Zaragoza. Describes 2173 mss. Index of authors (II, 367-76).

The same, Exposición de Códices miniados españoles, Catálogo. Madrid 1929. VI, 259 pp. and plates. p. 169-230: 197 mss. in different libraries.

B. Dudik, 'Archive im Königreiche Galizien und Lodomerien,' *Archiv für österreichische Geschichte* XXXIX (1868) 1-222. Lists some mss. at Cracow (34ff.), Tarnów (Sanguszko archive, 103ff.), Lwów (111 and 168ff.). Index (201ff.).

The same, *Forschungen in Schweden für Mährens Geschichte.* Brno 1852. 478 pp. Lists some mss. at Stockholm (198ff.), Upsala (318ff.), Strengnäs (351ff.), Linköping (356ff.), Lund (366ff.). Index (467ff.). (NN)

P. Durrieu, 'Manuscrits d'Espagne remarquables principalement par leurs peintures et par la beauté de leur exécution,' *Bibliothèque de l'École des Chartes* LIV (1893) 251-326.

The same, 'Notes sur quelques manuscrits français ou d'origine française conservés dans les bibliothèques d'Allemagne,' *Ibid.* LIII (1892) 115-43.

J. M. de Eguren, *Memoria descriptiva de los códices notables conservados en los Archivos Eclesiásticos de España.* Madrid 1859. xcix, 101 pp. Lists some mss. in various libraries, arranged by subjects. No index. (Pierpont Morgan Library)

M. Esposito, 'Hiberno-Latin Manuscripts in the Libraries of Switzerland,' *Proceedings of the Royal Irish Academy,* Section C, vol. XXVIII (1910) 62-95; XXX (1912) 1-14.

F. Falk, *Beiträge zur Rekonstruktion der alten Bibliotheca Fuldensis und Bibliotheca Laureshamensis.* (Centralblatt für Bibliothekswesen, Beiheft XXVI). Leipzig 1902. 112 pp. Lists mss. extant in different libraries. No index.

The same. *Die ehemalige Dombibliothek zu Mainz, ihre Entstehung, Verschleppung und Vernichtung.* (Centralblatt für Bibliothekswesen, Beiheft XVIII). Leipzig 1897. 175 pp. Lists mss. extant in different libraries. Index (166ff.).

J. Feifalik, 'Beiträge zur deutschen Handschriftenkunde aus mährischen Bibliotheken und Archiven' *Notizen-Blatt der historisch-statistischen Section der k.k. mährisch-schlesischen Gesellschaft zur Beförderung des Ackerbaues, der Natur- und Landeskunde* (Brno) 1857, no. 7, p. 53-56; no. 8, p. 61-64. Lists 43 German mss. Covers Olomouc, Rajhrad, Znojmo. Index p. 63-64. (British Museum; reprint 8 pp., NIC).

M. Férotin, *Histoire de l'abbaye de Silos.* Paris 1897. 369 pp. Lists about 100 mss. now at Silos or elsewhere. No index.

K. Fischer, *Die Buchmalerei in den beiden Dominikanerklöstern Nürnbergs.* Thesis, Erlangen. Nürnberg 1928. 87 pp. and plates. p. 5-9: Lists of mss. in Nürnberg and in other libraries.

C. Foligno, 'Codici di materia veneta nelle biblioteche inglesi,' *Nuovo Archivio Veneto,* N.S. X (1905) 89-128: XI, pt. 1 (1906) 171-86; pt. 2, 162-93. 105 mss. mainly in London. No index.

(France) Ministère de l'Instruction Publique et des Beaux-Arts. *Catalogue des Manuscrits conservés dans les Dépôts d'archives départementales communales et hospitalières.* Paris 1886. 467 pp. Index (373-455).

—*Catalogue des Manuscrits conservés aux Archives Nationales.* Paris 1892. 532 pp. 2913 mss. Index.

—*Catalogue Général des Manuscrits des Bibliothèques Publiques des Départements* (Quarto Series). I (1849) 1-40: Séminaire d'Autun by G. Libri. 153 mss. 41-255: Laon, by F. Ravaisson. 477 mss. 257-77:

Ville de Montpellier. 64 mss. 279-477:
École de médecine de Montpellier. 542
mss. 479-98: Albi. 102 mss. Index.
—II (1855) 1-1010: Troyes. 2427 mss.
1010-12: Hotel de Ville de Troyes. 3 mss.
1012-16: Trésor de la Cathédrale de Troyes.
4 mss. Index.
—III (1861) 1-386: Saint-Omer, by M.
Michelant. 842 mss. 387-471: Épinal.
204 mss. 473-505: Saint-Dié. 75 mss.
507-39: Saint-Mihiel. 73 mss. 541-602:
Sélestat. 137 mss. Not complete. Index.
—IV (1872) 1-426: Arras, by J. Quicherat.
1139 mss. 427-562: Avranches, by L. D.
246 mss. 563-699: Boulogne-sur-Mer, by
H. Michelant. 201 mss. Index.
—V (1879) 1-415: Metz, by Prost. 1029 mss.
417-536: Verdun. 396 mss. 537-677:
Charleville, by G. R. 284 mss. Index.
—VI (1878), 908 pp. Douai, by C. Dehaisnes.
1239 mss. Index.
—VII (1885). Introduction, by A. Molinier.
1-528: Toulouse. 887 mss. 529-666:
Nîmes. 365 mss. Index.
—*Catalogue général des Manuscrits des Bi-
bliothèques Publiques de France. Départe-
ments.* (Octavo Series). I (1886), 623 pp.
Rouen, by H. Omont. 2522 mss.
—II (1888) 1-270: Rouen, nos. 2523-3493 and
special collections. 271-83: Dieppe, by
Ch. Paray. 85 mss. 285-87: Eu, by H. O.
7 mss. 289-93: Fécamp, by H. O. 34 mss.
295-96: Elbeuf. 13 mss. 297: Gournay-en-
Bray. 3 mss. 299-346: Le Havre, by J.
Baillard. 396 mss. 347-54: Neufchâtel-en-
Bray, by E. Coyecque. 43 mss. 355:
Bernay. 1 ms. 357-62: Conches, by H.
Omont. 11 mss. 363: Gisors. 3 mss.
365-73: Louviers, by H. Omont. 36 mss.
375-77: Verneuil, by the same. 10 mss.
379-465: Évreux, by the same. 129 Latin
mss. 465-537: Alençon, by the same. 192
mss. 539-44: Montivilliers, by E. Coyecque. 49 mss. Index for I and II.
—III (1885) 1-68: Châlons-sur-Marne, by A.
Molinier. 337 mss. 69-172: Soissons, by
the same. 275 mss. 173-91: Moulins, by
H. Omont. 100 mss. 193-215: Ajaccio, by

A. Touranjon. 145 mss. 217-23: Agen,
by G. Tholin. 26 mss. 225-59: Saint-
Quentin, by A. Molinier. 182 mss. 261-
313: Provins, by the same. 269 mss. 315-
32: Beauvais, by H. Omont. 81 mss.
333-56: Meaux, by A. Molinier. 119
mss. 357-68: Melun, by the same. 87 mss.
369-76: Noyon, by the same. 40 mss.
377-80: Corbeil, by the same. 9 mss. 381-
87: Gap, by J. Roman. 36 mss. 389-92:
Bourbourg, by C. Couderc. 4 mss. 393-
490: Vendôme, by H. Omont. 370 mss.
—IV (1886) 1-91: Bourges, by H. Omont.
400 mss. 93-94: Issoudun, by J. de
Fréminville, 13 mss. 95-97: Brioude, by
L. Cadier. 7 mss. 99-100: Brive, by J. de
Fréminville. 13 mss. 101-03: Guéret, by
the same. 23 mss. 105-06: Chatellerault,
by S. Bougenot. 4 mss. 107-08: Dinan,
by the same. 3 mss. 109-112: Lamballe,
by H. Omont. 7 mss. 113: Clamecy, by J.
de Fréminville. 3 mss. 115-16: Apt, by
the same. 7 mss. 117-18: Libourne. 9
mss. 119: Bourmont, by J. de Fréminville,
2 mss. 121-299: Nancy, by J. Favier. 1137
mss. 301-08: Aire-sur-la-Lys, by H.
Loriquet. 40 mss. 309-10: Béthune, by
the same. 5 mss. 311-21: Calais, by the
same. 49 mss. 323-29: Saint-Pol, by the
same. 30 mss. 331-33: Hesdin, by the
same. 3 mss. 335-45: Roubaix, by Th.
Leuridan. 34 mss. 347: Privas, by Massip.
2 mss. 349-69: Laval, by D. Oehlert. 99
mss. 371-82: Mende, by F. André. 60
mss. 383-86: Saint-Amand (Nord) by S.
Bougenot. 28 mss. 387-435: Auch, by
L. Cadier. 81 mss.
—V (1889), 545 pp. Dijon, by Molinier,
Omont, Bougenot and Ph. Guignard. 1556
mss.
—VI (1887) 1-100: Auxerre, by Molinier.
269 mss. and special collections. 101-29:
Tonnerre, by the same. 70 mss. 131-34:
Avallon, by the same. 99 mss. 135-45:
Joigny, by the same. 70 mss. 147-204:
Sens, by the same. 289 mss. 205-10:
Fontainebleau, Palais, by the same. 24
mss. Now at Paris, Bibliothèque Natio-

nale. 211-13: Nemours, by the same. 11 mss. 215-34: Bourg, by Brossard. 69 mss. 235: Nantua, by the same. 1 ms. 237-38: Trévoux, by the same. 5 mss. 239: Pont-de-Vaux, by the same. 1 ms. 241-48: Chatillon-sur-Seine, by V. Croix. 32 mss. 249-92: Beaune, by Molinier. 279 mss. 293: Montbard. 1 ms. 295-328: Semur, by Molinier. 117 mss. 329-32: Auxonne, by J. Gauthier. 42 mss. 333-35: Autun, by S. Bougenot. 9 mss. 337-39: Charolles, by the same. 10 mss. 341-44: Cluny, by L. Lex. 20 mss. 345-58: Mâcon, by the same. 78 mss. 359-79: Chalon-sur-Saône, by S. Bougenot. 143 mss. 381-87: Tournus, by L. Lex. 34 mss. 389-99: Gray, by J. Gauthier. 32 mss. 401-61: Vesoul, by the same. 230 mss. 463-64: Baume-les-Dames, by the same. 5 mss.

—VII (1889), 803 pp. Grenoble, by P. Fournier, E. Maignien and A. Prudhomme. 2089 mss. and autographs.

—VIII (1889), 683 pp. La Rochelle, by G. Musset. 759 mss.

—IX (1888) 1-48: Salins, by Coste. 245 mss. 49: Lure, by Arnoux. 1 ms. 51-64: Pontarlier, by J. Gauthier. 58 mss. 65-77: Pau, by L. Soulice. 10 mss. 79-87: Bayonne, by L. Cadier. 22 mss. 89: La Ferté-Bernard, by V. Duchemin. 3 mss. 91-125: Narbonne, by L. Cadier. 163 mss. 127-51: Périgueux, by the same. 67 mss. 153-57: Digne, by Chaspoul. 34 mss. 159-84: Châteauroux, by L. Cadier. 81 mss. 185: Dreux. 3 mss. 187-89: Aurillac, by C. Couderc. 11 mss. 191-97: Cahors, by the same. 85 mss. 199-210: Saint-Germain en Laye. 28 mss. 211-17: Pontoise. 30 mss. 219-40: Rodez, by C. Couderc. 116 mss. 241-379: Versailles, by E. Delerot and A. Taphanel. 1187 mss. and autographs. 381: Lagny. 1 ms. 383-84: Coulommiers. 10 mss. 385-89: Hyères, by J. de Fréminville. 30 mss. 391-92: Corte, École Paoli, by the same. 8 mss. 393-405: Bastia, by the same. 52 mss. 407-41: Abbéville, by A. Ledieu. 205

mss. 443-44: Villeneuve-sur-Yonne. 4 mss. 445-65: Limoges, by L. Guibert. 39 mss. 467: Mirecourt. 4 mss.

—X (1889) 1-125: Avranches, by Omont. 254 mss. 127-35: Coutances, by the same. 54 mss. 137-50: Valognes, by the same. 219 mss. 151-203: Cherbourg, by G. Amiot. 225 mss. 205-33: Bayeux, by E. Coyecque. 251 mss. 235: Condé-sur-Noireau. 1 ms. 237-48: Falaise, by E. Coyecque. 47 mss. 249-50: Flers, by the same. 17 mss. 251: Domfront. 1 ms. 253-58: Argentan, by Christophle. 40 mss. 259-63: Lisieux, by Omont. 24 mss. 265: Honfleur, by Coyecque. 4 mss. 267: Saint-Lo. 3 mss. 269-70: Mortain, by Boulay. 8 mss. 271-400: Chapître de Bayeux, by E. Deslandes. 320 mss. 401-14: Pont-Audemer, by Coyecque. 63 mss. 415-58: Vire, by C. A. Fédérique. 236 mss.

—XI (1890). 573 pp. Chartres, by Omont, Molinier, Couderc and Coyecque. 1796 mss.

—XII (1889), 418 pp. Orléans, by Ch. Cuissard. 968 mss.

—XIII (1891) 1-65: Vitry-le-François, by G. Hérelle. 173 mss. 67-68: Rambervillers. 5 mss. 69-73: Pont-à-Mousson, by J. Favier. 21 mss. 75-76: Sedan, by J. Letellier. 17 mss. 77-131: Perpignan, by L. Cadier. 121 mss. 133: Cette. 2 mss. 135: Lectoure. 1 ms. 137: Oloron. 5 mss. 139: Saint-Geniès. 1 ms. 141-42: Saint-Chamond, by G. Lefebvre. 12 mss. 143: Moissac. 1 ms. 145-50: Valence, by A. Lacroix. 35 mss. 151: Thiers. 1 ms. 153: Tulle. 2 mss. 155: Uzès. 2 mss. 157: Mauriac. 4 mss. 159-60: Mamers. 8 mss. 161-66: Annonay, by E. Nicod. 11 mss. 167-253: Carcassonne, by L. Cadier. 300 mss. and authographs. 255-63: Saintes, by L. Audiat. 53 mss. 265: Fougères. 6 mss. 267-72: Morlaix, by A. Koscher. 28 mss. 273-74: Pithiviers. 6 mss. 275-78: La Roche-sur-Yon. 15 mss. 279-84: Belfort, by J. Gauthier. 18 mss. 285-336: Montbéliard, by the same. 212 mss. 337-52: Le Puy, by A. Chassaing. 49 mss.

353-55: Alais. 18 mss. 357-76: Saint-Brieuc. 115 mss. 377-455: Dôle, by J. Gauthier. 412 mss.

—XIV (1890) 1-213: Clermont-Ferrand, by C. Couderc. 787 mss. 215-380: Caen, by G. Lavalley. 599 mss. 381-92: Toulon, by J.-H. Albanès. 62 mss. 393-408: Draguignan, by the same. 41 mss. 409-21: Fréjus, by the same. 9 mss. 423-31: Grasse, by the same. 30 mss. 433-73: Nice, by the same. 122 mss. 475-76: Tarascon. 5 mss.

—XV (1892), 574 pp. Marseille, by Albanès. 1656 mss.

—XVI (1894), 728 pp. Aix, by the same. 1229 mss.

—XVII (1891), 593 pp. Cambrai, by Molinier. 1398 mss.

—XVIII (1893), 680 pp. Alger, by E. Fagnan. 1987 Arabic mss.

—XIX (1893), 615 pp. Amiens, by E. Coyecque. 932 and 121 mss.

—XX (1893) 1-252: Le Mans, by Couderc. 493 mss. 253-59: Château-Gontier, by the same. 12 mss. 261-65: Saint-Malo, by the same. 21 mss. 267: Villefranche (Rhône), by the same. 2 mss. 269-75: Vannes, by the same. 15 mss. 277: Guingamp, by the same. 3 mss. 279-84: Saint-Calais, by the same. 16 mss. 285-94: Saumur, by the same. 30 mss. 295-306: Angoulême, by the same, 58 mss. 307-309: Castelnaudary, by the same. 5 mss. 311: Castres, by the same. 3 mss. 313: Lavaur, by the same. 1 ms. 315-23: Béziers, by the same. 27 mss. 325-29: Nogent-Le-Rotrou, by the same. 20 mss. 331-38: Seilhac, by the same. 15 mss. 339-44: Avesnes, by the same. 25 mss. 345-520: Arles, by Albanès, 425 mss. 521-63: Mantes, by E. Grave. 36 mss. and autographs. 565-72: Montargis, by Couderc. 49 mss. 573-76: Cannes, by Pinatel. 35 mss. 577: Briançon. 1 ms.

—XXI (1893) 1-63: Chaumont, by J. Gauthier. 256 mss. 65-112: Langres, by the same. 138 mss. 113-21: Arbois, by the same. 33 mss. 123-30: Lons-le-Saunier, by the same. 20 mss. 131-36: Poligny, by the same. 11 mss. 137-51: Saint-Claude, by the same. 21 mss. 153: Sainte-Menchould. 1 ms. 155-56: Toul, by J. Favier. 2 mss. 157: Nogent-sur-Seine. 2 mss. 159-72: Remiremont. 50 mss. 173-91: Lunéville, by Mather. 179 mss. 193: Louhans. 1 ms. 195-212: Chambéry. 38 mss. 213-20: Annecy. 42 mss. 221-39: Rochefort-sur-mer, by G. Musset. 100 mss. 241-312: Saint-Étienne. 274 mss. 313: Pamiers. 1 ms. 315: Confolens. 1 ms. 317: Constantine, by E. Fagnan. 1 Arabic ms. 319-91: Châteaudun, by Hetté. 537 mss. 393-487: Cognac, by P. de Lacroix. 85 mss. 489-500: Montbrison, by E.-S. Bougenot. 59 mss. 501-15: Roanne, by the same. 84 mss. 517-24: Saint-Bonnet-le-Château, by J. de Fréminville. 40 mss. 525-70: Vienne, by E.-S. Bougenot. 162 mss.

—XXII (1893) 1-423: Nantes, by Molinier. 2211 mss. and autographs. (no. 1-123 in Latin). 425-41: Quimper, by the same. 41 mss. 443-74: Brest, by the same. 43 mss.

—XXIII (1894), 745 pp. Bordeaux, by Couderc. 1184 mss.

—XXIV (1894) 1-262: Rennes, by A. Vétault. 602 mss. 263: Lorient. 5 mss. 265: Lannion. 15 mss. 267-69: Vitré, by A. de La Borderie. 11 mss. 271: Montreuil-sur-mer. 3 mss. 273-78: Étampes, by Molinier. 52 mss. 279-88: Clermont-de-l'Oise, by E. Roussel. 66 mss. 289-92: Senlis, by Cultru. 40 mss. 293: Gien. 5 mss. 295-311: Fontainebleau, by Coyecque. 22 mss. 313-21: Château-Thierry, by the same. 20 mss. 323-80: Épernay, by the same. 220 mss. 381-414: Blois, by the same. 122 mss. 415-36: Loches, by the same. 40 mss. 437-51: Neufchâteau, by the same. 56 mss. 453-57: Bourbonne, by the same. 13 mss. 459-60: Condom, by the same. 12 mss. 461-506: Bar-le-Duc, by H. Dannreuther. 200 mss. 507-47: Nevers, by H. de Flamare and D'Asis-Guillissans. 21 mss. 549-89:

Compiègne, by Comte de Marsy. 86 and 14 mss. 591: Mont-de-Marsan, by H. Tartière. 2 mss.

—XXV (1894) 1-187: Poitiers, by A.-F. Lièvre. 547 mss. 189-533: Valenciennes. 1057 mss.

—XXVI (1897) 1-627: Lille, by H. Rigaux. 744 and 183 mss. 629-51: Dunkerque, by J. L'Hermitte. 87 mss. 653-73: Bergues, by the same. 74 mss. 675-705: Roye, by A. Ledieu. 44 mss. 707-14: Péronne, by the same. 41 mss. 715-17: Ham, by the same. 27 mss. 719: La Chatre. 1 ms.

—XXVII (1894). 645 pp. Avignon, by L.-H. Labande. 1500 mss.

—XXVIII (1895), 831 pp. Avignon, nos. 1501-2900.

—XXIX (1897), 679 pp. Avignon, nos. 2901-3861 and autographs. XXIX, pt. II (1901), p. 681-1563: Index for vols. XXVII-XXIX.

—XXX (1900), 800 pp. Lyon, by Molinier and Desvernay. 1964 and 637 mss. XXX pt. II (1900), p. 801-1391: nos. 638-1308 and 401 and 94 mss. Index.

—XXXI (1898) 1-144: Lyon, Palais des Arts, by J. Vaesen. 311 mss. Now in the Bibliothèque Municipale. 145: Briey. 1 ms. 147-52: Gien, by J. Doinel. 39 mss. 153: Confolens. 1 ms. 155-58: Riom, by L. de Sarrazin. 31 mss. 159: Gaillac. 1 ms. 161: Villeneuve-sur-Lot. 1 ms. 163-77: Lunel, by J. Berthelé and Th. Millerot. 42 mss. 179-88: Montauban, by F. Monziès. 51 mss. 189-618: Angers, by Molinier. 1928 mss. 619-41: Niort. 185 mss. 643-44: Orange, by L. Duhamel. 3 mss. 645: Saint-Hippolyte-sur-le-Doubs. 2 mss. 647-60: Tarbes, by P. Labrouche. 63 mss. 661-80: Baguères-de-Bigorre, by the same. 84 mss. 681-707: Foix, by Fontes and F. Pasquier. 67 mss. 709: Saint-Maudé. 1 ms. 711: Villefranche-de-Rouergue. 1 ms 713-15: Trie-sur-Baise, by P. Labrouche. 8 mss.

—XXXII (1897), 1015 pp. Besançon, by A. Castan. 1296 mss.

—XXXIII (1900), 711 pp. Besançon cont.

103 and 208 mss. XXXIII pt. II (1904), p. 713-1471. Besançon cont., 74 and 53 and 41 and 130 and 31 and 89 mss. Index.

—XXXIV (1901), 848 pp. Carpentras, by Duhamel. 1720 mss. XXXV (1899), 714 pp. Carpentras, by Duhamel and Liabastres. nos. 1721-1830. XXXVI (1902), 543 pp. Carpentras, by Liabastres, nos. 1831-2154. XXXVI pt. II (1903), p. 545-1156: Carpentras, Index, by L.-H. Labande.

—XXXVII (1900), 656 pp. Tours, by Collon. 905 mss.

—XXXVIII (1904), 864 pp. Reims, by H. Loriquet. 665 mss. XXXIX (1904), 750 pp. Reims, nos. 666-1538. XXXIX pt. II (1905), p. 751-1297. Reims, nos. 1539-2114 and autographs. Index. XXXIX bis (1909), 740 pp. Reims, Collection Tarbé, by L. Demaison.

—XL (1902), Supplément, vol. I, p. 1-38: Abbéville, by A. Ledieu. Nos. 206-329. 39-40: Agen, by Calvet. Nos. 27-34. 40-43: Aire-sur-la-Lys, by Vaast. Nos. 41-47. 43-83: Aix, by Gaudefroy-Demombynes. Nos. 1230-1351. 84-85: Aix-les-Bains, by Mauvert. 9 mss. 85-86: Ajaccio, by Marcaggi. Nos. 146-50. 86-87: Albi, by Ch. Portal. Nos. 103-11. 87-102: Albi, Bibliothèque Rochegude, by E. Jolibois and Ch. Portal. 109 mss. 103-04: Alençon, by Berthey. Nos. 193-96. 104-05: Alger (Ville), by Dujardin. 5 mss. 105-10: Amiens, by H. Michel. Nos. 933-91. 111-14: Annecy, by M. Le Roux. No. 43. 114-20: Annonay, by E. Nicod. Nos. 12-63. 121: Antibes. 1 ms. 121-25: Apt, by Sauve. Nos. 8-20. 125: Argentan, by Lévesque. No. 48. 125-49: Arles, by Martel. Nos. 426-83. 149-64: Arras, by Wicquot and P. Laroche. Nos. 1103-67. 164-429: Arras, Fonds Victor Advielle, by V. Advielle. 1186 mss. 429-31: Autun, by Latieule. Nos. 10-25. 431-48: Auxerre, by Porée. Nos. 270-384. 449: Auxonne, by Bernaud. Nos. 43-44. 449: Avallon, by Chambon. Nos. 100-02. 450-72: Avignon, by Labande. Nos. 3862-3943. 473: Ba-

guères-de-Bigorre, by Pépouey. No. 85.
473-92: Bagnols-sur-Cèze, by Mme. Garidel. 116 mss. 492-97: Bar-le-Duc, by Dannreuther. Nos. 201-16. 497-98: Bastia, by le Baron Cervoni. Nos. 53-58. 498-543: Bayeux, by A. Bénet. Nos. 178-461. 544-49: Bayonne, by L. Hiriart. Nos. 23-44. 549-57: Beaune, by Lambert. Nos. 280-313. 557: Beauvais. No. 82. 557: Béziers, by Barbier. No. 28. 558-76: Blois, by P. Dufay. Papiers Dupré. 259 mss. 576-622: Bordeaux, by Boucherie. Nos. 1185-1563. 622-30: Boulogne-sur-Mer, by E. Martel. Nos. 202-39. 631: Bourbonne-les-Bains, by Parison. No. 14. 631-33: Bourbourg. Nos. 5-11. 633-35: Bourg. Nos. 70-87. 636-40: Bourges, by P. Micon. Nos. 401-22. 640: Brest, by Marion. Nos. 44-45.

—XLI (1903), Supplément, vol. II. p. 1-9: Caen, by Lavalley. Nos. 600-35. 9-10: Cahors, by Cangardel. Nos. 86-97. 10-21: Calais, by Boucher. Nos. 50-97. 21-24: Cambrai, by Capelle. Nos. 1399-1421. 24-28: Cannes, by Pinatel. Nos. 36-66. 28-36: Carcassonne, by Massé. Nos. 301-62. 37: Castres, by Estadieu. Nos. 4-5. 37-81: Châlons-sur-Marne, by Mallet and Pélicier. Nos. 338-582, and other 63 and 26 mss. 82-100: Chambéry, by Perpéchon. Nos. 39-155. 100-21: Charleville, by Barbadeux. Nos. 285-445. 121-47: Chartres. Nos. 1797-1873. 147-50: Châteaudun, by Hetté. Nos. 538-49. 150: Château-Gontier, by Guillemain. No. 13. 150: Château-Thierry. Nos. 21-23. 151-85: Cherbourg, by Amiot. Nos. 226-310. 185-88: Clermont (Oise), by Ch. Pouillet. Nos. 67-80. 188-89: Clermont-Ferrand, by E. Vimont. Nos. 364-66 and 788-93. 190: Compiègne, by Ridoux. No. 87. 190: Conches. No. 12. 190-91: Condé-sur-Noireau, by A. Bénet. No. 2. 191-92: Condom, by Gardère. Nos. 13-17. 192: Constantine, by Hinglais. Nos. 2-3. 193-96: Corbeil by Dufour. Nos. 10-27. 197: Crépy-en-Valois. 3 mss. 197-204: Dijon, by Guignard. Nos. 171-485 (scattered

nos.). 205: Dinan, by Sabot. Nos. 4-7. 205-47: Douai, by Rivière. Nos. 1240-1478. 248: Épernay, by Brion. Nos. 221-23. 248-50: Étampes, by Sabatier. Nos. 53-66. 250-51: Fécamp, by Delabonde. Nos. 35-39. 251: Figeac. 4 mss. 252-53: Flers, by Murie. Nos. 18-37. 253-54: Fontainebleau, by Goujat. Nos. 23-27. 254-55: Fougères, by Bourdais. Nos. 7-14. 256: Gaillac. Nos. 2-3. 256: Gien. No. 40. 256-61: Grasse, by Doussan. Nos. 31-66. 261-67: Gray, by Jourdy. Nos. 33-65. 268-377: Grenoble, by E. Maignien. Nos. 2090-2485. 378: Hyères. No. 31. 378-79: Lagny, by Desgeans. Nos. 2-5. 379-84: Langres, by A. Baudouin. Nos. 139-56. 384-447: Laon, by Mestre and Houssart. Nos. 478-608 and autographs. 447-509: La Rochelle, by Musset. Nos. 760-1352. 509-17: La Roche-sur-Yon, by E. Louis. Nos. 16-60. 518-31; Laval, by Brou. Nos. 100-260. 531-43: Le Havre, by Millot. Nos. 397-459. 543-45: Le Mans, by Guérin. Nos. 494-500. 545-47: Le Puy. Nos. 50-58. 547-48: Libourne, by Saüe. Nos. 10-22. 548-637: Lille, by E. Desplanque. Nos. 745-986. 637-41: Limoges, by C. Leymarie. Nos. 40-49. 641-52: Lons-le-Saunier, by Bertrand. Nos. 21-58. 652-53: Lorient, by Colas. Nos. 6-9. 653-54: Louviers. Nos. 37-43. 654-57: Lunéville, by Monin. Nos. 180-96. 657: Luxeuil, by Nardin, 6 mss.

—XLII (1904), Supplément, vol. III. 1-278: Lyon, by Desvernay. Nos. 1965-2335, and 1010 autographs from the Charavay Collection. 278-86: Mâcon, by Lex. Nos. 79-158. 286-89: Marseille, by Barré. Nos. 1657-71. 290-91: Meaux, by Andrieux. Nos. 120-33. 291-95: Melun, by Leroy. Nos. 88-101. 295: Menton. 1 ms. 296: Mézières. 2 mss. 296: Mirecourt, by Tresse. No. 6. 296-97: Montbéliard, by Meunier. Nos. 213-24. 298: Mont-de-Marsan, by Teulet. No. 3. 298-303: Montdidier, by A. Ledieu. 46 mss. 304-52: Montpellier, by Gaudin. Nos. 65-117. 352-53: Morlaix, by Koscher. Nos. 29-39. 353-88:

Nancy, by Favier. Nos. 1138-1471. 388-93: Nantes, by Rousse. Nos. 2212-43, and 98 other mss. 393-416: Narbonne, by Tissier. Nos. 164-301. 417: Nemours. No. 12. 417: Neufchâtel. Nos. 44-47. 418-19: Nevers, by Duminy. Nos. 22-32. 420-560: Nîmes. Nos. 366-578. 560: Niort, by Chotard. No. 186. 561-62: Noyon, by Gandissart. Nos. 41-53. 563: Oloron, by Marque. Nos. 6-8. 563-649: Orléans, by Cuissard. Nos. 969-1386.

—XLIII (1904), Supplément, vol. IV. p. vii-xv: Liste des collaborateurs. p. xvii-xxiii: Liste des villes (for quarto and octavo series). 1-126: Paris, Bibliothèque de l'Arsénal, by H. Martin. Nos. 7601-7907. 126: Pau, by Soulice. Nos. 37-40. 126-29: Périgueux, by Caillac. Nos. 68-73. 130: Péronne, by A. Ledieu. No. 17. 131-33: Perpignan, by Vidal. Nos. 122-27. 133-39: Poitiers, by Ginot. Nos. 548-67. 139-45: Poligny, by Bonvalot. Nos. 54-59. 145-46: Pont-à-Mousson. Nos. 22-24. 146: Pont-de-Vaux, by Girardin. No. 2. 146-48: Provins, by Bellanger. Nos. 270-81. 148: Rambervillers, by Gardeur. Nos. 6-21. 149-54: Remiremont, by Denis. Nos. 51-66. 154-64: Roanne, by L. Dorez. 51 mss. 165: Rodez, by De Rouget. Nos. 117-20. 165-68: Romorantin, by G. Trouilliard. 15 mss. 168-226: Rouen, by H. Loriquet. 161 mss. 226-27: Roye, by Ledieu. Nos. 45-53. 227-28: Saint-Amand. No. 22. 228-29: Saint-Brieuc, by Petit. Nos. 116-22. 229-35: Saint-Calais, by Charbonnier. Nos. 17-44. 235-59: Saint-Dié, by Gerlach, Tremsel and L. Dorez. Nos. 76-104. 259-73: Saint-Étienne, by Maissiat. Nos. 236-306. 273-97: Saint-Germain, by Bonneau. Nos. 27-127. 297-98: Saint-Malo, by Lemoine. Nos. 22-25. 298-306: Saint-Omer, by Framezelle. Nos. 887bis-925. 307-09: Saint-Pol, by Robache and Edmond. Nos. 31-42. 309-40: Saint-Quentin, by Magnier. Nos. 183-291. 340-41: Saintes, by Audiat. Nos. 54-60. 341-45: Sens, by Morin de Champrousse. Nos. 290-319. 345-47: Soissons, by Judas.

Nos. 276-80. 347-67: Toulon. Nos. 63-64. 367-423: Toulouse, by Massip. Nos. 888-1020. 423-31: Tournus, by Martin. Nos. 35-100. 432: Le Tréport, by Ledieu. 3 mss. 433-650: Troyes, by L. Dorez. Nos. 2428-2920. 650-63: Tulle, by Godard and Gauthier. Nos. 3-93. 663-64: Valence, by Chirol. Nos. 36-37. 664-65: Valenciennes, by Hénault. Nos. 1089-94. 665-67: Vannes, by Laisné. Nos. 16-21. 667-72: Vendôme, by F. Bonnardot. Nos. 397-750. 750-52: Versailles, by Léonardon. Scattered nos. to 856 bis. 753: Vervins. 5 mss. 753-56: Vesoul, by Stouff. Nos. 231-43. 757: Vienne. Nos. 163-64. 757-58: Villefranche (Rhône) by Déresse. Nos. 3-5. 758: Villeneuve-sur-Lot, by P. Meyer. 2 mss. 758-59: Vire, by C.-A. Fédérique. Nos. 237-44. 760-62: Vitry-le-François, by Nicolle. Nos. 174-75. 762-64: Millau, by E. Lacroix. 10 mss. 764-65: Montélimar, by Fauque. 5 mss.

—XLIV (1911) 1-310: Caen, Collection Nancel, by R.-N. Sauvage. 306 mss. 311-486: Avignon, Deuxième Supplément, by L. H. Labande and J. Girard. Nos. 3944-4329.

—XLV (1915) 1-34: Paris, Bibliothèque de l'Arsenal, by P. Deslandres. Nos. 7466-9155. 35-55. Paris, Bibliothèque Mazarine, by P. Marais and A. D'Artois. Nos. 4529-61 and documents. 57-126: Paris, Bibliothèque Sainte-Geneviève, by Ch. Kohler. Nos. 3415-3585. 127-398: Besançon, by G. Gazier, M. Prinet and P. Nicolle. Nos. 1297-1875. 399-515: Aix, Deuxième Supplément. Nos. 1352-1612.

—XLVI (1924) 1-224: Bibliothèques de la Marine, Supplément, by Ch. de la Roncière. 225-348: La Rochelle, Deuxième Supplément, by G. Musset. Nos. 1353-2137. 349-419: Nancy, Deuxième Supplément, by J. Favier. Nos. 1472-2200.

—XLVII (1923), 936 pp. Strasbourg, Bibliothèque nationale et universitaire, by E. Wickersheimer. 4759 mss. (nos. 1-348 in Latin).

—XLVIII (1933) 1-225: Rouen, Deuxième Supplément, by H. Labrosse. Nos. 162-1300. 227-321: Amiens, Deuxième Supplément, by H. Michel. Nos. 992-1400. 323-35: Université de Lille, by L. Macaigne. Nos. 1-3, 101-13, 201-25. 336-59: Université de Nancy, by A. Kolb. 33 and 7 and 54 mss. 361-452: Metz, Supplément, by P. Marot. Nos. 1030-1475.

—XLIX (1951) 1-46: Aix-en-Provence, 3e Supplément, by B. Durand. Nos. 1613-1768. 47-133: Arles, 2e Supplément, by F. Benoit. Nos. 484-1014. 134-35: Avignon, 3e Supplément, by J. Girard. Nos. 4330-5844.

—L (1954). XIII-XXII, 1-159: Paris, Bibliothèque de l'Arsenal, 3e Supplément, by F. Calot and J. Boussard. Nos. 13000-14125. 161-86: Amiens, 3e Supplément, by P. Logié. Nos. 1401-1945. 187-218: Bayonne, 2e Supplément, by H. Jeanpierre. Nos. 45-380. 219-375. Bordeaux, 2e Supplément, by L. Desgraves. Nos. 1565-1883. 377-390: Dieppe, Premier Supplément, by A. Boudier. Nos. 86-202. 391-92: Palais de Fontainebleau, 1er Supplément, by J. Guignard. Notice of the transfer of the mss. to the Bibliothèque Nationale, Paris. 393-412: Nîmes, 2e Supplément, by R. Durand. Nos. 573-700. 413-58: Strasbourg, Bibliothèque Nationale et Universitaire, 1er Supplément, by E. Wickersheimer. Nos. 4760-5070.

—LI (1956). Archives Départementales. XIV, 551 pp. p. xi-xiii: survey of older mss. Index in each volume.

—*Catalogue général des Manuscrits des Bibliothèques Publiques de France.* Paris. I (1909), 607 pp. 1-109: Bibliothèque Municipale du XVIe Arrondissement de Paris, by E. Coyecque. 132 mss. 111-214: École des Beaux-Arts, by M. de Bengy-Puyvallée. 638 mss. 215-348: Faculté de Médecine, by A. Boinet. 767 mss. 349-428: Académie de Médecine, by the same. 551 mss. 429-53: Archives de l'Assistance Publique, by the same. 69 mss. 455-63: Archives de l'Hospice des Quinze-Vingts.

25 mss. 465-81: École Supérieure de Pharmacie. 72 mss. 483-89: Institution Nationale des Sourds-Muets. 5 mss. 491-92: Institution Nationale des Jeunes-Aveugles. 4 mss. 493-98: École Vétérinaire d'Alfort. 66 mss.

—II (1914). vii, 565 pp. iii-357: Muséum d'Histoire Naturelle, by A. Boinet. 2009 mss. 359-66: École des Mines, by the same. 29 mss. 367-455: École des Ponts et Chaussées, by the same. 353 mss. 457-65: École Polytechnique, by the same. 24 mss. Each volume indexed.

—*Catalogue des Manuscrits de la Bibliothèque de l'Arsénal,* by H. Martin. I (1885): Nos. 1-663. II (1886): Nos. 664-2387. III (1887): Nos. 2388-3800. IV (1888): Nos. 3801-5002. V (1889): Nos. 5003-6022. VI (1892): Nos. 6023-8807. VII (1896): Index of vols. I-VI. VIII (1899): 'Histoire de la Bibliothèque de l'Arsénal.' IX (1892): Archives de la Bastille, by F. Funck-Brentano. Nos. 10001-12727.

—*Bibliothèque de l'Institut. Ancien et Nouveau Fonds,* by M. Bouteron and J. Tremblot. Paris 1928. 758 pp. 3800 mss. and autographs.

—*Bibliothèque de l'Institut. Collection Godefroy,* by F. Gébelin. Paris 1914. 951 pp. 553 mss.

—*Bibliothèque de l'Institut. Musée Condé à Chantilly. Bibliothèque Thiers. Musées Jacquemart-André à Paris e à Chaalis.* Paris 1928. 497 pp. p. 1-275: Musée Condé à Chantilly, by G. Macon. 1480 mss. 277-354: Bibliothèque Thiers, by H. Malo. 1250 mss. 355-61: Musée Jacquemart-André à Paris. 23 mss. 363-370: Musée Jacquemart-André à Chaalis. 25 mss. 371-76: Bibliothèque Thiers, Supplément, by H. Malo. 586 documents. (NN)

—*Catalogue des Manuscrits de la Bibliothèque Mazarine,* by A. Molinier. I (1885): Nos. 1-1066. II (1886): Nos. 1067-3059. III (1890): Nos. 3060-4482. IV (1892-98): Supplément, Nos. 4483-94 and appendix. Index of vols. I-IV. Supplément 1898 (nos. 4495-4528).

—*Catalogue des Manuscrits de la Bibliothèque Sainte-Geneviève*, by Ch. Kohler. I (1893): Nos. 1-1382. II (1896): Nos. 1383-3414. Index of vols. I-II. Introduction (1898).
—*Bibliothèque du Senat*, by L. Engerand. Paris 1908. 597 pp. 1343 mss.
—*Chambre des Députés*, by E. Coyecque and H. Debraye. Paris 1907. 664 pp. 1546 mss.
—*Catalogue général des Manuscrits des Bibliothèques Publiques de France. Archives de la Guerre*, by L. Tuetey. I (1912): Nos. 1-1246. II (1915): Nos. 1247-1878. III (1920): Nos. 1879-2118. Index of vols. I-III.
—*Bibliothèques de la Guerre*, by J. Lemoine and others. Paris 1911. 547 pp.
— *Bibliothèques de la Marine*, by Ch. de la Roncière. Paris 1907. 558 pp.
—*Sociétés Savantes*, vol. I, Paris 1931. 623 pp. 1-70: Société des Antiquaires de Picardie à Amiens, by C. Brunel. 442 mss. 71-131: Société des Antiquaires de l'Ouest à Poitiers, by the same. 299 mss. 133-62: Société des Archives Historiques de Poitou à Poitiers, by the same. 192 mss. 163-94: Société libre d'agriculture, sciences, arts et belles-lettres d'Eure à Évreux, by H. Omont and L. Regnier. 5 Latin mss., 17 French mss. and documents. 195-255: Société Archéologique de Montpellier, by E. Bonnet. 80 mss. and documents. 257-320: Société d'archéologie lorraine à Nancy, by J. Favier and P. Laprevote. 315 mss. 321-467: Société de l'histoire du Protestantisme Français à Paris, by A. Mailhet and E.-G. Léonard. 933 mss.
— *Université de Paris et Universités des Départements. Paris* 1918. 803 pp. 1-368: Bibliothèque de l'Université de Paris, by Ch. Beaulieu. 1590 mss. and documents. 369-465: Bibliothèque Victor Cousin à la Sorbonne, by P. Deschamps. 261 mss. 467-91: Faculté de Droit de Paris, by P. Viollet. 140 mss. 493-99: Aix-Marseille, by G. Fleury and M. Godefroy. 25 mss. and documents. 499-501: École de Médecine de Besançon, by F. Prieur. 14 mss.

501-17: Bordeaux, by E. Bouvy. 178 mss. 517-22: Caen, by D. Bonnet. 56 mss. 522-23: Dijon, by L. Balland. 7 mss. 524: Grenoble, by O. Nicaud. 5 mss. 524-40 and 659-60: Lyon, by M. Dreyfus and E. Gaillard. 102 mss. 540-75: Montpellier, by H. Bel and L. Girard. Nos. 543-614. 575: Poitiers, by G. Vacher de Laponge. 1 ms. 575-606: Rennes, by H. Teulié. 247 mss. 606-58: Toulouse, by G. Ducos and L. Vié. 390 mss.

E. Franceschini, 'Le versioni latine medievali di Aristotele e dei suoi commentatori greci ed arabi nelle biblioteche delle Tre Venezie,' *Miscellanea di Scritti di Bibliografia ed Erudizione in memoria di Luigi Ferrari* (Florence 1952) 313-26. Covers Belluno, Novacella, Padua, S. Candido, S. Daniele, Trent, Treviso, Trieste, Venice.

G. Fransen, 'Manuscrits canoniques conservés en Espagne,' *Revue d'Histoire Ecclésiastique* XLVIII (1953) 224-234; XLIX (1954) 152-56. Arranged by subjects. Covers Barcelona, Burgo de Osma, Calahorra, Cordoba, Escorial, Granada, Leon, Madrid, Murcia, Oviedo, Pamplona, Pontevedra, Salamanca, Santander, Santiago de Compostela, Segovia, Sevilla, Sigüenza, Soria, Tarazona, Tarragona, Toledo, Tortosa, Tuy, Valencia, Valladolid, Vich, Zaragoza. (NNUT)

J. Frast, 'Merkwürdige Handschriften der österreichischen Stifte Altenburg, Herzogenburg und Heiligenkreuz,' *Jahrbücher der Literatur* XXIV (1823), *Anzeige-Blatt*, 38-41. No index.

W. H. Frere, *Bibliotheca Musico-Liturgica: A descriptive handlist of the musical and Latin-liturgical Mss. of the Middle Ages preserved in the libraries of Great Britain and Ireland.* 2 vols. in 4 fascicules. London 1894-1932. Covers London, Oxford, Canterbury, York, Durham, Bangor, Exeter, Hereford, Lincoln, Ripon, Salisbury, Truro, Worcester, Liverpool, Stonyhurst, Manchester, Edinburgh, Paisley, Stirling, Dublin, Cambridge. 1031 mss. Indices.

*A. Gabriel, *Nürnberger Handschriften in Ungarn.* (Etudes sur l'Europe Centre-Orientale 52). Budapest 1944. (OO)

L. Gachard, *Les Bibliothèques de Madrid et de l'Fscurial: Notices et Extraits des manuscrits qui concernent l'histoire de Belgique.* Brussels 1875. 678 pp.

E. Garin, 'Le traduzioni umanistiche di Aristotele nel secolo XV,' *Atti e Memorie dell' Accademia Fiorentina di Scienze Morali " La Colombaria ",* XVI (N.S.II) 1947-50 (Florence 1951) 55-104.

The same, 'Ricerche sulle traduzioni di Platone nella prima metà del sec. XV,' *Medioevo e Rinascimento: Studi in Onore di Bruno Nardi* I (Florence 1955) 339-74.

C. A. Garufi, *Catalogo illustrato del tabulario di S. Maria Nuova in Monreale* (Documenti per servire alla Storia di Sicilia, ed. Società Sicilⁱana per la storia patria, Ser. I vol. XIX). Palermo 1902. XXI, 271 pp. p. 133-43: 'Codici pergamenacei e cartacei.' 33 mss. p. 223-35: 'Codici e libri quattrocentini dell' ex Monastero di S. Maria Nuova di Monreale conservati nella Biblioteca di quel Comune.' 25 mss. Index (243 ff.). The first group of mss. is now in the Biblioteca Nazionale, Palermo.

Martini Gerberti . . . *Iter Alemannicum, accedit Italicum et Gallicum* . . . St. Blasien 1765. 519 pp. Lists mss. of S. Giorgio Maggiore in Venice (p. 452-58). Index inadequate. (NNUT)

Martin Gerberts... *Reisen durch Alemannien, Welschland und Frankreich...* Ulm, Frankfurt and Leipzig 1767. 478 pp. (DLC)

Phil. Wilh. Gercken, *Reisen durch Schwaben, Baiern, angränzende Schweiz, Franken, und die rheinischen Provinzen etc. in den Jahren 1779-1782* . . . 4 vols. Stendal 1783-88. Lists mss. at Heilbronn (I, 31ff.), Zwiefalten (69ff.), Ulm (97ff.), Wiblingen (111), Ochsenhausen (115), Weingarten (120ff.) Salmansweiler (151), Constance (155ff.), Reichenau (163ff.), Memmingen (181ff.), Ottobeuren (196), Augsburg (243ff.), Munich (329ff.), Freising (345ff.), Ingolstadt (356ff.), Polling (371), Benediktbeuren (377ff.), Tegernsee (390ff.), Salzburg (II, 17ff.), Ober-Altaich (75ff.), Windberg (79ff.), Regensburg (99ff.), Zürich (246ff.). St. Gall (273ff.), Würzburg (340ff.), Eberach (361ff.), Fulda (370ff.), Erlangen (377ff.), Ansbach (429ff.), Mainz (III, 37ff.), Mannheim (171ff.), Köln (307ff.), Trier (378), Arnstein (437), Dillenberg (459), Frankfurt (IV, 176ff.): Darmstadt (286ff.). No index. Largely superseded. (Newark Public Library).

Giornale delle Biblioteche. I (1867) 4-6; 28-29: 'Le Biblioteche di Genova.' Lists 41 mss. of Biblioteca Civica Berio, and a few of University Library. 6; 14; 23-24: 'Biblioteca della Cava dei Tirreni.' Lists 116 mss. 12-13: 'Elenco di Codici Manoscritti esistenti nella Regia Biblioteca di Parma.' Lists some older mss. 17-20: 'Biblioteca di Ferrara.' Lists some mss. 26-28: 'Biblioteca Vaticana, Manoscritti del Conte Giammaria Mazzuchelli.' Describes Vat. lat. 9260-71. 38-39: 'Elenco di codici antichi della Biblioteca Riccardiana.' 44-45; 61-63; 72: 'Manoscritti esistenti nella Biblioteca del Principe Baldassarre Boncompagni.' 93-94; 104; 119-20: 'Dei Manoscritti esistenti nella Biblioteca del Marchese Gino Capponi a Firenze.'

—II (1868) 37-38; 41-42; 62-64; 83-85; 109-110; 124-125: A. Dorange, 'Notice sur la Bibliothèque de la ville de Tours.' Lists 432 mss. 42-43: 'Biblioteca Communale di Savona.' Lists 17 mss. 55-56; 64; 75-76; 90-92; 112; 117-18; 126-27; 140-42; 187-89; III (1869) 21-22; 30-31; 51-52; 61-62; 68-69; IV (1870) 88: G. Benelli, 'Cenno storico della R. Biblioteca di Mantova.' Lists 121 mss. II 82-83; 89-90; 103-04; 125-26; 131-33: 'Biblioteca de' Missionari Urbani in Genova.' Lists mss. no. 41-157.

—III (1869) 105-06; 115-17; 137-38; IV (1870) 9-10; 17-18; 25-27; 34-36; 41-42; 51-52: 'Di alcuni manoscritti della Biblioteca Nazionale di Brera in Milano.' III (1869) 158-60; 175-76; 181-83; IV

(1870) 23-24: 'Memorie sulla Biblioteca di Rimini.' Lists some mss.

—IV (1870) 73-75; 92; 98-99; 107-08; 114-16; 122-23; V (1871) 53-54; 62-63; 76-78; 83-85; 93-94; VI (1872) 35-36; 41-42; 49-50; 61-62; VII (1873) no. 1 p. 7-8; no. 2 p. 4; no. 3 p. 5-6; no. 4 p. 4-6; no. 5 p. 2-3: 'Codici pregevoli della Biblioteca Bertoliana Comunale di Vicenza.' Lists many mss.

—IV (1870) 96; 111-12; 128; 176: A. Mainardi, 'Manoscritti della R. Biblioteca di Mantova.' Lists mss. no. 122-129.

—V (1871) 42-44: L. Longoni, 'Biblioteca Nazionale di Milano, Di un codice della Geografia di Francesco Berlinghieri.' 49-52; 57-60; 65-67: G.B.C. Giuliari, 'Delle emigrazioni letterarie italiane, ovvero alquanti Codici spariti, non è molto, da Verona.' Lists Saibante mss.

—VI (1872) 62-63: A. Meana, 'Biblioteca Comunale di Torino.' Lists 1 ms. No indices. (MnU)

P. Glorieux, *La littérature quodlibétique* (de *1260 à 1320*). 2 vols. Le Saulchoir 1925 and Paris 1935. (Bibliothèque Thomiste V and XXI). Each volume arranged alphabetically by first names of authors. Index of mss. (I, 379-80, and for both volumes: II, 336-39).

The same, *Répertoire des maîtres en théologie de Paris au XIII⁰ siècle*. (Études de philosophie médiévale XVII-XVIII). 2 vols. Paris 1933-34. Arranged by religious orders and by authors. Index of authors (II, 351-62) and of mss. (II, 463-503) for both volumes.

Cf. V. Doucet, 'Maîtres Franciscains de Paris. Supplément au "Répertoire des Maîtres en Théologie de Paris au XIIIᵉ siècle" de M. le Chan. P. Glorieux,' *Archivum Franciscanum Historicum* XXVII (1934) 531-64.

T. Gottlieb, *Mittelalterliche Bibliothekskataloge Österreichs*. I. Niederösterreich. Wien 1915. XVI, 615 pp. p. 289-414: Wien, Dominikanerkloster. This old catalogue is still partly valid. (NNC). Vol. II: *Register*, by A. Goldmann. 1929. IX, 167 pp. (NN)

M. Grabmann, *Mittelalterliches Geistesleben.* 3 vols. Munich 1926-56. Each volume has an index of mss.

(Great Britain) *Historical Manuscripts Commission. Report 1st*, London 1874 . . . *22nd Report*, 1946. Also many other volumes (to vol. 81, 1940). This series covers mostly private collections and lists mainly documents. Of special interest are: Everingham Park, by J. Stevenson (First Report, 1870, App., p. 45-46); Helmingham Hall, by A. J. Horwood, (60-61); College of St. Mary, Oscott, by J. Stevenson (89-90); College of St. Cuthbert, Ushaw, by the same (91-92); Wrest Park (Second Report, 1871, App., p. 4-9); Worthenbury (65-68); St. Lawrence's College, Ampleforth (109-110; 125-26); Stonyhurst College, First Report, by J. Stevenson, (143-46, 35 mss.); Dominican Friars, Woodchester (146-49); Catholic College, Blairs (201-203, 35 mss.); Second and concluding notice of the mss. preserved at Stonyhurst College, by J. Stevenson (Third Report, 1872, App., p. 334-41); The Manuscripts of the former College of Irish Franciscans, Louvain, by J. T. Gilbert (Fourth Report, 1874, p. 599-613); Oxford, Pembroke College, by H. T. Riley (Sixth Report, 1877, App., p. 549-51); Royal College of Physicians, London (Eighth Report, 1881, App., pt. 1, p. 226-35); The Manuscripts of the Earl of Ashburnham (pt. 3, p. 5-127); Eton College, by H.C.M. Lyte (Ninth Report, 1883, App., pt. 1, p. 349-58); Holkham Hall, by A. J. Horwood (p. 357-75); Library of the Inner Temple, by W. D. Macray (Eleventh Report, 1888, App., pt. 7, p. 227-308); Gloucester Cathedral Library, by W. H. Stevenson (Twelfth Report, 1891, App., pt. 9, p. 397-99). Also the following volumes of the whole series: *Report on Franciscan Manuscripts preserved at the Convent, Merchants' Quay, Dublin* (called vol. 65). Dublin 1906.

XII, 296 pp. (by G. D. Burtchaell and J. M. Rigg). Describes mss. D 1-4 only. Not complete. The library is now in Killiney. *Report on Manuscripts in Various Collections* (called vol. 55), vol. IV (1907), p. 23-95: Muniments and Library of the Dean and Chapter of Exeter, by R. L. Poole (esp. p. 28-34). *Report on the Manuscripts of Lord Middleton, preserved at Wollaton Hall, Nottinghamshire* (called vol. 69). London 1911. XV, 746 pp. (by W. H. Stevenson). p. 196-271: Manuscript Books. The collection is now deposited in Nottingham University Library.

Gyldne Bøger. Copenhagen 1952. 95 pp. and plates. 203 illuminated mss. from Danish and Swedish collections. Exhibition catalogue.

Gyllene Böcker. Stockholm 1952. 96 pp. and plates. 209 illuminated mss. from Danish and Swedish collections. Exhibition catalogue.

G. Haenel, *Catalogi librorum manuscriptorum qui in bibliothecis Galliae, Helvetiae, Belgii, Britanniae M., Hispaniae, Lusitaniae asservantur.* Leipzig 1830. 1238 coll. Mostly superseded. Of interest are the lists for Basel (513-660, arranged alphabetically); Lausanne (733); Muri (734); The Hague (769-70); Louvain (770); Glasgow, University Library (784-86); Lincoln Cathedral (799-801); Liverpool (802); London, St. Martin (802-03); Barcelona (919-20); Madrid (965-75); Segovia (977); Seville (979-83); Toledo (984-999); Lisbon (1014-36). Good index.

The same, 'Ungedruckte Handschriftenkataloge,' *Neue Jahrbücher für Philologie und Pädagogik*, Supplementband V (Archiv für Philologie und Pädagogik V, 1837) 591-639; VI (1840) 224-42; 423-61; 546-94; VII (1841) 594-617; VIII (1842) 437-58; 587-621. Covers collection Nic. Sen. Jankowich at the National Museum in Budapest (V-VI); Admont, mss. no. 428-783, by A. von Muchar (VI, 424-44); Clara Vallis Aust. (Zwettl; 444-52); Schaff-

hausen (452-459); Solothurn (459-60); Phillipps Collection (VI-VIII).

C. R. Haines, 'The Library of Dover Priory: Its Catalogue and Extant Volumes,' *The Library*, Fourth Ser. (Transcations of the Bibliographical Society, Second Ser.) VIII (1927-28) 73-118. Lists 19 mss. extant in different libraries. No index.

R. W. Hall Jr. and L. MacKinney, 'Microfilms and Photostats of European Manuscripts,' *Speculum* XXIX (1954) 336-38. p. 336-37: French Manuscripts destroyed during the war. p. 338: Italian Libraries in which Mss. were destroyed, damaged or lost during the war.

K. Halm, 'Verzeichnis der älteren Handschriften lateinischer Kirchenväter in den Bibliotheken der Schweiz,' *Sitzungsberichte der Kaiserlichen Akademie der Wissenschaften* [Vienna], *Philosophisch-Historische Classe* L (1865) 107-60. Covers Bern, Zurich, St. Gall, Schaffhausen, Basel, Einsiedeln.

Handschriftenverzeichnisse österreichischer Bibliotheken. Kärnten, Bd. I: Klagenfurt, Maria Saal, Friesach, by H. Menhardt. Vienna 1927. 353 pp. 1-82: Klagenfurt, Bischöfliche Bibliothek. Mss. XXIX a 1- XXXI c 15, and 14 other mss. 83-183: Studienbibliothek. Perg. Hs. 1-46, Pap. Hs. 1-251. 184-254: Geschichtsverein für Kärnten. Mss. 1/1-11/21. 255-59: Kapuzinerkloster. 36 mss. 260-61: Priesterseminar. 9 mss. 262-63: Private collections. 2 mss. 264-87: Maria Saal. 45 mss. 288: Friesach, Stadtpfarre. 3 mss. 288-89: Dominikanerkloster. 4 mss.

—*Steiermark, Bd. II: Die Handschriften der Universitätsbibliothek Graz*, vol. II, by A. Kern. Vienna 1956. 412 pp. mss. 713-2066. No index. (NN)

Th. D. Hardy, *Descriptive Catalogue of Materials Relating to the History of Great Britain and Ireland, to the end of the reign of Henry VII.* 3 vol. in 4, London 1862-71. Chronological list to 1327 A. D. of numerous mss. mainly in British collections.

J. L. Heiberg, 'Bibliotheksnotizen,' *Philo-*

logus LV (N.F. IX, 1896) 732-48. Mentions a few Latin mss. in Bergamo.

G. Heider and J. V. Haeufler, 'Archäologische Notizen gesammelt auf einem Ausfluge nach Herzogenburg, Göttweih, Melk und Seitenstätten im September 1849, *Archiv fürKunde österreichischer Geschichtsquellen*, year III (1850) vol. II p. 139-78; 523-606. Discusses only Herzogenburg and Göttweih.

A. De Hevesy, *La bibliothèque du roi Matthias Corvin*. Paris 1923. 103 pp. and plates. Lists 156 mss. extant in different libraries (59-86).

F. Hipler, 'Analecta Varmiensia,' *Zeitschrift für die Geschichte und Alterthumskunde Ermlands* V (1870-74) 316-488. Discusses mss. in Braunsberg (Braniewo), Uppsala (428-39), Linköping (439-57), Stockholm (Riksarkivet, 457-61), as well as in Prussia, Poland, France and Italy. (NN)

F. K. G. Hirsching, *Versuch einer Beschreibung sehenswürdiger Bibliotheken Teutschlands nach alphabetischer Ordnung der Städte*. 4 vols. Erlangen 1786-91. Lists mss. at Eberach (I, 101-02); Gaybach (131ff.); Würzburg (265 ff.); Altona (II, 22ff.); Augsburg (103ff.); Gaybach (333ff.); Neustadt an der Aisch (446ff.); Nuremberg (III, 30ff.); Prague (208ff.); Rebdorf (479ff.); Regensburg (580ff.); Bayreuth (IV, 71ff.); Nuremburg (114ff.); Kassel (223ff.); Giessen (246ff.); Prague (272ff.). Index in vol. IV.

Hispania Sacra I (1948) 183-206: 'Manuscritos españoles en Bibliotecas Extranjeras.' Copenhagen, by A. Fabrega Gran (184-90, 13 mss.). Rome, Biblioteca Angelica, by J. Rius Serra (191-206). II (1949) 221-31. Rome, Biblioteca Nazionale, by the same (73 mss.). III (1950) 216-22. The same cont. (18 mss.). V (1952) 181-96. Cava, Einsiedeln, Engelberg, Reichenau (Karlsruhe), by J. Rius Serra and J. Vives. VI (1953) 208-12. Erlangen, by J. Vives. VIII (1955) 447-51. 'Manuscritos Hispánicos en colecciones Inglesas,' by the

same. Covers London, Oxford, Bristol, Leeds. (NN)

—VIII (1955) 429-46. A. Olivar, 'Notas sobre manuscritos.' Covers Madrid, Escorial, Elna (scattered), Barcelona, Sigüenza; collection Capdevilla Rovira, Barcelona (440-46, 6 mss.). (NN)

P. Högberg, 'Manuscrits italiens dans les bibliotheques suédoises,' *Rivista delle Biblioteche e degli Archivi* XXV (1914) 44-81. Describes 39 mss. at Stockholm and Uppsala, of which several in Latin. No index.

The same, 'Manuscrits espagnols dans les bibliothèques suédoises,' *Revue Hispanique* XXXVI (1916) 377-474. Describes 27 mss. in Swedish libraries, including several Latin mss. in Stockholm. No index. See also: L. Pfandl, 'Ergänzungen zu Högbergs Katalog spanischer Handschriften in schwedischen Sammlungen,' *Archiv für das Studium der Neueren Sprachen und Literaturen*, year LXXVI, vol. CXLIV (N. S. XLIV, 1922) 241-49.

J. Huemer, 'Iter Austriacum,' *Wiener Studien* IX (1887) 51-93. Notes on many collections. No index.

Joseph Hunter, *Three Catalogues; describing the contents of the Red Books of the Exchequer, of the Dodsworth Mss. in the Bodleian Library, and of the Mss. in the Library of the Honourable Society of Lincoln's Inn*. London 1838. IX, 413 pp. p. 57: ' A Catalogue of the manusripts written or collected by that eminent antiquary Roger Dodsworth, and now deposited in the Bodleian Library.' Lists 161 mss. p. 251: 'A Catalogue of the manuscripts in the Library of the Honourable Society of Lincoln's Inn.' 486 mss. No index. (NN). The last part was also published separately, London 1838, 157 pp. (DLC)

Institut de Recherche et d'Histoire des Textes, *Bulletin d'Information* II (1953) 7-24: E. Pellegrin, 'Manuscrits des auteurs classiques latins de Madrid et du Chapître de Tolède.' III (1954) 7-32. The same, 'Manuscrits d'auteurs latins de l'epoque classique conservés dans les bibliothèques publiques de Suède.' Covers Stockholm, Skokloster, Strängnäs, Linköping, Lund, Växjö. IV (1955) 7-33. The same cont. Covers Uppsala. Index. III (1954) 111-16: M.-Th. Vernet, 'Les manuscrits de la Hessische Landesbibliothek de Darmstadt.' VI (1957) 7-40. The same, 'Notes de Dom André Wilmart sur quelques manuscrits latins anciens de la Bibliothèque Nationale de Paris.'

Inventare Schweizerischer Archive (Beilage zum Anzeiger für Schweizerische Geschichte). 2 pts., Bern 1895-99. Pt. 2, p. 1-110: Inventar des Staatsarchives des Kantons Zürich, by P. Schweizer. p. 118-84: Inventar des Stiftsarchivs St. Gallen, by J. Häne. (NN)

(Italy). Ministero dell' Interno. *Pubblicazioni degli Archivi di Stato.* In this series, note especially: II. Archivio di Stato di Firenze, *Archivio Mediceo avanti il Principato, Inventario.* Vol. I (Rome 1951). XXIX, 413 pp. Covers filze 1-20. Vol. II (1955). 547 pp. Covers filze 21-50. Vol. III (1957). 558 pp. Covers filze 51-100. IV. Archivio di Stato di Trento, *Archivio del Principato Vescovile, Inventario.* (Rome 1951). XXXII, 243 pp.

(Italy) Ministero dell' Istruzione Pubblica. *Indici e Cataloghi.* IV: *Cataloghi dei manoscritti della R. Biblioteca Nazionale Centrale di Firenze,* ed. A. Bartoli. *I Codici Palatini,* vol. I, by L. Gentile. Rome 1889. 736 pp. 448 mss. Index. *I codici palatini della R. Biblioteca Nazionale Centrale di Firenze,* vol. II, fasc. 1-6, 1890-99. 480 pp. Mss. no. 449-1006. *Indici,* by E. Rossi, Rome 1940. IV, 136 pp. *I manoscritti Palatini,* vol. III, fasc. 1-3, by P. L. Rambaldi and A. Saitta Revignas (1950-52). pp. 1-240. Mss. no. 1007-1107. No index.

—V: G. Mazzatinti, *Inventario dei manoscritti italiani delle biblioteche di Francia.* 3 vols., Rome 1886-88. I (1886): Paris, Bibliothèque Nationale, Fonds italien, mss.

1-1697. II (1887): mss. 1698-2000. Supersedes the catalogues of Marsand and Raynaud. III (1888). Other French libraries, including Paris libraries other than the Bibliothèque Nationale. Arranged alphabetically by cities.

—VII: *I codici Panciatichiani della R. Biblioteca Nazionale Centrale di Firenze.* Vol. I fasc. 1-3. Rome 1887-91. 240 pp. 148 mss. Fasc. 4, by B. Maracchi Biagiarelli (1953). pp. 241-347. Mss. no. 148-210. No index.

—VIII: *I codici Ashburnhamiani della R. Biblioteca Mediceo-Laurenziana di Firenze,* by C. Paoli. Fasc. 1-5, Rome 1887-1917. 400 pp. 243 mss. (NN). Fasc. 6, by E. Rostagno and T. Lodi (1948). pp. 401-480. Mss. no. 243-88. No index. The valid shelf marks are not the serial numbers of the catalogue, but the first numbers given in parentheses. The second numbers in parentheses are those of the printed list of 1884.

—X: A. Bianchi, *Relazione e Catalogo dei manoscritti di Filippo Pacini esistenti nella R. Biblioteca Nazionale Centrale di Firenze.* Rome, 1889. xxxvi, 288 pp. Modern material.

—XIII: F. Carta, *Codici, corali e libri a stampa miniati della Biblioteca Nazionale di Milano.* Rome 1891. 174 pp. 59 mss.

—XV: S. Morpurgo, *I manoscritti della R. Biblioteca Riccardiana di Firenze. Manoscritti italiani.* Vol. I fasc. 1-9, Rome 1893-1900. 713 pp. Describes Italian mss., no. 1002-1700. Covers a few Latin texts. (NN).

Nuova Serie II: *Catalogo dei manoscritti della Biblioteca Casanatense.* Vol. I (1949), by E. Moneti and others. VII, 169 pp. Mss. no. 1-100. II (1956), by M. Ceresi and E. Santovito. 105 pp. Mss. no. 101-200. III (1952), by M. Ceresi. 128 pp. Mss. no. 201-300. V (1958), by A. Moricca Caputi. 150 pp. Mss. no. 401-500. No index.

(Italy) Ministero dell' Educazione Nazionale. *Mostra delle biblioteche italiane. Acquisti e doni degli ultimi dieci anni.* Rome 1934. 232 pp. Lists 179 mss. (p. 3-51). No index.

Izložba Jugoslavenskih Rukopisa i Knjiga od XI.-XVIII. Stoljeća. Exposition des Manuscrits et des Livres du XIe au XVIIIe siècles. Zagreb 1954. 48 pp. and plates. Lists mss. from various Yougoslav libraries. Exhibition catalogue.

E. Jacobs, 'Die Handschriftensammlung Joseph Görres', *Zentralblatt für Bibliothekswesen* XXIII (1906) 189-204. p. 202-04: List of located mss. Most of them are in Berlin, but others are scattered.

M. R. James, *On the Abbey of S. Edmund at Bury.* (Cambridge Antiquarian Society, Octavo Publications, no. 28). Cambridge 1895. 220 pp. Lists mss. extant in different libraries, especially at Bury St. Edmund's, Ipswich, and Wisbech.

The same, 'Bury St. Edmunds Manuscripts,' *English Historical Review* XLI (1926) 251-60. Corrected list of 263 mss. extant in different libraries, including Bury St. Edmund's, Ipswich, and Wisbech. No index.

The same, 'The Library of the Grey Friars of Hereford,' *Collectanea Franciscana* I (British Society of Franciscan Studies, V; Aberdeen 1914) 114-23. Lists 18 mss. extant in different libraries.

The same, 'List of Manuscripts from the Cathedral Priory of Norwich now existing in English Libraries' (appendix to H. C. Beeching, 'The Library of the Cathedral Church of Norwich'), *Norfolk Archaeology* XIX, 1 (1915) 93-116. Lists 109 mss. extant in different libraries, including Norwich Cathedral (p. 103-04, 2 mss.). No index. (NN)

The same, *Lists of Manuscripts formerly in Peterborough Abbey Library* (Supplement to the Bibliographical Society's Transactions, no. 5). Oxford 1926. 104 pp. 15-17: Lists mss. extant in different libraries.

The same, 'Manuscripts from Essex Monastic Libraries,' *Transactions of the Essex Archaeological Society*, N. S. XXI (1937) 34-46. Lists mss. extant in different libraries. (NN)

The same, 'The Catalogue of the Library of the Augustinian Friars at York...,' *Fasciculus Joanni Willis Clark dicatus* (Cambridge 1909) 2-96. Present locations given for 4 mss. (p. 16).

(Thomas James) *Ecloga Oxonio-Cantabrigiensis* ... 2 pts. in 1, London 1600. Covers College libraries at Oxford and Cambridge. Superseded. (NNGr)

H. A. von Keller, *Verzeichnis altdeutscher Handschriften*, ed. E. Sievers. Tübingen 1890. V, 178 pp. (NN)

C. Kelly, 'Franciscan Scholarship in the Middle Ages,' *The Catholic Review* (Auckland) IV (1948-49) 665-89; 753-782; V (1949) 135-214. V 180-183: A Descriptive Catalogue of Franciscan Manuscripts. Lists 3 mss., apparently at the Auckland Public Library (cf. p. 137). 213-214: 1 more ms., apparently at the Kyancutta Museum, Kyancutta, South Australia. (DCU)

Neil R. Ker, *Medieval Libraries of Great Britain.* London 1941. 169 pp. Discusses many mss. extant in different libraries.

The same, 'More Manuscripts from Essex Monastic Libraries ...,' *Transactions of the Essex Archaeological Society*, N.S. XXII pt. II (1945) 298-310. (NN)

The same, *Fragments of Medieval Manuscripts used as Pastedowns in Oxford Bindings..* (Oxford Bibliographical Society, Publications, N.S. 5). Oxford 1954. XX, 278 pp. and plates. 2017 nos. and appendices. Index of libraries (p. 254-59). Covers Oxford and other British libraries.

M. Kos, *Codices aetatis mediae manu scripti qui in Slovenia reperiuntur. Srednjeveški rokopisi v Sloveniji.* Ljubljana 1931. 247 pp. Lists 159 mss. at Ljubljana, Kranj, Novo mesto, Maribor, Stari. (NN)

P. O. Kristeller, *Supplementum Ficinianum.* 2 vols. Florence 1937. Cites many humanistic mss. in Italian libraries (I, 109-35: II, 321-55). Index of names (II, 364-67) inadequate. No index of mss.

The same, *Studies in Renaissance Thought and Letters*. Rome 1956. XVI, 680 pp. p. 629-32: index of mss.

S. Kuttner, *Repertorium der Kanonistik (1140-1234). Prodromus Corporis Glossarum.* Vol. I, Vatican City 1937 (Studi e Testi 71). xx, 536 pp. p. 465-91: index of mss.

Ph. Labbeus, *Nova Bibliotheca manuscriptorum librorum* . . . Paris 1652-53. 515 pp. Contains list of mss. of some French collections. Superseded. (NN)

A. De La Fage, *Essais de diphthérographie musicale.* Paris 1864. 568 pp. Describes mss. in Rome, Florence, Pisa, Montecassino and Paris. (NN)

W. Lampen, 'Catalogus librorum abbatiae Sancti Adelberti Egmondanae,' *Antonianum* XVII (1942) 39-72. Lists a few mss. extant in different libraries (40-46). (NNUT)

The same, 'Mitteilungen über franziskanische Handschriften in Dänemark und Skandinavien,' *Miscellanea Historica P. Livario Oliger Septuagenario ab amicis et discipulis oblata = Antonianum* XX (1945) 439-58. Lists mss. in Kobnhavn, Linköping, Uppsala, Lund and Stockholm. No index. (NNUT)

**The same article, also in: *Kirchengeschichtliche Studien P. Michael Bihl O.F.M. als Ehrengabe dargeboten* (Kolmar 1944) 65-87.

*The same, 'Nomenclature et description de manuscrits franciscains,' *La France Franciscaine* XVII (1934) 217-26; 479-86; XVIII (1935) 443-49; XIX (1936) 269-79; XX (1937) 67-73. (DHN) Covers Amsterdam, Assisi, Avignon, Basel (5 mss.), Bruges (Séminaire, 2 mss.), Bruxelles, Chartres, Dresden, Erfurt, Essen (Stiftskirche), Firenze, Gent, 'sGravenhage (Royal Library, 3 mss.), Haarlem, Halle (1 ms.), Köln (Archiv der Stadt, 1 ms), London, Lüneburg (Ratsbuecherei, 13 mss.), Luxembourg, Luzern, Milano (Ambrosiana, 4 mss.; Braidense, 1 ms.), Montecassino, Monteprandone, Napoli (Nazionale, 4 mss.), Oristano (Cagliari, Cattedrale, 6 mss.; Conventuali, 4 mss.), Padova (Universitaria, 1 ms.) Paris, Roma (Casanatense, 1 ms.; Corsiniana, 1 ms.), Rostock (1 ms.), Sint Agatha (Kruisheren, 3 mss.), Utrecht, Vatican (6 mss.), Wien, Würzburg (Franziskaner, 1 ms.).

J. Leclercq, 'Les manuscrits des bibliothèques d'Espagne,' *Scriptorium* III (1949) 140-44.

The same, 'Textes et manuscrits de quelques bibliothèques d'Espagne,' *Hispania Sacra* II (1949) 91-118. Covers Santo Domingo de la Calzada (p. 103-04, 5 mss.) and Calahorra (105-06, 32 mss.).

The same, 'Manuscrits Cisterciens dans les Bibliothèques d'Italie,' *Analecta Sacri Ordinis Cisterciensis* V (1949) 94-108. Covers Florence, Lodi, Milan, Naples, Palermo, Pavia, Rome and Turin. (PU). VII (1951) 71-77. Covers Aosta (Biblioteca Capitolare), Como (Seminario Maggiore, 13 mss.), Torino (Seminario Metropolitano, 9 mss.). No index. (PU). X (1954) 302-07. Covers Bergamo, Bologna, Bressanone, Cesena, Ferrara, Foligno, Lucca, Mantua, Milan (Archivio di Stato), Modena, Novacella, Padua, Parma, Perugia, Pisa, Rome, Trent, Treviso, Venice, Verona, Vicenza. (NN)

The same, 'Recherches dans les manuscrits Cisterciens d'Espagne,' *ibid.* V (1949) 109-19. Covers Madrid, Pamplona (Diputación, p. 112-13), Tarragona, Seo de Urgel, Tarazona, Barcelona, Escorial, Seville, Toledo, León. (PU).

The same, 'Textes et manuscrits cisterciens en Suède,' *ibid.* VI (1950) 125-30. Covers Linköping, Stockholm, Uppsala. (PU)

The same, 'Les manuscrits Cisterciens du Portugal,' *ibid.* VI (1950) 131-39. Covers Arouca (Museu regional de arte sacra, p. 135-37, 7 mss.) and Lisbon (Arquivo nacional do Torre do Tombo, p. 137-39, 10 mss. from Lorvão). (PU)

The same, 'Textes Cisterciens dans les Bibliothèques d'Allemagne,' *ibid.* VII (1951) 46-70. Covers Aschaffenburg (Stiftsbibliothek), Cologne, Koblenz, Darmstadt, Dillingen, Düsseldorf, Frankfurt, Freiburg,

Fulda (Landesbibliothek and Priesterseminar), Heidelberg, Mainz, Munich, Nürnberg. Ottobeuren, Paderborn, Pommersfelden, Wolfenbüttel. (PU)

The same, 'Manuscrits cisterciens dans di-
verses bibliothèques,' *ibid.* XI (1955) 139-
48. Covers Frankfurt, Mainz (Priester-
seminar), Piesing (Schlossbibliothek), Trier
(St. Matthias), Würzburg, Linz, Salzburg
(St. Peter), Tarragona, Paris (École des
Beaux-Arts), Périgueux (Archives de la
Dordogne), Busto Arsizio, Padua, Clervaux
(Luxembourg), Aarau, Lausanne. (NN)

The same, 'Textes et manuscrits cisterciens
dans diverses bibliothèques,' *ibid.* XII
(1956) 289-310. Scattered mss. (NN)

P. Lehmann, 'Auf der Suche nach alten
Texten in nordischen Bibliotheken,' *Zentralblatt für Bibliothekswesen* LIV (1937)
261-86. Mentions a few mss. at København, Oslo, Göteborg, Strängnäs, Uppsala,
Stockholm and Helsinki, No index.

The same, 'Corveyer Studien,' *Abhandlungen
der Bayrischen Akademie der Wissenschaften. Philosophisch-Philologische und Historische Klasse* XXX no. 5 (1919). 83 pp.
p. 34-53: mss. extant in different libraries.

The same, 'Fragmente,' *Abhandlungen der
bayrischen Akademie der Wissenschaften,
Philosophisch-Historische Abteilung,* N.F.
XXIII (1944). 47 pp. Lists 46 frs. in
Wertheim, Würzburg, Munich.

The same, *Franciscus Modius als Hand-
schriftenforscher* (Quellen und Untersuchungen zur lateinischen Philologie des Mittelalters III, 1). Munich 1908. 152 pp.
p. 146-48: mss. extant in different libraries.

The same, 'Gerwin von Hameln und die
Andreasbibliothek in Braunschweig,' *Zentralblatt für Bibliothekswesen* LII (1935)
565-86. p. 578-81: Lists 21 mss. extant
in different libraries.

The same, 'Handschriften des Erfurter Benediktinerklosters St. Petri,' *Studien und
Mitteilungen zur Geschichte des Benediktinerordens,* N. F. XII-XIII (XLIII-XLIV,
1926) 14-31; 89-91. (NN)

The same, 'Holländische Reisefrüchte I-III,'

*Sitzungsberichte der philosophisch-philolo-
gischen und der historischen Klasse der
Bayrischen Akademie der Wissenschaften,*
1920, no. 13. 34 pp. Describes mss. at
Leyden, the Hague, Amsterdam, Groningen, Utrecht, Deventer and Venloe. No
index.

The same, *Johannes Sichardus und die von
ihm benutzten Bibliotheken und Handschriften* (Quellen und Untersuchungen
zur lateinischen Philologie des Mittelalters
IV, 1). Munich 1913. 237 pp. p. 222-27:
List of mss.

The same, 'Mitteilungen aus Handschriften
I,' *Sitzungsberichte der philosophisch-philo-
logischen und der historischen Klasse der
Bayerischen Akademie der Wissenschaften,*
1929, no. 1. 55 pp. Describes mss. at
Erfurt, Freiburg, Heidelberg, Innsbruck,
Karlsruhe, Leyden, Nuremberg, Paris,
Vatican, Stuttgart, Tübingen, Wolfen-
büttel and Würzburg.

—II, *Ibid.* 1930, no. 2. 55 pp. Covers the
Hague, Kassel, London, Oxford, Paris.
Index for I and II (p. 48-55).

—III, *Ibid.* 1931-32, no. 6. 66 pp. Describes
over 70 mss. of the Lobkowitz collection at
Prague, and 3 at Berlin.

—IV, *Ibid.* 1933, no. 9. 84 pp. Covers Berlin, Kassel, Lüneburg and Wolfenbüttel.

—V, *Ibid.* 1938, no. 5. 93 pp. Covers
Budapest, Hamburg and other libraries.

—VI, *Ibid.* 1939, no. 4. 57 pp. Covers
Budapest. Index for V-VI (45-56).

—VII, *Ibid.* 1942, no. 10. 45 pp.

—VIII, *Ibid.* 1944, no. 2. 34 pp. 'Zu den
sprachlogischen Traktaten des Mittelalters.' Alphabetical list of Incipits, with
references to mss.

The same, *Mittelalterliche Bibliothekskataloge Deutschlands und der Schweiz.* 3 vols.
in 5, Munich 1918-39. Vol. III is by P. Ruf.

The same, 'Skandinavische Reisefrüchte,'
I, *Nordisk Tidskrift för Bok- och Biblioteks-
väsen* XXI (1934) 165-76. Covers Stock-
holm, Copenhagen, Uppsala. II, *Ibid.*
XXII (1935) 1-24. Covers Göteborg,
Växjö. III, *Ibid.,* 103-31. Soest; index

(126-31). Neue Folge, *Ibid.* XXIII (1936) 13-22; 49-84. Covers Lund. Index (80-84). Erste Nachlese, *Ibid.* XXIV (1937) 103-20; 141-64. Oslo, Göteborg, Stockholm, Bergen. Index (161-64). Zweite Nachlese, *Ibid.* XXV (1938) 155-72; 243-58. Helsingfors. Arranged by topics, not by ibraries.

Cf. lT. Kleberg, 'Einige Bemerkungen zu Paul Lehmanns "Skandinavische Reisefrüchte,"' *Ibid.* XXVII (1940) 241-42. Covers Göteborg.

Abbé V. Leroquais, *Les Bréviaires manuscrits des bibliothèques publiques de France.* 6 vols. Paris 1934. Arranged by libraries. 1045 mss.

The same, *Les Pontificaux manuscrits des bibliothèques publiques de France.* 3 vols. Paris 1937. Arranged by libraries. 250 mss.

The same, *Les Psautiers manuscrits latins des bibliothèques publiques de France.* 3 vols. Mâcon 1940-41. Arranged by libraries. 498 mss. (MH)

The same, *Les Sacramentaires et les Missels manuscrits des bibliothèques publiques de France.* 4 vols. Paris 1924. Arranged by libraries. 914 mss. (NN)

W. Levison, 'Conspectus codicum hagiographicorum,' in: *Monumenta Germaniae Historica, Scriptores Rerum Merovingicarum* VII (1920) 529-706. Arranged alphabetically by cities.

Libraries Guests of the Vaticana during the Second World War. Vatican City 1945. 70 pp. 228 mss.

W. M. Lindsay, *Notae Latinae: An Account of Abbreviations in Latin Manuscripts of the Early Minuscule Period* (*c.* 700-850). Cambridge 1915. 500 pp. p. 444-94: Lists of mss. in different libraries.

Little, see Section C under Oxford.

K. Löffler, *Die Handschriften des Klosters Weingarten* (Zentralblatt für Bibliothekswesen, Beiheft XLI). Leipzig 1912. 185 pp. Lists mss. extant at Stuttgart, Fulda and other libraries (54-150).

G. Loewe and W. von Hartel, 'Bibliotheca Patrum Latinorum Hispaniensis,' *Sit-*

zungsberichte der Kaiserlichen Akademie der Wissenschaften [Vienna], *Philosophisch-Historische Classe* CXI (1886) 415-568; CXII (1886) 161-266; 689-737; CXIII (1886) 47-128; 215-84; 499-578. Lists many patristic and classical mss. at the Escorial and Madrid (Biblioteca Nacional and other collections). No index. For an index, see Grubbs, above Section A, under Richardson.

E. A. Lowe, *The Beneventan Script: A History of the South Italian Minuscule.* Oxford 1914. 384 pp. p. 334-70: List of mss. in Benevento (41 mss, p. 335-36) and in other libraries.

The same, *Codices Latini Antiquiores: A Palaeographical Guide to Latin Manuscripts Prior to the Ninth Century.* Vol. I, Oxford 1934. 44 pp. Covers the Vatican. 117 mss. Vol. II, 1935: Great Britain and Ireland. 53 pp. Mss. no. 118-277. Vol. III, 1938: Italy—Ancona-Novara. 48 pp. Mss. no. 278-406. Vol. IV, 1947: Italy—Perugia-Verona. xxviii, 40 pp. Mss. no. 407-516. Vol. V, 1950: France, Paris. viii, 63, pp. Mss. no. 517-703. Vol. VI, 1953. France—Abbéville-Valenciennes. xxx, 48 pp. Mss. no. 704-841. Vol. VII, 1956. Switzerland. xi, 61 pp. Mss. no. 842-1021. Vol. VIII, 1959: Germany—Altenburg-Leipzig. xii, 69 pp. Mss. no. 1024-1229.

The same, 'A Hand-List of Half-Uncial Manuscripts,' *Miscellanea Francesco Ehrle* IV (Studi e Testi 40, Rome 1924) 34-61. Lists 160 mss. in different libraries.

The same, *Scriptura Beneventana: Facsimiles of South Italian and Dalmatian Manuscripts from the Sixth to the Fourteenth Century.* 2 vols. Oxford 1929. Lists 100 mss.

T. De Luca, *Catalogo di una pregevole collezione di manoscritti e di libri a stampa delle più ricercate edizioni.* Venice 1816. 286 pp. p. 7-19: Alphabetical list of mss. Collection scattered.

A. Luchaire, *Études sur quelques manuscrits de Rome et de Paris.* (Université de Paris.

Bibliothèque de la Faculté des Lettres VIII). Paris 1899. 175 pp. Describes a few mss. at Paris and the Vatican.

F. Maassen, 'Bibliotheca latina iuris canonici manuscripta,' *Sitzungsberichte der Kaiserlichen Akademie der Wissenschaften* [Vienna], *Philosophisch-Historische Classe* LIII (1866) 373-427; LIV (1867) 157-288; LVI (1867) 157-212. Describes canonistic mss. in different libraries. No index.

J. Mabillon and M. Germain, *Museum Italicum seu Collectio Veterum Scriptorum ex Bibliothecis Italicis.* 2 vols. Paris 1687-89. Vol. I pt. I: 'Iter Italicum.' (Pierpont Morgan Library). 2nd ed. Paris 1724. (DCU)

J. Mabillon, *Vetera Analecta . . .* New ed. Paris 1723. 573 pp. p. 1-16: 'Itineris Germanici descriptio.' (NN)

David Mc Roberts, *Catalogue of Scottish Medieval Liturgical Books and Fragments.* Glasgow 1953. 28 pp. 156 mss. in different libraries. Gives no shelf marks, but references. (NN)

A. Malin, 'Studier i Vadstena klosters bibliothek,' *Nordisk Tidskrift för Bok- och Biblioteksväsen* XIII (1926) 129-53. Describes mss. now in Uppsala, Skokloster and elsewhere.

Manoscritti e libri rari notificati. Rome 1943. 344 pp. Lists 215 mss. and rare books in Italian private collections. Arranged by provinces.

—2nd. ed. Rome 1948. 378 pp. 239 nos.

Manoscritti e stampe Venete dell' Aristotelismo e Averroismo (Secoli X-XVI). Venice 1958. x, 205 pp. and plates. Exhibition catalogue. p. 29-82: List of mss., mostly in Venice and Padua. Index of mss. (p. 199-203).

T. De Marinis, *La Biblioteca Napoletana dei Re d'Aragona.* 4 vols. Milan 1947-52. Vol. II (1947) p. 3-179: List of mss., arranged alphabetically by authors. Collection scattered. The largest number is now in Paris and Valencia. (Pierpont Morgan Library).

E. Martène and U. Durand, *Voyage littéraire de deux religieux bénédictins de la Congrégation de Saint Maur.* 2 vols. in 1. Paris 1717.

J. B. Martin, 'Inventaire méthodique de manuscrits conservés dans des Bibliothèques privées de la Région Lyonnaise,' *Revue des Bibliothèques* VII (1897) 471-95. Arranged by subjects. Covers 160 mss. in Seminary and other church libraries in Annonay, Bourg, Clermont-Ferrand, Grande Chartreuse, Grenoble, Le Puy, Lons-le-Saulnier, Lyon, Montbrison, Saint-Antoine, Saint-Claude, Sainte-Foyles-Lyon. Index (492-495). 'Deuxième Série,' *Ibid.* IX (1899), App., 30 pp. Covers Seminary and other church libraries in Annecy, Avignon, Belley, Besançon, Dijon, Romans, Viviers. No index.

The same, 'Inventaire méthodique de manuscrits conservés dans diverses bibliothèques privées. *Ibid.* XI (1901) 181-234. Arranged by subjects. Covers Seminary and other church libraries in Annecy, Besançon, Bourges, Chambéry, Dijon, Lyon, Montbrison, Nevers, Orléans, Paris, Romans, Saint-Antoine, Sainte-Foye-les-Lyon, Sens, Viviers. Mostly late. No index. (NN)

(Mas Latrie) *Dictionnaire des manuscrits, ou recueil de catalogues de manuscrits existants dans les principales bibliothèques d'Europe, concernant plus particulièrement les matières ecclésiastiques et historiques.* (Migne, *Nouvelle Encyclopédie Théologique*, vol. XL-XLI). 2 vols. Paris 1853. I: France. II: Germany, England, Belgium, Holland, Spain, Italy, Portugal, Sweden, Switzerland, Malta and Istanbul. Mostly based on Montfaucon, Haenel and other older sources. Largely superseded. No index.

G. Mazzatinti, *La Biblioteca dei Re d'Aragona in Napoli.* Rocca S. Casciano 1897. clvii, 200 pp. Lists 629 mss. extant in different libraries.

The same, *Inventari dei Manoscritti delle Biblioteche d'Italia.* Vol. I fasc. 1, Turin 1887. 160 pp. (extra volume). p. 1-22: Imola, by B. Roncovassaglia. 161 mss.

23-28: Camerino, Biblioteca Valentiniana, by M. Santoni and D. Feliciangeli. 62 mss. 29: Empoli, by P. Lami. 1 ms. 30-35: Capua, Biblioteca Arcivescovile, by V. Bindi. 29 mss. 36-40: Aquila, Biblioteca Provinciale, by A. Faiani. 23 mss. 41-42: Rieti, by A. Bellucci. 8 mss. 43: Terni, by E. Sconocchia, 6 mss. 44: Narni, by G. Eroli. 1 ms. 45: Senigaglia, by D. Mantovani. 4 mss. 46-52: Crescentino, Biblioteca Gregoriana, by V. del Corno. 57 mss. 53: Sessa Aurunca, by A. Margutti. 5 mss. 54: Asti, Biblioteca del Seminario. 1 ms. 55: Reggio Calabria, Biblioteca Comunale and Museo, by L. Lofaro. 3 mss. 56-61: Alba, Biblioteca Comunale, Biblioteca del Seminario and Biblioteca dell' Accademia. 29 mss. 62-65: Piazza Armerina, by L. Nincheri. 28 mss. 66-75: Casale, Biblioteca del Seminario, by Comello, A. Bolla and G. Cerrato. 6 mss. 76-83: Siracusa, Biblioteca del Seminario, by S. Cipolla. 79 mss. 84-99: Cuneo, by Belli and Boccaccini. 124 mss. 100-60: Macerata. 157 mss. No index.

The same and A. Sorbelli, *Inventari dei Manoscritti delle Biblioteche d'Italia*. I (Forlì 1890) 1-83: Forlì, by Mazzatinti. 142 mss. and special collections. 85-120: Savignano, Comunale (i.e., Accademia), by the same. 76 mss. and letters. 121-54: Gubbio, Biblioteca Sperelliana (now at Archivio di Stato), by the same. 238 mss. and special collections. 155-159: Serrasanquirico, by D. Gaspari. 27 mss. (mostly sold afterwards). 161-229: Subiaco, Biblioteca dell' Abbazia, by L. Allodi. 435 mss. and documents. 231-237: Fabriano, by A. Zonghi. 92 mss. 237-238: Pinerolo, by A. Caffaro. 33 mss. 239-267: Pistoia, Biblioteca Forteguerri, by E. Gori and A. Zanelli. 253 mss. (A 1-E 401, valid shelf marks in parentheses). 268-77: Pistoia, Biblioteca Fabroniana, by A. Zanelli. 176 mss. 278-280. Bevagna, Biblioteca Comunale and Biblioteca dell' Orfanotrofio. 10 mss. and documents. 281-86: Forlì cont., by Mazzatinti. Ms. 143 and documents.

—II (1892) 3-100: Vicenza, Biblioteca Bertoliana. 639 mss. 100-101: Vicenza, Biblioteca della Cattedrale. 14 mss. 101: Vicenza, Museo Civico. 101-03: Vicenza, Biblioteca Trissino (now scattered). 103-11: Como, by F. Fossati. 81 mss. Shelf marks antiquated. 111: Cagli, 10 mss. 112-13: Nicosia, by A. Boffi. 10 mss. 113-17: Lodi, by F. Flamini. 46 mss. Shelf marks antiquated. 118-28: Belluno, Biblioteca Lolliniana, by F. Pellegrini. 59 mss. 128-31: Belluno, Museo Civico, by G. Padovan. 71 mss. 132-65: Rimini, by A. Tambellini. 176 mss. and special collections. Shelf marks antiquated. 166-70: Fonte Colombo (Rieti), by A. Bellucci. 11 mss. Now in Rieti. 171-79: Perugia, Biblioteca Dominicini, by A. Bellucci. 46 mss. 180-243: Volterra, Biblioteca Guarnacci, by G. Giannini. 348 mss. Valid shelf marks in parentheses. 244-50: Gubbio, Biblioteca Benveduti, by Mazzatinti. 7 mss.

—III (1893) 3-99: Rovigo, Biblioteca dell' Academia dei Concordi, by G. Tambara. 596 mss. 100-56: Sandaniele del Friuli, Biblioteca Communale Guarneriana, by Mazzatinti. 282 mss. and special collections. Some mss. recently lost . 156-159: Sandaniele, Biblioteca Concina, 35 mss. 161-72: Cividale, Biblioteca Ex-Capitolare and Archivio Ex-Capitolare, by Conte Alvise Zorzi and Mazzatinti. 113 mss. 173-238: Udine, by Mazzatinti. (173-209: Biblioteca Comunale, 289 mss. 210-15: Biblioteca Joppi, 66 mss. Now with the Comunale. 215-17: Biblioteca Florio, 16 mss. 217-34: Biblioteca Arcivescovile, 232 mss. 234-36: Biblioteca Bartolini, 62 mss. Now with the Arcivescovile. 237-38: Biblioteca Capitolare, 17 mss. It suffered some losses.) 239-46: Castronovo, Biblioteca Popolare, by G. Traina. 49 mss.

—IV (1894) 1-20: Ivrea, Biblioteca Capitolare, by A. Professione. 112 mss. 21-141: Assisi, Convento di San Francesco, (i.e. Biblioteca Comunale), by Mazzatinti and

L. Alessandri. 702 and 244 mss. 142-43: Foggia, by G. Villani. 15 mss. 144-254: Ravenna, Biblioteca Classense, by S. Bernicoli, 510 mss.

—V (1895) 3-47: Ravenna cont. Nos. 511-930 and documents. 48-55: Vigevano, by F. Pellegrini. 48-51: Istituto Roncalli, 7 mss. 51-53: S. Ignazio. 16 mss. 54: Biblioteca del Seminario. 5 mss. 54-55: Archivio Comunale, 3 mss. 56-297: Perugia, Biblioteca Comunale, by A. Bellucci. 1565 mss.

—VI (1896) 3-7: Ancona, by Mazzatinti. 73 mss. 8: Città di Castello, by the same. 19 mss. 9-12: Osimo, Biblioteca del Collegio Campana, by G. Cecconi. 73 mss. 13: Noto, by E. Potente. 3 mss. 13. Bosa, by Mazzatinti. 31 mss. (not listed). 14-21: Molfetta, by F. Carabellese. 30 mss. (14-19: Biblioteca del Seminario, 28 mss. 19-21: Archivio Comunale, 2 mss.) 22-46: Bitonto, by F. Carabellese (22-29: Conte E. Rogadeo, 25 mss. 29-36: Archivio Municipale, 7 mss. 37-42: Archivio Capitolare. 13 mss. 42-45: Ufficio del Registro, 2 mss. 45-46: Seminario Vescovile. 4 mss). 47-48: Sulmona, by G. B. Crovato (Biblioteca Comunale, 25 mss. 48: Prof. Piccirilli, 2 mss. Prof. De Nino, some autographs). 49-50: Bagnacavallo. 41 mss. 51-101: Novara, by N. Colombo. (51-64: Biblioteca Civica. 37 mss. 64-70: Biblioteca del Seminario. 19 mss. 70-101: Biblioteca Capitolare. 134 mss. Valid shelf marks in parentheses.) 102-05: Bitonto, Istituto C. Sylos. 10 mss. 106-08: Terlizzi (106-07: P. G. Morgese, 3 mss. 107-08: Archivio Capitolare. 2 mss.) 109-114: Trani. (109-112: Archivio Capitolare, 3 mss. 112-13: D. D'Alessandro, 3 mss. 113: F. Sarlo, 1 ms. 114: G. B. Beltrani. 1 ms.). 115-16: Andria. (115-16: Archivio Capitolare. 3 mss. 116: Biblioteca del Seminario. 1 ms.). 117-22: Barletta. (117: March. R. Bonelli, 2 mss. 117-18: Archivio della Cattedrale, 3 mss. 118: Biblioteca Municipale, 1 ms. 118-21: Chiesa di S. Sepolcro, 1 ms. 121-22: F. Vista, 4 mss.) 123-24: Canosa, Archivio Capitolare,

5 mss. 125-26: Bisceglie. (125: Archivio della Cattedrale, 2 mss. 125-26: Chiesa di S. Audoeno, 1 ms.) 127: Ruvo, Archivio della Cattedrale, by F. Carabellese. 1 ms. 128-50: Poppi, by G. Cipriani. 419 mss. 151-69: Longiano, by Mazzatinti. 47 mss. 170-241: Arezzo, Biblioteca della Fraternita di S. Maria (Fraternita dei Laici), by G. F. Gamurrini. 445 mss. 242-48: Faenza, by G. Camozzi. (242-47: Biblioteca Comunale. 137 mss. 247-48: Biblioteca Capitolare. 13 mss. 248: Biblioteca del Seminario. 1 ms.).

—VII (1897) 5-194: Milano, Biblioteca di Brera, Codici Morbio, by L. Frati. 156 mss. 195-205: Monteleone, Biblioteca Capialbi. 42 mss. The town is now called Vibo Valentia. 206-52: Firenze, Biblioteca Nazionale Centrale, Fondo Principale, by Mazzatinti. Ms. II-1 to II-232. — VIII (1898) 3-198: The same cont. Ms. II-233 to II-448; II.I.1-511; II.II.1-81.—IX (1899) 5-198: The same cont. Ms. II.II.82-560; II.III.1-213.—X (1900) 5-201: The same cont. Ms. II.III.214-508; II.IV.1-285.—XI (1901) 7-284: The same cont. Ms. II.IV.286-732; II.V.1-176; II.VI.1-139; II.VII.1-167; II.VIII.1-180; II.IX.1-115.—XII (1902-03) 7-176: The same cont. Ms. II.IX.116-176; II.X.1-193; II.XI.1-91; Magl. I.2-73; II.1-11; III.1-135; IV. 1-73; V.1-65; VI.1-248; VII.4-25.—XIII (1905-06) 7-208: The same cont. Ms. Magl. VII.25-1000.

—XIV (1909) 9-58: Bologna, Biblioteca Ambrosini, by R. Ambrosini. 355 mss. 59-81: Sassuolo, by N. Cionini. 83 mss. 83-130: Parma, by St. Lottici-Maglione. (83-95: Museo d'Antichità, 78 mss. 95-97: March. G. di Soragna. 17 mss. 98-125: Archivio Comunale. 184 mss. 125-128: Prof. A. del Prato. 23 mss. 128-30: Archivi privati. 15 mss.). 131-38: Cascia, by A. Morini. 39 mss. 139-67: Chiari, Biblioteca Morcelliana, by L. Rivetti. 174 mss. 169-73: Camurana (169-70: Archivio Comunale. 2 mss. 170-73: Libreria Bortolini. 8 mss.).

—XV (1909) 5-176: Bologna, R. Biblioteca Universitaria, by Lod. Frati. Italian mss. nos. 1 (I¹)—249 (166).

—XVI (1910) 5-37: Conegliano, by A. Vital. 136 mss. 39-48: Grosseto, Biblioteca Chelliana, by A. Segré. 39 mss. 49-60: Bologna, Biblioteca Arcivescovile, by G. Belvederi. 69 mss. 60-103: Bologna, Libreria Breventani, by the same. 114 mss. 105-47: Modena, Libreria Jacoli, by F. Jacoli. 164 mss. 149-99: S. Severino Marche, by V. Pirazzoli. 208 mss.

—XVII (1910-1911) 5-181: Bologna, Universitaria cont. Italian mss. no. 250 (167) - 494 (635).

—XVIII (Florence 1912) 5-180: Cortona, by G. Mancini. 350 mss. Valid shelf marks in parentheses.

—XIX (1912) 5-176: Bologna, Universitaria, cont. Italian mss. no. 495 (636)-826 (1243).

—XX (1913-1914) 5-95: Cortona cont. Mss. no. 351-630. 97-132: Parma, Archivio di Stato, by St. Lottici-Maglione. 139 mss. 133-48: Catania, R. Biblioteca Universitaria, by G. Tamburini. 138 mss. 149-164: Biblioteca Ventimigliana. 142 mss. Now with the Biblioteca Universitaria.

—XXI (1914) 5-192: Bologna, Universitaria cont. Italian mss. no. 827 (1249)-1227 (2021).

—XXII (1915) 5-209: Roma, R. Biblioteca Angelica, by E. Celani. Mss. no. 1544-1800.

—XXIII (1915) 5-164: Bologna, Universitaria cont. Italian mss. no. 1228 (2022)-1569(3677).

—XXIV (1916-1917) 5-68: Pisa, R. Biblioteca Universitaria, by G. Tamburini. 763 mss. 69-92: Pisa, Biblioteca Cateriniana del Seminario, by the same. 181 mss. 93-111: Argenta, by P. Antolini. 99 mss. 113-28: Pavullo, by A. Sorbelli. 100 mss.

—XXV (1916-1917) 5-216: Bologna Universitaria cont. Italian mss. no. 1570 (3678)-1817 (3935).

—XXVI (1918-1920) 5-99: Faenza, by P. Beltrami. 329 mss. 101-220: Castiglione Fiorentino, by G. Mischj. 465 mss. 220-

221: *Ibid.* Collegio Cosimo Serristori. 6 mss. 222: *Ibid.* PP. Cappuccini. Some papers.

—XXVII (1923) 5-167: Bologna, Universitaria cont. Italian mss. no. 1818 (3936) - 2057(4186).

—XXVIII (1922-1924) 5-196: Torino, Biblioteca Nazionale, by F. Cosentini. 1986 mss. Valid shelf marks in parentheses.

—XXIX (1923) 5-220: Pesaro, Biblioteca Oliveriana, by E. Viterbo. 241 mss.

—XXX (1924) 1-213: Bologna, Biblioteca Comunale dell' Archiginnasio, by C. Lucchesi. Mss. A 1-562.

—XXXI (1925) 1-72: Prato, Raccolta Guasti, by S. Nicastro. 336 mss. 73-128: Vercelli, Archivio Capitolare, by R. Pastè. 221 mss. 129-73: Novara, Biblioteca Negroni-Civica, by G. Bustico. 105 mss.

—XXXII (1925) 1-233: Bologna, Archiginnasio cont. Mss. A 563-1292.

—XXXIII (1925) 1-227: Pesaro cont. Mss. no. 242-375.

—XXXIV (1926) 1-123: Veroli, Biblioteca Giovardiana, by C. Scaccia-Scarafoni. 463 mss. 125-57: Urbania, by E. Liburdi. 141 mss. 159-70: Domodossola, Biblioteca Galletti, by G. Bustico. 64 mss.

—XXXV (1926) 1-222: Pesaro cont. Mss. no. 375-376.

—XXXVI (1926) 1-197: Bologna, Archiginnasio cont. Mss. A 1293-1865.

—XXXVII (1927) 1-221: Pesaro cont. Mss. no. 376-90.

—XXXVIII (1928) 1-195: Fano, Biblioteca Comunale Federiciana, by A. Mabellini. 444 mss.

—XXXIX (1929) 1-248: Pesaro cont. Mss. no. 391-455.

—XL (1929) 1-192: Bologna, Archiginnasio cont. Mss. A 1866-2181.

—XLI (1930) 1-187: Foligno, Biblioteca Jacobilli (del Seminario), by D. M. Faloci-Pulignani. 563 mss.

—XLII (1929) 5-227: Pesaro cont. Mss. no. 456-967.

—XLIII (1930) 1-211: Bologna, Archiginnasio cont., by A. Sorbelli. Mss. A 2182-2464.

—XLIV (1930) 5-132: Salò, Ateneo, by G. Lonati. 197 mss. 133-94: Castiglione Fiorentino cont. by A. Nunziati. Mss. no. 466-546.

—XLV (1930) 5-250: Pesaro cont. Mss. no. 968-1527.

—XLVI (1930-1931), 5-211: Udine, Biblioteca Comunale, by G. B. Corgnali. 111 mss.

—XLVII (1931) 1-196: Bologna Archiginnasio cont. Mss. A 2465-2833.

—XLVIII (1931) 5-268: Pesaro cont. Mss. no. 1528-1745.

—XLIX (1931) 5-201: Udine cont. Mss. no. 112-340.

—L (1931) 5-300: Bassano del Grappa, by P. M. Tua. 1593 mss.

—LI (1932) 1-196: Fano cont. 495 mss.

—LII (1933) 1-315: Pesaro cont. Mss. no. 1746-2000.

—LIII (1933) 1-208: Bologna, Archiginnasio cont. by L. Barbieri. Mss. B 1-180.

—LIV (1933) 1-215: Ferrara, Biblioteca Comunale, by G. Agnelli and G. Ravegnani. Mss. I. A.-H; I. 1-150.

—LV (1934) 1-242: Bassano cont. Mss. no. 1594-1861 and documents.

—LVI (1934) 1-289: Roma, Angelica cont. by S. Vitale. Mss. no. 1801-2190.

—LVII (1934) 1-269: Benedello, Raccolta di Cà d'Orsolino, by A. Sorbelli. 425 mss.

—LVIII (1934) 1-302: Bassano cont. Documents only.

—LIX (1935) 1-201: Benedello cont. Mss. no. 426-820.

—LX (1935) 1-97: Pescia, by G. Calamari. (1-78: Biblioteca Comunale, 155 mss. and special collections. 79-97: Biblioteca Capitolare, 92 mss.) 99-119: Modigliana, by R. Zanelli (99-115: Biblioteca Comunale, 93 mss. 117-19: Seminario Vescovile, 14 mss.) 121-24: Forlì, by the same. Documents only. 125-36: Trani, by the same. 23 mss. 137-200: Pinerolo, by the same. 192 mss.

—LXI (1935) 1-212: Benedello cont. Mss. no. 821-1450.

—LXII (1936) 1-180: Bologna, Biblioteca Carducciana. 134 mss. and documents.

—LXIII (1937) 1-145: Guastalla, Biblioteca Maldottiana, by A. Cerlini. 97 mss.

—LXIV (1937) 5-155: Guastalla, cont. 330 mss.

—LXV (1937) 1-170: Bologna, Biblioteca Gozzadini, by M. Cenacchi. 199 mss.

—LXVI (1937) 1-138: The same cont. Mss. no. 200-445 and documents.

—LXVII (1938) 1-196: Trento, Biblioteca Comunale, by I. Lunelli. 591 mss.

—LXVIII (1939) 1-212: Venezia, Museo Civico Correr, Manoscritti Morosini-Grimani, by M. Brunetti. 342 mss.

—LXIX (1939) 1-208: Bologna, Archiginnasio cont. Mss. B. 181-488.

—LXX (1939) 1-148: Cremona, Biblioteca Governativa, by V. Dainotti and V. Dainotti-Carini. 207 mss. 149-254: Cremona, Seminario Vescovile, by F. Zanoni. 395 mss.

—LXXI (1940) 1-196: Trento cont. Mss. no. 592-1382.

—LXXII (1940) 1-212: Benedello cont. Mss. no. 1451-1915.

—LXXIII (1941) 1-120: Roma, R. Archivio di Stato, Collezione degli Statuti, by O. Montenovesi. 799 mss. 121-44: Sassari, Biblioteca Universitaria, by G. Tamburini. 237 mss.

—LXXIV (1942) 1-141: Trento cont. Mss. no. 1383-2145.

—LXXV (1945) 1-132: Bologna, Archiginnasio cont. Mss. B. 489-1300.

—LXXVI (1948) 1-149: Roma, Angelica cont. by S. Vitale. Mss. no. 2191-2418.

—LXXVII (1950) 1-185: Venezia, Biblioteca Nazionale Marciana, by P. Zorzanello. Mss. Ital. VI 1-502.

—LXXVIII (1953) 5-152: Udine cont. by G. B. Corgnali. Mss. no. 341-479.

—LXXIX (1954) 1-103: Bologna, Archiginnasio cont. by F. Mancini. Mss. B 1301-1945.

—LXXX (1954) 5-245: Urbino, Biblioteca Universitaria, by L. Moranti. Fondo dell' Università 1-165; Buste 1-95. Fondo della Congregazione di Carità 1-56; Buste 1-54; Fondo del Comune 1-148; Buste 1-148.

—LXXXI (1956) 1-168: Venezia, Marciana cont. by P. Zorzanello. Mss. Ital. VII 1-500.

—LXXXII (1957) 1-128: Bologna, Archiginnasio cont. by F. Leonetti. Mss. B 1946-2795. Each volume indexed.

L. Meier, 'Iter Britannicum Scotisticum,' *Antonianum* XXVI (1951) 115-128. List of libraries (116-121). (NNUT)

The same, 'Iter Germanicum Scotisticum, *ibid.* XXIII (1948) 501-520. List of libraries (503-514). (NNUT)

G. Mercati, *Codici latini Pico Grimani Pio e di altra biblioteca ignota del s. XVI esistenti nell' Ottoboniana e i codici greci Pio di Modena* . . . (Studi e Testi 75). Vatican City 1938. 321 pp. Index of mss. (293ff.).

Messager des sciences et des arts de la Belgique, Ser. II, v (1837) 329-50: J. de Saint-Genois, 'Notice sur les manuscrits historiques, qui appartiennent au dépôt d'Archives de la Flandre Orientale, à Gand.' 58 mss.

Messager des sciences historiques de Belgique, 1843, 133-62: 'Rapport de M. Bethmann, de Hanovre, sur les résultats de ses recherches historiques dans les bibliothèques de la Belgique faites en 1839, 1840 et 1841.' Translated by Hallmann. 287-312: J. de Saint-Genois, 'Deuxième notice sur les manuscrits des Archives de la Flandre Orientale.' Mss. no. 64-120.

F. Michel, *Rapports à M. le Ministre de l'Instruction Publique sur les anciens monuments de l'histoire et de la littérature de la France qui se trouvent dans les Bibliothèques de l'Angleterre et de l'Ecosse.* Paris 1838. 280 pp. No index. (NjP)

A. Millares Carlo, *Nuevos estudios de paleografia española*, Mexico City (1941). ix. 175 pp. 35-125: 'Los códices visigóticos de la Catedral Toledana.' (also separately published, Madrid 1935, 95 pp.). Covers 29 mss. in Toledo and Madrid. 127-47: 'Ultimos estudios acerca de Códices Visigóticos.' 149-71: 'Los manuscritos visigóticos del fondo latino de la Biblioteca Nacional de París.' Index of mss. (167-71).

José M. Millás Vallicrosa, *Las traducciones orientales en los manuscritos de la Biblioteca Catedral de Toledo.* Madrid 1942. 371 pp. 52 mss. in Toledo and Madrid. Covers Latin versions of Aristotle and of Arabic authors. (NNUT)

Catalogo dei Codici Manoscritti posseduti dal Nobile Signore Conte Eugenio Minutoli Tegrimi in Lucca. Lucca 1871. 42 pp. 196 mss. Attributed to S. Bongi, but not signed. Collection scattered. (Walters Art Gallery)

J. B. Mittarellius, *Bibliotheca Codicum Manuscriptorum Monasterii S. Michaelis Venetiarum prope Murianum.* Venice 1779. 1257 and 491 coll. Arranged alphabetically by authors. Mss. now scattered, many at the Marciana and the Vatican.

E. Modigliani, *Catalogo della mostra degli oggetti d'arte e di storia restituiti dall' Austria - Ungheria.* Rome 1923. 100 pp. and plates. Covers mss. returned from Vienna to Naples (48-54, 24 nos.). (NN)

G. E. Mohan, 'Incipits of Logical Writings of the XIIIth-XVth Centuries,' *Franciscan Studies* XII (1952) 349-489.

B. Montfaucon, *Bibliotheca Bibliothecarum Manuscriptorum Nova.* 2 vols. Paris 1739. Vol. I p. xxi-ccli: Index for both volumes. Lists 2111 mss. Reginenses of Vatican (I, 14-61, antiquated shelf marks), some mss. of Vaticani latini (98-133), of Archivio di S. Pietro (156-59), S. Isidoro in Rome (159-70), Vallicelliana (170), Ottoboniani (183-91, antiquated shelf marks), Sessoriana (193), Monte Cassino (215-29), Badia in Florence (413-418), S. Marco in Florence (419-29, antiquated shelf marks), Annunziata in Florence (429), S. Maria degli Angeli in Florence (430), Ambrosiana in Milan (505-24), Escorial (616-25). Vol. II deals with France. Many of the other lists are antiquated or based on printed sources such as Bernardus.

The same, *Diarium Italicum.* Paris 1702. 526 pp.

Ambrosio de Morales, *Viage . . . por orden del Rey D. Phelipe II, a los reynos de León, y Galicia, y principado de Asturias. Para reconocer las reliquias de Santos, Sepulcros reales y libros manuscritos de las Cathedrales y monasterios.* Ed. by H. Florez. Madrid 1765. xxvi, 224 pp. Lists some mss. at Valladolid (9ff.), León (51ff.), Oviedo (93ff.), Celanova (155), etc. (NN)

C. Morbio, *Francia ed Italia ossia i manoscritti francesi delle nostre biblioteche.* Milan 1873. 322 pp. No index.

*Verzeichnis einer Sammlung wertvoller Handschriften und Bücher . . . aus der Hinterlassenschaft des Herrn Cavaliere Carlo Morbio in Mailand, welche am 24. Juni 1889 . . . in Leipzig. . . versteigert werden wird. Leipzig 1889. 141, 54 pp. Collection scattered. (NIC)

'Mostra bibliografica dell' Italia Meridionale e della Sicilia,' in: *Primo Congresso Mondiale delle Biblioteche e di Bibliografia,* Rome-Venice 1929, *Atti* VI (Rome 1933) 129-86. Also separately, Naples 1929. XI, 86 pp. and plates.

Mostra di Codici Autografici in onore di Girolamo Tiraboschi. Modena 1932. 131 pp. 275 mss. from Modena and other libraries.

Mostra storica nazionale della Miniatura, Catalogo. By G. Muzzioli. 2nd ed. Florence (1954). XXXIX, 528 pp. and plates. 748 nos.

R. A. B. Mynors, *Durham Cathedral Manuscripts to the End of the Twelfth Century.* Oxford 1939. x, 91 pp. and plates. Describes 155 mss. at Durham and other libraries.

Nachrichten von der Historischen Commission bei der Königlich Bayerischen Akademie der Wissenschaften, Zweiter Jahrgang, Zweites Stueck (*Beilage zur Historischen Zeitschrift* V, Munich 1861) 78-112: B. Erdmannsdoerfer, 'Bericht über eine im Auftrag der Historischen Commission unternommene Reise nach Italien.' Lists mss. in the Vatican, Rome, Lucca and other libraries concerning Charles IV and the Councils of Constance and Basel. Drittes Stueck (*Ibid.* 1861) 3-39: Th. v.

Kern, 'Reise durch Franken und Bayern im Sommer 1859, unternommen im Auftrage der Historischen Commission.' Lists mss. on local history in Bamberg, Schweinfurt, Kitzingen, Amberg, Neumarkt, Regensburg, Straubing, Passau, Landshut. Dritter Jahrgang, Viertes Stueck (*Ibid.* VII 1862) 107-135: The same, 'Verzeichnisse von Handschriften zur deutschen Städtegeschichte.' Covers Maihingen. 135-52: 'Handschriften des ungarischen Nationalmuseums zu Pest.'

P. Namur, *Histoire des bibliothèques publiques de la Belgique.* 3 vols. Brussels 1840-42. Lists 39 mss. at Louvain (II, 211ff.) and 46 at Liège (III, 79ff.). No index. (NN)

Neues Archiv der Gesellschaft für ältere deutsche Geschichtskunde. I (1876) 569-75: J. Merkel, 'Varia aus italienischen Bibliotheken.' 576-79: The same, 'Über die Bibliothek des Cistercienserklosters S. Croce in Gerusalemme in Rom.'

—II (1877) 29-46: 'Dr. H. Pabst's Reise nach Italien 1869/70.' 233-99: W. Arndt, 'Reisebericht.' Covers mostly hagiographical mss. in Belgian and French libraries. 301-24: J. Heller, 'Reise nach Lothringen, Nord-Frankreich und Belgien vom Oktober 1875 bis März 1876.' Covers Averboden. 325-81: G. Waitz, 'Reise nach Italien im Frühjahr 1876.' Covers Venice, Marciana (367ff.). 383-425: W. Wattenbach, 'Bericht über eine Reise durch Steyermark im August 1876.' Covers Reun, Vorau and Admont. 629-34. Index of libraries mentioned in *Archiv* vols. I-XII.

— III (1878) 77-138: H. Bresslau, 'Reise nach Italien im Herbst 1876.' 139-81; 319-83: P. Ewald, 'Reise nach Italien im Winter von 1876 auf 1877.' Covers Vatican and Rome. 216-18; 421-24: G. Waitz, 'Aus neuen Handschriften-Katalogen.' Covers Bern, St. Gall, Auxerre, Florence (Biblioteca Nazionale), Schaffhausen. 627-54: E. Winkelmann, 'Reisebericht.' Covers Palermo, Messina and Naples.

—IV (1879) 9-42: G. Waitz, 'Reise nach England und Frankreich im Herbst 1877.'

59-85: L. Weiland, 'Beschreibung einiger Handschriften der Universitäts-Bibliothek zu Giessen.' 323-93; 583-625: G. Waitz, 'Handschriften in englischen Bibliotheken.'
—V (1880) 9-30: E. Winkelmann, 'Bericht über eine Reise nach Italien 1878.' 220-21: W. Arndt, 'Über einige Handschriften in St. Petersburg.' 225: 'Handschriften der Landesbibliothek zu Fulda.' 241-65: K. Gillert, 'Lateinische Handschriften in St. Petersburg.' Lists 31 mss. 438-51: H. Bresslau, 'Handschriftliches aus Italien.' 457-65: W. Schum, 'Mittheilungen über die Fürstlich Metternichsche Bibliothek auf Schloss Königswart in Böhmen.' Lists 5 mss. 599-617: Gillert, cont.
—VI (1881) 217-398: P. Ewald, 'Reise nach Spanien im Winter von 1878 auf 1879.' Covers Escorial, Madrid, Toledo, Valladolid, Salamanca, Sevilla, Cordoba, Granada, Cadiz, Barcelona and Lisbon. No index. 473-96: G. Waitz, 'Pariser Handschriften.' 497-512: Gillert, cont.
—VII (1882) 169-86: Ph. Jaffé and W. Wattenbach, 'Geschichtliche Handschriften der Fürstlich Oettingen-Wallersteinschen Bibliothek in Maihingen.' Lists 41 mss.
—VIII (1883) 203-09: O. Holder-Egger, 'Handschriften der Gräflich Stolbergischen Bibliothek zu Wernigerode.' 285-98: W. Wattenbach, 'Nachricht von drei Handschriften in Eisleben.' 327-46: The same, 'Die Handschriften der Hamiltonschen Sammlung.'
—IX (1884) 225-34: Widmann, 'Mittheilungen aus Wiesbadener Handschriften.' 241-42: Wattenbach, 'Handschriften der Königl. Landesschule Pforta.' 389-441: O. Holder-Egger, 'Handschriften der Kgl. Bibliothek zu München.'
—X (1885) 213-39: O. Holder-Egger and G. Waitz, 'Reisen nach Frankreich, Belgien und Italien 1883.' 600-02 and XV (1890) 385-86: W. Heyd and Weiland, 'Handschriften der mit der kgl. öffentlichen Bibliothek in Stuttgart vereinigten vormaligen kgl. Handbibliothek.'
—XI (1886) 253-87: O. Holder-Egger, 'Bericht über eine Reise nach Italien 1885.' 408-12: E. Dümmler, 'Aus Darmstadter Handschriften.' Lists 5 mss. 619-28: Widmann, 'Kleine Mittheilungen aus Wiesbadener Handschriften.' Lists 18 mss.
—XIII (1888) 591-622: F. W. E. Roth and A. Schmidt, 'Mittheilungen aus Darmstadter Handschriften.'
—XV (1890) 437-73: E. Sackur, 'Reise nach Nord-Frankreich im Frühjahr 1889.' 475-95: H. Simonsfeld, 'Bericht über einige Reisen nach Italien.'
—XVII (1892) 461-524: O. Holder-Egger, 'Bericht über eine Reise nach Italien im Jahre 1891.' Covers Rome, Vatican, Cremona and Brescia. 601-11: H. V. Sauerland, 'Aus Handschriften der Trierer Seminarbibliothek.'
—XVIII (1893) 549-649; XIX (1894) 11-45: B. Krusch, 'Reise nach Frankreich im Frühjahr und Sommer 1892.'
—XXI (1896) 307-11: J. Loserth, 'Formularbücher der Grazer Universitätsbibliothek.'
—XXII (1897) 223-86; 335-415; 607-99: K. Hampe, 'Reise nach England vom Juli 1895 bis Februar 1896.' Covers Winchester Cathedral (696-97), Lincoln Cathedral (697), Exeter Cathedral (697) etc. 299-307: Loserth, cont. 501-41: O. Holder-Egger, 'Aus Handschriften des Erfurter St. Petersklosters.'
—XXIII (1898) 9-50; 291-374: J. Schwalm, 'Reiseberichte.' 375-417; 601-65: K. Hampe, 'Reise nach Frankreich und Belgien im Frühjahr 1897.' 751-61: Loserth, cont. Describes altogether 32 mss.
—XXV (1900) 717-66: J. Schwalm, 'Reise nach Italien im Herbst 1898.'
—XXVI (1901) 9-35: A. Werminghoff, 'Reise nach Frankreich und Belgien im Frühjahr 1899.' 299-347: A. Brackmann, 'Reise nach Italien vom März bis Juni 1900.' 679-706: O. Cartellieri, 'Reise nach Italien im Jahre 1899.' 707-41: J. Schwalm, 'Reise nach Italien im Herbst 1898.'
—XXVII (1902) 177-207: O. Holder-Egger, 'Aus Erfurter Handschriften.' 565-604:

A. Werminghoff, 'Reise nach Italien im Jahre 1901.' 695-733: J. Schwalm, 'Reise nach Oberitalien und Burgund im Herbst 1901.'

—XXVIII (1903) 485-501: Schwalm cont. Lists mss. of sequences in various Italian libraries. 711-16: F. Schneider, 'Reise nach Italien (1902).'

—XXIX (1904) 569-640: J. Schwalm, 'Reise nach Frankreich und Italien im Sommer 1903.'

—XXX (1905) 417-47: The same, 'Nachlese zu früheren Reiseberichten.'

—XXXII (1907) 17-26: M. Krammer, 'Reise nach Italien, Spanien und Frankreich im Herbst und Winter 1905.' 377-456: W. Levison, 'Aus englischen Bibliotheken.'

—XXXV (1910) 331-431: The same, cont.

—XXXVII (1912) 296-306: F. W. E. Roth, 'Aus Handschriften der Stadtbibliothek zu Luxemburg.'

—XXXVIII (1913) 503-24: W. Levison, 'Handschriften des Museum Meermanno-Westreenianum im Haag.' 572-80: F. W. E. Roth, 'Aus Handschriften der Mainzer Seminarbibliothek.' Lists 21 mss. 643-64: Levison, 'Aus englischen Bibliotheken,' cont.

—XLIII (1922) 605-09: E. Perels, 'Zur Wiederauffindung verschollener Handschriften der Biblioteca Vallicelliana.'

—XLV (1924) 102-12: P. Kehr, 'Aus der Bibliotheca Rossiana.'

—XLIX (1932) 524-49: F. Bock, 'Bericht über eine Reise nach Holland.' For the character of these articles, see above under *Archiv*, the predecessor of *Neues Archiv*.

J. Neuwirth, 'Datierte Bilderhandschriften österreichischer Klosterbibliotheken,' *Sitzungsberichte der Kaiserlichen Akademie der Wissenschaften* [Vienna], *Philosophisch-Historische Classe* CIX (1885) 571-630. Lists a few mostly liturgical mss. at Zwettl, Wilhering, Göttweih, Heiligenkreuz, Lilienfeld and Strahow.

The same, 'Studien zur Geschichte der Miniaturmalerei in Oesterreich,' *Ibid.* CXIII (1886) 129-211. Lists a few mss. at Lambach, Michaelbeuren, St. Florian, Herzogenburg, Melk and Salzburg.

The same, 'Italienische Bilderhandschriften in österreichischen Klosterbibliotheken,' *Repertorium für Kunstwissenschaft* IX (1886) 383-409. Lists some mss. at St. Florian, Kremsmünster, Salzburg, Göttweih, Melk, Wilhering, Lambach, Admont. No index.

Notices et Extraits des manuscrits de la Bibliothèque Nationale et autres bibliothèques, ed. Académie des Inscriptions et Belles-Lettres. XXIX, pt. II (1880) 363-403: L. Delisle, 'Notices sur plusieurs manuscrits de la Bibliothèque de Lyon.' 19 mss. No index.

—XXXI, pt. I (1884) 49-156: Ch. Fierville, 'Notices et Extraits des manuscrits de la Bibliothèque de St. Omer.' 157-356: L. Delisle, 'Notice sur les manuscrits disparus de la Bibliothèque de Tours pendant la première moitié du XIXᵉ siècle.' 357-440: The same, 'Notice sur plusieurs manuscrits de la Bibliothèque d'Orléans.' 32 mss.

—XXXII, pt. I (1886) 1-120: The same, 'Notice sur des manuscrits du fonds Libri conservés à la Laurentienne.' Studies on individual Latin mas. of the Bibliothèque Nationale by B. Hauréau are found in vols. XXIV pt. 2 (1876); XXXI pt. 2 (1886); XXXII pt. 1 (1886) and 2 (1888); XXXIII pt. 1 (1890); XXXIV pt. 1 (1891) and 2 (1895); XXXV pt. 1 (1896); XXXVIII pt. 2 (1906). Only the descriptions found in vols. XXXI, XXXII, XXXIII, and in XXXIV pt. 1 are reproduced in Hauréau's *Notices et Extraits* (see below, Section C, under Paris).

Notizenblatt. Beilage zum Archiv für Kunde österreichischer Geschichtsquellen. I (1851) 382-84: W. Wattenbach. 'Notizen aus Handschriften der Stadtbibliothek zu Lübeck.' 1 ms.

—II (1852) 25-26: H. J. Zeibig, 'Die Handschriften der Classiker in der Stiftsbibliothek zu Klosterneuburg.' 17 mss. 104-06;

135-38; 262-65: The same, 'Die histori-
schen Handschriften der Stiftsbibliothek
zu Klosterneuburg.' 325 mss.
—III (1853) 186-92: 201-12: J. Chmel,
'Auszug aus den Handschriften-Verzeich-
nissen der Bibliotheken zu Stuttgart und
Basel.'
*Nouvelles Archives des Missions Scientifiques
et Littéraires.* I (1891) 9-23: Ch. Joret,
'Rapport sur une mission en Allemagne.'
—II (1892) 1-322: A. Martin, 'Rapport sur
une mission en Espagne et en Portugal.'
Covers Greek mss.
—XVIII (1910) 175-538: G. Constant, 'Rap-
port sur une mission scientifique aux
Archives d'Autriche et d'Espagne.' Co-
vers the Council of Trent.
F. Novati, 'I manoscritti italiani d'alcune
biblioteche del Belgio e dell' Olanda,'
*Rassegna bibliografica della letteratura ita-
liana* II (1894) 43-51; 199-208; 242-48;
IV (1896) 18-26; 50-56; 135-44. Covers
Brussels, the Hague, Amsterdam, and
more shortly, Leiden, Haarlem, Utrecht.
Index (p. 144).
Nuernberger, 'Aus der litterarischen Hinterlassenschaft des hl. Bonifatius und des
hl. Burchardus,' 24. *Bericht der wissen-
schaftlichen Gesellschaft Philomathie in
Neisse* (1888) 133-80. Index of mss.
(178-180). Most of them are in Fulda and
Würzburg. (DLC)
Der Österreichische Geschichtsforscher II
(1841) Notizenblatt, p. xxix-xl: J. Chmel,
'Handschriften in der Bibliothek des
Klosters Göttweih.' 50 mss. No index.
p. li-lv: Mone, 'Handschriften in österreichischen Bibliotheken.' Covers St. Florian, Innsbruck, Klosterneuburg, Lambach,
Linz, Maria Saal, Salzburg and Vienna.
No index. lxxxiv-lxxxv: 'Handschriften
in dem Archive der Stadt Steyer.' (MH)
H. Omont, 'Recherches sur la Bibliothèque
de l'Église Cathédrale de Beauvais,' *Mémoires de l'Institut National de France.
Académie des Inscriptions et Belles-Lettres*
XL (1916) 1-93. Lists mss. extant in
different libraries.

The same, *Catalogue des manuscrits Ashburnham-Barrois récemment acquis par la
Bibliothèque Nationale.* Paris 1902. 124
pp. (also in: *Bibliothèque de l'École des
Chartes* LXII [1901] 555-610; LXIII [1902]
10-68). p. 106-18 (56-68): 'Concordance
des anciens numéros du fonds Barrois
avec les numéros du catalogue de vente
de 1901.' Indicates also the present location of the mss. in Paris, London, Oxford and other libraries.
The same, *Catalogue des manuscrits latins
et francais de la collection Phillipps acquis
en 1908 pour la Bibliothèque Nationale.*
Paris 1909. 269 pp. p. 185-239: 'Liste
numérique des Manuscrits Phillipps au-
jourd'hui conservés dans différentes bibliothèques d'Allemagne, Angleterre, Belgique, France et Pays-Bas.' Gives the
present locations of many Phillipps mss.
in Berlin, Bordeaux, Brussels, Cambridge,
Chantilly, The Hague, London, Oxford
and Paris.
(F.) Palacky, 'Italienische Reise im Jahre
1837,' *Abhandlungen der Königlichen Böhmischen Gesellschaft der Wissenschaften,*
Ser. V, vol. I (1841), *Historisch-philolo-
gischer Theil.* 123 pp. Covers mss. on
Bohemian history in the Vatican Library
(53-71), in Florence (Riccardiana, 71-72),
Milan (Ambrosiana, 72-75), Venice (Marciana, 77-78). No index. (NNM)
E. Pellegrin, 'Manuscrits de l'abbaye de
Saint-Victor et d'anciens Collèges de Paris
à la Bibliothèque de Berne, à la Bibliothè-
que Vaticane et à Paris,' *Bibliothèque de
l'École des Chartes* CIII (1942) 69-98.
Describes a few mss. No index.
The same, *La Bibliothèque des Visconti et
des Sforza.* Paris 1955. VII. 494 pp.
Lists many mss., chiefly at Paris.
Thomas Phillipps, *Catalogus manuscripto-
rum Magnae Britanniae.* 2 pts. Middle-
hill 1850. Covers several private collec-
tions, and a few mss. at the Bodleian
(I, 63-66) and at the College of Arms,
London (II, 1-4). No index. (DLC)
The following titles concern the Phillipps

collection, formerly in Cheltenham, England, and now scattered. See also *Archiv* VII-IX; Haenel (with Suppl.); Omont; Schenkl.

A. N. L. Munby, *The Catalogues of Manuscripts and Printed Books of Sir Thomas Phillipps*. Cambridge 1951. 40 pp. See esp. p. 13.

For a list of the sales catalogues, see S. De Ricci, *English Collectors of Books and Manuscripts* (Cambridge 1930) 126-127.

Catalogus librorum manuscriptorum in Bibliotheca D. Thomae Phillipps, Bart. Middlehill 1837 (-1871). 436 pp. 23837 mss. Not complete. No index. (NjP, photostat copy at Morgan Library)

Bibliotheca Phillippica: *A Catalogue of the Phillipps Manuscripts, Numbers 1388 to 2010*. Cheltenham 1886. Unpaged. Fuller than the large catalogue. (NjP)

Catalogue of Phillipps Manuscripts. An interleaved copy of the printed catalogue, with present locations, in 3 vols., continued in manuscript to no. 37028. (Mr. A. N. L. Munby, Cambridge)

Catalogue of Mss. in Thirlstaine Library that had never been catalogued by Sir Thos. Phillipps or had lost their Catalogue Numbers (by E. A. Bond). Mss. no. 23838-26179. (Mr. Munby).

Bibliotheca Phillippica (sales catalogues of Sotheby). VI (London 1893). Manuscripts pt. 1 (NN). VII (1895). Mss. pt. 2. (CtY). VIII (1896). Mss. pt. 3 (NN). IX (1897). Mss. pt. 4. (NN). X (1898). Mss. pt. 5 (NNC). XI (1899). Mss. pt. 6 (NN). XII (1903). Mss. pt. 7. (NN). XIII (1908). Mss. pt. 8 (NN). XIV (1910). Mss. pt. 9 (NN). XV (1911). Mss. pt. 10. (NN). XVI (1913). Mss. pt. 11. (NN). XVII (1919). Mss. pt. 12. (Morgan Library). XIX (1936). Mss. pt. 13 (Morgan Library). XX (1946). 34 mss. (NN). XXI (1946). Autograph letters and Documents (Morgan Library). The sales catalogues usually are in alphabetical order and fail to give the shelf marks.

In 1946, the remainder of the Phillipps collection was bought by William H. Robinson, London. See his catalogues 77 (1948) - 84 (no date, but after 1953), and especially: 77 (1948): *A selection of extremely rare and important printed books and manuscripts*; 81 (1950): *A selection of precious manuscripts, historic documents and rare books, the majority from the renowned collection of Sir Thomas Phillipps*. 83 (1953): *Rare books and manuscripts*.

C. Castellani, 'I manoscritti Veneti nella collezione Phillipps in Cheltenham', *Archivio Veneto*, N.S. XXXVII (1889) 199-248. (NN)

H. Omont, 'Manuscrits relatifs à l'histoire de France conservés dans la bibliothèque de Sir Thomas Phillipps à Cheltenham,' *Bibliothèque de l'École des Chartes* L (1889) 68-96; 180-217.

P. Durrieu, 'Les manuscrits à peintures de la bibliothèque de Sir Thomas Phillipps à Cheltenham.' *Ibid.* 381-432.

See also above under Omont.

R. Plancke, 'Répertoire des manuscrits de classiques latins conservés en Belgique,' *Revue des Études Latines* XVIII (1940) 141-86. Covers also Louvain.

A. Possevinus, *Apparatus Sacer*. 2nd ed. 2 vols. Cologne 1608. vol. II, Appendix: 'Catalogi Ms. Graecorum et aliorum etiam codicum, qui cum ad res sacras atque ecclesiasticas pertineant in antiquis et celebrioribus Bibliothecis asservantur, sive nunquam antea editi, sive integriores quam qui vulgati fuerunt ...' Covers some Latin mss. at Cesena (104), Cremona (106-07), Pesaro (107-08), Reggio (108-09), Frauenburg and Heilsberg (110-12). Antiquated. No index. (NNUT)

L. Prowe, *Mittheilungen aus schwedischen Archiven und Bibliotheken*. Berlin 1853. 64 pp. Concerns Copernicus and German history only. No index. (MH)

F. Van de Putte, 'Notice sur les bibliothèques modernes de la Flandre Occidentale,' *Annales de la Société d'Émulation pour l'Histoire et les Antiquités de la Flandre Occidentale* II (1840) 146-70; 246-70. Covers Bruges (Seminary and Episcopal Library) and Ypres. (NN)

P. Radó, 'Index codicum manu scriptorum liturgicorum Regni Hungariae,' *A Pannonhalmi Föapátsági Szent Gellert Föiskola Évkönyve*, N.S. I (1940-41) pp. 143-202. Lists 286 mss. in Eger, Budapest, Košice, Kolozsvár (Cluj), Kalocsa, Debrecin, Györ, Pannonhalma, Szombathely, Esztergom, Alba Julia, Bartfa, Bratislava and other libraries outside of Hungary. Also printed separately. (*Az Országos Széchényi Könyvtár Kiadványai* 14). Budapest 1941. 62 pp.

The same, *Libri liturgici manuscripti Bibliothecarum Hungariae.* Vol. I: *Libri liturgici manuscripti ad missam pertinentes.* (Az Országos Széchényi Könyvtár Kiadványai 26). Budapest 1947. 223 pp. 54 mss.

The same, 'Mittelalterliche liturgische Handschriften deutscher, italienischer und französischer Herkunft in den Bibliotheken Südosteuropas,' *Miscellanea Liturgica in Honorem L. Cuniberti Mohlberg* (2 vols., Rome 1948-49) II 349-92. Lists 83 mss. in Budapest, Cluj, Csorna, Debrecen, Eger, Esztergom, Györ, Kalocsa, Keszthely, Košice, Pannonhalma, Szombathely, Zirc. (NNG)

E. K. Rand, *Studies in the Script of Tours.* 2 vols. Cambridge Mass. 1929. Vol. I p. 81: 'A Summary Description of the Manuscripts of Tours.' Lists 231 mss. extant in different libraries. Index of mss. (209ff.).

The same and L. W. Jones, *Studies in the Script of Tours, II.* Cambridge Mass. 1934. 136 pp. p. 85: 'A Supplementary Description of Certain of the Manuscripts of Tours.' Index of mss. (123ff.).

G. Rathgen, 'Handschriften der Abtei Camp O.Cist.,' *Zentralblatt für Bibliothekswesen* LIII (1936) 114-34. Lists 26 mss. extant in different libraries.

F. Ravaisson, *Rapports au Ministre de l'Instruction Publique sur les Bibliothèques des Départments de l'Ouest.* Paris 1841. 418

pp. Lists mss. at Quimper (64ff.), Dol (104ff.), Avranches (114-94), Alençon (246ff.), Évreux (268ff.), Conches (279ff.) and Louviers (285ff.). Superseded. (DLC)

V. Redlich, *Tegernsee und die deutsche Geistesgeschichte im 15. Jahrhundert.* (Schriftenreihe zur bayerischen Landesgeschichte IX). Munich 1931. 268 pp. Lists mss. extant in different libraries (187-90). (NN)

A. Reifferscheid, 'Bibliotheca Patrum Latinorum Italica,' *Sitzungsberichte der Kaiserlichen Akademie der Wissenschaften* [Vienna], *Philosophisch-Historische Classe* XLIX (1865) 4-112; L (1865) 737-72; LIII (1866) 304-51; LVI (1867) 441-556; LIX (1868) 41-142; LXIII (1869) 567-749; LXVII (1871) 467-568; LXVIII (1871) 471-638; LXXI (1872) 5-168. Covers Verona, Rome (Sessoriana, S. Pietro, Barberini, Casanatense, Vallicelliana), Vatican, Milan (Ambrosiana), Turin (Biblioteca Nazionale, Archivio), Vercelli, Ivrea, Novara, Venice, Florence, Naples, Cava and Monte Cassino. Detailed descriptions of patristic mss. No index.

Repertorium Bibliographicum, or some account of the most celebrated British Libraries. London 1819. XLVIII, 673 pp. Mentions mss.

Revista de Archivos, Bibliotecas y Museos, I (1871) 39ff.: 'Codices de la Catedral de Avila destinados al Archivo histórico Nacional.' II (1872) 218ff.; 233ff.: G. F., 'Extracto del Catálogo de manuscritos de la Biblioteca del Escorial, hecho por D. Francisco Pérez Bayer.' III (1873) 87ff.; 104ff.: J. F. C., 'Catálogo de algunos códices y manuscritos del Archivo histórico de Toledo.' VI (1876) 14-16; 29-32; 69-72; 111-12; 199-200; 214-16; 230-232; 245-48; 262-64; 278-80; 294-96; 310-12: 'Indice de los manuscritos que poseyó la Biblioteca de San Isidro y fueron trasladados á la de las Córtes.' 713 mss. and documents. No index. Ser. II vol. IX (1883) 37ff.; 104ff.; 135ff.: J. Villa-Amil y Castro, 'Codices jurídicos de la Biblioteca de El Escorial.' (MH)

S. De Ricci, 'A Handlist of Latin Classical Manuscripts in American Libraries,' *Philological Quarterly* I (1922) 100-08. Arranged by authors.

The same and W. J. Wilson, *Census of Medieval and Renaissance Manuscripts in the United States and Canada.* 3 vols. New York 1935-40. Arranged alphabetically by states, cities and libraries. Includes many small private collections not listed here. I (1935) 3-9: Berkeley, *California*, University of California. 25 mss. and documents. 17-18: Los Angeles, Cal., University of Southern California. 7 mss. 20-21: Mrs. Edward L. Doheny. 8 mss. Now in Camarillo. 26-28: San Francisco, Cal., Adolph Sutro Library. 16 mss. 35-146: San Marino, Cal., Henry E. Huntington Library. 155: Thomas E. Marston. 4 mss. Some now at Yale University. 157-58: Hartford, *Connecticut*, Trinity College. 8 mss. 159: Ibid., Watkinson Library. 6 mss. 161-71: New Haven, Conn., Yale University. 54 mss. 179-266: Washington, *District of Columbia*, Library of Congress. 190 mss. and autographs. 267-450: Ibid., Folger Shakespeare Library. 451-53: Ibid., Army Medical Library. Now National Library of Medicine, Cleveland, Ohio. 12 mss. 454-61: Ibid., Catholic University. 32 mss. 470-84: Ibid., Holy Name College. 92 mss. 485-86: Ibid., Georgetown University. 11 mss. 488: Ibid., Smithsonian Institution. 17 mss. 493-95. Ibid., Senator David A. Reed. 12 mss. Now at Princeton University. 513-18: Chicago, *Illinois*, Art Institute. 522-50: Ibid., Newberry Library. 552-600: Ibid., University of Chicago. 674-90: Kenilworth, Ill., Roger W. Barrett. 153 mss. 696-711: Urbana, Ill., University of Illinois. 52 mss. 730-40: Trappist, *Kentucky*, Abbey of Gethsemani. 30 mss. 753-55: Baltimore, *Maryland*, Johns Hopkins University. 9 mss. 757-856: Walters Art Gallery, 557 mss. 862-64: *Ibid.* John Garrett. 14 mss. Now at Johns Hopkins University. 865-99:

Ibid. Robert Garrett. 167 mss. Now at Princeton University. 906-09: Woodstock College, Woodstock. 8 mss. 910-16: Boston, *Massachusetts*, Boston Medical Library. 25 mss. 917-29: *Ibid.*, Boston Public Library. 72 mss. 930-36: *Ibid.*, Gardner Museum. 42 mss. 937-41: *Ibid.*, Massachusetts Historical Society. 27 mss. 942-48: Ibid., Museum of Fine Arts. 42 mss. Ibid., 951-53: Harvey Cushing. 9 mss. 964-1020: Cambridge, Mass., Harvard College. 1021-1048: Ibid., Harvard Law School. 154 mss. 1052-1053: Harvard Business School. Has in deposit the Selfridge Collection. 1067-78: Wellesley, Mass., Wellesley College. 18 mss. and 30 Plimpton mss. 1081-86: Williamstown, Mass. Williams College. 23 mss. 1089-90: Worcester, Mass., Clark University. 11 mss. —II (1937) 1103-26: Ann Arbor, *Michigan*, University of Michigan. 208 mss. 1133-34: Detroit, Mich., Detroit Institute of Arts. 11 mss. 1137-39: Minneapolis, *Minnesota*, University of Minnesota. 9 mss. 1170-72: Madison, *New Jersey*, Drew Theological Seminary. 12 mss. 1174-84: Princeton, N. J., Princeton University. 61 mss. 1193-96: Brooklyn, *New York*, Brooklyn Museum. 18 mss. 1197-1201: Ibid., Long Island Historical Society. 25 mss. 1209-12: Buffalo, N.Y., Grosvenor Library. 28 mss. 1223-54: Ithaca, N.Y., Cornell University. 118 mss. 1258-79: New York, N.Y., Columbia University. 107 mss. 1280-82: *Ibid.*, Fordham University. 28 mss. 1284-87: *Ibid.*, General Theological Seminary. 15 mss. 1289-91: *Ibid.*, Grolier Club. 15 mss. 1292-1300: *Ibid.* Hispanic Society. 1301-05: Ibid., Jewish Theological Seminary. 13 mss. and documents. 1306-09: Ibid., Metropolitan Museum. 18 mss. 1310-13: Ibid., New York Academy of Medicine. 12 mss. 1314-45: New York Public Library. 152 mss. and autographs. 1347-58: Ibid., New York University. 206 mss. and documents. 1359-1636: Ibid., Pierpont Morgan Library. 839 mss. and autographs. 1637-49: Ibid., Union Theological Seminary. 68 mss. 1675-84: Ibid., Howard L. Goodhart. 40 mss. Some mss. went to Bryn Mawr. 1692-99: Ibid., Philip Hofer. 36 mss. Some mss. went to Harvard University. 1753-1808: Ibid., The late George A. Plimpton. 305 mss. Now at Columbia University. 1845-48: Ibid., The estate of Wilfrid M. Voynich. 16 mss. 1856-57: Poughkeepsie, *New York.* Vassar College. 8 mss. 1871-76: Rochester, N.Y., University of Rochester. 26 mss. 1877-78: Saint Bonaventure, N.Y, St. Bonaventure College. 6 mss. 1881-83: Staten Island, N.Y., Staten Island Institute of Arts and Sciences. 15 mss. 1889-1900: Tuxedo Park, N. Y., Grenville Kane. 58 mss. Now at Princeton University. 1907-09: Chapel Hill, *North Carolina*, University of North Carolina. 9 mss. 1910-11: Durham, N. C., Duke University. 15 mss. 1922-25: Cincinnati, *Ohio*, University of Cincinnati. 17 mss. 1928-32: Cleveland, Ohio, Cleveland Museum of Art. 24 mss. 1933-35: Ibid., Cleveland Public Library. 11 mss. 1972-77: Toledo, Ohio, Toledo Museum of Art. 36 mss. 1986-92: Bethlehem, *Pennsylvania*, Lehigh University. 16 mss. 2009-10: Philadelphia, Pa., College of Physicians. 8 mss. 2012-84: Ibid., Free Library. 426 mss. and documents. 2085-98: Ibid., Historical Society of Pennsylvania. 2103-05: Ibid., Library Company. 11 mss. 2106-10: Ibid., University of Pennsylvania. 19 mss. 2120-31: Titusville, Pa., John Hinsdale Scheide. 65 mss. Now deposited at Princeton University. 2140-42: Providence, *Rhode Island*, Brown University. 13 mss. 2143-52: Ibid., John Carter Brown Library. 33 mss. 2156-63: Austin, *Texas*, University of Texas. 39 mss. 2164-65: Houston, Tex., Houston Public Library. 8 mss. 2203-29: Montreal, Canada, McGill University. 209 mss. 2230-31: Ibid., David Ross McCord National Museum. 18 mss. 2235-37: Toronto, Can-

ada, Royal Ontario Museum of Archaeology. 17 mss.

—2239-2343: Errata and Addenda. Berkeley, University of California (2239-40). Mrs. Doheny. Mss. no 9-11 (2242-43). Huntington Library (2245-49). T. Marston (2249). Hartford, Conn., Case Memorial Library. 12 mss. (2249-51). Yale University (2251-55). Library of Congress (2256-59). Folger Shakespeare Library (2259-72). Georgetown University (2273). Newberry Library (2277-81). University of Chicago (2281-83). University of Illinois (2285-86). Johns Hopkins University. Ms. no. 10 (2288). Walters Art Gallery (2288-92). Robert Garrett. Mss. no. 168-171 (2295-96). Boston Museum (2298). Harvey Cushing (2298-99). Harvard University (2301-06). Wellesley College. Mss. no. 19-23 (2308-09). Drew Theological Seminary (2312). New York Public Library (2317-18). Pierpont Morgan Library (2318-19). Howard Goodhart (2339-40).

—III (1940): Indices.

Supplement to De Ricci's Census of Medieval and Renaissance Mss. 1 typed vol. Prepared by C. U. Faye and W. H. Bond. Deposited at the Harvard University Library, Cambridge, Mass.

Les Richesses de la Bibliophilie Belge. Brussels 1958. 80 pp. and plates. Describes mss. in various Belgian collections. Exhibition catalogue.

Rivista delle Biblioteche. II (1889) 91-94: G. Ottino, 'La Biblioteca comunale di Narni.' 25 mss. VI (1895) 115-17: A. Solerti, 'Notizie dei libri postillati da Torquato Tasso che si conservano nella Barberiniana di Roma.' Now at the Vatican. XXXIII (NS I, no. 1-2, 1923) 19-32: 'La Biblioteca Rossiana.' Lists many mss. Now at the Vatican.

U. Robert, *Inventaire sommaire des manuscrits des Bibliothèques de France dont les catalogues n'ont pas été imprimés.* Paris 1896. 606 pp. Arranged alphabetically by cities. Superseded. No index.

Rodney P. Robinson, 'Some newly discovered Fragments of Visigothic Manuscripts,' *Transactions and Proceedings of the American Philological Association* LX (1929) 48-56.

M. Rossetti, 'Notizie paleografiche e storiche di alcuni codici inediti in archivi della Provincia di Cuneo,' *Bollettino della R. Deputazione subalpina di storia patria, Sezione di Cuneo* XVI (1944) 82-99. Describes a few mss. in Alba (Seminario Vescovile, 1 ms., and Archivio Capitolare, 1 ms.), Mondovì (Archivio Capitolare, 3 mss.) and Saluzzo (Confraternita del Gonfalone, 1 ms.). (NN)

F. Rühl, 'Bemerkungen über einige Bibliotheken von Sicilien,' *Philologus* XLVII (N. F. I, 1889) 577-88. Covers Messina, Catania, Siracusa, Palermo and Naples.

J. Ruysschaert, *Les manuscrits de l'abbaye de Nonantola: Table de concordance annotée et index des manuscrits.* (Studi e Testi 182, Supplement). Vatican City 1955. 77 pp. 59-66: List of mss. with their present locations. Most of them are in the Biblioteca Nazionale, Rome, several at the Vatican. 3 mss. remain in Nonantola.

M. Salmi, *La miniatura italiana.* Milan 1955. 151 pp. 149-51: List of mss.

The same, *Italian Miniatures.* New York (1954). 214 pp.

A. Sanderus, *Bibliotheca Belgica manuscripta, sive elenchus universalis codicum manuscriptorum in celebrioribus Belgii coenobiis, ecclesiis, urbium, ac privatorum hominum Bibliothecis adhuc latentium.* 2 vols. in 1, Lille 1641-44. Covers numerous libraries. Largely superseded. No index. (DLC)

S. Sawicka, *Straty wojenne Zbiorów Polskich w Dziedzinie Rekopisów Iluminowanych.* Warsaw 1952. 99 pp. and plates. Surveys the illuminated mss. in Poland that were lost during the last war. (NN)

F. Saxl, 'Verzeichnis astrologischer und mythologischer illustrierter Handschriften des lateinischen Mittelalters,' *Sitzungsberichte der Heidelberger Akademie der Wissenschaften, Philosophisch-Historische Klasse,* VI (1915) no. 6-7, 143 pp.; XVI (1925-26) no. 2, 254 pp, Covers Vatican, Rome and Vienna.

The same and H. Meier, *Verzeichnis astrologischer und mythologischer Handschriften des lateinischen Mittelalters. III. Handschriften in englischen Bibliotheken. Catalogue of Astrological and Mythological Manuscripts of the Latin Middle Ages. III. Manuscripts in English Libraries.* 2 vols., ed. H. Bober. London 1953. Vol. I. 447 pp. Describes mss. in London, Kew (Sir Sydney Cockerell), Oxford, Cambridge, Durham. Vol. II. 65 pp. and plates. Indices, by E. Rosenbaum. p. 7-13: Index of mss. described and cited in the text. Among many mss. of better known collections, 1 ms. in Katowice is cited.

H. C. Scheeben, 'Handschriften,' *Archiv der Deutschen Dominikaner* I (1937) 149-202; II (1939) 134-214; III (1941) 201-25; IV (1951) 163-98. 12 mss. Covers Münster, Freiburg i. Br. (Stadtarchiv), Berlin, Soest, Munich, Vienna (Dominikaner). Index for pts. 1-3 in vol. III. (DCU)

H. Schenkl, 'Bibliotheca Patrum Latinorum Britannica,' *Sitzungsberichte der Kaiserlichen Akademie der Wissenschaften* [Vienna], *Philosophisch-Historische Classe.* CXXI (1890) no. 9, 80 pp.; CXXIII (1891) no. 5, 64 pp.; CXXIV (1891) no. 3, 48 pp.; CXXVI (1892) no. 6, 80 pp.; CXXVII (1892) no. 9, 78 pp.; CXXXI (1894) no. 10, 79 pp.; CXXXIII (1896) no. 7, 90 pp.; CXXXVI (1897) no. 5, 80 pp.; CXXXVII (1898) no. 8, 82 pp.; CXXXIX (1898) no. 9, 92 pp.; CXLIII (1901) no. 8, 49 pp.; CL (1905) no. 5, 78 pp.; CLVII (1908) no. 7, 89 pp. Covers Oxford, Cheltenham, Salisbury, Exeter, Canterbury, Bangor, Norwich, Wells, Chichester, Winchester, Westminster Abbey, Rochester, York, Lincoln, Edinburgh, Glasgow, St. Andrews, Aberdeen, Dublin, Holkham Hall, Cambridge, Hereford, Worcester, Durham, various London libraries, Blairs, Stonyhurst College, Oscott, Wisbech, Ipswich, Bury St. Edmunds, Plymouth, Manchester, Bristol, Gloucester, several private collections. Lists also many classical mss. Indispensable for many libraries. Indices in vol. CLVII.

F. Schillmann, *Wolfgang Trefler und die Bibliothek des Jakobsklosters zu Mainz*. (Zentralblatt für Bibliothekswesen, Beiheft XLIII). Leipzig 1913. 226 pp. Lists mss. extant in different libraries.

A. Schmidt, 'Handschriften der Reichsabtei Werden,' *Zentralblatt für Bibliothekswesen* XXII (1905) 241-264. Identifies mss. in Berlin, Düsseldorf, Münster, Darmstadt, Herzfeld a. d. Lippe (Kirchenbibliothek), Werden (Pfarrarchiv).

H. Schreiber, *Die Bibliothek der ehemaligen Mainzer Kartause: Die Handschriften und ihre Schicksale*. (Zentralblatt für Bibliothekswesen, Beiheft LX). Leipzig 1927. 234 pp. Lists mss. extant in different libraries.

F. Schulte, 'Die Rechtshandschriften der Stiftsbibliotheken von Göttweig . . ., Heiligenkreuz . . ., Klosterneuburg . . ., Melk . . ., Schotten in Wien . . .,' *Sitzungsberichte der Kaiserlichen Akademie der Wissenschaften* [Vienna], *Philosophisch-Historische Classe* LVII (1867) 559-616.

The same, 'Iter Gallicum,' *Sitzungsberichte der Kaiserlichen Akademie der Wissenschaften* [Vienna], *Philosophisch-Historische Classe* LIX (1868) 355-496. Covers Geneva (p. 366-67), Grenoble, Lyon, Carpentras, Avignon, Marseille, Nîmes, Montpellier, Toulouse, Tours, Angers, Alençon and Chartres. Describes 278 mss., mostly legal. Index of subjects, not of authors (491-96).

W. Schum, 'Erfurter Handschriften in auswärtigen Bibliotheken,' *Mittheilungen des Vereins für Geschichte und Alterthumskunde von Erfurt* VI (1873) 253-79. Lists mss. at Pommersfelden and Munich. (NN)

M. M. Schumpp, 'Über zwei dem hl. Albertus Magnus zugewiesene homiletische Traktate,' *Divus Thomas* (Freiburg) Ser. III,

vol. X (1932) 277-286. Cites mss., including one in Düsseldorf (Dominikanerkloster, p. 284). (NN)

Scriptorum veterum nova collectio e Vaticanis codicibus edita, ed. A. Mai. III (1828), pt. 1, p. 163-66: mss. in Montecassino and Cava.

E. Seckel, *Beiträge zur Geschichte beider Rechte im Mittelalter*. Tübingen 1898. 539 pp. Index of mss. (535-39).

Serapeum. I (1840) 104-11; 117-23: F. F. Oechsle, 'Nachricht von alten Handschriften der Stiftskirche zu Oehringen.' 9 mss. 177-85: 'Nachricht von der Auffindung einer Anzahl alter Handschriften des ehemaligen Domcapitels zu Havelberg.'

—II (1841) 24-32; 41-46; 52-59; 72-79; 318-30; III (1842) 140-44; 155-59; IV (1843) 353-64: E. G. Vogel, 'Über einige frühere italienische Bibliotheken.' Supplement to Blume's *Iter Italicum*.

—III (1842) 97-110: Hermann, 'Verzeichniss der Corveyer Handschriften zu Anfang des 19 Jahrhunderts.' 109 mss. No index.

—III (1842) 337-50; 365-68; V (1844) 113-22: F. Schmidt, 'Die Handschriften der gräflich Ortenburg'schen Bibliothek zu Tambach in Oberfranken.' 30 mss. No index. III (1842) 376-82: Reuss, 'Manuscriptenkatalog der vormaligen Dombibliothek zu Würzburg.' 183 mss. No index.

—IV (1843) 184-90; 205-08: Klüpfel, 'Die Handschriften der kgl. Universitäts-Bibliothek in Tübingen.' Lists 18 Latin mss. (188ff.). No index.

—VI (1845) 33-39: Bethmann, 'Einige Handschriften der Gräflich Schönborn'schen Bibliothek in Pommersfelde.'

—VII (1846) 193-204: 'Briefliche Mittheilung des Dr. G. Heine aus Berlin an Hofrat Hänel in Leipzig über spanische und portugiesische Bibliotheken.' Lists 7 mss. at S. Isidro de León (196-97) and 72 mss. at Cordoba Cathedral (201-04). 234-37: 'Handschriften und Urkunden in der Bibliothek des Herrn Hofrath Prof. Dr.

Gustav Hänel zu Leipzig.' Lists 61 Latin mss. (235-37). 337-42: F. Schmidt, 'Die Handschriften der Stadtbibliothek zu Memmingen in Schwaben.' 32 mss. No index.

—VIII (1847) 43-45: Hänel, 'Handschriften im Schlosse Liebenau bei Ravensburg.' 56 mss. No index. 78-80: 'Handschriften, welche Herr Dr. Heine in Berlin von seinen Reisen mitgebracht hat.' 26 mss. 81-95: 'Zweiter Bericht des Dr. G. Heine in Berlin über seine litterarische Reise in Spanien, gerichtet an Hofrath und Prof. Dr. Gustav Hänel...' Lists mss. at Barcelona (85-89), Vich (90-94), Roda (95). 103-05: 'Dritter Bericht des Dr. G. Heine in Berlin über seine litterarische Reise in Spanien, gerichtet an Hofrath und Prof. Dr. Gustav Hänel...' Lists mss. at Valladolid (103-04) and Aicalá (now Madrid) University (104-05). 289-94: F. Schmidt, 'Die Handschriften der ehemaligen Klöster zu Memmingen in Schwaben.' 27 extant mss.

—IX (1848) 145-57; 163-69: R. Naumann, 'Die Rats- oder Gymnasialbibliothek zu Zwickau.' 353-57: F. A. Schütz, 'Handschriften der Universitäts-Bibliothek zu Giessen.' 14 mss.

—X (1849) 266-70; XI (1850) 121-23: H. J. Zeibig, 'Aehrenlese merkwürdiger Inscripte aus den Handschriften der Stiftsbibliothek zu Klosterneuburg.'

—XI (1850) 129-37; 154-58; 173-76: F. Kritz, 'De Codicibus Bibliothecae Amplonianae Erfurtensis potioribus.' 50 mss. 161-73; 177-88; 193-202: F. L. Hoffmann, 'Ein Verzeichniss von Handschriften der ehemaligen Heidelberger Bibliothek.'

—XII (1851) 104-12: P. A. Dudik, 'Die Stifts-Bibliothek zu St. Paul in Kärnten.' 6 mss.

—XV (1854) 100-23: A. Ruland, 'Beitrag zur Kenntniss der Handschriften des Janus Gruterus' (Vat. Pal. lat.). 289-301; 305-20; 321-29: F. L. Hoffmann, 'Mittheilungen über die Handschriften-Kataloge öffentlicher Bibliotheken von welchen sich Abschriften in der hamburgischen Stadtbibliothek befinden.' Covers Berlin, Breslau, Erfurt, Escorial, Hamburg, Heidelberg, København, Leipzig, Mainz, Paris, Torino, Vienna and Zürich.

—XVII (1856) 129-35; 169-74; 177-84: W. T. Streuber, 'Handschriften der öffentlichen Bibliothek zu Basel.' 185-91; 193-235: A. Ruland, 'Zur Geschichte der alten nach Rom entführten Bibliothek zu Heidelberg.' Gives an old list of 610 mss. (212-24).

—XVIII (1857) 65-80; 81-91; 97-108: C. P. C. Schönemann, 'Zur Geschichte und Beschreibung der Herzogl. Bibliothek zu Wolfenbüttel.' 209-218: A. Ruland, 'Beiträge zur Kenntnis der Handschriften des Janus Gruterus.'

—XVIII (1857)-XXI (1860): Neigebaur, many articles on various Italian libraries. Lists a few mss. at Vercelli (XVIII, 167-68, 178-90), Parma (XIX, 1858, 356-57), Turin (XXI, 1860, 321-22).

—XXIV (1863) 113-16: F. Schmidt, 'Handschriften in Kempten.' 9 mss.

—XXV (1864) 353-65; 369-83; XXVII (1865) 24-31; 33-42; 49-59; 65-76; 81-89; 97-104: F. X. Kraus, 'Die Handschriften-Sammlung des Cardinals Nicolaus v. Cusa.' Superseded. With index (XXVII, 100-104).

—XXXI (1870) 273-83; 321-28; 337-51: H. Ratjen, 'Handschriften der Kieler Universitäts-Bibliothek.' Latin mss. no. K. B. 18-91. No index.

Serapeum; Intelligenz-Blatt. 1856, 153-57; 161-65; 169-73; 177-81; 185-89: 'Ausstellung von Cimelien der Stadtbibliothek zu Leipzig.' 83 mss.

—1858, 177-81; 185-89: 'Katalog der Bibliothek der Benedictiner-Abtei Zwiefalten.' Cont. through 1859 and 1860. With index (1860, 65ff.).

—1860-1865: Neigebaur, many articles on various Italian and German libraries. Mentions mss. at Aschaffenburg (1864, p. 83) and Turin (1865, 17-19).

—1861, 97-102; 105-11; 113-18; 121-27; 129-34; 137-43; 145-49; 153-57; 161-67: 'Ma-

nuscriptenkataloge aus R. K. von Sencken-
berg's Nachlasse.' Covers Munich, Ulm
and some private collections.

—1862, 137-42; 145-50; 153-58; 161-66:
'Auszug aus dem Catalogue of the Manuscripts at Ashburnham Place 1853.' 169-
72: G. Hänel, 'Einige von der Bodleian
Library seit 1828 erworbene Handschriften.' 177-83; 185-90: 'Auszug aus Phillipps Catalogus Librorum Manuscriptorum.'

—1863, 36-38: M. Alvin, 'Rapport triennal
sur la situation de la bibliothèque royale
pendant les années 1858-59, 1859-60 et
1860-61.' Lists mss. of Bruxelles, up to
no. 21818.

—1864, 169-75: F. Schmidt, 'Bruchstücke
aus Handschriften und alten Drucken der
Bibliotheken zu Memmingen und Tambach.'

—1866, 105-09; 113-17; 121-26: 'Katalog
der Handschriften in der Bibliothek der
regulirten Chorherren zu S. Salvatore in
Bologna.' 145-48; 153-59; 161-66; 169-
74; 177-82: H. S. Müller, 'Die Bilderhandschriften des Mittelalters in den Bibliotheken der Stadt und der Hauptschule zu
Bremen.' 20 mss. No index.

—1869, 25-29; 33-35: G. Parthey, 'Verzeichniss der griechischen und lateinischen
Handschriften in der Biblioteca Angelica
bei S. Agostino in Rom.' 35-36: The same,
'Verzeichniss der griechischen und lateinischen Handschriften in der Bibliothek der
Propaganda in Rom.' 24 mss.

—1870, 177-81: F. Schmidt, 'Nachricht von
Handschriften und alten Drucken in
Franken und Schwaben.'

Cf. R. Proctor, A Classified Index to the
Serapeum. London 1897. 159 pp. p. 103-
147: Alphabetical lists of public and private libraries.

A. Siegmund, Die Überlieferung der griechischen christlichen Literatur in der lateinischen Kirche bis zum zwölften Jahrhundert. München-Pasing 1949. 308 pp.
Index of mss. (289-302).

H. E. Sigerist, 'A Summer of Research in

European Libraries,' Bulletin of the Institute of the History of Medicine II (1934)
559-613. (NNN)

J. R. de Sinner, Voyage historique et littéraire
dans la Suisse occidentale. New ed. 2 vols.
Neuchatel 1787. No index.

L. de Sinner, Rapport adressé à M. le
Ministre de l'Instruction Publique . . . sur
un voyage historique et littéraire dans
quelques Cantons de la Suisse. Paris
(1846). 60 pp. Covers Luzern, Fribourg,
Solothurn, Basel, Bern, mostly for Swiss
and French history. (Bibliothèque Nationale, Paris).

Société française de reproductions de manuscrits à peintures. Bulletin. I (1911) 85-
106: Comte P. Durrieu, 'Notes sur quelques manuscrits à peintures d'origine
française ou flamande conservés en Italie.'
27 mss. at Vatican.

—II (1912) 5-53; III (1913) 5-55: R. Beer,
'Les principaux manuscrits à peintures
de la Bibliothèque Impériale de Vienne.'
II (1912) 55-107: H. Aubert, 'Les principaux manuscrits à peintures de la Bibliothèque Publique et Universitaire de
Genève.' 108-14: M. Bernath, 'Notice
sur quelques beaux manuscrits à peintures conservés en Allemagne.'

—IV (1914-20) 81-149: E. G. Millar, 'Les
manuscrits à peintures des Bibliothèques
de Londres.' Covers Soane's Museum and
Lincoln's Inn.

—V (1921) 160 pp. A. Boinet, 'Les manuscrits à peintures de la Bibliothèque Sainte-
Geneviève de Paris.'

—VI (1922) 5-30: The same, 'Choix de miniatures détachées conservées au Musée
de Cluny, à Paris.' 31-61: The same,
'Les principaux manuscrits à peintures de
la Bibliothèque de la Chambre des Députés à Paris.'

—VII (1923) 5-33: C. Oursel, 'Les manuscrits à miniatures de la Bibliothèque de
Dijon.'

—VIII (1924) 66 pp. Millar cont. (from
IV). Covers Lambeth Palace. IX (1925),
32 pp. The same cont.

—X (1926) 42-72: S. De Ricci, 'Les manuscrits de la Collection Henry Yates Thompson.' 108 mss. No index.

—XIV (1930) 35 pp. R. Dos Santos, 'Les principaux manuscrits à peintures conservés en Portugal.' Covers Lisbon, Oporto, Coimbra. No index.

—XV (1931) 124 pp. A. W. Byvanck, 'Les principaux manuscrits à peintures conservés dans les collections publiques du Royaume des Pays-Bas.' Covers Amsterdam, Arnhem, Culemborg, Groningen, Haarlem, 's Gravenhage, Leeuwarden, Leiden, Middelburg, Utrecht and Zwolle. No index.

—XVI (1933) 5-62: G. de la Batut, 'Les principaux manuscrits à peintures conservés à la Bibliothèque Mazarine de Paris.' No index.

—XVII (1933) 119 pp. Z. Ameisenowa, 'Les principaux manuscrits à peintures de la Bibliothèque Jagellonienne de Cracovie.'

—XVIII (1935) 204 pp. M. Jaroslawiecka-Gąsiorowska, 'Les principaux manuscrits à peintures du Musée des Princes Czartoryski, à Cracovie.' Covers also the Cathedral Library at Cracow. 36 mss.

—XIX (1938) 321 pp. S. Sawicka, 'Les principaux manuscrits à peintures de la Bibliothèque Nationale de Varsovie, du Château Royal et des Bibliothèques des Zamoyski à Varsovie, du Séminaire de Płock et du Chapître de Gniezno.' 38 mss.

—XX and XXI (1937-38): E. Trenkler and others, 'Les principaux manuscrits à peintures de la Bibliothèque Nationale de Vienne.'

Soupis Rukopisů Knihoven a Archivů Zemí Českých, Jakož i Rukopisných Bohemik Mimočeských. I (Prague 1910). A. Patera and A. Podlaha, *Soupis Rukopisů knihovny Metropolitní kapitoly Pražské*, vol. I. VIII, 513 pp. 846 mss.

II (1910) J. V. Šimák, *Rukopisy Majorátní Knihovny Hrabat z Nostitz a Rhienecka v Praze.* XI, 166 pp. 227 mss.

III (1915). A. Patera, *Bohemika Knížecí*

Dietrichsteinské Knihovny v Mikulově. 88 pp. 70 selected mss.

IV (1922). A. Podlaha, *Soupis Rukopisů knihovny Metropolitní kapitoly Pražské*, vol. II. 667 pp. Mss. no. 847-1702. Index for vols. I-II. (NN)

Soupis Rukopisů v Třeboni a v Českém Krumlove. Catalogus codicum manu scriptorum Trzebonae Crumloviique asservatorum. Prague 1958. 381 pp. and plates. 146 mss. 17-270: Třeboň, Statni Archiv, by J. Weber (i.e., J. Kadlec). 67 mss. (A 1-C 13). 271-302: Český Krumlov, Bibliotheca Capellanorum, by J. Třiška (nos. 68-103). 303-26: Cesky Krumlov, other libraries (Prelatura, City Archive, Museum, Provincial Archive), by P. Spunar (nos. 104-46).

Spicilegium Romanum, ed. A. Mai, V (1841) 237-42: 'Notitia codicum Sessorianorum.' 242-43: 'De codicibus quibusdam Vallicellianis.' 244-50: 'De nonnullis codicibus Bibliothecae Ambrosianae Mediolanensis, et primum de palimpsestis.' No index.

Th. Spizelius, *Sacra Bibliothecarum illustrium Arcana retecta, sive Manuscriptorum theologicorum in praecipuis Europae bibliothecis extantium designatio . . .* Augsburg 1668. 384 pp. Covers Augsburg (1ff.), Basel (17ff.), Vienna, Istanbul, Florence, Paris, Escorial, Leiden, Munich, Milan, Oxford, Padua, Vatican, Utrecht, Venice. Largely superseded. (MH)

C. F. Stälin, 'Zur Geschichte und Beschreibung alter und neuer Büchersammlungen im Königreich Würtemberg, insbesondere der Königlichen öffentlichen Bibliothek in Stuttgart und der mit derselben verbundenen Münz-, Kunst- und Alterthümer-Sammlung,' *Würtembergische Jahrbücher für vaterländische Geschichte, Geographie, Statistik und Topographie* 1837 (1838) 293-387. Surveys mss. at Stuttgart (307ff. and 350ff.), Tübingen (359ff.) and other cities in Württemberg. (NN)

R. Stauber, *Die Schedelsche Bibliothek.* (Studien und Darstellungen aus dem Gebiet der Geschichte VI, 2-3). Freiburg

1908. 277 pp. Lists mss. extant at Munich, Nuremberg and other libraries. (NN)

E. Steffenhagen and A. Wetzel, 'Die Kloster-bibliothek zu Bordesholm und die Gottorfer Bibliothek,' *Zeitschrift der Gesellschaft für Schleswig-Holstein-Lauenburgische Geschichte* XIII (1883) 65-142; XIV (1884) 1-156. Lists over 100 mss. now at Kiel (XIII, 127ff.) and 25 mss. now at København (XIV, 41ff.) (NN)

F. Stegmüller, 'Repertorium initiorum plurimorum in Sententias Petri Lombardi Commentariorum,' *Römische Quartalschrift* XLV (1937) 85-360. Index of mss. (342-56) and of authors (357-60).

The same, *Repertorium Commentariorum in Sententias Petri Lombardi.* 2 vols., Würzburg 1947. II 733-817: Index codicum, with many references to catalogues.

Cf. V. Doucet, 'Commentaires sur les Sentences: Supplément au Répertoire de M. Frédéric Stegmueller, *Archivum Franciscanum Historicum* XLVII (1954) 88-170; 400-427.

F. Stegmüller, *Repertorium Biblicum Medii Aevi.* 6 Vols. Madrid 1940 (i.e., 1950)-1959.

The same, 'Zur Literargeschichte der Philosophie und Theologie an den Universitäten Evora und Coimbra im XVI. Jahrhundert,' *Spanische Forschungen der Görresgesellschaft*, Erste Reihe, Bd. 3 (1931) 385-438. Lists mss. in Lisbon, Coimbra, Evora, Braga.

E. v. Steinmeyer and E. Sievers, *Die althochdeutschen Glossen.* 5 vols. Berlin 1879-1922. IV (1898) 371-686; V (1922) 50-86. Lists 751 mss.

S. Stelling-Michaud, *Catalogue des manuscrits juridiques (droit canon et droit romain) de la fin du XIIᵉ au XIVᵉ siècle conservés en Suisse.* Geneva 1954. 129 pp. Lists 187 mss. in Basel, Bern, Einsiedeln, Geneva (library and archive), Cologny (Bodmer), Lausanne, Luzern, St. Gall, Sion (Archives Cantonales and Bibliothèque du Chapître), Zuerich.

A. M. Stickler, 'Iter Helveticum,' *Traditio*

XIV (1958) 462-84. Lists 35 canonist mss. See below under *Traditio.*

A. Strittmatter, 'Liturgische Handschriften in amerikanischen Bibliotheken,' *Jahrbuch für Liturgiewissenschaft* XIV (1938) 224-30.

Studi italiani di filologia classica. V (1897) 429-40: M. Fava, 'Codices latini Catinenses.' Covers Catania, Biblioteca Universitaria (429-35) and Biblioteca Ventimiliana (435-40). No index.

—VIII (1900) 115-318: A. Mancini, 'Index codicum latinorum publicae bybliothecae Lucensis.' (Lucca, Biblioteca Governativa). Index (304ff.). 321-427: C. Vitelli, 'Index codicum latinorum qui Pisis in bybliothecis Conventus S. Catherinae et Universitatis adservantur.' (Pisa, S. Caterina and Biblioteca Universitaria). Index (423ff.).

—IX (1901) 489-94: A. Balsamo, 'Indice dei codici latini classici conservati nella Biblioteca Comunale di Piacenza.' 17 mss. No index. 508-12: C. Vitelli, 'Indicis codicum latinorum Pisis in Bybliotheca conventus S. Catherinae adservatorum Supplementum.' No index.

—X (1902) 323-58: L. Galante, 'Index codicum classicorum latinorum qui Florentiae in bybliotheca Magliabechiana adservantur.' 52 mss. from Classes I-VII. No index. 165-74: V. Ussani, 'Codices latini bybliothecae Universitatis Messanensis ante saec. XVI exarati.' 17 mss. No index.

—XI (1903) 165-388: R. Sabbadini, 'Spogli Ambrosiani latini.' Describes some classical mss. of the Ambrosiana at Milan. 401-31: N. Terzaghi, 'Index codicum latinorum classicorum qui Senis in bybliotheca publica adservantur. ' (Siena, Biblioteca Comunale). 75 mss. Index (428ff.).

—XII (1904) 1-9: A. Solari, 'Codici latini della biblioteca communale di Livorno anteriori al s. XVII.' 19 mss. No index.

—XIII (1905) 59-66: N. Pirrone, 'Codices latini qui in publica bybliotheca Drepanensi adservantur.' (Trapani, Biblioteca Comunale). 10 mss. No index.

—XIV (1906) 17-96: A. Beltrami, 'Index codicum classicorum latinorum qui in bybliotheca Quiriniana Brixiensi adservantur.' (Brescia, Biblioteca Queriniana). 44 mss. Index (91ff.). 362-73: A. Solari, 'Index codicum latinorum classicorum qui Lucae in bybliotheca Capituli Maioris Ecclesiae adservantur.' (Lucca, Biblioteca Capitolare). 29 mss. No index.
—XV (1907) 129-60: Galante cont. Florence, Mss. Magliab. no. 53-103. Covers classes VII-XL. Index for both parts (157ff.).
—XVI (1908) 103-432: L. Frati, 'Indice dei codici latini conservati nella R. Biblioteca Universitaria di Bologna.' ms. lat. 1 1 I-1077(2200). XVII (1909) 1-171. The same cont. Mss. no. 1078 (2202-3)-1628 (4030-31), 1629(701). Valid shelf marks in parentheses. Index for both parts (141ff.).
—XVIII (1910) 77-169: G. Funaioli, 'Index codicum latinorum qui Volaterris in bybliotheca Guarnacciana adservantur.' (Volterra, Biblioteca Guarnacci). Inadequate index (164ff.).
—XIX (1912) 19-23: A. Mancini, 'Codices latini publicae Bybliothecae Faventinae.' (Faenza, Biblioteca Comunale). Index (23). 24-52: G. Procacci, 'Index codicum latinorum classicorum qui Ferrariae in civica bybliotheca adservantur.' 44 mss. Index (50ff.).
—N. S. I (1920) 319-26: S. Ferri, 'Index codicum classicorum qui Pisauri in Bibliotheca Oliveriana adservantur.' (Pesaro). 24 Latin mss. No index.
H. Swarzenski, *Die lateinischen illuminierten Handschriften des XIII. Jahrhunderts in den Ländern an Rhein, Main und Donau.* 2 vols. Berlin 1936. 95 mss. in different libraries.
G. B. Tarallo, 'Catalogo dell' edizioni del secolo XV e dei Codici della Biblioteca dei PP. Benedettini Cassinesi, di Monreale,' *Giornale di Scienze Lettere e Arti per la Sicilia* LI (1835) 3-20; 132-49; LII (1835) 3-15; 129-43; 225-41; LIII (1836) 264-76; LV (1836) 252-78. (CtY). Also as a separate volume, Palermo 1836. 120 pp.

(Palermo, Biblioteca Nazionale). The mss. are listed in vol. LV (pp. 95-120 of the separate edition). They are now in Monreale and Palermo.
David M. Taylor, *The Oldest Manuscripts in New Zealand.* Wellington 1955. xx, 218 pp. and plates. Lists 77 Western mss. in Dunedin (University of Otago, Knox College, Dunedin Public Library, Selwyn College), Christchurch (Earlham Library), Wellington (Alexander Turnbull Library, British and Foreign Bible Society), Auckland (Auckland Central Library, Trinity Methodist Theological College, Dr. V. Heine). (NN)
A. Tenneroni, *Catalogo ragionato dei manoscritti appartenenti al fu Conte Giacomo Manzoni.* (Catalogo della Biblioteca del fu Conte Giacomo Manzoni, pt. 4). Città di Castello 1894. ix, 187 pp. 186 mss. Collection scattered. Many mss. now in Berlin and Rome (Biblioteca Nazionale).
J. Theele, *Die Handschriften des Benediktinerklosters S. Petri zu Erfurt.* (Zentralblatt für Bibliothekswesen, Beiheft XLVIII). Leipzig 1920. 220 pp. Lists mss. extant in different libraries.
L. Thorndike, 'Alchemical Writings in Vatican Palatine and Certain Other Continental Latin Manuscripts,' *Speculum* XI (1936) 370-83. 19 mss.
The same, and P. Kibre, *A Catalogue of Incipits of Mediaeval Scientific Writings in Latin.* (The Mediaeval Academy of America. Publications, no. 29). Cambridge, Mass. 1937. 926 pp. Index of authors (786ff.).
The same, 'Additional Incipits of Mediaeval Scientific Writings in Latin,' *Speculum* XIV (1939) 93-105. No index.
The same, and P. Kibre, 'More Incipits of Mediaeval Scientific Writings in Latin,' *Speculum* XVII (1942) 342-66. No index.
The same, 'Further Incipits of Mediaeval Scientific Writings in Latin,' *Speculum* XXVI (1951) 673-695.
The same, *A History of Magic and Experimental Science.* 8 vols. New York 1923-

58. Each volume has an index of authors and one of manuscripts. The indices in vol. 6 cover also vol. 5.

The same, 'Some Later Medieval Latin Medical Mss. at Bern and Prag,' *Annals of Medical History* N.S. VIII (1936) 427-32.

The same, 'Some Alchemical Manuscripts at Bologna and Florence,' *Ambix* V (1956) 85-110. No index.

H. Tietze, *Die Entführung von Wiener Kunstwerken nach Italien.* Vienna 1919. 57 pp. and plates. Lists mss. taken from Vienna to Trent and Naples (p. 47-57).

P. Toesca, *La pittura e la miniatura nella Lombardia dai più antichi monumenti alla metà del Quattrocento.* Milan 1912. 594 pp.

J. M. Octavio de Toledo, *Catálogo de la Libreria del Cabildo Toledano.* 2 vols. in 1, Madrid 1903-06. I, 207 pp.: 420 mss., arranged alphabetically. They are now partly in Toledo, partly in Madrid.

Traditio VII (1949-51) 444-449: Toni Schmid, 'Canon Law in Manuscripts from Medieval Sweden.'

—VIII (1952) 402-18: C. H. Talbot, 'A List of Cistercian Manuscripts in Great Britain.'

—XI (1955) 259-379: M. W. Bloomfield, 'A Preliminary List of Incipits of Latin Writers on Virtues and Vices.' 429-48: (S. Kuttner), 'Institute of Research and Study in Medieval Canon Law, Bulletin for 1955.' Includes S. Kuttner, 'An Interim Checklist of Manuscripts' (439-448).

—XII (1956) 557-622: The same, 'Bulletin for 1956.' Includes 'An Interim Checklist of Manuscripts,' pt. II (560-66); A. M. Stickler, 'Decretistica Germanica adaucta' (593-605); S. Kuttner, 'Manuscripts and Incunabula exhibited at the Inauguration of the Institute in 1956' (611-15). 457-555. W. J. Wilson, 'Manuscript Cataloging.'

—XIII (1957) 463-514: The same, 'Bulletin for 1957.' Includes 'An Interim Checklist of Manuscripts,' pt. III (467-71).

—XIV (1958) 457-512: The same, 'Bulletin for 1958.' Includes: A. M. Stickler, 'Iter Helveticum' (462-84). Describes 35 mss. in Basel, Bern, Genf, Luzern, St. Gall, Sion, Zurich.

See also Section A under Kristeller and Wilson.

L. Traube, *Vorlesungen und Abhandlungen* I (Munich 1909) 157-263: 'Die lateinischen Handschriften in Alter Capitalis und in Uncialis.' Lists 413 mss. in different libraries. No index.

Trésors des Bibliothèques d'Italie. Paris 1950. Unpaged. 468 nos. Exhibition Catalogue. (Morgan Library).

C. H. Turner, *Early Worcester Manuscripts.* Oxford 1916. lxxii pp. and plates. Lists 51 Latin mss. extant in different libraries (lxiii ff.).

Z. C. von Uffenbach, *Merkwürdige Reisen durch Niedersachsen, Holland und Engelland.* 3 vols. Ulm 1753-54. Index in vol. III inadequate.

B. L. Ullman, 'Latin Manuscripts in American Libraries,' *Philological Quarterly* V (1926) 152-56: VII (1928) 6-8. Each section arranged by classical authors.

Union Académique Internationale. *Catalogue des manuscrits alchimiques latins.* I (Brussels 1939): J. Corbett, *Manuscrits des Bibliothèques publiques de Paris antérieures au XVIIe siècle.* 9 mss.

—II (Brussels 1951): The same, *Manuscrits des Bibliothèques publiques des Départements français.* 200 pp. 50 mss.

—*Catalogue of Latin and Vernacular Alchemical Manuscripts in Great Britain and Ireland dating from before the XVIth Century,* by Dorothy Waley Singer. 3 vols. Brussels 1928-31. Arranged by texts. Index in vol. III.

—*Corpus Philosophorum Medii Aevi … Aristoteles Latinus.* Codices descripsit G. Lacombe (with A. Birkenmajer, M. Dulong, Aet. Franceschini). Pars prior. Rome 1939. 763 pp. Describes 1120 mss. of Aristotle and his commentators. Arranged by countries. No index.

—Pars Posterior, ed. L. Minio-Paluello. Cambridge 1955. pp. 769-1388. Mss. no. 1121-2012. Indices.

Van de Putte, see under P.

H. O. Vaubel, 'Die Miniaturenhandschriften der Giessener Universitätsbibliothek und der Gräfl. Solmsischen Bibliothek zu Laubach,' *Mitteilungen des Oberhessischen Geschichtsvereins* XXVII (1926), 94 pp. 13 mss.

Verzeichnis der Handschriften im Deutschen Reich. I: *Die Handschriften der Staats- und Universitätsbibliothek Breslau.* Preface signed by H. A. Krüss.

Vol. I fasc. 1-2 (1938-39) 160 pp. Mss. I F 1-155. No index. II: A. Kern, *Die Handschriften der Universitätsbibliothek Graz.* Vol. I (1939-42). 432 pp. 712 mss. No index. (fasc. 1-5 at NN; fasc. 6 seen in Graz). Cf. A. Teetaert a Zedelgem, 'De manuscriptis franciscanis sparsis in bibliothecis Germaniae et Austriae,' *Collectanea Franciscana* XIII (1943) 35-60. (DCU)

*A. Vetulani, 'Projet d'un catalogue des manuscrits juridiques du moyen-âge conservés dans les bibliothèques polonaises,' *Collectanea Theologica* XVIII (Lwow 1937). 436ff. Important for 2 mss of the Seminary in Płock (now lost). (DCU)

The same, "Une suite d'études pour servir à l'histoire du 'Décret' de Gratien," *Revue historique de droit français et étranger*, Ser. IV, vol. XV (1936) 343-58; XVI (1937) 461-79; 674-92. Describes 7 mss. in Cracow and Gniezno (XV 344-58).

The same 'Les Manuscrits du Décret de Gratien et des œuvres des décrétistes dans les bibliothèques polonaises,' *Studia Gratiana* I (Bologna 1953) 217-287. Describes 14 mss. in Cracow (University and Chapter) Gdansk, Gniezno (Chapter), Lublin (Catholic University), Płock (Seminary, now lost), Poznan (Chapter).

J. Villa-Amil y Castros, *Los Códices de las Iglesias de Galicia en la Edad Media.* Madrid 1874. 127 pp. Revised reprint from *Revista de Archivos* III-IV (1873-74). (Hispanic Society).

Jaime Villanueva, *Viage literario a las iglesias de España.* 22 vols. Madrid 1803-52. Lists mss. at Valencia (I, 88ff); S. Miguel de los Reyes (II, 124ff.); Segorve (III, 173 ff.); Portaceli (IV, 43ff.); Valencia (132ff.); Tortosa (V, 1ff. and 158ff.); Vique (VI, 67ff.); Barcelona (VIII, 1ff.); Serrateix (118ff.); Cervera (IX, 11ff.); Solsona (40ff.); Ager (125ff.); Urgel (XI, 163ff.); Gerona (XII, 101ff.); Lérida (XVI, 50ff.); Barcelona (XVIII, 84ff. and 176ff. and 208ff.); Belen (275ff.); Murta and other monasteries (XIX, 1ff.); Tarragona (99ff.); Santas Cruces (XX, 109ff.); Poblet (147ff.); Palma (XXI, 17ff.; XXII, 205ff.). Each volume indexed. (Hispanic Society).

C. Vivell, *Initia Tractatuum musicae.* Graz 1912. 352pp. (NN)

E. Volger, 'Mittheilungen aus Handschriften,' *Philologus* XIII (1858) 192-204; XIV (1859) 161-68. Covers Barcelona, Tarragona, Vich.

W. Wattenbach, 'Iter Austriacum 1853,' *Archiv für Kunde österreichischer Geschichts-Quellen* XIV (1855) 1-94.

R. Weiss, *Humanism in England during the fifteenth century.* Oxford 1941. xxiii, 190 pp. p. xiii-xiv: list of mss. at Ambrosiana, Tokyo, Vatican and other libraries.

—2nd ed. Oxford 1957. xxiii, 202 pp.

F. Wickhoff, ed., *Beschreibendes Verzeichnis der illuminierten Handschriften in Oesterreich.* 8 vols. in 22, Leipzig 1905-38. I (1905): J. Hermann, *Die illuminierten Handschriften in Tirol.* 275 mss. at Ambras, Bolzano, Bressanone, Fiecht, Gries, Innichen, Innsbruck, Chiusa, Merano, Novacella, Rovereto, Schwaz, Stams, Trento and Wilten.

—II (1905): H. Tietze, *Die illuminierten Handschriften in Salzburg.* 126 mss. at Salzburg, Mattsee and Michaelbeuren.

—III (1907): R. Eisler, *Die illuminierten Handschriften in Kärnten.* 98 mss. at Klagenfurt and St. Paul.

—IV (1911): P. Buberl, *Die illuminierten Handschriften in Steiermark.* 304 mss. at Admont and Vorau.

—V (1911): H. Tietze, *Die illuminierten Handschriften der Rossiana in Wien-Lainz.* (now at the Vatican). 381 mss.

—VI (1917) : H. Folnasics, *Die illuminierten Handschriften in Dalmatien.* 79 mss. at Zara, Sibenik, Archangelsk, Trogir, Split, Lesina, Dubrovnik, Kotor, Ercegnovi and Rab.

—VII (1917): The same, *Die illuminierten Handschriften im Österreichischen Küstenlande, in Istrien und der Stadt Triest.* 79 mss. at Trieste, Capodistria, Parenzo, Pirano, Buic, Dignano, Grisignana, Gorizia, Grado, Aquileia, Duino, Verbenico (Veglia) and Ossero.

—VIII (N. F. I): *Die illuminierten Handschriften und Inkunabeln der Nationalbibliothek in Wien.* I (1923): H. J. Hermann, *Die frühmittelalterlichen Handschriften des Abendlandes.* 80 mss. II (1926): The same, *Die deutschen romanischen Handschriften.* 262 mss. III (1927): The same, *Die romanischen Handschriften des Abendlandes mit Ausnahme der deutschen Handschriften.* 90 mss. IV (1937-38): P. Buberl, *Die byzantinischen Handschriften.* V (1928-30): H. J. Hermann, *Die italienischen Handschriften des Dugento und Trecento.* 121 mss. VI (1930-33): The same, *Die Handschriften und Inkunabeln der italienischen Renaissance.* 489 mss. VII (1935-38): The same, *Die westeuropäischen Handschriften und Inkunabeln der Gotik und Renaissance mit Ausnahme der niederländischen Handschriften.* 141 mss. Each vol. indexed.

T. W. Williams, 'Gloucestershire Mediaeval Libraries,' *Transactions of the Bristol and Gloucestershire Archaeological Society* XXXI (1908) 78-195. Describes many mss. now at Bristol, Wells and other libraries. Index (187-95). (NN)

The same, *Somerset Mediaeval Libraries and Miscellaneous Notices of Books in Somerset prior to the dissolution of the Monasteries.* Bristol 1897. 199 pp. Index of extant mss. (147ff.) and of authors (152ff.) (NN)

W. J. Wilson, 'Catalogue of Latin and Vernacular Alchemical Manuscripts in the United States and Canada,' *Osiris* VI (1939) 1-836. 79 mss.

B. Wirtgen, *Die Handschriften des Klosters St. Peter und Paul zu Erfurt bis zum Ende des 13. Jahrhunderts.* Diss. Berlin, Gräfenhainichen 1936. 138 pp. Lists mss. extant in different libraries.

R. Wolkan, 'Aus österreichischen Handschriftenkatalogen,' *Zeitschrift des österreichischen Vereins für Bibliothekswesen* II (XV, 1911) 69-73; III (XVI, 1912) 14-19; *Österreichische Zeitschrift für Bibliothekswesen* I (XVII, 1914) 2-7; 186-94. Covers Minoritenkloster and Dominikanerkloster, Vienna; Seitenstetten. No index.

Xenia Bernardina: Sancti Bernardi. . . octavos natales saeculares pia mente celebrantes Antistites et Conventus Cistercienses provinciae Austriaco-Hungaricae. Pars secunda. *Handschriften-Verzeichnisse. Die Handschriften-Verzeichnisse der Cistercienser-Stifte . . .* 2 vols. Vienna 1891. I, 1-114: Reun, by A. Weiss. 210 mss. Index (80ff.). 115-272: Heiligenkreuz, by B. Gsell. 550 mss. Index (232ff.). 273-91: Neukloster at Wiener-Neustadt, by E. Bill. 81 mss. Index (289ff.). 293-479: Zwettl, by St. Rössler. 420 mss. Index (440ff.). 481-561: Lilienfeld, by C. Schimek. 229 mss. Index (584ff.).

—II, 1-114: Wilhering, by O. Grillnberger. 224 mss. Index (84ff.). 115-64: Ossegg (Osek), by B. Wohlmann. 103 mss. Index (154ff.). 165-461: Hohenfurt (Vyšší Brod), by R. Pavel. 1210 mss. Index (347ff.). 463-79: Stams. 61 mss. Index (476ff.). 481-511: Schlierbach, by B. Hofinger. 100 mss. Index (505ff.). (MH).

F. A. Zaccaria, *Excursus literarii per Italiam ab anno 1742 ad annum* 1752. Venice 1754. 380 pp. Lists mss. at Pesaro (15ff.), Milan (121ff.), Arona (136ff.), Modena (152ff.), Pavia (212), Florence (213ff.), Osimo (252ff.). No index. (NN)

The same, *Iter litterarium per Italiam ab anno 1753 ad annum 1757 . . .* Venice 1762. 364 pp. Lists mss. at Lucca (2ff.), Florence

(46ff.), Reggio Emilia (82ff.), Cesena (93ff.) Modena (112ff.), Brescia (118ff.), Mantua (124ff.), Turin (137ff.), Bologna (146ff.), Ferrara (157ff.). Index (351ff.). (NN)

K. Zangemeister, 'Bericht über die im Auftrage der Kirchenväter-Commission unternommene Durchforschung der Bibliotheken Englands,' *Sitzungsberichte der Kaiserlichen Akademie der Wissenschaften* [Vienna], *Philosophisch-Historische Classe* LXXXIV (1876) 485-584. No index.

G. W. Zapf, *Reisen in einige Klöster Schwabens, durch den Schwarzwald und in die Schweiz im Jahr 1781*. Erlangen 1786. 260 pp. Lists mss. at Weingarten (11ff.), Salmansweil (54ff.), St. Blasien (67), Zurich (100ff.), Rheinau (127ff.). Largely superseded.

E. H. Zimmermann, *Vorkarolingische Miniaturen*. Berlin 1916. XII, 330 pp. With 4 vols. of plates.

A. Zingerle, 'Übersicht über philologische Handschriften aus Tirolischen Bibliotheken,' *Commentationes Aenipontanae* IV (1909) 1-4. 15 mss. at Innsbruck, Fiecht, Stams and Bressanone.

E. Zinner, *Verzeichnis der astronomischen Handschriften des deutschen Kulturgebietes*. Munich 1925. 544 mimeographed pages. Arranged by authors. 12563 entries. Index of libraries (2-12).

K. Zolnai, *Bibliographia bibliothecae regis Mathiae Corvini*. (Az Országos Széchényi Köynvtár Kiadványai 10). Budapest 1942. 161 pp. (NN)

SECTION C

Printed Catalogues and Handwritten Inventories of Individual Libraries, by Cities

*Aachen (Aix-la-Chapelle), West Germany. See *Archiv* XI.

**Catalog der Stadt-Bibliothek zu Aachen. Aachen 1834.

J. Greving, 'Geschichte des Klosters der Windesheimer Chorherren zu Aachen,' *Zeitschrift des Aachener Geschichtsvereins* XIII (1891) 1-122. p. 56-16: 'Die noch erhaltenen Handschriften des Klosters.' 10 mss. (NN)

O. Gutzweiler, *Die liturgischen Handschriften des Aachener Münsterstifts* (Liturgiegeschichtliche Quellen X) Münster 1926. 222 pp. (NNG)

Aarau, Switzerland. Kantonsbibliothek. See *Beiträge*; Haenel; Leclercq.

Rariora, Musik, Incunabeln, Manuscripte, Scrinium J.+K. Contains a topographical list of the manuscripts.

Manuscripte. An alphabetical list. Centuries not given.

Katalog der Aargauischen Kantons-Bibliothek. Aarau 1806. 325 pp. p. 300-304: Mss. alphabetically arranged. No shelf marks. No index. Not complete. (Aarau)

*Abbéville, France. See France, *Catalogue Général, Départements,* IX and XL.

A. Ledieu, *Catalogue analytique des manuscrits de la Bibliothèque d'Abbéville.* Abbéville 1885. lxxxiii, 222 pp. 329 mss.)

*Aberdeen, Scotland. See Schenkl.

M. R. James, *A Catalogue of the Medieval Manuscripts in the University Library Aberdeen.* Cambridge 1932. 148 pp. 1009 mss. of which only a part is described in detail.

Catalogue of the General Library of the University of Aberdeen. 2 vols. Aberdeen 1873-74. Vol. II, p. 785-803: Manuscripts.

Alphabetical. Antiquated shelf marks.) (NjP)

*Aberystwyth, Wales.

The National Library of Wales. *Catalogue of Manuscripts.* I (1921): J. H. Davies, *Additional Manuscripts in the Collections of Sir John Williams.* 381 pp. 446 mss. of which a few in Latin.

Handlist of Manuscripts in the National Library of Wales. (The National Library of Wales Journal. Supplement Series II). vols. I-III (pts. I--XV, 1940 ff.). 9165 nos. No index. Hardly pertinent. (Morgan Library).

Latin Mss. of the 14th-16th cent. in N. L. W. Typed list of 10 mss. kindly sent to me by the librarian.

Acireale (Catania), Italy. Biblioteca dell' Accademia Zelantea.

*Catalogo dei manoscritti. Ca. 1000 mss. (communication of the librarian).

*Card index (AB VI 487).

*Admont, Austria. Stiftsbibliothek. See *Archiv* VI and X; Haenel (Suppl.); *Neues Archiv* II; Wickhoff.

J. Wichner, 'Die Bibliothek der Abtei Admont mit besonderer Berücksichtigung des Zustandes derselben in der zweiten Hälfte des 14. Jahrhunderts,' *Mittheilungen des Historischen Vereins für Steiermark* XX (1873) 67-90. Lists a few mss. No index.

Catalogus codicum manu scriptorum Admontensis, by P. Jakob Wichner (1889). Mss. A-E, 1-960, and Appendix 1-43. Some mss. sold (microfilm seen at DLC).

*Agen, France. See France, *Catalogue Général, Départements,* III and XL.

*Ager, Spain. See Villanueva.

*Agira, Italy.

F. Moffa, 'Una biblioteca dimenticata,' *Archivio storico per la Sicilia Orientale* II (1905) p. 368-369: 30 mss. No index.

Notazione bibliografica degli Incunabuli conservati nella Biblioteca Comunale di Agira (Scuola di Bibliografia Italiana, Scritti 36). Reggio Emilia 1936. 20 pp. p. 19-20: 4 mss., by P. Sinopoli. (NN)

Agram, see **Zagreb**.

Agrigento, Italy. Biblioteca Lucchesiana. See Blume.

Typed card index, by Sig.ʳᵃ A. Daneu Lattanzi. 138 mss.

A. Mancini, 'Appunti e notizie di codici greci e latini di biblioteche di Sicilia I. Codici latini della Biblioteca Lucchesiana di Girgenti,' *Rassegna di Antichità Classica*, ed. G. M. Columba (Palermo 1898), 129-132. 5 mss. Printed but not published. Photostat in my possession, based on the copy belonging to the Palumbo family, kindly lent to me through Prof. G. Santangelo.

*Aire, France. See France, *Catalogue Général, Départements*, IV and XL.

*Aix, France. See France, *Catalogue Général, Départements* XVI, XL, XLV, XLIX; *Universités*.

L. G. Pélissier, 'Notes et Extraits de quelques manuscrits de la Bibliothèque Méjanes,' *Revue des Bibliothèques* IV (1894) 241-370.

*Aix-la-Chapelle, see **Aachen**.

*Aix-les-Bains, France. See France, *Catalogue général, Départements* XL.

*Ajaccio, Corsica. See France, *Catalogue Général, Départements* III and XL.

*Alais, France. See France, *Catalogue général*, Départements, XIII.

*Alba, Italy. See Mazzatinti (1887); Rossetti.

*Alba Julia (Karlsburg; Gyula-Féhervár), Rumania. Biblioteca diocesana Batthyaneum. See Radó.

A. Beke, *Index Manuscriptorum Bibliothecae Batthyanianae Dioecesis Transsylvaniensis.* K. Féhervar 1871. viii, 56 pp. 658 items. Index (p. v ff.). (ICU)

E. Varjú, 'A Gyulafejérvári Batthyány-Könyvtár' *Magyar Könyvszemle* N.S. VIII (1900), 17-55; 131-69; 228-49; 337-61; IX (1901) 24-52. 270 mss. (NN)

Catalogus concinnus librorum manuscriptorum Bibliothecae Batthyanianae Albae in Transsilvania. Editio secunda adaucta, by R. Szentiványi. Szombathely 1949. 164 pp. 702 mss. (DCU)

Catalogus concinnus librorum manuscriptorum Bibliothecae Batthyányanae. 4th ed., by R. Szentiványi. Szeged 1958. Offset printed. 366 pp. and plates. 709 mss.

*Albenga (Savona), Italy. Biblioteca Capitolare. 60 mss., mostly liturgical. See Comune di Savona.

*Albi, France. See France, *Catalogue Général, Départments*, I (Quarto Series) and XL.

*Alençon, France. See France, *Catalogue Général, Départments* II and XL.

*Alessandria, Italy.

L. Madaro, *Inventario dei manoscritti della Biblioteca Civica di Alessandria.* Alessandria 1926. 68 pp. 187 mss. (DLC)

*Altenburg, Austria. Stiftsbibliothek. See Frast.

**Manuscripta in Bibliotheca Altenburgens* (1844). 270 mss.

Die Handschriften des Stiftes Altenburg, by P. G. Schweighofer. 1 typed vol. 44 parchment mss., 339 paper mss. (micr. at DLC)

*Altenburg, East Germany. See *Archiv* VIII. The manuscripts are apparently lost.

**Chr. Fr. Wilisch, *Manuscripta si quae essent bibliothecae nostrae scholasticae quae lucem mereantur.* progr. Altenburg 1717

M. Geyer, *Verzeichniss der Handschriften in dem Archive der Gesellschaft.* (Mittheilungen der Geschichts- und Alterthumsforschenden Gesellschaft des Osterlandes. Erstes Ergänzungsheft) Altenburg 1901. 123 pp. 878 items. Hardly pertinent. (NN)

*Altenfurt (Nürnberg), West Germany. Freiherrlich von Scheurlsche Stiftung.

*Bibliothek. Inventory of mss. and edd.

*Archiv. Card file of letters and documents

(Communication of the owner)

*Altona, West Germany. See Hirsching.
M. J. F. Lucht, *Nachrichten über die Bibliothek des Gymnasiums und die in derselben
befindlichen Handschriften.* progr. Altona
1878. 34 pp. p. 3-20: 17 mss. No index.
(Erlangen, Universitätsbibliothek).
Joh. Clausen, *Nachrichten über die Bibliothek
nebst Verzeichnis ihrer Drucke aus dem
15. Jahrhundert.* progr. Altona 1897. 32
pp. p. 8-9: Summarizes and supplements
the list of Lucht. 17 mss. (Erlangen,
Universitätsbibliothek)
*Amberg, West Germany. Provinzialbi-
bliothek.
Manuscripte. Fol. 1-55; Qu. 1-87. (Photostat kindly supplied by the librarian)
*Ambras, Austria. See Wickhoff.
*Amiens, France. See France, *Catalogue
Général, Départments* XIX, XL, XLVIII,
L, and *Sociétés.*
(J. Garnier, *Catalogue déscriptif et raisonné
des manuscrits de la Bibliothèque Commu-
nale de la ville d'Amiens.* Amiens 1843.
lv, 563 pp. 572 mss.)
*Catalogue de la Bibliothèque de M. le Cte.
Charles de L'Escalopier.* 3 vols. Paris
1866-67. Mss. described with printed
books. Index of mss. (III 151, s.v.
Manuscrits). (NN)
*Ampleforth, England. See Great Britain,
Historical Manuscripts Commission.
Amsterdam, Holland. See Byvanck; Lehmann, *Holländische Reisefrüchte*; *Novati*;
Société française.
—Bibliotheek van de Remonstrants Gereformeerde Gemeente. Deposited in the
University Library.
P. Scheltema, *Catalogus van de handschriften en boeken behoorende tot de Bibliotheek der Remonstrantsch-gereformeerde Kerk te Amsterdam.* Amsterdam
1849. viii, 115 pp. p. 1-36: 320 mss.
alphabetically arranged. No index. (Paris, Bibliothèque Nationale)
(Jo. Tideman), *Catalogus der boeken en handschriften van de bibliotheek der Remonstrantsche Gemeente te Amsterdam.* Amsterdam 1877. II, 121 pp. p. 61-118:

mss. alphabetically arranged. No index
(Leiden, Bibliotheek der Rijksuniver-
siteit).
—Universiteits Bibliotheek.
*Bibliotheek der Universiteit van Amsterdam.
Catalogus der Handschriften.* 7 vols.
Amsterdam 1899-1923. Vol. I (1899): J.
Hellendoorn, *Schenking-Diederichs, Neder-
landsche Afdeeling.* Vol. II (1902): M.
B. Mendes da Costa, *De Handschriften der
Stedelijke Bibliotheek.* 1627 mss. Vol. III
(1903): Hellendoorn, *Schenking-Diede-
richs. Fransche Afdeeling.* Vol. IV (3 pts.
1911-19): *Brieven.* Vol. V (1913): T. P.
Sevensma, *Schenking-Diederichs, Kleinere
Afdeelingen.* (NNC). Vol. VI (1917):
Bertha M. v.d. Stempel, the same cont.
VII (1923): M. B. Mendes de Costa,
*De Handschriften van de Remonstrantsche
kerk*; J. Berg, *De Handschriften van het
Evangelisch-luthersche Seminarium en van
de Vereenigde Doopsgezindegemeente.*
M. Battistini, 'Documenti italiani nella Bi-
blioteca Universitaria d'Amsterdam,' *Ri-
vista storica degli Archivi Toscani* IV (1932)
109-139; 206-224.
Card index, arranged by subjects, in 4 trays.
Supplements the printed catalogue.
*Ancona, Italy. See Mazzatinti VI.
**M. Natalucci, *Il Tesoro e l'Archivio della
Cattedrale di Ancona.* Ancona 1938. 119
pp. p. 116-117: 8 mss.
*Andria, Italy. See Mazzatinti VI.
*Angers, France. See France, *Catalogue
Général, Départements* XXXI.
(A. Lemarchand, *Catalogue des manuscrits
de la Bibliothèque d'Angers.* Angers 1863.
VII, 511 pp., 1143 mss.) (MH)
X. Barbier de Montault, *Antiphonaires et
Lectionnaires manuscrits de la Bibliothè-
que Publique d'Angers.* (Angers 1897).
14 pp. 6 mss. No index. (CoDB)
The same, *Les livres d'heures de la Biblio-
thèque de la Ville d'Angers.* Angers 1889.
33 pp. 11 mss. No index. (Paris, Biblio-
thèque Nationale)
*Angoulême, France. See France, *Catalogue Général, Départements* XX.

*Annaberg, East Germany. See Cooper (Section A).

Chr. G. Wilisch, *Kurtze Nachricht von der Oeffentlichen Bibliotheque der Schulen zu St. Annenberg.* progr. St. Annenberg (1724). 14 unnumbered pages. 17 mss. No index. (Paris, Bibliothèque Nationale). The same, *Arcana Bibliothecae Annabergensis.* Leipzig 1730. 332 pp. Not a catalogue of mss. (DLC)

*Ann Arbor, Michigan, USA. See De Ricci.

*Annecy, France. See France, *Catalogue general, Departments* XXI; XL; Martin.

*Annonay, France. See France, *Catalogue Général, Départements* XIII and XL; Martin.

*Ansbach, West Germany. See Gercken. Th. Preger, *Die Handschriften des Historischen Vereins für Mittelfranken.* Ansbach 1907. 54 pp. 658 items. Hardly pertinent (MH)

*Antibes, France. See France, *Catalogue général, Departements* XL.

*Anvers (Antwerpen, Antwerp), Belgium. See *Catalogue général* V, and *Archivum Franciscanum Historicum* XLIX.

(*Bibliotheca Antverpiensis. Catalogue méthodique de la bibliothèque publique d'Anvers . . .*, by F. H. Mertens. 2 vols. Antwerp 1843-46, and 3 supplements, 1852-73. I, 48-54: Mss.) (NN; Supplements not located)

(S. De Ricci, 'Inventaire Sommaire des manuscrits du Musée Plantin à Anvers,' *Revue des Bibliothèques* XX [1910] 217-32. 181 mss. No index.)

Musaeum Plantin-Moretus. Catalogue des manuscrits, by J. Denucé. Antwerp 1927. 304 pp. 506 mss. Index.

*Aosta, Italy. See *Archiv* IX; Leclercq.

—*Biblioteca del Seminario Maggiore. No inventory. 250 mss. (Communication of Prof. A. Visalberghi).

—*Collegiata di S. Orso. Over 20 Mss. No information.

*Apt, France. See France. *Catalogue général, Départements* IV; XL.

Aquila, Italy. Biblioteca Provinciale 'S. Tommasi.' See Istituto Storico Italiano (Section A), and Mazzatinti (1887).

C. De Lollis, 'Ricerche Abruzzesi,' *Bullettino dell' Istituto storico italiano* III (1887) 53-100. p. 72-80: 'Descrizione di codici.' 19 mss.

(O. D'Angelo), *Sommario alfabetico dei Manoscritti e dei libri dell' Antico Archivio del Municipio Aquilano.* Aquila 1909. 52 pp. p. 9-48: 328 mss. Alphabetically arranged. No index.

Catalogo dei libri rari, manoscritti, incunaboli. 2 vols. (AB VI 63).

Alphabetical card file.

**E. Casti, *Antico archivio del Municipio Aquilano.* Aquila 1888. 46 pp.

E. Moschino, *La 'Tommasiana': Storia opere e funzioni della Biblioteca Provinciale di Aquila con l'Antico Archivio Aquilano.* Aquila 1931. 175 pp. p. 105-110: I manoscritti. Surveys modern mss. p. 147-153: I messali miniati. No index. (Vatican Library)

*Aquileia, Italy. See Wickhoff.

F. Spessot, 'I codici liturgici della Basilica Aquileiese,' *Aquileia nostra* II (1931) coll. 33-38; III (1932) 121-128. 2 mss. (DDO)

*Arbe, see Rab.

*Arbois, France, See France, *Catalogue général, Départements* XXI.

*Archangelsk, Yugoslavia. See Wickhoff.

Arezzo, Italy. Biblioteca della Fraternità dei Laici. See Mazzatinti VI.

Library copy of printed catalogue adds handwritten descriptions for mss. 446-545.

*Card index (AB V 106).

—Seminario. Charters only.

—*Archivio Vasariano.

A. Del Vita, *Inventario e Regesto dei manoscritti dell' Archivio Vasariano.* Rome 1938. 209 pp. (DLC)

*Argenta, Italy. See Mazzatinti XXIV.

*Argentan, France. See France, *Catalogue Général, Départements* X; XL.

*Arles, France. See France, *Catalogue Général, Départements* XX, XL, XLIX.

*Armagh, North Ireland.

J. Dean, *Catalogue of Manuscripts in the Pu-*

blic Library of Armagh. Dundalk 1928. 43 pp. Arranged alphabetically.

Arnhem, Holland. See *Société française. Catalogus van de openbare bibliotheek te Arnhem.* Arnhem 1858. 289 pp. p. 241-50: Mss. (DLC)

Arnsberg, West Germany. See *Archiv* XI.

Arona, Italy. See Zaccaria, *Excursus.*

Arouca, Portugal. See Leclercq.

Arras, France. See France, *Catalogue Général, Départements* IV (Quarto Series) and XL.

Th. Phillipps), *Codices manuscripti in bibliotheca Sti. Vedasti apud Atrebatiam.* (Paris) 1828. 76 pp. 1055 mss., and some additional groups. (OCl)

Catalogue des manuscrits de la Bibliothèque de la Ville d'Arras. Arras 1860. 703 pp. 1102 mss. Preface signed Caron.)

Aschaffenburg, West Germany. See *Serapeum, Intelligenzblatt* 1864.

-* Hofbibliothek.

, Merkel, *Die Miniaturen und Manuscripte der Kgl. Bayerischen Hofbibliothek in Aschaffenburg.* Aschaffenburg 1836. 16 pp. 32 mss. No index. (Pierpont Morgan Library)

E. Hock), *Handschriften der Hofbibliothek Aschaffenburg.* 51 mss. (Communication of the librarian)

-*Stiftsbibliothek. See Leclercq. 70 mss. No information.

K. W. Renz. *Die Inkunabeln der Stiftsarchiv-Bibliothek zu Aschaffenburg.* progr. Aschaffenburg 1908. 132 pp. (ICN)

scoli Piceno. Italy. Biblioteca Communale Card index (AB V 429).

ssisi, Italy. See *Archiv* XII; Mazzatinti IV.

. Ehrle, 'Zu Bethmanns Notizen über die Handschriften von St. Francesco in Assisi,' *Archiv für Litteratur- und Kirchengeschichte des Mittelalters* I (1885) 470-507. Discusses 33 historical mss.

ocietà Internazionale di Studi Francescani in Assisi. *Catalogo delle pergamene e degli antichi autografi dell' Archivio Comunale di Assisi.* Assisi 1903. 86 pp. No index. (MB)

*Asti, Italy. Biblioteca del Seminario. See Mazzatinti (1887). 30 mss. (Communication of the librarian.)

*Athenai (Athens), Greece.

I. and A. Sakkelion, Κατάλογος τῶν χειρογράφων τῆς ἐθνικῆς βιβλιοθήκης τῆς Ἑλλάδος. Athens 1892. 339 pp. 1856 mss. Latin mss. no 1603-42 (283-87), *Supplement to no. 3121 (1956). Copy at the Institut de Recherches et d'Histoire des Textes, Paris.

*Atri, Italy. Archivio Capitolare.

G. Jorio, 'Scorsa nell' Archivio Capitolare di Atri: Codici manoscritti ed incunaboli, *Rivista Abruzzese* IX (1894) 399-421. p. 402-417: 22 mss. No index. (MH)

*Auch, France. See France, *Catalogue Général, Départements* IV.

*Auckland, New Zealand. See also under Oxford, *Bodleian Library Record*, V. See Kelly; Taylor.

H. Shaw, *A Guide to the Principal Manuscripts, Early Printed Books, Autograph Letters etc. contained in the Auckland Free Public Library.* Auckland. 1908. 70 pp. Latin mss. no. 3-24 (p. 10-19). No index. (DLC)

Augsburg, Germany. Staats- und Stadtbibliothek. See *Archiv* IX. Gercken and Hirsching.

Placidus Braun, *Notitia historico-literaria de codibus manuscriptis in bibliotheca ... monasterii ... ad SS. Udalricum et Afram Augustae extantibus.* 6 pts. in 1. Augsburg 1791-96. Index in pt. 6. Shelf marks added in library copy. Some of the mss. are now in Munich, others are dispersed. (NN)

G. C. Mezger, *Geschichte der vereinigten Kgl. Kreis- und Stadt-Bibliothek in Augsburg.* Augsburg 1842. 132 pp. p. 53-128: 394 mss. including mss. Folio 1-247. No index. (NN)

Handschriften-Repertorium. Arranged by shelf marks, covers all mss. (3370 mss., plus letters and music).

Augustana Handschriften. Typed volume, arranged by subjects.

Verzeichnis der Handschriften der Staats-, Kreis- und Stadtbibliothek Augsburg. Fol. 1-572; Qu. 1-281; Oct. 1-202; Cod. adl(e-gati); Fragmenta; Autogramme. Superseded for Fol. 1-247 by Mezger.

Staats- Kreis- und Stadtbibliothek Augsburg, Verzeichnis der Handschriften (by Dr. Dobel).

Zettelkataloge. For codd. 2º, 4º, 8º, Augustana, Halder and Stetten mss.

—*Ordinariatsbibliothek.

B. Kraft, 'Die früh- und hochmittelalterlichen Handschriften der Bischöflichen Ordinariatsbibliothek in Augsburg,' *Das Schwäbische Museum* 1929, 120-49; 1930, 97-112; 1931, 129-55. No index. (MH)

B. Kraft, *Die Handschriften der Bischöflichen Ordinariatsbibliothek in Augsburg.* Augsburg 1934. 109 pp. 152 mss.

*Aurillac, France. See France, *Catalogue Général, Départements* IX.

*Austin, Texas, U.S.A. See De Ricci.

*Autun, France. See *Cabinet Historique; France, Catalogue Général, Departements* I (Quarto Series); VI; XL.

*Auxerre, France. See *Cabinet Historique; France, Catalogue Général, Départements* VI and XL.

H. Monceaux, G. Bonneau and F. Molard, 'Inventaire du Trésor actuel de la Cathédrale d'Auxerre, *Bulletin de la Société des sciences historiques et naturelles de l'Yonne* XLVI (Ser. III, vol. XVI, 1892) 194-282. p. 194-210: 25 mss. (NNM)

*Auxonne, France. See France, *Catalogue Général, Départements* VI; XL.

*Avallon, France. See France, *Catalogue Général, Départements* VI and XL.

*Avellino, Italy.

S. Pescatori and G. Gabrieli, 'I manoscritti Tafuri della Biblioteca Provinciale di Avellino,' *Japigia* I (1930). 472-85. 84 mss. (Vatican Library; micr. at NNC)

*Averboden (Everbode), Belgium. See Académie Royale, Commission (1885) and *Neues Archiv* II.

*Avesnes, France. See France, *Catalogue général, Départements*, XX.

*Avignon, France. See France, *Catalogue Général, Départements* XXVII-XXIX, XL, XLIV, XLIX; Martin.

(L.-H. Labande, *Catalogue sommaire des manuscrits de la Bibliothèque d'Avignon Musée Calvet.* Avignon 1892. 433 pp. 3093 mss.)

*Avranches, France. See France, *Catalogue Général, Départements* IV (Quarto Series) and X.

(Abbé Desroches, 'Notice sur les manuscrits de la Bibliothèque d'Avranches,' *Mémoires de la Société des Antiquaires de Normandie* Ser. II, vol. I, 1837-39 [1840] 70-156). (NN)

*Bagnacavallo (Ravenna), Italy. Biblioteca Comunale Giuseppe Taroni. See Mazzatinti VI.

*'Cataloghi speciali dei manoscritti entrat in Biblioteca dopo il 1900' (AB IV 550) Supplements Mazzatinti VI.

*Bagnols, France. See France, *Catalogue Général, Départements* XL.

*Baguères, France. See France, *Catalogue Général, Départements* XXXI and XL.

Baltimore, Maryland, USA. Dee De Ricci

*Bamberg, West Germany.

(H. J. Jaeck, *Vollständige Beschreibung de öffentlichen Bibliothek zu Bamberg.* 2 pts Nuremberg 1831-32. 2650 mss. No index.

F. Leitschuh and H. Fischer, *Katalog de Handschriften der kgl. Bibliothek zu Bam berg.* 3 vols. in 6 pts. Bamberg 1887-1912 Vol. I. Pt. 1 (1895-1906), 978 pp. Theolog and canon law. Pt. 2 (1895-1906), 595 pp Classics, history, philosophy, sciences, med icine, philology, mathematics, varia an jurisprudence. Pt. 3 (1908), VIII, 62, 20 pp. Additions and indices. Vol. II (1887) LIV, 201 pp. *Die Handschriften der Hel leriana.* Vol. III (1-2, 1912), 306 pp Local and miscellaneous mss.

Mittelalterliche Miniaturen aus der Staat lichen Bibliothek, Bamberg. 2 vols. Bam berg 1926-29. 5 mss.

*Bangor, Wales. Great Britain. See Frere Schenkl.

Barcelona, Spain. See Grubbs (unde Richardson, Section A); *Hispania Sacr

VIII; Kehr (Section A); Carini; Haenel; *Neues Archiv* VI; *Serapeum* VIII; Villanueva; Volger.

Las Bibliotecas de Barcelona y su provincia. Madrid 1952. 155 pp.

A. Cordoliani, 'Los manuscritos de cómputo eclesiástico en las Bibliotecas de Barcelona,' *Analecta Sacra Tarraconensia* XXIII (1950) 103-130.

—Archivo de la Corona de Aragon.

R. Beer, 'Die Handschriften des Klosters Santa Maria de Ripoll,' *Sitzungsberichte der Kaiserlichen Akademie der Wissenschaften* [Vienna] *Philosophisch-Historische Classe,* CLV (1908) no. 3. 112 pp. CLVIII (1908) no. 2. 117 pp. Not a catalogue. No index. (NNC) Also transl. Barnils y Giol, 'Los manuscrits del monastir de Santa Maria de Ripoll,' *Boletin de la R. Academia de Buenas Letras de Barcelona* V (1909-10) 137-70; 230-77; 299-320; 329-65; 492-520. (NN)

Z. Garcia, 'Bibliotheca Patrum Latinorum Hispaniensis, II. Band.' *Sitzungsberichte...* [Vienna] *Philos.-Hist. Classe* CLXIX (1915) no. 2. 98 pp. Describes 230 mss. of Santa Maria de Ripoll at the Archivo general de la Corona de Aragon. For an index, see Grubbs (under Richardson, Section A).

Francesc X. Miquel Rosell. *Catàleg dels llibres manuscrits de la Biblioteca del Monestir de Sant Cugat del Valles existents al' Arxiu de la Corona d'Aragó.* Barcelona, 1937 (from *Butlletí de la Biblioteca de Catalunya,* VIII and IX). 154 pp. 91 mss. The first part (to mss. no. 60) appeared in *Butlletí* VIII (1928-32, published 1934) 143-240. *Butlletí* IX was printed but never published. Card index of mss., arranged by provenance. Does not include the mss. of Ripoll and San Cugat, which have printed catalogues.

—*Biblioteca del Ateneo Barcelonés.

J. Massó Torrents, 'Manuscrits de la Biblioteca de l'Ateneu Barcelonés,' *Revista de bibliografíaca talana* I (1901) 12-67; 154-

226. 52 mss. Index (219ff.). (Pierpont Morgan Library)

—*Biblioteca del Cabildo.

J. Massó Torrents, 'Catàleg dels Manuscrits Catalans de la Biblioteca Capitular de Barcelona,' *Butlletí de la Biblioteca de Catalunya* I (1914) 145-155. 10 mss.

*Card index. 191 mss. (communication of L. Bertalot and E. Massa).

—Biblioteca Central (formerly de Catalunya).

J. Massó Torrents and J. Rubió i Balaguer, 'Caàleg dels manuscrits de la Biblioteca de Catalunya,' *Butlletí de la Biblioteca de Cat i nya* I (1914) 22-29; 49-121; 156-62; II (1915) 107-13; 158-78; III (1916) 93-122); IV (1917) 78-119; V (1918-19) 149-85; V I (1920-22) 238-312; VII (1923-27) 339-46. 154 mss. No index. (NN)

The acquisitions of the library are briefly listed in the section *Cronica* of the *Butlletí de la Biblioteca de Catalunya* : I (1914) 30-31 (no shelf marks); 133 (no. 343-346); 170 (347-351); II (1915) 118-119 (352-392); 184 (398-419); III (1916) 28-57 (La Biblioteca Dalmases, by R. d'Alós, nos. 456-677, with a concordance of shelf marks, p. 51, and an index, p. 52-57); 143-146 (nos. 421-454); IV (1917) 168-169 (678-703); V (1918-19, published 1920) 250-252 (nos. 705-754); VI (1920-22, published 1923) 404-408 (755-848); VII (1923-27, published 1932) 347-55 (849-966). The library has a volume of reprints, with shelf marks and centuries added in handwriting.

For more recent acquisitions see the *Anuario de la Biblioteca Central y de las Populares y Especiales*: 1941 (published 1942), p. 45-52 (nos. 967-1378); 1944 (1945) 48 (1490-1522); 1945 (1946) 49 (1523-59); 1946 (1947) 38 (1560-1600); 1947 (1948) 47-48 (1603-18); 1948-50 (1955) 60 (1619-60). These lists are summary and selective. (NN)

More complete are a card index by authors, in 7 bound volumes, and a card index by subjects, in 4 boxes.

—*Biblioteca del Seminario.

Biblioteca del Palacio episcopal.

*Indice de los manuscritos de la Biblioteca Episcopal (1887). Cf. Cordoliani, Analecta, p. 129-130.

Archivo del Palau.

I. Casanovas, 'Codecs de l'Arxiu del Palau,' Revista de bibliografia catalana VI (1906) 5-42. 16 mss. Index (39ff.). (Pierpont Morgan Library)

—Biblioteca Universitaria.

D. Angel Aguiló y Miró, 'Notas sobre algunos códices de la Biblioteca Provincial y Universitaria de Barcelona,' Universidad de Barcelona 1908 à 1909 (Anuario) 511-65; 1909 à 1910, 513-97. No index. In most instances, no shelf marks. (MH)

F. Miquel Rosell, 'Manuscritos de la Orden de Predicadores conservados en la Biblioteca de la Universidad de Barcelona,' Analecta Sacra Tarraconensia XV (1942) 325-359. 21 mss. No index.

The same, 'Manuscritos patristicos existentes en la Biblioteca de la Universidad de Barcelona,' Ibid. XVII (1944) 31-66. No index.

The same, 'Manuscritos biblicos y litúrgicos de la Biblioteca Universitaria de Barcelona, Estudios Biblicos VII (1948) 257-292; 407-440; VIII (1949) 5-46. Arranged by subjects. No index. (NNJ)

The same, 'Inventario de Manuscritos de la Biblioteca Universitaria de Barcelona, referentes a Órdenes religiosas,' Hispania Sacra II (1949) 209-220.

The same, 'Manuscritos hagiográficos de la Biblioteca Universitaria de Barcelona,' Revista Española de Teología XII (1952) 99-151. (PU)

Indices y catalogos por materias de los mss. que exsisten en la Biblioteca Universitaria y Provincial de Barcelona (1861). By subjects. Sketchy.

*Bardejow (Bartfa, Bartfeld). Czechoslovakia. See Radó.

J. Abel, A Bártfai Sz.-Egyed Temploma Könyvtárának Története. Budapest 1885. 206 pp. (Vatican Library). Cf. L. Hoffmann, 'Die Bibliothek der St. Egidius-Kirche zu Bartfeld,' Ungarische Revue

VI (1886) 555-66. 4 mss. (NN)

*Bari, Italy.

X. Barbier de Montault, 'Les manuscrits du trésor de Bari,' Analecta Iuris Pontificii XVI (1877) 226-30. (NNUT)

Barnabei, 'Le pergamene della cattedrale di Bari,' Rendiconti della Reale Accademie dei Lincei Ser. IV vol. II, pt. 1 (1886) 557-62.

*Bar-Le-Duc, France. See France, Catalogue Général, Départements XXIV and XL.

*Barletta, Italy. See Mazzatinti VI.

*Bartfa (Bartfeld), see Bardejow.

Basel, Switzerland. Oeffentliche Bibliothek der Universität. See Cooper (Section A) Archiv VII; Bernards. Esposito; Haene (shelf marks often wrong or antiquated) Halm; Lampen; Notizenblatt; Serapeum XVII; Sinner; Spizelius; Stelling-Michaud Traditio.

(Thomas Phillipps) Catalogue of some of the manuscripts in the Publick Library of Basl in Switzerland. n.d. (Middlehill 1824) 8 pp. (MH)

Die Handschriften der oeffentlichen Bibliothek der Universität Basel. Erste Abteilung. Die deutschen Handschriften. Vol. I (1907): G. Binz, Die Handschriften der Abteilung A. 437 pp. Lists some Latin texts.

K. Escher, Die Miniaturen in den Basler Bibliotheken, Museen und Archiven. Basel 1917. 278 pp.

Ph. Schmidt, 'Die Bibliothek des ehemaligen Dominikanerklosters in Basel,' Basler Zeitschrift für Geschichte und Altertumskunde XVIII (1919) 183-244: 499 mss. No index. (NIC)

G. Morin, 'A travers les manuscrits de Bâle Notices et extraits des plus anciens manuscrits latins,' Basler Zeitschrift für Geschichte und Altertumskunde XXVI (1927) 175-249. Index (242ff.). (NN)

L. Thorndike, 'Little Known Medical Work and Authors in Basel Manuscripts,' Annals of Medical History, Ser. III, vol. I (1940) 280-290.

Bericht über die Verwaltung der öffentlichen

Bibliothek der Universität Basel. Lists acquisitions.

E. Staehelin, *Johann Ludwig Frey, Johannes Grynaeus und das Frey-Grynaeische Institut in Basel.* Rektoratsprogramm, Basel 1947. 221 pp. p. 182-195: Summary list of the mss. of the Frey-Grynaeum (I 1 - X 12).

Old inventory in 5 vols. by Jo. Zvingerus (1672-80), by subjects, listing parchment and paper mss. separately. Each section arranged alphabetically by authors. I. *Catalogus librorum Theologicorum Manuscriptorum Academiae Basiliensis.* II: *Catalogus codicum iuridicorum.* III: *Catalogus codicum medicorum.* IV: *Catalogus librorum philosophicorum manuscriptorum.* V: *Catalogus codicum historicorum.* This is the source of Haenel's printed catalogue, but frequently fuller or more correct (cf. Born 225).

Handschriften des Mittelalters mit deutschen Sprachbestandteilen (by G. Binz, continuing his printed catalogue). ms. sheets in 4 boxes.

Ältere Theologie (by G. Meier). ms. sheets in 6 boxes. Covers the parchment mss. of class B. (Cf. Born 325?).

Medizin und Alchemie des Mittelalters (by G. Goldschmidt). ms. sheets in 5 boxes. Covers most of class D. (Cf. Born 326).

Sammlung des Remigius Faesch (by G. Binz). ms. sheets in 3 boxes. Covers class O.

Amerbach'scher Nachlass. 18 notebooks. Covers mss. C VI a 1-95; b 1-4 (some gaps).

Briefsammlung Mscr. G I 1-70. 1 typed vol. G II 1-33. 1 ms. vol. Not complete. (Untitled). 1 typed folder. Describes G² I 1-21; 34-37; II 6; 28-80 (with some gaps).

Verzeichnis der Erasmuslade. 1 typed vol.

Handschriften des Kirchenarchives. 1 typed vol. 239 mss.

Absenderverzeichnisse des Frey-Grynaeums. 3 ms. vols. (micr. at DLC).

Alphabetical card index of all letters, in 72 boxes.

Typed list of class B, by Mlle Lebreton (Institut de Recherches et d'Histoire des Textes, Paris).

*Bassano, Italy. See Mazzatinti L, LV and LVIII.

*Bastia, Corsica. See France, *Catalogue Général, Départements* IX and XL.

*Baume-les-Dames, France. See France, *Catalogue général, Départements* VI.

*Bautzen, East Germany.
'Alterthümer der Städte Laubau, Zittau, Löbau, Bauzen und Camenz,' *Neues Lausitzisches Magazin* VII (1828) 315-35; 465-501. 1 ms. (471-72). (NN)

—*Stadt- und Kreisbibliothek.
Handwritten catalogue of the von Gersdorff-Weicha collection. Over 100 mss. Selective list kindly supplied by the librarian.

*Bayeux, France. See France, *Catalogue Général, Départements* X and XL.

*Bayonne, France. See France, *Catalogue Général, Départements,* IX; XL; L.

*Bayreuth, West Germany. See Hirsching.
Catalog der Bücher und Manuscripte des Historischen Vereins für Geschichte und Alterthumskunde von Oberfranken... (with: *Archiv für Geschichte und Alterthumskunde von Oberfranken* XIII). Bayreuth 1875. 102 pp. Lists a few unimportant mss. (NN)

*Beaune, France. See France, *Catalogue Général, Départements* VI and XL.

*Beauvais, France. See France, *Catalogue Général, Départements* III and XL.

A. Salmon, 'Notice sur les manuscrits de la Bibliothèque du Tribunal de Beauvais,' *Revue des Bibliothèques* VIII (1898) 361-70. No index.

*Belfort, France. See France, *Catalogue Général, Départements* XIII.

*Belley, France. See Martin.

*Belluno, Italy. See Mazzatinti II.

L. Dolleonius, 'Catalogus Mss. Codicum Lollinianae Bellunensis Bibliothecae,' *Nuova Raccolta d'Opuscoli Scientifici e Filologici* (ed. Calogerà) IV (1758) 143-70. c. 60 mss. No index. (PPAP)

L. Alpago-Novello, 'La vita e le opere di Luigi Lollino vescovo di Belluno, *Archivio*

Veneto, Ser. V, vol. XIV (1933) 15-116; XV (1934) 199-304. Lists a few mss. (p. 259-261). No index.

*Benedello, Italy. See Mazzatinti LVII, LIX, LXI and LXXII.

Benevento, Italy. Biblioteca Capitolare. No inventory. See *Analecta Bollandiana* LI; Lowe.

X. Barbier de Montault, 'Le trésor de la cathédrale de Bénévent,' *Revue de l'art chrétien* XXVII (2nd ser. X, 1879) 62-94. p. 85-88: Liturgical mss. no. 63-73.

R. Andoyer, 'I codici liturgici della Biblioteca Capitolare di Benevento.' Benevento 1909. (reprint from *Settimana* X, 46). 16 pp. No index. (Prof. E. A. Lowe, Princeton, N. J.)

Bergamo, Italy. Biblioteca Civica. See Heiberg.

A. Tiraboschi, *Notizie storiche intorno alla Civica Biblioteca di Bergamo.* Bergamo 1880. 34 pp. Not a catalogue. (NNGr)

G. Cremaschi, 'Testi classici in manoscritti della Biblioteca Civica di Bergamo, *Atti dell' Istituto Veneto di Scienze, Lettere ed Arti* CXI, *Classe di Scienze Morali e Lettere* (1952-53) 133-51. Cf. the notes of the same on individual mss. or authors in *Bergomum* N.S. XX (anno 40, 1946) 21-29; XXI (41, 1947). Parte speciale, p. 18-28; XXV (45, 1951) fasc. 4, p. 1-7; XXVI (46, 1952) fasc. 1, p. 1-18; XXVIII (48, 1954), fasc. 1, p. 69-81; XXIX (49, 1955), fasc. 1, p. 9-37; and in *Aevum* XXVI (1952) 276-279; 369; 370; XXVIII (1954) 72-89; XXIX (1955) 88-94; XXX (1956) 550-555.

L'Archivio Silvestri in Calcio, Notizie e inventario-regesto, by G. Bonelli. 4 vols., Turin 1912-Milan 1935. (Bergamo)

Catalogo Generale della Pubblica Biblioteca Comunale della Regia Città di Bergamo, compilato per studio e fatica del Conte Bartolomeo Secco Suardo. Arranged alphabetically (cf. AB III 557). (micr. at DLC)

Card index (AB III 557).

Archivio Silvestri. Card file in 6 trays.

Archivio Stella, Letteratura. Card file (Scatola 42).

—Biblioteca del Clero di S. Alessandro in Colonna.

*Catalogo dei manoscritti. 300 mss. (Apolloni I 104). (micr. at DLC)

*Bergen, Norway. See Lehmann.

A. M. Wiesener, 'Katalog over Bergens Museums Manuskriptsamling,' *Bergens Museums Aarbok* 1913, no. 5. 170 pp. 524 items, not pertinent. (NN)

*Bergues, France. See *Archiv* XI, and France, *Catalogue Général, Départements* XXVI.

*Berkeley California, U.S.A. See De Ricci.

Berlin, Germany (East Berlin). Deutsche Staatsbibliothek (formerly Preussische Staatsbibliothek).

Many of the mss. are now at the Westdeutsche Bibliothek, Marburg, or at the Universitätsbibliothek, Tübingen. Some others are missing.

For the mss. in Marburg, see: *Signaturenverzeichnis der in der Westdeutschen Bibliothek vorhandenen Berliner Handschriften...* Reprint from *Jahresbericht 1955/56 der Westdeutschen Bibliothek Marburg.* 4 pp.

See *Archiv* I; VIII; XI; Diekamp; Jacobs; Lehmann, *Mitteilungen*; *Neues Archiv* VIII; Omont; Schmitt; Tenneroni.

J. C. V. Möhsen, *Dissertatio epistolica prima (secunda) de manuscriptis medicis quae inter codices Bibliothecae Regiae Berolinensis servantur.* Berlin 1746-47. 82 pp. numbered continuously. 9 mss. No index. (ICJ)

J. C. C. Oelrich, *Entwurf einer Geschichte der Königlichen Bibliothec zu Berlin.* Berlin 1752. 164 pp. Lists some Latin mss. No index.

F. Wilken, *Geschichte der Königlichen Bibliothek zu Berlin.* Berlin 1828. xiv, 242 pp. Lists many Latin mss. (218-42). No index.

Index librorum manuscriptorum et impressorum quibus Bibliotheca Regia Berolinensis aucta est anno 1835. Berlin n.d. p. 1:

14 mss. The same for 1836. p. 1-7: 156 mss. The same for 1837-38. p. xxxi-xxxvi: 92 mss. The same for 1839. p. 1-2: 21 mss. (DLC)

Verzeichniss der von dem verewigten Herrn Staatsminister Carl Friedrich von Savigny . . . der Kgl. Bibliothek zu Berlin vermachten Werke. Berlin 1865. 95 pp. p. 74-95: 46 mss. No index. (DLC)

W. Voege, 'Die Mindener Bilderhandschriftengruppe,' *Repertorium für Kunstwissenschaft* XVI (1893) 198-213. 9 mss.

L. Stern, 'Mitteilungen aus der Lübener Kirchenbibliothek,' in *Beiträge zur Bücherkunde und Philologie, August Wilmanns. . . gewidmet* (Leipzig 1903) 67-93.

Beschreibende Verzeichnisse der Miniaturen-Handschriften der Preussischen Staatsbibliothek zu Berlin. Vol. I (1926): J. Kirchner, *Die Phillipps-Handschriften.* Vol. V (1928): H. Wegener, *Die deutschen Handschriften bis 1500.*

Schöne Handschriften aus dem Besitze der Preussischen Staatsbibliothek. Berlin 1931. 135 pp. 77 mss. No index. (Pierpont Morgan Library).

V. Rose and F. Schillmann, *Verzeichnis der lateinischen Handschriften der kgl. Bibliothek zu Berlin.* (Die Handschriften-Verzeichnisse der Kgl. Bibliothek zu Berlin XII-XIV). 3 vols. Berlin 1893-1919. Vol. I (1893): *Die Meerman-Handschriften des Sir Thomas Phillipps.* 221 mss. and 57 other items. Vol. II: *Die Handschriften der Kurfürstlichen Bibliothek und der Kurfürstlichen Lande.* pt. 1 (1901): Mss. no. 222-610. pt. 2 (1903): Mss. no. 611-855. pt. 3 (1905): Mss. no. 856-1030, and other items, no. 58-291. vol. III (1919): *Die Görreshandschriften.* 192 mss. Each volume is indexed. Not complete; valid shelf marks in parentheses. See concordances in vol. II pt. 3 (1515-22) and vol. III (261-2)

Mitteilungen aus der kgl. Bibliothek [Berlin] II (1914): *Neue Erwerbungen der Handschriftenabteilung.* pt. 1: 'Lateinische und deutsche Handschriften erworben 1911.'

121 pp. Describes many Latin mss. (1-60). No index. III (1917). The same. pt. 2: 'Die Schenkung Sir Max Waechters 1912.' 164 pp. Several Latin mss. (1-37). No index.

IV (1918). (H. Morf), *Kurzes Verzeichnis der romanischen Handschriften.* II, 141 pp. p. 37-92: 'Italienische Handschriften.' Ital. Fol. 1-173; Q 1-81; Oct. 1-10; and a few others.

Codices manuscripti latini theologici. Vol. I: fol. 1-381; quarto 1-142; oct. 1-67; indices. Vol. II: fol. 382-737; quarto 143-378; oct. 68-189. Not completely superseded by the printed catalogue of Rose and Schillmann. (Partial micr. at DLC) Most of the mss. are now in Marburg and Tübingen.

Codices manuscripti latini. Vol. I: mss. fol. 1-486; quarto 1-398; oct. 1-137; index. Vol. II: fol. 487-938; quarto 399-951; oct. 138-433 (microfilm at DLC). Lists numerous mss. not described in printed catalogues. Most mss. are now in Marburg and Tübingen.

Manuscripta Borussica. mss. fol. 1-1081; quarto 1-514; oct. 1-128 (mostly late) (communication of the librarian).

Manuscripta Dieziana. B. Santeniana. mss. 1-148m; index. (micr. at DLC)

Manuscripta Dieziana. C. Codices manuscripti occidentales. mss. fol. 1-85; quarto 1-125; oct. 1-36; index. (micr. at DLC) (Hamilton Collection)

Some of the Hamilton mss. were sold (see the second entry), others were assigned to the Museum (Kupferstichkabinett, now in West Berlin; see below the catalogue by Wescher). The bulk of the collection, as described in the catalogue of 1882, remained in the Berlin library as a separate unit, and is still there.

Catalogue of the Hamilton Collection of Manuscripts. London 1882. 120 pp. 692 mss. No index. (Pierpont Morgan Library)

Catalogue of Ninety-One Manuscripts on Vellum. . . chiefly from the famous Hamilton Collection and till lately in the posses-

sion of the Royal Museum of Berlin. London 1889. 79 pp. 91 mss. No index. (Pierpont Morgan Library)

W. v. Seidlitz, 'Die illustrierten Handschriften der Hamilton-Sammlung zu Berlin,' *Repertorium für Kunstwissenschaft* VI (1883) 256-73; VII (1884) 78-89; 295-306; VIII (1885) 94-110. 181 mss. No index.

P. Hinschius, 'Die kanonistischen Handschriften der Hamilton'schen Sammlung im Kupferstich-Kabinett des Königlichen Museums zu Berlin,' *Zeitschrift für Kirchengeschichte* VI (1884) 193-246. 5 mss.

K. Müller, 'Kirchengeschichtliche Handschriften in der Hamilton-Sammlung,' *Ibid.* 247-82. Alphabetical list (247-53), and description of 4 mss.

Theinert, 'Die Hamilton'sche Handschriften-Sammlung im Berliner Museum und ihre Beziehungen zur Geschichte des Nachrichten- und Verkehrswesens,' *Archiv für Post und Telegraphie* XII (1884) 449-476. (NN)

L. Biadene, 'I manoscritti italiani della collezione Hamilton nel R. Museo e nella R. Biblioteca di Berlino,' *Giornale storico della letteratura italiana* X (1887) 313-355. Lists 17 mss. in the Museum, 79 mss. in the library, and 5 other Italian mss. in the library.

(Autographen-Sammlung)

Most of it is lost since the war.

Verzeichniss der von dem verstorbenen Preussischen General-Lieutenant J. von Radowitz hinterlassenen Autographen-Sammlung. 3 vols. in 1. Berlin 1864. 810 pp., numbered continuously, and Index. (DLC)

Königliche Bibliothek zu Berlin. Verzeichniss der Autographen-Sammlung von Professor Dr. Ludwig Darmstaedter. Berlin 1909. 377 pp. Alphabetical list. Shelf marks corrected in library copy. (Morgan Library)

Die Autographa der Königlichen Bibliothek zu Berlin. 6 ms. vols. Arranged alphabetically.

(Musikabteilung) *Mus. ms. autogr. theor. Mus. ms. theor. Nachlässe.* Card file which includes an alphabetical list of mss. containing musical treatises.

Mus. ms. theor. 1 typed folder, listing the preserved mss. of this group.

—*Hauptarchiv (formerly Preussissches Geheimes Staatsarchiv, Berlin-Dahlem).

Übersicht über die Bestände des Geheimen Staatsarchivs zu Berlin-Dahlem. (Mitteilungen der Preussischen Archivverwaltung XXIV-XXVI). 3 vols. Leipzig 1934-39. Relevant are Repositur 94 (mss., vol. I, p. 133) and 94 A (autographs, p. 133-134). The mss. are now partly lost, partly preserved in Merseburg, Deutsches Zentralarchiv.

—*Kupferstichkabinett.

Beschreibendes Verzeichnis der Miniaturen—Handschriften und Einzelblätter—des Kupferstichkabinetts der Staatlichen Museen, Berlin. (By P. Wescher.) Leipzig 1931. 246 pp.

—*Institut für Geschichte der Medizin.

J. Ruska, 'Katalog der orientalischen und lateinischen Originalhandschriften, Abschriften und Photokopien des Instituts für Geschichte der Medizin und der Naturwissenschaften in Berlin,' *Quellen und Studien zur Geschichte der Naturwissenschaften und der Medizin* VII, 2-3 (1939) 1-149. 27 Latin mss. (126-45).

*Bern, Switzerland. Bürgerbibliothek. See Buchon; Pellegrin; Sinner; Stelling-Michaud; Thorndike; *Traditio* XIV.

H. Hagen, *Catalogus codicum Bernensium* (*Bibliotheca Bongarsiana*). Bern 1875. 662 pp. 722 mss.

(J. R. Sinner, *Catalogus codicum Manuscriptorum bibliothecae Bernensis.* 3 vols., Bern 1760-72. 636 pp.)

(The same, *Bibliothecae Bernensis codicum manuscriptorum syllabus* . . . Bern 1773. 116 pp.)

*Handwritten supplement to Hagen's printed catalogue by H. Bloesch. Describes mss. 723-824. Mostly late. (Communication of the librarian, cf. Born 348).

—*Schweizerische Landesbibliothek. No mss. (Communication of the librarian). Cf. Born 339.

*Bernay, France. See France, *Catalogue Général, Départements* II.

*Beromünster, Switzerland. Stiftsbibliothek.

M. Estermann, *Die Stiftsschule von Bero-Münster* . . . Lucerne 1876. vi, 224 pp. Lists 9 mss. (19-28). No index. (IU)

K. A. Kopp, *Die Stiftsbibliothek von Beromünster.* 2 vols. Lucerne 1903-04. II, p. 3-23: mss. No shelf marks. No index. (IU)

*Besançon, France. See France, *Catalogue Général, Départements* XXXII, XXXIII and XLV; *Universités*; Martin.

*Bethlehem, Pennsylvania, U.S.A. See De Ricci.

*Béthune, France. See France, *Catalogue Général, Départements* IV.

*Beuron, West Germany. Erzabtei. No inventory. Some Latin mss. (Communication of the librarian).

*Bevagna, Italy. See Mazzatinti I.

*Béziers, France. See France, *Catalogue Général, Départements* XX; XL.

*Biberach, West Germany. Spitalarchiv. *Findbuch der Abteilung B* (Bände). 1 typed vol. Section XV (Bücherei) describes mss. B 3513-41. Partial copy kindly supplied by the archivist.

*Binasco. See under Pavia.

*Bisceglie, Italy. See Mazzatinti VI.

*Bitonto, Italy. See Mazzatinti VI.

*Blairs, Great Britain. See Great Britain, *Historical Manuscripts Commission.*

*Blois, France. See France, *Catalogue Général, Départements* XXIV and XL.

*Bludov, Czechoslavakia.

M. Boháček and F. Čáda, 'Žerotínské Rukopisy Bludovské. Codices Zierotiniani manu scripti Bludovienses,' *Sborník Národního Musea v Praze.* Acta Musei Nationalis Pragae. Rada C. Literárni historie. Series C. Historia litterarum. Vol. III, num. 3-4 (1958) 45-221. 250 mss., mostly late.

*Böhmisch Krummau. See Český Krumlov.

Bologna, Italy. See *Analecta Bollandiana* XLII; *Archiv* V; XII; Blume; Mazzatinti XIV-XVII; XIX; XXI; XXIII; XXV; XXVII; XXX; XXXII; XXXVI; XL; XLIII; XLVII; LIII; LXII; LXV; LXVI LXIX; LXXV; LXXIX; LXXII; *Serapeum, Intelligenzblatt* 1866; *Studi Italiani.* XVI-XVII; Thorndike.

M.-H. Laurent, *Fabio Vigili et les Bibliothèques de Bologne au début du XVIe siècle d'après le Ms. Barb. Lat. 3185.* (Studi e Testi CV). Vatican City 1943. xlviii, 416 pp. Describes many mss. now in the Collegio di Spagna and in other Bologna libraries.

—*Archivio di Stato.

F. Malaguzzi Valeri, 'Le pergamene, i codici miniati e i disegni del R. Archivio di Stato di Bologna,' *Atti e Memorie della R. Deputazione di Storia Patria per le provincie di Romagna,* Ser. III, vol. XVI (1897-98, published 1899) 52-142. 110 nos. Index (140-142).

—*Biblioteca Arcivescovile.

La Sala Breventani nella Biblioteca arcivescovile di Bologna: Relazione e Indice dei Manoscritti. Bologna 1909. xiv, 34 pp. Report signed G. Belvederi and A. Manaresi. No index.

—Biblioteca Comunale dell' Archiginnasio. See Mazzatinti XXX; XXXII; XXXVI; XL; XLIII; XLVII; LIII; LXIX; LXXV; LXXIX; LXXXII.

C. Lucchesi, 'Manoscritti della Biblioteca Comunale dell' Archiginnasio di Bologna contenenti opere di Lettori dello Studio di Padova,' *Studi e Memorie per la Storia dell' Università di Bologna* VII (1922) 33-54. Arranged chronologically. No index.

F. Mancini, 'Consistenza e stato attuale dei manoscritti della Biblioteca Comunale dell' Archiginnasio,' *L'Archiginnasio* XLVI-XLVII (1951-52) 25-65. p. 26-33: List of lost and damaged mss. of the main collection (groups A and B). p. 35-65:

Inventario dei Fondi Speciali. Summary list of 146 groups of mss. and of the Archivio Gozzadini.

Card index in 20 boxes, supplements the printed catalogue (AB IV 248).

—Biblioteca Universitaria. See *Studi Italiani* XVI-XVII; Mazzatinti XV; XVII; XIX; XXI; XXIII; XXV; XXVII.

F. Cancellieri, *Notizie della vita e delle miscellanee di Monsignor Pietro Antonio Tioli* . . . Pesaro 1826. 160 pp. p. 83-143: Summary table of contents of the 36 vols. of the Miscellanea Tioli (ms. 2948) which is not described in Mazzatinti or in *Studi Italiani*. Indices (p. 145-160).

F. Zambrini, 'Descrizione di codici manoscritti che si conservano nella R. Biblioteca dell' Università di Bologna,' *Il Propugnatore* I (1868) 121-36; 251-72; 384-97; 505-13. 13 Italian mss.

L. Frati, *Catalogo dei manoscritti di Ulisse Aldrovandi.* Bologna 1907. 288 pp.

The same, 'Catalogo dei manoscritti di Luigi Ferdinando Marsili, conservati nella Biblioteca Universitaria di Bologna,' *Bibliofilia* XXVII (1925-26) 185-215; 263-85; 370-85; 447-51; XXVIII (1926-27) 50-56; 193-200; 291-301; 405-13; XXIX (1927-28) 46-54; 298-312; 404-19; XXX (1928-29) 120-39.

Catalogo dei Manoscritti della Biblioteca Universitaria di Bologna. 4 ms. vols. I: 1-500. II. 501-1500. III: 1501-3645. IV: 3646-4245. Supplements the printed catalogue for a few omitted mss. and for recent acquisitions. (AB II 2 p. 52 no. 15).

—Collegio di Spagna.

E. Orioli, *Elenco dei libri del cardinale Albornoz donati al collegio di Spagna in Bologna.* Bologna, per nozze, 1893. 15 pp. (Vatican Library)

C. Piana, 'Descriptio codicum Franciscalium necnon S. Thomae Aquin. in Bibliotheca Albornotiana Collegii Hispani Bononiae asservatorum,' *Antonianum* XVII (1942) 97-132. Index (p. 132). (NNUT)

Bibliotheca Albornotiana continet Manuscriptos Codices qui adservantur in Regali ac Majori Collegio Hispanorum gratia ab eximio Card. Albornotio Bononiae erecto... (1748). Arranged by subjects. *Ca.* 290 mss. (micr. at DLC)

—Conservatorio di Musica G. B. Martini.

G. Gaspari, *Catalogo della Biblioteca del Liceo Musicale di Bologna.* 4 vols. Bologna 1890-1905. I, p. 157-268: 347-356: Alphabetical list of mss. and edd. containing musical treatises. Shelf marks added in library copy. (NN)

—*Istituto Rizzoli.

La Raccolta Vittorio Putti: Antiche opere di medicina manoscritte e stampate lasciate all' Istituto Rizzoli di Bologna. Milan 1943. 109 pp. p. 3-7: 17 mss. No index. (MH)

—*Museo di S. Petronio.

A. Gatti, *Catalogo del Museo di S. Petronio.* Bologna 1893. 48 pp. Lists a few choirbooks (p. 41-47). No index. (Morgan Library)

L. Frati, *I corali della Basilica di S. Petronio in Bologna.* Bologna 1896. 106 pp. p. 33-80: 15 mss. (Morgan Library)

Bolzano-Bozen, Italy. See Wickhoff.

—*Padri Minori Francescani. Franziskanerbibliothek. Typed list of 31 mss. kindly supplied by the librarian.

—*Benedettini di Muri-Gries. 96 mss. See Wickhoff. See under Sarnen.

Bonn, West Germany. Universitätsbibliothek. See *Archiv* XI.

(J. H. Withof, *Kritische Anmerkungen über Horaz und andere römische Schriftsteller, nebst einer Beschreibung der lateinischen Handschriften in der Duisburgischen Universitäts-Bibliothek* von H. A. Grimm. Vol. I, Düsseldorf 1791. p. 95ff.: 2 mss. Vol. II [1791] p. 145ff.: 2 ms. Vol. III [1793] p. 153ff.: 1 ms.) (PU)

(The same, *Conjecturen über verschiedene lateinische Dichter und Prosaiker, gesammelt und nebst einer Beschreibung und Vergleichung der Duisburgischen Handschriften* hrsg. von H. A. Grimm. 3 vols. Düsseldorf 1798-1801. Vol. I [1798] p. 155ff.: 2 mss. II [1799] p. 149ff.: 1 ms. [ICU]. **Vol. III [1801] not located).

Catalogi Chirographorum in Bibliotheca Academica Bonnensi servatorum particula I, by A. Klette. Bonn 1858. 42 pp. 178 mss. Fasciculus II, 1859. p. 43-76. Mss. no. 179-299. Index (p. 63-64). Fasciculus III, 1860. p. 77-100. Mss. no. 300-59. Fasciculus IIII, 1862. p. 101-20. Mss. no. 360-411. Fasciculus V, 1863. p. 121-42. Mss. no. 412-76. (NjP). Fasciculi VI pars I, 1865. p. 143-59. Mss. no. 477-532. (PU). Fasciculi VI pars II, by J. Staender, 1875-76. p. 161-86. Mss. no. 533-711. Vol. II, 1876. p. 187-250. Mss. no. 712-856. Index (215ff.). (MH). Fasciculi VII-XIII cover Oriental mss. (DLC). (No complete set located).

**Rheinische Handschriften der Universitätsbibliothek Bonn. Bonn 1941. 35 pp. Cf. Historisches Jahrbuch LXII-LXIX (1942-49) 889-890.

*Handwritten continuation of printed catalogue was lost, along with many mss., during the war. There is a photostat copy of it, but it is difficult to read. (Communication of the librarian).

*Bordeaux, France. See France, Catalogue Général, Départements XXIII, XL and L. Universités; Omont.

J. Gómez Perez, 'Manuscritos españoles en Burdeos,' Revista de Archivos, Museos y Bibliotecas LX (1954) 477-510. 118 mss.

Archives Municipales de Bordeaux. Catalogue des manuscrits. By X. Védère. Bordeaux 1938. XXII, 317 pp. 830 mss., mostly modern. (NN)

(Bordeaux, Bibliothèque Municipale. Catalogue des manuscrits. Vol. I, Bordeaux 1880. xxxiii, 462 pp. Preface signed by J. Delpit.) 842 mss. No index. (OCI)

*Borgonovo, Italy.

C. Piana, 'I codici della Biblioteca del convento di S. Bernardino di Borgonovo Val Tidone,' Bollettino Storico Piacentino XLVIII (1953) 10-16. 3 mss.

*Bosa, Italy. See Mazzatinti VI.

Boston, Mass., USA, see De Ricci.

J. F. Ballard, A Catalogue of the Medieval and Renaissance Manuscripts and Incunabula in the Boston Medical Library. Boston 1944. xx, 246 pp. 52 mss. (p. 1-28).

—Boston Public Library.

Z. Haraszti, 'Medieval Manuscripts in the Library,' More Books, The Bulletin of the Boston Public Library, Ser. VI. vol. III (1928) 57-75. Arranged by languages. No shelf marks. No index.

*Boulogne, France. See France, Catalogue Général, Départements IV (Quarto Series) and XL.

*Bourbonne, France. See France, Catalogue général, Départements XXIV; XL.

*Bourbourg, France. See France, Catalogue général, Départements III; XL.

*Bourg, France, See France, Catalogue Général, Départements VI and XL; Martin.

*Bourges, France. See France, Catalogue Général, Départements IV and XL; Martin.

*Bourmont, France. See France, Catalogue général, Départements IV.

*Bozen, see Bolzano.

*Braga. Portugal. See Stegmüller.

M. G. da Costa, Inéditos de filosofia em Portugal. Oporto 1949. 143 pp. Lists 118 mss. in the Biblioteca Pública in Braga (p. 30-118) and 12 more in the Biblioteca da Faculdade de Filosofia. Concordance of shelf marks. Index. (NN)

—*Biblioteca Pública e Arquivo Distrital. 993 mss. described in handwritten inventories. Older mss. are all covered by the printed lists. (Communication of the librarian)

*Brandenburg, East Germany.

E. Köpke, Mittheilungen aus den Handschriften der Ritter-Akademie zu Brandenburg a.H. I. Johannes von Hildesheim. progr. Brandenburg 1878. 35 pp. (NNC)

**II. Jacobus de Cessolis. 1879 (not located).

*Braniewo, Poland. See Hipler.

O. Meinertz, Die Handschriften und alten Drucke der Gymnasial-Bibliothek zu Braunsberg. progr. Braunsberg 1880-82. 20 pp. 5 mss. (p. 4-6). No index. (MH)

*Bratislava (Poszonyi, Pressburg), Czechoslovakia. See Radó. See also under Szombathely.

F. Knauz, *A Poszonyi Káptalannak Kéziratai. (Codices manuscripti capituli Posoniensis).* Reprinted from *Különnyomat a Magyar Sion* IV-VII. Strigonii (Esztergom) 1870. 324 pp. 248 mss. No index. The mss. are now divided between the Archív mesta Bratislavy and the Státny slovenský ustredný archív. Some mss. are lost. (microfilm at NNC)

—*Slovenská akadémia vied, Ústredná Knížnica, správa Lyceálnje Knižnice.

K. Harmath, A pozsonyi evang. lyceum kéziratgyüjteményének ismertetése. progr. Pozsony 1879. 35 pp. 73 nos. No index.

*Braunsberg, see Braniewo.

*Braunschweig, West Germany.

H. Nentwig, *Die mittelalterlichen Handschriften in der Stadtbibliothek zu Braunschweig.* Wolfenbüttel 1893. 202 pp. 184 mss.

(A. Rhamm), *Verzeichnis der bis zum Jahre 1815 erschienenen Drucksachen und der Handschriften der Landschaftlichen Bibliothek zu Braunschweig.* Braunschweig 1907. viii, 205 pp. Arranged by subjects, mss. listed with edd., mostly late. No Index. (Erlangen Univ. Library).

E. Henrici, 'Zum Handschriftenkatalog der Braunschweiger Stadtbibliothek,' *Zentralblatt für Bibliothekswesen* XXV (1908) 158-61.

The same, 'Bruchstücke mittelalterlicher Handschriften in der Braunschweiger Stadtbibliothek,' *Ibid.* XXVII (1910) 356-63.

*Bremen, West Germany. Staatsbibliothek. See *Serapeum, Intelligenzblatt* 1866.

Verzeichnis der handschriftlichen Bücher und einiger alten Drucke der Bremischen Öffentlichen Bibliothek. (By H. Rump). Bremen 1834. 52 pp. Fol. 1-130; Qu. 1-98; Oct. 1-54. No index.

H. A. Müller. *Die Bilderhandschriften des Mittelalters in den Bibliotheken der Stadt und der Hauptschule zu Bremen.* progr. Bremen 1863. 18 pp. 20 mss. No index.

Standortskatalog der Manuscriptsammlung. Mss. a 1-225; b 1-232; c 1-133. Partly superseded by Rump's printed catalogue of 1834. Some of the mss. were lost during the war (communication of the librarian).

Seit Rumps Handschriftenverzeichnis von 1834 neu hinzugekommene lateinische Handschriften der Staatsbibliothek Bremen. Typed list kindly supplied by the librarian. Many mss. are missing since the last war.

Brescia, Italy.

E. Calabi, 'Giovanni Pietro da Birago e i Corali miniati dell' antica Cattedrale di Brescia,' *La Critica d'Arte* III (1938) 144-51. 18 mss.

The same, 'I corali miniati di S. Francesco a Brescia,' *ibid.* 57-67.

—Biblioteca Civica Queriniana. See *Neues Archiv* XVII; *Studi Italiani* XIV; Zaccaria *Iter.*

**A. Valentini, *I manoscritti della collezione Di Rosa.* Brescia 1890. 61 pp.

Catalogo Manoscritti, Biblioteca Queriniana. 2 vols. Centuries not given. Arranged alphabetically. I: A-L. II: M-Z. At the end, a list of the older mss. by centuries. (Cf. AB IV 171). (micr. at DLC)

Card index in 6 boxes (AB IV 171-72). (micr. at DLC)

Breslau. See Wrocław.

Bressanone-Brixen, Italy. Archivio del Seminario (Seminararchiv). See Wickhoff; Zingerle.

Catalogus Manuscriptorum (microfilm kindly supplied by the archivist). 77 mss. Inventory on loose Sheets.

*Brest, France. See France, *Catalogue Général, Départements* XXII; XL.

*Bretten (Baden), West Germany. Melanchthonhaus.

K. A. Meissinger, 'Die Urkundensammlung des Melanchthonhauses,' *Archiv für Reformationsgeschichte* XIX (1922) 48-71; XXIV (1927) 22-97. 450 mss. (NNG)

*Briançon, France. See France, *Catalogue Général, Départements* XX.

*Brieg. See Brzeg.

*Briey, France. See France, *Catalogue Général, Départements* XXXI.

*Brindisi, Italy.

Elenco dei Manoscritti esistenti nella Biblioteca Arcivescovile De Leo di Brindisi. Typed list of 99 mss. Copy kindly sent by the librarian.

*Brioude, France. See France, *Catalogue Général, Départements* IV.

*Bristol, England. See Bernardus; *Hispanic Sacra* VIII; Schenkl; Williams.

N. Mathews, *Early Printed Books and Manuscripts in the City Reference Library, Bristol.* Bristol 1889. 84 pp. 10 mss. (p. 59-70).

*Brive, France. See France, *Catalogue Général, Départements* IV.

Brixen, see **Bressanone**.

Brno, Czechoslovakia. Statni Archiv. See *Archiv* IV; X; Burdach; Feifalik.

W. Schram, *Katalog der Handschriften des Franzens-Museums in Brünn.* Brünn 1890. IV, 36 pp. Arranged alphabetically. New shelf marks added in archive copy. (Brno, Statni Archiv)

B. Dudik, *J. P. Ceroni's Handschriftensammlung.* Brno 1850. (Mährens Geschichts-Quellen I). 510 pp.

Die Cerroni'sche Handschriften-Sammlung (by J. H. Czikann). Lists 413 mss.

Německy Historický Spolek (Geschichtsverein), Sbírka rukopisů (by Dr. J. Radimsky, 1947). 1 typed vol. 589 nos.

For the main collection of the archive (StAB), there is an alphabetical card file in 8 boxes.

—Archiv Města.

J. Dřímal, *Archiv Města Brna.* Prague 1956. 268 pp. and plates. (Brno)

Inventar Rukopisů Archivu Zemského Hlavniho Města Brna. 6 ms. vols. 7922 nos.

Rukopisy, inventář.. 1 typed vol. 618 mss. (Brno, Statni Archiv).

Jakob Sv., rukopisy a inkunabule, inventář. 1 typed vol. in German. 113 mss. (Brno, Statni Archiv)

Catalogus antiquissimae bibliothecae ecclesiae ad S. Jacobum Brunae Moravorum (by A. Habrich O.S.B. and M. Simonius O. Capuc., 1782-1805). 125 mss.

Bibliothek an der Pfarrkirche zu St. Jacob in Brünn. 132 mss.

Die Handschriften und. . . . Druckwerke der S. Jacobs Bibliothek in Brünn. 125 mss.

—Universitní Knihovna. It acquired some of the mss. from Mikulov, Nova Říša, Rajhrad and Veselí, as well as those of several local monasteries.

M. Kinter, 'Die Bibliothek des Stiftes Raigern,' *Archiv für Bibliographie* I (1926) 204-213. Surveys the mss.

B. Dudik, 'Handschriften der Fürstlich Dietrichsteinschen Bibliothek zu Nikolsburg in Mähren,' *Archiv für österreichische Geschichte* XXXIX (1868) 417-534. 108 mss. of which no. 24-57 (p. 472ff.) are Latin. Index (525ff.).

Soupis Rajhradskych Rukopisů uložených v Zemské a universitní knihovně v Brně.. (By V. Dokoupil.) I, 106 pp. R 1-723. Indices. Mimeographed.

Soupis Rukopisů knihovny starobrněnskych augustiniánů. (By V. Dokoupil). III, 65 pp. Mimeographed list. A 1-117.

Soupis Rukopisů knihovny brněnskych minoritů. (By V. Dokoupil). II, 34 pp. Mimeographed list (1953). Mn 1-58.

Soupis Rukopisů knihovny novořišskych premonstrátů. (By V. Dokoupil). 47 pp. Mimeographed list (1954). NR 1-77.

Soupis Rukopisů mikulovské dietrichsteinské knihovny, uložených v Universitní knihovně v Brně. (By V. Dokoupil). VIII, 164 pp. Mimeographed list (1954). Mk 1-116.

Soupis Rukopisů byvalé zamecké knihovny hrabat Chorinskych ve Veselí n. Mor., uložených v Universitní knihovně v Brně. (By V. Dokoupil). II, 68 pp. Mimeographed list (1954). H 1-103; mostly late (Brno).

Soupisy rukopisných fondů Universitní knihovny v Brně. Catalogi codicum manu scriptorum in Bibliotheca Universitatis Brunensis asservatorum. I. Soupis Rukopisů Knihovny Augustiniánů na St. Brně. Catalogus codicum manu scriptorum Bibliothecae Monasterii Eremitarum S. Au-

gustini Vetero-Brunae. By V. Dokoupil. Brno 1957. 144 pp. and plates. 135 mss.
—II. *Soupis Rukopisů Mikulovské Dietrichsteinské Knihovný. Catalogus codicum manu scriptorum Bibliothecae Dietrichsteinianae Nicolspurgensis.* By the same. Brno 1958. 277 pp. and plates. 116 mss. (out of the former collection of 459 mss.)
—III. *Soupis Rukopisů z Knihovny Minoritů v Brně, Františkánů v Moravske Třebově a Premonstratů v Nové Říši. Catalogus codicum manu scriptorum, qui in Bibliothecis Fratrum Minorum Brunensium, Fratrum Ordinis Sancti Francisci Moravotriboviensium, Fratrum Ordinis Praemonstratensis Neoreischensium asservabantur.* By V. Dokoupil. Prague 1959. 163 pp. and plates. Mss. Mn 1-60; MT 1-35; N R 1-77. Some of the mss. formerly in Nova Říše are lost.
*Brooklyn, New York, U.S.A. See De Ricci.
Brugge (Bruges), Belgium. See *Analecta Bollandiana* X; *Archiv* VIII; *Catalogue général*; Van de Putte.
*—Bibliothèque de la ville.
(P. J. Laude, *Catalogue méthodique, descriptif et analytique des manuscrits de la Bibliothèque Publique de Bruges.* Bruges 1859. 552 pp. 562 mss.)
A. De Poorter and M. Alliaume, 'Catalogue des manuscrits mathématiques et astronomiques de la Bibliothèque de Bruges,' *Annales de la Société d'Émulation de Bruges* LXV (1915-22) 13-50. (MH)
A. De Poorter, 'Les manuscrits de l'abbaye bénédictine d'Oudenbourg à la Bibliothèque de Bruges,' *Revue des Bibliothèques* XXXIII (1923) 375-94. 13 mss. No index.
The same, 'Catalogue des manuscrits de médecine médiévale de la bibliothèque de Bruges,' *Ibid.* XXXIV (1924) 271-306. No index.
The same, 'Catalogue des manuscrits de grammaire latine médiévale de la bibliothèque de Bruges,' *Ibid.* XXXVI (1926) 103-37. No index.
The same, 'Catalogue des manuscrits de

prédication médiévale de la bibliothèque de Bruges,' *Revue d'Histoire Ecclésiastique* XXIV (1928) 62-124. No index. (NNUT)
The same and J. Brys, 'Les manuscrits de droit médiéval de l'ancienne abbaye des Dunes à Bruges,' *Ibid.* XXVI (1930) 609-57. Describes many mss. in the Bibliothèque de la Ville (611-656) and 3 mss. at the Grand Séminaire (656-7). No index. (NNUT)
A. De Poorter, 'Les manuscrits de sophistique de la bibliothèque de Bruges, *Revue Néoscolastique de Philosophie* XXXIV (1932) 57-65. No index.
The same, 'Manuscrits de philosophie aristotélicienne à la Bibliothèque de Bruges,' *Ibid.* XXXV (1933) 56-95.
The same, 'Catalogue des livres d'Heures et de Prières de la Bibliothèque de Bruges,' *Revue d'Histoire Ecclésiastique* XXIX (1933) 344-364. (NNUT)
—Grand Séminaire. See Lampen; Van de Putte.
Tentoonstelling van Miniaturen en Boekbanden, Geillustreerde Catalogus. Bruges 1927. 159 pp., and plates. 140 mss. (Morgan Library)
Handwritten list without title, in 3 vols. I: mss. 1-66. II: 67-133. III: 134-196. (Kindly sent on loan by Prof. E. H. Janssens de Bisthoven). Sketchy.
Catalogus cod. Mss. Seminarii Maioris Brugensis. Typed, in Flemish. mss. 1/2-197/122. Suppl. 1-150.
—Bibliothèque de l'Évêché. Deposited in the Grand Séminaire. No inventory. Ca. 50 mss.
Brünn, see **Brno**.
Bruxelles (Brussels), Belgium.
See *Archiv* VII; VIII; XI; Novati; Omont; *Serapeum, Intelligenzblatt* 1863.
—Bibliothèque Royale
Le Baron de Reiffenberg. *Notices et Extraits des Manuscrits de la Bibliothèque dite de Bourgogne, relatifs aux Pays-Bas.* Vol. I, Brussels 1829. 135 pp. No index. (NjP)
Bibliotheca Hulthemiana ou Catalogue Méthodique de la riche et précieuse collection

de livres et de manuscrits délaissés par
M. Ch. Van Hulthem. 6 vols. Ghent
1836-37. Vol. VI: Manuscrits. 223 pp.
1016 mss. (NN)
Catalogue des manuscrits de la Bibliothèque
Royale des Ducs de Bourgogne. 3 vols.
Brussels 1842. Vol. I: 18000 mss. The
numbering refers to texts rather than to
volumes. Index (separately paged, dated
1857). Vols. II-III: Table of subjects.
Inventaire des Manuscrits de l'ancienne Bibliothèque Royale des Ducs de Bourgogne,
Brussels 1839. xix, 360 pp. Preface
signed by J. Marchal. Lists 18000 mss.
This is an earlier edition of vol. I of the
catalogue of 1842. The main part is identical, but the introduction is much shorter.
(NN)
Annuaire de la Bibliothèque royale de Belgique. 12 vols. Brussels 1840-51. Contains reports on acquisitions of mss., and
a section entitled 'Notices et extraits des
Manuscrits de la Bibliothèque Royale.'
Catalogue des accroissements de la bibliothè-
que royale en livres imprimés, en cartes,
estampes et en manuscrits. 2 series in
15 pts., Brussels 1843-56. pt. 1 (1843)
129-33: 77 mss. pt. 2 (1843) p. 59-64:
Mss. no. 78-149. pt. 3 (1844) 119-22:
Mss. no. 150-88. pt. 4 (1844) 111-16:
Mss. no. 189-234. pt. 5 (1844) 117-19:
Mss. no. 235-96. pt. 6 (1845) 142-47:
Mss. no. 297-375. pt. 7 (1846) 142-44:
Mss. no. 376-403. pt. 8 (1847) 125-36:
Mss. no. 404-509. pt. 9 (1848) 173-78:
Mss. no. 510-55. pt. 10 (1849) 105-06:
Mss. no. 556-60. pt. 11 (1850) 117-24:
Mss. no. 561-618. Ser. II pt. 1 (1853)
223-50: 270 mss. pt. 2 (1854) 173-79: Mss.
no. 271-332. pt. 3 (1855) 169-72: Mss. no.
233-71. pt. 4 (1856) 145-58: 155 mss.
No index. Serial numbers go up to 21370.
(NN)
Bibliothèque Royale de Belgique. Catalogue
de la Bibliothèque de F. J. Fétis acquise par
l'État Belge. Brussels 1877. 946 pp. In-
cludes several mss. (612ff.). (NN)
Catalogus codicum hagiographicorum Biblio-

thecae Regiae Bruxellensis. Pars I: Codices Latini Membranei. 2 vols. Brussels
1886-89. 235 mss. (NNUT)
P. Thomas, Catalogue des manuscrits de
classiques latins de la Bibliothèque Royale
de Bruxelles. (Université de Gand. Recueil de Travaux. Publiés par la Faculté de Philosophie et Lettres. no. 18).
Ghent 1896. 110 pp. 349 mss. Index (p.
xi-xiv).
J. Van den Gheyn and others, Catalogue des
manuscrits de la Bibliothèque Royale de
Belgique. 13 vols. Brussels 1901-48. Vol.
I (1901): Bible and liturgy. 900 mss.
Vol. II (1902): Church Fathers. Mss. no.
901-1533. Vol. III (1903): Theology. No.
1534-2491. Vol. IV (1904): Jurisprudence
and Philosophy. No. 2492-3046. Vol. V
(1905): History and hagiography. No 3047-
3594. Vol. VI (1906): Church History.
No. 3595-4559. Vol. VII-XI (1907-27):
History of individual countries (XI also
geography and travel). No. 4560-7450.
Vol. XII (1936): Heraldics. No. 7451-
7621. Vol XIII (1948): Heraldics and
Genealogy, by F. Lyna. No. 7622-8506.
No indices. Not complete. Serial numbers differ from those of 1842. Valid shelf
marks in parentheses.
C. Gaspar and F. Lyna, Les principaux manuscrits à peintures de la Bibliothèque Royale
de Belgique. 2 vols, Paris 1937-47. (Pier-
pont Morgan Library).
H. Michel, 'Les manuscrits astronomiques
de la Bibliothèque Royale de Belgique,'
Ciel et Terre LXV (1949) 199-204. Arranged by subjects. No index.
E. Mikkers, 'Cisterciensia in de Koninklyke
Bibliotheek te Brussel,' Cîteaux in de
Nederlanden I (1950) 47-50. Offset printed.
Section des Manuscrits. Inventaire, 18001
à 22487. Actually goes to no. 23000.
Supplements printed catalogue of 1842
and covers acquisitions to 1870 (Cf. Born
35).
Bibliothèque Royale. Inventaire. 5 vols. Co-
vers acquisitions for 1870-1952. I: IIe
série, mss. 1-825. II: 826-3053. III:

3054-4979. IV: 4980-7415. V: 7416-7848.
—Société des Bollandistes. See *Analecta Bollandiana* XXIV.
Catalogue de nos manuscrits. A pack of ms. sheets arranged by shelf marks. 1063 mss. Card file in 2 trays. Not accessible to the public.

Bryn Mawr, Pennsylvania, U.S.A. Bryn Mawr College. See De Ricci.
Typed list of mss. Includes some from the Goodhart collection.

*****Brzeg**, Poland. See *Archiv* XI.

*****Bucuresti**, Rumania. Biblioteca Academiei Republicii Populare Romîne.
*Inventory of Latin mss.
*Inventory of Italian mss. Typed list of 13 older Latin mss. and of 4 Italian mss. kindly supplied by the librarian.

*****Budapest**, Hungary. See *Archiv* VI; *Bibliotheca Corvina*; Haenel (Supplement); Hevesy; Lehmann, *Mitteilungen*; Radó.
Könyv-Kiállítási Emlék. Budapest 1882. 263 pp. 324 mss. (p. 1-112). (NNGr)
—*Egyetemi Könyvtár (University Library).

Catalogus manuscriptorum Bibliothecae Regiae Scientiarum Universitatis Budapestiensis. A Budapesti Magyar Kir. Egyetemi Könyvtár Kéziratainak Czimjegyzéke. (éd. S. Szilágyi and others). 2 vols. in 5. Budapest 1881-1910. Vol. I: *Catalogus codicum Bibliothecae Universitatis R. Scientiarum Budapestinensis. A Budapesti M. Kir. Egyetemi Könyvtár Codexeinek Czimjegyzéke*, 1881. 155 pp. 116 Latin mss. (NjP) Vol. II, pt. 1. *Catalogus librorum manuscriptorum.* 1889. (MH). pt. 2. *Catalogus litterarum originalium ac Collectionis Hevenessianae et Praganae.* 1894. (MH). * pt. 3. (*Catalogus collectionis Kaprinayanae*) and 4 (*Indices*) not located.
*Card catalogue.
—*Magyar Tudományos Akadémia Könyvtára (Academy of Sciences).
*Card catalogue.
—*Országos Széchényi Könyvtár (Szechenyi Library of the National Museum).

Catalogus manuscriptorum Bibliothecae Nationalis Hungaricae Széchényiano-Regnicolaris. 3 vols. Sopronii 1814-15. Appendix signed J. F. Miller de Brasso. Arranged alphabetically by authors or titles I: A-C. II: D-M. III: N-Z. Mostly late material. No general index. (NN)

G. Heinrich, 'Die heimgekehrten Bände der « Corvina »,' *Literarische Berichte aus Ungarn* I (1877) 321-40. 34 mss. No index. (NN)

A. v. Török, *XXXV Handschriften.* (Geschenk des Sultans Abdul Hamid II). Budapest 1878. 52 pp. No index.

L. Zambra, 'I manoscritti italiani nella Biblioteca Széchényi del Museo Nazionale Ungherese di Budapest,' *Bibliofilia* XII (1911) 94-102. Arranged chronologically. No index.

E. Hoffmann, *A Nemzeti Múzeum Széchényi Könyvtárának Illuminált Kéziratai.* (Országos Széchényi Könyvtár Tudomanyos Kiadványai 1). Budapest 1928. 137 pp. and plates. Not a catalogue. (Morgan Library)

Emma Bartoniek, *Codices latini medii aevi.* (Catalogi Bibliothecae Musaei Nationalis Hungarici XII). Budapest 1940. XVII, 528 pp. 449 mss.

Helga J. Hajdu, 'A kézirattár állományának gyarapodása a felszabadulás óta,' *Az Országos Széchényi Könyvtár Evkönyve* 1957 (Budapest 1958) 108-126. Surveys the acquisitions since 1945.

*****Buffalo**, New York, U.S.A. See De Ricci.

*****Burgo de Osma**, Spain. See Grubbs (Section A, under Richardson).

T. Rojo Orcajo, *Catálogo descriptivo de los códices que se conservan en la santa iglesia catedral de Burgo de Osma.* Madrid 1929. 305 pp. 204 mss. (NNC). Also in: *Boletín de la Real Academia de la Historia* XCIV (1929) 655-792; XCV (1929) 152-314. (NN)

*****Burgos**, Spain. See *Anuario* II.

—*Biblioteca de la Catedral.

D. Mansilla, *Catalogo de los codices de la Catedral de Burgos.* Madrid 1952. 205 pp.

and plates. 61 mss. 87 choirbooks and 7 inventories.

—*Biblioteca Pública Provincial. No inventory. Typed list of 81 mss. kindly sent by the librarian.

*Burgsteinfurt, West Germany. K. Hamann, *Beschreibung der Handschriften und alten Drucke der Bbibliothek des alten Arnoldinums. Erste Folge.* progr. Burgsteinfurt. Iserlohn 1877. 43 pp. p. 14-20: 2 Latin mss. No index. (Erlangen, University Library)

*Bury St. Edmunds, England. See M. R. James; Schenkl.

*Busto Arsizio, Italy. Biblioteca Capitolare. See Leclercq.
I codici medioevali della Biblioteca Capitolare di Busto Arsizio, by P. Mancarella (1 typed vol., a thesis of the Università Cattolica written in 1946, kindly shown to me by Prof. E. Franceschini).

C, see also under K.

*Caceres, Spain. Biblioteca publica. See *Anuario.* Typed list of 13 mss. kindly supplied by the librarian.

*Cadiz, Spain. See *Neues Archiv* VI. J. A. de Aldama, 'Manuscritos teológicos postridentinos de la biblioteca provincial de Cádiz,' *Archivo teologico Granadino* II (1939) 25-33. (DCU)

*Cadouin, France. Suzanne Corbin, 'Le fonds manuscrit de Cadouin,' *Bulletin de la Société historique et archéologique du Périgord* LXXXI (1954), Supplément, 34 pp. 24 mss. (NN)

*Caen, France. See France, *Catalogue général, Départements* XIV; XLI; XLIV; *Universités.*
(G. Lavalley, *Catalogue des manuscrits de la Bibliothèque Municipale de Caen . . .* Caen 1880. LIX, 274 pp. 522 mss. Index: p. 247-63). (MH)

*Cagli, Italy. See Mazzatinti II.

*Cagliari, Italy. Biblioteca Comunale.
Elenco sommario dei manoscritti (AB VI 552).

*—Biblioteca Universitaria.
Catalogo dei manoscritti (AB I 5-6 p. 102).

*Cahors, France. See France, *Catalogue Général, Départements* IX; XLI.

*Calahorra, Spain. See Fransen; Leclercq.

*Calais, France. See France, *Catalogue Général, Départements* IV; XLI.

*Camarillo, California, U.S.A. St. John's Seminary. See De Ricci.
Catalogue of Books and Manuscripts in the Estelle Doheny Collection. 3 vols. Los Angeles 1940-55. I (1940) 3-6; II (1946) 3-5; III (1955) 3-8: mss.

*Cambrai, France. See France, *Catalogue Général, Départements* XVII; XLI.
(A. Le Glay, *Catalogue descriptif et raisonné des Manuscrits de la Bibliothèque de Cambrai.* Cambrai 1831. 256 pp.) (NN). Also in: *Mémoires de la Société d'Émulation de Cambrai* XII (1830) 117-368. 1046 mss. No index. (NN)

Ch.-A. Lefebvre, 'Catalogue descriptif et analytique de la 2me Série des manuscrits de la Bibliothèque Communale de Cambrai (Nos. 1047 à 1156)' *Ibid.* XXVII, 2 (1862) 401-88. Mss. no. 1047-1158. Index (455ff.). (NN)

Cambridge, England. See Bernardus; Omont; Schenkl.

—University Library.
(J. O. Halliwell, *The Manuscript Rarities of the University of Cambridge.* London 1841. 175 pp. Covers mss. Dd. I. 1-Ff. V. 48. No index.)

A Catalogue of the Manuscripts Preserved in the Library of the University of Cambridge. 6 vols. Cambridge 1856-67. I (1856): 889 mss. II (1857): Nos. 890-1395. III (1858): Nos. 1396-2129. IV (1861): Nos. 2130-3429. V (1867): Baumgartner papers, Baker mss., Additional mss. 3773-4109. VI (1867): Index. Not complete.

A Catalogue of Adversaria and Printed Books containing Manuscript Notes preserved in the Library of the University of Cambridge. Cambridge 1864. (By H. R. Luard). 100 pp. (NN)

Additional Manuscripts. 7208 mss. (Cf. Born 44).

Subject-Index, 2 vols.

—Other Libraries.

M. R. James, *A Descriptive Catalogue of the Western Manuscripts in the Library of Christ's College, Cambridge.* Cambridge 1905. vi, 36 pp. 12 mss. No index.

The same, *A Descriptive Catalogue of the Western Manuscripts in the Library of Clare College, Cambridge.* Cambridge 1905. viii, 51 pp. 31 mss. No index.

The same, *A Descriptive Catalogue of the Manuscripts in the Library of Corpus Christi College, Cambridge.* 2 vols. Cambridge 1912. I: No. 1-250. II: Nos. 251-538. Index.

(*Catalogus librorum manuscriptorum in Bibliotheca Collegii Corporis Christi in Cantabrigia quos legavit Matthaeus Parkerus Archiepiscopus Cantuariensis.* London 1722. 112 pp. Mss. A.1-D.12. Misc. A-Z and 1-28. 44 other mss.)

(J. Nasmith, *Catalogus librorum manuscriptorum quas collegio Corporis Christi et B. Mariae Virginis in Academia Cantabrigiensi legavit... Matthaeus Parker, Archiepiscopus Cantuariensis.* Cambridge 1777. 429 pp. 482 mss.)

M. R. James, *The Western Manuscripts in the Library of Emmanuel College: A Descriptive catalogue.* Cambridge 1904. xiv, 178 pp. 264 mss.

The same, *A Descriptive Catalogue of the Manuscripts in the Fitzwilliam Museum.* Cambridge 1895. l, 472 pp. 239 mss.

The same, *A Descriptive Catalogue of the McClean Collection of Manuscripts in the Fitzwilliam Museum.* Cambridge 1912. xxxii, 410 pp. 202 mss.

(W. G. Searle, *The Illuminated Manuscripts in the Library of the Fitzwilliam Museum, Cambridge.* Cambridge 1876. lxxiv, 195 pp. 149 mss.)

F. Wormald and P. M. Giles, 'A Handlist of the Additional Manuscripts in the Fitzwilliam Museum,' *Transactions of the Cambridge Bibliographical Society,* vol. I, pt. 3 (1951) 197-207 (nos. 1-65). pt. 4 (1952) 297-309 (nos. 66-133); pt. 5 (1953) 365-375 (nos. 134-182); vol. II, pt. 1 (1954)

1-13 (index).

M. R. James, *A Descriptive Catalogue of the Manuscripts in the Library of Gonville and Caius College.* 2 vols. Cambridge 1907-08. I: Nos. 1-354. II: Nos. 355-721. Index.

The same, *Supplement to the Catalogue of Manuscripts in the Library of Gonville and Caius College.* Cambridge 1914. xxiv, 56 pp. Nos. 722-809. (NN)

(J. J. Smith, *A Catalogue of the Manuscripts in the Library of Gonville and Caius College, Cambridge.* Cambridge 1849. viii, 330 pp. 700 mss.) (NN)

M. R. James, *A Descriptive Catalogue of the Manuscripts in the Library of Jesus College, Cambridge.* London and Cambridge 1895. 122 pp. 77 mss.

The same, *A Descriptive Catalogue of the Manuscripts Other than Oriental in the Library of King's College, Cambridge.* Cambridge 1895. x, 87 pp. 41 mss.

The same, *A Descriptive Catalogue of the Manuscripts in the College Library of Magdalene College, Cambridge.* Cambridge 1909. x, 59 pp. 33 mss. No index.

Bibliotheca Pepysiana: *A Descriptive Catalogue of the Library of Samuel Pepys.* 4 pts. London 1914-40. pt. 1 (1914): '"Sea" Manuscripts,' by J. R. Tanner. pt. 2 (1923): 'Mediaeval Manuscripts,' by M. R. James. 128 pp. Also in Magdalene College.

M. R. James, *A Descriptive Catalogue of the Manuscripts in the Library of Pembroke College, Cambridge.* Cambridge 1905. xl, 314 pp. 308 mss. and some other pieces. With a hand list of printed books to 1500, by E. H. Minns (p. 281-295).

The same, *A Descriptive Catalogue of the Manuscripts in the Library of Peterhouse.* Cambridge 1899. xxxii, 389 pp. 280 mss.

The same, *A Descriptive Catalogue of the Western Manuscripts in the Library of Queen's College, Cambridge.* Cambridge 1905. 29 pp. 34 mss. No index.

The same, *A Descriptive Catalogue of the Manuscripts in the Library of St. Catharine's College, Cambridge.* Cambridge 1925. 27 pp. 18 mss. No index.

The same, *A Descriptive Catalogue of the Manuscripts in the Library of St. John's College, Cambridge.* Cambridge 1913. xx, 389 pp. 507 mss.

(M. Cowie, *A Descriptive Catalogue of the Manuscripts and Scarce Books in the Library of St. John's College, Cambridge.* Cambridge 1842. 162 pp. Mss. A.1-T.18. Also in *Publications of the Cambridge Antiquarian Society, Quarto Series*, I nos. 6 and 8, 1842-43)

M. R. James, *A Descriptive Catalogue of the Manuscripts in the Library of Sidney Sussex College, Cambridge.* Cambridge 1895. viii, 132 pp. 106 mss.

The same, *The Western Manuscripts in the Library of Trinity College, Cambridge: A Descriptive Catalogue.* 4 vols. Cambridge 1900-04. I (1900): Class B. 417 mss. II (1901): Class R. Nos. 418-1024. III (1902): Class O. Nos. 1025-1506. IV (1904): Index.

The same, *A Descriptive Catalogue of the Manuscripts in the Library of Trinity Hall.* Cambridge 1907. viii, 46 pp. 31 mss. No index.

Cambridge, Mass., USA. See De Ricci.
—Harvard University Library.

(Harvard College Library). *Illuminated and Calligraphic Manuscripts.* Cambridge, Mass. 1955. 45 pp. and plates.

The Houghton Library, Report of Accessions. Annual report published since 1941/42, which lists the acquisitions of mss. for each year.

—*Harvard School of Business Administration.

Gertrude R. B. Richards, *Florentine Merchants in the Age of the Medici.* Cambridge Mass. 1932. x, 342 pp. Treats the Selfridge Collection of Medici papers.

Camerino, Italy, Biblioteca Valentiniana e Comunale. See Mazzatinti (1887).

Alphabetical card index, typed.

Catalogo di Manoscritti. 1 folder, arranged alphabetically.

New typed catalogue, by Prof. G. Boccanera. 214 mss.

*Camurana, Italy. See Mazzatinti XIV.

*Cannes, France. See France, *Catalogue Général, Départements* XX; XLI.

*Canosa, Italy. See Mazzatinti VI.

*Canterbury, England. See Bernardus; Schenkl.

H. J. Todd, *Some Account of the Deans of Canterbury . . . to which is added a Catalogue of the Manuscripts in the Church Library.* Canterbury 1793. 298 pp. p. 259-98: 'Catalogue of the Manuscripts in the Church Library.' No index. (CtY)

Catalogue of the Books, both Manuscript and Printed, which are preserved in the Library of Christ Church, Canterbury. (By H. J. Todd.). 1802. cii, 131 pp. Index (p. I-CII). Catalogue of the Manuscripts (p. 109-31). (NNGr)

M. R. James, *The Ancient Libraries of Canterbury and Dover.* Cambridge 1903. xcv, 552 pp. Lists some extant mss. of the Dean and Chapter Library (530ff.). Important. No index.

C. Eveleigh Woodruff, *A Catalogue of the Manuscript Books . . . in the Library of Christ Church, Canterbury.* Canterbury 1911. 60 pp. 106 mss. (Prof. R. A. B. Mynors, Oxford)

The same, *Memorials of the Cathedral and Priory of Christ in Canterbury.* London 1912. 490 pp. Lists a few mss. (402ff.). No shelf marks.

*Capestrano, Italy. See Chiappini.

V. De Bartholomaeis, 'Ricerche Abruzzesi,' *Bullettino dell' Istituto Storico Italiano* VIII (1889) 75-173. p. 77-113: 'I codici capestranesi.' 61 mss. No index.

*Capodistria, Italy. Convento di S. Anna and Biblioteca Civica. See Wickhoff.

B. Ziliotto, 'Codici capodistriani con particolare riflesso a un codice della Batracomiomachia,' *Archeografo Triestino* Ser. III vol. II (1906) 3-39. 3 Latin mss.

*Capua, Italy. See Mazzatinti (1887).

*Carcassonne, France. See France, *Catalogue Général, Départements* XIII; XLI.

Ch. Fierville, 'Étude sur les Manuscrits de la Bibliothèque publique de Carcassonne,'

Mémoires de la Société des arts et des sciences de Carcassonne III (1870) 119-328. Describes 57 mss. (136-179). Indices (315-321). (NN)

*Carignano (Torino), Italy. Conte Ademaro Barbiellini Amidei.

G. Rodolfo, *Di manoscritti e rarità bibliografiche appartenuti alla Biblioteca dei Duchi di Savoia.* Carignano 1912. 97 pp. and plates. No index. The collection was then in the possession of Cav. Ademaro Mola-Boursier dei Conti di Larissè in Carignano. It has since been partly lost or dispersed. (Communication of the owner)

*Carlisle, England. See Bernardus.

*Carpentras, France. See France, *Catalogue Général, Départements* XXXIV-XXXVI.

(C.-G.-A. Lambert, *Catalogue descriptif et raisonné des manuscrits de la Bibliothèque de Carpentras.* 3 vols. Carpentras 1862. I: 645 mss. II: Peiresc collection, 70 mss. III: Others collections. No index of authors.)

Casale Monferrato, Italy. Biblioteca del Seminario. See Mazzatinti (1887).

G. Manacorda, *Alcuni codici notevoli della Biblioteca del Seminario in Casale.* Casale Monferrato 1906. 21 pp. 5 mss. No index. (Casale; micr. at NNC).

G. Cerrato, 'Biblioteca storica del Seminario Vescovile di Casale,' *Revista Storica Italiana* II (1888) 923-25. 18 mss.

Biblioteca del Seminario di Casale Monferrato, Elenco dei Manoscritti. 1 ms. folder. More detailed descriptions of some selected mss. in 2 ms. folders.

Inventario dei codici e manoscritti più importanti di questa Biblioteca, by Sac. Pietro Richetta, Ms a 1-26; b 1-20; c 1-21; d 1-25; e 1-34; f 1-30; g 1-26; MS' a 1-13; b 1-16; c 1-17; d 1-16; e 1-13. (Copy kindly sent by the librarian).

—*Biblioteca Municipale.

G. Manacorda, *I manoscritti della Biblioteca Municipale Leardi in Casale Monferrato.* Casale Monferrato 1905. 31 pp. 37

mss. Index (29-31). Mostly late. (Milan, Biblioteca Nazionale Braidense).

P. D'Ancona, 'Due preziosi cimeli miniati nel Duomo di Casale Monferrato,' *L'Arte* XIX (1916) 85-87. 2 mss.

*Cascia, Italy. See Mazzatinti XIV.

A. Morini, *I manoscritti e gli incunaboli della Biblioteca Comunale di Cascia.* Cascia 1925. 17 pp. 53 mss. (p. 1-11). No Index. (Vatican Library)

*Castelnaudary, France. See France, *Catalogue Général, Départements* XX.

*Castelnuovo, see **Ercegnovi**.

*Castiglione Fiorentino, Italy. See *Manoscritti*; Mazzatinti XXVI; XLIV.

*Castres, France. See France, *Catalogue Général, Départements* XX; XLI.

*Castronovo, Italy, See Mazzatinti III.

Catania, Italy. See Mazzatinti XX; Rühl; *Studi Italiani* V.

—Biblioteca Universitaria. Fondo Universitario.

Ministero della Pubblica Istruzione. Inventario dei Manoscritti della R. Biblioteca Universitaria di Catania, by Nicolò Sardo (1914). Supplements the printed catalogue in Mazzatinti for mss. 139-166 (cf. AB I 5-6 p. 95).

—Fondo Ventimiliano.

F. Strano, *Catalogo ragionato della Biblioteca Ventimilliana esistente nella Regia Università degli Studi di Catania.* Catania 1830. 580 pp. 567-78: Alphabetical list of mss. (DLC)

G. Tamburini, 'I manoscritti della R. Biblioteca Ventimiliana di Catania,' *Archivio Storico per la Sicilia Orientale* VIII (1911) 241-57; IX (1912) 245-76; X (1913) 237-44; 425-32. 118 mss. No index. Incomplete.

Inventario de' Manoscritti Ventimiliani. Centuries not given. Supplements Mazzatinti and the other printed catalogues for mss. 143-153.

—Biblioteche Riunite 'Civica e A. Ursino-Recupero.'

1 ms. folder: *Civica, Mss. de' Fondi vecchio e nuovo, Inventario.* Inside: *Biblioteca*

Civica di Catania. Inventario dei Manoscritti. Mss. A 1-72; B 1-87; C 1-86; D 1-114; E 1-114; F 1-109. Nuovo Fondo A 301-17; B 301-28; C 301-16; D 301-09; E 301-09; F 301-09 (cf. AB VI 550: 481 mss.).

1 ms. folder: *Biblioteca Ursino-Recupero, Inventario dei Manoscritti.* Mss. A 1-70; B 1-79; C 1-77; D 1-42; E 1-100; F 1-69.

*Cattaro, see Kotor.

Cava, Italy. See *Giornale* I; Istituto Storico, *Guida* (Section A); Reifferscheid.

Lettre de l'Abbé de Rozan à *Mr. le Bibliothécaire de la Bibliothèque du Roi à Naples, Naples 1800, Avec la traduction italienne en Aagard (sic)* par le P. Morcaldi. Naples 1822. 204 pp. Discusses a few mss. (DLC)

Codex Diplomaticus Cavensis. 8 vols. Naples 1873-93. Vol. I (1873) App.: 'I manoscritti membranacei della Biblioteca della SS. Trinità di Cava de' Tirreni,' descritti per D. Bernardo Gaetani d'Aragona O.S.B. Biblical mss. Vol. II (1875) App.: The same cont. 2 Patristic mss. Vol. III (1876) App. Mss. of Lombard laws. Vol. IV (1877) App. Frankish laws. Vol. V (1878) App. Bede, etc. Each volume in its appendix describes one or few mss.

P. Guillaume, *Essai historique sur l'Abbaye de Cava.* Cava 1877. 454, clxiv pp. p. cxiii-cxxi: 'Liste des manuscrits de l'Abbaye de Cava.' Lists 76 mss. on parchment and 127 on paper. No index.

L. Mattei-Cerasoli, *Codices Cavenses.* Pars I: *Codices membranacei.* Cava 1935. vii, 132 pp. 65 mss. Not complete.

*Cento, Italy.

A. Pellegrini, *Cenni storici sulla Biblioteca Comunale di Cento.* Lucca 1901. 61 pp. 8 mss. (p. 7-11). No shelf marks. No index.

*Cervera, Spain. See Villanueva.

Cesena, Italy. Biblioteca Malatestiana. See Italy *Statistica* (Sect. A).

J. M. Mucciolus, *Catalogus codicum manuscriptorum Malatestianae Caesenatis Bibliothecae.* 2 vols. in 1. Cesena 1780-84. Vol. I: Plut. I Dextr. 1-XXIX.4. Vol. II:

Plut. II Sin.1-XXIX.4. Each vol. indexed.

R. Zazzeri, *Sui codici e libri a stampa della Biblioteca Malatestiana di Cesena.* Cesena 1887. xxxii, 586 pp. I D1-S XXIX 33. (ICN, micr. at NNC)

Catalogo dei Manoscritti della Biblioteca Comunitativa (1897). 1 ms. vol. cod. 164. 1-167.169.

Catalogo della Biblioteca Piana di Cesena (by R. Zazzeri, 1872). 1 ms. vol. mss. 3.145-377.

*Český Krumlov, Czechoslovakia. See *Soupis.*

*Cette, France. See France, *Catalogue Général, Départements* XIII.

*Chaalis, France. See France, *Catalogue Général, Paris, Institut.*

*Châlons-sur-Marne, France. See France, *Catalogue Général, Départements* III; XLI.

*Chalon-sur-Saône, France. See France, *Catalogue Général, Départements* VI.

*Chambéry, France. See France, *Catalogue Général, Départements* XXI; XLI; Martin.

*Chantilly, France. See France, *Catalogue Général, Paris, Institut*; Omont.

Institut de France, Musée Condé, Chantilly. *Le Cabinet des Livres. Manuscrits.* 3 vols. Paris 1900-1911. I: 427 mss. II: Nos. 428-697. III: Nos. 698-1480. No index. (Morgan Library)

J. Meurgey, *Les principaux manuscrits à peintures du Musée Condé à Chantilly.* Paris 1930. 231 pp. and plates.

*Chapel Hill, North Carolina. See De Ricci.

*Charleville, France. See France, *Catalogue Général, Départements* V (Quarto Series); XLI.

*Charolles, France. See France, *Catalogue Général, Départements* VI.

*Chartres, France. See *Analecta Bollandiana* VIII; France, *Catalogue Général, Départements* XI; XLI. For recent losses, see *Speculum* 24 (1954) 336-7.

(*Catalogue des manuscrits de Bibliothèque de la ville de Chartres.* Chartres 1840. xii, 211 pp. 653 mss. and documents).

Y. Delaporte, *Les manuscrits enluminés de la Bibliothèque de Chartres*. Chartres 1929. xii, 190 pp. 300 mss.

*Châteaudun, France. See France, *Catalogue Général, Départements* XXI; XLI.

*Château-Gontier, France. See France, *Catalogue Général, Départements* XX; XLI.

*Châteauroux, France. See France, *Catalogue Général, Départements* IX.

(*Catalogue des livres imprimés et manuscrits de la Bibliothèque de la Ville de Châteauroux.* (By J. Patureau). Châteauroux 1880. 379 pp. p. 377-379: mss.) (OCl)

*Château-Thierry, France. See France, *Catalogue Général, Départements* XXIV; XLI.

*Chatellerault, France. See France, *Catalogue Général, Départements* IV.

*Chatillon-sur-Seine, France. See France, *Catalogue Général, Départements* VI.

*Chatsworth, England.

Catalogue of the Library at Chatsworth. 4 vols. London 1879. (By J. P. Lacaita). IV 319-30: Alphabetical list of mss. (NNGr)

*Chaumont, France. See France, *Catalogue Général, Départements* XXI.

*Chełmno (Kulm), Poland.

R. Dabel, *Nachricht über die auf der Lehrer-Bibliothek der höheren Bürgerschule zu Kulm vorhandenen Handschriften und alten Drucke.* progr. Kulm 1877. 21 pp. p. 3-7: 1 ms. (Heidelberg, Univ. Library.)

*Chemnitz, see Karl-Marx-Stadt.

*Cherbourg, France. See France, *Catalogue Général, Départements* X; XLI.

*Chiari, Italy. See Mazzatinti XIV.

*Chicago, Ill., USA. See De Ricci.

E. J. Goodspeed and M. Sprengling, *A Descriptive Catalogue of Manuscripts in the Libraries of the University of Chicago.* Chicago (1912). xi, 128 pp. 100 mss. (Nos. 1-44 in Latin).

—The Newberry Library.

The Newberry Library Bulletin (1944ff.). Covers acquisitions of mss. See esp. vol. III, no. 5. (1954) 156; no. 8 (1955) 249; vol. IV, no. 3 (1956) 78-83 ('Manuscript Acquisitions in 1955' by H. Baron).

H. Baron, 'Newberry Library, Acquisitions,' *Renaissance News* VII (1954) 146-150, esp. 146-147.

Typed list of mss. before 1500.

Typed descriptions of mss. of the 16th century.

*Chichester, England. See Schenkl.

Chieti, Italy.

E. Carusi, 'Notizie su codici della Biblioteca Capitolare di Chieti e sulla collezione canonica Teatina del cod. Vat. Reg. 1997,' *Bullettino della R. Deputazione Abruzzese di storia patria* Ser. III vol. IV (1913) 7-90. 4 mss. (p. 10-22). (CtY)

A. Balducci, *Regesto delle Pergamene della Curia Arcivescovile di Chieti.* 2 vols. Casalbordino 1926-29. II: 'Regesto delle pergamene e codici del Capitolo Metropolitano di Chieti.' 69 pp. p. 57: Codici. 5 mss. (DLC)

F. Di Pretoro, 'Pergamene e scritture antiche dell' archivio municipale e manoscritti vari del comune di Chieti conservati nella Biblioteca Provinciale "A. C. De Meis",' *Convegno Storico Abruzzese-Molisano 25-29 marzo 1931, Atti e Memorie* II (1935) 857-61. Not a catalogue. (NN)

*Chiusa (Klausen), Italy. See Wickhoff.

Chiusi, Italy, Museo del Duomo.

Several liturgical mss. See *Mostra Storica Nazionale della Miniatura.*

G. Di Cocco, 'I corali miniati di Monteoliveto Maggiore conservati nella Cattedrale di Chiusi,' *Bollettino d'Arte del Ministero della P(ubblica) Istruzione* IV (1910) 458-80. Mss. A-Y.

P. Lugano, 'Corali e minii di Monte Oliveto Maggiore a Chiusi,' *Rivista Storica Benedettina* VI (1911) 36-55.

*Chojnice (Konitz), Poland.

**H. Deiters, *Die Handschriften und alten Drucke der hiesigen Gymnasialbibliothek.* progr. Conitz. 1875. 32 pp.

*Christchurch, New Zealand. See Taylor.

*Chur, Switzerland.

**Katalog der Kantons-Bibliothek von Graubünden.* I (Chur 1886): *Rhaetica et Helvetica.* 473 pp. Mss.: p. 51-65; 183-230;

470-73. Latin mss. p. 193-230. No index. (NIC)

*Cincinnati, Ohio, U.S.A. See De Ricci.

*Città di Castello, Italy. See Mazzatinti VI.

*Cividale, Italy. See Mazzatinti III.

A. Zorzi, *Notizie, guida e bibliografia dei RR. Museo Archeologico, Archivio e Biblioteca già Capitolari ed Antico Archivio Comunale di Cividale del Friuli.* Cividale 1899. vii, 275 pp. p. 182-201; 214-217: mss. No index. (DLC)

*Clamecy, France. See France, *Catalogue Général, Départements* IV.

*Clermont de l'Oise, France. See France, *Catalogue Général, Départements* XXIV; XLI.

*Clermont-Ferrand, France. See France, *Catalogue Général, Départements* XIV; XLI; Martin.

*Clervaux, Luxembourg. See Leclercq.

Cleveland, Ohio, U.S.A. See De Ricci.

—*National Library of Medicine.

Dorothy M. Schullian and Francis E. Sommer, *A Catalogue of Incunabula and Manuscripts in the Army Medical Library.* New York, n.d. (1948?). XIII, 361 pp. p. 213-262: Alphabetical list of Western mss.

*Clongowes, Ireland. See also under Naas.

*Aubrey S. Gwynn, 'Some Old Books and Manuscripts in the Museum and Library,' *The Clongownian* 1939, 17-21.

*The same, 'Some More Notes about Manuscripts in the Clongowes Library,' *Ibid.* 1944, 11-15.

*Cluny, France. See France, *Catalogue Général, Départements* VI.

Coburg, West Germany. Landesbibliothek. See *Archiv* VIII; *Société française.*

Verzeichnis und Beschreibung der aus der Herzogl. Hof- und Staatsbibliothek herrührenden Handschriften (by Dr. Thilo Krieg 1922). Arranged by subjects. ca. 100 mss.

—Gymnasium Casimirianum. Mss. deposited in the Landesbibliothek. No inventory.

*Cognac, France. See France, *Catalogue Général, Départements* XXI.

Coimbra, Portugal, Biblioteca Geral da Universidade. See *Société française*; Stegmüller.

'Catálogo dos manuscriptos da Bibliotheca da Universidade de Coimbra,' in: *Bibliotheca da Universidade de Coimbra, Archivo Bibliographico* I (1901) 9-12; 41-44; 57-61; 73-76; 89-91; 109-12; 125-28; 137-40; 153-56; 169-72; 185-88 (90 mss.); II (1902) 9-12; 25-28; 41-44; 57-61; 73-78; 89-92; 105-08; 121-24; 153-56; 169-71; 185-89 (Nos. 91-156); III (1903) 10-14; 33-36; 49-53; 65-69; 81-84; 89-92; 105-09; 121-24; 137-40; 153-57; 169-73; 185-90 (Nos. 157-244); IV (1904) 9-12; 25-28; 41-44; 58-60; 73-76; 89-92; 105-09; 121-25; 137-40; 153-56; 169-73; 185-88 (Nos. 245-345); V (1905) 9-12; 26-28; 41-44; 61-64; 77-80; 93-96; 109-12; 125-28; 141-44; 159-62; 179-82; 197-200 (Nos. 346-98); VI (1906) 9-11; 25-28; 41-44; 57-60; 73-76; 89-92; 121-24; 137-40; 153-55; 169-72; 185-88 (Nos. 399-455); VII (1907) 9-12; 25-28; 41-44; 57-59; 137-40; 153-56; 169-72; 185-88 (Nos. 455-69); VIII (1908) 9-12; 25-28; 41-43; 57-61; 73-77 (Nos. 469-78); IX (1909) 9-12; 26-29; 41-44; 57-60; 74-76; 89-91 (Nos. 479-88); X (1910) 25-28; 41-43; 57-59; 105-07; 121-22; 137-40; 153-56; 169-72; 185-86 (Nos. 488-90); XI (1911) 9-11; 25-26; 41-43; 57-59; 73-75; 89-91; 105-08; 121-24; 137-40; 153-55; 169-71; 185-87 (Nos. 490-99); XII (1912) 129-32; 141-44 (Nos. 500-04); XIII (1913) 9-12; 21-24; 33-36 (Nos. 504-05). (NN)

'Catálogo dos manuscritos da Biblioteca da Universidade de Coimbra.' In: *Boletim Bibliográfico da Biblioteca da Universidade de Coimbra* I (1914) 24-27; 74-77; 136-39; 181-83; 227-29; 285-87; 324-25; 370-75; 422-25; 468-69; 514-18; 562-65 (Nos. 505-07); II (1915) 1-4; 33-36; 65-68; 89-92; 117-20; 145-48; 169-72; 233-25; 265-68; 293-95; 325-28 (Nos. 507-10); III (1916) 1-3; 45-49; 114-18; *236-40 (Nos. 510-12); IV (1917) 61-65; 143-49 (Nos.

512-16); V (1918) 1-11 (Nos. 516-18); VI (1919-21) 43-49 (No. 519); VII (1922-25) 69-80 (Nos. 520-25, by A. Mendes Simões de Castro); VIII (1927) 89-130; 299-322 (Nos. 526-28, by A. Gomes da Rocha Madahil); IX (1928-30) 145-80; 440-65 (Nos. 529-38); X (1932-33) 250-308 (Nos. 539-47); XI (1933-34) 111-94 (Nos. 548-55, by A. A. Ferreira da Cruz). No index. (NN, set incomplete; more complete at MH).

A. G. da Rocha Madahil, 'Os Codices de Santa Cruz de Coimbra.' *Ibid.* VIII (1927) 379-420 (7 mss.); IX (1928-30) 192-229; 352-83 (Nos. 8-53); X (1932-33) 55-105 (Nos. 54-95 and chart. 1-12); XI (1933-34) 50-96 (Nos. 13-50). No index. (NN)

Boletim da Biblioteca da Universidade. Suplemento ao vol. XII. Catálogo de Manuscritos. Códices N.os 556 a 630. Coimbra 1935. 215 pp.—*Códices N.os 631 a 705.* 303 pp.—*Códices N.os 706 a 821.* 224 pp. —*Códices N.os 822 a 1080.* 224 pp.—*Códices N.os 1081 a 1311.* 223 pp.—*Códices N.os 1312 a 1431.* 224 pp.—*Códices e Maços N.os 1432 a 1511.* Coimbra 1936. 195 pp. No index. (NN)

—*Suplemento ao vol. XIII. Códices e Maços N.os 1512 a 1634.* 1936. 175 pp.—*N.os 1635 a 1708.* 1937. 213 pp. No index.

Publicações da Biblioteca da Universidade. Catálogo dos manuscritos da restauracão da Biblioteca da Universidade de Coimbra, by A. A. Ferreira da Cruz. Coimbra 1936. 79 pp. Late historical material.

Publicações da Biblioteca Geral da Universidade. Catálogo de manuscritos (Códices 1 a 250), by A. M. Simões de Castro. Coimbra 1940. 258 pp. (*Códices 251 a 555*). 1945. 750 pp.—(*Códices 1709 a 1833*), by C. Pegado. 1941. 158 pp. —(*Códices 1931 a 2046*). 1946. 199 pp. No index.

—(*Códices 2205 a 2309*), by A. Lopes de Almeida e Sousa. Coimbra 1942. xi, 287 pp.—(*Códices 2529 a 2625*). Coimbra 1946. 372 pp.

(Faculdade de Letras da Universidade de Coimbra, Instituto de Estudios Clássicos).

Catálogo dos manuscritos da Biblioteca Geral da Universidade de Coimbra relativos à antiguidade Clássica, by A. da Costa Ramalho and J. de Castro Nunes. Coimbra 1945. XXIII, 116 pp. No index. Card indices by authors and subjects. *Ca.* 3000 mss. The printed catalogues are not yet complete.

Colmar, France. See *Archiv* VIII.
—Bibliothèque de la Ville.

A.-M.-P. Ingold, 'Les manuscrits des anciennes maisons religieuses d'Alsace,' *Le Bibliographe Moderne* I (1897) 209-215; 375-385; II (1898) 113-124; 255-272. Describes many mss. now in the Colmar library.

J. Leclercq, 'Textes cisterciens à la Bibliothèque de Colmar,' *Analecta Sacri Ordinis Cisterciensis* X (1954) 308-313. (NN)

Manuscrits de Colmar. Ms. inventory, arranged by subjects. 717 nos. (with some gaps).

—*Bibliothèque du Consistoire.

(*Catalogue de la Bibliothèque du Consistoire de Colmar et de la Bibliothèque Théologique des Pasteurs du Haut-Rhin.* Preface signed by A. Schaeffer and L. Horst. Colmar 1868. VI, 126 pp. Arranged by subjects. Mss. listed among the printed books.) (NN)

F. Landmann, 'Die spätmittelalterliche Predigt der Franziskaner-Konventualen nach den Handschriften der Konsistorialbibliothek zu Colmar,' *Archiv für Elsässische Kirchengeschichte* V (1930) 19-88. No index. (MH)

The same, 'Drei Predigt- und Seelsorgsbüchlein von Konrad Dreuben,' *Ibid.* VIII (1933) 209-240. (MH)

P. Bolchert, 'Catalogue de la Bibliothèque du Consistoire de l'Église de la Confession d'Augsbourg à Colmar: Manuscrits,' *Annuaire de Colmar* V (1955) 14-37. 55 mss.

*Colocza, see **Kalocsa**.

Cologne, see **Köln**.

Como, Italy. Biblioteca Comunale. See Mazzatinti II.

Biblioteca Comunale di Como, Manoscritti, Catalogo di posizione (by F. Fossati, 1888).

More detailed than Mazzatinti who used it. Shelf marks added in red ink.

Codici latini fino al sec. XVI (1953). Typed list, contains a few additional mss.

Catalogo dei manoscritti di proprietà di D. Santo Monti ora di proprietà del dottor Ingegnere Alberto Riva, entrati nella Biblioteca Comunale di Como il 5 dicembre 1947.

—Seminario Maggiore. See Leclercq. 18 mss. mostly from Morimondo. No inventory. Mss. 2-8 are listed on a piece of card board.

*Compiègne, France. See France, *Catalogue Général, Départements* XXIV and XLI.

*Conches, France. See *Cabinet Historique*; France, *Catalogue Général, Départements* II and XLI.

*Condé-sur-Noireau, France. See France, Catalogue *Général, Départements* X; XLI.

*Condom, France. See France, *Catalogue Général, Départements* XXIV; XLI.

*Conegliano, Italy. See Mazzatinti XVI.

*Confolens, France. See France, *Catalogue Général, Départements* XXI; XXXI.

*Constantinople, see Istanbul.

Copenhagen, see København.

*Corbeil, France. See France, *Catalogue général, Départements* III; XLI.

Cordoba, Spain. Archivo Catedralicio (Biblioteca del Cabildo.)

See Beer (Section A); Fransen; *Neues Archiv* VI; *Serapeum* VII.

R. Criado, 'Nota sobre los manuscritos teológicos postridentinos de las bíbliotecas públicas de Cordoba,' *Archivo teológico Granadino* IX (1946) 115-25 (DCU)

Alphabetical card file, more complete than the printed lists.

*Corte, Corsica. See France, *Catalogue Général, Départements* IX.

Cortona, Italy. See Mazzatinti XVIII; XX.

(G. Mancini, *I manoscritti della Libreria del Comune e dell' Accademia Etrusca di Cortona.* Cortona 1884. xxxi, 284 pp. 447 mss.) (MH)

*Corvey, Germany. See *Archiv* IV; VIII; Lehmann, *Corveyer Studien*: *Serapeum* III.

*Coulommiers, France. See France, *Catalogue Général, Départements* IX.

*Courtrai, Belgium. See *Catalogue général* III.

**Catalogue des livres et manuscrits de la Bibliothèque de feu M. Goethals-Vercruysse.* Courtrai 1875. 354 pp. Mss.: p. 291-344. (*Catalogue de la Bibliothèque de M. F.-V. Goethals. Manuscrits,* by A. Pinchart. Brussels 1878. 467 pp. 2335 items. Late material.) (MH)

*Coutances, France. See France, *Catalogue Général, Départements* X.

*Coventry, England. See Bernardus.

The Grammar School Library is now dispersed. Cf. Mary D. Harris, 'The Manuscripts of Coventry,' *Transactions of the Bristol and Gloucestershire Archaeological Society* XXXVII (1914) 187-193. (NN)

Cremona, Italy. See Mazzatinti LXX; *Neues Archiv* XVII.

—*Archivio Storico Comunale.

Isabella Pettenazzi, 'A proposito del ritrovamento di frammenti di codici nell' Archivio Storico Comunale,' *Bollettino Storico Cremonese* XIX (1954) 170-172. (NN)

The same, 'Di un frammento del « Brutus » del sec. XV,' *Ibid.* XX (1955-57) 83-97. (NN)

—Biblioteca Governativa.

S. Bassi, 'Di un recente prezioso acquisto di codici e incunabuli per la Libreria Çivica...' *Annali della Biblioteca Governativa e Libreria Civica di Cremona* I (1948, published 1949) 23-33. Lists 16 mss. transferred from the Museo Civico. No index.

Fondo Libreria Civica, Manoscritti. Alphabetical card index. 1 box (AB II 3 p. 52). The printed catalogue in Mazzatinti LXX covers only the Fondo Governativo.

*Inventario dei manoscritti della Libreria Civica. 1 ms. vol. Summary list of 907 mss. (Communication of the librarian)

—*Duomo.

V. Dainotti, 'I corali della Cattedrale di Cremona,' *Accademie e Biblioteche d'Italia* XIII (1939) 26-44.

I corali del Duomo di Cremona e la miniatura cremonese nel quattrocento (Annali della Biblioteca Governativa e Libreria Civica di Cremona VIII 1955). Pt. II (1956): F. Zanoni, 'Catalogo descrittivo comprendente i Corali di S. Agata.' cx pp. and plates. p. xli-lxxxvii: 28 mss. of the Duomo, and 3 mss. of S. Agata.

*Crépy-en-Valoîs, France. See France, *Catalogue Général, Départements* XLI.

*Crescentino, Italy. See Mazzatinti (1887).

Cues, Germany. See Kues.

*Culemborg, Holland. See *Société française*.

*Cuneo, Italy. See Mazzatinti (1887).

*Danzig. See Gdańsk.

Darmstadt, West Germany. Hessische Landes- und Hochschulbibliothek. See *Archiv* VIII; Bernards, Gercken· Institut de recherches, Leclercq; *Neues Archiv*, XI, XIII; Schmïdt.

Ph. A. F. Walther, *Beiträge zur näheren Kenntniss der Grossherzoglichen Hofbibliothek zu Darmstadt*. Darmstadt 1867. 158 pp. Lists 50 mss. (p. 126-43). No index. (NIC)

The same, *Neue Beiträge zur näheren Kenntniss der grossherzoglichen Hofbibliothek in Darmstadt*. Darmstadt 1871. 168 pp. p. 93-128: 'Mittheilungen über Handschriften.' Lists 184 mss. (DLC)

F. W. E. Roth, 'Lateinische Gedichte des XII.-XIV. Jahrhunderts. Aus Darmstadter Handschriften,' *Romanische Forschungen* VI (1891) 9-16.

The same, 'Mittheilungen zur Literatur des Mittellateins. Aus Darmstadter Handschriften,' *Ibid.* 17-56.

The same, 'Mittheilungen aus mittellateinischen Handschriften der Hofbibliothek zu Darmstadt,' *Ibid.* 239-70.

The same, 'Mittheilungen aus lateinischen Handschriften zu Darmstadt, Mainz, Coblenz und Frankfurt a. M.' *Ibid.* 429-61. No indices.

Standortsverzeichnis der Handschriften der Landesbibliothek Darmstadt. 1 typed volume. 3967 mss. Sketchy. Centuries not given.

Zettelkatalog. By subjects. 10 boxes. (Cf. Born 205).

Verfasserregister. 6 boxes. (Cf. Born 206). New handwritten catalogue in 4 boxes. Arranged by subjects.

Typed notes taken by Mme. Vernet in 1951 are available at the Institut de Recherches et d'Histoire des Textes in Paris.

*Debrecen, Hungary. See Radó.

A. Gabriel, 'A debreceni könyvtar középκori kéziratai,' *Magyar Könyvszemle*, Ser. III, vol. LXVI (1942) 345-63. 2 mss.

****Z. Varga, *A debreceni református föiskola nagykönyvtára irásban és képben.* 2 vols. Debrecen 1934. I p. 15-22: mss.

*Card file.

*Děčín, Czechoslovakia. See under Praha.

Dessau, East Germany. Landesbibliothek.

Katalog der Herzoglichen Hofbibliothek zu Dessau. 15 vols. Dessau 1829-1919. Lists a few mss. among the printed books. (DLC)

Katalog der Herzoglich Anhaltischen Behoerden-Bibliothek zu Dessau. Dessau 1896. VII, 800, 237 pp. Mss. listed among the printed books, marked with a blue cross in the library copy. (DLC)

Georgsbibliothek. Alphabetical card file in 4 boxes, covers mss. and edd.

Ausgelagerte Bestaende. Typed lists.

Typed list of mss. returned from Russia in 1958. There are no inventories for the Georgsbibliothek or the Hofbibliothek.

Detmold, West Germany. Lippische Landesbibliothek.

F. W. Wellner, *Erster Versuch einer Nachricht von der Hochgräfl. Lipp. öffentl. Bibliothek zu Detmold worinn zugleich einige Handschriften auf Pergament nä*her *beschrieben werden.* Progr. Lemgo, 1773, 20 pp. 4 mss. (Detmold)

The same, *Fortgesetzte Anzeige der auf der Hochgräfl. Lipp. Öffentlichen Bibliothek befindlichen Pergamen und anderer Handschriften.* Progr. Lemgo, 1774. 15 pp. mss. no. 5-12 (Detmold)

Katalog der Manuscripte der öffentl. Bibliothek zu Detmold (1841-64). 154 mss.

*Detroit, Michigan, U.S.A. See De Ricci.

*Deventer, Holland.

Catalogus der Handschriften berustende op de Athenaeum-Bibliotheek te Deventer. Deventer 1892. 80 pp. 113 mss. before 1600. Preface signed by J.C.V.S. No index. (NN)

(*Catalogus Bibliothecae publicae Daventriensis.* 4 vols. Deventer 1832-80. I, p. 235-254; II 1864, p. 260-261; III 1872, p. 215; IV, p. 274-280: mss.) (DLC)

*Diebau, see Dybowo.

*Dieppe, France. See France, *Catalogue Général, Départements* II.

*Dignano, Italy. See Wickhoff.

*Digne, France. See France, *Catalogue Général, Départements* IX.

*Dijon, France. See France, *Catalogue Général, Départements* V; XLI; *Universités*; *Sociétés*; Martin.

Dillingen, West Germany. Kreis- und Studienbibliothek. See Leclercq.

Standkatalog XV. Manuscripte. 1 ms. folder. 254 mss., mostly in Latin.

*Dinan, France. See France, *Catalogue Général, Départements* IV; XLI.

*Dôle, France. See France, *Catalogue Général, Départements* XIII.

*Domfront, France. See France, *Catalogue Général, Départements* X.

*Domodossola, Italy. See Mazzatinti XXXIV.

G. Bustico, *Catalogo descrittivo dei manoscritti della biblioteca Galletti di Domodossola.* Domodossola 1910. 20 pp. 57 mss. No index. (Milan, Bibl. Naz. Braidense)

—Monte Calvario. See under Stresa.

*Donaueschingen, West Germany.

K. A. Barack, *Die Handschriften der Fürstlich Fürstenbergischen Hofbibliothek zu Donaueschingen.* Tübingen 1865. 666 pp. 925 mss. A few mss. were sold.

*Nachtrag des Handschriften-Katalogs. A folder of ms. sheets, arranged by subjects. Describes 300 mss. and frs. (Communication of the librarian)

*Dorpat. See Tartu.

*Dortmund, West Germany. Stadt- und Landesbibliothek. See *Archiv* XI.

*Ca. 50 Latin mss. before 1600, listed in: *Aus 1000 Jahren (900-1900): Kostbarkeiten in Handschrift und Buchdruck* (Dortmund 1929), VI, 38 pp. p. 1-4: mss.

*Douai, France. See *Analecta Bollandiana* XX; France, *Catalogue Général, Départements* VI (Quarto Series); XLI.

H. R. Duthillœul, *Catalogue descriptif et raisonné des manuscrits de la Bibliothèque de Douai* . . . Douai 1846. xxxix, 548 and viii, 135 pp. 955 mss. Index: p. 526ff. (NN)

*Downside Abbey, England.

A. Watkin, 'Some Manuscripts in the Downside Abbey Library,' *The Downside Review* LVIII (N.S. XXXIX, 1940) 438-451 (3 mss.); LIX (N.S. XL, 1941) 75-92 (nos. 4-5). (NN)

The same, 'Note on a Salisbury Missal,' *Ibid.* LX (N.S. XLI, 1942) 105-106. (NN)

*Draguignan, France. See France, *Catalogue Général, Départements* XIV.

*Dresden, East Germany. See Bruck.

F. Schnorr von Carolsfeld and L. Schmidt, *Katalog der Handschriften der Kgl. öffentlichen Bibliothek zu Dresden.* 4 vols. Leipzig 1882-1923. I (1882): A.1-H.206. II (1883): J.1-M.299. III (1906): N.1-R.310 and a.1-d.101. IV (1923): e.1-n. app. 1-183 and music 1-176. Each volume indexed.

(*Die Merckwürdigkeiten der kgl. Bibliothek zu Dresden.* 3 vols. Dresden 1743-46. By J. Chr. Götze. Each vol. indexed.) (NN)

(F. A. Ebert, *Geschichte und Beschreibung der kgl. öffentlichen Bibliothek zu Dresden.* Leipzig 1822. 358 pp. p. 263-90: Latin mss. nos. 104-95).

(K. Falkenstein, *Beschreibung der Königlichen öffentlichen Bibliothek zu Dresden.* Dresden 1839. IV, 887 pp. p. 173-467: List of mss., by subjects.) (NN)

The library recently acquired most of the mss. from Moritzburg.

O. Meltzer, *Mittheilungen über die Bibliothek der Kreuzschule.* progr. Dresden 1880. XXVIII, 35 pp. p. xxiii-xxv: 11 mss. (Erlangen, University Library). This Library was destroyed during the last war.

*Dreux, France. See France, *Catalogue Général, Départements* IX.

Dublin, Ireland. See *Analecta Bollandiana* XLVI; *Archivum Franciscanum* VII, Bernardus; Frere; Great Britain, *Historical Manuscripts Commission*; Schenkl. See also under Killiney.

T. K. Abbott, *Catalogue of the Manuscripts in the Library of Trinity College, Dublin...* Dublin 1900. 606 pp. 1711 mss. and other collections. Valid shelf marks in a concordance. (p. xvi-xxvi). (NN)

M. Esposito, 'Classical Manuscripts in Irish Libraries,' *Hermathena* XIX (1922) no. 42 (1920) 123-40. 23 mss. at Trinity College.

Western Illuminated Manuscripts from the Library of Sir Chester Beatty. Exhibited in the Library of Trinity College, Dublin. Dublin 1955. Unpaged. 42 mss. including a few belonging to Trinity College. No index.

Catalogue of T.C.D., by Monck Mason. 5 ms. vols. More detailed than Abbott, but does not cover recent acquisitions.

—Franciscan Library. See under Killiney.

—Jesuits' Library. No inventory.

—*Marsh' Library.

J. R. Scott and N. J. D. White, *Catalogue of the Manuscripts Remaining in Marsh's Library, Dublin.* Dublin 1913. 137 pp. Mostly modern.

*Dubrovnik (Ragusa), Yugoslavia. See Wickhoff.

—*Knjižnica Male Braće (formerly Franciscan Library).

Biblioteca di Fra Innocenzo Ciulich nella libreria dei RR.PP. Francescani di Ragusa. Supplemento all' Osservatore Dalmato. Zara 1860. 427 pp. (by G. A. Casnacich). p. 1-209: 1132 mss. (DLC)

M. Brlek, *Rukopisi Knjižnice Male Braće u Dubrovniku.* Vol. I (all published). Zagreb 1952. 328 pp. and plates. 293 mss. Not complete.

—*Dominikanski Samostan.

K. Vojnović, 'Prilozi k arhivalnijem pabircima dubrovačkijem,' *Starine* XXVIII

(1896) 1-96. 82 mss. (p. 1-31). No index. (NN)

K. Balić, 'Alte Handschriften der Dominikanerbibliothek in Dubrovnik/Ragusa,' in: *Aus der Geisteswelt des Mittelalters* (Beiträge zur Geschichte der Philosophie und Theologie des Mittelalters, Supplementband III pt. 1; Münster 1935) p. 3-18. No index.

*Chirographotheca Coenobii S. Dominici de Ragusio ordinis Praedicatorum, sive Codices MSS. qui in Bibliotheca eiusdem Coenobii asservantur (by P.S.M. Cerva, 1751). 328 mss. Some of them now lost. (Communication of the librarian).

**Card file. 217 mss. (Communication of the librarian)

—*Naučna Biblioteka.

S. Kastropil, *Rukopisi Naučne Biblioteke u Dubrovniku.* Vol. I (all published). Zagreb 1954. 432 pp. and plates. Covers 418 (out of 880) mss.

*Duino, Italy. See Wickhoff.

*Dulwich, England. See under London.

*Dunedin, New Zealand. See Taylor.

*Dunkerque, France. See France, *Catalogue Général, Départements* XXVI.

*Durham, England. See Holtzmann (Section A); Bernardus; Mynors; Schenkl.

—*Cathedral Library.

T. Rud, *Codicum manuscriptorum ecclesiae Cathedralis Dunelmensis catalogus classicus.* Durham 1825. 456 pp.

—*University Library.

Catalogi veteres librorum ecclesiae cathedralis Dunelmensis. (Publications of the Surtees Society no. VII.) London 1838. 238 pp. p. 136-91: 'Mss. in Bishop Cosin's Library, Durham.'

J. Conway Davis, 'Bishop Cosin's Manuscripts,' *The Durham Philobiblon*, Vol. I, no. 2 (1949) 10-16. 32 mss.

*A Catalogue of Manuscripts constituting the collections known under the name of the Mickleton and Spearman mss. presented by the Rev. George Wasey, A.M. to the Honourable & Right Reverend Shute (Barrington) *Lord Bishop of Dur-*

ham and by him presented in the year one thousand eight hundred and seventeen to the Library founded by Bishop Cosin at Durham. 107 mss. (Communication of the librarian).

*Durham, North Carolina, U.S.A. See De Ricci.

Düsseldorf, West Germany. See *Archiv* XI ; Bernards ; Leclercq; Schmidt; Schumpp.

***Bibliotheca Vossiana bibliothecae gymnasii Dusseldorpiensis adiuncta . . .* Düsseldorf 1851. p. 29-33: mss.

Studien zur niederrheinischen Geschichte: Festschrift zur Feier des Einzugs in das neue Schulgebäude des Königlichen Gymnasiums. progr. Düsseldorf 1906. 62 pp. p. 14-24: K. Bone, 'Zwei illuminierte Manuskripte der Bibliothek des Königl. Gymnasiums zu Düsseldorf.' p. 25-35: H. Willemsen, 'Die Handschriften der Gymnasialbibliothek.' 5 mss. No index. (Erlangen, University Library.)

—Landes- und Stadtbibliothek.

Illustrierte Handschriften und Frühdrucke aus dem Besitz der Landes- und Stadtbibliothek Düsseldorf. (By E. Galley). Düsseldorf 1951. 16 pp.

Katalog der illustrierten Handschriften und ausgewählter Frühdrucke aus der Landes- und Stadtbibliothek Düsseldorf. (Düsseldorf 1951). 16 pp. p. 1-14: 77 mss.

Katalog der Handschriften. Mss A 1-18; B 1-206; C 1-106; D 1-37; E 1-28; F 1-38; G 1-77.

*Dybowo, Poland. See *Archiv* XI.

*Dzikow. See under Kraków.

Edinburgh, Scotland. See *Analecta Bollandiana* XLVII; Schenkl.

—National Library of Scotland.

For the Advocates' manuscripts, there is a complete list in the Old Folio Catalogue in 9 vols., arranged by subjects (Charters, Chartularies, Genealogical and Heraldic, Historical, Law, Miscellaneous, Northern, Poetry and Romance, State Papers). (Cf. Born 296-97?).

A Catalogue of the Mediaeval Manuscripts in the Library of the Faculty of Advocates at Edinburgh..., by Catherine Robina Borland (1906-08), 3 ms. vols. I: Theology. II: Law, History, Chartularies. III: Poetry and Romance; Classics; Science. More detailed than the old folio catalogue, but selective.

Index to Folio Catalogues of Advocates' Mss. 2 typed vols. I: A-L. II: M-Z. (Cf. Born 295 and 298?)

National Library of Scotland. Catalogue of Manuscripts Acquired since 1925. I, Edinburgh 1938. 551 pp. 1800 mss. Not complete.

National Library of Scotland. Catalogue of Manuscripts acquired since 1925. 3 typed vols. I: mss. 1801-2740. II: 2741-3216. III: 3217-3873. Supplements the printed catalogue of 1938. Cf. Born 299.

—*New College.

Catalogue of the Printed Books and Manuscripts in the Library of the New College Edinburgh. Edinburgh 1868. (By J. Laing). 939 pp. p. 935-37: alphabetical list of Latin mss. (NNUT)

—*Royal Observatory.

Catalogue of the Crawford Library of the Royal Observatory Edinburgh. Edinburgh 1890. viii, 499 pp. p. 485-497: Alphabetical list of mss. No shelf marks. No index.

—University Library.

Catherine R. Borland, *A Descriptive Catalogue of the Western Medieval Manuscripts in Edinburgh University Library.* Edinburgh 1916. 359 pp. 230 mss. Shelf marks in parentheses. Not complete.

List of Manuscript Books in the Collection of David Laing, LL.D. (by the Rev. John Anderson, privately printed, with ms. additions). Mostly superseded by Miss Borland's catalogue. I 1-350, II 1-716, III 1-821. (micr. at NNC)

Shelf Catalogue. 3 ms. vols. Section I: Laing mss. (La III 1-821). Section II: Non-Laing mss. Vol. I: Da-Dc (most Latin mss. are in section Db). Vol. II: Dd-Do (lists some mss. and many edd.).

*Eger, Hungary. See Radó.

***Az egri érseki könyvtar szakszerü cimje-
gyzéke.* (By M. Michalek). 2 vols. Eger
1893, and supplements of 1894 and 1900.
Mss. described in vol. I, pt. 2.

E. Varjum, 'Adatokaz egri érsekmegyei
könyvtár ismertetéséhez,' *Magyar Könyvszemle*, Ser. II, vol. X (1902) 27-49. (NN)

Eichstätt, West Germany. See Cooper
(Section A); *Archiv* IX.

J. Lechner, *Die spätmittelalterliche Hand-
schriftengeschichte der Benediktinerinnen-
abtei St. Walburg/Eichstätt* (*By*) (Eich-
stätter Studien II). Münster 1937. 103 pp.
p. 9-19: 7 Latin mss. (NjP)

—Seminarbibliothek.

*Handschriften der Seminarbibliothek Eich-
stätt nach Nummern.* 1 box of ms. sheets.
426 mss.

—Staatliche Bibliothek.

*Handschriften der Staatlichen Bibliothek
Eichstätt nach der Reihenfolge der Nummern.* 1 box of typed sheets. 768 mss.

Einsiedeln, Switzerland. Stiftsbibliothek.
See *Archiv* I; VII; VIII; Bruckner I and
V; Buchon; Haenel; Halm; Stelling-Mi-
chaud.

Gabr. Meier, *Catalogus codicum manu scriptorum qui in Bibliotheca Monasterii Ein-
sidlensis O.S.B. servantur.* I, Einsiedeln
1899. 422 pp. 500 mss. Not complete.
(NN)

Morel, 'Einsiedler Handschriften der lateinischen Kirchenväter bis zum IX. Jahrhundert,' *Sitzungsberichte der Kaiserlichen
Akademie der Wissenschaften* [Vienna],
Philosophisch-Historische Classe LV (1867)
243-61. Arranged alphabetically by authors.

Gabr. Meier, *Heinrich von Ligerz, Biblio-
thekar von Einsiedeln im 14. Jahrhundert.*
(Centralblatt für Bibliothekswesen, Beiheft XVII). Leipzig 1896. 68 pp. Describes many mss. (p. 42-66). No index.

*Catalogus codicum manuscriptorum Bibl.
Monrii. Eins.* III: mss. 502-774. Supplements printed catalogue.

(No title). A pack of typed sheets. Describes mss. 759-1000.

*Eisleben, East Germany. See *Neues Archiv* VIII.

*Elbeuf, France. See France, *Catalogue Général, Départements* II.

*Elbląg (Elbing) Poland. See *Archiv* XI.

****J. A. Merz, progr. Elbing 1840.

Katalog der Stadtbibliothek zu Elbing. (By
L. Neubaur.) 2 vols. Elbing 1893-94. II
563-97: Mss. arranged by subjects and
alphabetically. (Mon. Germ. Hist. Munich)

*Emden, West Germany.

***Verzeichniss sämmltlicher Bücher, die auf
dem Saal der grossen Kirche zu Emden vorhanden sind.* pt. 3 (Emden 1852) p. 184-
88: mss.

*Emmerich, West Germany. Gymnasiumsbibliothek.

***1200 Jahre Gymnasium Emmerich, Festschrift aes Staatlichen Gymnasiums zu
Emmerich zur Jahrhundertfeier der Wie-
deraufrichtung verbunden mit der Zwölf-
hundertjahrfeier des Bestehens.* Ed. H.
Disselbeck. Emmerich 1932. (340 pp.,
numbered irregularly, and plates). pt. III,
p. 3-17: Gleumes, 'Die Handschriften.'
2nd ed. Emmerich 1958. (7), XII, 333 pp.
and plates. p. 215-28: Gleumes, 'Die
Handschriften.' 19 mss. No index. (Revised by Dr. Reis). (NNC)

*Empoli, Italy. See Mazzatinti (1887).

*Engelberg, Switzerland. See Bruckner
VIII.

B. Gottwald, *Catalogus codicum manuscriptorum qui asservantur in Bibliotheca Monasterii O.S.B. Engelbergensis in Helvetia.*
Freiburg i. Br. 1891. 327 pp. 914 mss.

*Épernay, France. See France, *Catalogue
Général, Départements* XXIV; XLI.

*Épinal, France. See France, *Catalogue
Général, Départements* III (Quarto Series).

*Ercegnovi (Castelnuovo), Yugoslavia. See
Wickhoff.

Erfurt, East Germany. See *Archiv* VIII; XI;
Neues Archiv XXII; XXVII; Wirtgen.

—Domarchiv.

Card file. Mss. Th. 1-59; Liturg. 1-23; Erf.
1-39; Philol. 1-16; Med. 1-7; Ius 1-27;
Hist. 1-12; Fragmenta latina 1-105.

—Wissenschaftliche Bibliothek der Stadt.
F. Kritzius, *De codicibus Bibliothecae Amplonianae Erfurtensis potioribus...* progr. Erfurt 1850. 50 pp. p. 1-25: 50 mss. No index. Cf. *Serapeum* XI.
W. Schum, *Beschreibendes Verzeichnis der Amplonianischen Handschriften-Sammlung zu Erfurt.* Berlin 1887. 1010 pp. 957 mss. The same, *Exempla codicum Amplonianorum Erfurtensium.* Berlin 1882. 28 pp. and plates. 55 mss.
Codices Erfurtenses. Card file in 3 bound vols. I: CE 2° and 4°. II: 8°. III: Mss. transferred to Berlin or to the archive in Erfurt.

*Erlangen, West Germany.
Katalog der Handschriften der Universitätsbliothek Erlangen. Neubearbeitung. Vol. I (Erlangen 1928): H. Fischer, *Die lateinischen Pergamenthandschriften.* 634 pp. 436 mss. Vol. II (1936): The same, *Die lateinischen Papierhandschriften.* xxix, 699 pp. 1209 mss. Vol. VI (1936): E. Lutze, *Die Bilderhandschriften.* 285 pp. (Pierpont Morgan Library.)
(J. C. Irmischer, *Handschriften-Katalog der Kgl. Universitäts-Bibliothek zu Erlangen.* Frankfurt 1852. 472 pp. 1911 mss.)
(E. von Steinmeyer), *Die jüngeren Handschriften der Erlanger Universitätsbibliothek.* Erlangen 1913. iv, 241 pp. (Vatican Library)

Escorial, El, Spain. See Grubbs (Section A under Richardson); Carini; Gachard; Haenel; Loewe and Hartel; *Revista.*
F. Mateu y Llopis, 'Los catalogos de manuscritos de la Biblioteca del Escorial,' *Hispania Sacra* III (1950) 223-230.
G. Antolín, *Catálogo de los códices latinos de la Real Biblioteca del Escorial.* 5 vols. Madrid 1910-23. Vol. I (1910): a I 1-d IV 32. Vol. II (1911): e I 1-k III 31. Vol. III (1913): L I 2-R III 23. Vol. IV (1916): S I 1-Z IV 22 and others. Vol. V (1923) p. 504-12: Additional mss. Each vol. (except the last) is indexed.
(A. Llacayo y Santa María, *Antiguos manuscritos de historia, ciencia y arte militar*

medicina y literarios existentes en la Biblioteca del Monasterio de San Lorenzo del Escorial. Seville 1878. 344 pp. No index.) (DLC)
*F. Rozanski, *Relación sumaria sobre los códices y manuscritos del Escorial.* Madrid 1888. 100 pp. 14 mss. No index. (NIC). Also in: *Revista Contemporánea* LXXI (1888) 113-27; 272-86; 387-405; 474-85; 615-27; LXXII (1888) 58-70; 187-94; 237-48. (NN)
G. Antolín, 'Real Biblioteca del Escorial: Códices latinos procedentes de Venecia,' *La Ciudad de Dios* CXVIII (1919) 402-16; 452-62; 'Códices latinos procedentes de Flandes,' *Ibid.* CXIX (1919) 37-45; 'Códices latinos procedentes de Roma,' *Ibid.* 125-33; 'Códices... de la librería de D. Diego Hurtado de Mendoza,' *Ibid.* 374-84; 'Códices ... de Francia,' *Ibid.* CXX (1920) 106-16; 'Códices ... de D. Silvestre Maurolico,' *Ibid.* 339-49; 'Códices ... de Gonzalez Pérez,' *Ibid.* CXXI (1920) 117-28; 'Códices ... de la Capilla real de Granada,' *Ibid.* 282-91. (DLC)
Iole Ruggeri, 'Manoscritti italiani nella Biblioteca dell' Escuriale,' *Bibliofilia* XXXII (1930) 421-441; XXXIII (1931) 138-149; 201-209; 308-318; XXXIV (1932) 52-61; 127-139; 245-255; 381-392; XXXV (1933) 20-28. No index.
*A. Cordoliani, 'Les manuscrits de comput ecclésiastique de la Bibliothèque de l'Escorial,' *La Ciudad de Dios* CLXIII (1951) 277-317. (MH)

*Essen, West Germany. See Lampen.
*Este (Padova), Italy. Biblioteca Comunale.
A few liturgical and theological mss. Apparently no inventory. (Communication of the Sindaco). Cf. *Aevum* XXIX (1955) 291.

*Esztergom (Gran), Hungary. See Radó.
'Az Esztergomi Föegyházi Könyvtár Kéziratai,' *Magyar Könyvszemle* VII (1882) 306-35. (By J. Csontosi). 338 mss. No index. (DLC)
P. Lehmann, 'Handschriften und Handschriftenbruchstücke des 8.-15. Jahr-

hunderts in Esztergom,' *Egyetemes Philo-logiai Közlöny* (*Archivum Philologicum*) LXII (1938) 165-172.

P. Radò, 'Esztergomi Könyvtárak liturgikus Kéziratai,' *A Pannonhalmi Föapátsági Szent Gellért Föiskola Évkönyve*, N. S. I (1940-41) 86-142.

**Magyarország müemléki topográfiája. I. kötet. Esztergom müemlekei. I. rész.* Budapest 1948. p. 287-371: illuminated mss.

*Card catalogue.

**Catalogus bibliothecae Joannis cardinalis Simor.* Esztergom 1887. p. 178-83: mss.

*Étampes, France. See France, *Catalogue Général, Départements* XXIV; XLI.

*Eton, England. Eton College Library.

M. R. James, *A Descriptive Catalogue of the Manuscripts in the Library of Eton College.* Cambridge 1895. 125 pp. 193 mss.

The library copy of James' catalogue adds handwritten descriptions for mss. 194-255. Typed copy kindly supplied by the librarian.

List of Phillipps and humanistic Mss. in Eton College library subsequent to Ms. no. 255. Typed list kindly supplied by the librarian.

*Eu, France. See France, *Catalogue Général, Départements* II.

*Everbode, see Averboden.

*Évora, Portugal. See Stegmüller.

J. H. da Cunha Rivara, *Catálogo dos manuscritos da Bibliotheca Pública Eborense.* 4 vols. Lisbon 1850-71. Each vol. except the last is indexed. Arranged by subjects. (NN)

L. Silveira, *Manuscritos de filologia latina da Biblioteca Pública e Arquivo Distrital de Évora.* Evora 1940. 161 pp. 36 mss. (NN)

M. Gonçalves da Costa, 'Inéditos de Filosofia da Biblioteca de Evora,' *A Cidade de Evora* VIII, (1951) no. 23-24, p. 7-43; no. 25-26, p. 298-397. 162 mss. arranged chronologically. No index of authors. (NN)

*Évreux, France. See France, *Catalogue Général, Départements* II; *Sociétés.*

Exeter, England. Cathedral Chapter Library. See Holtzmann (Section A); Ber-

nardus; Frere; Great Britain, Hist. Manuscripts Commission. *Neues Archiv* XXII; Schenkl.

M. P. Crighton, *A Catalogue of the Medical Books and Manuscripts, including a selection of the scientific works, in Exeter Cathedral Library.* (Birmingham) 1934. 38 pp. p. 36-37: 8 mss. No Index.

A Calendar of the Archives of the Dean and Chapter of the Cathedral Church of Exeter (by Stuart A. Moore, 1873). In serial order. Ms. books appear under nos. 3500-3549.

*Fabriano, Italy. See Mazzatinti I.

Faenza, Italy. See Mazzatinti VI; XXVI; *Studi Italiani* XIX.

*Falaise, France. See France, *Catalogue Général, Départements* X.

*Falconara, Italy. See *Archivum Franciscanum Historicum* XLV; XLVIII.

*Fano, Italy. See Mazzatinti XXXVIII; LI.

(A. Mabellini, *Manoscritti, incunabuli, edizioni rare del s. XVI esistenti nella Biblioteca Comunale Federiciana di Fano.* Fano 1905. 167 pp. No index.) (DLC)

A. Zonghi, *Repertorio dell' Antico Archivio Comunale di Fano.* Fano 1888. xxi, 565 pp. Section X (Archivio Amiani) includes a few literary mss. (MH)

*Farfa, Italy. See *Archiv* XII.

*Fécamp, France. See France, *Catalogue Général, Départements* II; XLI.

Fermo, Italy. Biblioteca Communale. See *Archiv* IX; XII.

F. Raffaelli, *La biblioteca comunale di Fermo: relazione storica, bibliografica, artistica.* Recanati 1890. 209 pp.

A. Mancini, 'Una Biblioteca Provinciale: Fermo,' *Reale Accademia d'Italia, Rendiconti della Classe di Scienze Morali e Storiche*, Ser. VII, vol. II (1941) 471-489.

Serafino Prete, 'Catalogo dei Manoscritti della Biblioteca Comunale di Fermo,' *Studia Picena* XXII (1954) 123-142 (nos. 1-15); XXIII (1955) 21-15 (nos. 16-40); XXIV (1956) 31-63 (nos. 41-70). No index. Not complete.

Card file, known as 'Schedario Raffaelli' (cf. AB V 516).

Ferrara, Italy. Biblioteca Comunale Ariostea. See *Archiv* XII; Costabili; *Giornale* I; Mazzatinti LIV; *Studi Italiani* XIX.

G. Antonelli, *Indice dei manoscritti della Civica Biblioteca di Ferrara*. pt. I, Ferrara 1884. 311 pp. 608 mss. Not complete.

G. Agnelli, *Saggio di un catalogo dei codici di autori non ferraresi che si conservano nella Biblioteca Comunale di Ferrara*. Florence 1891. 32 pp. Describes selected mss. No index. (MiU)

P. Antolini, *Manoscritti relativi alla storia di Ferrara*. (Argenta) 1891. 52 pp. 136 nos. Lists also some mss. in other libraries. Alphabetically arranged.

H. Stein, 'Une visite à la Bibliothèque Communale de Ferrare,' *Le Bibliographe Moderne* XI (1907) 232-43. No shelf marks or index.

Library copy of Antonelli's catalogue adds ms. descriptions for mss. I 609-812.

Codici Manoscritti. Classe Ia Ferraresi. IIa Esteri. (Inside); *Codices Manuscripti Bibliothecae Pub. Ferrariensis binas in partes distributi, in quarum prima codices ad scriptores Ferrarienses pertinentes, in altera codices exterorum scriptorum recensentur (1815)*. Pars altera (describing class II, that is, the non-Ferrarese authors) supplements the printed catalogue of Antonelli. Alphabetical. (Cf. AB IV 545.)

Collezioni Antonelli e Antolini. Catalogo dei Manoscritti della Collezione Antonelli. Describes mss. Antonelli 1-967 and Antolini 1-188. (Cf. AB IV 545).

Autografi. 1 ms. vol. Alphabetical list of 3104 items. (micr. at DLC)

—*Museo Schifanoia.

A. Venturi, 'La miniatura ferrarese nel secolo XV e il "Decretum Gratiani": Per l'inaugurazione del Museo della miniatura nel salone di Schifanoia in Ferrara,' *Le Gallerie Nazionali Italiane* IV (1899) 187-209. (NN)

Fiecht, Austria. Stiftsbibliothek. See Wickhoff; Zingerle.

Inventar des Klosterarchivs, by H. Bachmann (1938). 1 typed vol. Comprises the 533 manuscript books. Arranged by subjects. (Micr. at DLC)

*Fiesole, Italy.

**D. Brunoni, *Il seminario die Fiesole: memoria storica, con prefazione di L. Candali*. Fiesole 1925. 331 pp.

*Figeac, France. See France, *Catalogue Général, Départements* XLI.

Firenze (Florence), Italy. See *Archiv* V; XII; *Archivum Franciscanum*; Ashburnham; Blume; *Giornale* I; La Fage; Mazzatinti VII-XIII; Italy, *Indici e Cataloghi* IV; VII; VIII; X; XV; Montfaucon; *Neues Archiv*; *Notices et Extraits*; Palacky; Reifferscheid; *Studi Italiani* X; XV; Thorndike; Zaccaria, *Excursus* and *Iter*.

S. and G. Camerani, 'Bibliografia degli Archivi Fiorentini,' *Archivio Storico Italiano* CXIV (1956) 304-319.

L. Passerini, 'Notizie sui Manoscritti Rinucciani acquistati dal Governo Toscano e nuovamente distribuiti tra gli Archivi e le Biblioteche di Firenze,' *Ibid.*, *Appendice* VIII (1850) 205-215.

R. Blum, *La Biblioteca della Badia Fiorentina e i Codici di Antonio Corbinelli* (Studi e Testi CLV). Vatican City 1951. xii, 190 pp. Identifies many mss. at Laurenziana and Nazionale and in libraries outside of Florence.

S. Orlandi, *La biblioteca di S. Maria Novella in Firenze dal sec. XIV al sec. XIX*. Florence 1952. 131 pp. and plates. Identifies many mss. at Laurenziana and Nazionale.

—Accademia della Crusca.

R. Accademia della Crusca, *Repertorio di Mss. e Incunaboli*. 72 mss., mostly late.

—Archivio di Stato.

See Italy, Pubblicazioni degli Archivi di Stato.

Elenco dei manoscritti e codici letterari esistenti nel R. Archivio di Stato di Firenze. 1 typed volume. 408 mss.

Inventario dei Manoscritti. 842 mss.

Archivio Mediceo avanti al Principato. In-

dice alfabetico dei mittenti. 1 typed vol. by R. Sartini and R. Barbadoro (1915).

Le carte Strozziane del R. Archivio di Stato in Firenze Inventario, Serie prima. 2 vols. Florence 1884-91. I: Filze 1-149. II: Filze 150-371 (of the first series). The archive has a typed index for vol. I, and a hand-written index for vol. II. (micr. at DLC)

Le carte Strozziane del R. Archivio di Stato in Firenze. Inventario. Printed proof-sheets, 592 pp. Covers Series II (148 nos) and III (nos. 1-205).

Inventario dei Manoscritti Strozziani esis-tenti nell' Archivio della nobil famiglia Uguccioni-Gherardi nel 1851. 292 mss. of series III.

Inventario dell' Archivio Strozzi- Uguccioni posseduto dalle eredi del Cav. Tommaso Uguccioni-Gherardi (by A. Gherardi). 1 ms. vol. Covers Carte Strozziane, Series IV.

Carte Strozziane. List of Series V. (micr. at DLC)

Carte Strozziane. Tavole di raffronto delle vecchie colle nuove segnature (comprese fra quest' ultime quelle della R. Biblioteca Na-zionale e della R. Galleria Uffizi).

F. Dini, 'Archivio Gianni-Mannucci già Leo-netti,' *Archivio Storico Italiano,* Ser. V, vol. XI (1893) 349-377.

Archivio Leonetti-Mannucci-Gianni. 1 vol. Appendix: *Codici e Pergamene.* 54 mss.

Repertorio delle filze, libri etc. esistenti nell' Archivio della nobil famiglia Cerchi. At the end, a list of the manuscript books of the collection.

—Biblioteca Marucelliana.

Inventario dei Manoscritti della R. Biblio-teca Marucelliana. 3 vols. I: Class A. II: B. III: C (cf. AB II 4-5 p. 92).

Catalogo dei manoscritti Redi e Cestoni (Cf. AB II 4-5 p. 92).

Catalogo dei Manoscritti Martelli Carraresi ecc. (Cf. AB II p. 92).

*Card index, 6 boxes (AB II 4-5 p. 92).

—Biblioteca Medicea Laurenziana.

A. M. Bandinius, *Catalogus codicum lati-norum Bibliothecae Mediceae Laurentianae.*

5 vols. Florence 1774-78. Vol. I (1774) Plut. XII.1-XXVII.1. Vol. II (1775) XXIX.1-LXVIII.29. Vol. III (1776) LXXI.4-LXXXIV.29; Laur. Gadd. LXXXIX sup. 1-XCI sup. 50. Vol. IV (1777): Laur. Gadd. XCI inf. 1-17; S. Croce I Sin. 1-XXXVI Dext. 13. Vol. V (1778): Italian mss. Index.

The same, *Bibliotheca Leopoldina Lauren-tiana seu Catalogus manuscriptorum qui iussu Petri Leopoldi . . . in Laurentianam translati sunt . . .* 3 vols. Florence 1791-93. Vol. I (1791): Aedilium, 224 mss.; Fratrum Minorum de Nemore, 18 mss.; Monte Amiata, 7 mss. Vol. II (1792): Gaddi, 235 mss.; Segni, 21 mss; Biscioni, 36 mss; Strozzi, 184 mss; Fiesole, 59 mss. Vol. III (1793): Fiesole, mss. no. 60-227; Mediceo-Palatini, 244 mss; Index for vols. I-III. (NN)

Schedario alfabetico dei Fondi Minori. Covers the Fondo Conventi Soppressi and some of the others, but not Ashburnham nor Acquisti e Doni. Card index.

Fondo Conventi Soppressi.

Supplementum alterum ad Catalogum codi-cum Graecorum, Latinorum, Italicorum etc. Bibliothecae Medicae Laurentianae... Catalogus codicum manuscriptorum Grae-corum, Latinorum, Italicorum etc. qui a saeculo XVIII exeunte usque ad annum MDCCCXLVI saeculi insequentis in Bi-bliothecam Mediceam Laurentianam trans-lati sunt cura et studio Francisci De Furia eiusdem Bibliothecae Regii Prae-fecti digestus atque illustratus. 4 vols. Careful descriptions. Not in alphabetical or topographical order. Supplements the printed catalogues of Bandini and covers the Fondo Conventi Soppressi of the Laurenziana. Arranged according to the monasteries from which the mss. came. Vol. 1: Badia. II: SS. Annunziata, S. Ma-ria Novella, S. Maria del Carmine, S. Ma-ria Maggiore, S. Maria delle Selve (Signa). III: Vallombrosa, Camaldoli. IV (which comprises acquisitions to 1856): S. Marco, S. Spirito, S. Paolino, S. Maria degli

Angioli, Ognissanti, Bosco ai Frati, S. Croce, S. Domenico di Fiesole, S. Lucia a Signa, S. Ambrogio, Monte Oliveto, Madonna de' Ricci, S. Jacopo Oltrarno, Castellina, and some mss. of the Fondi Redi and Acquisti. (Cf. AB III p. 60-61). (micr. at DLC)

Fondo S. Marco.

A. A. Björnbo, 'Die mathematischen S. Marcohandschriften in Florenz,' *Bibliotheca Mathematica* Ser. III vol. IV (1903) 238-45; VI (1905) 230-38. 4 mss. No index.

Index Manuscriptorum Bibliothecae FF. Ordinis Praedicatorum Florentiae ad S. Marcum (1768) (cod. Laur. S. Marco 945.) Arranged by classes, not in topographical order. 861 mss. Covers the Fondo S. Marco. List of the original S. Marco collection in which the mss. now in the Laurenziana are distinguished by the stamp of the library, whereas those now in the Nazionale or dispersed are marked otherwise (Cf. AB III p. 62). (Micr. at NN)

Codici di S. Marco consegnati alla Laurenziana nel 1883. 194 mss. (Cf. AB III p. 62). (micr. at DLC)

Fondo Scioppiano.

Indice dell' opere di Gasparo Scioppio Conte di Chiaravalle, che quasi tutte originali si conservano nella Biblioteca dell' Ill.mo Sig. Conte Gio. Michele Pierucci acquistata dal R. Erario per la Libreria Laurenziana (1816). 1 typed folder. 30 mss.

Fondi Redi, Tempi, Rinuccini.

Inventario dei codici Redi, Tempi e Rinuccini. Describes mss. Redi 1-225, Tempi 1-8, Rinuccini 1-24. (Cf. AB III 62).

Fondo Antinori.

Inventario di libri a penna e stampa venduti dal March. G. Antinori alla R. Biblioteca Laurenziana (1884). Mss. 1-255; then printed books with ms. notes, nos. 256-326 (Cf. AB III 62).

Fondo Ashburnham. See Ashburnham; *Indici e Cataloghi; Notices et Extraits.*

(Italy) *Camera dei Deputati, Legislatura XV. Sessione 1882-86. Raccolta degli Atti . . .*

vol. XVII (Rome 1886) no. 225, 85 pp.: 'Disegno di legge presentato alla Camera dal Ministro della Pubblica Istruzione (Coppino) di concerto col Ministro delle Finanze, interim del Tesoro (Magliani). Acquisto e trasporto dei codici italiani della Biblioteca Ashburnham. Seduta del 12 giugno 1884.' Lists 1826 mss. and 10 of appendix. No index. (DLC)

(Italy) *Ministero della pubblica Istruzione. Bollettino ufficiale* X no. 8 (Aug. 1884) 390-95; 9 (Sept. 1884) 478-88; 10 (Oct. 1884) 555-66; 11 (Nov. 1884) 626-42; 12 (Dec. 1884) 709-23: 'Relazione alla Camera dei Deputati e disegno di legge per l'acquisto di Codici appartenenti alla biblioteca Ashburnham descritti nell' annesso catalogo.' Then: 'Catalogo dei codici Ashburnham-Place in Londra, Fondo Libri.' Lists 1826 mss. and 10 of appendix. No index. (NN)

Library copy of the printed list of the Fondo Ashburnham (*Relazione alla Camera dei Deputati... 1884*, with the actual shelf marks entered in red ink (Cf. AB III 61-62). Partly superseded by the printed catalogue in progress.

E. Narducci, 'Indici alfabetici per autori e per soggetti e classificazione per secoli dei codici manoscritti della collezione Libri-Ashburnham ora nella Biblioteca Mediceo-Laurenziana di Firenze per uso del catalogo pubblicatosene in Italia premessavi la nota dei codici sopra numerari e dei posteriormente ritrovati,' *Il Buonarroti* Ser. III vol. II (1884) 289-326. Lists mss. app. 1827-1926 (p. 293-98). Index for all mss. (p. 299ff.).

Fondo Acquisti e Doni.

Inventario dei codici Laurenziani Acquisti e Doni.' 446 mss. (Cf. AB III 62).

*Fondo Martelli (acquired in 1958). Summary list. 77 mss. (Communication of the librarian)

—Biblioteca Moreniana (annexed to the Riccardiana).

(Provincia di Firenze), *I Manoscritti della Biblioteca Moreniana,* by C. Nardini,

A. Gigli, A. Badiani and B. Maracchi Biagiarelli. 2 vols. Florence 1903-59. I (1903-44), 17 fascicules, 601 pp. Manoscritti Moreni 1-396. Index (521-601). II (1912-59), 14 fascicules, 448 pp. Manoscritti Pecci 1-136 (p. 1-130). Manoscritti Frullani 1-43 (p. 131-191). Autografi Frullani 1-1995 (p. 192-316). Manoscritti Bigazzi 1-32 (p. 317-448). No index.

Inventario dei Manoscritti, 2 vols. Supplements the printed catalogue. Vol. I: Manoscritti Palagi, 430 mss. II: Carteggio Libri; Manoscritti Bigazzi, 357 mss.; Manoscritti Bigazzi (Cassette), B 1-128; Manoscritti Acquisti diversi, 166 mss.

—Biblioteca Nazionale Centrale.

D. Fava, *La Biblioteca Nazionale Centrale di Firenze e le sue insigni raccolte*. Milan 1939. xix, 242 pp. p. 194-197: mss. No shelf marks.

A. Bartoli, *I manoscritti italiani della Biblioteca Nazionale di Firenze*. 4 vols. Florence 1879-85. I (1879). IX, 382 pp. (NNC). II (1881). 387 pp. (NNC). III (1883). 384 pp. (NN). *IV, fasc. 1 (1885). 64 pp. (Biblioteca Nazionale, Rome)

Fondo Principale. See Mazzatinti VII-XII.

Fondo Magliabecchiano.

Fondo Magliabecchiano. Inventario dei Manoscritti (by Giov. Targioni Tozzetti). 11 vols. Vol. I: Classes I-VI. Vol. II: VII 1-951. Vol. III: VIII 1-1367. Vol. IV: IX 1-119; X 1-70; XI 1-113; XII 1-46. Vol. V: XIII 1-65; XIV 1-39; XV 1-174; XVI 1-139. Vol. VI: XVII 1-29; XVIII 1-34; XIX 1-69; XX 1-51; XXI 1-114; XXII 1-17; XXIII 1-90. Vol. VII: XXIV 1-146. Vol. VIII: XXV 1-484. Vol. IX: XXVI 1-163; XXVII 1-113; XXVIII 1-46; XXIX 1-160; XXX 1-222. Vol. X: XXXI 1-59; XXXII 1-28; XXXIII 1-11; XXXIV 1-69; XXXV 1-168; XXXVI 1-61. Vol. XI: XXXVII 1-272; XXXVIII 1-98; XXXIX 1-59; XL 1-37. With 3 vols. of indices (Cf. AB II 6 p. 102-03, where a list of the subjects covered by the 40 classes is given). The first two volumes are superseded by Mazzatinti XII-XIII. (Micr. of vols. 3-11 at DLC)

Catalogo dei Codici della Libreria Strozziana comprati dopo la morte di Alessandro Strozzi da S.A.R. Pietro Leopoldo Granduca di Toscana e passati alla Pubblica Libreria Magliabechiana... Compilato dal Bibliotecario Prof. Ferdinando Fossi nel 1789 e trascritto da Antonio Montelatici... 'In questo Catalogo sono notati oltre gli Strozziani quelli che sono venuti dopo la morte del Bibliotecario D. Giovanni Targioni o non notati nel primo Catalogo.' 2 vols. Continues the inventory in 11 vols. and completes the description of the actual Fondo Magliabecchiano, covering the higher numbers in each class (often cited as Magl. Strozz.). Vol. I: Class I-VI; VII 950bis-1231; VIII 1368-1456; IX 120-144; X 71-78; XI 114-71; XII 47-60; XIII 66-94; XIV 40-49; XV 175-201; XVI 140-46; XVII 30-34; XIX 70-200; XX 52-61. Vol. II: XXI 115-71; XXII 18-28; XXIII 91-156; XXIV 146bis-166; XXV 485-707; XXVI 164-84; XXVII 114-20; XXVIII 47-59; XXIX 161-206; XXX 223-49; XXXI 59bis-66; XXXII 29-50; XXXIII 12-21; XXXIV 70-80; XXXV 169-278; XXXVI 62-79; XXXVII 273-329; XXXVIII 99-150; XXXIX 60-96; XL 38-49. Superseded by Mazzatinti XII-XIII for classes I-VI and VII 950-1000. (Micr. at DLC)

Catalogo analitico dei Manoscritti della Biblioteca Nazionale di Firenze, by D. Carbone (1864). More detailed description of 37 selected mss. of the Fondo Magliabecchiano (VIII-IX) and of 12 mss. of the Fondo Nazionale (AB II 6 p. 103).

Repertorio numerico Manoscritti Fondo Magliabechi (*Vacchetta*). Indispensable concordance for the Fondo Magliabecchiano which indicates the items missing since the last century and gives the actual shelf marks for those transferred to the Fondo Nazionale (completely described in Mazzatinti VII-XII) or other collections. It also lists at the end of each class some mss. not described in the inventories.

Magl. VIII. Appendix of letters. 27 vols. in 4 series. Mostly transferred from other mss. of the Fondo Magliabecchi. No inventory.

Fondo Palatino.

G. Molini, *Codici Manoscritti Italiani dell' I. e R. Biblioteca Palatina di Firenze.* Florence 1833. 88 pp. 39 mss. No index. (NN)

F. Palermo, *I manoscritti Palatini di Firenze.* 3 vols. Florence 1853-68. I (1860): 572 mss. II (1860): Mss. no 573-628. III (1868): 3 mss. Each volume indexed. Covers some Latin mss.

Inventario dei manoscritti trovati nella già Biblioteca Palatina di Firenze in questo giorno 1 febraio 1862... Sketchy list of the Fondo Palatino, which does not follow the actual topographical order and is superseded to no. 1006 by the printed catalogue in progress. See Italy, *Indici e Cataloghi,* IV. It is followed by summary lists of the following collections annexed to the Fondo Palatino: Baldovinetti (258 mss.), Capponi (214 mss. known as Palatino-Capponi and different from the Fondo Gino Capponi, which has a printed catalogue by Milanesi), Targioni (189 mss.), Panciatichi (369 mss., partly superseded by the printed catalogue in progress, See Italy, *Indici e Cataloghi,* VII), Graberg (39 mss.), Del Furia (84 mss.), Bandinelli (12 mss.), Sinner (39 mss.), Raccolta delle opere di Galileo (12 filze). (Cf. AB II 6 p. 103). With an alphabetical card index in 2 boxes. (Micr. at DLC)

Repertorio numerico Mss. Fondo Palatino (Vacchetta). Table of correspondence for the Fondo Palatino, indicating the mss. transferred to other collections.

A. Favaro, *Per la edizione nazionale delle opere di Galileo Galilei: Indice alfabetico e topografico del commercio epistolare.* Florence 1889. 23 pp.

The same, *Per la edizione nazionale delle opere di Galileo Galilei: Indice cronologico del Carteggio Galileiano.* Florence 1896. 101 pp. (MB)

L. Andreani, 'I manoscritti di Galileo e della sua scuola nella Biblioteca Nazionale Centrale di Firenze...,' *Bibliofilia* XI (1909-10) 44-61. No shelf marks.

Indice generale dei Manoscritti scientifici dall' epoca di Galileo all' altra dell' Accademia del Cimento inclusive (by Fontani). 306 mss. (AB II 6 p. 104).

Indice analitico dei manoscritti Galileiani nella Biblioteca Naz. di Firenze. 3 vols. (AB II 6 p. 104). 335 mss.

O. Tommasini, *La vita e gli scritti di Niccolò Machiavelli,* 2 vols. Turin 1883 - Rome 1911. II 1257-1407: 'Elenco dei documenti relativi al Machiavelli contenuti nelle sei Buste della Biblioteca Nazionale di Firenze.' Arranged chronologically.

Autografi Palatini (Carte Machiavelli ecc.). 6 mss.

*Inventario dei carteggi (including the *autografi Palatini*). 1 ms. folder. Topographical.

Schedario dei carteggi (Autografi). Alphabetical card index in many trays.

Raccolta Gonnelli (autografi). Alphabetical card index in 7 boxes.

Fondo Conventi Soppressi.

Catalogo dei mss. dei Conventi soppressi. Summary topographical list of the Fondo Conventi Soppressi. Describes Classes A I-IX, B I-IX, C I-IX, D I-IX, E I-VIII, F I-IX, G I-IX, H I-IX, J I-X. The serial numbers of the individual mss. are not in continuous order. Class J contains the mss. from S. Marco. (Micr. at DLC)

Indice dei Manoscritti scelti nelle Biblioteche Monastiche del Dipartimento dell' Arno dalla Commissione degli Oggetti d'Arti e Scienze, e dalla medesima rilasciati alla Pubblica Libreria Magliabechiana. Alphabetical index of the Fondo Conventi Soppressi. More detailed than the inventory, but without indication of centuries (Cf. AB II 6 p. 104: 2227 mss.).

Conventi soppressi da riordinare. 519 mss., mostly late, and ca. 20 mss. marked SMN. No inventory.

Inventario dei Manoscritti, carte ecc. appartenenti alla Libreria degli ex-Filippini di San Firenze. 1 ms. folder. 98 mss. (AB II 6 p. 104).

Fondo Rossi-Cassigoli. See Pistoia.

Inventario de' Mss. della collezione Rossi-Cassigoli. A: Codici. 437 mss. B: Miscellanee. 36 nos. C: Cassette. XXII nos. Cᵃ: Musica. XXIII nos. See Chiapelli, under Pistoia.

*Catalogo dei manoscritti della Collezione pistoiese Rossi-Cassigoli. Card index in 5 boxes. 479 ms. vols. (AB II 6 p. 105).

Fondo Gino Capponi.

C. Milanesi, *Catalogo dei manoscritti posseduti dal marchese Gino Capponi.* Florence 1845. 268 pp. 2114 items, alphabetically arranged.

Fondo Rinuccini. 27 filze. No inventory.

Fondo Tordi.

Inventario dei Manoscritti Tordi. 570 mss.

Fondo Landau.

Catalogue des livres manuscrits et imprimés composant la bibliothèque de M. Horace de Landau. 2 vols. Florence 1885-90. (By F. Roediger). I: Covers 33 mss. II p. 1-144: Mss. no. 34-295. (IU)

Cf. A. Mondolfo, 'La Biblioteca Landau Finaly,' in *Studi di bibliografia e di argomento romano in memoria di Luigi De Gregori* (Rome [1949]) 265-85.

Inventario Landau Finaly. Ms. folder. 310 mss.

Manoscritti Landau Finaly: Concordanze tra le segnature del Catalogo Roediger e le attuali. 1 ms. folder.

Elenco dei manoscritti, libri ed oggetti d'arte legati alla Città di Firenze dal Signor Horace Finaly. 1 typed vol.

Card file (of the Fondo Landau).

Fondo Nuovi Acquisti.

Nuovi Acquisti e accessioni di mss., carteggi, libri rari ecc. 1905... 3 ms. vols. I: 1-482. II: 485-771. III (*Registro dei Manoscritti Nuovi Acquisti*): 772-967. (Micr. at DLC)

Nuovi Acquisti. Card index in 2 boxes (Cf. AB II 6 p. 105).

Fondo Banco Rari.

Inventario del Banco Rari. Arranged by old shelf marks.

Alphabetical card index. Covers 350 mss. and printed editions transferred from other collections. (Cf. AB II 6 p. 107).

*Fondo Postillati. 98 mss. Topographical card file, and alphabetical catalogue by authors and annotators. (Communication of the librarian)

Società Colombaria.

U. Dorini, 'Inventario dell' archivio e degli altri manoscritti della Società Colombaria,' *Atti della Società Colombaria di Firenze dall' anno 1910 all' anno 1920* (1921) 265-356. (fasc. for 1913-1914 [1915] p. 29-120). Also published separately (Florence 1915, 92 pp.). Mss. III 1-IV IV 25. No index. Many mss. were lost during the war. The remainder is deposited in the Biblioteca Nazionale.

(No title). Summary list of the extant mss. and of their actual (changed) shelf marks.

—Biblioteca Riccardiana.

J. Lamius, *Catalogus codicum manuscriptorum qui in Bibliotheca Riccardiana Florentina adservantur.* Livorno 1756. 436 pp. Arranged by authors. Shelf marks antiquated.

Inventario e stima della Libreria Riccardi: Manoscritti e edizioni del s. XV. Florence 1810. 225 pp. p. 1-61: summary list of 3590 mss. No index.

Maria Luisa Scuricini Greco, *Miniature Riccardiane.* Florence 1958. 317 pp. 325 mss.

Library copy of printed *Inventario e stima* (1810), contains ms. changes and additions. The shelf marks have been changed for nos. 2992-3868, and the numbering goes now to 3955.

Typed concordance, giving the actual shelf marks corresponding to the old ones used in Lami's printed catalogue of 1756.

Catalogo dei Mss. Riccardiani. One large ms. volume serving as an author's index to all mss. of the library (Cf. AB III 66). (micr. at DLC)

Schedario. Card index for all mss. in serial order.

—Galleria degli Uffizi, Biblioteca, Manoscritti. *Elenco dei Manoscritti, Biblioteca Gallerie.* Typed list. 357 mss. Centuries not given.

—Private archives and libraries. *Inventario Biblioteca Principe Ginori Conti.* Mss. 0048-0229.

R. Ridolfi, 'Le lettere dell' Archivio Bartolini-Salimbeni,' *Bibliofilia* XXIX (1927) 193-226. Index.

The same. 'L'Archivio della famiglia da Verrazzano. *Ibid.* XXX (1928) 20-39. No index.

The same, 'Gli Archivi de' Gondi,' *Ibid.* XXX (1928) 81-119. No index.

The same, 'L'Archivio della famiglia Guicciardini,' *Ibid.* XXX (1928) 449-470; XXXI (1929) 14-37; 295-309; XXXII (1930) 10-22; 285-310; 458-473. No index. (NNC) Also in a separate revised edition, Florence 1931. VII, 145 pp. (NN).

The same, *Gli archivi delle famiglie fiorentine.* Florence 1934. V, 249 pp. Separate edition of all articles first published in *Bibliofilia.*

P. Toesca, 'Manoscritti miniati della Biblioteca del Principe Corsini a Firenze,' *Rassegna d'Arte* XVII (1917) 117-28.

*Flers, France. See France, *Catalogue Général, Départements* X; XLI.

Florence, see Firenze.

*Foggia, Italy. See Mazzatinti IV.

*Foix, France. See France, *Catalogue Général, Départements* XXXI.

Foligno, Italy. Biblioteca Comunale.

Comune di Foligno. *Inventario dei manoscritti* by Don Angelo Messini (1940), with additions. Mss. C 1-176; F 1-365; M 1-171.

—Biblioteca Jacobilli. See Mazzatinti XLI.

*Fondi, Italy. Cattedrale. Has a few liturgical mss.

*Fontainebleau, France. See France, *Catalogue Général, Départements* VI; XXIV; XLI.

*Fonte Colombo, see under Rieti.

Forlì, Italy. Biblioteca Comunale. See Mazzatinti I and LX.

G. Mazzatinti, 'I manoscritti storici della Biblioteca Comunale di Forlì,' *Rivista storica italiana* VI (1889) 658-61. 38 mss. No index.

A. Servolini, 'I corali e gli offizi miniati della Bibliotheca Comunale di Forlì,' *Gutenberg-Jahrbuch* 1944-49, 18-34. 39 mss., most of them not listed by Mazzatinti. Card index in 1 box, supplements the printed list in Mazz. I. (Cf. AB IV 554).

Fondo Piancastelli.

A. Mambelli, *Un umanista della Romagna: Carlo Piancastelli.* Faenza 1938. XI, 262 pp. p. 134-136: Autografi.

D. Fava, 'Le raccolte romagnole di Carlo Piancastelli', *Accademie e Biblioteche* XVI (1941-42) 12-22. Mentions some mss.

Biblioteca Piancastelli, Romagna. Mscr. Alphabetical card index of the Codici Piancastelli, in 2 bound volumes. I: A-L. II: M-Z.

Collezione di autografi del Dottor Carlo Piancastelli dal secolo XII al XVIII. Alphabetical index of the autographs. No dates are given.

—Biblioteca del Seminario. Ca. 40 mss. No information.

*Fougères, France. See France, *Catalogue Général, Départements* XIII; XLI.

*Franeker, Holland. See under Leeuwarden.

Frankfurt a.M., West Germany. See Bernards; Cooper (Section A); *Archiv* I; II; Gercken; Leclercq.

G. Swarzenski and Rosy Schilling, *Die illuminierten Handschriften und Einzelminiaturen des Mittelalters und der Renaissance in Frankfurter Besitz.* 2 vols. Frankfurt 1929. 219 mss.

Stadt- und Universitätsbibliothek.

J. J. Lucius, *Catalogus Bibliothecae Publicae Moeno-Francofurtensis . . .* 11 pts. in 1, Frankfurt 1728. pt. 11 p. 433-50: Mss. arranged alphabetically. (MH).

E. Kelchner, 'Die von Uffenbach'schen Manuscripte auf der Stadtbibliothek zu

Frankfurt a.M.,' *Archiv für Frankfurts Geschichte und Kunst* N.F. I (1860) 335-53. Only of local interest. (NN)

Stadtbibliothek Frankfurt am Main: *Handschriften, Einbände, Formschnitte und Kupferstiche des 15. Jahrhunderts* . . . Frankfurt 1920. 94 pp. Lists a few Latin mss. No index.

Stadtbibliothek Frankfurt a.M., Handschriftenkatalog. 2 vols. I: *Codices manu exarati in antiquissima Imp. Ecclesiae S. Bartholomaei Francofurtensis Bibliotheca reperti eoque quo in forulis modo sunt positi ordine recensiti* (1776). Ms. Barth. I-CLXXV, and Appendix I-V. II: *Catalog über Handschriften* (63-175) *der ehemaligen Dombibliothek* (1872-73); *Catalog der Handschriften der ehemaligen Praedicatoren- oder Dominikaner-Bibliothek* (Praed. 1-190); *Catalog von Handschriften der Stadt-Bibliothek* (II 1-54; III 1-54). (No title). 3 small ms. folders. Describe Cod. lat. fol. 1-8; quart. 1-65; oct. 1-123 (Cf. Born 215).

*Gymnasiumsbibliothek.

H. Rumpf, *De foliis quibusdam manu scriptis, quae in bibliotheca gymnasii Francofurtensis adservantur*. progr. Frankfurt 1868, 40 pp. p. 1-18: 22 mss. No index. (Mss. apparently lost.)

Frankfurt a.O., East Germany. See *Archiv* XI.

R. Schwarze, *Die alten Drucke und Handschriften der Bibliothek des Königl. Friedrichs-Gymnasiums zu Frankfurt a.O.* progr. Frankfurt a.O. 1877. XIV 30 pp. p. 23-30: 22 mss. No index (Erlangen Univ. Library)

Frascati, Italy. Archivio della Congregazione di Monte Corona.

J. Leclercq, *Un humaniste ermite, Le Bienheureux Paul Giustiniani*. Rome 1951. 182 pp. p. 147-176: 14 mss.

*Frauenburg, see Frombork.

*Frauenfeld, Switzerland.

**Katalog der Thurgauischen Kantonsbibliothek*. Frauenfeld 1858, 96 pp. p. 90-96: mss. Also supplements 1864, 1867 and 1870.

Katalog der Thurgauischen Kantonsbibliothek. Frauenfeld 1887. 824 pp. p. 151-54: Alphabetical list of 193 mss. (DLC)

Freiberg, East Germany. See *Archiv* VIII.

**Sam. Moller, *Manuscripta ad rem sacram, ad iura, ad philosophiam atque ad historiam pertinentia*. progr. Freiberg 1727.

Katalog der Freiberger Alterthumsvereins-Bibliothek (with: *Mittheilungen des Freiberger Alterthumsvereins* VIII, 1870). 92 pp. p. 1-19: Mss. Only late and local material. Supplements with X (1873) 93-108; XVI (1879) 109-38; XXX (1893) 139-70. (DLC)

—*Bibliothek der Oberschule.

F. A. Hecht, *Litterarische Nachricht von einigen Handschriften und vielen typographischen Seltenheiten in der Freyberger Schulbibliothek*. Freyberg (1803). 8 pp. p. 2-3: 10 mss. No index. (Paris, Bibliothèque Nationale).

M. Rachel, *Über die Freiberger Bibelhandschrift nebst Beiträgen zur Geschichte der vorlutherischen Bibelübersetzung. Beigefügt sind Proben aus dem neuangelegten Handschriftenkatalog der Freiberger Gymñasialbibliothek*, by R. Kade. progr. Freiberg 1886. 31 pp. p. 23-31: 7 mss. (NjPT)

**Ed. C. Heydenreich, *Die Hyginhandschrift der Freiberger Gymnasialbibliothek*. progr. Freiberg 1878. 28 pp.

*Handschriften-Catalog, by R. Kade and P. Krenkel. Card file arranged by subjects. 285 mss. and frs. (Communication of the librarian)

Freiburg i.B., West Germany. *Stadtarchiv. See Scheeben.

Handschriftenverzeichnis, a card file. Describes ca. 300 mss. (Communication of the archivist)

—Universitätsbibliothek. See *Archiv* VIII; Leclercq.

H. Amann, *Praestantiorum aliquot codicum manuscriptorum qui Friburgi servantur ad iurisprudentiam spectantium notitia*. 2 pts. progr. Freiburg 1836-37. 49 and 72 pp. 4 mss. (DLC)

Handschriftenkatalog. 2 typed folders, the first alphabetical, the second by subjects. Card index, in 3 boxes, entitled *Handschriften*. By subjects and authors. (Cf. Born 218).

*Fréjus, France. See France, *Catalogue Général, Départements* XIV.

Fribourg, Switzerland. Bibliothèque Cantonale et Universitaire. See Sinner.

Catalogue de la Bibliothèque cantonale de Fribourg. By Meinrad Meyer, J. Gremaud and others. 4 vols. Fribourg 1852-86. II (1855) p. 593-614: 216 mss. No index. Alphabetical. (Fribourg)

(No title). 2 typed vols. I: mss. 1-223. II: 224-896 (Cf. Born 353).

—Couvent des PP. Capucins. No inventory.

A. Wagner, *Peter Falcks Bibliothek und humanistische Bildung* (Bibliothek des Schweizer Bibliophilen II 2). Bern 1926. XVI, 221 pp. p. 104-113: 14 mss. (5 are at the Couvent des Capucins). (NN)

—*Couvent des PP. Cordeliers. Ca. 120 mss.

*Handwritten inventory. (Communication of the librarian).

B. Fleury, 'Un moine bibliophile au XVe siècle: Le P. Jean Joly, Cordelier de Fribourg,' *Zeitschrift für Schweizerische Kirchengeschichte* VI (1912). 27-33. Lists *ca.* 30 mss. out of a total of *ca.* 140. (MH)

The same, 'Le Couvent des Cordeliers de Fribourg au Moyen Age,' *Ibid.* XV (1921) 26-44; 93-121; 193-206; 279-302. (NN). Also printed separately. Fribourg 1922. 90 pp. Mentions some mss.

—*Société Économique.

W. J. Meyer, 'Catalogue des manuscrits de la Bibliothèque de la Société Économique de Fribourg,' *Archives de la Société d'Histoire du Canton de Fribourg* X, fasc. 2 (1915) 297-379. Indices. (NN)

*Fritzlar, West Germany. See under Fulda.

*Frombork, Poland. See *Archiv* XI; Possevinus.

*Friesach, Austria. See *Handschriftenverzeichnisse*.

Fulda, West Germany. Landesbibliothek. See *Archiv* I; VIII; Christ; Falk; Gercken;

Leclercq; Loeffler; *Neues Archiv* V; Nürnberger.

**N. Kindlinger, 'Katalog und Nachrichten von der ehemaligen aus lauter Handschriften bestandenen Bibliothek in Fulda,' *Buchonia* I, 2 (1811) 117-61. Also separately, Leipzig 1812. 88 pp.

Festgabe zum Bonifatius-Jubiläum 1905. Fulda 1905. LXXVI, 37 pp. and plates. p. 1-37: G. Scherer, 'Die Codices Bonifatiani in der Landesbibliothek zu Fulda.' 3 mss. (MH)

Catalogi Publicae Fuldensis Bibliothecae Tomus I. continns Manuscripta, confectus et descriptus ab Amando Keitz anno 1850-1851.

—*Bibliothek des Bischöflichen Priesterseminars. 123 mss. from Fritzlar. No further information.

*Fürstenstein, see Książ.

***Gaeta**, Italy. Cattedrale. Has a few liturgical mss.

***Gaillac**, France. See France, *Catalogue Général, Départements* XXXI; XLI.

Gand, see Gent.

***Gap**, France. See France, *Catalogue Général, Départements* III.

***Gdańsk**, Poland (Danzig). Biblioteka Gdańska Polskiej Akademii Nauk. See Aland. (Sect. A.); Archiv XI; Vetulani.

Katalog der Danziger Stadtbibliothek. 6 vols. in 5, Danzig 1892-1921. Vol. I (1892): *Die Danzig betreffenden Handschriften*, by A. Bertling. 782 mss. Vol. II (1903): *Katalog der Handschriften, Teil 2*, by O. Günther. Mss. no. 783-1667 (with some gaps). Vol. III (1909): The same, *Teil* 3. Nos. 1750-2529, and addenda to vols. I-II. Vol. IV (1911): The same, pt. 4. Mss. no. 4001-42; St. Katherinen; St. Johann; no. 4205-10. V (1921). The same, pt. 5, by the same: *Die Handschriften der Kirchenbibliothek von St. Marien in Danzig.* Each vol. indexed.

E. Steffenhagen, 'Romanistische und canonistische Handschriften in Danzig,' *Zeitschrift für Rechtsgeschichte* X (1872) 296-308. 22 mss.

List of lost Mss kindly supplied by the librarian.

Genève, Switzerland. See *Archiv* VII; Buchon; *Société française*; Stelling-Michaud; *Traditio.*

—*Archives d'État.

Archives d'État de Genève. Catalogue de la Collection des manuscrits historiques. (By Paul-E. Martin). Geneva 1936. 211 pp. 230 mss.

*Handwritten supplement for later acquisitions. (Communication of the archivist).

—Bibliothèque Publique et Universitaire.

J. Senebier, *Catalogue raisonné des manuscrits conservés dans la Bibliothèque de la ville et république de Genève.* Geneva 1779. 478 pp. 125 Latin mss. (p. 51-292).

H. Aubert, 'Notice sur les manuscrits Pétau conservés à la bibliothèque de Genève (fonds Ami Lullin)' *Bibliothèque de l'École des Chartes* LXX (1909) 247-302; 470-522; LXXII (1911) 279-313; 556-99. Latin mss. (LXX, 256-302). No index.

B. Gagnebin, 'Le Cabinet des Manuscrits de la Bibliothèque de Genève,' *Genava*, N.S. II (1954) 73-125. Surveys the catalogues. (NN)

Récolement des Manuscrits de la Bibliothèque de Genève. Covers Latin mss. 126-141.

Inventaire des Manuscrits grecs, latins, français Jallabert, Rocca, Bonnet, Cramer, Constant, Dumont. Covers Latin mss. 141-332.

*Catalogue of the ecclesiastic correspondence by L. Micheli. Handwritten inventory for mss. lat. 106-121 and franc. 401-413. (Communication of the librarian).

*Card file for all letters.

*New catalogue of all mss. in preparation.

Genève-Cologny, Switzerland. Bibliothèque Bodmer. See Stelling-Michaud.

*Card file.

Genova, Italy. See *Archives des Missions* XX; Blume; *Giornale* I; II.

Ch. L. Livet, 'Bibliothèques publiques de Gênes: Manuscrits relatifs à l'histoire de France,' *Le Cabinet Historique* XXVI 2 (1880) 193-221.

—Archivio di Stato. Fondo Manoscritti *Pandetta della collezione Manoscritti e Libri rari.* Nos. 1-846, I-CI. Centuries not given.

—Archivio Storico Comunale.

Archivio storico. 1649 nos. Centuries not given.

—Biblioteca Civica Berio.

Card index of mss. (AB VI 554). Lost during the war.

Typed lists of preserved items. Available at the Palazzo Rosso in 1949.

—Biblioteca Civica Brignole Sale.

Catalogo delle opere conservate nella Camera dei Manoscritti e Libri Rari della Biblioteca Brignole Sale De Ferrari (1875). Arranged alphabetically. Includes editions. Centuries not always given. Some mss. were sold, others lost during the war.

—Biblioteca della Congregazione de' RR. Missionari Urbani.

Inventory lost during the war. Preserved mss. are kept in the Biblioteca Franzoniana. The most important mss. are listed in G. Bianchero's *Guida di Genova*, Genoa, 1846, pt. I, 497-523.

—Biblioteca Franzoniana.

Catalogo della Biblioteca Franzoniana compilato per ordine d'autore (1900). At the end: III. *Manoscritti* (8 pages). Alphabetical. Centuries not given.

—Biblioteca Universitaria.

Bibliothecae Universitatis Genuensis repertorium codicum manuscriptorum (1870). Topographical inventory (AB II 1 p. 65).

Index codicum manuscriptorum qui in Regii Genuensis Athenei Bibliotheca adservantur ordine alphabetico dispositus anno domini MDCCCLVIII. Alphabetical. Centuries not always given (Cf. AB II 1 p. 65-66).

Inventario dei Manoscritti. 1 typed vol. Over 1409 mss., marked A I 1 - G VII 7 (Cf. AB II 1 p. 65). (micr. at DLC)

Fondo Gaslini.

A. Cutolo, 'La donazione "Gerolamo Gaslini,"' *Accademie e Biblioteche* XVI (1941-42) 215-224. p. 220-221: Summary list of the 61 mss. No valid shelf marks. No index.

Manoscritti Gaslini (acquired 1943). 61 mss. (micr. at DLC)

—Società Ligure di Storia Patria.

Manoscritti. Card index in 1 box, alphabetical.

—Marchesa Matilde Negrotto Cambiaso Giustiniani (Biblioteca Durazzo).

Catalogo della Biblioteca di un amatore bibliofilo. Italia (*sic*), s.l.a., 251 pp. Alphabetical catalogue of printed editions and manuscripts. Shelf marks of mss. are entered in the library copy. Many mss. come from the library of the Duc de La Vallière and are better described by G. de Bure (*Catalogue des livres de la bibliothèque de feu M. le duc de La Vallière, Première partie,* 3 vols. Paris 1783.)

G. L. Oderico, 'Osservazioni. . . sopra alcuni codici della libreria di G. F. Durazzo,' *Giornale Ligustico* VII-VIII (1881) 3-27; 49-64; 94-120; 142-56; 180-94; 236-47; 273-88; 299-316; 331-62. 41 mss. No index.

Gent (Gand Ghent), Belgium. See *Analecta Bollandiana* III; IV; *Archiv* VIII; *Catalogus codicum hagiographicorum.*

—Bibliothèque de l'Évêché. Deposited in the Cathedral. See *Archiv* VIII (1843) 552-553 (6 mss.). No shelf marks.

—Bibliothèque Universitaire (Bibliotheek der Rijksuniversiteit).

Baron Jules de Saint-Genois, *Catalogue méthodique et raisonné des manuscrits de la Bibliothèque de la ville et de l'université de Gand.* Ghent 1849-52. 499 pp. 686 nos., 642 mss. (NN)

(J.-A. Walwein de Tervliet, *Catalogue des Manuscrits de la Bibliothèque Publique de la ville de Gand.* Ghent 1816. xii, 56 pp. 234 mss. No index.)

Bibliotheek der Rijksuniversiteit te Gent. Census van de Handschriften. Unnumbered filing cards, offset printed. Prefaces signed by U. Stuyck and K. G. van Acker. 5 parts, Gent 1955-57. Pt. 1 (1955): Mss. no. 643-665; 2 (1955) 666-698 (with some gaps) and index for parts 1-2; 3 (1956): 678-706 (with some gaps, and a few others); 4 (1957): 707-734 (gaps); 5 (1957): 713-752 (gaps).

Bibliothèque Gand. Manuscrits. 3057 nos. Largely superseded by the published catalogues.

(Section Gantoise). Card file in 3 trays.

*Gerona, Spain. See Cordoliani; Kehr (Section A); Villanueva.

—*Biblioteca Provincial.

*Catalogo razonado de los codices góticos incunables y de los manuscritos que existen en la biblioteca provincial de Gerona, by D. Nicolas Magan (1857). *Ca.* 100 mss., mostly Latin. (A. Cordoliani in *Hispania Sacra* IV, 1951, p. 366).

—*Biblioteca Capitular.

A. Brutails, 'Bible de Charles V et autres manuscrits du chapître de Girone,' *Bibliothèque de l'École des Chartes* XLVII (1886) 637-45.

*Handwritten catalogue. *Ca.* 130 mss. (Cordoliani *ibid., p.* 368).

Ghent, see Gent.

*Gien, France. See France, *Catalogue Général, Départements* XXIV; XXXI; XLI.

*Giessen, West Germany. See *Archiv* IX; Hirsching; *Neues Archiv* IV; *Serapeum* IX; Vaubel.

J. V. Adrian, *Catalogus codicum manuscriptorum Bibliothecae Academicae Gissensis.* Frankfurt 1840. 400 pp. 1268 mss.

The same, *Additamenta ad catalogum codicum manuscriptorum Bibliothecae Academicae Gissensis.* 1862. 18 pp. No index. (DLC)

Verzeichniss der den Druckwerken der Grossherzoglichen Universitäts-Bibliothek zu Giessen beigebundenen Handschriften. n.d. 11 pp. No index. (MH)

F. G. Otto, *Commentarii critici in codices bibliothecae academicae Gissensis Graecos et Latinos philologicos et medii aevi historicos ac geographicos. . .* Giessen 1842. lvii, 332 pp. Index (p. xiii ff.). Latin mss. (p. 3-108). (NN)

*Gijon, Spain.

J. Somoza de Montsorin, *Catálogo de manuscritos e impresos notables del Instituto de Jove-Llanos en Gijon.* Oviedo 1883. 257 pp. Late copies.

Girgenti, see Agrigento.

*Gisors, France. See France, *Catalogue Général, Départements* II.

*Glarus, Switzerland.

***Katalog der Landesbibliothek in Glarus.* Glarus 1879, and supplement of 1886. Mss.: p. 141-47 and suppl. p. 47.

Katalog der Landesbibliothek in Glarus. Näfels 1903. 347 pp. p. 281-90: mss. Arranged alphabetically. Late material only. (NN)

Glasgow, Scotland. See Haenel; Great Britain, *Historical Manuscripts Commission*; Schenkl.

J. Young and H. Aitken, *A Catalogue of the Manuscripts in the Library of the Hunterian Museum in the University of Glasgow.* Glasgow 1908. 566 pp. 649 mss.

Glasgow University Library, Catalogue of Manuscripts. Pt. 1: 'List of manuscripts belonging to the General Collection and to the Ewing Collection.' Pt 2: 'List of manuscripts belonging to the Hamilton Collection.' Each part arranged alphabetically. Supplements the printed catalogue of the mss. of the Hunterian Museum deposited in the same library.

*Glatz, see Kłodzko.

*Gloucester, England. See Schenkl; Great Britain, Historical Manuscripts Commission.

*Gniezno, Poland. See *Archiv* XI; *Société française*; Vetulani.

—*Biblioteka Kapitulna.

T. Trzciński, 'Sredniowieczne rękopisy biblioteki kapitulnej w Gnieźnie,' *Roczniki Towarzystwa Przyjaciół Nauk Poznańskiego* XXXV (1909) 169-320. 196 mss. Arranged chronologically. No index. (NN) Also printed separately under the title: *Katalog Rękopisów Biblioteki kapitulnej w Gnieźnie aż do poczatku wieku XVI. Catalogus codicum manuscriptorum usque ad initium saeculi decimi sexti qui in Bibliotheca Almae Ecclesiae Metropolitanae*

Gneznensis asservantur. Poznan 1910. xvi, 136 pp. and plates. (British Museum; micr. at NN)

—*Biblioteka Seminarium.

*(T. Trzciński), 'Krótkie wiadomości z bibliotek gnieźnieńskich II,' *Przegląd Kościelny Poznań* VI (1904) 212-228; 282-306. Also separately printed under the title: *Katalog rękopisów biblioteki seminaryjnej w Gnieźnie aż do wieku XVI włącznie*, 42 pp. 49 mss. (Cracow, Biblioteka Jagiellonska)

Biblioteka Seminaryum Duchownego w Gnieźnie. I. Katalog Rekopisów aż do roku 1725. Preface signed by T. Trzciński. Poznań 1909. III, 80 pp. 159 mss. Arranged chronologically. No index. (British Museum; micr. at NN). Enlarged edition of the preceding catalogue.

*Gorizia, Italy. See Wickhoff.

B. Ziliotto, 'Alla ricerca dei codici manoscritti del Seminario di Gorizia,' *Memorie storiche Forogiuliesi* XXXVIII (1942) 91-94.

The mss. were lost during the first world war.

*Görlitz, East Germany. See under Wrocław.

*Gorzów, Poland.

F. A. Wagler, *Bericht über die Bibliothek des Gymnasiums zu Landsberg a.W.* progr. Landsberg 1877. 16 pp. p. 3: 2 mss. (Erlangen, Universitätsbibliothek)

*Goslar, West Germany. Stadtarchiv.

U. Hoelscher, *Verzeichnis der in der Marktkirche zu Goslar ... aufbewahrten alten Druckwerke. Mit einem Verzeichnis der im Archive zu Goslar vorhandenen alten Handschriften und einem kurzen Vorworte über die Geschichte der Marktkirchen-Bibliothek.* pt. I: *Lateinische Werke.* progr. Goslar 1896. 51 pp. p. 4-5: 10 mss. and some fragments. No index. (Vatican Library)

*Göteborg, Sweden. See Lehmann.

Göteborgs Stadsbibliothek 1891-1941: *Minneskrift.* Göteborg 1941. Contains: T. Kleberg, 'Catalogus codicum Graecorum et latinorum Bibliothecae Gotoburgensis,' 48 pp. 30 Latin mss. (p. 14ff.).

Gotha, East Germany. Landesbibliothek. See *Archiv* VI; VIII.

E. S. Cyprianus, *Catalogus codicum manuscriptorum Bibliothecae Gothanae.* Leipzig 1714. 124 pp. 531 mss. Shelf marks partly changed.

F. Jacobs and F. A. Ukert, *Beiträge zur ältern Litteratur oder Merkwürdigkeiten der Herzoglichen Öffentlichen Bibliothek zu Gotha.* 3 vols. Leipzig 1835-43. Miscellaneous work, with frequent mention of mss. Vol. I no. 2 (1835) 197-278: 'Scriptores Graeci et Latini manuscripti.' Arranged alphabetically by authors. Vol. II no. 1 (1836) 1-158; no. 2 (1837) 333-70: Theological mss. Vol. III no. 1 (1838) 3-66: Latin poets and prose works of the Middle Ages. No. 2 (1843) 259-356: History and letters. Index (vol. III 379-404). (NN)

G. Rathgeber, *Bibliotheca Gothana: Section der abendländischen, mit Gemälden geschmückten Handschriften.* Gotha 1839. X, 32 pp. 1 ms. (Bibl. Nat. Paris)

L. Traube and R. Ehwald, 'Jean-Baptiste Maugérard, Ein Beitrag zur Bibliotheksgeschichte,' *Abhandlungen der Historischen Classe der Kgl. Bayerischen Akademie der Wissenschaften* XXIII (LXXVI, 1906) 301-87. Describes 50 mss. at Gotha. No index.

Handwritten inventory, in 2 vols. I: Codices membranacei et chartacei A. Mss. I 1-181; II 1-232; A 1-2073. II: Codices chartacei formae minoris. Mss. B 1-2071.

Sachkatalog, in *ca.* 50 vols. It includes the Briefkatalog, an alphabetical list of the senders of all letters in the collection.

H. Habich, *Codicem miscellaneum bibliothecae gymnasii Gothani descripsit et ex eo Reineri Alemannici poema Phagifacetum sive Thesmophagiam emendatius edidit.* progr. Gotha 1860. 32 pp. (PU)

R. Ehwald, *Beschreibung der Handschriften und Inkunabeln der Herzoglichen Gymnasialbibliothek zu Gotha.* progr. Gotha 1893. 20 pp. 10 mss.

M. Schneider, *Die Gelehrtenbriefe der Gothaer Gymnasialbibliothek aus dem XVI. und XVII. Jahrhundert.* progr. Gotha 1897. 35 pp. p. 4-25: Alphabetical list of authors for mss. 6-8, (Gotha, micr. at NNC) The mss. of the Gymnasialbibliothek are now in the Landesbibliothek, except for mss. 3 and 4, which are lost.

*Göttingen, West Germany. See *Archiv* VI. *Verzeichniss der Handschriften im preussischen Staate. I. Hannover.* 1 *Göttingen.* 3 vols. Berlin 1893-94. Arranged by subjects. Includes 121 mss. from St. Michael, Lüneburg (II). Index in vol. III.

*Göttweig, Austria. Stiftsbibliothek. See Cooper (Section A): *Archiv* VI; X; Heider; Neuwirth; *Der Oesterreichische Geschichtsforscher;* Schulte.

H. Jaeck, 'Verzeichniss der brauchbarsten Handschriften, welche sich in der Bibliothek der Abtey Göttweich befinden,' *Isis* 1822, *Litterarischer Anzeiger,* coll. 189-90. 49 mss. *Ibid.* 1824 no. 7, cover: The same, 'Über Handschriften.' 6 Göttweig mss. (NNM)

H. Mužik, 'Die Göttweiger Handschriften zu Classikern,' *Zeitschrift für die österreichischen Gymnasien* XLVII (1896) 398-400. *Manuscripten-Catalog der Stifts-Bibliothek zu Göttweig,* by V. Moeli (1844). 3 ms. vols. (microfilm at DLC). I: mss. 1-457. II: 458-910. III: Index. Shelf marks changed, and some mss. lost since 1844. (Communication of the librarian).

*Gouda, Holland. Stedelijke Librije.

D. Van Heel, *Handschriften berustende in de Goudse Librye.* Gouda 1949. 47 pp. 24 mss. No index.

*Gournay-en-Bray, France. See France, *Catalogue Général, Départements* II.

*Grado, Italy. See Wickhoff.

*Gran, see **Esztergom**.

Granada, Spain. Biblioteca Universitaria y Provincial. See Grubbs (Section A under Richardson); *Anuario; Neues Archiv* VI.

J. M. Caparrós, 'Indice de manuscritos de la Biblioteca Universitaria y Provincial de Granada,' *Revista del Centro de Estudios*

histéricos de Granada y su Reino VI (1916)
309-14. 122 mss. Index in Grubbs. (NN)
Card catalogue for mss. and incunabula, arranged by shelf marks.

—Duque de Gor.

Catálogo de la Biblioteca del Excmo. Sr. Duque de Gor (by E. Manuel de Villena).
Granada 1907. 254 pp. p. 5-18: mss., arranged by subjects. (Granada, Duque de
Gor, perhaps a privately printed, unique
copy).

*Grande Chartreuse**, France. See Martin.

*Grasse**, France. See France, *Catalogue
Général, Départements* XIV; XLI.

's Gravenhage (The Hague), Holland. See
Analecta Bollandiana VI; XXXI; *Archiv*
VII; VIII; Byvanck; Delisle; Haenel;
Lampen; Lehmann, *Holländische Reisefrüchte*; Lehmann, *Mitteilungen* II; *Neues
Archiv* XXXVIII, Novati; Omont; *Société
française.*

A. W. Byvanck, *Les principaux manuscrits à
peintures de la Bibliothèque Royale des
Pays-Bas et du Musée Meermanno-Westreenianum à la Haye.* 2 vols. Paris 1924.
vol. I: 48 mss.

—Koninklijke Bibliotheek.

A. Jubinal, *Lettres à M. le Comte de Salvandy
sur quelques-uns des manuscrits de la Bibliothèque Royale de la Haye,* Paris 1846. 262
pp. No index. (NN)

*De Oranje Nassau-boekerij en de Oranjepenningen in de Koninklijke bibliotheek en
in the Koninklijk penning-kabinet te
's Gravenhage.* 2 pts. in 1, Haarlem 1898.
pt. I lists 186 mss.

Catalogus codicum manuscriptorum Bibliothecae Regiae. vol. I: *Libri Theologici.*
Hague 1922. IX, 336 pp. 959 mss. (DLC)

Koninklijke Bibliotheek, Verslag. Hague
1867ff. Annual report in which the acquisitions of mss. are mentioned. (DLC,
incomplete.)

*Koninklijke Bibliotheek. Catalogus van de
Handschriften der Koninklijke Nederlandsche Akademie van Wetenschappen, in
bruikleen in de Koninklijke Bibliotheek.*
By D. J. H. Ter Horst. Hague 1938.

66 pp. 343 mss. Index.
Card index by authors (Cf. Born 276).
Card index by subjects. 3 boxes. (Cf. Born
275).

Stand Catalogus. Card index by shelf marks,
in 5 drawers.

—Museum Meermanno-Westreenianum.
Card index, 1 box.

Catalogus van de handschriften in het Museum Meermanno-Westreenianum, by A.
F. Dekker and Vermeeren. Typed catalogue ready for the press. Copy at the
Royal Library. (Communication of the
librarian)

*Gray**, France. See France, *Catalogue Général, Départements* VI; XLI.

Graz, Austria. See *Archiv* X; *Neues Archiv* XXI-XXIII.

—Universitätsbibliothek. See *Verzeichnis
der Handschriften* (for mss. no. 1-712);
Handschriftenverzeichnisse (for mss. no.
713-2066).

Zahn, 'Verzeichniss der Handschriften der
k.k. Universitäts-Bibliothek zu Gratz,'
Beiträge zur Kunde steiermärkischer Geschichtsquellen I (1864) 17-46. (NN)

—Steiermärkisches Landesarchiv.

Katalog der Handschriften, by J. v. Zahn
and A. Mell (Publicationen aus dem Steiermärkischen Landesarchive. Abtheilung A.
Kataloge. Kataloge des Steiermärkischen
Landesarchives. I. Johanneumsarchiv. 1.
Handschriften). Graz and Leipzig, 1898.
xi, 242 pp. 1460 mss.

Katalog der Handschriften. 1683 mss. Continued in another folder to no. 1823.
Superseded to no. 1456 (1460) by the
printed catalogue.

Greifswald, East Germany. See *Archiv*
XI; Hulshof (below under Rostock).

—Universitätsbibliothek.

H. Müller, 'Verzeichnis der Lateinischen
Handschriften in der Kgl. Universitäts-Bibliothek zu Greifswald,' *Neuer Anzeiger für Bibliographie und Bibliothekswissenschaft* 1875, 169-71; 198-204; 228-34; 269-74.

The same, 'Verzeichnis der Theologischen

Handschriften in der Kgl. Universitäts-Bibliothek zu Greifswald,' *Ibid.* 1875, 312-17; 346-49; 377-80; 1876, 13-19. No index.

The same, 'Die Manuscripta Borussica der Königlichen Universitäts-Bibliothek zu Greifswald,' *Zeitschrift für Preussische Geschichte und Landeskunde XIII* (1876) 217-220. 19 late mss. (MH)

The same, 'Die Manuscripta Pomeranica der Königlichen Universitäts-Bibliothek zu Greifswald,' *Baltische Studien* XXVII (1877) 1-167.

Handwritten inventory, in 7 vols., arranged by subjects. This is the source of Müller's printed catalogues, but the shelf marks have been changed, and some additions made. I: Borussica; Pomeranica; Italica; Francica; Batava. II: Orientalia; Latina; Germanica; Theologica. III: Suecica. IV: Kosegarten, Höfer, etc. (Nachlässe). V: Neuzugänge. (VI:): Kriegsbriefe. (VIII) K. Adam, *Katalog der Odebrechtschen Familienbibliothek im Rathaus der Stadt Greifswald* (1882-83, copied 1910; covers mss. and edd.)

—Bibliothek des Geistlichen Ministeriums (in der Nikolaikirche).

Th. Pyl, *Die Rubenow-Bibliothek: Die Handschriften und Urkunden der von Heinrich Rubenow 1456 gestifteten Juristen- und Artisten-Bibliothek zu Greifswald, aus der Nicolai-Kirche zu Greifswald herausgegeben.* Greifswald 1865. 196 pp. 93 mss. No index. (NjP)

The same, 'Die Handschriften und Urkunden in der Bibliothek der Nicolai-Kirche zu Greifswald,' *Baltische Studien* XX, 2 (1865) 148-95; XXI, 1 (1866) 1-148. Describes many mss. No index. (NN)

A. Reifferscheid, *Mitteilungen aus Handschriften der St. Nikolaikirchenbibliothek zu Greifswald.* progr. Greifswald 1902. 16 pp. 1 ms.

R. Lühder, 'Die Handschriften der Bibliothek des geistlichen Ministeriums zu Greifswald, in Fortsetzung von Dr. Th. Pyls " Rubenow-Bibliothek " 1865,' *Pommer-sche Jahrbücher* VII (1906) 263-336. No index. (MH)

*Grenoble, France. See France, *Catalogue Général, Départements* VII; XLI; *Universités*; Martin.

*Gries, Italy. See Bolzano.

*Grisignano, Italy. See Wickhoff.

*Groningen, Holland. See *Archiv* VIII; Byvanck; Lehmann, *Holländische Reisefrüchte*; *Société française.*

H. Brugmans, *Catalogus codicum manuscriptorum Universitatis Groninganae Bibliothecae.* Groningen 1898. 396 pp. 594 mss. and other collections. Nos. 2-214 are Latin (p. 2-100).

*Grosseto, Italy. See Mazzatinti XVI.

*Grottaferrata, Italy.

A. Rocchi, *Codices Cryptenses seu Abbatiae Cryptae Ferratae in Tusculano.* Tusculani 1883. 540 pp. 666 mss. mostly in Greek.

*Guadalajara, Spain.

I. Montiel, 'Incunables, impresos del siglo XVI y manuscritos en la Biblioteca Pública Provincial de Guadalajara,' *Revista Bibliográfica y Documental* III (1949) 141-161. p. 157-161: 48 mss. No index.

The same, 'Manuscritos de la Biblioteca Pública de Guadalajara,' *Revista de Archivos, Bibliotecas y Museos* LVIII (Ser. IV, vol. V, 1952) 61-69. 48 mss.

*Guadalupe, Spain. Monasterio de los PP. Franciscanos.

A. Barrado Manzano, 'Manuscritos franciscanos de la Biblioteca de Vicente Barrantes,' *Archivo Ibero-Americano*, Ser. II, vol. IX (1949) 211-237. Alphabetical list of 51 late mss. (NN)

*Guastalla, Italy. See Mazzatinti LXIII-LXIV.

*Gubbio, Italy. See *Archiv* XII; Mazzatinti I-II.

The mss. of the Biblioteca Sperelliana have been transferred to the Sottosezione Archivio di Stato.

G. Castelfranco, 'I corali miniati di S. Domenico di Gubbio,' *Bollettino d'Arte*, Ser. II, vol. VIII (1928-29) 529-555. 11 mss.

*Guéret, France. See France, *Catalogue Général, Départements* IV.

*Guingamp, France. See *ibid.* XX.

*Györ, Hungary. Püspöki Papnevalöintézet Könyvtará. See Radó.

A Györi Püspöki papnevelöintézet könyvtárának czimjegyzéke. By L. Zalka. Györ 1893. viii, 950 pp. p. 1-4: mss. (OCI)

*Gyula-Fehérvár. See Alba Julia.

Haarlem, Holland. See *Archiv* VIII; Byvanck; *Société française.*

—Stads-Bibliotheek en Leeszaal.

Catalogus Bibliothecae Publicae Harlemensis. Haarlem, 1848. 5 and 661 pp. p. 1-21: mss. mbr. in folio 1-22; in quarto 1-3; cart. in quarto 1-3. No index. (NN). New shelf marks added in library copy.

Lijst van Handschriften aanwezig op de Stadsbibliotheek en Leeszaal te Haarlem. (Haarlem n.d.). Offset printed. 29 pp. Arranged alphabetically.

—*Bisschoppelijk Museum.

B. Kruitwagen O. F. M., *Catalogus van de Handschriften en Boeken van het Bisschoppelijk Museum te Haarlem.* Amsterdam 1913. xix, 326 pp. 144 mss. Index (130ff.). (MH)

The Hague, see **'s Gravenhage**.

*Haguenau (Hagenau), France. Bibliothèque Municipale.

Catalogue sommaire des manuscrits conservés aux Archives-Bibliothèques de la Ville de Haguenau. Typed list of 13 mss., kindly supplied by Mlle J. Vielliard.

*Halberstadt, East Germany. See *Archiv* VIII; XI; Diestelkamp. See also under Halle.

Gustav Schmidt, *Die Handschriften der Gymnasial-Bibliothek.* 2 pts. progr. Halberstadt 1878-81. 38 and 32 pp. 235 ms. No index.

*Hall, Austria. Bibliothek der Franziskaner.

*Standortskatalog, vol. VII: mss.

Typed list of older mss. kindly supplied by Dr. H. Bachmann (Innsbruck).

Handwritten list of additional mss. kindly supplied by P. D. Gmeiner.

Halle, East Germany. See *Archiv* VI; XI; Diestelkamp; Lampen; *Neues Archiv* VIII.

**B. Weissenborn, *Der hallische Handschriftenschatz in Auswahl.* Halle 1939. 30 pp. Covers Universitätsbibliothek and Marien-Bibliothek. Cf. *Zentrallbatt für Bibliothekswesen* LVII (1940) 430-432.

—Archiv der Francke'schen Stiftungen.

Johannes Schmidt, (Wilhelm) Schum and August Müller, *Die Manuscripte der Waisenhaus-Bibliothek.* progr. Halle 1876. 64 pp. p. 17-37: 102 mss. of which only 15 mss. are Western (p. 17-23). No index. (NIC)

K. Weiske, 'Mitteilungen über die Handschriftensammlung der Hauptbibliothek der Franckeschen Stiftungen zu Halle a.d.S.,' in: *Aus der Hauptbibliothek der Franckeschen Stiftungen: Zur Begrüssung der 47. Versammlung Deutscher Philologen und Schulmänner in Halle a.s. dargebracht von dem Kollegium der Lateinischen Hauptschule* (progr. Halle 1903, 63 pp.) 7-24. 60 mss. No index.

—Bibliothek der Marienkirche.

Verzeichnis der auf der Marien-Bibliothek zu Halle befindlichen Handschriften (by Dr. F. K. Knauth, 1847). 2 ms. vols. I: Mss. no. 1-166. II: 167-285.

—Universitäts- und Landesbibliothek.

Aus alten Büchern der Hallischen Universitäts-Bibliothek. Halle 1900. (By M. Perlbach). 79 pp. Gives ms. notes from early printed books. No index. (NNGr)

Real-Katalog Ya-Yl. Handschriften. Arranged by shelfmarks and subjects. Complete for the old nucleus of the collection.

E. Förstemann, *Die Gräflich Stolbergische Bibliothek zu Wernigerode.* Nordhausen 1866. viii, 167 pp. p. 73-102: 89 Latin mss. Index (157ff.). Not complete. (DLC)

The nucleus of this collection, including both mss. listed and not listed in the printed catalogue, is now in Halle. The remainder is scattered.

The library also acquired many mss. from Halberstadt, Koethen, Magdeburg, Quedlinburg, Stendal, and other places of the region. The cataloguing of these acquisitions is in progress, and they have only temporary shelf marks so far.

Card file in 2 trays. I: 7 A 1-20 H 2. II: 25 C 1-27 B 27. Covers these new acquisitions. Not complete.

Verzeichnis der L-B-Listen. Typed lists of the libraries which were absorbed by the Halle library after the last war.

H. Reinhold, 'Die Handschriftensammlung der Ungarischen Nationalbibliothek in Halle,' *Zentralblatt für Bibliothekswesen* XXX (1913) 490-99. 105 mss. Mostly modern material. No index.

*Ham, France. See France, *Catalogue Général, Départements* XXVI.

Hamburg, West Germany. Staats- und Universitäts-Bibliothek.

Many mss. have been missing since the last war, and at least some of them have been recently reported to be in Berlin.

See Cooper (Section A); *Archiv* VI; IX; (Académie Royale) Commission; Lehmann, *Mitteilungen* V.

C. Petersen, *Geschichte der Hamburgischen Stadtbibliothek.* Hamburg 1838. xviii, 254 pp. p. 190-251: 'Nachweisung der wichtigsten bereits gedruckten Nachrichten über die in der Hamburgischen Stadtbibliothek vorhandenen Handschriften...'. Surveys also the content of some mss.

Bibliotheca Uffenbachiana Universalis sive Catalogus librorum tam typis quam manu exaratorum quos ... collegit Zach. Conradus ab Uffenbach, nunc vero ... venales prostant. 4 vols. Frankfurt 1729-31. Vol. III (1730): *Bibliothecae Uffenbachianae Universalis tomus III. exhibens integrum mssstorum tam vet. quam recent. adparatum ...* 758 pp. Index at the end. Vol. IV (1731): *... exhibens libros collatos ac manu cl. virorum illustratos.* 1382 pp. Index. (NN)

Bibliotheca Uffenbachiana seu catalogus librorum quos ... collegit ... Zach. Conradus ab Uffenbach. 4 vols. in 1, Frankfurt 1735. Vol. III lists books with mss. notes. No index.

Bibliotheca Uffenbachiana Mssta seu Catalogus et recensio msstorum codicum qui in Bibliotheca Zachariae Conradi ab Uffenbach

Traiecti ad Moenum adservantur ... priores Jo. Henricus Maius ... recensuit reliquas possessor ipse digessit ... 2 vols. in 1, Halle 1720. Vol. II lists many Latin mss. (NN)

Catalogus manuscriptorum codicum Bibliothecae Uffenbachianae. Frankfurt 1747. 320 pp. No shelf marks. No index. (MH) Not all of the Uffenbach mss. went to Hamburg. Many others were scattered.

Conspectus supellectilis epistolicae et literariae manu exaratae quae exstat apud Jo. Christophorum Wolfium ... Hamburg 1736. 463 pp. (DLC)

N. Staphorst, *Historia ecclesiae Hamburgensis diplomatica, das ist Hamburgische Kirchengeschichte.* 2 parts in 5 vols. Hamburg 1723-31. Part I, vol. III (1727) 138-486: 'Nachricht von der Bibliothec zu St. Petri.' Describes mss. no. 4-60 (p. 182-486; nos. 1-3 are edd.). (MH)

J. J. Rasch, *Historische Beschreibung der öffentlichen Kirchen-Bibliothec zu St. Jacobi in Hamburg.* (Hamburg 1754). 40 pp. p. 25-32: 9 mss. No index. (Paris, Bibliothèque Nationale).

The same, *Fortgesetzte historische Beschreibung der öffentlichen Kirchen-Bibliothek zu St. Jacobi in Hamburg.* Hamburg 1755. 48 pp. p. 18-26: 13 mss. Two further continuations (1756-57) contain nothing on mss. (Paris, Bibliothèque Nationale)

F. L. Hoffmann, 'Relevé des manuscrits se rattachant aux Pays-Bas et à la Belgique ... qui se trouvent à la bibliothèque publique de la ville de Hambourg,' *Le Bibliophile Belge* XVIII (1862) 343-54; XX (1864) 22-36. No index.

F. Eyssenhardt, 'Die spanischen Handschriften der Stadtbibliothek,' *Jahrbuch der Hamburgischen Wissenschaftlichen Anstalten* XIV (1896, published 1897) 1-21. 42 mss. No index. Not complete. (NN)

The same, 'Die italienischen Handschriften der Stadtbibliothek I,' *Ibid.* XVIII (1900, published 1901) 19-100. 24 mss. No index. Not complete. (NN)

Philologica Hamburgensia: *Für die Mitglieder der 48. Versammlung Deutscher Philologen und Schulmänner ausgestellt von der Stadtbibliothek zu Hamburg*. (By R. Münzel). Hamburg 1905. 58 pp. Summary list of selected 277 mss. No index.

Catalog zum Scrinium angelegt 1921. 254 mss.

The old ms. inventory, which usually fails to give the century, comprises the following 13 unnumbered volumes: *Codices Mssti Theologic* I-II. (III:) *Codices Mssti. Philologia* (IV:) *Cod. Mssti. Philosophici argumenti*; *Mathesis*. (V:) *Ars medica, chemia alchemia, magia*. (VI-VII:) *Katalog der Historischen Manuscripte* I; II. (VIII:) *Hist. litt., Hist. Art.* (IX:) *Geogr.* (X:) *Jur.* (XI:) *Thesaurus Epistolicus* (*Index voluminum quae Joh. Christoph. Wolfii conspectui supellectilis epistolicae et literariae sunt addita*. (XII:) *Verzeichnis slavischer Handschriften*, by S. v. Arseniew (1906). (XIII:) *Katalog der musikalischen Handschriften*.

Handschriften-Katalog der Hanseatica, 8 vols.

The mss. of St. Petri, St. Jacobi, Convent St. Catharinen have no inventories, yet see above.

Conspectus supellectilis epistolicae Uffenbachii et Wolfiorum in Bibliotheca publica Hamburgensi asservatae by A. de Dommer, 2 vols. I: List of senders. II: List of addressees.

*Hameln, West Germany.

E. Bachof, *Die Handschriften und älteren Drucke der Gymnasialbibliothek*. progr. Hameln 1876. 24 pp. 12 mss.

*Hannover (Hanover), West Germany. See *Archiv* I; VIII; Diekamp.

C. L. Grotefend, *Verzeichniss der Handschriften und Incunabeln der Stadt-Bibliothek zu Hannover*. 3 pts. Hanover 1844. I p. 1-30: 142 mss. of Stadt-Bibliothek, 100 of Kreuzkirche. No index. (MH)

E. Bodemann, *Die Handschriften der kgl. öffentlichen Bibliothek zu Hannover*. Hanover 1867. 656 pp. 1262 mss. (NN)

H. Graeven, 'Die drei ältesten Handschriften im Michaeliskloster zu Lüneburg,' *Zeitschrift des historischen Vereins für Niedersachsen* 1901, 276-318. 3 mss. now at Hanover. (NN)

—*Kestner-Museum. Over 120 mss.

Cf. *Führer durch das Kestner-Museum*. 2nd ed. Section II. Hannover 1904. 159 pp. p. 137-42: Mss. and autographs.

Schloss Harburg (Kreis Donauwörth), West Germany. Fürstlich-Oettingen-Wallerstein'sche Bibliothek. See *Neues Archiv* VII.

G. Schepss, *Zwei Maihinger Handschriften*. progr. Dinkelsbühl 1878. 28 pp. (MH)

The same, *Sechs Maihinger Handschriften*. progr. Dinkelsbühl 1879. 26 pp. (Harburg, Schlossbibliothek)

Öttingen-Wallersteinische Sammlungen in Maihingen. Handschriften-Verzeichnis. I. Hälfte, by G. Grupp. Nördlingen 1897. 36 pp. 968 mss. No index. Not complete.

F. Zoepfl, 'Maihinger mittelalterliche Handschriften und Inkunabeln aus dem Besitze von Weltgeistlichen der Diözese Augsburg,' *Archiv für die Geschichte des Hochstifts Augsburg* VI (1929) 745-65. Arranged by owners. No index. (MH)

(*Standortskatalog*). 1 ms. vol. Complete. Some mss. were sold some time ago.

*Card file, arranged by subjects.

*Hartford, Connecticut, U.S.A. See De Ricci.

*Hasselt, Belgium.

G. Remans, 'Handschriften in de Boekerij der Minderbroeders te Hasselt,' *Het Oude Land van Loon* IV (1949) 173-176. 18 mss. No index. (Brussels, Bibliotheque Royale; micr. at NNC)

*Havelberg, East Germany. See *Serapeum* I.

Heidelberg, West Germany. Universitätsbibliothek. See *Archiv* I; IX; Buchon; Leclercq; Lehmann, *Mitteilungen* I.

F. Wilken, *Geschichte der Bildung, Beraubung und Vernichtung der alten Heidelbergischen Büchersammlungen. Nebst einem ... Verzeichniss der ... von ... Pius VII. der Universität Heidelberg zurückgegebenen Handschriften...* Heidelberg 1817.

552 pp. Index of authors not complete (p. v-vii). p. 273: 'Verzeichniss der aus der pfälzischen Bibliothek im Vatikan an die Universität Heidelberg zurückgegebenen Handschriften.' Includes several Latin mss. (p. 291-303).

A. von Oechelhäuser, *Die Miniaturen der Universitäts-Bibliothek zu Heidelberg*. 2 vols. Heidelberg 1887-95. 45 mss.

Katalog der Handschriften der Universitätsbibliothek in Heidelberg. I (1887): *Die altdeutschen Handschriften*, by K. Bartsch. (NNC) II (1903): *Die deutschen Pfälzer Handschriften*, by J. Wille. Covers only German mss. (DLC)

Catalogus alphabeticus Bibl. Acad. Heidelberg. Cod. Heid(elbergenses). 9 vols. Centuries not given. I: A-Bons. II: Bontenock-Cyprianus. III: Dagobert-Geibel. IV: Geiler-Justiniani. V: Kahle-Mendoza. VI: Menologio-Quedlinburgische. VII: R-Souvenir. VIII: Spaeth-Tychsen. IX: Uchteman-Zwinger. (micr. at NN and DLC)

Codices Salemitani. 2 vols. I: Abbo-Justinian. II: Karinga-Zwingerus. (micr. at. NN and DLC)

Druckwerke mit Bemerkungen. 2 vols.

*Heilbronn, West Germany. See Gercken.

*Heiligenkreuz, Austria. See *Xenia Bernardina*.

S. Grill, 'Nachtrag zum Handschriftenverzeichnis der Stiftsbibliothek Heiligenkreuz,' *Sancta Crux* (Jubilaeums-Festausgabe 1935) 62-67. (Vienna, Nationalbibliothek; micr. at NNC). Reprinted in *Collectanea Ordinis Cisterciensium Reformatorum* XII (1950) 49-56. Mss. no. 551-581. No index. (Abbey of Gethsemani, Trappist, Ky.)

*Heilsberg, see Lidzbark Warminski.

*Helmingham Hall, England. Earl of Tollemache. See Great Britain, *Historical Manuscripts Commission*. See also under London, British Museum.

*Helsinki (Helsingfors), Finland. See Lehmann.

T. Haapanen, *Verzeichnis der mittelalterli-*

chen Handschriftenfragmente in der Universitätsbibliothek zu Helsingfors. (Helsingin Yliopiston Kirjaston Julkaisuja. Helsingfors Universitetsbiblioteks Skrifter IV; VII; XVI). 3 vols. Helsingfors 1922-32. Only liturgical mss.

*Hereford, England. See Holtzmann (Section A); Bernardus; Schenkl.

A. T. Bannister, *A Descriptive Catalogue of the Manuscripts in the Hereford Cathedral Library*. Hereford 1927. viii, 190 pp. Index at the beginning. Introduction by M. R. James. Mss. O. 1.I-O.9.XI; P.1.I-P.9.VI (NN)

*Herford, West Germany. See *Archiv* XI.

*Herrnstein über Siegburg, West Germany. Gräflich Nesselrode'sche Bibliothek. Formerly in Herten, Westfalen. Mss. lost during the war. (Communication of the owner)

*'s Hertogenbosch, Holland.

P. J. Ridder Van der Does de Bije, *Analytische Catalogus der Oorkonden met opgave der Handschriften berustende in de Boekerij van het Provinciaal Genootschap van Kunsten en Wetenschappen in Noord-Brabant*. 's Hertogenbosch 1875. 127 pp. p. 106-127: 534 mss. Mostly late material. (DLC)

A. F. O. van Sasse van Ysselt, *Nieuwe Catalogus der Oorkonden en Handschriften berustende in de Boekerij van het Provinciaal Genootschap van Kunsten en Wetenschappen in Noord-Brabant*. 'sHertogenbosch. 1900. 252 pp. p. 167ff.: 662 mss.

The same, *Eerste Supplement*. 's Hertogenbosch 1915. 426 pp. p. 341ff.: Mss. no. 10a-666. No index.

*Herzfeld, West Germany. Kirchenbibliothek. See Schmidt.

*Herzogenburg, Austria. Stiftsbibliothek. See Frast; Heider; Neuwirth.

Katalog der Handschriften der Stiftsbibliothek Herzogenburg. Typed list based on a fuller inventory. 428 mss. (microfilm at DLC).

*Hesdin, France. See France, *Catalogue Général, Départements* IV.

Hildesheim, West Germany.

J. M. Kratz, *Der Dom zu Hildesheim.* pt. II-III in 1 vol. Hildesheim 1840. pt. II p. 103-30: 6 mss. No index. (NNUT)

R. Herzig, *Der Dom zu Hildesheim und seine Kunstschätze.* Hildesheim 1911. 107 pp. Lists 11 mss. in the Domschatz. (NNUT)

—8th ed. Hildesheim and Leipzig 1925. 55 pp. and plates. Lists 10 mss. (CtY)

—Beverin'sche Bibliothek (Dombibliothek) Card file, arranged by subjects and numbers. 765 mss. Some of them were lost during the last war.

Jos. God. Müller, *Nachricht über die Bibliothek des Gymnasii Josephini und die auf derselben vorhandenen Handschriften und alten Drucke.* progr. Hildesheim 1876. 44 pp. p. 1-15: 76 mss. No index. (NIC)

H. Nentwig, 'Die mittelalterlichen Handschriften und die Wiegendrucke in der Stadtbibliothek zu Hildesheim,' *Centralblatt für Bibliothekswesen* XI (1894) 345-68. 12 mss. No index.

*Hof, East Germany.

H. Hommel, 'Die Handschriften der Stadtbibliothek Hof,' *Archiv für Schreib- und Buchwesen* IV (1930) 47-60. 50 mss. No index. (Pierpont Morgan Library)

*Hohenfurt, see Vyšší Brod.

Holkham Hall, Wells, Norfolk, England. Library of the Earl of Leicester. See *Archiv* IX; Great Britain, *Historical Manuscripts Commission;* Schenkl.

R. Förster, 'Mittheilungen aus Handschriften. 1. Handschriften in Holkham,' *Philogus* XLII (1884) 158-167. Lists à few Latin mss. (p. 165-167).

L. Dorez, *Les manuscrits à peintures de la Bibliothèque de Lord Leicester à Holkham Hall, Norfolk.* 2 vols. Paris 1908. (NN)

S. de Ricci, *A Handlist of Manuscripts in the Library of the Earl of Leicester at Holkham Hall, abstracted from the catalogues of William Roscoe and Frederick Madden* (Supplements to the Transactions of the Bibliographical Society no. 7). Oxford 1932. 64 pp. 771 mss. No index.

W. O. Hassall, *A Catalogue of the Library of Sir Edward Coke* (Yale Law Library Publications 12). London and New Haven 1950. xxvii, 98 pp. 1227 nos. No index. Covers mss. and edd. States whether the book remains at Holkham, but gives no shelf marks.

Catalogue of Manuscripts in the Library at Holkham Hall in the County of Norfolk belonging to Thomas William Coke Esq. M.P., compiled and arranged by William Roscoe, collated and enlarged by Frederic Madden (1815-28). 8 vols. Much fuller than De Ricci's printed catalogue, which is entirely based on this inventory. I: mss. 1-68. II: 69-112. III: 113-203. IV: 204-262. V: 263-371. VI: 372-512. VII: 513-788. VIII: Introductory Notices and Illustrations. Data supplied by W. O. Hassell.

Some of the mss. were recently transferred to the British Museum and to the Bodleian Library.

*Honfleur, France. See France, *Catalogue Général, Départements* X.

*Houston, Texas. U.S.A. See De Ricci.

*Höxter, West Germany.

K. Honselmann, 'Verzeichniss der Handschriften der Dechaneibibliothek zu Höxter,' *Zeitschrift für vaterländische Geschichte und Altertumskunde* (ed. Verein für Geschichte und Altertumskunde Westfalens) LXXXIV (1927) pt. 2 p. 161-62. 45 mss. No index. (NN)

*Huesca, Spain. See *Anuario;* Cordoliani.

R. del Arco, 'Libros corales, códices y otros manuscritos de la Catedral de Huesca (Noticias inéditas),' *Linajes de Aragón* VI (1915) 242-54. Survey article, not a catalogue. Discusses several mss. No shelf marks. No index. (NNFr)

I. Montiel, 'Manuscritos de la Biblioteca Pública Provincial de Huesca,' *Revista de Archivos, Bibliotecas y Museos* LV (Ser. IV, vol. III, 1949) 57-70. Alphabetical list of 131 vols. Mostly late. No index. No shelf marks.

*Hyerès, France, See France, *Catalogue Général, Départements* IX; XLI.

Iesi, Italy. Biblioteca Comunale.

(Fondo Principale). *Manoscritti.* Alphabetical list of 147 mss. (Cf. AB V 509; VI 555).

Card index.

(Fondo Planettiano).

C. Annibaldi, 'Una Biblioteca Umbra a Iesi,' *Bollettino della Regia Deputazione di Storia Patria per l'Umbria* XIX, no. 1 (1915) 183-189. Survey. No index. (NN)

Ms. folder containing an incomplete list of the mss.

—*Conte Aurelio Baldeschi-Balleani. See *Manoscritti e Libri rari notificati.*

M. Vattasso, 'Un codice antico e sconosciuto dell' Agricola di Tacito,' *Bollettino di filologia classica* IX (1902-03) 107.

*Ilfeld, East Germany.

Freyer, *Verzeichniss der in der Bibliothek der Ilfelder Klosterschule vorhandenen älteren Drucke und Handschriften.* progr. Ilfeld, Nordhausen 1876. 63 pp. 17 mss. (p. 35-47). No index. (NIC)

*Imola, Italy. Biblioteca Comunale. See Mazzatinti (1887).

R. Galli, *I manoscritti e gli incunaboli della Biblioteca Comunale di Imola.* Imola 1894. cxxii, 94 pp. Index (p. cxix ff.). 173 mss. (p. xxix ff.).

*Library copy of printed catalogue with ms. addidtions for acquisitions after 1894. (AB IV 409-10).

Cf. F. Mancini, 'I fondi speciali manoscritti della Biblioteca Comunale d'Imola,' *Studi Romagnoli* VI (1955) 103-128.

Innichen, see San Candido.

*Innsbruck, Austria. Staatsarchiv. See under Trento.

—*Universitätsbibliothek. See also under Novacella.

See Lehmann, *Mitteilungen* I; *Der Oesterreichische Geschichtsforscher*; Wickhoff; Zingerle.

F. Wilhelm, 'Die historischen Handschriften der Universitäts-Bibliothek in Innsbruck,' *Mittheilungen des österreichischen Vereines für Bibliothekswesen* V (1901) 61-66; 135-38; 209-12; VI (1902) 34-39; 67-74; 106-10. No index. (NN)

'Die Rechtshandschriften der Universitätsbibliothek in Innsbruck' (By A. Wretschko) in: *Beiträge zur Rechtsgeschichte Tirols. Festschrift herausgegeben vom Ortsausschuss des 27. Deutschen Juristentages* (Innsbruck 1904) 173-213. Also separately (Innsbruck 1904, 41 pp.). No index.

A. Zingerle, *Beiträge zur Geschichte der Philologie. I. Theil. De carminibus latinis saeculi XV. et XVI. ineditis.* Innsbruck 1880. LXI, 151 pp. Describes Innsbruck ms. 664 (and Vienna, ms. 3506).

A. Stara, 'Wiltner Handschriften in der Innsbrucker Universitätsbibliothek,' *Analecta Praemonstratensia* XVIII (1942) 144-145.

Handschriften Zettelkatalog. 1155 mss. At the end, a list of the mss. turned over to Italy in 1921 (microfilm at DLC).

Handschriften, Bandkatalog. Alphabetical index (microfilm at DLC).

—*Servitenkloster. 500 mss. No information.

—*Tiroler Landesmuseum Ferdinandeum. 500 mss. No information.

*Ipswich, England. See M. R. James; Schenkl.

M. R. James, 'Description of the Ancient Manuscripts in the Ipswich Public Library,' *Proceedings of the Suffolk Institute of Archaeology and Natural History* XXII (1936) 86-103. 9 mss. No index. (NN)

*Isny, West Germany. Bibliothek der Nikolaikirche.

I. Kammerer and G. Kopp, *Die Nikolaikirche in Isny und ihre Bibliothek.* Isny 1949. 31 pp. Surveys 70 mss. (p. 22-23). (NN)

Handschriftenkatalog der Nikolaikirchenbibliothek Isny, by K. O. Müller. Typed volume. Describes ca. 80 mss. (Communication of the librarian)

*Issoudin, France. See France, *Catalogue Général, Départements* IV.

*Istanbul (Constantinople), Turkey. See *Archiv* IX.

F. Blass, 'Die griechischen und lateinischen Handschriften im alten Serail zu Konstantinopel,' *Hermes* XXIII (1888) 219-33; 622-25.

A. Deissmann, *Forschungen und Funde im Serai.* Berlin 1933. 144 pp. p. 37-135: 'Verzeichnis der nichtislamischen Handschriften der Serai-Bibliothek.' 135 mss. of which some in Latin. (NN)

*Ithaca, New York, USA. See De Ricci.

*Ivrea, Italy. See *Analecta Bollandiana* XLI; *Archiv* IX; Mazzatinti IV; Reifferscheid.

—*Biblioteca Capitolare.

*Library copy of Mazzatinti adds 10 mss. (Communication of the librarian).

Jena, East Germany. Universitätsbibliothek. See *Archiv* III; VIII.

B. G. Struvii . . . 'Historia et memorabilia Bibliothecae Ienensis,' in: *De Bibliothecis accessio altera collectioni Maderianae adiuncta,* Helmstedt 1705, p. 279-292. Lists a few mss. (286-88).

J. Chr. Mylius, *Memorabilia Bibliothecae academicae Jenensis sive designatio codicum manuscriptorum . . . et librorum impressorum plerumque rariorum . . .* Jena 1746. 640 pp. p. 300-410: 'De codicibus Bibliothecae Electoralis manuscriptis.' 125 mss. Index (411ff.). Shelf marks partly changed. (NN)

Universitäts-Bibliothek Jena, Katalog der Handschriften. Typed copy by Dr. E. Brandenburg (1931-32) from the lost handwritten catalogue. Electorales Fol. 1-100; Q 1-21; Q Phil 1-5; O 1-2. Bose Fol 1-8; Q 1-30; O 1-9. Sagittarius Fol 1-18; Q 1-27; O 1-16. Recens Fol 1-10; O 1-4. Appendix 1-30. Birkneriana theol 1-4; Fol. 1-3. Other collections.

Manuscripta Buderiana, Bosiana et Sagittariana, befindlich in der Bibliothek zu Jena. Typed copy by Dr. Brandenburg (1931) from the handwritten catalogue of Christ. A. Vulpius (1819). Buder Fol 1-395; Q 1-115; O 1-14. In spite of the title, the volume does not describe the Bose mss., or all of the Sagittarius mss.

Universitäts-Bibliothek Jena. Katalog der Handschriften der Gruppe 'Provisorisch.'

1 typed vol. Mss. Fol 1-161; Q 1-110; O 1-41.

Griechische Handschriften der Universitätsbibliothek Jena. Typed list which covers also translations from the Greek.

A card index covering the continuation of the group 'Provisorisch' and the 'Goethe-Bibliothek' (the collection of Goethe's grandsons) is lost.

Jesi, see **Iesi**.

*Joigny, France. See France, *Catalogue Général, Départements* VI.

*Kaliningrad, USSR. See *Archiv* XI.

**Jo. Dan. Metzger, *Medicinischer Briefwechsel.* 1785. Contains: 'Verzeichniss der medicinischen Handschriften auf der kgl. Bibliothek zu Königsberg.'

R. J. Bock, 'Nachrichten über Handschriften und alte Druckwerke der Gräfl. von Wallenrodtischen Bibliothek zu Königsberg i. Pr.,' *Preussische Provincial-Blätter* II (1829) 505-18. 40 mss. No index.

E. J. H. Steffenhagen, *Catalogus codicum manuscriptorum Bibliothecae Regiae et Universitatis Regimontanae.* 2 vols. Königsberg 1861-72. Covers 415 juristic and historical mss. Each volume indexed. Not complete. (NN)

A. Seraphim, *Handschriften-Katalog der Stadtbibliothek Königsberg i. Pr.* (Mitteilungen aus der Stadtbibliothek zu Königsberg i. Pr. I). Königsberg 1909. 411 pp. There is no information about the fate of these collections.

*Kalocsa (Colocza), Hungary. See *Archiv* VI; Radó.

J. Csontosi, 'A kalocsai föegyházi könyvtárat Kéziratai,' *Magyar Könyvszemle* VIII (1883) 275-308. 280 mss. (DLC)

**P. Winkler, *A kalocsai érseki kastély és föszékesegyházi könyvtár története.* Kalocsa 1932. p. 32 and 40-42: mss.

*Card file.

*Kamenz, East Germany.

Munde, 'Die alte Bibliothek der Hauptkirche St. Marien in Kamenz,' *Neues Lausitzisches Magazin* LXXV (1899) 290-92. Discusses mss. (NN)

*Kamienna Gora, Poland.

Th. Langner, *Katalog der von Wallenberg-Fenderlin'schen Bibliothek zu Landeshut i. Schl.* Landeshut 1881. x, 136 pp. p. 112-36: 26 mss. arranged alphabetically. (Schwenckfelder Historical Library, Pennsburg, Pa.)

H. Pohl, *I. Nachtrag zu dem Katalog der von Wallenberg-Fenderlin'schen Bibliothek zu Landeshut i. Schl.* Landeshut 1902. 15 pp. p. 15: 5 mss. (Schwenckfelder Historical Library). The fate of the collection is not known.

*Kampen, Holland. Archief der Gemeente. Several Latin mss. List of some mss. kindly supplied by the librarian.

*Karl-Marx-Stadt (Chemnitz), East Germany. Bezirksbibliothek.

M. Lehnerdt, 'Zu den Briefen des Leonardo Bruni von Arezzo,' *Zeitschrift für vergleichende Litteraturgeschichte* N.F. V (1892) 459-466. Describes ms. 2411a.

Karlsruhe, West Germany. Badische Landesbibliothek.

See Cooper (Section A); *Archiv* XI; Buchon; Gercken; Lehmann, *Mitteilungen* I.

Die Handschriften der Grossherzogl. Badischen Hof- und Landesbibliothek in Karlsruhe. 9 vols. Karlsruhe 1895-1932. Vol. I (1891): W. Brambach, history of the collection. Vol. II (1892): Oriental mss. Vol. III (1895): A. Holder, *Die Durlacher und Rastatter Handschriften.* 263 and 328 mss. Vol. IV (1896): W. Brambach, *Die Karlsruher Handschriften.* 1299 mss. and other items. Vol. V (1906): A. Holder, *Die Reichenauer Handschriften; Die Pergamenthandschriften.* 267 mss. Vol. VI (1914): The same cont. *Die Papierhandschriften.* 164 mss. and 193 fragments. Vol. VII (1918): The same cont. Index. Vol. VIII (1926): K. Preisendanz, *Die Karlsruher Handschriften,* cont. Mss. no. 1300-2000. Vol. IX (1932): The same, *Die Handschriften der Klosters Ettenheim-Münster.* 460 mss. Each volume indexed.

Beilage II: 1894. 49, XIII, 117, xx pp. *Romanische Handschriften* by F. Lamey (49 pp., 7 ms.). *Deutsche Handschriften,* by T. Längin (Paris, Bibliothèque Nationale)

Beilage III: E. Ettlinger, *Die ursprüngliche Herkunft der Handschriften, die aus Kloster-, Bischöflichen und Ritterschafts-Bibliotheken nach Karlsruhe gelangt sind.* Heidelberg 1901. 93 pp. This covers Allerheiligen (7 mss.), Gengenbach (2 mss.), Güntersthal (17 mss.), Lichtenhal (142 mss.), Oehningen (1 ms.), Offenburg (1 ms.), St. Blasien (117 mss.), St. Georgen (111 mss.), St. Märgen (12 mss.), St. Trudpert (4 mss.), Schuttern (5 mss.), Schwarzach (19 mss.), Thennenbach (10 mss.), Wonnenthal (17 mss.), Bruchsal (11 mss.), Meersburg (5 mss.), Kraichgau-Heilbronn (5 mss.), Ortenau-Offenburg (12 mss.). The index (p. 74-92) covers also Ettlinger's list of the St. Peter mss. and his list of the 447 Ettenheim-Münster mss.

E. Ettlinger, 'Geschichte der Bibliothek von St. Peter im Schwarzwalde unter besonderer Berücksichtigung des Handschriftenbestandes,' *Zeitschrift für die Geschichte des Oberrheins* LIV (N.F. XV, 1900) 611-641. 123 perg. and 48 pap. mss. (NN)

F. Molter, *Beiträge zur Geschichte und Litteratur: Aus einigen Handschriften der Markgräflich Baadischen Bibliothek.* Frankfurt 1798. xlvi, 270 pp. 5 mss. No index. (ICU)

H. Ehrensberger, *Bibliotheca liturgica manuscripta: Nach Handschriften der grossherzoglich Badischen Hof- und Landes-Bibliothek.* Karlsruhe 1889. ix, 84 pp.

E. Ettlinger, 'Studien über die Urprovenienzen von Handschriften der Grossherzoglichen Hof- und Landesbibliothek zu Karlsruhe,' *Centralblatt für Bibliothekswesen* XVI (1899) 437-69. Lists 447 mss. from Ettenheim-Münster.

Th. Raschl, 'Zur Geschichte der Blasianer Handschriften,' *Ibid.* XXXVI (1919) 243-56.

The library has more complete and more detailed inventories of all the collections listed above. Moreover, there is an inventory of recent acquisitions, in 4 vols., entitled *Karlsruher Hs.* (I: 1880-2056, superseded to no. 2000 by the printed catalogue; II: 2057-2316; III: 2317-2451; IV: 2452-2639). *Mss. Unbestimmter Herkunft* (36 mss., of which nos. 23-36 have been transferred to the Ettenheim-Münster collection, cf. the printed catalogue). *Fragmente unbestimmter Herkunft* (35 mss.). *Fragmenta Augiensia* (nos. 194-212, cf. the printed catalogue vol. VI).

—*Generallandesarchiv.

Inventare des Grossherzogl. Badischen General- Landesarchivs. 4 vols. Karlsruhe 1 901-11. I (1901) 193-290: Mss. 1-1161. II (1907) 324-346: Mss. 1162-1350. (WU)

Veröffentlichungen der Staatlichen Archivverwaltung Baden-Württemberg. Gesamtübersicht der Bestände des Generallandesarchivs Karlsruhe. By M. Krebs. 2 pts. Stuttgart 1954-57. 576 pp. Part I, p. 155-181: 2720 mss. More complete, but less detailed than the older inventory.

*Karlův Týn** (Karlstein), Czechoslovakia.

F. M. Bartoš, 'Rukopisy děkanství karlštejnského' (Les manuscrits du décanat au château de Karlův Týn), *Věstník Královské České Společnosti Nauk, Třída Filosoficko-Historicko-Filologicka,* 1944 (published 1946), no. 5 (1945). 18 pp. 23 mss.

*Karlsburg**, see **Alba Julia**.

*Kaschau**, see **Košice**.

Kassel, West Germany. Landesbibliothek. See Coope r (Section A); *Archiv* I; VI; Hirsching; Lehmann, *Mitteilungen* II and IV.

Schubart, 'Zwei italienische Handschriften der Landesbibliothek in Kassel,' *Serapeum* XXIV (1863) 36-41.

W. Hopf, ed., *Die Landesbibliothek Kassel,* 1580-1930. 2 vols. in 1, Marburg 1930. pt. II, 127 pp.: G. Struck, *Handschriftenschätze der Landesbibliothek Kassel.* Describes 20 selected Latin mss. No index.

Handschriften Katalog. 2 vols. I: Mss. Theol. Fol. 1-170, Theol. Qu. 1-130, Theol. Oct.

1-42; Iur. (76,43, and 2 mss. respectively); Med. (12,23,12); Physica (15,10,3); Oec. (1,14,0); Chemica (22,106,40); Philos. (34,34,9); Math. (61,54,22); Astron. (16, 17,4); Philol. (28,123,16); Hist. (135,81, 23); Hist. Litterariae (34,36,15); Poetica (31,29,17); Theatralia (8,30,5). II: *Manuscripta Hassiaca.* Fol. 1-659; Qu. 1-324; Oct. 1-125.

—*Friedrichs-Gymnasium.

(Carl Friedrich Weber), 'Fragmenta codicum manuscriptorum in bibliotheca Gymnasii Cassellani servata,' progr. Cassel 1846 (IV, 44 pp.) 32-39. 2 mss. (Heidelberg, University Library, partial micr. at NNC) The mss. are in the Landesbibliothek. (Communication of the Landesbibliothek Kassel)

*Katowice**, Poland. Biblioteka Śląska. See Saxl and Meier.

*Kempten**, West Germany. See *Serapeum* XXIV.

*Kenilworth**, Illinois, U.S.A., See De Ricci.

*Kew**, England. Sir Sydney Cockerell. See Saxl and Meier.

Sir Sydney Cockerell, 'Signed Manuscripts in my Collection,' *Book Handbook* I, no. 6-9 (1948-50) 321-338; 402-404; 429-449; II, no. 1 (1951) 13-26. *Book Collector* I, no. 2 (1952) 77-91. 14 mss. Some of them have been recently sold.

*Kiel**, West Germany. Universitätsbibliothek. See *Serapeum* XXXI; Steffenhagen.

H. Ratjen, *Verzeichniss der Handschriften der Kieler Universitätsbibliothek welche die Herzogthümer Schleswig und Holstein betreffen.* 3 vols. Kiel 1858-66. I (1858): S.H. 1-186. II (1858): S.H. 187-576A. Index. (NNC). III (1865-66). Local material only. (DLC) Vol. I-II were first published as supplements of *Nordalbingische Studien* I, V and VI (1847-54). (Communication of the librarian in Kiel).

The same, *Zur Geschichte der Kieler Bibliothek.* 2 pts. progr. Kiel 1862-63. 136 pp. p. 40-60; 65-116: 'Ehemalige Bordesholmer Handschriften der Kieler Universitätsbibliothek.' 121 mss. Index (127ff.). (NjP)

The same, *Verzeichniss von Handschriften der Kieler Universitäts-Bibliothek. Abtheilung* 1-4. progr. Kiel 1873. 65 pp. Mss. K.B. 1-217. No index. (DLC)

The same, 'Nachträge zu meinem Verzeichniss der Handschriften der Kieler Universitätsbibliothek, welche die Herzogthümer Schleswig, Holstein, Lauenburg, sowie Hamburg und Lübeck betreffen,' *Zeitschrift der Gesellschaft für Schleswig-Holstein-Lauenburgische Geschichte* V (1875) Beilage, 599-634. No index. (NN)

Handschriften der Kieler Universitäts-Bibliothek. Abteilung V-IX (1909). Abteilung IX (69 mss.) contains some old fragments. (Communication of the librarian).

Killiney, Ireland. Dun Mhuire, Franciscan Library. See *Analecta Bollandiana* XLVI; Great Britain, *Historical Manuscripts Commission.*

Catalogue of Irish Mss. in Franciscan Library Merchants Quay. 1 typed folder. Mss. A 1-38.

(No title). A pack of ms. sheets. Mss. B 1-109 (literary mss.)

For the other groups there is no inventory.

*Klagenfurt, Austria. See *Handschriftenverzeichnisse*; Wickhoff.

*P. Dudik, 'Merkwürdige Handschriften der K. K. Bibliothek zu Klagenfurt,' *Neues Archiv für Geschichte, Staatenkunde, Literatur und Kunst* II (1830) 757-58. (MH)

**The same, 'Handschriften der K. K. Bibliothek zu Klagenfurt, '*Österreichische Blätter für Literatur* 1845, p. 648 and 671.

H. Menhardt, 'Die Handschriftensammlung der bischöflichen Bibliothek in Klagenfurt,' *Zentralblatt für Bibliothekswesen* XXXIX (1922) 363-81. 231 mss. No index.

*Klausen, see Chiusa.

*Kleve, West Germany. See *Archiv* XI.

*Kłodzko, Poland.

E. Beck, *Handschriften und Wiegendrucke der Gymnasial-Bibliothek in Glatz.* pt. I, progr. Glatz 1892. 31 pp. 4 mss. (NNC). *pt. II, progr. Glatz 1893. 36 pp. Late material. (CSmH)

Klosterneuburg, Austria. Stiftsbibliothek. See *Archiv* VI; X; *Notizenblatt*; *Der Oesterreichische Geschichtsforscher*; Schulte; *Serapeum* X; XI.

H. Pfeiffer and B. Černik, *Catalogus codicum manuscriptorum qui in Bibliotheca Canonicorum Reg. S. Aug. Claustroneoburgensi asservantur.* 2 vols. in 1, Vienna 1922-31. I: 260 mss. II: Mss. no. 261-452. Index in each volume. Not complete.

*Typed continuation of the printed catalogue, by B. Černik.

Catalogus Bibliothecae Claustroneoburgensis, Pars. I Codices Manuscripti qui extant in Bibliotheca Claustroneoburgensi (by M. Fischer, 1808). 1419 mss. Superseded to no. 452 by the printed catalogue.

København (Copenhagen), Denmark. See *Archiv* VII; Dudik, *Forschungen*; *Hispania sacra* I; Lampen; Lehmann; Steffenhagen.

(M. Mackeprang), *Greek and Latin Illuminated Manuscripts, X-XIII* [sic] *Centuries, in Danish Collections.* Copenhagen and London 1921. 51 pp. and plates. Covers Royal Library and National Museum.

—Kongelige Bibliotek.

Carl S. Petersen, *Det Kongelige Biblioteks Handskriftsamling.* Copenhagen 1943. 56 pp. Contains a bibliography of the catalogues (p. 41-42).

The following catalogues cover several of the separate collections of the library:

Aarsberetninger og Meddelelser fra det Store Kongelige Bibliothek, vol. III (1874-89, published 1890) 3-297: Chr. Bruun, 'De illuminerede Handskrifter i det Store Kongelige Bibliothek.' (NN)

P. Högberg, 'Notices et extraits des manuscrits espagnols de Copenhague,' *Revue Hispanique* XLVI (1919) 382-99. Describes 22 mss. from Spain, partly in Latin.

The same, 'Les manuscrits italiens de Copenhague,' *Études Italiennes* II (1920) 85-96; 154-171. No index. Not complete.

Ellen Jørgensen, *Catalogus codicum latinorum medii aevi Bibliothecae Regiae Haf-

niensis. Copenhagen 1926. 536 pp. Describes the Latin mss. to 1500 from several collections of the library. Concordance of shelf marks (p. 530-536).

Kongelige Bibliotheks Haandskriftsamling. 13 ms. vols., arranged by subjects. Centuries not always given.

Alphabetical card index in 24 trays. It covers both the main collections of the library (1-16) and the mss which formerly belonged to the University Library (17-24). 4 more trays cover the Rigsarkivet and other Scandinavian collections.

Old Royal Collection.

J. Erichsen, *Udsigt over den gamle Manuscript-Samling i det store Kongelige Bibliothek.* Copenhagen 1786. 141 pp. (NN). Shelf marks added in library copy.

Catalogus Manuscriptorum Bibliothecae Regiae in Folio (1784). 2 ms. vols. Covers Gl. kgl. Sml. 2º 1-1215.

Catalogus Manuscriptorum Bibliothecae Regiae in Quarto (1784-86) 2 mss. vols. Covers Gl. kgl. Sml. 4º 1306-3374; 8º 3375-3677.

New Royal Collection.

Catalogus Manuscriptorum in Collectione Nova Regia. 4 ms. vols. Covers Ny kgl. sml. 2º 1-1443; 4º 1-224; 8º 1-415.

Haandskrift-Samlingen. Ny Kgl. Samlings Accession. Lists of acquisitions, beginning in 1891.

Accessionen. Covers the period 1924-45.

Handskriftsamlingen. Accessionsprotokol 1946-.

Thott Collection.

Catalogus Bibliothecae Thottianae. 7 vols. in 12. Copenhagen 1788-95. Vol. VII (1795) p. 273-537: 'Index codicum manuscriptorum.' (NN, incomplete; ICN, complete). The library has an interleaved copy with ms. additions.

Kall Collection.

Bibliotheca Kalliana sive Index librorum quos possidebat Beatus Abrahamus Kall. 2 parts. Copenhagen 1822. Part I, p. i-xliv: 688 mss. (NN)

The following catalogue describes most of the collections formerly belonging to the University Library and now transferred to the Royal Library:

A. Krarup, *Katalog over Universitetsbibliotekets Handskrifter.* 2 vols. Copenhagen 1929-35.

Cf. *Petri Johannis Resenii Bibliotheca Regiae Academiae Hafniensi donata...* Copenhagen 1685, 368 pp. p. 343-49: 172 mss. No index. (MH)

Fabricius Collection, also transferred from the University to the Royal Library.

Bibliotheca J. A. Fabricii, 4 vols. Hamburg 1738-41. Vol. IV (1741) p. 173-218: 'Designatio auctorum veterum cum codd. mss. collatorum, item codicum manu exaratorum vett. et recentiorum qui haeredibus Fabricianis servabuntur.' (Copenhagen; reference verified by the librarian, Mr. Kåre Olsen).

'Designatio auctorum veterum cum codd. mss. collatorum, item codicum manu exaratorum vett. et recentiorum ex bibliotheca J. A. Fabricii superstitum,' s.l.a., p. 195-240. (Copenhagen, Royal Library). I have been unable to identify the source of this reprint. In the library copy, the actual shelf marks have been added.

Fabricius'ske Haandskrifter. 1 typed vol.

—*Universitetsbiblioteket.

(Arnamagnaeanske Legat. *Katalog over den Arnamagnaeanske Handskriftsamling.* 2 vols. Copenhagen 1889-94. Mostly Scandinavian mss.

E. Gigas, 'Lettres inédites de quelques savants espagnols du XVIe siècle,' *Revue Hispanique* XX (1909) 429-58. Describes 12 mss. from Spain, mostly in Latin, in the Arnamagnaean collection.

Koblenz, West Germany. Staatsarchiv. See *Archiv* VII; VIII; XI; Bernards; Leclercq.

E. Dronke, *Über die Gymnasialbibliothek und einige in derselben aufbewahrten Handschriften.* progr. Koblenz n. d. (1832). 26 pp. No index. (NN)

The same, *Beiträge zur Bibliographie und Literaturgeschichte oder Merkwürdigkeiten der Gymnasial- und der städtischen Biblio-*

thek zu Koblenz. Erstes Heft, Koblenz 1837. 124 pp. p. 83-124: 21 mss. No index.

Index librorum manu scriptorum, qui adservantur in bibliotheca gymnasii regii Confluentini primum compositus a. 1822, curis secundis elaboratus 1831 et 1832 ab Ernesto Dronke. 232 mss., and some Fragments.

701. *Handschriften.* Inventory of all manuscript books in the archive, including those of the Gymnasial-Bibliothek.

Koburg, see **Coburg.**

Köln (Cologne), West Germany. See *Analecta Bollandiana* LXI; *Archiv* XI; Bernards; Gercken; Lampen; Leclercq.

Kl. Loeffler, *Kölnische Bibliotheksgeschichte im Umriss.* Cologne 1923. 86 pp. p. 66-82: Lists extant mss. (MH)

—*Dombibliothek.

J. Hartzheim, *Catalogus historicus criticus codicum manuscriptorum Bibliothecae Ecclesiae Metropolitanae Coloniensis.* Cologne 1752. 162 pp. (NNUT)

Ph. Jaffé and G. Wattenbach, *Ecclesiae Metropolitanae Coloniensis codices manuscripti.* Berlin 1874. x, 166 pp. 218 mss. No index. (DLC)

P. Heusgen, 'Der Gesamtkatalog der Handschriften der Kölner Dombibliothek,' *Jahrbuch des Kölnischen Geschichtsvereins E.V.* XV (1933) 1-78. Describes mss. no. 219-414 as a supplement to Jaffé (p. 2-47). Index covers also Jaffé (p. 48-78). (NN)

A. Decker, 'Die Hildebold'sche Manuskriptensammlung des Kölner Doms,' *Festschrift der 43. Versammlung deutscher Philologen und Schulmänner dargeboten von den Höheren Lehranstalten Kölns* (Bonn 1895) 215-51. Lists some extant mss. (229-51). No index.

Leslie Webber Jones, *The Script of Cologne from Hildebald to Hermann.* (The Mediaeval Academy of America. Publications, no. 10). Cambridge Mass. 1932. 98 pp. and plates. p. 29-73: 28 mss., mostly at Cologne.

—Erzdiözesanbibliothek (formerly Priesterseminar).

Handschriften-Verzeichnis der Bibliothek des Erzbischöflichen Priesterseminars in Cöln... 352 mss. Some of them are lost.

—Historisches Archiv der Stadt Köln.

Katalog der Handschriften des Historischen Archivs der Stadt Köln. Pt. I: *Alphabetisches Register.* Pt. II: *Beschreibender Katalog,* in 12 vols., arranged by subjects; the subjects are listed by K. Menne, *Deutsche und niederländische Handschriften,* pt. I, Cologne 1931, p. vi-vii (Mitteilungen aus dem Stadtarchiv von Köln, Sonderreihe: Die Handschriften des Archivs, Heft X Abt. I). Vols. I-IX describe theological mss., vol. X contains humanism, poetry and jurisprudence, vol. XI philosophy, rhetoric, classics, and medicine, vol. XII the sciences and music. The mss. include the following collections: GB (Hss. der früheren Gymnasialbibliothek, 213 in folio, 272 in quarto, 209 in octavo); W (Wallraf'sche Sammlung, 384 mss.); W* (Älterer Bestand, and acquisitions, 391 mss.); Geschichtliche Hss. (343 mss., cf. 'Chroniken und verwandte Darstellungen im Stadtarchiv,' *Mittheilungen aus dem Stadtarchiv von Köln,* vol. VII nᵒ 20 [1892] 67-86); Geistliche Abteilung (cf. H. Kelleter, 'Handschriften der geistlichen Abteilung,' 238 mss., *ibid.* IX 24 [1894] 1-44); Farragines Gelenii (cf. *ibid.,* III 9 [1886] 141-67).

***Kolozsvár,** Hungary. See Radó.

***Königsberg,** see Kaliningrad.

***Königswart,** see Lazne Kynzwart.

***Konitz,** see **Chojnice.**

***Konstanz,** West Germany. See Buchon; Gercken.

F. Weisgerber, *Index ac recensio aliquot codicum manuscriptorum in lycei Constantiensis bibliotheca repositorum . . .* progr. Constance 1832. 16 pp. (Erlangen Univ. Lib.)

*Card index. Gives new shelf marks. 81 mss. (Communication of F. Stegmüller)

Kórnik, Poland. Biblioteka Kórnicka Polskiej Akademii Nauk.

Inwentarz rękopisów Bibljoteki Kórnickiej

(1930). Mimeographed list of 1612 mss. (micr. at NN). The library copy has handwritten additions to no. 1788.

*Košice, Czechoslovakia. See Radó.

V. Récsei, *A Kassai Püspökségi Könyvtár Codexeinek és Incunabulumainak Jegyzéke.* Budapest 1891. XII, 109 pp. p. 3-14: 12 mss. in the episcopal library. (Vatican Library)

*Köslin. See Koszalin.

*Koszalin, Poland. See *Archiv* XI.

*Köthen, East Germany. See under Halle.

*Kotor (Cattaro), Yugoslavia. See Wickhoff.

Kraków, Poland. See Aland (Section A); Dudik, 'Archive'; *Société française*; Vetulani.

—*Archivum Kapituly Metropolitalnej.

J. Polkowski, 'Katalog rękopisów kapitulnych Katedry Krakowskiej,' *Archiwum do dziejów literatury i oświaty w Polsce* III (1884) 1-168. 228 mss. No index, except that of the volume.

—Biblioteka Jagiellońska.

W. Wisłocki, *Catalogus codicum manuscriptorum Bibliothecae Universitatis Jagellonicae Cracoviensis. Katalog Rękopisów Biblijoteki Universytetu Jagiellońskiego.* 2 vols. Cracow 1877-81. 1: 1875 mss. II: Mss. no. 1876-4176. Index. (NN)

Bibljoteka Jagellońska. Katalog Wystawy Rękopisów i Druków Polsko-Węgiorskich, XV i XVI Wieku. Cracow 1928. 38 pp. and plates. Exhibition catalogue. p. 13-18: 13 mss., including some from the Czartoryski collection. (NN)

Z. Ameisenowa, *Minjatury włoskie Bibljoteki Jagiellońskiej. Trecento.* Cracow 1929. 59 pp. and plates. (NN)

Katalog wystawy iluminowanych rękopisów włoskich. Cracow 1934. 56 pp. and plates. 87 nos. (NN)

Z. Ameisenowa, *Rękopisy i Pierwodruki Iluminowande Biblioteki Jagiellońskiej.* Wrocław and Cracow 1958. 236 pp. and plates. 215 illuminated mss and early edd.

A. Chmiel 'Rękopisy biblioteki w Dzikowie hr. Tarnowskich,' *Przewodnik bibliogra-*

ficzny XXX (1907) 115-16; 141-42; 163-64; 198-99; 223-24; 253-54; 280-82; XXXI (1908) 23-24; 50-51. Also separately, Cracow 1908, 31 pp. This collection was recently acquired by the Biblioteka Jagiellónska. No index. (NN)

Inwentarz rękopisów Biblioteki Jagiellóns-kiej Nr. 4175-6000 (1938). 2 typed vols. continuing Wisłocki. (micr. at NN).

(No title). 1 typed vol. Covers mss. 6001-6200 (micr. at NN)

(No title). 1 ms. folder. Covers mss. 6201-7758.

Biblioteka Jagiellońska w Krakowie, Oddział Rękopisów, Ksiega Przybutków. List of accessions, with temporary numbers, beginning in 1945.

Opisy katalogowe Rkp. 5 typed folders. Cover mss. 8001-9424.

—Biblioteka Muzeum Narodowego w Krakowie, Oddział Zbiory Czartoryskich.

J. Korzeniowski and St. Kutrzeba, *Catalogus codicum manu scriptorum Musei Principum Czartoryski Cracoviensis.* 2 vols. Cracow 1887-1913. Vol. 1, fasc. 1-4, 385 pp. 917 mss. Vol. II, fasc. 1-4, 385 pp. Mss. no. 918-1681. (MH).

C. Piotrowicz, *Index nominum et Rerum quorum in volumine primo (secundo) Catalogi codicum manu scriptorum Musei Principum Czartoryski Cracoviensis mentio fit.* 2 vols. I: Cracow 1928, 200 pp. II: Tessin 1931, 199 pp. (Cracow, Biblioteka Jagiellonska; microfilm at NN).

Inwentarz rękopisów Bibl. Czartoryskich, Nr. 1681-5999. 1 typed vol. (micr. at NN)

(No title). Handwritten inventory of acquisitions, in 3 vols. 3347 nos. (temporary shelf marks). Mostly late.

—*Biblioteka Polskiej Akademii Nauk.

J. Czubek, *Katalog Rękopisów Akademii Umiejętności w Krakowie*, Cracow 1906. V, 313 pp. 1588 mss.

The same, *Dodatek* (Supplement) *I.* Cracow 1912. 167 pp. Mss. no. 1589-1810.

—*Wojewodskie Archiwum Panstwowe.

B. Gorczak, *Katalog Rękopisów Archiwum X.X. Sanguszków w Sławucie.* Sławuta

1902. XL., 488 pp. 1127 mss., mostly documents. (MH)

*Kranj, Yugoslavia. See under Ljubljana.

*Kremnica, Czechoslovakia.

(A. Ipolyi), 'Egy középkori magyar plébános könyvtara,' *Magyar Könyvszemle* I (1876) 229-41. 26 mss. No index. (Miu; micr. at NNC)

*Kremsier, see **Kroměříž**.

*Kremsmünster, Austria. Stiftsbibliothek. See *Archiv* VI; Neuwirth.

Hugo Schmid, *Catalogus codicum Manuscriptorum in Bibliotheca Monasterii Cremifanensis Ord. S. Bened. asservatorum . . .* vol. I fasc. 1-3; Linz 1877-81, 192 pp. Mss. no. 1-10. Not complete. No index.

W. Neumüller, 'Zur mittelalterlichen Bibliotheksgeschichte Kremsmünsters,' in *Festschrift zum 400 jährigen Bestande des öffentlichen Obergymnasiums der Benediktiner zu Kremsmünster.* Herausgegeben vom Professorenkollegium (Wels 1949, VII, 369 pp.), p. 265-312. Indices of names and authors (p. 304-311). Index of mss. (p. 311-312). (MH)

Bibliotheca Cremifanensis, Catalogus Manuscriptorum. Excerpt by P. Beda Lehner from a draft by P. Hugo Schmid. 416 mss., plus 19 'im Schatzkasten' (Microfilm at DLC).

*Bibliotheca Cremifanensis, Catalogus Manuscriptorum, Codices novi. Mss. No. 1-1358. Mostly late (communication of the librarian).

*Kroměříž, Czechoslovakia.

B. Dudik, *Bibliothek und Archiv im fürsterzbischöflichen Schlosse zu Kremsier.* Vienna 1870. xxi, 134 pp. Index (p. v ff.). p. 44-53: 9 Latin mss. (MH)

*Książ (Fürstenstein) Poland. See *Archiv* XI.

Kues, West Germany. See *Archiv* VIII; XI; *Serapeum* XXV; XXVII.

J. Marx, *Verzeichnis der Handschriften-Sammlung des Hospitals zu Cues bei Bernkastel a. Mosel.* Trier 1905. 332 pp. 314 mss. Index (p. 308-313).

*Kulm, see **Chełmno**.

*Kwidzyn, Poland.

**E. Brocks, *Bericht über die Geschichte und die Handschriften und alten Drucke der Gymnasial-Bibliothek.* progr. Marienwerder 1875. 23 pp.

*Kyancutta, Australia. See Kelly.

*La Chatre, France. See France, *Catalogue Général, Départements* XXVI.

*La Ferté-Bernard, France. See France, *Catalogue Général, Départements* IX.

*Lagny, France. See *ibid.* IX; XLI.

Laibach, see **Ljubljana**.

*Lambach, Austria, Stiftsbibliothek. See Neuwirth; *Der Oesterreichische Geschichtsforscher.*

Handschriften-Katalog Lambach. IIter Tomus Iter Band... enthält I. Manuscripte. II. Incunabeln. Opus est P. Felicis Resch. 'Dieser alte Catalog wurde mit den Codices verglichen und diese Codices nach diesen Ziffern neu numerirt im J. 1827.' Lists 197 Codices Membranei and 553 Codices chartacei. (Microfilm at DLC). Some mss. have been sold.

*Lamballe, France. See France, *Catalogue Général, Départements* IV.

*Landeshut, see Kamienna Góra.

*Landsberg, see Gorzów.

*Langres, France. See France, *Catalogue Général, Départements* XXI; XLI.

*Lannion, France. See France, *Catalogue Général, Départements* XXIV.

*Laon, France. See France, *Catalogue Général, Départements* I (Quarto Series); XLI.

*La Roche, France. See France, *Catalogue Général, Départements* XIII; XLI.

*La Rochelle, France. See France, *Catalogue Général, Départements* VIII; XLI; XLVI.

*Laubach, West Germany. Gräfl. Solms-Laubach'sche Bibliothek. See Vaubel.

Typed list of some older mss. kindly supplied by the librarian.

*Lausanne, Switzerland. Bibliothèque Cantonale et Universitaire. See Haenel; Leclercq; Stelling-Michaud.

*Few Latin mss., mostly described among the printed books in the printed catalogues: *Catalogue de la Bibliothèque Cantonale Vaudoise*, 7 vols. Lausanne 1853-56. *Supplément* 1856-86, Lausanne 1887. *Supplément* 1886-1902, 2 vols. Lausanne 1905 (DLC). There are also summary lists of all mss., on typed sheets or index cards. (Communication of the librarian).

*Laval, France. See France, *Catalogue Général, Départements* IV; XLI.

*Lavaur, France. See France, *Catalogue Général, Départements* XX.

*Lazne Kynzwart (Königswart), Czechoslovakia. See *Neues Archiv* V.

*Lecce, Italy.

Biblioteca Provinciale di Lecce. Catalogo Bibliografico delle opere di Scrittori Salentini raccolte fino al maggio 1929 . . . (By P. Marti). *In appendice: Elenco dei manoscritti*, by A. Foscarini, Anno 1927. Lecce 1929. 203, lxxx pp. 126 late mss. (p. i ff.). No index. (MH)

*Lectoure, France. See France, *Catalogue Général, Départements* XIII.

*Leeds, England. See *Hispania Sacra* VIII.

The Brotherton Library. A Catalogue of Ancient Manuscripts and Early Printed Books collected by Edward Allen Baron Brotherton of Wakefield, by J. A. Symington. Leeds 1931. 300 pp. p. 3-33: Mss. No index.

A Catalogue of the Manuscripts and Printed Books collected by Thomas Brooke ... 2 vols. London 1891. 761 pp. numbered continuously. Arranged alphabetically. Mss. listed among edd. Most mss. went to the Yorkshire Archaeological Society. (NN)

Catalogue of Manuscripts in the Library of the Yorkshire Archaeological Society, by W. T. Lancaster. Leeds 1912. III, 52 pp. 350 mss., and deeds. (NN)

Catalogue of Manuscripts and Deeds in the Library of the Yorkshire Archaeological Society, at 10, Park Place, Leeds. By E. W. Crossley. 2nd ed. Leeds 1931. IX, 109 pp. p. 1-64: Catalogue of the Manuscripts. 520 modern mss. (NN)

List of Manuscripts and Deeds added to the Society's Collections, 1931-1933 (Leeds 1933), 10 pp.; 1933-35, 12 pp.; 1935-37, 7 pp.; 1937-39, 5 pp. The mss. go up to no. 670. (NN)

*Leeuwarden, Holland. Provinciale Bibliotheek van Friesland. See *Archiv* VIII; *Société française*.

Systematische Catalogus der Provinciale Bibliotheek van Friesland. 6 vols. Leeuwarden 1871-81. Vol. V (1881) p. 1761-1944: 962 mss. (Partial microfilm at NNC). Copy kindly sent on loan by the librarian. Index in vol. VI. Many mss. from Franeker. The same, Supplement. Leeuwarden 1897. 518 pp. p. 387-429: Mss. (late). (DLC)

***M. P. van Buijtenen, *Catalogus van de boeken en handschriften van de Jezuïtenstatie te Leeuwarden*. Leeuwarden 1941.

*Leghorn, see **Livorno**.

*Legnica, Poland. See also under Wrocław. See *Archiv* XI.

E. Pfudel, *Mittheilungen über die Bibliotheca Rudolfina der Königl. Ritter-Akademie zu Liegnitz*. 3 pts. progr. Liegnitz 1876-78. 130 pp. p. 115-122: 26 musical mss. Index (125-130). (Schwenckfelder Historical Library)

The same, *Die Musik-Handschriften der Königl. Ritterakademie zu Liegnitz*. (Musik-Handschriften auf öffentlichen Bibliotheken, ed. R. Eitner. Beilage zu den Monatsheften für Musikgeschichte, I) Leipzig 1886. 74 pp. Only musical compositions. (NN)

*Le Havre, France. See France, *Catalogue Général, Départements* II; XLI.

*Leicester, England.

John J. Jeaffreson, *An Index to the Ancient Manuscripts of the Borough of Leicester, Preserved in the Muniment Room of the Leicester Town Hall*. Westminster (1878). 94 pp. p. 10: 17 manuscripts books. No index. (NN)

Leiden, Holland. Bibliotheek der Rijksuniversiteit. See *Archiv* VII; VIII; Lehmann, *Holländische Reisefrüchte*; Lehmann, *Mitteilungen* I; *Société française*. (*Nomenclator autorum omnium quorum libri vel manuscripti, vel typis expressi exstant* *in Bibliotheca Academiae Lugduno-Batavae.* Preface signed by P. Bertius. Leiden 1595. Fols. A 1-M 3. No pagination). (Leiden, University Library).

Catalogus Bibliothecae Publicae Lugduno-Batavae. Leiden 1640. 216, 21 pp. Lists some mss. No shelf marks.) (Leiden, University Library).

Catalogus Bibliothecae Publicae Lugduno-Batavae noviter recognitus. Leiden 1674. 426 pp. p. 391-419: Mss.) (ICN)

Catalogus librorum tam impressorum quam manuscriptorum Bibliothecae Universitatis Lugduno-Batavae, by W. Senguerd, J. Gronovius, and J. Heyman. Leyden 1716. 500 pp. p. 324-494: Mss. (NN)

Supplementum Catalogi librorum tam impressorum quam manuscriptorum Bibliothecae Universitatis Lugduno-Batavae ab anno 1716 usque ad annum 1741. Leyden 1741. p. 529-34: Mss. No index. (NN)

J. Geel, *Catalogus librorum manuscriptorum qui inde ab anno 1741 Bibliothecae Lugduno-Batavae accesserunt.* Leyden 1852. 306 pp. 1015 mss. of which nos. 312-1015 (p. 76-297) in Latin.

F. Momlot, 'Les manuscrits latins de Melchisédec Thévenot à la Bibliothèque de l'Université de Leyde,' *Revue des Bibliothèques* IV (1894) 107-26. 54 mss. now among Vossiani. No index.

Bibliotheca Universitatis Leidensis. Codices manuscripti. Vol. I (by P. C. Molhuysen, Leiden 1910): *Codices Vulcaniani.* 65 pp. 109 mss. Vol. II (1910): *Codices Scaligerani (praeter orientales).* 40 pp. 77 mss. Vol. III (1912): *Codices Bibliothecae Publicae Latini.* 225 pp. 2012 mss. Each volume indexed. Vol. IV (by T. P. Sevensma, 1946): *Codices Perizoniani.* ix, 146 pp. F. 1-85; Q 1-111; O 1-60. Vol. V (1948): *Codicum in finibus Belgarum ante annum 1550 conscriptorum qui in Bibl. universitatis asservantur Pars I. Codices 168-360 Societatis cui nomen Maatschappij der Nederlandsche Letterkunde,* by G. I. Lieftinck. XXII, 236 pp. Vol. VI (1955); *Codices Vossiani Graeci et Mis-*

cellanei, by K. A. de Meyier. XXIV, 319 pp. The Miscellanei include Latin texts.

Bibliotheca Academiae Lugduno-Batavae. Catalogus. Deel 14, Leyden 1932. *Inventaris van de Handschriften,* Eerste Afdeeling. 197 pp. Short list of Vossiani, Perizoniani, Bibliotheca Publica and many other groups. Deel 22, 1934; The same, Tweede Afdeeling, Eerste Heft. 247 pp. Index epistolarum. Deel 26, 1935. The same, Tweede Heft. 133 pp. Index of addressees of letters. Deel 35, 1936. The same, Derde Afdeeling. 159 pp. Index of letters at the Maatschappij der Nederlandsche Letterkunde. Deel 37, 1937. The same, Vierde Afdeeling. 105 pp. Mss. of the Maatschappij. Title (beginning with pt. 2) also: *Catalogus compendiarius continens omnes codices manuscriptos qui in Bibliotheca Academiae Lugduno-Batavae asservantur.*

M. Battistini, 'Documenti italiani nella Biblioteca Universitaria di Leida,' *Giornale storico della letteratura italiana* CXIV (1939) 209-220.

K. A. de Meyier, *Paul en Alexandre Petau en de Geschiedenis van hun handschriften (voornamelijk op grond van de Petau-Handschriften in de Universiteitsbibliotheek te Leiden).* thesis Leiden 1947. XIII, 239 pp. Index of mss. (DLC)

(*Catalogus van de Bibliotheek der Maatschappij van Nederlandsche Letterkunde te Leiden.* Eerste Deel, Leyden 1847. p. 1-96: Mss. *Bijvoegsel over de Jaren 1848-52.* Leyden 1853. p. 1-8: Mss. *Bijvoegsel over de Jaren 1853-57.* Leyden 1857. p. 1-8: Mss.)

Catalogus Manuscriptorum Bibliothecae Lugduno Batavae. 6 ms. vols. I: Bibliotheca Vossiana; II: Smaller collections; III: Bibliotheca Publica Graeca; IV-VI: Bibliotheca Publica Latina, Belgica, Gallica cet. (1-1250; 1251-2250; 2251-2605). Mostly superseded by printed catalogues, except for mss. P.B.L. 2013-2605. Yet it fills some gaps in the catalogues of 1932, or gives fuller descriptions.

Alphabetical card catalogue (Communication of the librarian, cf. Born 285).

Leipzig, East Germany. See Cooper (Section A); *Archiv* VI; Bruck; *Serapeum* VII and *Intelligenzblatt 1856*; *Société française.*

—Stadtbibliothek.

A. G. R. Naumann, *Catalogus librorum manuscriptorum qui in Bibliotheca Senatoria Civitatis Lipsiensis asservantur.* Grimma 1838. 562 pp. 937 mss. of which no. 33-108 (p. 11-32) in Latin.

R. Naumann, 'Die Malereien in den Handschriften der Stadtbibliothek zu Leipzig,' *Archiv für die zeichnenden Künste...* I(1855) 233-335. 18 mss. No index. (NNC) Also separately published (Leipzig 1855, 103 pp.). (DLC)

M. Bernath, *Studien über die Miniaturhandschriften der Leipziger Stadtbibliothek.* I. Diss. Fribourg, Borna-Leipzig 1912. 43 pp. 3 mss. (Pierpont Morgan Library)

Zuwachs-Verzeichnis der Handschriften. 2 ms. vols. I: 1-457. II: 458-532. The valid shelf marks are given in parentheses.

—Universitätsbibliothek.

J. Feller, *Catalogus codicum manuscriptorum bibliothecae Paulinae in Academia Lipsiensi.* Leipzig 1686. 450 pp. Arranged by subjects. No index. No shelf marks.

Katalog der Handschriften der Universitäts-Bibliothek zu Leipzig. Section IV: *Die Lateinischen und deutschen Handschriften.* Vol. I: *Die Theologischen Handschriften.* pt. 1, 1926-35, by R. Helssig. 815 pp. 500 mss. No index. Vol. III, 1905: *Die juristischen Handschriften*, by the same. 371 pp. Mss. no. 870-1113 and Haeneliani 1-58. Index. Not complete.

Handschriften-Katalog der Universitäts-Bibliothek Leipzig (by Ebert). 2 ms. vols. Arranged alphabetically. Photostatic copy at Berlin, State Library.

H. Klemm, *Beschreibender Catalog des Bibliographischen Museums. Erste und zweite Abtheilung*: *Manuscripte und Druckwerke des 15. und 16. Jahrhunderts . . .* Dresden 1884. viii, 509 pp. p. 1-6: 51 mss. No index.

A. Schramm, *Das Deutsche Buchmuseum zu*

Leipzig, 1885-1925. Leipzig 1925. 102 pp. Hardly relevant.

*Le Mans, France. See *Analecta Bollandiana* XII; France, *Catalogue Général, Départements* XX; XLI.

*Lemberg, see Lwów.

*Lemgo, West Germany.

F. Gerlach, *Aus mittelalterlichen Klosterbüchereien und Archiven.* (Lemgo 1934). 30 pp. 23 mss. No index. (Pierpont Morgan Library)

Leningrad (St. Petersburg), U.S.S.R.

—*Archiv Akademii Nauk SSSR. It has the scientific mss. formerly preserved at the Astronomical Observatory in Pulkovo.

—Archiv Leningradskogo Otdelenija Instituta Istorii Akademii Nauk SSSR.

Putevoditel po Archivu Leningradskogo Otdelenia Instituta Istorij. Moscow and Leningrad 1958. 603 pp. p. 451-515 : Western European collections.

—Biblioteka Akademii Nauk SSSR.

Istoricheskii ocherk i obzor fondov rukopisnogo otdela Biblioteki Akademii Nauk. 2 vols. Moscow and Leningrad 1956-58. Especially vol. II, p. 205-271: 'Sobranije inostrannykh rukopisej' (by E. Bobrova). Catalogue in progress.

—Gosudarstvennyj Ermitazh. Otdelenije risunkov.

The Department of Drawings of the Hermitage Museum has a small but important collection of illuminated mss. Handwritten list.

—Publichnaja Biblioteka im. M. E. Saltykova-Shchedrina (the former Imperial Library, often wrongly referred to as Hermitage Library). See Cooper (Section A); *Archiv* VI; XI; Clossius; *Neues Archiv* V; VI. For mss. turned over to Poland after 1921, see also under Warszawa.

T. P. Voronova, 'Western Manuscripts in the Saltykov-Shchedrin Library,' *The Book Collector* V (1956) 12-18.

Ochety Imperatorskoj publichnoj biblioteki. Reports of the library for the years 1808-1912 (published 1917) where the acquisitions of mss. are mentioned. (NN)

Catalogus codicum Bibliothecae Imperialis Publicae Graecorum et Latinorum, by E. de Muralto. fasc. 1, St. Petersburg 1840: Codices Graeci. 32 coll. No more published. (NN)

A. de Lamothe, 'Principaux manuscrits latins et français conservés dans la Bibliothèque Impériale et dans celle de l'Ermitage, à Saint-Pétersbourg,' *Bibliothèque de l'École des Chartes* XXV (1864) 162-68. 73 mss. No index.

B. Dudik, 'Historische Forschungen in der kaiserlichen öffentlichen Bibliothek zu St Petersburg,' *Sitzungsberichte der kaiserlichen Akademie der Wissenschaften* [Vienna] *Philosophisch-Historische Classe* XCV (1880) 329-82. Important survey of the collection. 223 Latin mss (336-380). No index.

A. Blumenstok, 'Wiadomość o Rekopisach Prawno-Historycznych Biblioteki Cesarskiej w Petersburgu,' *Archiwum Komisyi Historycznej* VI (Cracow 1891) 379-463. (NN)

A. Halban-Blumenstok, 'Die canonistischen Handschriften der kaiserlichen öffentlichen Bibliothek in St. Petersburg,' *Deutsche Zeitschrift für Kirchenrecht* Ser. III vol. V (1895) 219-312. Arranged by authors. (NNUT)

A. Staerk, *Les manuscrits latins du Ve au XIIIe siècle conservés à la Bibliothèque impériale de Saint-Pétersbourg*. 2 vols. St. Petersburg 1910. I: 141 mss. No index. II: plates.

V. Zabughin, 'Tre codici umanistici Petersburghesi,' *Giornale storico della letteratura italiana* LXIV (1914) 259-261.

(Leningrad. Publichnaia biblioteka. Srednevekovie. v rukopisiakh). *Analecta Medii Aevi*. Vol. II (1927) p. 3-60: O. Dobiaš-Roždestvensky, 'Quelques inaperçus.' Discusses a few early Latin mss. p. 143ff.: V. Chichmaref, 'Quelques traces de la « librairie » du roi René dans le fonds manuscrit de la Bibliothèque Publique: Notices et extraits des manuscrits romans de la Bibliothèque de Leningrad.' (NN) Vol. III (1929): O. Dobiaš-Roždestvensky, *Les anciens manuscrits latins de la Bibliothèque Publique de Leningrad*. pt. 1: *V-VII siècles*. 64 pp. and plates. 15 mss. No index. (ICU; micr. at NN).

O. Dobiaš-Roždestvenskaïa, *Codices Corbeienses Leninopolitani: Histoire de l'atelier graphique de Corbie de 651 à 830 reflétée dans les Corbeienses Leninopolitani*. (Académie des sciences de l'URSS. Travaux de l'Institut de l'histoire de la science et de la technique, Ser. II fasc. 3). Leningrad 1934. 173 pp. 36 mss. (p. 107-66). (NN)

A. Comte de Laborde, *Les principaux manuscrits à peintures conservés dans l'ancienne Bibliothèque impériale publique de Saint-Pétersbourg*. 2 vols. Paris 1936-38. 195 mss. No index.

Gosudarstvennaja ordena Trudovogo Krasnogo Znameni Publichnaja Biblioteka im. M. E. Saltykova Shchedrina, Kratkij ochet rukopisnogo otdela za 1914-1938 gg. So vstupitel'nym istoricheskim ocherkom, ed. T. K. Ukhmylovoj and V. G. Gejmana. Leningrad 1940. 302 pp. See esp. p. 241-244 for the Latin mss. acquired between 1914 and 1938.

A. D. Lublinskaja, 'Zapadnyje rukopisi v Leningradskoj Publichnoj Biblioteke,' *Sovetskaja Nauka* 1940, no. 9, p. 96-107.

T. V. Luizova, 'Sobranje rukopisej P. P. Dubrovskogo v Gosudarstvennoj Publichnoj Biblioteki imeni M. E. Saltykova-Shchedrina,' *Voprosy Istorii* 1952, no. 8, p. 150-154.

The same, 'Ob istoricheskikh uslovijakh vozniknovenija tak nazyvajemogo goticheskogo pis'ma,' *Srednije Veka* V (1954) 269-286.

The same, 'Rannegoticheskije rukopisi Publichnoj Biblioteki,' *Trudy, Gosudarstvennaja Publichnaja Biblioteka imeni M. E. Saltykova-Shchedrina* I (IV) 1957, 237-264 and plates. (MH)

P. Lehmann, 'Reste der Klosterbibliothek Weissenau,' *Zentralblatt für Bibliothekswesen* XLIX (1932) 1-11. 34 mss. of the so-called Hermitage Collection.

Katalog latinskich rukopisej. 3 ms. vols. I: Class I. II: Classes II-XIII. III: Classes XIV-XVIII; Classici latini. The mss. turned over to Poland after the first World War are marked with red ink notations.

Latinskije. 1 ms. folder. Describes Latin acquisitions.

Katalog italijanskim ispanskim i portugalskim rukopisjam. Contains descriptions of the Italian mss., in 18 classes.

Italjanskije. 1 ms. folder. Describes Italian acquisitions.

Katalog raznojazychnykh rukopisej (Manuscripta diversis linguis exarata). Mostly late.

Catalogue des manuscrits de l'Ermitage Impérial. 1 ms. folder. Describes a special collection. Arranged by languages. 41 Latin and 13 Italian mss.

Obshecheje sobranije avtografov. Alphabetical list of the general collection of autographs. An inserted separate folder describes the Baehr Collection (arranged by names).

Sobranije Dubrovskogo. Collection of autographs for which there is an inventory, an alphabetical card file, and a chronological card file.

Katalog Avtografov Kolektsii Grafa Sukhtelena (Suchtelen Collection). Arranged by countries and names.

Sobranije Vakselja. Arranged by names.

Lettere ms. al Padre Calogerà. 30 vols., with an index volume.

*León, Spain. See Grubbs (Section A, under Richardson); *Serapeum* VII.

Biblioteca Provincial Legionense: Su origen y vicisitudes . . ., by D. Ramon A. De la Braña. León 1884. 91 pp. p. 55-60: Alphabetical list of 36 mss. (Hispanic Society)

R. Alvarez de la Braña, *Catálogos de la Biblioteca Provincial de León.* 2nd ed. 2 vols. León 1897. vol. I, p. 671-675: 37 mss., arranged alphabetically.

R. Beer and J. Elroy Diaz Jimenez, *Noticias bibliográficas y catálogo de los códices de la Santa iglesia Catedral de León.* Leon 1888.

xxxiv, 44 pp. 40 mss. No index. (Hispanic Society)

Z. García Villada, *Catálogo de los códices y documentos de la Catedral de León.* Madrid 1919. 263 pp. 53 mss. (Pierpont Morgan Library)

J. Perez Llamazares, *Catálogo de los códices y documentos de la Real Colegiata de San Isidoro de León.* Leon 1923. 183 pp. 119 mss. (p. 1-86). No index (Index in Grubbs, see above, Section A, under Richardson)

E. Díaz-Jiménez y Molleda, *Datos para la historia de la Biblioteca de San Isidoro de León.* Madrid 1925. 42 pp. 36 mss. No index. (Pierpont Morgan Library)

*Le Puy, France. See France, *Catalogue Général, Départements* XIII; XLI; Martin.

U. Ronchon, 'La bibliothèque Philippe Jourde au Puy: Ses manuscrits,' *Revue des Bibliothèques* XVII (1907) 284-88. Modern material.

—Chapître de la Cathédrale. Has a few uncatalogued mss. (Communication of Giles Constable)

*Lerida, Spain. See Beer (Section A); Cordoliani; Villanueva.

*Lesina, Italy. See Wickhoff.

*Le Tréport, France. See France, *Catalogue Général, Départements* XLIII.

Leuwen, see **Louvain**.

*Libourne, France. See France, *Catalogue Général, Départements* IV; XLI.

*Lichfield, England. See Bernardus.

J. Charles Cox, *Catalogue of the Muniments and Manuscript Books pertaining to the Dean and Chapter of Lichfield . . .* Lichfield 1881-86. xvii, 230, xxi pp. p. 86-103: Manuscript Books. Charters only. (DLC)

A Catalogue of the Printed Books and Manuscripts in the Library of the Cathedral Church of Lichfield. London 1888. VIII, 120 pp. p. 119-120: 33 mss. No shelf marks. No index, (Paris, Bibliothèque Nationale)

*Lidzbark Warmiński (Heilsberg), Poland. See Possevinus.

*Liebenau, West Germany. See *Serapeum* VIII.

Liège (Luik), Belgium. See *Analecta Bollandiana* V; *Archiv* VIII; *Archivum Franciscanum* IV; V; VII; Catalogus Codicum Hagiographicorum; Namur.

G. Fransen, 'Manuscrits de Décrétistes dans les Bibliothèques Liégeoises,' *Studia Gratiana* I (Bologna 1953) 289-302. Describes 2 mss. at the Seminary and 2 at the University Library.

—*Bibliothèque Centrale de la Ville.

H. Helbig and M. Grandjean, *Catalogue des Collections léguées à la Ville de Liége par Ulysse Capitaine.* 3 vols. in 1, Liége 1872. III p. 1-47: 226 mss. and autugraphs. No index. (NNGr)

—*Bibliothèque de l'Université.

Bibliothèque de l'Université de Liége. Catalogue des manuscrits. Liége 1875. (By M. Grandjean). 589 pp. 888 mss. (DLC)

Société des Bibliophiles Liégeois. Bulletin II (1884-85) 185-231: (Grandjean) 'Tables analytiques de 425 pièces tant manuscrits qu'imprimées portant les numéros 1015-1035 annexées aux six volumes in-folio manuscrits intitulés: Mémoires pour servir à l'histoire ecclésiastique du pays et du diocèse de Liége par Francois-Jean-Baptiste Delvaux'; 232-248: (The same) 'Renseignements sur les manuscrits déposés à la Bibliothèque de l'Université de Liége, 28 septembre 1875'; 249-80: (the same) 'Supplément au Catalogue des manuscrits de la Bibliothèque de l'Université de Liége publié en 1875.' — Describes some mss. numbered c. 1100-1300. No index. (NN). Also printed separately, Liège, n.d. 96 pp. (MiU). VII (1905) 33-97: J. Brassinne, 'Annexes au catalogue des manuscrits de la Bibliothèque de l'Université de Liége.' Mss. no. 1314-33. No index. (NN)

J. Brassinne, *Catalogue des manuscrits légués à la Bibliothèque de l'Université de Liége par le Baron Adrien Wittert.* Liége 1910. xv, 243 pp. 117 mss.

—Grand Séminaire.

Catalogi Bibliot. Major. Semin. Leod. vol. 6 Pars I re (sic). *Manuscripta. Pars 2 me*
(sic). *Typographiae Incunabula.* 1 ms. vol. Arranged by subjects.

*Liegnitz, see Legnica.

*Lilienfeld, Austria. See *Archiv* VI; *Xenia Bernardina.*

*Lille, France. See France, *Catalogue Général, Départements* XXVI; XLI; XLVIII.

(*Catalogus Manuscriptorum in Bibliotheca Publica apud Lille in Gallia,* by T. P. [i.e. Thomas Phillipps]. Middlehill 1828. 16 pp. No index.) (NN)

(M. Le Glay, *Catalogue descriptif des manuscrits de la Bibliothèque de Lille.* Lille 1848. xxxvi, 443 pp. 391 mss.)

*Limoges, France. See France, *Catalogue Général, Départements* IX; XLI.

L. Guibert, *Les Manuscrits du Séminaire de Limoges: Notice et Catalogue.* Limoges 1892. 107 pp. 205 mss. No index. (MH)

*Lincoln, England. See Holtzmann (Section A); Haenel; Michel; M. R. James; *Neues Archiv* XXII; Schenkl.

G. F. Apthorp, *A Catalogue of the Books and Manuscripts in the Library of Lincoln Cathedral.* Lincoln 1859. 288, xxx pp. p. 277-85: Alphabetical list of mss. (MH)

R. M. Woolley, *Catalogue of the Manuscripts of Lincoln Cathedral Chapter Library.* Oxford 1927. xxiv, 190 pp. 298 mss.

*Lindau, West Germany. Stadtbibliothek. See Archiv IX.

Verzeichnis der Handschriften, by Gumcke (1949). mss. A I 61 - P IV 136. Few Latin mss. (communication of the librarian).

*Lingen, West Germany.

K. A. Fricke, *Verzeichniss der in der hiesigen Gymnasialbibliothek befindlichen Handschriften und selteneren Drucke aus dem 15., 16. und 17. Jahrhundert.* progr. Lingen 1876. 18, 10 pp. p. 14-15: 6 mss. Hardly relevant. No index. (Erlangen, University Library).

Linköping, Sweden. Stifts- och Landsbiblioteket. See Barwinski; Hipler; Institut de Recherches; Lampen; Leclercq.

Linköpings Bibliotheks Handlingar. 2 vols. 1793-95. I, 1-140: 56 mss. in folio. II, 1-177: 83 mss. in quarto. By P. Kylander.

Not complete. Each volume indexed, though inadequately. Does not give actual shelf marks.

Förteckning öfwer Handskrifter i Linköpings Kongl. Gymnasii- och Stiftsbibliothek, by Elof Tegnér (1873). 1 typed vol. By subjects.

*Linz, Austria, Studienbibliothek.

—See *Archiv* X; Leclercq; *Der österreichische Geschichtsforscher.*

Die Handschriften der Oeffentl. Studienbibliothek in Linz, by K. Schiffmann (1935). 1 typed vol. 504 mss. plus autographs and fragments (microfilm at DLC).

Lisboa, Portugal. See Erdmann (Section A); Haenel; Leclercq: *Neues Archiv* VI; *Société française*; Stegmüller.

M. A. Machado Santos, 'Manuscritos de Filosofia do século XVI existentes em Lisboa,' *Boletim da Biblioteca da Universidade de Coimbra* XIX (1950) 241-382; XX (1951) 295-525. Alphabetical list of 150 mss. in the libraries in Lisbon. No index. Also separately printed, Coimbra 1951. XV, 384 pp. Indices added.

—Academia das Ciencias.

Catalogo Alphabetico dos Manoscriptos da Livraria do Convento de Nossa Senhora de Jezus de Lisboa. (Inside:) *Catalogo dos Manuscriptos da Livraria do Convento de N. Snr.ª de Jezus de Lisboa pertencente a os Religiozos da Terceiro Ordem da Penitencia*, by N. P. S. Francisco (1826). 2 vols. Centuries not given. I: A-L. II: M-Z.

—Arquivo Nacional da Torre do Tombo.

Manuscritos da Livraria. Card index in 2 boxes, each alphabetical. I: Manuscritos Proprios. II: Manuscritos Comuns.

Miscellanea Manuscrita. Alphabetical card index.

—Biblioteca de Ajuda.

C. A. Ferreira, 'Iluminuras, Aguarelas, Ornatos e Desenhos à pena dos Manuscritos da Biblioteca da Ajuda,' *Boletim da Biblioteca da Universidade de Coimbra* XVIII (1948) 295-352.

Biblioteque Royal (sic) *d'Ajuda, Catalogue des manuscrits* (par matières). Copie des fiches de Cardozo de Bethencourt. 1 typed volume. By subjects, largely limited to Portuguese history. Gives shelf marks, but no titles.

Indice geral dos Manuscriptos da Bibliotheca da Coroa, disposto alfabeticamente (1813). By subjects, and alphabetical in each section.

Large card file, arranged topographically.

—Biblioteca Nacional.

Fundo Alcobaça.

Index codicum Bibliothecae Alcobatiae. Lisbon 1775. 213 pp. 476 mss.

Fr. Joaquim de S. Agostinho, 'Memoria sobre os Codices Manuscritos, e Cartorio do Real Mosteiro de Alcobaça,' *Memorias de litteratura portugueza*, ed. Academia Real das Sciencias de Lisboa V (1793) 297-362. No index. (NN)

Fr. Fortunati a D. Bonaventura . . . *Commentariorum de Alcobacensi mstorum* [sic] *Bibliotheca libri tres.* Coimbra 1827. 191 pp. No index. (Hispanic Society)

Biblioteca Nacional de Lisboa. Inventario dos codices alcobacenses. 5 pts. in 1 vol. Lisbon 1930-32. 428 pp. 456 mss. No index.

Fundo Pombal.

Bibliotheca Nacional de Lisboa. Inventario. Secção XIII—Manuscritos. Colleção Pombalina. (By J. A. Moniz). Lisbon 1889 (on cover: 1891). 204 unnumbered pages, and 143 pp. 758 mss., mostly modern. (Hispanic Society).

Fundo Illuminades.

G. P. (Pereira), 'Bibliotheca Nacional de Lisboa, Codices em Pergaminho com Illuminuras,' *Boletim da Real Associação dos Architectos Civis e Archeologos Portuguezes* Ser. III vol. VII, 11 (1897) 161-66. 151 mss. No index. (DLC)

Gabriel Pereira, *A colleção dos codices com illuminuras da Bibliotheca Nacional de Lisboa.* Lisbon 1904. 16 pp. 155 mss. No index. (Photostat at NNC).

Biblioteca Nacional, Lisboa. Collecção dos livros de coro dos conventos extinctos. By G. Pereira. Lisbon 1904. 24 pp. (Lisbon, Biblioteca Nacional)

Manuscriptos Illuminades. Card index in 2 bound vols. Over 138 mss. Vol. I is arranged by shelf marks, vol. II, alphabetically.

Codices d'Alcobaça. Concordancia de anumeração. Appendix: *Mss. Illuminados.* 186 mss. Superseded by the printed list of Pereira to no. 155.

Fundo Geral

Bibliotheca Nacional de Lisboa. Inventario. Secção XIII. Manuscriptos. Lisbon 1896. Unpaged. No index. Describes mss. 1-739 of the Fundo Geral.

Large alphabetical card file.

Inventario dos Manuscriptos. (Inside:) *Inventario dos documentos da vitrina.* 52 nos. Then title page: *Inventario da Secção XIII. da Bibliotheca Nacional de Lisboa. Collecção Geral dos manuscriptos,* by Manuel Luiz Ferreira (1895). Sketchy. 10677 mss. Superseded by the printed list to no. 739.

*Lisieux, France. See France, *Catalogue Général, Départements* X.

*Litoměřice (Leitmeritz), Czechoslovakia. Narodni Archiv.

**Státní archiv v Litoměřicích: Průvoce po archivních fondech.* Prague 1956. A survey. (Prague, University Library)

No further information.

Liverpool, England. See Haenel; Ker.

A Catalogue of the Books, printed and in manuscript, bequeathed by the late Thomas Glazebrook Rylands of Highfields Thelwall Cheshire, Esquire, to the Library of University College Liverpool. By J. Sampson. Liverpool 1900. IX, 113 pp. p. 1-19: Mss. Shelf marks added in library copy. No index.

Handlist of Manuscripts (Ancient, Medieval and Modern) in the University Library, Liverpool. 2 typed folders, arranged by subjects. 38 Latin mss. before 1600.

—City of Liverpool Public Museums. Their collection is deposited in the University Library.

Liverpool Corporation, Free Public Museum, Catalogue of Mediaeval and later Antiquities contained in the Mayer Museum... by Charles T. Gatty. Liverpool 1883. 108 pp. and plates. p. 6-11: 130 mss., including 27 Latin mss. before 1600. No index.

There is a more complete handwritten list kept in the University Library.

Livorno, Italy. Biblioteca Labronica. See *Giornale* I; *Studi Italiani* XII.

*Card index (AB V 100).

Ljubljana (Laibach), Yugoslavia. See Kos.

—Narodna in Univerzitetna Knjižnica. *Codices manu scripti Ms 1-Ms 1059.* More complete than Kos.

—Državni arhiv. It now has the mss. described by Kos for the Narodni Museum.

—*Škofijski arhiv. It now has the mss. formerly preserved at Kranj, Župnišče. Cf. Kos.

—Franciscan Monastery. Completely described by Kos.

—Seminary Library. Completely described by Kos.

*Loches, France. See France, *Catalogue Général, Départements* XXIV.

Lodi, Italy. Biblioteca Civica. See Mazzatinti II.

L. Cremascoli and A. Novasconi, *I Corali Palavicino.* (Lodi) 1955. 55 pp.

**Schedario manoscritti storia locale* (AB III 559), apparently more complete than Mazzatinti II. New catalogue in preparation (Communication of the Librarian).

Inventario provvisorio.

Lonato (Brescia), Italy. Fondazione Ugo da Como.

Manoscritti. 1 typed folder. 444 mss.

London, England. See Holtzmann (Section A); Bernardus; Foligno; Haenel; Great Britain, *Historical Manuscripts Commission*; Hunter; Omont; Phillipps; Schenkl; *Société française*; Zangemeister.

L. M. Harrod, *The Libraries of Greater London.* London 1951. VII, 252 pp.

—*Alleyn's College, Dulwich.

G. F. Warner and F. B. Bickley, *Catalogue of the Manuscripts and Muniments of Alleyn's College of God's Gift at Dulwich.*

2 vols. London 1881-1903. 136 mss. and charters. Each volume indexed.

—British Museum.

R. Sims, *Handbook to the Library of the British Museum*. London 1854. XII, 414 pp. Lists the collections and their catalogues (p. 19-80). Lists some of the Additional manuscripts (65-80).

Julius P. Gilson, *A Student's Guide to the Manuscripts of the British Museum*. London 1920. 48 pp. Lists the collections and their catalogues (p. 41-44).

'The Catalogues of the British Museum, 2. Manuscripts,' by T. C. Skeat, *The Journal of Documentation* VII (1951) 18-60. Also printed separately as: *British Museum, The Catalogues of the Manuscript Collections*. London 1951. 43 pp. A complete and annotated list of all printed and unpublished catalogues of the various collections.

Catalogue of Ancient Manuscripts in the British Museum. (By E. Maunde Thompson and G. F. Warner). 2 vols. London 1881-84. II: Latin mss.

A. Palma di Cesnola, *Catalogo di Manoscritti Italiani esistenti nel Museo Britannico di Londra*. Turin 1890. 209 pp. 1679 nos. No index.

G. Fanchiotti, *I Mss. Italiani in Inghilterra descritti in forma popolare*. Serie I. Londra, II Museo Britannico. 3 vols., London 1899 - Caserta 1902. Only vol. III is indexed. (DLC)

Illuminated Manuscripts in the British Museum, ed. G. F. Warner. 4 series in 1 vol. London 1903. No index.

Cotton mss.

Th. Smith, *Catalogus Librorum manuscriptorum Bibliothecae Cottonianae*. Oxford 1696. 159 pp.

A Catalogue of the Manuscripts in the Cottonian Library deposited in the British Museum. (By J. Planta). London 1802. 618 pp. Julius A. I-Faustina F.X., and appendix 1-45.

Royal and King's mss.

(D. Casley, *A Catalogue of the Manuscripts of the King's Library*. London 1734. 360 pp.)

British Museum. Catalogue of Western Manuscripts in the Old Royal and King's Collections, by Sir George F. Warner and Julius P. Gilson. 4 vols. London 1921. Vol. I: Royal mss. 1.A.I-11.E.XI. Vol. II: Royal mss. 12.A.I-20.E.X and appendix 1-89. Vol. III: King's mss. 1-446. Index for I-III. Vol. IV: Plates.

Harley mss.

(*A Catalogue of the Harleian Collection of Manuscripts ... Preserved in the British Museum*. 2 vols. London 1759-63. By H. Wanley and others.) (DLC)

A Catalogue of the Harleian Manuscripts in the British Museum. (By R. Nares and others) 4 vols. London 1808-12. I: Mss. no 1-1309. II: No. 1310-3099. III: No. 3100-7639. IV: Indices. Ms. additions in library copy.

Arundel and Burney mss.

(*Bibliotheca Norfolciana sive Catalogus libb. manuscriptorum et impressorum ... quos ... Henricus Dux Norfolciae etc. Regiae Societati Londinensi ... donavit*. London 1681. 175 pp. p. 126-53: Mss.)

Catalogue of Manuscripts in the British Museum. New Series. (By J. Forshall). 3 pts. in 1, London 1834-40. pt. 1, 168 pp. 550 Arundel mss. pt. 2, 159 pp. 524 Burney mss. pt. 3: Index.

Hargrave mss.

A Catalogue of Manuscripts formerly in the possession of Francis Hargrave ... now deposited in the British Museum. London 1818. 188 pp. 499 mss., mostly late. Hardly relevant. Ms. additions in library copy (NN)

Stowe mss.

Ch. O'Conor, *Bibliotheca Ms. Stowensis: A Descriptive Catalogue of the Manuscripts in the Stowe Library*. 2 vols. Buckingham 1818-19. Arranged by subjects. Each volume, as well as the appendix to vol. I, are indexed. (NN)

Catalogue of the Important Collection of Manuscripts from Stowe. London 1849. 252 pp. 996 mss. Index (p. ixff.). (NN)

Catalogue of the Stowe Manuscripts in the British Museum (By Edward J. L. Scott). 2 vols. London 1895-96. Mostly modern. Index in vol. II.

Lansdowne mss.

A Catalogue of the Lansdowne Manuscripts in the British Museum (By H. Ellis and F. Douce). 2 pts. in 1, London 1819. 1245 mss. mostly late.

Cole mss.

G. J. Gray, *Index to the Contents of the Cole Manuscripts in the British Museum.* Cambridge 1912. 170 pp. Mostly late material.

Sloane, Additional and Egerton mss.

S. Ayscough, *A Catalogue of the Manuscripts preserved in the British Museum hitherto undescribed.* 2 vols. in 1, London 1782. XVI, 909, (160) pp. Covers Sloane mss. (1-4100) and additional mss. no. 4101-5017.

**Annual List of Donations and Bequests to the Trustees of the British Museum*, 1828. London 1830. 45 pp. p. 3-12: mss. (Skeat 8).

**The same, 1829. London 1831. 31 pp. p. 3-18: mss. (Skeat 9).

**The same, 1830. London 1831. 32 pp. p. 3-9: mss. (Skeat 10).

***List of Additions made to the Collections in the British Museum in the Year 1831*. London 1833. 126 pp. p. 1-26: mss. (Skeat 11).

**The same, 1832. London 1834. 160 pp. p. 1-22: mss. (Skeat 12).

**The same, 1833. London 1835. 223 pp. p. 1-33: mss. (Skeat 13).

**The same, 1834. London 1837. 439 pp. p. 1-13: mss. (Skeat 14).

**The same, 1835. London 1839. 478 pp. p. 1-35: mss. (Skeat 15).

Index to the Additional Manuscripts with those of the Egerton Collection, preserved in the British Museum, and acquired in the years 1783-1835. London 1849. (By F. Madden and others.) 514 pp. Arranged alphabetically. Covers Additional mss. no. 5018-10018 and Egerton 1-606.

List of Additions to the Manuscripts in the British Museum, 1836-40. London 1843. Covers additional mss. 10019-11748 and Egerton 607-888.

Catalogue of Additions to the Manuscripts in the British Museum, 1841-45. London 1850. Additional mss. 11749-15667 and Egerton 889-1139.

The same, *1846-47*. London 1864. Additional mss. 15668-17277 and Egerton 1140-49.

The same, *1848-53*. London 1868. Additional mss. 17278-19719 and Egerton 1150-1636. (NN)

The same, *1854-75*. 3 vols. London 1875-80. Additional mss. 19720-29909 and Egerton 1637-2399. Index in vol. III.

The same, *1876-81*. London 1882. Additional mss. 29910-31896 and Egerton 2400-2600.

The same, *1882-87*. London 1889. Additional mss. 31897-33344 and Egerton 2601-78.

The same, *1888-93*. London 1894. Add. mss. 33345-34526 and Egerton 2679-2790.

The same, *1894-99*. London 1901. Add. mss. 34527-36297 and Egerton 2791-2826.

The same, *1900-05*. London 1907. Add. mss. 36298-37232 and Egerton 2827-61.

The same, *1906-10*. London 1912. Add. mss. 37233-38091 and Egerton 2862-89.

The same, *1911-15*. London 1925. Add. mss. 38092-39255 and Egerton 2890-2909.

The same, *1916-20*. London 1933. Add. mss. 39256-40015 and Egerton 2910-3030.

The same, *1921-25*. London 1950. Add. mss. 40016-41295 and Egerton 3031-3038. Each volume indexed.

Edward I. L. Scott, *Index to the Sloane Manuscripts in the British Museum.* London 1904. 583 pp. The Sloane mss. are Add. mss. 1-4100.

Catalogue of Fifty Manuscripts and Printed Books bequeathed to the British Museum by Alfred H. Huth. (By F. G. Kenyon). London 1912. xvi, 130 pp. 13 mss. (p. 1-20), now add. mss. 38114-26. (NN)

The British Museum Quarterly I (1926) ff. Contains regular reports on acquisitions of mss. See especially: IV (1929-30) 82-83: 'Kenelm Digby Papers,' by R. F.

VIII (1933-34) 17-18: 'Three Manuscripts from the Chester Beatty Collection,' by E. G. M. XII (1937-38) 128-129: 'Manuscripts of the Royal Historical Society,' by B. Schofield. Now mss. Add. 45122-36. XV (1952) 18-35: 'Manuscripts acquired during the years 1941-50.' XVI (1951-52) 4-6: 'The Yates Thompson Manuscripts,' by F. Wormald. XVII (1952) 23-40: 'Manuscripts and printed books from the Holkham Hall Library.' 'The Manuscripts,' by T. C. Skeat (25-33). XVIII (1953) 4-10. 'The Sloane Collection of Manuscripts.' XIX (1954) 3-9: 'The Yelverton Manuscripts,' by B. Schofield. Now mss. Add. 48000-48196. XX (1955-56) 28-30: 'The Medici Papers, by K. W. Gransden. XXI (1957-58) 63-66: 'More Manuscripts from Holkham,' by B. Schofield.

Catalogus Librorum Manuscriptorum Bibliothecae Sloanianae. 1 vol. of printed sheets (1837-40). Covers mss. Sloane 1-1091 (Skeat 3).

Catalogue of Additional Manuscripts. 9 ms. vols. Mss. Sloane 1091-4100 (Skeat 4, cf. Born 56).

Catalogue of the Sloane, Birch and Additional Mss. in the British Museum (1782). Cuttings from Ayscough's printed catalogue, with ms. additions and corrections, listing mss. 1-5017 in numerical order. (Cf. Skeat 2).

A Catalogue of the Additions made to the Library of Manuscripts in the British Museum since the Publication of Mr. Ayscough's Catalogue. 5 ms. vols. in 2 (1817-27). Add. mss. 5018-6665 (Skeat 6).

Catalogue of the Additions made to the Department of Manuscripts since the publication of Mr. Ayscough's Catalogue in 1782. 24 ms. vols. (1831-37). Add. mss. 5018-7079 (Skeat 7, cf. Born 59).

Catalogue of Additional Manuscripts, Nos. 6666-10018 (1830-39). 1 vol. of printed cuttings from the annual Lists of Additions (Skeat 16, cf. Born 60).

Catalogue of the Egerton Manuscripts. Nos. 1-606. 1 vol. of printed cuttings from the annual Lists of Additions for the same period (Skeat 46, cf. Born 54).

All these lists give fuller information on the Sloane and Additional mss. than the printed Catalogue by Ayscough (1782) and the printed Index (1849).

Catalogue of Additions 1926-27. Add. mss. 41296-41476. Volume of proof sheets (Cf. Skeat 34, Born 61).

Hand-List of Recent Accessions (1927-36). Typed volume. Add. mss. 41477-44919 and Egerton 3039-3141 (Cf. Skeat 36).

Hand-List of Recent Accessions (1937-...). Add. mss. 44920-48590 and Egerton 3142-3722 (Cf. Skeat 37).

Handlist of Yates Thompson Mss. Typed list. 31 mss. (Cf. Skeat 53).

Helmingham Hall Library (Tollemache Trust). Typed list. 78 mss. (Cf. Skeat 89). The mss. are no longer in the British Museum.

Class Catalog of Manuscripts. By subjects. 110 vols. of printed cuttings from various catalogues (Born 52; Skeat 161).)

—*College of Arms.

Catalogue of the Arundel Manuscripts in the Library of the College of Arms. (By W. H. Black). London 1829. 136 pp. 64 mss.

—*Dutch Austin Friars.

A Catalogue of Books, Manuscripts, Letters etc. belonging to the Dutch Church Austin Friars, London. London 1879. 184 pp. 47 mss. (p. 155-64). (CtY).

Ecclesiae Londino-Batavae Archivum, ed. J. H. Hessels. 3 vols. in 4. Cambridge 1887-97. Contains a list of the collection, and presents the text of most of its documents. (NN)

A part of the collection was recently sold, see· Catalogue of the highly important correspondence of Abraham Ortelius.... presented.. to the Dutch Church in London (and now sold by Order of the Trustees. London (Sotheby) 1955. 32 pp. 99 nos. (NN) The remainder is deposited in the Guildhall Library.

—*Gray's Inn. See Bernardus.

A Catalogue of the Ancient Manuscripts belonging to the Honourable Society of Gray's Inn. (By Alfred J. Horwood). London 1869. VIII, 22 pp. 24 mss. Index (p. vii-viii).

*Typed catalogue. (Communication of the Librarian.)

—*Inner Temple.

A Catalogue of Printed Books in the Library of the Inner Temple; to which is prefixed the Manuscripts therein. London 1806. 172 pp. p. 149-172: Mss. (British Museum; partial micr. at NNC)

A Catalogue of the Printed Books and Manuscripts in the Library of the Inner Temple. London 1833. IV, 289 pp. p. 263-289: Manuscript Books. Charters only. No index. (NN)

—*Lambeth Palace.

A Catalogue of the Archiepiscopal Manuscripts in the Library at Lambeth Palace. By H. J. Todd. London 1812. 270 pp. 1221 mss.

M. R. James and Cl. Jenkins, *A Descriptive Catalogue of the Manuscripts in the Library of Lambeth Palace.* 5 vols. in 1, Cambridge 1930-32. 871 pp. 1214 mss. Yet many mss. are skipped.

—*Lincoln' Inn. See Hunter.

A Catalogue of the printed books, to which is prefixed o short account of the Manuscripts, in the Library of Lincoln's Inn. London 1835. 215 pp. Contains only a short survey of the 479 mss. on 3 unnumbered pages at the beginning. (DLC)

—*Medical Society.

Warren R. Dawson, *Manuscripta Medica: A Descriptive Catalogue of the Manuscripts in the Library of the Medical Society of London.* London 1932. 140 pp. 140 mss. (NNN)

—*Middle Temple. Typed List of Latin mss. kindly supplied by the Librarian.

—*Royal College of Surgeons.

Victor G. Plarr, *Catalogue of Manuscripts in the Library of the Royal College of Surgeons of England.* (London) 1928. 76 pp. Arranged alphabetically. Modern material only.

—*Royal Society.

J. O. Halliwell, *A Catalogue of the Miscellaneous Manuscripts, preserved in the Library of the Royal Society.* London 1840. 38 pp. 145 and 34 mss., mostly modern. Index (p. 31-32).

W. E. Schuckard, *Catalogue of Manuscript Letters in the Possession of the Royal Society.* London 1840. 179 pp. Arranged alphabetically. All modern.

—*St. Paul's Cathedral.

W. Sparrow Simpson, *S. Paul's Cathedral Library: A Catalogue of Bibles, Rituals, and Rare Books; Works relating to London and especially to S. Paul's Cathedral. . . .* London 1893. xxii, 281 pp. p. 66-68: 14 mss.

—*Sion College.

Guil. Reading, *Bibliothecae Cleri Londinensis in Collegio Sionensi Catalogus.* London 1724. Unpaged. At the end (fol. Ppppp): Libri manuscripti. 119 mss. No index.

—*Sir John Soane's Museum. See *Société Française.*

—Society of Antiquaries.

A Catalogue of Manuscripts in the Library of The Society of Antiquaries of London (by H. Ellis). London 1816. 92 pp. 216 mss.

List of Manuscripts (by M. Stephenson and C. V. Deane). 3 mss. vols. I: 217-500. II: 501-760. III: 761-799.

—University of London Library.

R. A. Rye, *Catalogue of the Manuscripts and Autograph Letters in the University Library . . . of London.* London 1921. 132 pp. 181 mss. and autographs. Hardly relevant.

University of London, Catalogue of the Manuscripts and Autograph Letters in the University Library. Supplement 1921-1930. (By Reginald A. Rye). London 1930. 47 pp. Covers mss. 155 and 182-243. Index (p. 41ff.).

Catalogue of Manuscripts and Autograph Letters, Supplementary Entries. Typed list. Mss. 244-407.

Dorothy K. Coveney, *A Descriptive Catalogue of Manuscripts in the Library of*

University College, London. London 1935. 121 pp. 20 Latin mss.

—Victoria and Albert Museum.

South Kensington Museum. Dyce Collection. A Catalogue of the Printed Books and Manuscripts bequeathed by the Reverend Alexander Dyce. 2 vols. London 1875. I p. 1-9: Mss.

South Kensington Museum. Forster Collection. A Catalogue of the Paintings, Manuscripts, Autograph Letters, Pamphlets etc. bequeathed by John Forster. London 1893. 261 pp. p. 21-57: Mss. and letters. Index (p. 58-72). Modern material only.

Catalogue of the Circulating Collection of Illuminated Manuscripts (Leaves and Cuttings) Selected from the Victoria and Albert Museum, South Kensington. London 1908. 16 pp.

Victoria and Albert Museum, Department of Circulation. List of Illuminated Leaves and Cuttings in the Travelling Series. London 1924. VIII, 24 pp. and plates. p. 17-24: 76 nos.

Catalogue of Illuminated Mss. 2 typed vols. The general card index of the library has a section for mss., arranged by languages.

—Wellcome Historical Medical Library.

Alphabetical card index.

Cross index of older mss. for nos. 1-2000. Many mss. were sold after the last war.

—*Westminster Abbey.

J. A. Robinson and M. R. James, *The Manuscripts of Westminster Abbey.* Cambridge 1909. 108 pp. 34 mss. (p. 63-92). (NN)

*Longiano, Italy. See Mazzatinti VI.

*Lons-le-Saunier, France. See France. *Catalogue Général, Départements* XXI; XLI; Martin.

*Lorient, France. See France, *Catalogue Général, Départements* XXIV; XLI.

Los Angeles, California, U.S.A. See De Ricci.

—University of Southern California Library.

The Seeley Wintersmith Mudd Special Collection in the Hoose Library of Philosophy. Los Angeles 1940. 39 pp. p. 14-17: Alphabetical list of 16 mss. Shelf marks added in Library copy.

*Louhans, France. See France, *Catalogue Général, Départements* XXI.

*Louvain (Leuwen), Belgium. See *Archiv* VIII; Haenel; Namur; Plancke.

E. de Moreau, *La Bibliothèque de l'Université de Louvain ' 1636-1914.'* Louvain 1918. 114 pp. Lists 154 mss. (p. 50-80). No index. Said to be a reprint from *Revue des Questions Scientifiques,* but never published in that periodical which did not appear between 1914 and 1920.

M.-Th. Vernet-Boucrel, 'Quelques manuscrits de classiques latins à la Bibliothèque Universitaire de Louvain,' *Mélanges dédiés à la mémoire de Félix Grat* II (Paris 1949) 351-386. Describes 14 mss. lost in 1940.

A list of some mss. recently acquired was kindly supplied by the librarian.

*Louviers, France. See *Cabinet Historique*; France, *Catalogue Général, Départements* II; XLI.

*Löwenberg, see **Lwówek Slaski.**

Lübeck, West Germany. Stadtbibliothek. See *Archiv* III; *Notizenblatt.*

J. H. v. Melle, *Typographische Monumente und Handschriften der ehemaligen Domstifts-Bibliothek zu Lübeck.* Lübeck 1807. VIII, 23 pp. Lists a few theological mss. No index. (Paris, Bibl. Nat.)

C. Curtius, 'Über Pliniushandschriften in Lübeck,' in: *Historische und Philologische Aufsätze Ernst Curtius zu seinem siebenzigsten Geburtstag am zweiten Sept. 1884 gewidmet.* Berlin 1884, p. 325-37.

P. Hagen, *Die deutschen theologischen Handschriften der Lübeckischen Stadtbibliothek* (Veröffentlichungen der Stadtbibliothek der freien und Hansestadt Lübeck, Erstes Stück, Teil 2). Lübeck 1922. VIII, 101 pp. 152 mss. Covers some Latin texts.

P. Karstedt, 'Eine Erfurter Handschriftenwerkstatt im ausgehenden Mittelalter,' *Zentralblatt für Bibliothekswesen* LIII (1936) 19-29. Lists 7 mss. in Lübeck, Stadtbibliothek.

Manuscripta Philologica (by F. Weber, 1937). 37 mss.

Manuscripta theologica latina et philosophica (by the same, 1934-36). 240 and 36 mss.

Lubecensien Handschriften (by P. Hagen, 1936).

Historische Handschriften. 127 mss.

Mathematische, naturwissenschaftliche und technologische Handschriften (by P. Hagen and G. Sack, 1932), 21, 16, 6 mss.

Naturwissenschaftliche und Medizinische Handschriften. Mss. Nat. 17-18; R(ost) 1-69; Med. 1-28.

Juristische Handschriften und Nachlass Dreyer. 265 mss.

(No title). Mss. Hamb. 1-39; Brem. 1-5; geogr. 1-12; lit. germ. 1-34.

Most of the mss. have been missing since the last war.

***Lüben**, see under Berlin.

***Lublin**, Poland. See Vetulani.

—*Biblioteka Publiczna im. Łopacińskiego.

A. Jaworowski, *Katalog Rękopisów Biblioteki Publicznej im. Łopacińskiego w Lublinie.* Lublin 1913. 147 pp. 1314 nos.

The same, *Dodatek* 1. Lublin 1917. 78 pp. Mss. no. 1315-1728. (Cracow, Biblioteka Jagiellonska, micr. at NN)

—*Biblioteka Seminarium Duchownego.

L. Zalewski, *Bibljoteka seminarjum duchownego w Lublinie...* Warsaw 1926. XV, 303 pp. Historical study. (Cracow, Biblioteka Jagiellonska; micr. at NN)

The library has not been reorganized since the war.

—*Biblioteka Uniwersytecka Katolickiego Uniwersytetu Lubelskiego.

Library not yet completely reorganized.

Lucca, Italy. See *Archiv* XII; Blume; *Studi Italiani* VIII; XIV. Zaccaria, *Iter.*

—Archivio Arcivescovile.

A. Mancini, 'Codici latini ignoti a Lucca,' *Rivista di filologia* XXXVI (1908) 518-23. No index.

Catalogo general dei libri di proprietà della R.ma Mensa Arcivescovile di Lucca, by Paolo Quinto Giusti and Ant. Petrini. 35 mss.

—Archivio di Stato.

Inventario del R. Archivio di Stato in Lucca.

4 vols. Lucca 1872-88. Vol. IV, 809-53: 128 mss. (NN)

—Biblioteca Capitolare Feliniana.

Catalogus antiquae Bibliothecae Illustrissimorum et Reverendissimorum DD. Maioris Lucanae Ecclesiae Canonicorum..., by Bernardinus Baronius (1757). Nos. 1-619 and A.-H. Includes some early editions.

Card index of the Fondo Giuseppe Martini (acquired 1946). Includes mss. and edd.

—Biblioteca Governativa.

F. V. Di Poggio, *Notizie della libreria de' padri domenicani di S. Romano di Lucca.* Lucca 1792. 216 pp. p. 168-213: 100 mss. They are now partly in the Biblioteca Governativa. No index. (MH)

Repertorio Generale ossia Catalogo descrittivo di tutti i manoscritti della Biblioteca Pubblica di Lucca, by Leone Del Prete (1877). 3 vols. I: Mss. 1-2737. II-III: Indices (Cf. AB II 4-5 p. 84). (micr. at DLC)

Appendice al Catalogo generale dei manoscritti della Pubblica Biblioteca di Lucca (1883). Mss. 2738-3341 (Cf. AB II 4-5 p. 84). (micr. at DLC)

***Lugano**, Switzerland. Biblioteca Cantonale.

R. Sabbadini, 'Manoscritti di Cicerone, San Zenone e Paolo Veneto nella Biblioteca Cantonale di Lugano,' *Bollettino Storico della Svizzera Italiana* XXX (1908) 79-82. 3 mss. No shelf marks. (NN)

**Catalogo generale della Biblioteca Cantonale.* Lugano 1912. p. 37-47: Mss. (Lugano)

Manoscritti posseduti dalla Biblioteca Cantonale di Lugano anteriori al 1600. Typed list kindly supplied by the librarian. 5 mss. There is no separate inventory of the mss.

Lugo, Italy. Biblioteca Comunale Trisi.

A. Bongiovanni, *La Biblioteca Trisi-Comunale di Lugo dall' origine ai nostri giorni.* Lugo 1898. 263 pp. p. 223-245: Alphabetical list of 144 mss. No index. (NN)

G. Mambelli, *Di alcuni codici, frammenti e libri a stampa miniati che si conservano nella Biblioteca Comunale Trisi di Lugo.* Lugo 1920. 19 pp. 7 mss. No index. (Milan, Biblioteca Nazionale Braidense)

Catalogo dei mss. (Apolloni III 123).

*Card index (AB IV 417).

Luik, see **Liège**.

Lund, Sweden. Universitetsbiblioteket. See Barwiński; Dudik, *Forschungen*; Institut de Recherches; Lampen; Lehmann.

P. Wieselgren, *Catalogus manuscriptorum Bibliothecae Academiae Lundensis.* Section I, pt. 1, respondente Petro E. Oseen. Lund 1830. 16 pp. Describes the catalogues of the library. (MB). Pt. 2 (1830), respondente J. P. Janzon, p. 17-36. Section II, pt. 1 (1830), respondente A. C. Sjöbeck, p. 1-16; pt. 2 (1830), respondente P. J. Björner, p. 17-32. Describes a few mss (Lund, University Library).

Medeltids-Handskrifter. Typed card index. 45 mss.

Large card index for all mss., arranged by subjects. Mostly modern.

Lüneburg, West Germany. Ratsbücherei. See Archiv XI; Lampen; Lehmann, *Mitteilungen* IV.

Handschriften der Ratsbücherei. 1 typed volume.

*Lunel, France. See France, *Catalogue Général, Départements* XXXI.

*Lunéville, France. See France, *Catalogue Général, Départements* XXI; XLI.

M. Rousset, 'Catalogue des manuscrits de la Bibliothèque Municipale de Lunéville, Deuxième Supplément,' *Le Bibliographe Moderne* XX (1920-21) 28-33. Mss. no. 197-210, all modern.

*Lure, France. See France, *Catalogue Général, Départements* IX.

*Luxembourg. See *Archiv* VIII; *Neues Archiv* XXXVII.

Clasen, *Catalogue des livres et des manuscrits de la Bibliothèque de Luxembourg.* Luxembourg 1846. p. 255-64: Mss. alphabetically arranged. (DLC)

N. van Werveke, *Catalogue descriptif des manuscrits de la Bibliothèque de Luxembourg* (Supplément du Catalogue de la Bibliothèque de Luxembourg. Troisième Partie.) Luxembourg 1894. 509 pp. 262 mss. No index. (DLC)

N. van Werveke, 'Catalogue descriptif des manuscrits conservés à la Bibliothèque de la Section historique de l'Institut G.-D.,' *Publications de la Section Historique de l'Institut Grand-Ducal de Luxembourg* XLV (1896) 221-244; XLVI (1898) 219-284; XLIX (1899-1901) 268-373; LI (1903) 165-289. 382 mss. Mostly late. (NN)

*Luxeuil, France See France, *Catalogue Général, Départements* XLI.

Luzern, Switzerland. Zentralbibliothek. See Sinner; Stelling-Michaud; *Traditio* XIV.

Katalog der Bürgerbibliothek in Luzern, (by L. Keller). Luzern 1840, (and Supplements 1845, 1851, 1856 and 1866.) XX, 610, liv pp. p. 431-553: 288 local mss. p. 555ff.: 'Verzeichnis von Inkunabeln, seltenen alten Hss. und anderen Merkwürdigkeiten.' (Vatican Library)

Standorts-Repertorium (1915). Covers Bürger-Bibliothek und supplements the printed catalogue of 1840.

Bücher-Verzeichniss der Kantons-Bibliothek in Luzern, 3 vols. Luzern 1835-36. Vol. III, p. 157-66: 204 mss, alphabetically arranged.

Schöne Miniaturen aus Handschriften der Kantonsbibliothek Luzern, ed. Jos. Schmid. Luzern 1941. 36 pp. and plates. (NN)

Handschriften-Katalog. Covers Kantons-Bibliothek, and adds many items to the printed catalogue of 1836.

Large card index of all mss.

*Lwów, see under Wrocław.

*Lwówek Śląski (Löwenberg), Poland. See *Archiv* XI.

*Lyon, France. See France, *Catalogue Général, Départements* XXX; XXXI; XLII; *Universités*; Martin; *Notices et Extraits.*

A. F. Delandine, *Manuscrits de la Bibliothèque de Lyon* ... 3 vols. Paris 1812. 1518 mss. (in Latin: nos. 56-634, I p. 150-395). Index in vol. III.

E. Caillemer, 'Notices et Extraits de Manuscrits de la Bibliothèque de Lyon,' *Mémoires de l'Académie des Sciences, Belles-Lettres et Arts de Lyon, Classe des Lettres*

XX (1881-82) 39-88. 7 mss. No index. (NN)

The same, *Les manuscrits Bouhier, Nicaise et Peiresc du Palais des Arts de Lyon.* Lyon 1880. 48 pp. 6 late mss. No index. (CtY)

E. A. Lowe, *Codices Lugdunenses antiquissimi.* (*Documents paléographiques, typographiques, iconographiques de la Bibliothèque de Lyon,* fasc. 3-4). Lyons 1924. 52 pp. and plates.

The Bibliothèque Municipale now owns the manuscripts formerly preserved at the Palais des Arts.

*Maastricht, Holland.

Catalogus der Stadsbibliotheek van Maastricht, by A. J. Flament. 2 vols. Maastricht 1888-94. I, 1-12: 58 nos.

List of 7 additional mss. kindly supplied by the librarian.

Macerata, Italy. Biblioteca Comunale. See Mazzatinti (1887).

Per la storia della Biblioteca Comunale Mozzi-Borgetti di Macerata: Notizie e documenti. (By C. Capotosti and A. Menchini). Macerata 1905. 180 pp. p. 47-70: mss. Corrects Mazzatinti on many points.

Library copy of Mazzatinti (1887) adds descriptions for mss. 518-604.

*Mâcon, France. See France, *Catalogue général, Départements* VI; XLII.

L. Lex, 'Nouvelles acquisitions de la Bibliothèque de la ville de Mâcon (1889-94), *Revue des Bibliothèques* IV (1894) 398-99. Mss. no. 86-96, all modern.

*Madison, New Jersey, U.S.A. See De Ricci.

Madrid, Spain. See Beer (Section A); Grubbs (Section A, under Richardson); *Anuario; Archiv* VIII; Carini; Cordolani; Dominguez Bordona; Gachard; Haenel; Loewe and Hartel; Mas Latrie; *Hispania Sacra* VIII; Institut de Recherches; Millares Carlo; Millas Vallicrosa; *Neues Archiv* VI; *Revista; Serapeum* VIII; Octavio de Toledo.

Guia de las Bibliotecas de Madrid. Madrid 1953. XII, 556 pp.

A. Cordoliani, 'Inventaire des manuscrits de comput ecclésiastique conservés dans les Bibliothèques de Madrid,' *Hispania Sacra* VII (1954) 111-43; VIII (1955) 177-208. (NN) Cf. also *Revista de Archivos, Museos y Bibliotecas* LVII (1951) 5-35; LXI (1955) 135-82. (NNC)

—Academia de la Historia.

'Noticia de los codices pertinecientes a los monasterios de San Millán de la Cogolla y San Pedro de Cardeña remitidos á la Real Academia de la Historia por la Dirección general de fincas del Estado,' *Memorial histórico Español* II (1851) pp. ix-xix. 77 mss. No index. (NN)

Cristóbal Pérez Pastor, 'Indice por títulos de los códices procedentes de los monasterios de San Millán de la Cogolla y San Pedro de Cardeña, existentes en la Biblioteca de la Real Academia de la Historia,' *Boletin de la Real Academia de la Historia* LIII (1908) 469-512; LIV (1909) 5-19. 77 mss. Index in LIV. (NN)

Indice general de manuscritos, by A. Rodriguez Villa. Alphabetical. Describes mss. different from the ones listed in the printed catalogues.

Sección de 'Fondos Antiguos,' by Félix Gomez Centurión y Morato (1915). Several typed vols. Alphabetical.

Card index, typed.

*Catálogo de obras impresas o manoscritas que se atesoran en la Biblioteca de la Real Academia de la Historia con sus correspondientes signaturas y resúmenes claros y precisos. (Communication of J. García Morales).

—Archivo Historico Nacional.

Guia de la Seccion de Codices. 1 typed vol. A pack of index cards, arranged by subjects.

—*Biblioteca Municipal.

Ayuntamiento de Madrid. Revista de la Biblioteca, Archivo y Museo I (1924) 127-28; 265-68; 414-16; 548-53; II (1925) 321-22; 457-58; III (1926) 129-30; 266-68; IV (1927) 248-50: A. Andarias, 'Catálogo de los manuscritos de la Biblioteca Municipal.' 31 recent mss. No index. Not complete.

—Biblioteca del Palacio.

Catálogo de la Real Biblioteca. V: *Manu-*

scritos. *Crónicas generales de España*, by
R. Menéndez Pidal. 1st ed. Madrid 1898.
164 pp. 3rd ed. Madrid 1918. 238 pp.
Covers Spanish chronicles only.

*Indice de los Codices y mss. de la Bibl.ca
particular de la Reina N.ra S.ra D.a
Isabel 2a.* 8 vols. Alphabetical. Fails
to give actual shelf marks. I: A-B. II:
C. III: D-F. IV: G-L. V: M-O. VI:
P-R. VII: S. VIII: T-Z.
Large card index.

*Relacion de los Ms. que procedentes de los
Colegios Mayores de Salamanca, se con-
servan en la Biblioteca Real.* 1 ms. folder.
Concordance of old and new shelf marks.
Not complete.

A large group of mss. was transferred in
1954 to the Biblioteca Universitaria in
Salamanca.

—Biblioteca Nacional

*Madrid. Biblioteca Nacional. Catálogo de
códices latinos.* I, Madrid 1935. By M. de
la Torre and P. Longás. 203 Biblical mss.
Index. Not complete.

*Inventario General de Manuscritos de la
Biblioteca Nacional.* Vols. I-IV. (By R.
Paz Remolar and J. Lopez de Toro).
Madrid 1953-58. I: Mss. no. 1-500. II:
(1956): 501-896. III (1957): 897-1100. IV:
1101-1598.

B. J. Gallardo, *Ensayo de una biblioteca
española de libros raros y curiosos.* 4 vols.
Madrid 1863-89. II (1866), Appendix of
179 pp.: 'Indice de manuscritos de la
Biblioteca Nacional.' Alphabetically arranged. Mostly in Spanish.

J. M. Rocamora, *Catálogo abreviado de los
manuscritos de la Biblioteca del Excmo.
Señor Duque de Osuna é Infantado.* Madrid 1882. 138 pp. 212 mss. (p. 3-51) arranged alphabetically, and other items.
(Pierpont Morgan Library)

M. Schiff, *La bibliothèque du Marquis de
Santillana* (Bibliothèque de l'École des
Hautes Études, Sciences Historiques et
Philologiques 153). Paris 1905. XCI, 509
pp. Discusses 71 groups of mss. Most of
them are among the mss. of the Biblioteca

Nacional that came from the Duque de
Osuna. Antiquated shelf marks.

P. Roca, *Catálogo de los manuscritos que
pertenecierón a D. Pascual de Gayangos
existentes hoy en la Biblioteca Nacional.*
Madrid 1904. 401 pp. 1155 mss., mostly
modern.

M. de Barcelona, 'Notes descriptives dels manuscrits franciscans medievals de la Biblioteca Nacional de Madrid,' *Estudis Franciscans* XLV (1933) 337-404. (MH)

*Biblioteca Nacional, Madrid. Departamento
de Manuscritos. Catálogo de 'Tomos de
varios.'* Vol. I, by J. Paz. Madrid 1938.
vii, 343 pp. Describes mss. 2345-2393.
Hardly relevant.

*R. Fernandez Pousa, 'Los manuscritos vi-
sigóticos de la Biblioteca Nacional,' *Ver-
dad y Vida* III (1945) 376-423. 29 mss.
(NStC)

H. Anglés and J. Subirá, *Catálogo musical de
la Biblioteca Nacional.* 3 vols. Barcelona
1946-51. Vol. I: 234 mss. (NN)

J. Anguita Valdivia, *Manuscritos concepcio-
nistas en la Biblioteca Nacional.* Madrid
1955. 125 pp. and plates. 121 mss. dealing with the Immaculate Conception.
Index. (NN)

Library copies of printed catalogues by
Rocamora, Octavio de Toledo, Schiff,
Loewe-Hartel, Roca, with shelf marks
added in handwriting.

Inventario topografico antiguo. Large card
index which follows antiquated shelf
marks.

Inventario topografico nuevo. Large card
index which follows the actual shelf
marks and has some gaps.

Concordance for the old and new shelf
marks, 1 vol.

Indice, 4 vols. Alphabetical. Titles in Spanish. Not complete for recent acquisitions.
I: A-C. II: D-K. III: L-Q. IV: R-Z.

Equivalencias for the mss. from Toledo.
Several typed sheets.

—Instituto Valencia de Don Juan.

Inventario de los Manuscritos de la Biblioteca.
3 ms. sheets. 77 mss.

—Biblioteca de la Universidad.

J. Villa-Amil y Casto, *Catálogo de los manuscritos existentes en la Biblioteca del Noviciado de la Universidad Central (procedentes de la antigua de Alcalá).* pt. 1: *Códices.* Madrid 1878. 73 pp. 160 mss. Some mss. lost during the Civil War and marked in library copy.

*Magdeburg, East Germany. See *Archiv* XI. See also under Halle.

A. Göring, *Notitia codicis manuscripti e L. A. Senecae epistolis, Diogenis Laertii X libris, et D. Justiniani institutionibus excerpta continentis.* progr. Lübeck 1823. 12 pp. (NN)

K. Knaut, *Die Handschriften und ältesten Drucke der Kloster-Bibliothek.* progr. Magdeburg 1877. 48, 23 pp. p. 37-39: 9 mss. No index. (Erlangen, University Library.) Many mss. lost.

H. Dittmar, *Die Handschriften und alten Drucke des Dom-Gymnasiums.* 3 pts. progr. Magdeburg 1878-80. pt. 1: 51 pp. 100 mss. pt. 3: 112 pp. Mss. no. 101-285. Index for both parts (p. 105ff.). (ICU)
The mss. are now partly in Berlin, partly in Halle, partly lost.

—*Stadtbibliothek. Mss. lost.

*Maihingen, see under **Harburg**.

Mainz, West Germany. See Falk, *Die ehemalige Dombibliothek*; Bernards; Gercken; Leclercq; *Neues Archiv* XXXVIII; Schreiber.

—Priesterseminar. See Leclercq.

Handschriften-Katalog (by Dr. Stock, 1906). Arranged by subjects.

New typed list (not yet completed in 1955).

—Stadtbibliothek.

G. C. Braun, 'Über einige Handschriften auf der Öffentlichen Bibliothek zu Mainz,' *Kritische Bibliothek für das Schul- und Unterrichtswesen*, ed. Seebode, II, 2 (1820) 773-74. 9 mss. (ICU)

Verzeichnis der Handschriften. (Inside:) *Catalogus codicum Manuscriptorum Bibliothecae Moguntinae.* Centuries not given. Mss. 1-650; II 1-485; III 1-71; IV 1-94. Card index. Alphabetical.

*Malines (Mecheln), Belgium. See *Catalogue Général* IV.

*Malvern, England.

Sir George Warner, *Descriptive Catalogue of Illuminated Manuscripts in the Library of C. W. Dyson Perrins.* 2 vols. Oxford 1920. I: 135 mss. (Pierpont Morgan Library)

The collection is now being dispersed. See: *The Dyson Perrins Collection, Part I. Catalogue of Forty-Five exceptionally important Illuminated Manuscripts... the property of the late C. W. Dyson Perrins.* London (Sotheby) 1958. 108 pp. (Morgan Library)

*Mamers, France. See France, *Catalogue Général, Départements* XIII.

Manchester, England. See Bernardus; Schenkl.

—Chetham Library.

Bibliotheca Chethamensis sive Bibliothecae publicae Mancuniensis ab Humfredo Chetham armigero fundatae catalogus. 6 vols. Manchester 1791-1883. II (1791) 618-22: Mss. no. 6680-6723. III (1826) 165-74: Mss. no. 7995-8029. Index for vols. I-III. IV (1862) 424-49: Mss. no. 11362-11398. V (1863): Index for vols. I-IV. VI (1883) 367-82: Mss.

J. O. Halliwell, *An Account of the European Manuscripts in the Chetham Library, Manchester.* Manchester 1842. 26 pp. Mss. no. 6680-6723; 7995-8042. No index. (NN)

A Catalogue of the Library of the late John Byrom... (By B. R. Wheatly). (London) 1848. Privately printed. 249 pp. p. 239-249: Mss. No shelf marks. No index. Descriptions fuller than in *Bibliotheca Chethamensis*, vol. VI.

**Accession Registers*, 3 ms. vols. I: a. 1655-1880. II: 1880-1933. III: 1921 - current date. Printed books and manuscripts together. Not complete.

*Gift Books, 4 ms. vols. I: 1694-1853. II: 1853-78. III: 1878-1909. IV: 1909-date. Printed books and manuscripts together.

New typed catalogue in progress.

—John Rylands Library.

Second International Library Conference. List of Manuscripts, Printed Books and Examples of Bookbinding Exhibited to the American Librarians on the Occasion of their Visit to Haigh Hall. Aberdeen 1897. 76 pp. 263 mss. of which nos. 10-54 (p. 2-9) in Latin. No index. (NN)

Bibliotheca Lindesiana. List of Manuscripts and Examples of Metal and Ivory Bindings Exhibited to the Bibliographical Society at the Grafton Galleries 13th June 1898 by the President. Aberdeen 1898. 46 pp. 265 mss. No index. (Pierpont Morgan Library).

'List of Manuscripts . . . from the Bibliotheca Lindesiana. Exhibited to the Bibliographical Society . . . by the President, Lord Crawford,' *Transactions of the Bibliographical Society* IV (1898) 213-32. 265 mss. No index.

(*Catalogue of the Printed Books and Manuscripts in the John Rylands Library, Manchester.* 3 vols. Manchester 1899. Vol. III, p. 1983-1986: Alphabetical list of mss.)

M. R. James, *A Descriptive Catalogue of the Latin Manuscripts in the John Rylands Library at Manchester.* 2 vols. Manchester 1921. I, 328 pp.: 183 mss. II: Plates.

R. Fawtier, 'Hand-List of Additions to the Collection of Latin Manuscripts in the John Rylands Library, 1908-1920,' *Bulletin of the John Rylands Library* VI (1921-22) 186-206. Mss. no. 184-332. No index.

M. Tyson, 'Hand-List of Additions to the Collection of Latin Manuscripts in the John Rylands Library, 1908-1928,' *Ibid.* XII (1928) 581-609. Mss. no. 184-395. Index (605-09).

The same, 'Hand-List of the Collections of French and Italian Manuscripts in the John Rylands Library, *Ibid.* XIV (1930) 563-628. 69 Italian mss.

F. Taylor, *Supplementary Hand-List of Western Manuscripts in the John Rylands Library.* Manchester 1937. 49 pp. Latin mss. no. 396-447 (p. 7-21).

Hand-List of Additions to the Collection of

Latin Manuscripts in the John Rylands Library (by F. Taylor, 1937 to date). Mss. no. 448-468 (1955).

—University Library.

Catalogue of the Christie Collection, by Charles W. E. Leigh. Manchester, 1915. XV, 536 pp. p. 461-69: Manuscripts. Arranged alphabetically. Shelf marks added in library copy.

*Mannheim, West Germany. Schlossbücherei.

**Inventory lost during the war. Few Latin mss. (Communication of the librarian).

*Mantes, France. See France, *Catalogue Général, Départements* XX.

Mantova, Italy. See *Giornale* II-IV; Zaccaria, *Iter.*

—*Archivio di Stato.

L'Archivio di Stato di Mantova. Vol. I, by P. Torelli, Ostiglia 1920. Vol. II, by A. Luzio, Verona 1922. (Pubblicazioni della R. Accademia Virgiliana di Mantova. Ser. I, Monumenta, vol. 1-2). Summary list.

Mittenti delle lettere della Serie E (Corrispondenza Estera) e della Serie F II 8 (Lettere da Mantova e Paesi dello Stato). Notebooks by Davari. (Micr. at DLC)

—Biblioteca Comunale.

G. G. Orti, 'Lettera al.... Gio. Batt. Vermiglioli,' *Poligrafo, Giornale di Scienze, Lettere ed Arti,* N.S. IV (Verona 1834) 221-232. Describes a few mss. of the Biblioteca Comunale, Mantua. No index. (Venice, Biblioteca Marciana)

Catalogo dei Manoscritti secondo la sede che occupano negli scaffali. Centuries not always given. A I 1-J II 14. Over 1000 mss. (micr. at DLC)

*Card index (AB III 552).

T. Bertotti, *Saggio per uno studio dei codici letterari latini della Biblioteca Comunale di Mantova.* Thesis, Università Cattolica, Milan 1946-47.

—*Marchese Castiglioni. See *Manoscritti e libri rari.*

Marburg, West Germany. *Universitätsbibliothek.

Car. Fr. Hermann, *Catalogus codicum manuscriptorum, qui in Bibliotheca Academica Marburgensi asservantur, Latinorum.* Marburg 1838. xii. 104 pp. (MH)

The same, *Analecta Catalogi codicum bibliothecae academicae latinorum.* progr. Marburg 1841. 40 pp. No index. (PU)

Katalog der Handschriften. 773 mss. Lists many Latin mss. not described in Hermann's printed catalogue. (Communication of the librarian, cf. Born 230).

—Westdeutsche Bibliothek. See under Berlin.

*Maria Saal, Austria. See *Handschriftenverzeichnisse.*

*Maribor, Yugoslavia. See Kos.

*Mariemont, Belgium. Musée Warocqué. See *Les Richesses.*

M. Battistini, 'Documenti italiani nel Belgio,' *Giornale Storico della letteratura italiana* XCVII (1931) 296-317.

*Marienthal, East Germany. See Bruck.

*Marienwerder, see Kwidzyn.

*Marseille, France. See France, *Catalogue Général, Départements* XV; XLII.

*Mattsee, Austria. See *Archiv* X; Wickhoff.

*Mauriac, France. See France, *Catalogue Général, Départements* XIII.

*Maynooth, Ireland. See *Analecta Bollandiana* XLVI.

*Meaux, France. See France, *Catalogue Général, Départements* III; XLII.

*Mecheln, see Malines.

*Meersburg, West Germany. See *Archiv* VIII.

*Meiningen, East Germany. Landesbibliothek. See *Archiv* VIII.

'Verzeichnis einiger auf der Herzogl. Bibliothek zu Meiningen befindlichen Handschriften und Codices,' *Historisch-litterarisch-bibliographisches Magazin* VII-VIII (1794) 160-81. 9 mss. No index.

Grobe, *Die Schätze der Herzoglichen Öffentlichen Bibliothek zu Meiningen.* progr. Meiningen 1896. 18 pp. List a few mss. (DLC)

The mss. are all lost.

*Melbourne, Australia. Public Library of Victoria. 24 mss. No separate catalogue. List of 5 mss. kindly supplied by the librarian.

*Meldorf, West Germany.

F. Hestermann, *Biblische und liturgische Handschriften-Fragmente des Dithmarscher Landesmuseums in Meldorf.* (Jahrbuch des Vereins für Dithmarscher Landeskunde XI [1932], Supplement). Heide (1932). 36 pp. 32 nos. (Meldorf; micr. at NNC)

*Melk, Austria. Stiftsbibliothek. See Cooper (Section A); *Archiv* VI; X; Neuwirth; Schulte.

M. Kropff, *Bibliotheca Mellicensis.* Vienna 1747. 682 pp. p. 13-75: Mss. (NNUT) New shelf marks added in Library copy.

Catalogus codicum manuscriptorum qui in Bibliotheca Monasterii Mellicensi O.S.B. servantur. I, Vienna 1889. 362 pp. 234 mss. Not complete.

O. Holzer, *Die geschichtlichen Handschriften der Melker Bibliothek.* progr. Melk 1896. No index. 54 pp.

Catalogus Codicum Manu Scriptorum qui in Bibliotheca Monasterii Mellicensis O.S.B. servantur. I, Vienna, 1889 (printed): mss. 1-234. II: 238-707. III: 708-1854. Current shelf-marks added in red in all three volumes. (Communication of the librarian; micr. at DLC). Some mss were sold.

*Melun, France. See France, *Catalogue Général, Départements* III; XLII.

*Memmingen, West Germany. Stadtbibliothek. See Gercken; *Serapeum* VII; VIII and *Intelligenzblatt* 1864.

*Fachkatalog und Verfasserkartei. 28 mss. before 1600. Information and list of mss. kindly supplied by the librarian.

*Mende, France. See France, *Catalogue Général, Départements* IV.

*Menton, France. See France, *Catalogue Général, Départements* XLII.

*Merano-Meran, Italy. See Wickhoff.

Merseburg, East Germany. See *Archiv* VIII; XI.

A. Assmus, *Mittheilung über die Bibliothek des Gymnasiums, namentlich über die*

Handschriften und die selteneren Druck-werke. progr. Merseburg 1879. 51 pp. p. 29-33: 64 late mss. No index. (Erlangen, Univ. Library)

—Archiv des Domkapitels.

Katalog der Kapitelsbibliothek zu Merseburg. Abtheilung I (Handschriften). 1 ms. vol. (1917). 207 mss.

—*Deutsches Zentralarchiv.

It has some of the mss. of the former Preussisches Geheimes Staatsarchiv. See also under Berlin.

Messina, Italy. Biblioteca Universitaria. See Blume; Italy, *Statistica* (Section A); Rühl; *Studi Italiani* X.

Catalogo dei Manoscritti. 3 ms. vols. I: Fondo Antico Sez. I nos. 1-264. II: Fondo Antico Sez. II nos. 265-502. III: Fondo Nuovo, nos. 503-539 (Cf. AB I 5-6 p. 99).

*Metelen, West Germany. Pfarrbibliothek.

W. Lampen, 'Codices liturgici Metellienses,' *Ephemerides liturgicae* XLI (1927) 334-348. 3 mss. (NNG)

*Metz, France. See France, *Catalogue Général, Départements* V (Quarto Series) and XLVIII.

Catalogue des manuscrits de la Bibliothèque de Metz. (By V. J., i.e., Jacob). Metz 1875. 178 pp. (OCI)

E. Paulus, 'Supplément au Catalogue des manuscrits de la bibliothèque de la ville de Metz: Collection Salis,' *Le Bibliographe Moderne* VII (1903) 401-16. 118 mss. No index.

Some mss. were lost during the last war. List kindly supplied by Mlle J. Vielliard.

*Mexico, Mexico. Biblioteca Nacional.

No information. Cf. A. M. Carreño, *Manuscritos, incunables y libros raros en la Biblioteca nacional de Mexico.* Mexico 1950. 74 pp. (NN)

*Mézières, France. See France, *Catalogue Général, Départements* XLII.

Michaelbeuern, Austria. Sitftsbibliothek. See Neuwirth; Wickhoff.

Catalogus librorum, qui in Bibliotheca monasterii Michaelis in Beurn O.S.B. asser-vantur. I. Pars, continens Manuscripta et incunabula, by P. Michael Filz (1825). 14 Pergamenthss., 122 Papierhss.

Catalogus manuscriptorum et incunabulorum et his aetate proximorum, by the same (1846). 9 Pergamenthss., 113 Papierhss.

Zettelkatalog, by P. Dionys (ca. 1930). 401 nos.

New catalogue in progress, by P. Werigand. Goes to ms. cart. 108 (1955).

The shelf marks have been changed, and many mss. have not yet received definitive numbers.

*Michelstadt, West Germany.

A. Klassert, *Mitteilungen über die Michelstädter Kirchenbibliothek.* 2 pts. progr. Michelstadt 1902 and 1905. 20 and 12 pp. pt. 1: 'Rückblick auf die Geschichte der Bibliothek, Zusammenstellung der Handschriften, Erstlingdrucke und einiger anderer interessanten Werke.' Lists a few mss. No index. (Hebrew Union College, Cincinnati, Ohio). Pt. 2 (University Library, Heidelberg, microfilm at NNC)

*Mikulov (Nikolsburg) Czechoslovakia. See Dietrichstein (Section B). See also under Brno.

Milano, Italy. See *Analecta Bollandiana* XI; *Archiv* V; IX; XII; Bernards; Blume; Leclercq; *Giornale* III; Italy, *Indici e Cataloghi* XIII; Lampen; Mazzatinti VII; Montfaucon; Palacky; Reifferscheid; *Spicilegium*; *Studi italiani* XI; Zaccaria, *Excursus.*

Le biblioteche Milanesi. (Preface signed by G. Bognetti). Milan 1914. XII, 583 pp. Describes all collections, including the Seminary library, now in Venegono Inferiore. Mentions some mss.

Liana Montevecchi, 'Catalogo dei codici epigrafici delle biblioteche milanesi,' *Epigraphica* I (1959) 53-79.

—*Archivio Borromeo.

A. Rivolta, 'Epistolario giovanile di S. Carlo Borromeo,' *Aevum* XII (1938) 253-280. Mss. L V 26-27.

The same, 'Corrispondenti di S. Carlo Borromeo,' *Ibid.* XIII (1939) 65-116. Mss. L V 20-25.

—Archivio Capitolare della Basilica di S. Ambrogio.

G. Nicodemi, 'I codici miniati nell' Archivio della Basilica Ambrosiana,' *Rassegna d'arte* XIII (1913) 191-194.

The same, 'I codici miniati dell' Archivio Santambrosiano,' *ibid.* XIV (1914) 91-96.

Basilica Ambrosiana, Archivio Capitolare, Elenco Codici membranacei. Privately printed (pro Manuscripto). No date. 4 unnumbered pages. 55 mss.

For the paper mss., there is no inventory. They are said to be mostly late or liturgical.

—Archivio di Stato.

Personaggi più notevoli (shelf mark 159).

Autografi (shelf mark 662). Summary alphabetical list which gives the actual shelf marks.

A new alphabetical inventory is in progress, which gives fuller data.

—Biblioteca e Archivio Capitolare del Capitolo Metropolitano.

Elenco dei Codici, Manoscritti, Incunabuli e altri libri rari. 1 ms. vol. Mss. D 1.1-F 3.39.

—Biblioteca Ambrosiana.

A. Saba, 'La Biblioteca Ambrosiana (1609-1632),' *Aevum* VI (1932) 531-620. A bibliographical survey. See especially pp. 560-605, for the mss.

A. Ceruti, *Lettere inedite di dotti italiani del secolo XVI tratte dagli autografi della Biblioteca Ambrosiana.* Milan 1867. 127 pp.

A. Martini and D. Bassi, *Catalogus codicum graecorum Bibliothecae Ambrosianae.* 2 vols. Milan 1906. 1297 pp. continuously numbered. 1093 mss. Index in vol. II. Describes many mss. with Latin or Italian parts, but does not always fully cover the latter.

A. Amelli, 'Indice dei codici manoscritti della Biblioteca Ambrosiana, *Rivista delle Biblioteche e degli Archivi* XX (1909) 142-72; XXI (1910) 39-46; 58-78; 151-58; 183-92. Mss. A inf. 1-I inf. 38; A sup. 1-157. No index. Incomplete.

M. Magistretti, 'Due inventari del Duomo di Milano del secolo XV,' *Archivio Storico Lombardo* Ser. IV vol. XII (1909) 285-362. 50 mss at Ambrosiana identified.

M. Grabmann, 'Mitteilungen über scholastische Funde in der Biblioteca Ambrosiana zu Mailand,' *Theologische Quartalschrift* XCIII (1911) 536-550. No index. (NNUT)

P. Revelli, *I Codici Ambrosiani di contenuto geografico* (Fontes Ambrosiani I 1). Milan 1929. 196 pp. 575 mss No index. (MH)

A. Rivolta, 'Catalogo di codici Pinelliani dell' Ambrosiana,' *Aevum* III (1929) 481-512. 70 mss.

The same, *Catalogo dei codici pinelliani dell'Ambrosiana.* Milan 1933. civ, 253 pp. Index (p. lxxxi-civ). 269 mss.

A. Saba, *La Biblioteca di S. Carlo Borromeo* (Fontes Ambrosiani XII). Florence 1936. xxvii, 113 pp. p. 71-76: 'Elenco dei Codici Ambrosiani provenienti dalla Biblioteca Capitolare di Milano.' 76 mss. (CtY)

Inventario Mss. (called Inventario Ceruti). 33 vols. I: A 1 inf. - A 275 inf. II: B 1-58 inf. III: C 1-158 inf. IV: C 159-320 inf. V: D 1-266 inf. VI: D 267-551 inf. VII: E 1-89 inf. VIII: F 1-260 inf. IX: G 1-306 inf. X: H 1-269 inf. XI: J 1-261 inf. XII: A 1 sup. - A 188 sup. XIII: B 1-174 sup. XIV: C 1-125 sup. XV: D 1-120 sup. XVI: E 1-154 sup. XVII: F 1-150 sup. XVIII: G 1-98 sup. XIX: H 1-118 sup. XX: J 1-121 sup. XXI: L 1-119 sup. XXII: M 1-95 sup: XXIII: N 1-351 sup. XXIV: O 1-249 sup. XXV: P 1-276 sup. XXVI: Q 1-126 sup. XXVII: R 1-126 sup. XXVIII: S 1-158 sup. XXIX: T 1-191 sup. XXX: V 1-35 sup.; X 1-39 sup. XXXI: Y 1-195 sup. XXXII: Z 1-251 sup. XXXIII: & 1-204 sup.; † 1-50 sup. (micr. at DLC)

Manuductio ad reperiendos Mss.os Codices Ambrosianos ordine alphabetico. Centuries not always given. Alphabetical index. I: A-E. II: F-O. III: P-Z (micr. at DLC)

Appendix, by M. Cogliati (1938). Alphabetical. Centuries not given. Covers the acquisitions not described in the other catalogues and known as Sussidio. (micr. at DLC)

Inventario Peritale dei mss. Trivulzio-Belgioioso-Trotti. 611 mss., not listed in serial order. Only about 400 of them are in the Ambrosiana. The others were scattered, and are marked with the sign d(eest). (micr. at DLC)

Card index.

*Archivio della Curia Arcivescovile, Archivio Spirituale, Sezione XIV. Libreria Manoscritti. This collection is deposited in the Ambrosiana. Cf. A. Sala, *Documenti circa la vita e le gesta di S. Carlo Borromeo* I (1857), p. xl-lxxxv, where a summary account of this collection is given. (PU)

—Biblioteca Nazionale Braidense.

I. Ghiron, 'Bibliografia Lombarda: Catalogo dei manoscritti intorno alla storia della Lombardia esistenti nella Biblioteca Nazionale di Brera,' *Archivio Storico Lombardo* VI (1879) 155-74; 367-97; 576-98; VII (1880) 41-72; IX (1882) 698-714; X (1883) 736-68. Arranged alphabetically.

Ai Soci dell' 'Atene e Roma' riuniti a Milano pel III Convegno Nazionale... la Biblioteca Nazionale di Brera. Milan 1908. 43 pp. p. 1-27: R. Sabbadini, 'Da codici Braidensi.' p. 29-43: D. Fava, 'La biblioteca della Certosa di Pavia.'

Biblioteca Nazionale di Brera, Milano. Catalogo descrittivo della mostra Bibliografica. Milan 1929. (By T. Gnoli). 60 pp. and plates. 32 mss. (p. 7-20).

Primo Congresso Mondiale delle Biblioteche e di Bibliografia (Rome Venice 1929), *Atti* VI (Rome 1933) 359-412: 'Mostra Bibliografica della R. Biblioteca Nazionale Braidense di Milano.' Preface signed by T. Gnoli. p. 368-381: 32 mss. and illuminated books.

Inventario della Biblioteca Nazionale di Milano. Manoscritti (1875-76). Mss. AD IX 1 - XV 22; AE IX 1 - XIV 27; AF IX 1 - XIV 20; AG IX 1 - XIV 11, and several more scattered mss.

Manoscritti della Biblioteca di Brera. 4 vols. Alphabetical index .I: A-C. II: D-L.

III: M-P. IV: Q-Z (Cf. AB II 1 p. 69). *Fondo Castiglioni.* Summary list of *ca.* 25 mss. recently given to the library.

—Biblioteca Trivulziana.

G. Porro, *Catalogo dei codici manoscritti della Trivulziana.* (Biblioteca Storica Italiana II). Turin 1884. 532 pp. Arranged alphabetically. 2276 mss.

C. Santoro, *Codices Trivultiani Antiquiores* (*ab VIII usque ad XII saeculum*). Milan 1950. 55 pp. and plates. 11 mss.

The same, *Codici miniati del Rinascimento Italiano.* Milan 1952. 71 pp. and plates. 60 mss.

The same, *I codici miniati della Biblioteca Trivulziana.* Milan 1958. xix, 169 pp. and plates. 134 mss.

Typed checklist of preserved mss. Many mss. listed in the printed catalogue of Porro were retained by the Trivulzio family, or lost during the last war.

The mss. retained by the Trivulzio family are also listed in *Manoscritti e Libri rari notificati* (2nd ed., 1948), p. 99-100, no. 69.

—*Seminario Arcivescovile. See under Venegono Inferiore.

—Società Storica Lombarda.

Elenco degli scritti lasciati da Francesco Novati (by G. Cesari, 1916). Alphabetical list. A few mss. were lost during the last war.

—*Conte Sola Gabiati. See *Manoscritti e libri rari.*

—*Principe Trivulzio. See *ibid.*

—*Conte Visconti di Modrone. See *ibid.*

C. Varischi da Milano, 'Catalogo dei codici della Biblioteca del Convento di San Francesco dei Minori Cappuccini in Milano,' *Aevum* XI (1937) 237-74; 461-503. 54 mss. No index.

Millau, France. See France, *Catalogue Général, Départements* XLIII.

Minneapolis, Minnesota, U.S.A. See De Ricci.

Mirecourt, France. See France, *Catalogue Général, Départements* IX; XLII.

Modena, Italy. See *Archiv* V; XII; *Archivum Franciscanum* I; II; V; Blume;

Hinschius; Mazzatinti XVI; *Mostra di codici autografici*; Zaccaria, *Excursus* and *Iter*.

—*Archivio del Comune.

Manoscritti di pregio esistenti nell' Archivio del Comune di Modena. (By O. Raselli). Modena 1875. 21 pp. p. 13-15: 'Lavori letterari e storici.' 21 nos. p. 16-19: 'Lettere.' No index. (Florence, Biblioteca Nazionale)

—Archivio di Stato.

Indice. Archivi per materia. Fasc. 14. Letterati. Alphabetical list.

Regesta di corrispondenze letterarie (by Campi). Arranged alphabetically.

—*Biblioteca Capitolare.

Lettera I (II) sopra i codici della Libreria Capitolare di Modena scritta dal P. F. A. Z. (Zaccaria) al . . . Abate Gaetano Marini,' *Biblioteca antica e moderna di storia letteraria* II (Pesaro 1767) pt. 1 p. 377-98; 399-426. No index. (DLC)

A. Dondi, *Notizie storiche ed artistiche del Duomo di Modena.* Modena 1896. 301 pp. p. 269-83: 'Appendice. Catalogo dei codici antichi e moderni dell' Archivio Capitolare di Modena.' 71 mss. No index.

—Biblioteca Estense.

**Cenni storici del museo annesso alla R. Biblioteca Estense.* Modena 1873. 12 pp.

C. Frati, 'Saggio di un catalogo dei codici Estensi,' *Revue des Bibliothèques* VII (1897) 1-25; 107-25; 177-227; 268-84; 305-40; 425-70. Index (454-64). Lists a few mss.

G. Bertoni, *La biblioteca Estense e la coltura ferrarese ai tempi del Duca Ercole I (1471-1505).* Turin 1903. 307 pp.

D. Fava, *La Biblioteca Estense nel suo sviluppo storico.* Modena 1925. 389 pp. 121 illuminated mss. (p. 229-87).

The same, *Catalogo della Mostra permanente della R. Biblioteca Estense.* Modena 1925. ix, 145 pp. p. 1-61: 121 illuminated mss. (NN). Apparently a separate edition of the second part of the preceding work (p. 225-364), with a new pagination and some minor changes.

The same, and M. Salmi, *I manoscritti miniati della Biblioteca Estense di Modena.* Vol. I (all published). Florence (1950.) 233 pp. and plates. 100 mss.

The same, 'I corali degli Olivetani di Bologna,' in *Miscellanea di scritti di bibliografia ed erudizione in memoria di Luigi Ferrari* (Florence 1952), 277-86.

Manuscriptorum codicum Bibliothecae Atestinae Catalogus in quinque partes tributus ... secundum Pluteorum et ipsorum codicum ordinem. 2 vols. I: 87 codices Orientales; 253 codices Graeci; 1289 codices Latini. II: 2032 codices Italici; 140 codices linguarum exterarum. The actual shelf marks are added in the margin (Cf. AB II 2 p. 60). (micr. at DLC)

Catalogus codicum latinorum Bibliothecae Atestinae. 4 vols. Mss. 1-1124 (AB II 2 p. 60-61).

Conspectus codicum italorum qui asservantur in Bibliotheca Atestina. Mss. 1-1224 (AB II 2 p. 61).

L. Lodi, *Catalogo dei codici e degli autografi posseduti dal Marchese Giuseppe Campori.* 5 pts. in 1 vol. 2nd ed. Modena 1895. 699 pp. 2213 mss. (IU)

R. Vandini, *Appendice prima (seconda) al catalogo dei codici e manoscritti posseduti dal Marchese Giuseppe Campori.* 2 pts. in 1 vol. Modena 1886-94. 973 pp. 2869 mss. (IU)

Elenco dei Manoscritti dati in deposito dal Collegio S. Carlo di Modena alla Biblioteca Estense. Typed list of 34 mss. Copy kindly supplied by the librarian.

*—Marchesa Molza-Viti. See *Manoscritti e Libri rari.*

Modigliana, Italy. See Mazzatinti LX.

Mogiła, Poland. Biblioteka O. O. Cystersów.

K. Kaczmarczyk and G. Kowalski, *Katalog Archiwum Opactwa Cystersów w Mogile.* Mogila 1919. XXXIV, 435 pp. 1024 mss. and documents.

Moissac, France. See France, *Catalogue Général, Départements* XIII.

Molfetta, Italy. See Mazzatinti VI.

F. Samarelli, 'La Biblioteca del Seminario di Molfetta e la provenienza di alcuni suoi codici e manoscritti,' *Rivista delle Biblioteche e degli Archivi* XXVIII (1917) 75-85. 28 mss. No index.

*Mondovì, Italy. Biblioteca Civica. See Rossetti.

Catalogo dei manoscritti, inventari ecc. (1905). 205 mss. (AB IV 180)

*Monnickendam, Holland. Gemeentearchief.

E. M(ikkers), 'Het handschrift van Klein-Galilea,' *Cîteaux in de Nederlanden* II (1951) 24-29. Mimeographed.

Monreale, Italy. Biblioteca Comunale. See Garufi, Tarallo.

Elenco dei manoscritti. 1 ms. sheet. 42 mss.

*Mons, Belgium. See *Analecta Bollandiana* IX; *Archiv* VIII; *Catalogus codicum hagiographicorum.*

P. Faider, *Catalogue des manuscrits de la Bibliothèque publique de la ville de Mons* (Universiteit te Gent. Werken uitgegeven door de Faculteit der Wijsbegeerte en Letteren, 65). Ghent 1931. XLVI, 646 pp. 1199 mss. Index subdivided by subjects.

*Montargis, France. See *Cabinet historique;* France, *Catalogue Général, Départements XX.*

*Montauban, France. See France, *Catalogue Général, Départements XXXI.*

*Montbard, France. See France, *Catalogue Général, Départements VI.*

*Montbéliard, France. See France, *Catalogue Général, Départements XIII; XLII.*

*Montbrison, France. See France, *Catalogue Général, Départements XXI;* Martin.

*Mont-de-Marsan, France. See France, *Catalogue Général, Départements XXIV; XLII.*

*Montdidier, France. See France, *Catalogue Général, Départements XLII.*

Monte Cassino, Italy. Biblioteca dell'Abbazia. See *Archiv* XII; Blume; La Fage; Montfaucon; Reifferscheid.

L. Tosti, *Storia della badia di Monte Cassino.* 3 vols. Naples 1842-43. I, 265ff.; II, 312ff. for mss. prior to the thirteenth century. No index.

A. Caravita, *I codici e le arti a Monte Cassino.* 3 vols. in 2, Monte Cassino 1869-71. Lists many mss. down to the nineteenth century. No index.

Bibliotheca Casinensis seu codicum manuscriptorum qui in Tabulario Casinensi asservantur series . . . 5 vols. Monte Cassino 1873-94. I (1873): 45 mss. II (1875): Mss. no. 46-109. III (1877): Mss. no. 110-71. IV (1880): Mss. no. 172-246. V (1894): Mss. no. 247-358.

Paul Guillaume, *Description historique et artistique du Mont-Cassin... avec la traduction italienne en regard.* Monte Cassino 1874. 290 pp. p. 186-204: Mss. No index. (MB)

The same, *Descrizione storica e artistica di Monte-Cassino.* Monte Cassino 1879. 284 pp. p. 198-222: Mss. No index. (NIC)

Codicum Casinensium manuscriptorum catalogus, by M. Inguanez. 3 vols. Monte Cassino 1915-41. I (1915): 200 mss. II (1928-34): Mss. no. 201-400. III (1940-41): Mss. no. 401-600. No index.

Bibliothecae Casinensis Mss. Tom. VI, by Placido Federici: mss. 501-700 (superseded to no. 600 by the printed catalogue). VII: 701-874.

*Montefalco, Italy.

**P. Pambuffetti, *Elenco dei manoscritti appartenenti alla Biblioteca Comunale di Montefalco.* 1938.

*Monteleone, see Vibo Valentia.

*Montélimar, France. See France, *Catalogue Général, Départements XLIII.*

*Monteprandone, Italy. See Caselli.

A. Crivellucci, *I Codici della Libreria raccolta da S. Giacomo della Marca nel Convento di S. Maria delle Grazie presso Monteprandone.* Livorno 1889. 110 pp. 60 mss. No index. (MH)

*Montevergine, Italy. Biblioteca dell'Abbazia. List of the older mss. kindly supplied by the librarian.

*Montivilliers, France. See France, *Catalogue Général, Départements II.*

*Montpellier, France. See *Analecta Bollandiana* XXXIV-XXXV; France, *Cata-

logue Général, Départements I (Quarto series); XLII; *Sociétés; Universités.*

*Montréal, Quebec, Canada. See De Ricci.

*Montreuil, France. See France, *Catalogue Général, Départements* XXIV.

*Montserrat, Spain. Biblioteca del Monasterio. See Grubbs (Section A under Richardson).

A. M. Albareda, 'Manuscrits de la Biblioteca de Montserrat,' *Analecta Montserratensia* I (1917-18) 3-99. 72 mss. For an index, see Grubbs (Section A under Richardson).

*Card catalogue for mss. 74-1058, mostly late. (Communication of the librarian).

*Monza, Italy. See *Archiv* V; XII.

A. F. Frisi, *Memorie storiche di Monza e sua corte.* 3 vols. Milan 1794. III, 19-251: 'Biblioteca Monzese ossia catalogo, e descrizione de' codici manoscritti, membranacei, latini, custoditi nell' Archivio della insigne, e Reale Basilica di Monza.' 245 mss. No index.

*Handwritten catalogue. (Communication of Dr. L. Bieler)

*Moravská Třebová (Mährisch-Trubau), Czechoslovakia. See under Brno.

*Moritzburg, East Germany. Schlossbibliothek. See under Dresden.

*Morlaix, France. See France, *Catalogue Général, Départements* XIII; XLII.

*Mortain, France. See *ibid.* X.

Moskva, USSR. Biblioteka SSSR imeni V.I. Lenina. See Clossius.

S. Zhitomirskaja, 'Zapadnoje srednevekovie v Rukopisjakh gosudarstvennoj Biblioteki SSSR im. V. I. Lenina,' *Srednije Veka* X (1957) 285-305.

Opis rukopisnykh knig na zapadnoevropejskich jazykakh. A handwritten list of European mss., in Russian. Nos. 1-2723 (with gaps). Shelf marks added.

List of Norov manuscripts. 1 typed volume.

*Moulins, France. See France, *Catalogue Général, Départements* III.

*Mount Sinai, Egypt. St. Catherine's Monastery.

Kenneth W. Clark, *Checklist of Manuscripts in St. Catherine's Monastery, Mount Sinai,*

microfilmed for the Library of Congress, 1950. Washington 1952. XI, 53 pp. 1 Latin ms. (p. 21).

E. A. Lowe, 'An Unknown Latin Psalter on Mount Sinai,' *Scriptorium* IX (1955) 177-199.

*Mühlhausen, East Germany. See *Archiv* XI.

München (Munich), West Germany. See P. Braun (under Augsburg); Cooper (Section A); *Archiv* VII; Gercken.

—Bayrische Staatsbibliothek

I. C. von Aretin, *Beyträge zur Geschichte und Literatur, vorzüglich aus den Schätzen der pfalzbaierischen Centralbibliothek zu München.* 9 vols. Munich 1803-07. I, 2 p. 75-96: Abt Maillot, 'Nachricht von den Manuscripten, welche in der Bibliothek des Petrus Victorius vorhanden waren, und jetzt in der Hofbibliothek zu München aufbewahrt werden.'

Chmel, 'Bericht über die von ihm im Frühjahr und Sommer 1850 unternommene literarische Reise,' *Sitzungsberichte der kaiserlichen Akademie der Wissenschaften* [Vienna], *Philosophisch-Historische Classe* V (1850) 361-450; 591-728.

A. Ruland, 'Geschichtliche Nachricht über die ehemalige Domstiftsbibliothek zu Augsburg, mit einer kurzen Beschreibung der in München noch vorhandenen Handschriften derselben,' *Archiv für die Geschichte des Bisthums Augsburg* I (1856) 1-142. p. 42-136: 205 mss. Index (137-42). (MH)

Halm, 'Über die handschriftliche Sammlung der Camerarii und ihre Schicksale,' *Sitzungsberichte der philophisch-philologischen und historischen Classe der k.b. Akademie der Wissenschaften zu München* III (1873) 241-72.

G. M. Thomas, 'Miscellen aus lateinischen Handschriften der Münchener Bibliothek,' *Ibid.* 1875, II, 209-40.

Catalogus Codicum manu scriptorum Bibliothecae Regiae Monacensis, Tomus VII. Codices Gallicos, Hispanicos, Italicos, Anglicos, Suecicos, Danicos, Slavicos, Esthnicos,

Hungaricos complectens. Munich 1858. X, 420 pp. p. 93-314: Italian mss. 1-585 (nos. 620-1103). Shelf marks in parentheses. (DLC)

Catalogus codicum latinorum Bibliothecae Regiae Monacensis, by C. Halm, G. Laubmann and others. 2 vols. in 7 pts. Munich 1868-81. (*Catalogus codicum manuscriptorum Bibliothecae Regiae Monacensis* III-IV). Vol. I, 1 (1868): 2329 mss. Vol. I, 2 (1871): Mss. no. 2501-5250. Vol. I, 3 (1873): Mss. no. 5251-8100. Vol. II, 1 (1874): Mss. no. 8101-10930. Index (p. 169ff.). Collectio Cameraria, no. 10351-10428 (189ff.) with its index (369ff.). Vol. II, 2 (1876): Mss. no. 11101-15028. Vol. II, 3 (1878): Mss. no. 15121-21213. Vol. II, 4 (1881): Mss. no. 21406-27268. Each part indexed. (NNFr, microfilm at NN)

Catalogus codicum latinorum Bibliothecae Regiae Monacensis. 2nd ed. Vol. I pts. 1-2, Munich 1892-94. Mss. no. 1-5250. Each part indexed. Incomplete.

G. Leidinger, *Verzeichnis der wichtigsten Miniaturen-Handschriften der Kgl. Hof- und Staatsbibliothek München.* Munich 1912. 56 pp. 252 mss. No index.

O. Hartig, 'Die Gründung der Münchener Hofbibliothek durch Albrecht V und Johann Jakob Fugger,' *Abhandlungen der K. Bayerischen Akademie der Wissenschaften, Philosophisch-philologische und Historische Klasse* XXVIII, 3 (1917), 412 pp. Discusses 11 illuminated mss. (338ff.).

Codices Latini Monacenses. Nos. 27269-28546 (continues the printed catalogue).

Typed notes on the mss. acquired after 1881 taken by Mme Vernet in 1954 are available at the Institut de Recherches et d'Histoire des Textes, Paris.

*Card files of authors and subjects.

Verzeichnis der lateinischen und deutschen Handschriftenfragmente. CLM 29000-29199. Arranged by subjects.

Libri impressi cum notis manuscriptis. 1 ms. vol. Fol. 1-80; Qu 1-100; Oct 1-229; 90 books of Caspar Bruschius. (Communication of the librarian).

Codd. Mon. Angl. Gall. Hisp. Lusit. Ital. Slav. 1 ms. vol. Describes Italian mss. 487-672.

Initia prosaica latina (11 boxes); *Initia metrica latina* (6 boxes). Begun by Joh. Andr. Schmeller, and continued since. (Communication of the librarian). Cf. Born 232.

—*Bayrisches Nationalmuseum.

P. Lehmann, 'Mittelalterliche Handschriften des K. B. Nationalmuseums zu München,' *Kgl. Bayerische Akademie der Wissenschaften zu München, Sitzungsberichte der Philosophisch-philologischen und der historischen Klasse* 1916 no. 4, 66 pp.

—Dominikanerkloster S. Kajetan.

It has a few mss. from the Dominican Library in Vienna. No inventory.

—Universitätsbibliothek.

P. Ruf. 'Eine Ingoldstädter Bücherschenkung v. J. 1502: Mit einem beschreibenden Verzeichnis der erhaltenen Handschriften und Drucke,' *Sitzungsb. d. Bay. Akad. d. Wiss., Phil.-Hist. Abteilung* 1933, no. 4, 87 pp.

The same, 'Der älteste Handschriftenbestand der Ingolstädter Artistenfakultät,' *Aus der Geisteswelt des Mittelalters* (Beiträge zur Geschichte der Philosophie und Theologie des Mittelalters, Supplementband 3) pt. 1 (Münster 1935) 91-110. No index.

P. Lehmann and O. Glauning, *Mittelalterliche Handschriftenbruchstücke der Universitätsbibliothek und des Georgianum zu München* (Zentralblatt für Bibliothekswesen, Beiheft LXXII). Leipzig 1940. 187 pp. 125 Latin mss.

Handschriften-Standort-Katalog. Sheets in 7 boxes. I: 2⁰ 1-200. II: 2⁰ 201-524. III: 2⁰ 525-778. IV: 4⁰ 1-500. V: 4⁰ 501-820. VI: 4⁰ 821-979. VII: 8⁰ 1-476 (Cf. Born 245).

Typed notes taken by Mme Vernet in 1954 are available at the Institut de Recherches et d'Histoire des Textes, Paris.

*Münster, West Germany. Universitätsbibliothek. See *Archiv* IV; XI.

Verzeichniss der Büchersammlung des Vereins für Geschichte und Alterhtumskunde Westfalens. Abtheilung Münster. Münster 1881. 225 pp. p. 192-211: 186 mss., mostly modern. No index. (NN)

J. Staender, *Chirographorum in Regia Bibliotheca Paulina Monasteriensi Catalogus.* Breslau 1889. 197 pp. 761 mss. (Pierpont Morgan Library)

Most mss. listed in the catalogue by Staender were lost during the last war (communication of Rev. P. Boehner).

*Murano, Italy.

(V. Zanetti) *Codici, pergamene, manoscritti ... appartenenti al Museo Comunale di Murano.* Venice 1873. 11 pp. p. 1-3; 48 mss. No index. (Venice, Biblioteca Marciana).

*Murcia, Spain. See Fransen.

*Muri, Switzerland. See under Aarau.

*Naas, Ireland. Clongowes Wood College.

Aubrey Gwynn, 'Some Old Books and Manuscripts in the Museum and Library,' *The Clongownian* XV, 2 (1939) 17-21; 'Some More Notes about Manuscripts in the Clongowes Library,' *ibid.* XVII, 1 (1944) 11-15. 7 medieval mss. (in vol. XVII), and some later mss. (Dublin, National Library; micr. at NNC)

*Namur, Belgium. See *Analecta Bollandiana* I-II; *Archiv* VIII; *Archivum Franciscanum* VI; *Catalogue Général* I; *Catalogus codicum hagiographicorum.*

*Nancy, France. See France, *Catalogue Général, Départements* IV; XLII; XLVI; XLVIII; *Sociétés.*

Inventaire sommaire des Manuscrits de la Bibliothèque Publique de Nancy. Nancy 1872. 17 pp. 2 coll. 612 mss. (OCl)

J. Favier, 'Catalogue des manuscrits de la Société d'Archéologie Lorraine,' *Mémoires de la Société d'Archéologie Lorraine et du Musée Historique Lorrain*, Ser. III, vol. XV (1887), pt. II, p. 1-82. 257 mss., mostly late. Index (77-82). (NN)

*Nantes, France. See France, *Catalogue Général, Départements* XXII; XLII.

Catalogue de la bibliothèque du Musée Thomas Dobrée. 2 vols. Nantes 1903-04. I

(1904): *Manuscrits,* by G. Durville. 700 pp. 26 mss. (DLC)

Musée Th. Dobrée. Catalogue général des collections, by P. De Lisle du Dreneuc. Nantes 1906. 1019 pp. p. 401-09: 26 mss. No index. (NNMM)

*Nantua, France. See France, *Catalogue Général, Départements* VI.

Napoli, Italy. See *Analecta Bollandiana* XXX; *Archiv* V; XII; Blume; Chiappini; Coggiola; Hinschius; Lampen; Modigliani; Reifferscheid; Tietze.

—*Archivio di Stato.

Inventario dei codici e dei manoscritti già esistenti presso l'Archivio di Stato di Napoli. 1 typed vol. 113 mss. (Micr. at DLC). The mss. were all lost during the last war.

— Biblioteca Nazionale.

I Quaderni della R. Biblioteca Nazionale Vittorio Emanuele III, Napoli. Ser. I, no. 1 (1938). *Mostra di Cimeli bibliografici.* 16 pp. and plates. 31 mss. (p. 7-11). Ser. II, no. 1 (1940). *Cenno Storico-Bibliografico della Biblioteca* (by G. Guerrieri). 29 pp. Discusses the various collections (p. 11ff.), their inventories (p. 10) and catalogues (p. 27-29), and some mss. (p. 24-25). Ser. II, no. 2. G. Guerrieri, *Il Fondo Farnesiano* (1941). 55 pp. Lists some mss. (p. 22-27). No index.

G. Guerrieri, 'Note sulla raccolta dei manoscritti della Biblioteca Nazionale di Napoli,' in *Studi di bibliografia e di argomento romano in memoria di Luigi De Gregori* (Rome [1949]) 192-200.

Fondo Principale.

Cataldus Iannellius, *Codex Perottinus manuscriptus Regiae Bibliothecae Neapolitanae...* Naples 1809. 287 pp. (NjP)

S. Cyrillus, *Codices Graeci Mss. Regiae Bibliothecae Borbonicae.* 2 vols. in 1. Naples 1826-32. 360 mss. He usually skips the Latin sections of the mss.

Cataldus Iannellius, *Catalogus Bibliothecae Latinae veteris et classicae manuscriptae quae in Regio Neapolitano Museo Borbonico adservatur.* Naples 1827. XII, 302 pp.

434 mss. Not complete. (Pierpont Morgan Library)

Sc. Volpicella, 'De' manoscritti della Biblioteca Nazionale di Napoli,' *Rendiconto delle Tornate dell' Accademia Pontaniana* 1866, 84-104. 2 mss. (NN). Also in his *Studi di letteratura storia ed arti* (Naples 1876, 536 pp.) 19-36: 'Di due manoscritti l'uno d'Angelo di Costanzo l'altro di Tiberio Carafa principe di Chiusano.' (Mi U)

Notizia della Biblioteca Nazionale di Napoli. (By V. Fornari, Naples 1872). 95 pp. Lists some mss. (p. 39ff.). No shelf marks. No index. (DLC)

V. Fornari, *Notizia della Biblioteca Nazionale di Napoli.* Naples 1874. 119 pp. Lists some mss. (39ff.). No shelf marks. No index. (NN)

A. Miola, *Le Scritture in volgare dei primi tre secoli della lingua ricercate nei codici della Biblioteca Nazionale di Napoli.* Vol. I (all published), Bologna 1878. 396 pp. Arranged by shelf marks. Goes from ms. I A 23 to XII F 57. No index (Morgan Library). Also in *Il Propugnatore* XI (1878) pt. 2, 292-345; 408-423; XII (1879) pt. 1, 133-152; pt. 2, 370-387; XIII (1880) pt. 1, 105-130; pt. 2, 70-86; 393-418; XIV (1881) pt. 1, 372-416; pt. 2, 141-167; XV (1882) pt. 1, 139-175; pt. 2, 191-233; XVI (1883) pt. 1, 352-385; pt. 2, 281-300; XVII (1884) pt. 2, 259-278; XVIII (1885) pt. 2, 98-117; XX (1887) pt. 1, 65-96; pt. 2, 237-253; N.S. I (1888) pt. 2, 131-151; IV (1891) pt. 2, 276-306. The sections beginning with vol. XVIII add descriptions not contained in the volume, and go to ms. XIII C 9.

T. Kaeppeli, 'Handschriftliche Mitteilungen über Werke von Dominikanerschriftstellern in der Biblioteca Nazionale in Neapel,' *Divus Thomas* (Freiburg) Ser. III, vol. XI (1933) 445-456. 6 mss. No index. (NNUT)

H. van Crombruggen, 'Note sur quelques manuscrits de la Bibliothèque Nationale de Naples, '*Bulletin de l'Institut Historique Belge de Rome* XXIX (1955) 161-175.

4 mss., mostly late.

Inventario Generale di tutti i Codici Manoscritti della Biblioteca Nazionale. 5 vols. Vol. I: I A 1 - V H 398 (over 2300 mss.). Vol. II: VI A 1 - XIV G 28 (over 3200 mss.). Vol. III (Aggiunte 1): I AA 39 - XI F 43. Vol. IV (Aggiunte 2): XII A 37 - XV G 41. Vol. V (Inventario dei Manoscritti Scaff. XVI-): XVI A 1-73; C 1-53; XVII 1-29; XVIII 1-49; XIX 1-34; XX 1-49. This last volume covers the recent acquisitions and also some mss. from S. Martino not listed in Padiglione's printed catalogue (micr. DLC)

(No title). Extra inventory for mss. VI A 1 - VII Aa 48.

Catalogo dei Manoscritti. 6 vols. Alphabetical index (Cf. AB I 4 p. 85).

Catalogo di monoscritti storici, by S. Volpicella. 2 vols. Covers shelves X and XI (AB I 4 p. 80).

Catalogo di Libri a stampa con note e aggiunte mss. cominciato dall' Assistente Alfonso Miola (AB I 4 p. 89).

Fondo Brancacciano.

Manuscriptorum quae in Bibliotheca Brancatiana S. Angeli ad Nilum adservantur catalogus. Naples 1750. 32 pp. Alphabetical list of mss. to letter J. (Naples, Biblioteca Nazionale)

A. Miola, *Catalogo topografico-descrittivo dei manoscritti della R. Biblioteca Brancacciana di Napoli.* I, 1918-21 (Appendix to *Bollettino del Bibliofilo* I-III). 194 pp. Mss. I A 1-II A 10. No index. Not complete.

Catalogo topografico descrittivo dei Manoscritti della Biblioteca Brancacciana (Cf. AB I 4 p. 90). 3 vols. I (1899): I A 1 - II C 14. Superseded to II A 10 by Miola's printed catalogue. II (1900): II D 1 - III E 15 (138 mss.). III (1900): III F 1 - VII B 14 (276 mss.).

Fondo S. Martino.

C. Padiglione, *La Biblioteca del Museo Nazionale nella Certosa di S. Martino in Napoli ed i suoi manoscritti . . .* Naples 1876. xcii, 808 pp. 381 mss. (p. 1-406), mostly late, arranged alphabetically, and other collections. For additional 88 mss. of this collection see above under Fondo Principale.

Manoscritti già Viennesi.

E. Martini, 'Sui codici Napoletani restituiti dall' Austria,' *Atti della Reale Accademia di Archeologia, Lettere e Belle Arti* N. S. IX (1926) 157-82. 72 Latin and Italian mss. (168-82). No index.

—*Biblioteca Governativa dei Girolamini (Biblioteca Oratoriana).

E. Mandarini, *I codici manoscritti della Biblioteca Oratoriana di Napoli.* Naples 1897. 401 pp. 283 mss. Antiquated shelf marks.

Concordance of new and old shelf marks. Typed copy kindly supplied by the librarian.

—Biblioteca Universitaria.

Catalogo Mss. Alphabetical card index. 111 mss., mostly modern.

—Società Napoletana di Storia patria.

Inventario dei Manoscritti appartenenti alla Società Napoletana di Storia patria (1905). Mss. XX A 1 - XXXII D 14.

Indice dei Manoscritti. 2 ms. vols.

*Narbonne, France. See France, *Catalogue Général, Départements* IX; XLII.

*Narni, Italy. See Mazzatinti (1887); *Rivista delle Biblioteche.*

*Neisse, see Nysa.

*Nemours, France. See France, *Catalogue Général, Départements* VI; XLII.

*Neuchâtel, Switzerland. Bibliothèque Publique de la ville.

Catalogue de la Bibliothèque de Neuchâtel. Neuchâtel 1861. XXIV, 592 pp. Includes the first supplement. *Second Supplément.* 1869. 730 pp. *Troisième Supplément.* 1879. 598 pp. Lists mss. with edd. (DLC)

Manuscrits latins. Typed list kindly supplied by the librarian.

*Neufchâteau, France. See France, *Catalogue Général, Départements* XXIV.

*Neufchâtel, France. See France, *Catalogue Général, Départements* II; XLII.

*Neunhof bei Lauf an der Pegnitz, West Germany. Freiherrlich von Welsersche Familienstiftung.

List of relevant mss. kindly supplied by the owner. See also below under Nürnberg, Metanchthon-Gymnasium.

*Neureisch, see Nova Rise.

*Neustadt a.d. Aisch, West Germany. See Hirsching.

Georg M. Schnizer, *Die Kirchenbibliothek zu Neustadt an der Aysch.* 6 pts. Nuremberg 1782-87. Lists many mss. No index. (DLC)

Neustift, see Novacella.

*Neustrelitz, see under Rostock.

*Nevers, France. See France, *Catalogue Général, Départements* XXIV; XLII; Martin.

*Newcastle, England.

A Catalogue of the Manuscripts, Books, . . . Belonging to The Society of Antiquaries of Newcastle-upon-Tyne. Newcastle 1839. 95 pp. p. 65-70: mss. etc. No index. Hardly relevant (British Museum)

A Catalogue of the Library belonging to the Society of Antiquaries of Newcastle-upon-Tyne, inclusive of the Manuscripts, Drawings, Prints, and Maps. Newcastle 1863. 108 pp. A few late mss. (p. 78-80). (ICN)

New Haven, Conn., USA. See Allen; De Ricci.

— Yale University Library.

Yale Iniversity Library Gazette I (1926)ff. Lists the acquisitions of mss. See especially: XXV (1951) 37: T. E. M. (i.e., Thomas E. Marston), 'Medieval Manuscripts and Printed Books.' XXIX (1955) 9-12: The same, 'The Collection of Henry Fletcher.' 99-112: 'Eight Medieval Manuscripts.'

Supplement to De Ricci's Census of Medieval and Renaissance Manuscripts. Typed list.

New York, N. Y., USA. See Allen; De Ricci.

—Columbia University Library.

G. A. Plimpton, 'Grammatical Manuscripts and Early Printed Grammars in the Plimpton Library,' *Transactions and Proceedings of the American Philological Association* LXIV (1933) 150-178. 18 mss. (150-155).

S. A. Ives, 'Corrigenda and Addenda to the Descriptions of the Plimpton Manuscripts as recorded in the De Ricci Census,' *Speculum* XVII (1942) 33-49.

Manuscript Collections in the Columbia University Libraries: A Descriptive List. (Preface signed by R. Baughman). New York 1959. 97 pp. 294 nos. Mostly late. Does not cover the manuscript books before 1600 owned by the library.

Medieval and Renaissance Mss. since De Ricci or not listed in De Ricci, by Miss A. Bonnell. A pack of index cards.

Catalogue of Western Manuscripts in the Plimpton Library, Columbia University (by S. Ives). 2 typed folders. Arranged alphabetically.

Plimpton mss. 1 folder. Arranged alphabetically.

De Ricci Census Supplement. 1 typed folder.

—New York Public Library.

S. De Ricci, 'Medieval Manuscripts in the New York Public Library,' *Bulletin of the New York Public Library* XXXIV (1930) 297-322. 116 mss., and 22 mss of the Spencer Collection. No index.

The New York Public Library, The Spencer Collection of Illustrated Books. Preface signed by Henry W. Kent. New York 1928. XV, 88 pp. Alphabetical list of mss. and edd.

(Spencer Collection). *Manuscripts.* Card file, arranged by countries. Includes mss. not listed by De Ricci.

—Pierpont Morgan Library.

Catalogue of Manuscripts and Early Printed Books from the Libraries of William Morris, Richard Bennett, Bertram, Fourth Earl of Ashburnham, and other sources, now forming portion of the Library of J. Pierpont Morgan. 4 vols. London 1906-07. I (1906): 115 mss., and five other mss.

H. Omont, 'Catalogue de manuscrits de la Bibliothèque de M. Pierpont Morgan à New York,' *Bibliothèque de l'École des Chartes* LXIX (1908) 412-22. 115 mss. No index.

The Pierpont Morgan Library. Review of the Activities and Acquisitions of the Library from 1936 through 1940. New York 1941. xiii, 127 pp. p. 29ff.: Illuminated mss. no. 795-810 and autographs.

Italian Manuscripts in the Pierpont Morgan Library. By M. Harrsen and G. K. Boyce. New York 1953. XII, 79 pp. and plates. 125 mss.

Central European Manuscripts in the Pierpont Morgan Library. By M. Harrsen. New York 1958. X, 86 pp. and plates. 64 mss.

The Pierpont Morgan Library. Morgan Mss. 771-893. Typed supplement to De Ricci.

—Mrs. Phyllis Goodhart Gordan.

Manuscripts. Typed list. 148 mss.

*Nice (Nizza), France. See France, *Catalogue Général, Départements* XIV.

*Nicosia, Italy. See Mazzatinti II.

Nijmegen, Holland. *Oud-Archief der Gemeente.

*Catalogus van het Museum van Oudheden te Nijmegen, by J. V.W. Krul van Stompwijk and J. H. A. Scheers. Nijmegen 1864.

*—2nd ed., by J. H. A. Scheers and Th. H. A. J. Abeleven. Nijmegen 1873.

—3d ed., by Th. H. A. Abeleven and A. M. van Voorthuysen. 1890. XX, 644 pp. p. 415-419: 31 mss., and letters. (ODW)

—4th ed., by Th. H. A. J. Abeleven and C. G. J. Bijleveld. 1895. XIX, 494 pp. p. 312-315: 33 mss., and letters. (MH)

—Rooms Katholieke Universiteit.

Card file. 266 mss.

*Nikolsburg, see **Mikulov**.

*Nîmes, France. See France, *Catalogue Général, Départements* VII (Quarto Series); XLII; L.

Catalogue des livres de la Bibliothèque de Nismes, by I.-E. Thomas de Lavernède. 2 vols. Nîmes 1836. Vol. II, p. 504-23: Mss. (13697-13903). (Paris, Bibliothèque Nationale)

Catalogue de la Bibliothèque de Nîmes, Second supplément, by A. A. Liotard. Nîmes 1861. XV, 568 pp. p. 510-513: mss. (3030-48). (Paris, Bibliothèque Nationale.

*Niort, France. See France, *Catalogue Général, Départements* XXXI; XLII.

*Nizza, see Nice.

*Nocera, Italy.

G. Mazzatinti, ' I manoscritti della Biblioteca Vescovile di Nocera,' *Archivio Storico per le Marche e per l'Umbria* I (1884) 541-56. 29 mss. No index.

*Nogent-Le-Rotrou, France. See France, *Catalogue Général, Départements* XX.

*Nogent-sur-Marne, France. See under Paris, Bibliothèque Nationale.

*Nogent-sur-Seine. See France, *Catalogue Général, Départements* XXI.

*Nonantola, Italy. See Ruysschaert.

*Nordhausen, East Germany. See *Archiv* XI.

*Nordkirchen, West Germany. See *Archiv* VI.

*Norwich, England. See Bernardus; M. R. James; Schenkl.

—*City Library.

G. A. Stephen, *Three Centuries of a City Library*. Norwich 1917. IV, 86 pp. p. 27-28: 8 mss.

*Noto, Italy. Biblioteca Comunale. See Mazzatinti VI.

Catalogo Alfabetico della Biblioteca Comunale di Noto. Preface signed by Sac. Puglisi. Noto 1889. XIV, 367 pp. p. 339-340: Alphabetical list of mss. Centuries not given.

Catalogo manoscritto. Adds a few mss.

List of 6 mss. kindly supplied by the librarian.

*Nottingham, England. See Great Britain, *Historical Manuscripts Commission*.

Novacella (Neustift), Italy. Convento dei Canonici Regolari (Augustiner-Chorherrenstift). See Wickhoff.

Card index in serial but not continuous order. The numbers are those of the Innsbruck University Library, to which the mss. belonged until 1921, beginning with 4 and ending with 931. 112 mss.

Novara, Italy. See *Analecta Bollandiana* XLIII; Andres; *Archiv* XII; Mazzatinti VI; XXXI; Reifferscheid.

—Archivio di S. Gaudenzio.

F. Curlo, 'L'Archivio di S. Gaudenzio di Novara,' *Bollettino storico-bibliografico subalpino* XIII (1908) 97-154; XIV (1909) 96-118. p. 140-154: 50 mss. No index. (NNC). Also printed separately, Asti 1909, 107 pp. (Milano, Biblioteca Nazionale Braidense).

The archive has been rearranged since the compilation of this catalogue, and the ms. books seem to have been lost since the last war.

—*Biblioteca Civica e Negroni.

A. Viglio, 'Archivi Novaresi: Catalogo dei manoscritti pergamenacei e cartacei dell' Archivio del Museo Civico,' *Bollettino storico per la provincia di Novara* XIX (1925) 32-53; 142-156. (ICN)

*Nova Riše, see under Brno.

*Novo mesto, Yugoslavia. See Kos.

*Noyon, France. See France, *Catalogue Général, Départements* III; XLII.

Nürnberg (Nuremberg), West Germany. See *Archiv* VII; IX; Fischer; Hirsching; Leclercq; Lehmann, *Mitteilungen* I; Stauber.

Chr. G. von Murr, *Beschreibung der vornehmsten Merkwürdigkeiten in des H. R. freyen Stadt Nürnberg und auf der hohen Schule zu Altdorf* ... Nuremberg 1778. 762 pp. Lists mss. of Stadtbibliothek (65ff.), Solgerische Bibliothek (127ff.), Ebnerische Bibliothek (428ff.)etc. No index. (NNMM)

The same, *Memorabilia Bibliothecarum Publicarum Norimbergensium et universitatis Altdorfinae*. 3 vols. Nuremberg 1786-91. I: City Library and Solger Library. II (1778): Dilherr, Chapter, Fenizer, Ebner. III: Marperger, Academy, Chapter of St. Aegidius, Welser etc. No index. (NN)

K. Mannert, *Miscellanea meist diplomatischen Inhalts*. Nürnberg 1795. 124 pp. Describes mss. of the Ebner Collection (now scattered) and of the Stadtbibliothek.

—Germanisches National-Museum.

K. Bartsch, 'Die Handschriftensammlung des Germanischen Museums,' *Anzeiger für Kunde der deutschen Vorzeit* N. F. V. (1858) 176-77; 212-15; 253-54; 292-95. 7 mss.

E. W. Bredt, *Katalog der mittelalterlichen Miniaturen des Germanischen National-museums.* Nuremberg 1903. 150 pp. 367 mss. (Pierpont Morgan Library)
Card index, alphabetical.

*Merkel collection. Handwritten inventory. A selected list kindly supplied by the director of the museum.

Autographen. Handwritten list, arranged by professional groups of senders. Selective list kindly supplied by the director of the museum.

Typed notes on the collection are available at the Institut de Recherches et d'Histoire des Textes, Paris.

—*Melanchthon-Gymnasium.

L. Krauss, *Mitteilungen über die Zusammensetzung der Lehrerbibliothek des Alten Gymnasiums...* 2 pts. progr. Nürnberg 1910-11. pt. 1, p. 57-59: 3 liturgical mss. pt. 2, p. 4-7: 6 mss. in the Familienarchiv Welser, Neunhof.

L. Früchtel, 'Der codex Norimbergensis (Ebnerianus) des Persius,' *Philologus* XCVI (N.F.L, 1944) 108-18. (Berlin, University Library; micr. at NNC)

—Staatsarchiv.

Nürnberger Handschriften. List of over 400 mss. (Communication of the archivist).

—Stadtbibliothek.

Bibliotheca sive supellex librorum impressorum... et codicum manuscriptorum... quos... collegit... Adamus Rudolphus Solger... 3 pts. Nürnberg 1760-62. Pt. I, p. 209-260: mss. (NN)

Georg Andreas Will, *Bibliotheca Norica Williana,* 8 pts., Nürnberg 1772-93. Indices in pt. VI (1778). Lists local mss. with edd. (MH)

Index rarissimorum aliquot librorum manuscriptorum saeculoque XV typis descriptorum quos habet Bibliotheca publica Noribergensis. (ed. F. G. Ghillany). Nuremberg 1846. 96 pp. 11 mss. and autographs. (NN)

K. Bartsch, 'Über die Handschriften der Nürnberger Stadtbibliothek,' *Anzeiger für Kunde der deutschen Vorzeit,* N.F.V (1858) 46-49: 77-79.

Catalogue des manuscrits de la succession de Wilibald Pirckheimer faisant partie de la collection de Monsieur le Baron Sigismond Chret. Joaquim Haller de Hallerstein... qui seront vendus à l'enchère et au comptant le 28 janvier 1861 et les jours suivants à Nüremberg sous la direction de l'antiquaire et commissaire spécialement chargé Fr. Heerdegen. (Nürnberg 1861). 32 pp. 551 nos. (Nürnberg, Stadtbibliothek)

Katalog der Stadtbibliothek in Nürnberg. Erste Abtheilung. Schwarz-Amberger'sche Norica-Sammlung. Nürnberg 1876. VI, 162 pp. p. 1-38: Alphabetical list of local mss. (Nürnberg, Stadtbibliothek)

Standort-Katalog (by Dr. E. Bock). 1 tray of index cards. Cent. I 1 - VIII 17; Solger 2º 1 - 12º 4; Hertel 1-92.

Typed notes on the collection are available at the Institut de Recherches et d'Histoire des Textes, Paris.

Autographen. Alphabetical card index in 2 boxes.

—*Freiherr Siegfried von Scheurl. See also under Altenfurt.

Archiv. Card index.

Bibliothek. Inventory in 1 ms. vol. (Communication of the owner).

*Nysa. See under Wrocław.

Ober-Altaich. Austria. See Gercken.

Oehringen. West Germany. See *Serapeum* I.

*Oelenberg, France.

E. M(ikkers), 'Cisterciensia uit de Nederlanden in de abdybibliotheek van Oelenberg,' *Cîteaux in de Nederlanden* I (1950) 45-46. Lists 11 selected mss., mostly late. Mimeographed.

Olesnica (Oels), Poland. See *Archiv* XI.

Oldenburg. West Germany. Landesbibliothek.

(L. W. C. von Halem), *Bibliographische Unterhaltungen.* 2 pts. s.l.a. (1794-95). 192 pp. 28 items of which 1 ms. No index. (OCl)

J. F. L. Th. Merzdorf, *Bibliothekarische Unterhaltungen*, 2 vols. Oldenburg 1844-50. Lists several mss. (DLC)

Cimelien. 302 mss. of which nos. 9-65 are in Latin.

Olomouc (Olmütz), Czechoslovakia. See *Archiv* IX; X; Burdach; Feifalik.

—Kapitolní knihovna. Now in the Statni Archiv.

B. Dudik, 'Handschriften der Bibliothek des Metropolitan-Capitels in Olmütz,' *Archivalische Zeitschrift* V (1880) 126-34. No index. Not complete.

Card file, arranged by shelf marks. 639 mss.

—Universitní Knihovna.

R. Beer, 'Mittheilungen über die Kaiserl. Kgl. Studienbibliothek in Olmütz,' *Centralblatt für Bibliothekswesen* VII (1890) 474-81. No index.

Alphabetical card file, in 2 trays.

Catalogus codicum Manuscriptorum Caesareo-Regiae Bibliothecae Olomucensis (by J. E. Karmaschek, 1800). Arranged by languages and subjects.

Repertorium der Handschriften. A concordance of the old and new shelf marks, with short titles

*Oloron, France. See France, *Catalogue Général, Départements* XIII; XLII.

*Opava, Czechoslovakia.

****J. Zukal, *Aus der Troppauer Museums-Bibliothek*. progr. 1880-81.

M. Boháček and F. Čáda, *Soupis Rukopisů Slezské Studijní Knihovny v Opavě Catalogus codicum manu scriptorum qui in Bibliotheca studiorum Silesiacorum Opaviae asservantur*. (Slezský Studijní Ústav, Publikace 13). Opava 1955. 127 pp. 81 mss.

*Oporto (Porto), Portugal. See *Société française*.

Catalogo da Bibliotheca Publica Municipal do Porto. Indice preparatorio do Catalogo dos manuscriptos. 10 pts. Oporto 1879-96. pt. 1 (1879): 144 vellum mss. pt. 2 (1885): Geographical mss., no. 145-260. pt. 3 (1888): Heraldic

mss., no. 261-334. pt. 4 (1892-93): Historical mss., no. 335-505. pt. 5 (1893): Military mss., no. 506-62. pt. 6 (1893): Literary mss., no. 600-731. pt. 7 (1896): Theology, no. 732-931. pt. 8 (1896): Law, no. 932-1011. pt. 9 (1896): Philosophy, no. 1012-77. pt. 10 (1896): Science, no. 1078-1183. Each part indexed (DLC has pt. 1-4 and 6; pt. 5 and 7-10 seen at the British Museum)

J. A. de Aldama, 'Manuscritos teológicos postridentinos de la Biblioteca Municipal de Porto,' *Archivo Teológico Granadino* I (1938) 7-26. Index (25-26) (DCU)

Biblioteca Pública Municipal do Porto. Catálogo dos Manuscritos (Códices N.os 1225 a 1364). By A. Cruz. Oporto 1952. XLIII, 205 pp. p. xxiv-xli: Concordance between old and new numbers. (NN)

*Orange, France. See France, *Catalogue Général, Départements* XXXI.

*Orense, Spain.

****B. Fernandez Alonso, 'Codices e incunables de la Catedral de Orense,' *Boletín de la Comisión Provincial de Monumentos de Orense* V (1916-17) 241-47; 293-94; 297-304; XIII (1941) 11-35.

*Orihuela, Spain. See *Anuario* II.

*Oristano, Italy. See Lampen.

*Orléans, France. See France, *Catalogue Général, Départements* XII; XLII; Martin; *Notices et Extraits*.

(A. Septier, *Manuscrits de la Bibliothèque d'Orléans ou Notices sur leur ancienneté...* Orleans 1820. 287 pp. 486 mss. of which nos. 4-302 [p. 33-173] in Latin.)

(Ch. Cuissard, *Inventaire des manuscrits de la Bibliothèque d'Orléans. Fonds de Fleury*. Orléans 1885. xxxvi, 274 pp. c. 400 mss.) (NN)

Orvieto, Italy. Biblioteca Civica.

Sezione Tordi. Catalogo dei manoscritti membranacei, by G. Buccolini (1936). 1 typed vol. 423 nos.

Catalogo dei manoscritti cartacei. 1 typed vol. 476 nos.

*Oscott, England. See Great Britain, *Historical Manuscripts Commission*; Schenkl.

*Osek (Ossegg), Czechoslovakia. See *Xenia Bernardina*; see under Praha.

Osimo, Italy. See Mazzatinti VI.

*Oslo, Norway. See *Archives* V; Lehmann.

—Riksarkivet.

S. A. Sørensen, 'Middelalderske Latinske Membranfragmenter i det Norske Rigsarkiv,' (Norsk) *Historisk Tidsskrift*, Ser. IV, vol. VI (1910) 23-47.

—*Universitetsbiblioteket.

* *Universitetsbibliotekets Handskriftavdeling. Tilvekstforteguelse over manuskripter.* 4 vols. for Octavo mss., 3 for Quarto, 3 for Folio mss. *Ca.* 6000 mss. of which only *ca.* 30 are in Latin. (Communication of the librarian).

*Osnabrück, West Germany. See *Analecta Bollandiana* LV.

L. Thyen, *Die Bibliothek des Gymnasii Carolini.* 2 pts. progr. Osnabrück 1875-76. 89 mss., and summary list of a few more. (pt. 1 not seen or located; pt. 2 seen at Erlangen, University Library).

R. Kuhlenbeck, *Die Bibliothek des Rathsgymnasiums, ihre Handschriften und alten Drucke*, 3 pts. progr. Osnabrück 1878-80. pts. 1-2 list 49 local mss. pt. 2 also lists 1 other ms., and pt. 3, 12 other mss. No index. (Erlangen, University Library.)

*Ossegg, see Osek.

*Ossero, Italy. See Wickhoff.

Ottobeuren, West Germany. Archiv des Benediktinerstiftes. See Leclercq.

Manuscripta. 167 mss. (Microfilm seen at NNC)

*Oviedo, Spain. See *Anuario*; Fransen.

A. Sierra Corella, 'Ligeras noticias sobre el Archivo y la libreria gótica de la Catedral de Oviedo,' *Revista de Archivos, Bibliotecas y Museos* LI (Ser. III, year XXXIV, 1930) 123-140. Gives a list of the mss, made in 1860 (p. 129-130).

Oxford, England. See Bernardus; Daremberg; Hunter; Ker; Omont; Phillipps; Schenkl; Zangemeister. See also Morelli under Venezia.

A. G. Little, *Initia Operum Latinorum quae saeculis XIII. XIV. XV. attribuuntur*

secundum ordinem *Alphabeti disposita.* Manchester 1904. xiii, 215 pp. Based on mss. in Oxford, and on printed sources. No index of authors or of mss.

—Bodleian, Library.

H. H. E. Craster, *The Western Manuscripts of the Bodleian Library.* London 1921. 48 pp. Lists catalogues (p. 24-33) and collections (34-48).

Bodleian Library, Instructions to Readers of Western Manuscripts (1950). 4 pp.

W. Huddesford, *Catalogus librorum manuscriptorum... Antonii a Wood Being a minute Catalogue of each particular contained in the manuscript Collections of Antony a Wood deposited in the Ashmolean Museum at Oxford.* Oxford 1761. 84 pp. Mss. no. 8463-8589. Mostly late material. No index. (NN)

**The same work, Middlehill 1824.

Codices manuscripti et impressi cum notis manuscriptis olim d'Orvilliani qui in Bibliotheca Bodleiana apud Oxonienses adservantur. Oxford 1806. 100 pp. (NN)

Catalogus sive notitia manuscriptorum qui a cel. E. D. Clarke comparati in Bibliotheca Bodleiana adservantur. 2 vols. in 1, Oxford 1812-15. (By T. Gaisford). Vol. I lists 17 Latin mss. No index. (NN)

(*Catalogue of the Printed Books and Manuscripts Bequeathed by Francis Douce, Esq., to the Bodleian Library.* Oxford 1840. 311 and 90 pp. The second part lists 393 mss.)

(Quarto Series). *Catalogi codicum manuscriptorum Bibliothecae Bodleianae. Pars secunda Codices Latinos et Miscellaneos Laudianos complectens*, by H. O. Coxe. 2 fascicules, Oxford 1858-85. 534 coll. and index of 29 pp. 875 mss. (NNC)

—*Pars tertia Codices Graecos et Latinos Canonicianos complectens*, by the same. Oxford 1854. 872 coll. and pp. 873-918. 1212 Latin mss. (DLC)

—*Pars quarta Codices... Thomae Tanneri.. complectens*, by A. Hackman. Oxford 1860. 794 coll. and pp. 796-1176. 467 mss. (NNC)

—*Partis quintae fasciculus primus viri munificentissimi Ricardi Rawlinson . . . codi-*

cum classes duas priores ad rem historicam praecipue et topographicam spectantes complectens, by Gul. D. Macray. Oxford 1862. 738 coll Mss A 1-B 520. . . . Fasciculus secundus . . . codicum classem tertiam, in qua libri theologici atque miscellanei, complectens. 564 coll. and pp. 565-992. 1878. Mss. C 1-989, and index for fasc. 1-2. . . . Fasciculus tertius . . . codicum classis quartae partem priorem (libros sc. miscellaneos octingentos et sexaginta) complectens. 1893. 684 coll. Mss. D 1-860. . . . Fasciculus quartus . . . codicum classis quartae partem alteram (libros sc. miscellaneos sexcentos et quinquaginta sex) complectens. 1898. 525 coll. Mss. D 861-1516. . . . Fasciculus quintus . . . codicum classis quartae indicem continens. 1900. pp. 527-778. Index for fasc. 3-4. (NNC)
—Pars Nona, Codices a . . . Kenelm Digby . . . donatos, complectens, by G. D. Macray. Oxford 1883. 254 coll. and pp. 257-87. 236 mss. Each part indexed. (NNC)

W. H. Black, A Descriptive Analytical and Critical Catalogue of the Manuscripts Bequeathed unto the University of Oxford by Elias Ashmole Esq. Oxford 1845. 1522 coll. 1828 mss.

W. D. Macray, Index to the Catalogue of the Manuscripts of Elias Ashmole, formerly preserved in the Ashmolean Museum, and now deposited in the Bodleian Library, Oxford. Oxford 1866. 188 pp. Index to the preceding catalogue.

These two volumes, though published separately, were later treated as Part X of the Quarto Series.

A. Mortara, Catalogo dei manoscritti italiani che sotto la denominazione di Codici Canoniciani Italiani si conservano nella Biblioteca Bodleiana a Oxford. Oxford 1864. xiv pp., 315 coll. 299 mss., with an appendix on 5 Spanish mss.

This volume, though published separately, was later treated as pat XI of the Quarto Series.

F. Madan, H. H. E. Craster and N. Denholm-Young, A Summary Catalogue of Western Manuscripts in the Bodleian Library at Oxford which have not hitherto been described in the Quarto Series, with references to the Oriental and other Manuscripts. 7 vols. Oxford 1895-1953. Vol. I (1953): Historical Introduction and Conspectus of shelf marks, by R. W. Hunt. Vol. II, 1 (1922): Mss. no. 1-3490. Vol. II, 2 (1937): Mss. no. 3491-8716. Vol. III (1895): Mss./ no. 8717-16669. Vol. IV (1897): Mss. no. 16670-24330. Vol. V (1905): Mss. no. 24331-31000. Vol. VI (1924): Mss. no. 31001-37299 (Accessions 1890-1915). Vol. VII (1953): Index, by P. D. Record. Refers to older catalogues where available.

E. Gómez, 'Catálogo de los manuscritos de escritores dominicos en la Universidad de Oxford,' Ciencia Tomista XLIV (1931) 53-68. Lists 23 mss. of the Bodleian Library. No index.

The same, cont., Divus Thomas (Piacenza) XXXV (1932) 62-69; 177-184; 399-404. Lists more mss. (no. 24-49) of the Bodleian Library. No index. (DCU).

Bodleian Quarterly Record I (1914) ff. Contains reports on acquisitions of mss. See also: I (1914-16) 53-56; 162; 344-349: 'Early Latin Bodleian Manuscripts.' 157-162: 'Early Oxford College Manuscripts'. 193-196; 323-326; 350-351: 'Twelfth-Century Latin Bodleian Mss.' II (1917-19) 253-258: 'Catalogue of Classical Mss. exhibited in the Bodleian Library.' III (1920-22) 19-22: 'Latin Bodleian Manuscript Fragments.' VII (1932-34) 169-173: 'Dated Western Manuscripts in the Bodleian.' 368-373: J. R. L., 'The Illuminated Manuscripts of the Douce Collection.' VIII (1935-37) 157-164 (cf. 234-235): R. Weiss, 'The Library of John Tiptoft, Earl of Worcester.'

The Bodleian Library Record I 1938ff. Continues the Bodleian Quarterly Record. See especially: I (1938-41) 37-38: 'Notable Accessions.' 45-50: 'Manuscripts exhibited in Arts End.' III (1950-51) 6: 'Fragments of Medieval Manuscripts in Bindings.' 13-34: R. W. Hunt, 'The Manuscript Collection of University College, Oxford: Origins and Growth.' Lists mss. 189-208, not described by Coxe (p. 31-34). 68-82: The same, 'The Lyell Bequest.' Lists 100 mss. No index. 155-164: C. Kirschberger, 'Bodleian Manuscripts relating to the Spiritual Life, 1500-1750.' IV (1952-53) 279-285: 'Manuscripts purchased from the Lyell Collection.' 65 mss. V (1954-56) 25-27: J. A. W. Bennett, 'A Medieval Manuscript in New Zealand.' Describes a ms. in the Auckland Public Library. VI (1957-59) 340-41· 'Medieval Manuscripts from Holkham.' Not a list. 348-369: R. W. Hunt, 'List of Phillipps Manuscripts in the Bodleian Library.' 459-515: N. R. Ker, 'Oxford College Libraries in the Sixteenth Century.'

Card index in 2 parts, one referring to the printed *Summary Catalogue*, the other to the acquisitions since 1916. (Cf. *Instructions* p. 2). Pt. 1 has now been printed.

Summary Catalogue of Western Mss. in the Bodleian Library. Accessions 1916-1918. 1 typed vol. Mss. 37300-40358 (Cf. *Instructions* p. 2).

Summary Catalogue of Western Manuscripts in the Bodleian Library. Accessions 1919-1921. 1 typed vol. Mss. 40359-41538 (Cf. *Instructions* p. 2).

Summary Catalogue of Western Manuscripts in the Bodleian Library. Accessions 1922-1923. 1 typed vol. Mss. 41539-42021.

Handlist of Manuscripts. Several ms. vols., arranged by subjects, which cover acquisitions since 1922.

Western Manuscripts. Accessions 1945... 1 typed vol. (Cf. *Instructions* p. 2).

Catalogue of Legal Mss. in Bodley, by H. Kantorowicz. Unfinished.

—College Libraries.

H. O. Coxe, *Catalogus codicum manuscriptorum qui in collegiis aulisque Oxoniensibus hodie adservantur.* 2 vols. in 8 and 11 pts. Oxford 1852. Vol. I: Universitatis (University College), 51 pp. 188 mss. — Balliolensis (Balliol), 116 pp. 363 mss. —

Mertonensis (Merton), 132 pp. 327 mss.— Exoniensis (Exeter), 46 pp. 184 mss.— Orielensis (Oriel), 28 pp. 82 mss.—Reginensis (Queen's), 91 pp. 390 mss.—Novi (New College), 123 pp. 344 mss.—Lincolniensis (Lincoln), 54 pp. 120 mss. —Vol. II: Omnium Animarum (All Souls), 78 pp. 297 mss.—B. Mariae Magdalenae (Magdalen), 99 pp. 247 mss.—Aenei Nasi (Brasenose), 7 pp. 22 mss.—Corporis Christi (Corpus Christi), 186 pp. 393 mss. —S. Trinitatis (Trinity), 37 pp. 89 mss.— S. Johannis Baptistae (St. John's), 74 pp. 212 mss.—Jesu (Jesus), 45 pp. 141 mss.— Wadhamensis (Wadham), 11 pp. 53 mss. —Vigorniensis (Worcester), 17 pp. 60 mss.—Aulae B. Mariae Magdalenae (Magdalen Hall), 7 pp. 6 mss. Index for both volumes, 117 pp.

(*Catalogue of Manuscripts in the Library of All Souls College*, by H. O. Coxe. Oxford 1842. vi, 99 pp. 296 mss.)

G. W. Kitchin, *Catalogus codicum manuscriptorum qui in Bibliothecae Aedis Christi* [Christ Church] *apud Oxonienses adservantur.* Oxford 1867. 82 pp. 345 mss. of which no. 87-144 (p. 41-50) in Latin.

The mss. of Corpus Christi, Jesus, Lincoln, New, Oriel, Trinity and University College are deposited in the Bodleian Library.

The Bodleian copy of Coxe has added handwritten lists of additional mss. for All Souls and Corpus Christi College.

Balliol College has a typed catalogue of accessions (not seen).

Hertford College Mss. and Brasenose and Lincoln Mss. not in Coxe. Ms. list (Bodleian Library).

F. M. Powicke, *The Medieval Books of Merton College.* Oxford 1931. XI, 287 pp. Identifies extant mss. at Merton College and in other libraries.

—*Pembroke College (not listed in Coxe). No inventory. Has 19 Latin mss. before 1600. (Communication of the Librarian). Cf. Great Britain, *Historical Manuscripts Commission.* A few mss. are also listed in the following catalogue:

Catalogue of the Aristotelian and Philosophical Portions of the Library of the late Henry William Chandler... Preserved in the Library of Pembroke College, Oxford. Oxford 1891. 182 pp. (PU)

—University College. See above, *Bodleian Library Record* III.

—Wadham College.

Catalogue of Books confined in U 9-16 and in A. Lists a few mss. not described by Coxe.

Paderborn, Germany. See *Analecta Bollandiana* LV; *Archiv* XI; Leclercq.

—Erzbischöfliche Akademische Bibliothek (Theodoriana).

(Hülsenbeck, *Die Theodorianische Bibliothek zu Paderborn: Kurze Geschichte und Statistik derselben nebst Verzeichniss der darin vorhandenen Handschriften, Incunabeln und seltenen Werke.* progr. Paderborn 1877. 27 pp. p. 6-14: 145 mss. No index. Erlangen, Univ. Library)

Wilh. Richter, *Handschriften-Verzeichnis der Theodorianischen Bibliothek zu Paderborn.* 2 pts. progr. Paderborn 1896-97. 36 and 62 pp. 290 mss. Index (pt. 2 p. 57-62). Typed addenda in Library copy.

B. Stolte, *Das Archiv des Vereins für Geschichte und Alterthumskunde Westfalens, Abteilung Paderborn.* I: *Codices und Akten.* II: *Urkunden.* Paderborn 1899-1905. 626. pp. 176 mss. (p. 5-63 and 127-28). (MH)

Handschriften der Akademischen Bibliothek. 1 ms. vol. 62 mss. Mostly late.

There is no inventory for the fourth group of mss., the so-called Fuerstenbergiana.

Padova, Italy. See *Archiv* XII; Blume; *Giornale* I; *Manoscritti e Stampe Venete*; Montfaucon.

Jac. Phil. Tomasinus, *Bibliothecae patavinae manuscriptae publicae et privatae.* Udine 1639. 142 pp. Covers Biblioteca Capitolare (p. 3-8), S. Antonio (p. 52-64) and many collections now scattered or transferred to the Biblioteca Marciana.

V. Forcella, *Catalogo dei manoscritti riguardanti la storia di Roma che si conservano nelle biblioteche di Padova pubbliche e private.* Vol. V (as appendix to a similar work on the Vatican library), Rome 1885. 187 pp. Covers Biblioteca Universitaria, Antoniana, Civica, Capitolare and del Seminario. (DLC)

L. Suttina, 'I codici francescani delle Biblioteche di Padova. I. Biblioteca Antoniana,' *Bullettino critico di cose francescane* I (1905) 14-21. 6 mss. No index. 'II. Codici e antiche stampe della Biblioteca del Seminario,' *Ibid.* 71-78. 2 mss. No index. (III). 'I manoscritti francescani della Regia Biblioteca Universitaria di Padova,' *Ibid.* 144-166. 21 mss. (MB)

—Biblioteca Antoniana.

L. M. Minciotti, *Catalogo dei codici manoscritti esistenti nella Biblioteca di Sant' Antonio di Padova.* Padua 1842. 161 pp. 617 mss. Index subdivided by subjects. (Pierpont Morgan Library)

A. M. Josa, *I codici manoscritti della Biblioteca Antoniana di Padova.* Padua 1886. 263 pp. Arranged alphabetically.

L. Guidaldi, *I più antichi codici della Biblioteca Antoniana di Padova (Codici del sec. IX).* Padua 1930. 38 pp. and plates. (Prof. E. A. Lowe, Princeton, N. J.)

—Biblioteca Capitolare.

A. Barzon. *Codici miniati, Biblioteca Capitolare della Cattedrale di Padova,* 2 vols., Padova, 1950. 85 mss.

E. Govi, 'La Biblioteca di Jacopo Zeno,' *Bollettino dell' Istituto di patologia del libro* X (1951) 34-118. 320 mss., most of them identified at the Biblioteca Capitolare. Index (112-118).

Index codicum manuscriptorum qui in Bibliotheca Reverendissimi Capituli Cathedralis Ecclesiae Patavinae asservantur, by Ferdinandus Com. Maldura (1830). Mss. A 1-72; B 1-66; C 1-112; D 1-63. A few acquisitions since 1830 are described in the appendix.

—Biblioteca Comunale (in the Museo Civico).

**L. Rizzoli, *Manoscritti della Biblioteca Civica di Padova riguardanti la storia Nobiliare Italiana.* Rome 1907. 126 pp.

A. Moschetti, *Il Museo Civico di Padova*. 2nd ed. Padua 1938. 525 pp. and plates. p. 53-88: Biblioteca. Surveys the collections, and lists many mss.

Manoscritti e incunaboli (vol. C of the inventory). Describes 935 mss. of the Fondo C M. (micr. at DLC)

Raccolta Padovana. 3 vols., describing mss. and printed books of the Fondo B P together. I: nos. 1-1668. II: 1629-2293. III: 2294-5658. Centuries not given.

*Card index. 11 boxes (AB III 359).

—Biblioteca del Seminario.

J. Valentinelli, 'Die Bibliothek des Seminariums zu Padua,' *Oesterreichische Blätter für Literatur und Kunst* II (1845) 537-540; 551-552; 556-560; 564-568; 573-576. Mentions many mss. (OCU)

Della Biblioteca del Seminario di Padova. Preface signed by G. Valentinelli. Venice 1849. II, 48 pp. Mentions many mss. (British Museum, microfilm at NNC)

Illustrazione Mmss. (by Coi). 771 mss. (micr. at DLC)

Ubicazione dei M.s.s. illustrati e contenuti nell' indice del Bibliotecario Coi. 1097 mss. Centuries not given. (micr. at DLC)

Catalogo MMSS. (1829). Alphabetical (communication of D. Schullian; micr. at DLC)

—Biblioteca Universitaria.

A. Avetta, *Contributo alla storia della R. Biblioteca Universitaria di Padova*. Padua 1908. 31 pp. Discusses several mss. (p. 8ff.). (NjP)

The same, *Manoscritti di Etica della Universitaria di Padova*. Padua, per nozze, 1909. xix pp. No index. (Milan, Biblioteca Nazionale Braidense)

Bibliotheca Regia Patavina Manuscripta. 2 vols. in 1, and 2 vols. of indices. I: mss. 1-1676. II: 1677-2276. Centuries not given. Superseded to no. 1181 by the *Catalogo* (AB II 3 p. 55-56). (Micr. at DLC)

Catalogo dei Manoscritti della Biblioteca Universitaria. Mss. 1-1181 (Cf. AB II 3 p. 56). (Micr. at DLC)

Catalogo dei Mss. al numero provvisorio. 220 mss. (Cf. AB II 3 p. 56) (Micr. at DLC)

*Card index (AB II 3 p. 56).

Paisley, Scotland. See Frere.

Palermo, Italy. See Blume; Garufi; Rühl; Tarallo.

V. Di Giovanni, 'Di due codici in volgare del secolo XIV,' *Il Borghini* II (1864) 139-48; 'Di tre codici in volgare del secolo XV esistenti nella Biblioteca Comunale e nella Nazionale di Palermo,' *ibid.*, 577-84. (CtY)

L. Castelli, 'I manoscritti esistenti nella Biblioteca di S. Martino delle Scale prima del 1866,' *Nuove Effemeridi Siciliane* Ser. III vol. IV (1876) 66-73; 183-204. 60 mss. No index. The mss. are now divided between the Biblioteca Comunale and Nazionale. (MH)

—*Archivio della Cattedrale.

L. Boglino, *I codici della Cattedrale di Palermo esistenti al secolo XV*. Palermo 1904. 31 pp. Lists 13 mss., mostly liturgical, found in 1881. No index. (Palermo, Biblioteca Nazionale)

—Biblioteca Comunale.

I manoscritti della Biblioteca Comunale di Palermo. 3 vols. in 4, Palermo 1873-1934. Vol. I (1873), by Gaspare Rossi. 388 pp. Mss. Qq.A.1-Qq.F.1. Vol. I pt. 2 (1894), by Gioacchino Di Marzo. 382 pp. Mss. Qq.F.232-H.284. Vol. II pt. 1 (1934), by E. Stinco. 244 pp. Mss. 2.Qq.A.1-G.40. III (1878), by G. Di Marzo. 385 pp. Mss. 3.Qq.A.1-4.Qq.D.81. No index. Not complete.

L. Boglino, *I manoscritti della Biblioteca Comunale di Palermo*. 4 vols. Palermo 1884-1900. Arranged alphabetically by subjects. I (1884): A-C. II (1889): D-L. III (1892): M-Q. IV (1900): R-Z. V (supplement) announced but not published.

**P. Revelli, *I manoscritti di carattere o d'interesse geografico della Biblioteca Comunale di Palermo*. Venice 1909. 64 pp.

Continuazione Indice Manoscritti. Mss. 2 Qq A 47-84; B 64-131; C 160-262; D 138-59; E 94-155; F 60-174; G 41-165; H 1-253. Supplements the printed catalogues.

—Biblioteca Nazionale.

Ministero della Pubblica Istruzione, Inventario dei Manoscritti della R. Biblioteca Nazionale di Palermo (1914). 2 vols. I: mss. I A 1 - VII F 4. II: Fondo Monreale 1-33; mss VII F 5 - X D 14. (micr. at DLC)

Catalogo Topografico dei Manoscritti della Biblioteca Nazionale di Palermo. Mss. I A 1 - XV H 8. Superseded to X D 14 by the *Inventario* (Cf. AB I 5-6 p. 94). (micr. at DLC)

Deposito Museo Nazionale. Summary list on 1 sheet. 13 mss.

*Indice alfabetico dei Manoscritti della Biblioteca Nazionale di Palermo (AB I 5-6 p. 94). (micr. at DLC)

—Società Siciliana per la Storia Patria.

C. Trasselli, ' I manoscritti Fitalia,' *Archivio Storico Siciliano* N.S. LII (1932) 425-431. A survey. No shelf marks.

The Fondo Fitalia has 128 mss. No inventory.

*Palma, Majorca, Spain. See *Anuario*; Villanueva.

P. Bohigas, 'Fondos manuscritos de Bibliotecas de Mallorca,' *Biblioteconomia* I (1944) 80-89. Discusses many different libraries and lists their mss.

J. M. Quadrado, 'Códices del Archivo General de Mallorca,' *Museo Balear de Historia y Literatura, Ciencias y Artes*, Ser. II, vol. IV (1887) 161-70. Surveys 40 mss. No index. (MH; micr. at NNC)

—Biblioteca Provincial.

**Card index. Over 1000 mss. (Communication of D. P. Lockwood).

*Pamiers, France. See France, *Catalogue Général, Départements* XXI.

*Pamplona, Spain. See Grubbs (Section A, under Richardson); Leclercq.

A. S. Hunt, ' The Library of the Cathedral of Pamplona,' *Centralblatt für Bibliothekswesen* XIV (1897) 283-90. 70 mss. Index in Grubbs.

*Pannonhalma, Hungary. See Radó.
**Card catalogue.

*Parenzo, Italy. See Wickhoff.

Paris, France. See Delisle; France, *Catalogue Général, Archives Nationales*; Départements XLIII; XLV; XLVI; L; *Paris*; *Sociétés*; *Universités*; Italy, *Indici e Cataloghi* V; Lowe; De Marinis; Martin; Millares Carlo; *Notices et Extraits*; Pellegrin; *Société française*; *Union Académique Internationale*.

A. Marsand, *I manoscritti italiani della Regia Biblioteca Parigina.* 2 vols. Paris 1835-38. Covers 896 Italian mss. at the Bibliothèque Nationale, and 160 mss. at the Bibliothèque de l'Arsenal, Ste. Geneviève and Mazarine. Shelf marks antiquated.

A. Sarfatti, *I codici Veneti delle biblioteche di Parigi.* Rome 1888. XI, 199 pp. Covers the same four libraries. No index.

—*Académie de Médecine.

**Handwritten supplement to the printed catalogue (Born 90).

—*Archives Nationales.

M. François, 'Les plus beaux manuscrits à peintures conservés aux Archives Nationales,' *Les Trésors des Bibliothèques de France* VI (1938) 163-85.

—Bibliothèque de l'Arsenal.

For the main catalogue, see France, *Catalogue Général.*

G. Molini, *Notizia dei Manoscritti Italiani o che si riferiscono all' Italia esistenti nella Libreria dell' Arsenale in Parigi.* Florence 1836. 25 pp. 47 mss.

H. Martin and Ph. Lauer, *Les principaux manuscrits à peintures de la Bibliothèque de l'Arsénal à Paris.* Paris 1929. 72 pp. and plates.

**Handwritten supplement to the printed catalogue (Born 113).

—*Bibliothèque de la Faculté des Lettres et de la Faculté des Sciences (Sorbonne).

**Inventory, 2 vols. (Born 111).

—*Bibliothèque de la Faculté de Médecine.

(A. Franklin, *Recherches sur la bibliothèque de la Faculté de médecine de Paris.* Paris 1864. 179 pp. Lists some mss., p. 139ff.)

—*Bibliothèque de l'Institut de France.

(F. Bournon, *Catalogue des manuscrits de la Bibliothèque de l'Institut.* Paris 1890. 56 pp. 543 mss. No index.)

*Handwritten supplement to the printed catalogue (Born 180).

—*Bibliothèque de l'Université.

(E. Chatelain, *Catalogue des Manuscrits de la Bibliothèque de l'Université*. Paris 1892. 36 pp. 1556 mss. No index.) (ICU)

E. Chatelain, 'Les manuscrits de l'ancien Collège du Trésorier,' *Revue des Bibliothèques* I (1891) 17-23. Now at University Library and others. No index.

—*Bibliothèque de la ville.

F. Bournon, *Catalogue des manuscrits de la Bibliothèque de la Ville de Paris*. Paris 1893 (cover 1894). 48 pp. 527 mss., mostly modern. No index.

Ville de Paris, Bulletin de la Bibliothèque et des Travaux Historiques II (1907), 129 pp.: G. Henriot, 'Catalogue des manuscrits entrés à la Bibliothèque de 1903 à 1905.' 106 mss. Vol. IV (1909) 35-137: '. . . de 1906 à 1908.' Nos. 107-46. Vol. V (1911), 208 pp.: '. . . de 1906 à 1910.' Nos. 147-488. Each part indexed. (NN)

—Bibliothèque Mazarine.

For the main catalogue, see France, *Catalogue Général*.

The library copy of the *Deuxième Supplement* (*Départements* XLV, p. 35-55) has handwritten additions for mss. 4562-4584.

Inventaire de la donation faite à la Bibliothèque Mazarine par Monsieur Paul Fatalicq (1954). Typed sheets describing 409 nos., mostly edd.

—Bibliothèque Nationale.

Bibliothèque Nationale, Département des Manuscrits, Catalogue alphabétique des livres imprimés mis à la disposition des lecteurs dans la salle de travail, suivi de la liste des catalogues usuels du Département des Manuscrits. 4th ed. Paris 1933. 142 pp. p. 121-140: 'Catalogues usuels mis à la disposition des lecteurs dans la salle de travail.'

Les Catalogues imprimés de la Bibliothèque Nationale. Liste, Description, Contenu. Paris 1943. 205 pp. p. 1-57: Manuscrits. (NN)

Fonds Latin

Catalogus codicum manuscriptorum Bibliothecae Regiae. 4 vols. Paris 1739-44. III (1744): Latin mss. no. 1-4793. IV (1744): Latin mss. no. 4794-8822; 233A-8818A; index for both volumes. (NN)

Bibliothèque Nationale. Catalogue général des manuscrits latins. 3 vols. Paris 1939-52. I: Mss. no. 1-1438. II: Mss. no. 1439-2692. III: Mss. no. 2693-3013A. Vols. I-II edited by P. Lauer.

L. Delisle, 'Inventaire des manuscrits conservés à la Bibliothèque Impériale sous les Nos. 8823-11503 du fonds latin,' *Bibliothèque de l'École des Chartes* XXIII (1862) 277-308; 469-512; XXIV (1863) 185-236. No index.

The same, 'Inventaire des manuscrits latins de Saint-Germain-des-Prés,' *Ibid.* XXVI (1865) 185-214; XXVIII (1867) 343-76; 528-56; XXIX (1868) 220-60. Mss. no. 11504-14231. No index.

The same, 'Inventaire des manuscrits latins de Saint-Victor conservés à la Bibliothèque Impériale sous les numéros 14232-15175,' *Ibid.* XXX (1869) 1-79. No index.

The same, 'Inventaire des manuscrits latins de la Sorbonne, conservés à la Bibliothèque Impériale sous les nos. 15176-16718 du fonds latin,' *Ibid.* XXXI (1870) 1-50; 135-61. No index.

The same, 'Inventaire des manuscrits latins de Notre Dame et de divers petits fonds conservés à la Bibliothèque Nationale sous les nos. 16719-18613 du fonds latin,' *Ibid.* 463-565. No index.

The same, 'État des manuscrits latins de la Bibliothèque Nationale au 1er août 1871,' *Ibid.* XXXII (1871) 20-62. Lists Nouvelles acquisitions latines nos. 111-52; 1143-72; 2074-85; 2503-05 (p. 50-59). No index.

The same, 'Inventaire des manuscrits latins de la Bibliothèque Nationale insérés au fonds des nouvelles acquisitions, du 1er août 1871 au 1er mars 1874,' *Ibid.* XXXV (1874) 76-92. Lists Nouvelles acquisitions latines nos. 153-88; 1173-1230; 2086-2127. No index.

The same, 'La Bibliothèque Nationale en 1875,' *Ibid.* XXXVII (1876) 65-111.

The same, 'La Bibliothèque Nationale en 1876,' *Ibid.* XXXVIII (1877) 193-256.

The same, 'Manuscrits légués à la Bibliothèque Nationale par Armand Durand.' *Ibid.* LV (1894) 627-60.

U. Robert, 'Inventaires des manuscrits latins de la Bibliothèque Nationale insérés au fonds des nouvelles acquisitions du 1er mars 1874 au 31 décembre 1881,' *Le Cabinet Historique* XXVIII (N.S. I, 1882) 52-74; 164-90; 293-96: Nos. 189-326; 1231-1429; 2128-2242; 2506-27. No index.

Bibliothèque Nationale. Manuscrits latins et français ajoutés aux fonds de Nouvelles Acquisitions pendant les années 1875-1891. Inventaire alphabétique, by L. Delisle. 2 vols. Paris 1891. LXXXVIII, 856 pp. Covers nos. 189-498; 1231-1679; 2128-2344; 2506-68; (cf. p. xxxiv-xxxv).

H. Omont, 'Nouvelles acquisitions du département des manuscrits de la Bibliothèque Nationale pendant l'année 1891-92,' *Bibliothèque de l'École des Chartes* LIII (1892) 333-82. Lists Nouvelles acquisitions latines nos. 499-548; 1680-88; 2345-52; 2569. No index. p. 364-66: Supplément grec, no. 1101-18. p. 368-79: Manuscrits italiens, no. 2001-66 (by L. Auvray).

The same, 'Nouvelles acquisitions... pendant les années 1892-93,' *Ibid.* LV (1894) 61-114; 241-58: Nos. 549-64; 1689-1711; 2353-64; 2570-72. Index inadequate (p. 62-64).

The same, 'Nouvelles acquisitions... pendant les années 1894-1895,' *Ibid.* LVII (1896) 161-96; 339-72: Nos. 565-612; 1712-47; 2365-76; 2573. Index inadequate (p. 162-66).

The same, 'Nouvelles acquisitions... pendant les années 1896-1897,' *Ibid.* LIX (1898) 81-135: Nos. 613-50; 1748-75; 2377-82; 2574-76. Index (p. 82-85).

The same, 'Manuscrits récemment entrés dans les Collections de la Bibliothèque Nationale (1891-1900) et exposés dans la Galerie Mazarine,' *Ibid.* LXI (1900) 243-247. 29 mss. of which nos. 1-9 in Latin. No index.

Bibliothèque Nationale. Nouvelles Acquisitions du Département des manuscrits pendant les années 1898-1899. Inventaire sommaire, by H. Omont. Paris 1900. 93 pp. Nos. 651-709; 1776-1805; 2383-85; 2577. Index (p. 4-7). (NN)

H. Omont, 'Catalogue des manuscrits Ashburnham-Barrois récemment acquis par la Bibliothèque Nationale,' *Bibliothèque de l'École des Chartes* LXII (1901) 555-610; LXIII (1902) 10-68: Nouv. acq. lat. nos. 725-33; 1824-27. Also printed separately, Paris 1902. 124 pp. With index.

The same, 'Liste des manuscrits de la Collection Barrois récemment acquis pour la Bibliothèque Nationale,' *Revue des Bibliothèques* XI (1901) 161-68. No index. (NN)

The same, 'Nouvelles acquisitions... pendant les années 1900-1902,' *Bibliothèque de l'École des Chartes* LXIV (1903) 5-30; 221-58: Nos. 710-73; 1806-68; 2380-89; 2578. Index (p. 7-10).

The same, 'Manuscrips de la Bibliothèque de Sir Thomas Phillipps récemment acquis pour la Bibliothèque Nationale,' *Ibid.* 490-553: Nouv. acq. Lat. nos. 778-825; 1873-76. Index (p. 549-53). The same also printed in *Revue des Bibliothèques* XIII (1903) 189-206.

The same, 'Nouvelles acquisitions... pendant les années 1903-1904,' *Bibliothèque de l'École des Chartes* LXVI (1905) 5-69: Nos. 774-856; 1869-88; 2390-2403; 2579-85. Index (p. 7-10).

The same, 'Nouvelles acquisitions... pendant les années 1905-1906,' *Ibid.* LXVIII (1907) 5-74: Nos. 857-905; 1889-1910; 2404-10. Index (p. 7-12).

The same, 'Nouvelles acquisitions... pendant les années 1907-1908,' *Ibid.* LXX (1909) 5-72: Nos. 906-55; 1911-77; 2411-24; 2586-93. Index (p. 7-11).

The same, 'Manuscrits de la Bibliothèque de Sir Thomas Phillipps récemment entrés a la Bibliothèque Nationale, '*Revue des Bibliothèques* XVIII (1908) 113-41: Nouv. acq. lat. nos. 925-51; 1921-70; 2412-23; 2586-87. Index (p. 138-41).

The same, *Catalogue des manuscrits latins et français de la collection Phillipps acquis en 1908 pour la Bibliothèque Nationale.* Paris 1909. 269 pp. Nouv. acq. lat. nos. 925-51; 1921-73; 2412-23; 2586-93.

The same, 'Nouvelles acquisitions... pendant les années 1909-1910,' *Bibliothèque de l'École des Chartes* LXXII (1911) 5-56: Nos. 956-1028; 1978-2038; 2425-33; 2594. Index (p. 7-9).

Bibliothèque Nationale. Nouvelles acquisitions du Département des Manuscrits pendant les années 1891-1910. Répertoire alphabétique des manuscrits latins et français, by H. Omont. Paris 1912. cxxxix, 300 pp. p. lxiv-lxx: Supplément grec no. 1282-1329. p. xcvi-cxi: Italian mss. 2067-2199. p. cxxiii-cxxxiii: 'Catalogues usuels du Département des Manuscrits.'

H. Omont, 'Nouvelles acquisitions . . . pendant les années 1911-1912,' *Bibliothèque de l'École des Chartes* LXXIV (1913) 5-66: Nos. 1029-61; 2039-58; 2434-37. Index (p. 8-11).

The same, 'Nouvelles acquisitions... pendant les années 1913-1914.' *Ibid.* LXXVI (1915) 5-96; 331-404: Nos. 1062-90; 1101-06; 2059-73; 2438-47; 2595-97. Index (p. 11-16).

The same, 'Nouvelles acquisitions... pendant les années 1915-1917,' *Ibid.* LXXVIII (1917) 221-68: Nos. 1091-1100; 1107-11; 2448-50; 2598-2600. Index (p. 224-27).

The same, 'Nouvelles acquisitions... pendant les années 1918-1920,' *Ibid.* LXXXII (1921) 117-56: Nos. 1112-23; 2451-54; 2601-02. Index (p. 119-22).

The same, 'Nouvelles acquisitions... pendant les années 1921-1923,' *Ibid.* LXXXV (1924) 5-57: Nos. 1-78; 1124-42; 2455-62. Index (p. 8-11).

The same, 'Nouvelles acquisitions... pendant les années 1924-1928,' *Ibid.* LXXXIX (1928) 240-98: Nos. 79-110; 2463-67; 3001-03. Index (p. 243-46).

The same, 'Nouvelles acquisitions... pendant les années 1929-1931,' *Ibid.* XCII (1931) 354-85: Nos. 2468-76; 3004-13. Index (p. 356-58).

Ph. Lauer, 'Nouvelles acquisitions latines et françaises du Département des manuscrits de la Bibliothèque Nationale pendant les années 1932-1935,' *Ibid.* XCVI (1935) 205-45: Nos. 2477-85; 3014-32. Index (p. 207-13).

The same, 'Nouvelles acquisitions... pendant les années 1936-1940,' *Ibid.* CII (1941) 156-210: Nos. 2486-2607; 3033-64. Index (p. 159-67).

J. Porcher, 'Nouvelles acquisitions latines et françaises du Département des Manuscrits de la Bibliothèque Nationale pendant les années 1941-1945,' *Ibid.* CVI (1945-46) 225-281: Nos. 2608-13; 3065-81. Index (229-235).

S. Solente, 'Nouvelles acquisitions latines et françaises du Département des Manuscrits de la Bibliothèque Nationale pendant les années 1946-1950,' *Ibid.* CXII (1954) 182-246: Nos. 2614-16; 3082-85. Index (186-194).

H. Omont, *Inventaire sommaire des manuscrits du Supplément Grec de la Bibliothèque Nationale.* Paris 1883. xvi, 135 pp. Lists a few Latin mss. (DLC)

The same, *Concordances des numéros anciens et des numéros actuels des manuscrits latins de la Bibliothèque Nationale, précédées d'une notice sur les anciens catalogues.* Paris 1903. xlvii, 195 pp.

Table des manuscrits latins du nouveau fonds. 4 vols. Alphabetical index of authors for all mss. not described in the printed catalogue of 1744.

Initia operum latinorum, by B. Hauréau (Cod. N. acq. lat. 2392-2402). 11 vols. (Communication of Mlle M. Th. d'Alverny, cf. Born 141).

*Ms. folders describing recent acquisitions (Born 143).

Répertoire alphabétique général des Fonds des

Nouvelles Acquisitions Latines de la Bibliothèque Nationale, 1868-1940 (by M. Duchemin). 1 typed vol.

(The following catalogues list groups of mss. most of which are also described in the preceding, indispensable catalogues).

Note sur le Catalogue Général des manuscrits des Bibliothèques des Départements, suivie du Catalogue de 50 manuscrits de la Bibliothèque Nationale. (By L. Delisle). Paris 1873. 53 pp. No index.

L. Delisle, *Inventaire des manuscrits de la Bibliothèque Nationale. Fonds de Cluni.* Paris 1884. xxv, 413 pp. 226 mss. No index. (DLC)

L. Delisle and M. de Fréville, *Collection de M. Jules Desnoyers. Catalogue des manuscrits anciens et des chartes.* Paris 1888. 84 pp. 49 mss. No index. (NN)

Bibliothèque Nationale. Catalogue des manuscrits des fonds Libri et Barrois, by L. Delisle. Paris 1888. 330 pp. 180 mss.

Bibliothèque Nationale. Catalogue des manuscrits du fonds de la Trémoïlle, by L. Delisle. Paris 1889. 51 pp. 49 mss. No index.

Bibliothèque Nationale. Catalogue des manuscrits grecs, latins, français et espagnols et des portulans recueillis par feu Emmanuel Miller, by H. Omont. Paris 1897. 137 pp. 6 Latin mss. (p. 68-73). (NN)

Catalogus codicum hagiographicorum latinorum antiquiorum saeculo XVI qui asservantur in Bibliotheca Nationali Parisiensi. 3 vols. Brussels 1889-93. 885 mss. Index in vol. III. (NNUT)

B. Hauréau, *Notices et Extraits de quelques manuscrits latins de la Bibliothèque Nationale.* 6 vols. Paris 1890-93. I (1890): Par. lat. 363-8650 (scattered numbers). II (1891): 8876-14193. III (1891): 14246-14929. IV (1892): 14932-15163. V (1892): 15265-17990. VI (1893): 18081-18570; Nouv. acq. lat. 202-1544. Each volume indexed. Part of this material appeared also in *Notices et Extraits...* ed. Académie des Inscriptions (see above, Section B).

A. Noyon, 'Notes pour servir au catalogue du fonds latin de la Bibliothèque Nationale: Inventaire des écrits théologiques du XIIe siècle non insérés dans la Patrologie Latine de Migne.' *Revue des Bibliothèques* XXII (1912) 277-333; XXIII (1913) 297-319; 385-418. Par. lat. up to no. 12019 (scattered numbers). No index.

V. Leroquais, *Les livres d'heures manuscrits de la Bibliothèque Nationale.* 2 vols. Paris 1927. 313 mss.

The same, *Supplément aux Livres d'Heures manuscrits de la Bibliothèque Nationale (Acquisitions récentes et donation Smith-Lesouëf).* Mâcon 1943. xxvii, 72 pp. and plates.

L. Thorndike, 'Notes on some astronomical, astrological and mathematical manuscripts of the Bibliothèque Nationale, Paris,' *Journal of the Warburg and Courtauld Institutes* XX (1957) 112-172.

Fonds Italien.

See above, Marsand. Superseded.

G. Raynaud, 'Inventaire des manuscrits italiens qui ne figurent pas dans le catalogue de Marsand,' *Le Cabinet Historique* XXVII (N.S.I, 1881), pt. 2, p. 132-164; 225-343. Also printed separately, Paris 1882, 152 pp. No. 7-1697 (with gaps). No index. Superseded.

See Mazzatinti under Italy, *Indici e Cataloghi* V, for mss. 1-2000.

See above, Omont, *Bibliothèque de l'École des Chartes* LIII (1892) 368-379, for mss. 2001-2066.

See above, *Bibliothèque Nationale, Nouvelles Acquisitions, Répertoire alphabétique* (1912), p. xcvi-cxi, for mss. 2067-2199.

L. Auvray, 'Inventaire de la Collection Custodi... conservée à la Bibliothèque Nationale (Mss. Italiens 1545-66),' *Bulletin italien* III (1903) 308-335; IV (1904) 149-155; 244-256; 316-327; V (1905) 73-89; 146-159; 349-79. Not relevant.

The same, 'La collection Armingaud à la Bibliothèque Nationale,' *Études Italiennes* I (1919) 168-180; 215-222. Covers

Italian mss. 2242-2260. Not relevant.
Fonds français.
Bibliothèque Nationale, Catalogue des Manuscrits latins du fonds français. 3 typed vols. (Paris, Institut de Recherches et d'Histoire des Textes)
Collections diverses.
L. Auvray and R. Poupardin, *Catalogue des manuscrits de la collection Baluze.* Paris 1921. 652 pp. 398 mss., mostly copies of documents. Rich index (471ff.) (NN)
Bibliothèque Nationale. Catalogue de la collection Dupuy. By L. Dorez. 2 vols. Paris 1899. Table alphabétique, by S. Solente. Paris 1928. 958 mss. Mostly charters, a few Latin letters. (NN)
Bibliothèque Nationale. Inventaire des manuscrits de la Collection Moreau. By H. Omont. Paris 1891. xiv, 282 pp. 1834 nos. Mostly concerning French history. (Morgan Library)
Catalogue des Livres composant la Bibliothèque de feu M. le Baron James de Rothschild. 5 vols. Paris 1884-1920. 89 mss. listed among the edd. Cf. index (vol. V, p. 503-504). Shelf marks added in library copy.
Lettres autographes et manuscrits de la collection Henri de Rothschild. Vol. I: Moyen Age - XVIᵉ siècle. Textes publiés et annotés par R. Gaucheron. Paris 1924. IV, 374 pp. (NN)
Inventaire sommaire des manuscrits anciens de la Bibliothèque Smith-Lesouëf à Nogent-sur-Marne (by P. Champion and S. De Ricci), Paris (1930). 16 pp., where 129 mss. are listed, of which nos. 1-51 in Latin.
*Handwritten list of over 200 mss. of the Bibliothèque Smith-Lesouëf, by P. Champion.
—Bibliothèque Sainte-Geneviève. See France, *Catalogue général,* Paris.
A. Boinet, 'Catalogue des miniatures des manuscrits de la Bibliothèque Sainte-Geneviève,' *Revue des Bibliothèques* XVIII (1908) 142-80. Index (p. 146-49).
*Handwritten supplement to the printed

catalogue (Born 163).
Parma, Italy. See *Archiv* XII; Blume; *Giornale* I; Mazzatinti XIV; XX; *Serapeum* XIX.
—*Archivio di Stato. See Mazzatinti XX.
G. Drei, *L'Archivio di Stato di Parma, Indice generale storico descrittivo ed analitico* (Bibliothèque des Annales Institorum 6). Rome 1941. ix, 283 pp.
Archivio di Stato di Parma, Biblioteca, Manoscritti. Card file, listing 50 mss.
* *Raccolta di Manoscritti* (shelf mark 119). Typed list of 143 mss.
Epistolaric Scelto (shelf mark 116). Alphabetical list of senders.
(Information kindly supplied by the archivist).
—Biblioteca Palatina.
Mss. Codices Hebraici Biblioth. I. B. De-Rossi . . . accurate ab eodem descripti et illustrati. Accedit Appendix qua continentur Mss. Codices reliqui al. linguarum. 3 vols. Parma 1803. III, 175-90: 86 Latin mss. 190-98: 31 Italian mss. Index (p. 220ff.).
F. Odorici, 'Memorie storiche della Nazionale Biblioteca di Parma,' *Atti e Memorie delle RR. Deputazioni di storia patria per le provincie modenesi e parmensi* I (1863) 349-80; II (1864) 443-69; III (1865) 397-464. The appendix (III, 425-42; 447-54) gives a selected list of mss. No index. (NN)
The same, *La Nazionale Biblioteca di Parma: Relazione.* Turin 1873. 91 pp. Gives a selected list of mss. (p. 33-48). No index. (Parma; micr. at NNC)
G. Catalano and C. Pecorella, 'Inventario ragionato dei manoscritti giuridici della Biblioteca Palatina di Parma,' Studi Parmensi V (1955) 311-394. No index. Also printed separately, Milan 1955, 100 pp. Indices added (85-100).
Fondo Palatino. Regia Biblioteca di Parma. Catalogo dei Manoscritti. Tomo unico. Arranged alphabetically (Cf. AB II 1 p. 75). (micr. at DLC)
Fondo Parmense. Regia Biblioteca di Parma. Catalogo dei Manoscritti. 8 vols.

(Cf. AB II 1 p. 75). Arranged alphabetically. I: A-B. II: C-F. III: G-L. IV: M (including Miscellanea). V: N-R. VI: S-St. VII: Storia. VIII: Stoss-Z; Manoscritti orientali e di altre lingue De Rossi e Stern. (Micr. at DLC)

Carteggio di Lucca (Autografi Palatini). 6 boxes of autographs. No inventory.

—*Chiesa di S. Giovanni Evangelista.

L. Testi, 'I corali miniati della chiesa di San Giovanni Evangelista in Parma,' *Bibliofilia* XX (1918-19) 1-30; 132-52. 11 mss.

Passau, West Germany. Staatliche Bibliothek.

Bibliothecae Regiae Passaviensis Incunabula typographica et Manuscripta (by J. Winkelmann, 1843). 123 mss. Some of them were lost during the last war.

*Pau, France. See France, *Catalogue Général, Départements* IX; XLII.

Pavia, Italy. See *Archiv* XII; Zaccaria, *Excursus.*

L. Colombo, *I codici liturgici della diocesi di Pavia* (Fontes Ambrosiani 24). Milan 1947. 114 pp. Describes mss. at the Capitolo del Duomo, S. Michele, S. Salvatore, S. Maria del Carmine, Seminario, Certosa, Binasco, and Biblioteca Universitaria. (NN)

—Biblioteca Universitaria.

(*Manuscriptorum codicum series apud Petrum Victorium Aldinium in I. Ticinensi Universitate . . . illustrata.* Pavia 1840. 74 pp. 355 mss.) (IU)

L. De Marchi and G. Bertolani, *Inventario dei manoscritti della R. Biblioteca Universitaria di Pavia.* Vol. I, Milan 1894. 408 pp. Covers Fondo Aldini, 582 mss.

Catalogo alfabetico dei Manoscritti. Arranged alphabetically. Centuries given in most cases. Describes the Manoscritti Ticinesi.

*Card index (AB II 1 p. 73).

—Museo Civico.

Alphabetical card file.

*Pavullo, Italy. See Mazzatinti XXIV.

*Pecs, Hungary. Egyetemi Könyvtár.

*Card catalogue.

*Pelplin, Poland. Biblioteka Seminarium Duchownego.

G. Sommerfeldt, 'Handschriftliches aus der Bibliothek des Klerikalseminars zu Pelplin,' *Zeitschrift für katholische Theologie* XXXIX (1915) 582-600. Describes a few theological mss. (NNUT)

Of the original collection of 640 mss., some were lost during the last war. Cf. A. Liedtke, 'Biblioteka Seminarium Duchownego w Pelplinie,' *Zapiski Towarzystwa Naukowego w Toruniu* XIII (1947) 89-92. (NN)

*Perelada (Gerona), Spain. Biblioteca del Palacio.

A few mss. are listed in the *Anuario de la Biblioteca Central y de las Populares y Especiales* (Barcelona) 1943 (1944) 389-391; 1944 (1945) 375-376. The collection is private and belongs to Sr. Miguel Mateu Pla.

*Périgueux, France. See France, *Catalogue Général, Départements* IX; XLIII.

*Péronne, France. See France, *Catalogue Général, Départements* XXVI; XLIII.

A. Ledieu, *Catalogue des manuscrits de la bibliothèque de Péronne.* Paris 1897. 13 pp. 42 mss. No index. (OCl)

*Perpignan, France. See France, *Catalogue Général, Départements* XIII; XLIII.

Perugia, Italy. See Mazzatinti II; V; *Archiv* V.

—Badia di San Pietro.

S. De Stefano, *Regesto in Transunto dell' Archivio di S. Pietro in Perugia.* Perugia 1902. 96 pp. p. 78-88: Libri manoscritti. No shelf marks. No index. Based on the handwritten inventory of A. Cappelli. (Micr. at NNC)

Catalogo Inventario, by Adriano Cappelli (1890). p. 111-209: Codici manoscritti. (Communication of the librarian)

Inventario delle Carte e Libri conservati nell' Archivio della Badia di S. Pietro in Perugia e riordinati da Don C. M. Lamberti (1930-34).

—Biblioteca Comunale (Augusta).

For mss. 1-1565, see Mazzatinti V.

There are 2 folders with typed descriptions

of mss. 1566-2322, and another for the 281 mss. of the Fondo Nuovo (Cf. AB V 286).

—*Museo dell' Opera. (Biblioteca Dominicini). See Mazzatinti II 171.

Museo dell' Opera del Duomo di Perugia, Catalogo. Perugia n.d. 18 pp. p. 3-11: 'Indice-Inventario dei manoscritti posseduti in proprietà dai Canonici della Metropolitana di Perugia.' 47 mss. No index. (Prof. E. A. Lowe, Princeton, N.J. micr. at NNC)

G. Cernicchi, *L'Acropoli Sacra di Perugia e suoi archivi al principio del secolo XX.* Perugia 1911. 138 pp. p. 115-120: 'Indice-Inventario dei manoscritti posseduti in proprietà dei Canonici della Metropolitana di Perugia.' 46 mss. p. 126-127: 11 more mss. of Biblioteca Dominicini. No index. (Prof. Augusto Campana, Rome)

Pesaro, Italy. See Mazzatinti XXIX; XXXIII; XXXV; XXXVII; XXXIX; XLII; XLV; XLVIII; LII; *Studi Italiani,* N.S.I. For recent acquisitions of mss., see *Studia Oliveriana* I (1953) ff. See especially: I (1953) 109-114: Mss. no. 2003-2006; 2009-2013; 2018-2021 (described by I.Z., i.e., Italo Zicari); II (1954) 137-139: no. 2001-2002; 2007-2008; 2014-2017; III (1955) 91-92: no. 2022-26; *IV-V (1957) 203; VI (1958) 88-89: no. 2029-2030.

*Pescia, Italy. See Mazzatinti LX.

*Pforta, East Germany. See *Archiv* XI; *Neues Archiv* IX.

P. Böhme, *Nachrichten über die Bibliothek der Königl. Landesschule Pforta.* pt. 2: 'Handschriften einschliesslich Urkunden.' progr. Pforta, Naumburg 1883. 40 pp. 211 mss. and documents. No index.

Philadelphia, Pennsylvania, USA. See De Ricci.

—Free Library.

E. Wolf II, *A Descriptive Catalogue of the John Frederick Lewis Collection of European Manuscripts in the Free Library of Philadelphia.* Philadelphia 1937. 219 pp. 200 mss.

Typed list of acquisitions.

—University of Pennsylvania Library. See De Ricci.

Acquisitions are mentioned in *The University of Pennsylvania Library Chronicle* I (1933) ff., continued as *The Library Chronicle* with vol. XIV (1947) ff. Note especially: XIV (1947) 15-19: A. C. Howland, 'Some Manuscripts in the Lea Library.' XXI (1955) 51-60: L. Donati, 'A Manuscript of « Meditationes Johannis de Turrecremata » (1469).' XXII (1956) 86-95; XXIII (1957) 16-31; 63-81; XXIV (1958) 37-53; 83-103: Lyman W. Riley, 'Aristotle Texts and Commentaries to 1700 in the University of Pennsylvania Library: A Catalogue of Books and Manuscripts.' Contains: 'Manuscripts,' by Norman P. Zacour (XXIV 1958, 94-98). 36 mss. Index (99-103).

Typed list and card file for numerous manuscripts recently acquired.

Piacenza, Italy. See *Archivum Franciscanum* V; *Studi Italiani* IX.

—Biblioteca Capitolare.

E. Nasalli-Rocca, 'L'Archivio e la biblioteca della Cattedrale di Piacenza,' *Studi storici in Memoria di Mons. Angelo Mercati* (Fontes Ambrosiani 30, Milan 1956) 251-261. Lists 69 mss. (259-261).

Handwritten list of 71 mss.

—Biblioteca Comunale Passerini-Landi.

A. Balsamo, *Catalogo dei manoscritti della Biblioteca Comunale di Piacenza, Parte I.* (Biblioteca Storica Piacentina I). Piacenza 1910. 91 pp. 117 mss. Not complete.

A. Nasalli Rocca, 'I manoscritti veleiati della Biblioteca Comunale di Piacenza,' *Aevum* X (1936) 105-114. Lists 7 late mss. concerning Veleia.

Card index in 2 boxes. Centuries not given. I: Manoscritti B. Palastrelli; mss. Landiani. II: mss. Comunali; mss. Vitali; mss. dei Frati di Campagna e dei Cappuccini; mss. Angelo Genocchi. Each section is alphabetically arranged (Cf. AB IV 547). The printed catalogue of Balsamo has better descriptions, but covers only a part of the collection.

*Piazza Armerina, Italy. See Mazzatinti (1887).

*Pienza, Italy. Museo.

G. B. Mannucci, 'I preziosi codici miniati del Museo di Pienza,' *Arte Cristiana* XXV (1927) 135-141. Not a catalogue. Mentions several liturgical mss.

*Piesing, West Germany. Schlossbibliothek. See Leclercq.

*Pieve di Cadore, Italy. Comunità Cadorina. See *Manoscritti e libri rari.*

*Pilchowice, Poland.

** *Verzeichniss der Bücher, Kupferwerke und Manuscripte, welche sich in der Majorats-Bibliothek von Pilchowitz befinden.* Ratibor 1835. p. 606-13: mss.

*Pinerolo, Italy. See Mazzatinti I; LX.

*Pirano, Italy. See Wickhoff.

*Pirna, East Germany.

R. Schmertosch von Riesenthal, 'Die Pirnaer Kirchenbibliothek mit ihren Handschriften und Inkunabeln,' *Centralblatt für Bibliothekswesen* XX (1903) 265-73. Lists a few mss. (267-71).

Pisa, Italy. See *Archiv* XII; La Fage; Mazzatinti XXIV; *Studi Italiani* VIII; IX.

—*Archivio Universitario.

P. E. Arias, 'Carte Quattrocentesche dello Studio Pisano,' *Rivista Storica degli Archivi Toscani* II (1930) 1-28.

—Biblioteca Universitaria.

C. Vitelli, 'Catalogo dei codici che si conservano nell' Archivio Roncioni in Pisa' *Studi Storici* XI (1902) 121-76. 88 mss. Index (174ff.).

Inventario dei manoscritti. (Inside:) *R. Biblioteca Universitaria di Pisa. Manoscritti Roncioni.* Covers mss. 680-736, also described in the printed catalogues of Mazzatinti and Vitelli, but with different shelf marks. Then descriptions of mss. 737-924, and again of mss. 1-946 (Cf. AB II 4-5 p. 88).

Card index of mss. (AB II 4-5 p. 88).

—Seminario Arcivescovile, Biblioteca Cateriniana. See Mazzatinti XXIV; *Studi Italiani* VIII; IX.

F. Pelster, 'Die Bibliothek von Santa Caterina zu Pisa, eine Büchersammlung aus den Zeiten des hl. Thomas von Aquin,' *Xenia Thomistica* III (Rome 1925) 249-280. Identifies and discusses some extant mss. No index.

Elenco dei Manoscritti. Typed list, largely superseded by the printed catalogues.

Pistoia, Italy. See Istituto Storico, *Guida* (Section A) ; Mazzatinti I.

L. Chiappelli, 'I manoscritti giuridici di Pistoia,' *Archivio Giuridico* XXXIV (1885) 201-275; XXXV (1885) 61-110. Covers Biblioteca Forteguerriana (4 mss.), Archivio Capitolare del Duomo (15 mss.), Biblioteca Fabroniana (1 ms.), Collezione Rossi-Cassigoli (1 ms., now at the Biblioteca Nazionale, Florence), Seminario Vescovile (1 ms.), Archivio dello Spedale del Ceppo (2 mss.), Archivio Comunale (2 mss.).

F. A. Zaccaria S. J., 'Ad Hieronymum Lagomarsinum de Mss. codicibus qui in Bibliotheca Pistoriensis ut aiunt Sapientiae adservantur Epistola,' *Raccolta d'Opuscoli Scientifici e Filologici*, ed. Calogerà, XXX (1744) 435-86. Surveys extant mss. (464ff.) No index or shelf marks.

The same, *Bibliotheca Pistoriensis.* Turin 1752. 408 pp. Lists mss. of Archivio Vescovile, Archivio Capitolare and Sapienza (p. 1-57). Index (p. 58-59).

—Archivio Capitolare del Duomo.

The manuscript books are listed by A. Chiti, 'Archivio Capitolare del Duomo' in G. Mazzatinti, *Gli Archivi della Storia d'Italia* III (Rocca S. Casciano 1900-01), p. 63-69 (nos. 40-181; nos. 1-39 are incunabula).

—Biblioteca Fabroniana.

Catalogo mss. Centuries not given. 415 mss. (Mazzatinti I lists only 176 mss.)

—Biblioteca Forteguerriana.

Catalogo dei Manoscritti della Biblioteca Forteguerri, by Vittorio Capponi (1873). Alphabetically arranged. Largely superseded by Mazzatinti I (Cf. AB V 104).

—*Biblioteca del Seminario Vescovile.

List of 8 mss. before 1600 kindly supplied by the librarian.

*Pithiviers, France. See France, *Catalogue Général, Départements* XIII.

*Płock, Poland, See *Société française*; Vetulani.

*Plymouth, England. See Schenkl.

J. O. Halliwell-Phillipps, *A Brief Description of the Ancient and Modern Manuscripts Preserved in the Public Library, Plymouth.* London, 1853. 239 pp. 143 mss. (p. 1-32). No index.

*Poitiers, France. See France, *Catalogue Général, Départements* XXV; XLIII; *Sociétés*; *Universités*.

*Poligny, France. See France, *Catalogue Général, Départements* XXI; XLIII.

*Pommersfelden, West Germany. Graeflich Schönbornsche Bibliothek. See *Archiv* IX; Hirsching; Leclercq; Schum; *Serapeum* VI.

J. Fr. Degen, *Beitrag zu Nachrichten von alten Handschriften.* 2 pts. progr. Onolzbach 1785-90. Lists a few mss. No index. (Erlangen, University Library)

Katalog der Handschriften der Gräflich von Schönbornschen Bibliothek zu Pommersfelden. 4 typed vols. I: 1-100. II: 101-200. III: 201-300. IV: 301-372. (Copy seen at the Monumenta Germaniae Historica, Munich)

*Pont-à-Mousson, France. See France, *Catalogue Général, Départements* XIV; XLIII.

*Pontarlier, France. See France, *Catalogue Général, Départements* IX.

*Pont-Audemer, France. See France, *Catalogue Général, Départements* X.

*Pont-de-Vaux, France. See France, *Catalogue Général, Départements* VI; XLIII.

*Pontevedra, Spain. See Fransen.

*Pontoise, France. See France, *Catalogue Général, Départements* IX.

*Poppi, Italy. See Mazzatinti VI.

O. Fanfani, *Inventario dei manoscritti della Biblioteca Comunale di Poppi.* Florence 1925. 32 pp. 432 mss. No index. (Prof. A. Campana, Rome)

*Porto, see **Oporto**.

Posen, see **Poznań**.

*Poszonyi, see **Bratislava**.

*Pöttmes, West Germany.

E. Krausen, *Archiv der Freiherren v. Gumppenberg zu Pöttmes* (Inventare nichtstaatlicher Archive Bayerns. I. Reg.-Bez. Oberbayern. 1. Landkreis Aichach). Munich 1950. Mimeographed. Appendix II: Handschriften, by B. Bischoff. 7 mss.

*Poughkeepsie, New York, U.S.A. See De Ricci.

Poznań, Poland. See Aland (Section A); *Archiv* XI; Vetulani.

—Biblioteka Głowna Uniwersytetu im. Adama Mickiewicza.

W. Schwartz, *Schulnachrichten.* progr. Posen 1875. 14 pp. p. 11: Note on ms. 3. — progr. Posen 1876. 23 pp. p. 20: Note on mss. 1-2. — progr. Posen 1877. 27 pp. p. 22-23: More detailed note on the same 3 mss. (by Kohlmann). (Poznan, Biblioteka Głowna; partial micr. at NNC)

Card file for older mss. Most of them come from local school and church libraries.

—*Biblioteka Seminaryjna.

A. Lisiecki, 'Katalog rekopisów biblioteki seminaryjnej w Poznaniu aż do wieku XV włącznie,' *Przeglad kościelny* VII (1905) 285-296; VIII (1905) 47-56; 119-127. Also published separately, Poznan 1905, 31 pp. 63 mss. Arranged chronologically. No index. (Cracow, Biblioteka Jagiellonska; micr. at NN)

—Miejska Biblioteka Publiczna im. Edwarda Raczyńskiego.

Katalog Biblioteki Raczyńskich w Poznaniu. (*Katalog der Raczyńskischen Bibliothek in Posen*). By M. E. Sosnowski and L. Kurtzmann. 3 vols. Poznan 1885. Vol. I, p. i-cccxxv: 359 mss. Index inadequate. (NN)

Katalog *Bibljoteki Raczyńskich w Poznaniu* 1885-1931. Vol. I, Poznan 1932. C, 496 pp. p. v-lxxxii: Mss. no. 360-499, mostly modern. Index (p. lxxxiii-xcvi). (NN)

Inwentarz rękopisów. A card file in 2 trays, supplementing the printed catalogues. I: 500-1080; 1455-1700. II: 1701-1996.

(No title). 1 ms. vol. Describes mss. no. 1081-1454.

Praha (Prague), Czechoslovakia. See *Archiv* IX; X; Balbinus; Burdach; Hirsching; Lehmann, *Mitteilungen* III; Thorndike.

J. Kelle, 'Die klassischen Handschriften bis herauf zum 14. Jahrhundert in Prager Bibliotheken,' *Abhandlungen der kgl. Böhmischen Gesellschaft der Wissenschaften*, Ser. VI vol. V (1872) no. 1, 39 pp.

F. Schulte, 'Die canonistischen Handschriften der Bibliotheken in Prag,' *Ibid*. Ser. VI vol. II (1868) no. 2, 115 pp. Index (p. 5-12).

—*Archiv hlavniho města Prahy.

*J. Čelakovský, *Soupis rukopisů chovaných v archivu král. hlav. města Prahy*, vol. I (no more published). Prague 1907, 124 pp. 122 mss. (Prague, University Library)

—*Knihovna Metropolitní Kapituli. See *Soupis Rukopisů Knihoven* I and IV.

A. Podlaha, *Die Bibliothek des Metropolitankapitels*. (Topographie der Historischen und Kunst-Denkmale im Königreiche Böhmen... II 2). Prague 1904. 304 pp. 184 mss.

The same, *Catalogus codicum manu scriptorum qui in Archivio Capituli Metropolitani Pragensis asservantur*. (Editiones Archivii et Bibliothecae S. F. Metropolitani Capituli Pragensis XVII). Prague 1923. 328 pp. 211 mss., only documents. (MH)

*The same, *Doplňky a opravy k soupisu rukopisů knihovny metropolitní kapitoly pražské*. (Editiones archivii et bibliothecae S. F. metropolitani capituli Pragensis XXII). Prague 1928. 54 pp. (Prague, Univ. Library)

—Narodni Museum.

F. M. Bartoš, *Catalogus codicum manu scriptorum Musaei Nationalis Pragensis. Soupis Rukopisů Národního Musea v Praze.* 2 vols. Prague 1926-27. I: 1818 Bohemian mss. II: Mss. no. 1819-4061 of which many are in Latin. No index. (NN)

The Museum now has the Nostitz collection, now called the Josef Dobrowsky library. See *Soupis Rukopisů Knihoven* II.

J. V. Simak, *Die Handschriften der Graf Nostitz'schen Majoratsbibliothek in Prag.* Prague 1910. 170 pp. 227 mss., mostly late. (DLC)

The library also has the mss. from Osek (Ossegg). See *Xenia Bernardina.*

The other ms. acquisitions of the library are listed in an alphabetical card file.

—Universitní knihovna.

(J. A. Hanslik, *Geschichte und Beschreibung der Prager Universitätsbibliothek.* Prague 1851. 633 pp. p. 593ff.: a few mss. listed. No index). (MH)

(J. Hanuš, *Zusätze und Inhaltsverzeichnisse zu Hanslik's 'Geschichte und Beschreibung der k.k. Prager Universitäts-Bibliothek.'* Prague 1863. viii, 92 pp. ICJ)

(J. Truhlář, 'Verzeichnis der neugeordneten handschriftlichen Cimelien der Universitäts-Bibliothek in Prag,' *Mittheilungen des österreichischen Vereines für Bibliothekswesen* V [1901] 102-06; 147-56.) (NN)

The same, *Catalogus codicum manuscriptorum latinorum qui in C. R. Bibliotheca Publica atque Universitatis Pragensis asservantur.* 2 vols. Prague 1905-06. I: 1665 mss. II: Mss. no. 1666-2830, and index for both volumes. Apparently not complete.

The same, *Katalog Českých Rukopisů c.k.. Veřejné a Universitní Knihovny Pražské.* Prague 1906. xi, 196 pp. 432 mss. including 135 Latin items which are covered by a separate index (p. 194-196).

E. Urbankova, 'Přírůstky rukopisného oddéleni Universitní knihovny od vydání tištených katalogů,' *Vědecko-Theoretický Sborník Knihovna* (Prague 1957) 41-64. Surveys the acquisitions made after the publication of Truhlář's catalogue.

The same, *Rukopisy a Vzácné Tisky Pražske Universitní Knihovny.* (Prague) 1957. 112 pp. and plates.

Rukopisy. Alphabetical card index in 3 trays, covering manuscript acquisitions not described in Truhlář's printed catalogue. The third tray contains a separate section describing the mss. from the Lobkowitz collection in Roudnice (Raudnitz): Mss. VI E b 16 - VI F g 73.

Německ rukopisy, Lobkovické rukopisy. Alphabetical card index in one tray. It covers the former Lobkowitz collection in Prague, the former Thun collection in Děčín, and a group of recent acquisitions, arranged by languages and authors.

For the Thun mss., see also:

J. Kapras, 'Rukopisy Děčínské,' *Časopis Musea Království Českého* LXXVIII (1904) 340-344; 423-430. 273 mss. (some numbers skipped). No index. (NN)

—Strahovska Knihovna (Památník Národního Písemnictví). See Neuwirth.

E. Weyrauch, *Geschichte und Beschreibung der königl. Stift Strahöwer Bibliothek.* Prague 1858. 41 pp. p. 17-26: 'Wichtigere Handschriften.' 64 mss. No index. (MiU)

A. Stara, 'Die theologischen Strahover Handschriften,' *Analecta Praemonstratensia* X (1934) 111-112.

Alphabetical card file in 11 bound vols. Rukopisy Strahovski knihovny. 1 ms. folder. Mss. D A I 1 - D S I 29.

Prato, Italy. See Mazzatinti XXXI.

—Biblioteca Roncioniana.

C. Guasti, 'I manoscritti italiani che si conservano nella Biblioteca Roncioniana di Prato,' *Il Propugnatore* II (1869) pt. 2, 451-461; III (1870) pt. 1, 412-426; pt. 2, 505-523; IV (1871) pt. 2, 428-462; V (1872) pt. 1, 319-365; pt. 2, 452-462; VI (1873) pt. 1, 151-167. 73 mss. (with gaps). No shelf marks.

*Alphabetical card index (Communication of the librarian).

*Pressburg, see **Bratislava**.

Princeton, New Jersey, U.S.A. See De Ricci.

—Princeton University Library.

The acquisitions are mentioned in *The Princeton University Library Chronicle* I (1939) ff.

See especially: III (1941-42) 123-130: D. D. Egbert, 'The Western European Manuscripts' (of the Robert Garrett collection). XI (1949-50) 37-44: Dorothy Miner, 'The Manuscripts in the Grenville Kane Collection.' XIX (1957-58) 159-190: A. P. Clark, 'The Manuscript Collections of the Princeton University Library: An Introductory Survey.' It has a section on Medieval and Renaissance Manuscripts (p. 161-163).

Typed lists of mss. not described in De Ricci.

The Scheide Library of Titusville is now deposited at Princeton.

*Privas, France. See France, *Catalogue Général, Départements* IV.

*Providence, Rhode Island, U.S.A. See De Ricci.

*Provins, France. See France, *Catalogue Général, Départements* III; XLIII.

*Przemyśl, Poland. See Dudik, *Archive*.

*Pulkovo, U.S.S.R. See under **Leningrad**.

*Quedlinburg, East Germany. See *Archiv* VIII; XI. See also under Halle.

—*Kreis- und Stadtbibliothek.

Tobias Eckhardus, *Codices Manuscripti Quedlinburgenses* . . . Quedlinburg 1723. 92 pp. 128 mss. (p. 4-56).

Tobias Eckhard, Kurtze Nachricht von den Öffentlichen Bibliothequen zu Quedlinburg. Quedlinburg 1715. 34 pp. Lists a few mss. (NN)

A. Düning, *Die deutschen Handschriften der Königlichen Stifts- und Gymnasialbibliothek bis zum Jahre 1520*. progr. Quedlinburg 1906. 23 pp. States that the library then had 78 mss. Describes 13 German mss.

—*Stadtarchiv.

Repertorium II 33. Typed volume. p. 45-54: Handschriftensammlung. Describes 9 mss. and 124 frs. (partial micr. at NNC)

*Quimper, France. See France, *Catalogue Général, Départements* XXII.

*Rab, Yugoslavia. See Wickhoff.

*Ragusa, see Dubrovnik.

*Rájec (Raitz), Czechoslovakia. Former Salm collection. *Knihovna Státního zámku v Rájei nad Svitavon. Bibliotheca Castelli Rájec prope Brunam in Moravia.* (Sborník Národního musea v Praze. Acta Musei Nationalis Pragae. Series C, Historia litterarum, vol. I, Supplementum). Prague 1957. 68 pp. and plates. p. 13-68: F. Čáda, 'Rukopisy knihovny Státního Zámku v Rájec nad Svitavon. Codices manuscripti qui in Bibliotheca Castelli Rájec prope Brunam asservantur.' 86 mss., mostly late. Index (64-68).

*Rajhrad, see under Brno.

*Rambervilliers, France. See France, *Catalogue Général, Départements* XIII; XLIII.

*Rastatt, West Germany.

Jak. Koehler, *Die Handschriften und Inkunabelndrucke der Rastatter Gymnasiumsbibliothek.* progr. Rastatt 1886. 24 pp. 14 mss., mostly German. (DLC)

*Rathenow, East Germany.

G. Weisker, *Bericht über die Rathenower Schulbibliothek.* progr. Rathenow 1877. 16 pp. p. 14-16: 3 ms. frs. (Heidelberg, Univ. Library)

Ratisbon, see Regensburg.

*Raudnitz, see **Roudnice**.

Ravenna, Italy. Biblioteca Classense. See Mazzatinti IV; V.

(A. Cappi, *La Biblioteca Classense illustrata ne' principali suoi codici e nelle più pregevoli sue edizioni del secolo XV.* Rimini 1847. 118 pp. p. 7-46: Mss. Index, p. 113-17). (MH)

Inventario dei codici mss. della Biblioteca Classense. 650 mss. Superseded to no. 625 by Mazzatinti V. After that number, the actual shelf marks differ (Cf. AB IV 405).

*Index in 2 vols. (AB IV 405).

*Recanati, Italy.

Libri manoscritti esistenti nella Libreria Leopardi in Recanati. (By M. Leopardi). Recanati 1826. 21 pp. 72 mss. No index. (MH)

*Redlynch House near Salisbury, England. Major J. R. Abbey. Important collection of mss. (seen when in Storrington). No inventory.

Regensburg (Ratisbon), West Germany. See Hirsching.

Joseph Schmid, *Die Handschriften und Inkunabeln der Bibliothek des Kollegiat-* *stiftes U. L. Frau zur Alten Kapelle in Regensburg.* Ratisbon 1907. 77 pp. p. 1-37: 57 mss. Index (p. 38-39). (NNGr)

—*Kreisbibliothek. Catalogue in progress. (Communication of the librarian)

—Fürstl. Thurn und Taxis'sche Hofbibliothek.

Katalog der Manuskripte der Fürstlich Thurn und Taxis'schen Hofbibliothek. 23 mss. on parchment and 207 on paper.

Typed notes taken by Mme Vernet in 1954 are available at the Institut de Recherches et d'Histoire des Textes, Paris.

Reggio Calabria, Italy. See Mazzatinti (1887)

—Biblioteca Comunale.

Catalogo-Inventario. 71 mss. and rare editions (AB VI 276-77).

Reggio Emilia, Italy. See Possevinus; Zaccaria, *Iter.*

—Biblioteca Capitolare. No information.

—Biblioteca Municipale.

G. Semprini, 'La Biblioteca Municipale di Reggio-Emilia,' *Bibliofilia* XXVII (1925-26) 121-30. Discusses some mss.

V. Mazzelli, 'I manoscritti di autori e di argomento francescani nella Biblioteca Municipale di Reggio nell' Emilia,' *Bollettino Francescano storico-bibliografico* I (1930) 228-43. Published as a supplement to the periodical *Frate Francesco.* 63 mss., mostly late. (Florence, Biblioteca Nazionale)

**G. Grasselli, *Tra i manoscritti della Municipale.* Reggio Emilia 1936. 29 pp.

B. Fava, 'Elenco descrittivo di 30 codici quattrocenteschi della Biblioteca Municipale di Reggio Emilia,' *Atti e Memorie della Deputazione di storia patria per le antiche provincie modenesi,* Ser. VIII, vol. VII (1955) 156-186. 30 mss. No index. (NN).

Schedario Vecchio. 4 boxes (Cf. AB IV 257). *Schedario Nuovo.* Many boxes.

*Reims, France. See France, *Catalogue Général, Départements* XXXVIII; XXXIX.

*Rein (Reun), Austria. See *Xenia Bernardina.*

(A. Weis, 'Handschriftenverzeichniss der Stiftsbibliothek zu Rein,' *Beiträge zur Kunde steiermärkischer Geschichtsquellen* XII, 1875, 1-142. 210 mss. Index, p. 130-32)

*Remiremont, France. See France, *Catalogue Général, Départements* XXI; XLIII.

*Rennes, France. See France, *Catalogue Général, Départements* XXIV; *Universités*.

D. Maillet, *Description, notices et extraits des manuscrits de la Bibliothèque Publique de Rennes.* Rennes 1837. xvi, 241 pp. 220 mss., arranged by subjects. Index. (NN)

*Reun, see Rein.

*Reval, see Tallinn.

*Rheims, see Reims.

Rieti, Italy. Biblioteca Comunale. See Mazzatinti (1887); Mazzatinti II.

E. Monaci, 'Codici rinvenuti nell' ex-convento di Sant' Antonio del Monte (Rieti),' *Bollettino ufficiale dell' Istruzione* XVIII, 2 (1891) 31-36. 58 mss. Index (p. 36). (NN)

*Riga, USSR. Latvijas PSR Zinatnu Akademija Fundamentala Biblioteka.

List of 14 Latin mss. kindly supplied by the librarian.

Rimini, Italy. Biblioteca Civica 'Gambalunga.' See *Giornale* III; IV; Mazzatinti II.

Indice ragionato delle cose più riservate della Biblioteca Gambalunga di Rimino, by Luigi Nardi (1828; shelf mark: 4 F I 19; cf. AB IV 415-16). More complete than Mazzatinti.

(Fondo Zefirino Gambetti). Schedario Gambetti: Alphabetical card file comprising mss. and edd. together.

Spoglio Manoscritti (by C. Lucchesi). Alphabetical card index, in 6 bound vols.

*Rinteln, West Germany.

Pulch (Paul), *Die alten Handschriften* (Mitteilungen aus der Bibliothek des Gymnasiums I). progr. Rinteln 1888. 37 pp. p. 1-17: 3 mss. No index. (Erlangen, Univ. Library)

*Rio de Janeiro, Brazil. Biblioteca Nacional.

J. de Saldanha da Gama, *Catalogo da Exposição Permanente dos Cimelios da Bibliotheca Nacional.* Rio de Janeiro 1885. xi, 1061 pp. p. 455-552: 68 mss. Index (551-552).

*Riom, France. See France, *Catalogue Général, Départements* XXXI.

*Ripon, England.

J. T. Fowler, 'Ripon Minster Library and its Founder,' *Yorkshire Archaeological and Topographical Journal* II (1873) 371-402. 7 mss. (p. 377-81).

*Roanne, France. See France, *Catalogue Général, Départements* XXI; XLIII.

*Rochefort, France. See France, *Catalogue Général, Départements* XXI.

*Rochester, England. See Schenkl.

*Rochester, New York, U.S.A. See De Ricci.

*Roda, Spain. See *Serapeum* VIII.

*Rodez, France. See France, *Catalogue Général, Départements* IX; XLIII.

Roma, Italy (see also Vaticano). See Andres; *Archiv* V; XII; *Archives* I; V; XXI; XXVIII; XXIX; Blume; Hinschius, *Hispania Sacra* II; III; Istituto storico, *Guida* (Section A); Italy, *Indici e Cataloghi*; La Fage; *Il Libro* (Section A); Mazzatinti XXII; LVI; LXXIII; LXXVI; Montfaucon; *Neues Archiv*; Reifferscheid; Saxl; *Serapeum, Intelligenzblatt* 1869; *Spicilegium*; Tenneroni; Ruysschaert.

Guide-Manuel des Bibliothèques de Rome (Bibliothèque des Annales Institutorum I). Revised edition. Rome 1932. 100 pp. Covers also the Vatican.

L. Pastor, 'Le biblioteche private e specialmente quelle delle famiglie principesche di Roma,' *Atti del Congresso Internazionale di Scienze Storiche*, Rome 1903, vol. III (1906) 123-130.

G. Brom, *Archivalia in Italie belangrijk voor de geschiedenis van Nederland.* (Rijks-Geschiedkundige Publikatiën. Kleine Serie II; VI; IX; XIV) 4 vols. Hague 1908-14. Covers Vatican and various Roman libraries.

B. Dudik, *Iter romanum* (*Im Auftrage des Hohen Maehrischen Landesausschusses in den Jahren 1852 und 1853 unternommen und veröffentlicht*). 2 pts. in 1 vol. Vienna 1855. pt. 1 (xx, 367 pp.): 'Historische Forschungen.' Describes many mss. in the Vatican and various Roman libraries. (NN)

Kervyn de Lettenhove, 'Les bibliothèques de Rome: Notes et Extraits,' *Académie Royale des Sciences, des Lettres et des Beaux-Arts de Belgique, Bulletins* Ser. II vol. IX (1860) 306-45. Describes some mss. in the Vatican and various Roman libraries. No index.

A. Poncelet, *Catalogus codicum hagiographicorum Latinorum Bibliothecarum Romanarum praeter quam Vaticanae.* Brussels 1909. 523 pp. Covers also several collections now in the Vatican. (NNUT)

—Abbazia di S. Paolo. No inventory.

—Archivio di Stato.

A. Lodolini, *L'Archivio di Stato in Roma e l'Archivio del Regno d'Italia, Indice generale storico descrittivo ed analitico* (Bibliothèque des Annales Institutorum II). Rome 1932. 251 pp. p. 41-42: Manoscritti.

A. Rota, 'Un fondo giuridico ignorato nell' Archivio di Stato in Roma: I codici dell' Arciospedale del SS.mo Salvatore ad Sancta Sanctorum,' *Archivi*, Ser. II, vol. II (1935) 155-177. 4 mss.

The same, 'Un brano del commento di S. Bonaventura alle Sentenze di Pier Lombardo,' *Ibid.* vol. III (1936) 82-90.

L. Sandri, 'Una bibbia latina del s. XIV ed un fondo di codici liturgici nell' Archivio di Stato di Roma, *Ibid.*, vol. IV (1937) 87-99.

O. Montenovesi, 'Una raccolta di Manoscritti nell' Archivio di Stato in Rome,' *Notizie degli Archivi di Stato* II (1942) 25-29. (DLC)

Catalogo alfabetico, Manoscritti. Card index in 2 bound vols.

Inventario degli Archivi degli Ospedali di Roma (ms. I 144).

—Biblioteca Alessandrina (Universitaria).

E. Narducci, *Catalogus codicum manuscriptorum praeter orientales qui in bibliothcea*

Alexandrina Romae adservantur. Rome 1877. 184 pp. 235 mss.

Library copy of Narducci's printed catalogue adds handwritten descriptions for mss. 236-361 (Cf. AB I 2 p. 68).

—Biblioteca Angelica. See Mazzatinti XXII; LVI; LXXVI.

E. Narducci, *Catalogus codicum manuscriptorum praeter Graecos et Orientales in Bibliotheca Angelica olim coenobii S. Augustini de Urbe.* Rome 1893. 662 pp. 1543 mss. (NNC). Index, paged 663-78 and printed Città di Castello 1913. (Micr. at NNC)

L. G. Pélissier, 'Manuscrits de Gilles de Viterbe, à la Bibliothèque Angélique (Rome),' *Revue des Bibliothèques* II (1892) 228-40.

Catalogus Chartarum quae in libris continentur. (Inside:) *Catalogo dei Manoscritti contenuti ne' libri a stampa dell' Angelica,* by E. Celani (Cf. AB I 3 p. 73).

—Biblioteca Casanatense. See Italy, *Indici e Cataloghi*; La Fage.

Grazia Salvoni Savorini, 'Di alcuni codici miniati della Biblioteca Casanatense,' *Bibliofilia* XXXVI (1934-35) 61-78. No index.

Inventario dei Manoscritti. 5440 mss. Superseded to no. 300 by recent printed catalogue.

Index manuscriptorum bibliothecae Casanatensis a P. M. Agnani ... concinnatus, deinde a p. Lectore Brini aliisque prosecutus et anno 1844 a... p... Hyacintho de Ferrari ... absolutus. 3 vols. (AB I 3 p. 76). (micr. at DLC)

—Biblioteca Corsiniana (Accademia dei Lincei).

L. G. Pélissier, 'Un inventaire des Manuscrits de la Bibliothèque Corsini à Rome dressé par La Porte Du Theil,' *Mélanges d'Archéologie et d'Histoire* IX (1889) 389-429. Lists a few mss. (411-29).

The same, 'Catalogue annoté de quelques manuscrits de la Bibliothèque Corsini (Rome) (Série 33 A 1 à 22),' *Annales de la Faculté des Lettres de Bordeaux* 1890, 113-46. 16 late mss.

The same, 'Inventaire sommaire de soixante-deux manuscrits de la Bibliothèque Corsini (Rome),' *Centralblatt für Bibliothekswesen* VIII (1891) 176-202; 297-324. 62 mss. Index (314-24).

Biblioteca Corsiniana. Manoscritti. Inventario. (Inside:) *Indice generale de' libri manoscritti che si conservano nella Libreria dell' Ecc.ma Casa Corsini diviso in tre parti...* (1738). 3 ms. vols. I: Topographical list. 2600 mss. Shelf marks added in the margins. II: Alphabetical list of authors. III: Index of subjects. Centuries not given. Sketchy. (micr. at DLC)

Catalogus selectissimae Bibliothecae Nicolai Rossii. . . Rome 1786. 259 pp. p. 17-41: 415 mss., now constituting the Fondo Niccolò Rossi at the Biblioteca Corsiniana. No index. Shelf marks added in Library copy. (NN)

—Biblioteca Lancisiana.

Bibliothecae Lancisianae Index Aut. ex Marchon. Ciojae Praeceptoris iussu emendatus et iterum confectus, Tom. I (1837). Begins with an alphabetical list of mss. Centuries and shelf marks are not given.

—Biblioteca Nazionale Centrale Vittorio Emanuele II. See Istituto storico, *Guida* (Section A); *Il Libro* (Section A).

G. Bourgin, 'Inventaire analytique et extraits des manuscrits du Fondo Gesuitico de la "Biblioteca Nazionale Vittorio Emanuele" de Rome, concernant l'histoire de France (XVIᵉ-XIXᵉ siècle),' *Revue des Bibliothèques* XVI (1906) 5-80. Index (p. 78-80).

O. Schaefer, 'Descriptio codicum franciscalium in Bibliotheca centrali nationali Romae asservatorum,' *Antonianum* XXIII (1948) 347-380. 18 mss. of the Fondo S. Bonaventura. No index. (NNUT)

Il quattrocento negli autografi e negli incunabuli della Biblioteca Nazionale di Roma. (Rome) 1950. 128 pp. and plates. Exhibition catalogue. Index of autographs (p. 12). No shelf marks. Index. (NN)

J. Gomez Perez, *Manuscritos Españoles en la Biblioteca Nacional Central de Roma. Catalogo.* Rome 1956. 282 pp. 454 mss. Arranged by subjects. (CtY)

Catalogo dei Manoscritti. Fondo Sessoriano. 590 mss. (Cf. AB I 3 p. 86). (micr. at DLC)

Catalogo dei Manoscritti Gesuitici. 1672 mss. (Cf. AB I 3 p. 86). (micr. at DLC)

Catalogo dei Manoscritti. Fondi Minori. 2 vols. I: S. Pantaleo, 125 mss.; Farfa, 28 mss.; S. Maria della Vittoria, 102 mss.; S. Gregorio, 110 mss.; Fondo 'Varia,' 304 mss.; S. Lorenzo in Lucina, 201 mss.; S. Andrea della Valle, 132 mss.; S. Martino ai Monti, 16 mss.; Traspontina, 48 mss.; Cappuccini di Roma, 18 mss.; SS. Apostoli, 44 mss.; Eborense, 33 mss. II: Gesù e Maria, 56 mss.; S. Francesco di Paola, 29 mss.; S. Maria Maddalena, 26 mss.; S. Onofrio, 155 mss.; S. Francesca Romana, 16 mss.; SS. Giovanni e Paolo, 20 mss.; S. Bonaventura, 58 mss.; S. Maria della Scala, 45 mss.; S. Francesco a Ripa, 54 mss.; Di provenienza claustrale varia, 12 mss.; mss. musicali, 162 mss. (Cf. AB I 3 p. 86). (micr. at DLC)

Catalogo dei Mss. Vittorio Emanuele. 3 vols. I: mss. 1-585. II: 586-1157. Superseded for nos. 1008-80 (Fondo Capilupi) by the printed catalogue of T. Gasparrini Leporace. See Istituto Storico Italiano (Section A). III: 1158-1201 (in continuation) (Cf. AB I 3 p. 86). (micr. at DLC)

Archivio Maffei. 8 boxes. No inventory.

Autografi. Over 26000 letters.

*Card file.

**Catalogo inventario.* In serial order.

—Biblioteca Romana Sarti (Accademia di S. Luca).

Inventario Topografico. Manoscritti. Mss. A 1-50.

—Biblioteca Vallicelliana.

Inventario. Descriptions on loose sheets in boxes.

Inventarium omnium codicum Manuscriptorum Graecorum et Latinorum Bibliothe-

cae Vallicellianae (1749). 3 vols. Vol. I: mss. I-XXVI; A 1-45; B 1-142; C 1-136; D 1-63; E 1-63; F 1-114. Vol. II: G 1-105; H 1-80; J 1-85; K 1-49; L 1-40; M 1-31. Vol. III: N 1-102; O 1-118; P 1-213; Q 1-78; R 1-113; S 1-74 (Cf. AB I 3 p. 82). (Micr. at DLC)

Index alphabeticus universalis cognominum, nominum auctorum, sanctorum et virorum illustrium ... quae in codicibus manuscriptis graecis et latinis Bibliothecae Vallicellianae continentur (1749). 2 vols. (AB I 3 p. 82). (micr. at DLC)

*Index materiarum... (1749) (AB I 3 p. 82).

*Supplemento a tutti i cataloghi dei codici. Supplements the other catalogues, but hardly of interest for Latin mss. (Communication of the librarian, cf. AB I 3 p. 82).

—Collegio di S. Isidoro.

Card index, by shelf marks. 2 boxes. Centuries not given. Mss. 1/1-1/164. 2/1-2/106.

—S. Gregorio Magno al Celio.

(G. Valentinelli, 'Biblioteca di San Gregorio al Monte Celio in Roma,' *Archivio Veneto* III (1872) 152-156. Lists many mss. that are no longer there.)

The library once had the bulk of the collection from S. Michele di Murano. These mss. are now scattered. The mss. which are left are mostly late. There is no inventory.

—*S. Maria sopra Minerva, Padri Domenicani. 17 mss. Cf. C. Ottaviano, 'Materiale bibliografico ricuperato alla scienza,' *Sophia* III (1935) 291. No further information.

—Pontificio Ateneo Antoniano (Collegio di S. Antonio).

Manoscritti. 1 typed notebook. 203 mss.

—Università Gregoriana.

Schedario, in 2 boxes. Arranged by shelf marks. Covers the 2301 mss. of the Archivum Pontificiae Universitatis Gregorianae.

Manoscritti della Soffitta. 1 folder of typed sheets. Covers the 2259 mss. of the Fondo Curia.

Catalogo di codici e stampe acquistati dalla Biblioteca Vaticana nel 1913. 1 ms. folder.

*Romans, France. See Martin.

*Romorantin, France. See France, *Catalogue Général, Départements* XLIII.

*Rossleben, East Germany.

H. Steudener, *Die Handschriften und älteren Drucke der Klosterbibliothek.* progr. Rossleben 1878. 13 pp. 3 mss.

Rostock, East Germany. Universitätsbibliothek.

Catalogus Bibliothecae Olai Gerhardi Tychsen (by A. T. Hartmann). Rostock (1817). VIII, 452, 46 pp. p. 32-33 (of last section): 15 late Latin mss. (NN)

Bibliotheca Kaemmeriana. Vermächtniss des wail. Geh. Hofrathes, Professors Ferdinand Kämmerer an die Universitäts-Bibliothek zu Rostock. Rostock 1843. IV, 339, 344 pp. Includes some mss. (DLC)

Catalog der Grossherzoglichen Bibliothek in Neustrelitz (by v. Bernstorff). 3 vols. Neustrelitz 1862. Mostly edd. (Rostock, University Library)

Katalog der Landes-Bibliothek — Bibliothek der Mecklemb. Ritter- und Landschaft- zu Rostock, by F. H. Danckelmann. 2 pts. Rostock 1905-1909. Mss. listed with edd. Index in vol. II. (Rostock, University Library; vol. I at NN)

A. Hulshof, *Verslag van een Onderzoek te Rostock naar Handschriften, Drukwerken en Bescheiden belangrijk voor de Geschiedenis van Nederland.* Hague 1909. 90 pp. Covers also Greifswald.

Catalogus Manuscriptorum. 4 ms. vols., arranged by subjects.

*Rottenburg a. N., West Germany. Priesterseminar.

*Handwritten inventory. Lists 42 mss. (Communication of the librarian)

*Rotterdam, Holland.

—*Bibliotheek der Gemeente.

(J. Clarisse), *Catalogus librorum quos complectitur Bibliotheca publica ad aedem S. Laurentii Roterodami.* (Rotterdam) 1814. 24 pp. p. 24: 5 mss. No index (Leiden, University Library).

A. Horawitz, 'Erasmus von Rotterdam und Martinus Lipsius, *Sitzungsberichte der Kaiserlichen Akademie der Wissenschaften* [Vienna], *Philosophisch-Historische Classe* C (1882) 665-799. The ms. described is now in Rotterdam, known as codex Horawitz.

Overzicht van de werken en uitgaven van Desiderius Erasmus aanwezig in de Bibliotheek der Gemeente Rotterdam (by F. Kossmann). Rotterdam 1937. IV, 84 pp. p. iii-iv: mss. (NN)

D. van Heel, *Middeleeuwse Handschriften op godsdienstig gebied in het bezit van de Bibliotheek der Gemeente Rotterdam.* Rotterdam 1948. x, 203 pp. Scattered shelf marks.

—*Bibliotheek der Remonstrants Gereformeerde Gemeente. This collection is now deposited in the Bibliotheek der Gemeente.

Catalogus van Handschriften op de Bibliotheek der Remonstrantsch-Gereformeerde Gemeente te Rotterdam (By H. C. Rogge and P. A. Tiele). Amsterdam 1869. 166 pp. 2198 mss., mostly late. (PU; micr. at NNC)

*Roubaix, France. See France, *Catalogue Général, Départements* IV.

*Roudnice, Czechoslovakia. See under **Praha**.

*Rouen, France. See *Analecta Bollandiana* XXIII; France, *Catalogue Général, Départements* I; II; XLIII; XLVIII.

*Rovereto, Italy. See Wickhoff.

—Biblioteca Civica.

E. Benvenuti, *I manoscritti della Biblioteca Civica di Rovereto descritti.* Parte I (s. XIV-XVII). Rovereto 1908. 39 pp. 24 mss. No index. (Florence, Biblioteca Nazionale; microfilm at NNC).

—Parte II, fascicolo I (s. XVIII-XIX). Rovereto 1909. 56 pp. Mss. no. 25-200. No index. (Rome, Biblioteca Nazionale).

*Catalogo dei manoscritti. The printed catalogue of Benvenuti is not complete (Apolloni II 148).

Rovigo, Italy. Biblioteca Comunale e Concordiana. See Mazzatinti III. Shelf marks added in library copy.

*Handwritten list of additional mss.

*Roye, France. See France, *Catalogue Général, Départements* XXVI; XLIII.

*Ruvo, Italy. See Mazzatinti VI.

*Saint-Amand, France. See France, *Catalogue Général* IV; XLIII.

P. Lauzun, *Les manuscrits de la Bibliothèque de Saint-Amans.* Agen 1889. 52 pp. A survey, not a catalogue.

Saint Andrews, Scotland. University Library. See Schenkl.

University Library St. Andrews. Alphabetical List & Index of Western Manuscripts. 2 typed vols., arranged alphabetically.

*Manuscript Collection. A card index, arranged by shelf marks.

*Saint-Antoine, France. See Martin.

*Saint Bonaventure, New York, U.S.A. See De Ricci.

*Saint-Bonnet-le-Château, France. See France, *Catalogue Général, Départements* XXI.

*Saint-Brieuc, France. See France, *Catalogue Général, Départements* XIII; XLIII.

*Saint-Calais, France. See *ibid.* XX; XLIII.

*Saint-Chamond, France. See *ibid.* XIII.

*Saint-Claude, France. See *ibid.* XXI; Martin.

*Saint-Dié, France. See France, *Catalogue Général, Départements* III (Quarto Series); XLIII.

E. Froment, 'Notes sur quelques Manuscrits de la Bibliothèque Municipale de Saint-Dié,' *Bulletin de la Société Philomathique Vosgienne* LIII-LIV 1927-28, (published 1929) 119-128. Detailed description of 3 mss. (DLC)

*Sainte-Foy-les-Lyon, France. See Martin.

*Sainte-Menchould, France. See France, *Catalogue Général, Départements* XXI.

*Saintes, France. See France, *Catalogue Général, Départements* XIII; XLIII.

*Saint-Étienne, France. See France, *Catalogue Général, Départements* XXI; XLIII.

*Saint-Geniès, France. See *ibid.* XIII.

*Saint-Germain, France. See France, *Catalogue Général, Départements* IX; XLIII.

*Saint-Hippolyte, France. See *ibid.* XXXI.

*Saint-Lo, France. See *ibid.* X.

*Saint-Malo, France. See *ibid.*, XX; XLIII.

*Saint-Maude, France. See *ibid.* XXXI.

*Saint-Mihiel, France. See France, *Catalogue Général, Départements* III (Quarto Series).

*Saint-Omer, France, See *Analecta Bollandiana* XLVII; France, *Catalogue Général, Départements* III (Quarto Series); XLIII; *Notices et Extraits*.

Catalogue sommaire des manuscrits de la Bibliothèque de la ville de Saint-Omer. s.l.a. (1828?). 32 pp. Alphabetical list. No shelf marks. (NN)

Saint Petersburg, see Leningrad.

*Saint-Pol, France. See France, *Catalogue Général, Départements* IV; XLIII.

*Saint-Quentin, France. See France, *Catalogue Général, Départements* III; XLIII.

Salamanca, Spain. Biblioteca Universitaria. See *Anuario*; Haenel; *Neues Archiv* VI.

F. Ruiz de Vergara y Alava, *Historia del Colegio viejo de S. Bartholome, mayor de la celebre Universidad de Salamanca* . . . 2nd ed. by J. de Roxas y Contreras, Marques de Alventos . . . 3 vols., Madrid 1766-70. Vol. III p. 308-41: Alphabetical list of mss. No shelf marks. (Bodleian Library)

Catálogo de los libros manuscritos que se conservan en la Biblioteca de la Universidad de Salamanca . . . (by Vicente de la Fuente and Juan Urbina). Madrid 1855. 75 pp. Arranged alphabetically. No shelf marks. (OCI)

R. Fernandez Pousa, 'Catalogo de los codices clasicos latinos de la Biblioteca Universitaria de Salamanca,' *Revista de la Universidad de Madrid* II (1942), fasc. 1, p. 168-189. 19 mss. No index. (IU; reprint seen at the Hispanic Society of America, New York)

Julio González, *El Maestro Juan de Segovia y su Biblioteca.* (Colección Bibliográfica VI). Madrid 1944. 213 pp. Identifies

12 mss. now at Salamanca (p. 135).

Manuscritos de la Biblioteca Salmantina. Indice de los libros manuscritos que se conservan en la Biblioteca de la Universidad de Salamanca formado en 1855 de orden del Sr. Rector D. Pablo Gonzalez Huebra por los Doctores D. Vicente de La Fuente ... y D. Juan Urbina... This alphabetically arranged inventory corresponds to the printed catalogue of 1855, but gives the shelf marks and adds three appendices covering acquisitions since 1855.

Card index in a large file.

In 1954, a large group of mss. was transferred to Salamanca from the Biblioteca del Palacio, Madrid. There is an alphabetical card index for this collection, and also a concordance of shelf marks: *Correlacion de Manuscritos de la Signatura de la Biblioteca de Palacio a la de la Biblioteca Universitaria de Salamanca.* A few typed pages.

Salerno, Italy. Biblioteca Provinciale.
—See *Archiv* XII. No inventory.

*Salins, France. See *Cabinet historique*; France, *Catalogue Général, Départements* IX.

*Salisbury, England. See Holtzmann (Section A); Bernardus; *Neues Archiv* XXII; Schenkl.

A Catalogue of the Library of the Cathedral Church of Salisbury. London 1880. viii, 334 pp. Preface signed S. M. Lakin, who says that the manuscript section was prepared by Maunde Thompson. p. 1-36: 'Catalogue of the Manuscripts in the Cathedral Library of Salisbury.' 187 mss. Index (p. 37-43). (PU; micr. at NNC)

*Salò, Italy. See Mazzatinti XLIV.

(G. Bustico, 'I manoscritti della Biblioteca dell' Ateneo di Salò,' *Commentari dell' Ateneo di Scienze, Lettere ed Arti in Brescia per l'anno 1911*, p. 178-96. Arranged alphabetically. Mostly late material). (NN)

*Saluzzo, Italy. See Rossetti.

Salzburg, Austria. See *Archiv* IX; X; Bernards; Cooper (Section A); Gercken;

Leclercq; Neuwirth; *Der österreichische Geschichtsforscher*; Wickhoff.

—*Museum Carolino-Augusteum.

Katalog über die in der Bibliothek des städtischen Museums Carolino-Augusteum vorhandenen Salisburgensia (Beilage zum Jahresbericht). Salzburg 1870. 117 pp. p. 98-109: Alphabetical list of mss. No shelf marks. (DLC)

—Stiftsbibliothek St. Peter. Some mss. were sold.

Katalog der Handschriften des Stiftes St. Peter in Salzburg, by P. Augustin Jungwirth (1910-12). Arranged alphabetically. Centuries not given. 1339 mss.

—Oeffentliche Studienbibliothek.

Standortskatalog und Signaturenkonkordanz der Handschriften (1946). 1003 mss.

Fachgruppen-Katalog der Hss. Sammlung der Oeffentlichen Studienbibliothek zu Salzburg. 1 typed vol. Arranged by subjects and chronologically.

Zettelkasten (1924). Alphabetical card index.

*Salzwedel, East Germany.

Herm. Hempel, *Die Handschriften und alten Drucke der Gymnasialbibliothek zu Salzwedel.* progr. Salzwedel 1878. 20 pp. p. 2-7: 13 mss. of which nos. 1-3 (p. 2) are Latin. No index. (Erlangen, University Library).

San Candido — Innichen, Italy. Biblioteca Collegiata (Stiftsbibliothek). See Wickhoff.

J. Rubió y Balaguer, 'Investigacions Lulianes en la Biblioteca de Innichen,' *Institut d'Estudis Catalans, Anuari* V (1913-14) 1915, pt. II, p. 742-745.

The same, 'Los códices Lulianos de la Biblioteca de Innichen (Tirol),' *Revista de filología española* IV (1917) 303-40. 14 mss.

L. Ferrari, 'Doctor Nicolaus Pol, la Collegiata di S. Candido ed i suoi Incunaboli.' *Atti del Reale Istituto Veneto di Scienze, Lettere ed Arti* XCVI (1936-37), pt. 2, p. 109-169.

M. Fisch, *Nicolaus Pol Doctor 1494. With a Critical Text of his Guaiac Tract.* Edited with a Translation by Dorothy M. Schullian. New York (1947). 246 pp. p. 135-235: 'Inclusive List of Books and Manuscripts known to have belonged to Nicolaus Pol.' Describes several mss., and manuscript parts bound with incunabula, in S. Candido.

Anna Maria Stua, *I manoscritti latini della Biblioteca Capitolare di S. Candido (Innichen).* Thesis, Università Cattolica, Milan. Discusses 28 mss.

Catalogus librorum bibliothecae Collegii Inticensis, by C. Standacher and A. Bergmann (1898). 65 mss. Does not indicate the ms. parts bound with incunabula.

*San Daniele, Italy. See Blume; Mazzatinti III. Some mss. were stolen in 1948.

*San Francisco, California, U.S.A. See De Ricci.

*Sangerhausen, East Germany. See *Archiv* XI.

San Gimignano, Italy. Biblioteca Comunale.

Inventario-Manoscritti. 1 ms. folder. Sketchy. Shelf marks do not correspond.

*Sankt Florian, Austria. Augustiner-Chorherren Stift.

A. Czerny, *Die Handschriften der Stiftsbibliothek St. Florian.* Linz 1871. 334 pp. 732 mss.

Nachtrag zum Handschriftenkatalog (1932). 1 typed vol. Describes ca. 150 mss. acquired since 1871, mostly late, supplementing the printed catalogue. (micr. at DLC)

*Sankt Gallen, Switzerland. See *Archiv* V; IX; Bruckner; Buchon; J. Clark; Esposito; Gercken; Halm; Stelling-Michaud; *Traditio* XIV.

—*Stiftsarchiv.

(Pfävers collection). See *Archiv* IX 593-599; Bruckner; *Inventare.*

**Verzeichnis der Pfäverser Hss.*, by G. Scherrer. 1 ms. vol. 30 mss.

—*Stiftsbibliothek.

Verzeichnis der Handschriften der Stiftsbibliothek von St. Gallen. (By G. Scherer). Halle 1875. 650 pp. 1725 mss.

—*Vadianische Bibliothek.

Verzeichniss der Manuscripte und Incunabeln der Vadianischen Bibliothek in St. Gallen. (By G. Scherer). St. Gall 1864. xiii, 352 pp. p. 1-138: c. 500 mss. Index (p. viiff.).

Sankt Georgenberg, Austria. See Fiecht.

***Sankt Paul im Lavanttal**, Austria. Stiftsbibliothek. See *Serapeum* XII; Wickhoff.

F. X. Kraus, 'Die Schätze St. Blasiens in der Abtei St. Paul in Kärnten,' *Zeitschrift für die Geschichte des Oberrheins* N.F. IV (1889) 46-68. Lists some mss. (p. 50-63). No index. (NN)

A. Trende, 'Die Stiftsbibliothek in St. Paul,' *Carinthia I: Geschichtliche und volkskundliche Beiträge zur Heimatkunde Kärntens, Mitteilungen des Geschichtsvereins für Kärnten* CXLII (1952) 609-668. p. 649ff.: Mss. No shelf marks. No index. (NN)

Catalogus codicum manuscriptorum ex monasteriis S. Blasii in nigra silva et Hospitalis ad Pyrhum montem in Austria nunc in monast. S. Pauli in Carinthia. Mss. A 1-90; B 1-291; C 1-126; D 1-376 (micr. at DLC.)

Sankt Pölten, Austria. Bischöfl. Alumnats-Bibliothek (des Priesterseminars). Typed list of 197 mss. and edd.

San Marino, California, U.S.A. See De Ricci.

San Severino, Italy. See Mazzatinti XVI.

***Santander**, Spain.

M. Artigas, *Catálogo de los manuscritos de la Biblioteca Menéndez y Pelayo.* Santander (1930). 447 pp. 377 mss. Index. Mostly Spanish mss. (NNC). Also (up to ms. no. 376 and without index) in: *Boletín de la Biblioteca Menéndez y Pelayo* IV (1922) 85-96; 185-92; 282-88; 378-84; V (1923) 77-96; 173-96; 289-92; 375-88; VI (1924) 87-104; 187-200; 280-96; VII (1925) 105-12; 200-08; 293-304; 424-32; VIII (1926) 85-96; 185-92; 264-88; 364-84; IX (1927) 81-96; 275-88; 376-84; X (1928) 164-92; 267-88; 375-410; XI (1929) 67-96; 168-88; 340-47. (NN)

***Santiago** (Compostela), Spain. See Fransen.

***Santo Domingo de la Calzada**, Spain. See Leclercq.

Saragossa, See Zaragoza.

***Sarnano**, Italy.

G. Abate, 'Antichi manoscritti ed incunaboli dell' ex-biblioteca O.F.M. Conv. di S. Francesco ora Biblioteca Comunale di Sarnano (Marche),' *Miscellanea Francescana* XLVII (1947) 478-529. p. 484-522: Lists 76 older mss., omitting many later mss. (p. 522). No index.

***Sarnen**, Switzerland. Bibliothek des Kollegiums. See Bruckner; Wickhoff (under Muri-Gries).

***Sárospatak**, Hungary.

*Card catalogue. (Communication of Dr. H. Hajdu)

Sarzana, Italy. Biblioteca comunale.

Esposizione Circondariale di Spezia 1887. Indice delle più importanti pergamene storiche, dei codici e dei libri antichi d'amministrazione che si conservano nell' Archivio Comunale di Sarzana. (Sarzana 1887). 10 pp. 28 mss. No index. (IU)

Mostra delle Antichità di Luni e dell' Archivio Storico della Città di Sarzana: Indice delle più importanti pergamene storiche, dei diplomi, codici e libri antichi d'amministrazione che si conservano nell' Archivio Comunale di Sarzana. (Sarzana) 1949. 6 unnumbered pp. 20 mss.

Catalogo della Biblioteca Comunale di Sarzana (1899). 1 ms. vol. Contains 2 sections on mss.

*Card index (Communication of the librarian).

***Sassari**, Italy. Biblioteca Universitaria. See Mazzatinti LXXIII.

*Card index (AB I 5-6 p. 103).

***Sassuolo**, Italy. See Mazzatinti XIV.

***Saumur**, France. See France, *Catalogue Général, Départements* XX.

Savignano, Italy. Biblioteca dell' Accademia dei Filopatridi (Rubiconia). See Mazzatinti I. Some mss. were lost during the last war.

Savona, Italy. Biblioteca Civica. See *Giornale* II.

Comune di Savona, Mostra codici, pergamene, incunabuli, libri antichi. (Savona) 1950. Unpaged. Exhibition catalogue.

Manoscritti. Alphabetical card index in 2 bound vols.

*Schaffhausen, Switzerland. See Bruckner; Haenel (supplement); Halm.

(*Bibliotheca Ministerii Sacri Scaphusiensis* . . . [Schaffhausen] 1820. 148 pp. p. 3-13: 113 mss. No index. British Museum).

H. Boos, *Die Handschriften der Ministerialbibliothek zu Schaffhausen.* Schaffhausen 1877. viii, 15 pp. 148 mss. No index. (MH)

Verzeichnis der Inkunabeln und Handschriften der Schaffhauser Stadtbibliothek (by H. Boos). Schaffhausen 1903. 157 pp. p. 65-105: 'Verzeichnis der Handschriften.' 105 mss. and local material. Index (p. 106-07).

*Schlägl, Austria.

G. Vielhaber and G. Indra, *Catalogus codicum Plagensium manuscriptorum.* Linz 1918. 417 pp. 269 mss.

Schlettstadt, see **Sélestat**.

*Schleusingen, East Germany.

G. Weicker, *Nachricht über die Geschichte der Bibliothek des Hennebergischen Gymnasiums zu Schleusingen.* progr. Schleusingen, Meiningen, 1878. 17, 24 pp. Mentions a few mss. No index. (Erlangen, University Library).

*Schlierbach, Austria. See *Xenia Bernardina.*

*Schneeberg, East Germany.

E. Heydenreich, 'Mitteilungen aus den Handschriften der alten Schneeberger Lyceymsbibliothek,' in *Festschrift des Königlichen Gymnasiums mit Realklassen zu Schneeberg durch welche zu der am 30. Oktober stattfindenden Einweihung des Neuen Schulgebäudes... einladet Prof. Dr. Walther Gilbert, Rektor* (progr. Schneeberg 1891; X, 79 pp.) p. 40-48. (Heidelberg, University Library; partial micr. at NNC)

The same, 'Mitteilungen zur sächsisch-thüringischen Geschichte aus den Handschriften der alten Schneeberger Lyceumsbibliothek,' *Neues Archiv für sächsiche Geschichte und Altertumskunde* XIII (1892) 91-107.

*Schwaz, Austria. Franziskanerkloster. See Wickhoff.

*Card index. (Communication of the librarian)

*Schweidnitz, see Świdnica.

*Schweinfurt, West Germany. Stadtbibliothek.

*Verzeichnis der Handschriften der Stadtbibliothek Schweinfurt. 322 mss. of which 11 are Latin mss. before 1600 (Communication of the librarian). List of 11 Latin mss. kindly supplied by the Librarian.

*Schwerin, East Germany. See under **Rostock**.

*Sebenico, see Šibenik.

*Sedan, France. See France, *Catalogue Général, Départements* XIII.

*Segorve, Spain. See Villanueva.

Segovia, Spain. Biblioteca de la Catedral. See Fransen; Haenel.

Typed catalogue, by Don Cristino Valverde. 100 mss. Not yet complete (1955).

*Seilhac, France. See France, *Catalogue Général, Départements* XX.

*Seitenstetten, Austria, Stiftsbibliothek. See *Archiv* VI; Wolkan.

J. Chmel, 'Bericht über eine im Jahre 1831 unternommene kleine Reise zum Behufe der Oesterr. Geschichts-Quellen-Sammlung,' *Oesterreichische Zeitschrift für Geschichts- und Staatskunde* II (1836) 369-371; 376; 379-380; 383-384; 388; 392; 395-396; 404; 407-408. Gives excerpts from the handwritten catalogue of mss. in Seitenstetten. 52 mss. No index. (MH)

Codicum Manuscriptorum Bibliothecae Seitenstettensis tomus I (mss. 1-200) and *tomus II* (mss. 201-305; index). (micr. at DLC)

Sélestat (Schlettstadt), France. Bibliothèque Municipale. See France, *Catalogue Général, Départements* III (Quarto Series).

Catalogue des Manuscrits de la Bibliothèque de Sélestat. A pack of ms. folders, arranged by subjects. More complete than the printed catalogue.

*Semur, France. See France, *Catalogue Général, Départements* VI.

*Senigallia, Italy. See Mazzatinti (1887).
**A. Menchetti, *I codici del Vescovado di Sinigaglia dei secoli XIV e XV*. Iesi 1910. 26 pp.
The same, 'L'Antico Archivio dei Vescovi di Sinigaglia,' *Atti e Memorie della R. Deputazione di Storia Patria per le Marche* N.S. X (1915) 125-130. Not a catalogue. Mostly charters.

*Senlis, France. See France, *Catalogue Général, Départements* XXIV.

*Sens. France. See France, *Catalogue Général, Départements* VI; XLIII; Martin.

*Seo de Urgel, Spain. Biblioteca Capitular. See Beer (Section A); Cordoliani; Kehr (Section A); Leclercq; Villanueva.

Breve summarium librorum Antichorum (sic) *manuscriptorum in Archivio publico Domus Capitularis ... Capituli sedis Urgellitanae reconditorum et per me fratrem Guillermum Costa ... extractorum, die 2 aprilis 1660*. Lists 157 mss.

*Serra San Quirico, Italy. See Mazzatinti I. Many mss. were sold in 1912.
V. Fanelli, *La Biblioteca Comunale di Serra San Quirico*. Serra San Quirico 1954. 22 pp. Lists about 30 mss. that remain (p. 11), and those that were sold (p. 19-22). (DLC)

*Sessa Aurunca, Italy. See Mazzatinti (1887).

Sevilla, Spain. See *Anuario* II; *Archiv* VIII; Haenel; *Neues Archiv* VI.
—Biblioteca Colombina.
Cl. Boutelou, 'Códices ilustrados de la Biblioteca Colombina,' *Museo Español de Antigüedades* I (1872) 149-62. 4 liturgical mss.
(Sección Colombina). *Indice de todos los Codices Manuscriptos que se conservan en la Biblioteca de la Santa Patriarchal Yglesia de Sevilla, D. D. Didacus de Galvez direxit (1780), Rafael Tabares scripsit*. Alphabetical. Apparently the basis of Haenel's list who lists only a part of this collection and does not give the actual shelf marks.
Card index in 1 box.

(Sección Capitular). *Catálogo de Manuscritos de la Capitular*. 1 typed vol., arranged by subjects. Shelf marks incomplete.
Card index in 5 boxes. Alphabetical.
—Biblioteca Universitaria.
Card index in 4 boxes.

*Sheffield, England. Ruskin Museum.
A Descriptive Catalogue of the Library and Print Room of The Ruskin Museum, Sheffield. London 1890. Preface signed by W. White. XII, 95 pp. p. 1-7: 7 mss. (NN)
L. Bron, 'Un nouvel homiliaire en écriture Wisigothique,' *Hispania Sacra* II (1949) 147-191.

*Shrewsbury, England.
S. Leighton, 'The Early Manuscripts belonging to Shrewsbury School,' *Transactions of the Shropshire Archaeological and Natural History Society*, 2nd Series, vol. IX (1897) 285-308. Includes: J. A. Herbert, 'Catalogue of the Early Manuscripts of Shrewsbury School' (p. 293-304); F. G. Kenyon, 'Report on the Manuscripts of Shrewsbury School' (p. 304-306). 36 mss. No index. (NN)

*Šibenik, Yugoslavia. See Wickhoff.
K. Stošić, 'Rukopisni kodeksi samostana sv. Frane u Šibeniku' (Codices manuscripti monasterii S. Francisci Sibenici), *Croatia Sacra* III (1933) 18-61. Describes mss. 1-144 (with gaps). No index. (DDO)

Siena, Italy. Biblioteca Comunale. See *Archiv* XII; *Studi Italiani* XI.
L. Ilari, *La Biblioteca Pubblica di Siena disposta secondo le materie*. 7 vols., Siena 1844-48. A subject catalogue. No index. Mss. are listed among the printed books. Hard to use. Not complete.
N. Terzaghi, 'De codibus latinis philologicis qui Senis in Bibliotheca publica adservantur,' *Bullettino Senese di storia patria* X (1903) 392-410. (NN)
Inventario dei Manoscritti. 3 vols. (Cf. AB V 98). Vol. I: A I 1 - E IX 25 (over 1000 mss.). Vol. II: F I 1 - J XI 57 (nearly 1500 mss.). Vol. III: K I 1 - Z II 38 (over 1000 mss.).

Inventario dei Manoscritti, Appendice. 4 ms. vols. Vol. I: A I 1 - A XI 47. Vol. II: B I 1 - H XI 67. Vol. III: J II 44 - L XI 52. IV: P I₂ 1 - Z₂ I 1. (Cf. AB V 98).

*Card index for *Appendice* in 6 boxes (AB V 98).

—Biblioteca Piccolomini.

Has a few liturgical mss.

—Convento dell' Osservanza.

E. Bulletti, 'Il Museo « Aurelio Castelli » dell' Osservanza,' *Rassegna d'Arte Senese* XVII (1924) 32-54. Lists 15 mss. and a few Codici Bernardiniani (p. 34-51). (NN)

The same, *Il Convento dell' Osservanza (Siena): Cenni storici e guida.* Florence 1925. 72 pp. p. 39-59: Mss.

V. Doucet, 'Cinq manuscrits dominicains conservés au couvent de l'Observance de Sienne,' *Antonianum* VIII (1933) 229-234. 5 mss. (NNUT)

Breve Inventario dei manoscritti dell' Osservanza (by P. M. B., that is, Martino Bertagna, 1953). Handwritten list of 57 mss. Not complete.

*Sigmaringen**, West Germany. Some mss. were sold.

(W. Wattenbach, 'Beschreibung einiger Handschriften der fürstlich hohenzollern'-schen Bibliothek in Sigmaringen,' *Anzeiger für Kunde der deutschen Vorzeit* N. F. XIV [1867] 235-39. 5 mss. No index)

Fürstlich Hohenzollern'sches Museum zu Sigmaringen. Verzeichniss der Handschriften, by F. A. Lehner. Sigmaringen 1872. 119 pp. 357 mss.

*Sigüenza**, Spain. Catedral. See Fransen.

J. Rius Serra, 'Inventario de los manuscritos de la Catedral de Sigüenza,' *Hispania Sacra* III (1950) 431-65. *ca.* 100 mss. No index.

*Silos**, Spain. See Grubbs (Section A, under Richardson); Férotin.

Walter Muir Whitewill, Jr., and Justo Pérez de Urbel, 'Los manuscritos del Real Monasterio de Santo Domingo de Silos,' *Boletín de la Real Academia de la Historia* XCV (1929) 521-601. c. 50 mss. Index in Grubbs. (NN)

*Sinigaglia**, see Senigallia.

*Sint Agatha**, Holland. See *Archivum Franciscanum Historicum* XLIX; Lampen.

*Sion**, Switzerland. See Stelling-Michaud; *Traditio* XIV.

—*Archive du Chapître.

Ca. 125 mss. not yet catalogued. (Communication of the archivist)

—*Bibliothèque et Archives Cantonales.

A few ms. books are found in its archival collections and summarily described in their inventories. (Communication of the librarian)

Siracusa, Italy.

Biblioteca Alagoniana. See Blume; Mazzatinti (1887); Rühl.

G. Cannarella, 'La Biblioteca Alagoniana di Siracusa,' *Accademie e Biblioteche d'Italia* I (1928), no. 4, p. 77-83.

The same, *La Biblioteca Alagoniana e il suo fondatore.* Siracusa 1929. 20 pp. p. 16-17: Mss. No shelf marks.

Indice dei Libri della Pubblica Biblioteca del Vescovil Seminario di Siracusa, by Vinc. Bajona (1843). Includes: 'Mss. preziosi della Libreria del Vescovile Seminario di Siracusa,' 22 mss. 'Mss. di data recente della Libreria del Vescovile Seminario di Siracusa' (this last section arranged alphabetically).

*Sitten**, see **Sion**.

*Skara**, Sweden.

C. Nordenfalk, *Romanska bokmålningar i Skara stiftsbibliotek* (Göteborgs högskolas årsskrift 47, 20). Göteborg 1941. 31 pp. and plates.

*Skokloster**. See under Stockholm.

*Slawuta**, see under **Krakow**.

Soest, West Germany. Stadtbibliothek. See *Archiv* XI; Lehmann.

Catalog der Handschriften der Stadtbibliothek (by Vogeler and Kindervater, 1896-1949). 1 folder of typed sheets. 90 mss.

Card index.

*Sofia**, Bulgaria. Narodna Biblioteka 'Wassil Kolarow.'

Typed list of 5 Latin mss. kindly supplied by the librarian.

*Soissons, France. See France, *Catalogue Général, Départements* III; XLIII.

Solothurn, Switzerland. Zentralbibliothek. See Haenel (supplement); Sinner.

A. Schönherr, *Verklungene Welten: Was alte Handschriften der Zentralbibliothek Solothurn erzählen.* Solothurn 1954. 22 pp. Lists some mss.

Zentralbibliothek Solothurn, Mittelalterliche Handschriften (by A. Schönherr). 3 typed vols.

Standortskatalog. Very summary.

*Solsona, Spain. See Cordoliani; Villanueva.

*Soria, Spain. See Fransen.

**T. Rojo, *Revista Eclesiástica* I (1929) 196-219. Lists 34 mss.

*Sorrento, Museo Correale.

Elenco dei manoscritti antichi. Typed list of 17 mss. kindly supplied by the librarian.

*Sovetsk, USSR.

**H. Pöhlmann, *Nachricht über die auf der Lehrerbibliothek des kgl. Gymnasiums zu Tilsit vorhandenen Handschriften und alten Drucke.* progr. Tilsit 1875. 36 pp.

*Speyer, West Germany. Staatliches Gymnasium.

Catalog der Lyceumsbibliothek zu Speier. 2 vols. Speyer 1866-73. Vol. I, p. 3-6: 15 mss.

*Split (Spalato), Yugoslavia. See Wickhoff.

Spoleto, Italy. Biblioteca Comunale.

*Inventario dei manoscritti (Communication of the librarian). Card index.

*Stams, Austria. See Wickhoff; *Xenia Bernardina*; Zingerle.

*Stargard, Poland. See *Archiv* XI.

Jo. Carl Conr. Oelrich, *Historisch-Diplomatische Beyträge zur litterarischen Geschichte, fürnehmlich des Herzogthums Pommern*... 2 pts. Berlin 1790. pt. 1 p. 121-34: 'Catalogus codicum Msctorum Bibliothecae Marianae Stargardensis.' 51 mss. No index. (NjP)

T. Pyl, *Die Rubenow-Bibliothek* (Greifswald 1865, see above under Greifswald) p. 178-179: Lists 15 mss. after Oelrichs.

R. Kuhnke, *Bericht über die auf der Bibliothek des Königlichen und Gröning'schen Gymnasiums zu Stargard in Pommern vorhandenen* . . . *Handschriften und alten Drucke.* progr. Stargard 1877. 37 pp. p. 5-9: 51 Latin mss. No index (Erlangen, University Library).

*Stari, Yugoslavia. See Kos.

*Staten Island, New York, U.S.A. See De Ricci.

*Stendal, East Germany. See under Halle.

*Sterzing, see Vipiteno.

*Stettin, see Szczecin.

*Stirling, Scotland. See Frere.

Stockholm, Sweden. See *Archives* IV; Barwiński; Collijn; Dudik, *Forschungen*; Hipler; Högberg; Institut de Recherches; Lampen; Leclercq; Lehmann; Malin.

—Kungl. Biblioteket.

G. P. Lilieblad, *Ecloga sive catalogus librorum tum MS.orum tum Impressorum Hispanici praesertim Idiomatis, quibus Regiam Bibliothecam Stockholmensem adauxit Vir Illustris Joh. Gabriel Sparfwenfeldt.* Stockholm 1706. 96 pp. p. 3-14: mss. No shelf marks. No index. (Stockholm.)

L. Hammarsköld, 'Försök till en Bibliografi öfver de Manuscripter och Litterära Rariteter som finnas i det Kongl. Allmänna Biblioteket i Stockholm,' *Lyceum* II (1811) 155-180. Lists some mss. No shelf marks. (NN)

Handlingar ur Hans Excellence, Stats-Ministerus, m.m. Herr Grefve L. v. Engeströms Bibliothek. 4 parts, Stockholm 1809-24. Pt. IV (1824): *Förtekning öfver Handkrifts-Samlingen uti Hans Excellence, Stats-Ministern, Academie-Canzlern, m.m. Herr Grefve L. v. Engeströms Bibliothek.* VIII, 150 pp. No shelf marks. No index. (Ct Y)

G. Stephens, *Förteckning öfver de förnämsta Brittiska och Fransyska Handskrifterna uti Kongl. Biblitheket i Stockholm.* Stockholm 1847. XII, 205 pp. No shelf marks. *Öfversigt af Utställningen i Visningssalen* (Kongl. Bibliothekets Handlingar VII).

Stockholm 1885. IV, 58 pp. Exhibition catalogue. No shelf marks. No index.

O. Wieselgren, 'Manoscritti Italiani esistenti nella Regia Biblioteca di Stoccolma,' *Primo Congresso Mondiale delle Biblioteche e di Bibliografia*, Rome and Venice 1929, *Atti* III (Rome 1931) 227-38. Lists several Latin mss. No index.

The same article also in *Nordisk Tidskrift för Bok- och Biblioteksväsen* XVI (1929) 94-103.

Catalogue of an Exhibition of Medieval Illuminated Manuscripts in the Royal Library at Stockholm. Stockholm 1933. 15 pp. 46 mss. No shelf marks. No index. (Morgan Library)

Kungl. Bibliotheket, Stockholm, Handskriften. Inventory on loose in sheets in 82 boxes, arranged by subjects, not by shelf marks. The following are of special interest: 13. Ekonomi, Filosofi. 14. Fornkunskap. 21-22. Historia. 32-33. Kyrkohistoria. 41. Kyrkolag. 42. Litteraturhistoria, Magi, Matematik, Astronomi. 43. Medicin. 44. Naturwetenskap. 45. Polygrafer. 57. Undervisning. 75. Klassiska författare. Krigsvetenskap. Kyrkohistoria. 72. Historia Ital. Sp(anish). Portug. 73. Historia Fr(ench). Engl. Nederl. Ty. 74. Historia Ry o Fi. Österl. Amer. 76. Lag. 77. Vitterhet. 79-82. Codices theologici medii aevi.

Signaturschema för Kungl. Bibliothekets handskriftsavdelning. 1 typed folder.

Översikt av Handskriftsavdelningens realkatalog. A table of contents of the large inventory, posted in the loan room.

Alfabetiskt Index till Handskriftskatalogen. A large card index.

—Riksarkivet. Collection of Skokloster, property of Friherre Rutger von Essen and deposited in the Riksarkivet.

Jo. H. Schröder, *Catalog öfver Manuscripterna . . . i Grefliga Braheska Bibliotheket på Skokloster*, with: *Handlingar rörande Skandinaviens Historia* XII-XV (1825-30). 116 pp. 397 mss. and documents. No index. (NN)

Catalog öfver manuscripterna m.m.i biblioteket på Skokloster. 2 vols. I: Fol. 1-228; Qu. 1-155; Oct. 1-29. II: Letters.

*Stonyhurst College, England. See Great Britain, *Historical Manuscripts Commission*; Schenkl.

Storrington, England. See under **Redlynch House** near Salisbury.

Strahov, Czechoslovakia. See Praha.

*Stralsund, East Germany. Stadtbibliothek. See *Archiv* XI; Dudik, *Forschungen.*

Die Bibliothek der Nikolai-Kirche in Stralsund. Preface signed by F. B. Droysen. (Stralsund) 1817. 48 pp. p. 17ff.: 28 mss. (microfilm at NNC)

T. Pyl, *Die Rubenow-Bibliothek* (Greifswald 1865, see above under Greifswald). p. 178: Lists 28 mss. after Droysen.

5 mss. were lost during the last war. List of a few additional mss. supplied by the Librarian.

Strängnäs, Sweden. See Dudik, *Forschungen*; Institut de recherches; Lehmann, *Auf der Suche.*

H. Aminson, *Bibliotheca Templi Cathedralis Strengnesensis. Supplementum, continens codices manu scriptos et libros, quos Johannes Matthiae, episcopus Strengnesensis templo dono dedit.* Stockholm 1863. clix pp. Alphabetical list of mss. (p. i-lix and clvii). Shelf marks not always clear ca. 20 mss.

*Strasbourg (Strassburg), France. See *Archiv* VIII; France, *Catalogue Général Départements* XLVII; L.

J. Gass, *Strassburgs Bibliotheken.* Strasbourg 1902. VIII, 82 pp. (DLC)

**The same, *Die Bibliothek des Priesterseminars in Strassburg.* Strasbourg 1902 35 pp.

P. Ristelhuber, 'Catalogue des manuscrit de la Bibliothèque Municipale créée er 1872,' *Bibliographie alsacienne*, 4th serie (1873) 130-140. 45 late mss. (NN)

J. Rathgeber, *Die handschriftlichen Schätz der früheren Strassburger Stadtbibliothek* Gütersloh 1876. viii, 216 pp. A survey not a catalogue. (MH)

*Stresa, Italy. Archivio Rosminiano.

R. Sabbadini, 'Frammenti di poesie volgari musicate,' *Giornale storico della letteratura italiana* XL (1902) 270-272.

The same, 'Un biennio umanistico,' *Giornale storico della letteratura italiana, Supplemento* VI (1903) 74-119. p. 117-118: describes Stresa, cod. 22.

Gianfranco Contini, 'Un manoscritto ferrarese quattrocentesco di scrittura popolareggiante,' *Archivum Romanicum* XXII (1938) 281-319.

Pergamene e Codici. Typed list of 28 mss. Copy kindly supplied by the librarian.

Stuttgart, West Germany.

—*Hauptstaatsarchiv.

Collection J 1-3. 381 nos. Described in a ms. inventory, 2 vols. and 1 index volume. Mostly modern.

Collection A 63 (church affairs). Handwritten inventory. 146 bundles. Contain many letters of the 16th century. (Communication of the archivist)

—Württembergische Landesbibliothek. See *Archiv* I; V; Gercken; Lehmann, *Mitteilungen* I; Löffler; *Neues Archiv* X; XV; *Notizenblatt*; *Serapeum, Intelligenzblatt* 1858-60 (under Zwiefalten); Stälin.

F. D. Gräter, 'Über die Merkwürdigkeiten der Bibliothek des ehemaligen Ritterstiftes Comburg am Kocher,' *Bragur* VIII (1812) 224-375. p. 249-64: 'Handschriften der ehemaligen Comburger Bibliothek (nunmehr in der Königl. Grossen Bibliothek zu Stuttgart befindlich).' 132 mss. No index.

'Gefällige Mittheilung des kön. Bibliothecariats zu Stuttgard an das kön. Bibliothekariat zu Bamberg,' *Isis* 1824, coll. 697-702. Lists Latin classical mss. (NNM)

W. von Heyd, *Die historischen Handschriften der kgl. öffentlichen Bibliothek zu Stuttgart.* 2 vols. in 1, Stuttgart 1889-91. I: Folio 1-753. II: Quarto 1-317; Oktavo 1-87; index for both volumes.

K. Löffler, *Die Handschriften des Klosters Zwiefalten* (Archiv für Bibliographie, Buch- und Bibliothekswesen, Beiheft VI). Linz 1931. 116 pp. 236 mss. now at Stuttgart. Handwritten inventory in 25 vols. (Cf. Born 251). (I): (1a) Biblia; (1b) Breviaria. (II-VIII): (1c) Theol. et Philos. (II): 4º 1-624; 8º 1-191 (probably superseded by vols. (III-VIII); (III-IV): Fol. 1-341; (V-VII): 4º 1-627; (VIII): 8º 1-193. (IX): (2a) Jurid. Fol. 1-301, 4º 1-184; (2b) Mathem. Fol. 1-36, 4º 1-63, 8º 1-26. (X): (3a) Med. et phys. Fol. 1-50, 4º 1-128, 8º 1-30; (3b) Orient.; (3c) Cameralia et Oeconomica. (XI): (4a) Militaria; (4b) Miscellanea. (XII-XIV): (5a) Poetica et Philologica. (XII): Fol. 1-91. (XIII): 4º 1-185. (XIV): 4º 186-203; 8º 1-75. (XV-XVI): (5 b and c) Musica. (XVII-XXI): (6) Historica. 'Fortsetzung des gedruckten Katalogs'. (XVII-XVIII): Fol. 754-998. (XIX-XX): 4º 318-579. (XXI): 8º 88-198. (XXII-XXV): 'Handschriften ehemals im Besitze der Kgl. Hofbibliothek.' (XXII): Codices ascetici (Hb I 1-249), biblici (II 1-60), dogmatici et polemici (III 1-59). (XXIII): Codices hermeneutici (Hb IV 1-36), historici (V 1-105), iuridici et politici (VI 1-139), Patres (VII 1-71). (XXIV): Codices philologici (Hb VIII 1-30), arabici (IX), philosophici (X 1-30), physic., medic., mathem. etc. (XI 1-56), Poetae (XII 1-23), Poetae germanici (XIII), Vitae Sanctorum (XIV 1-28), Codices Wirtembergici (XV 1-124), militares (XVI 1), musici (XVII). (XXV): Codices musici continued.

Typed notes taken by Mme Vernet in 1951 are available at the Institut de Recherches et d'Histoire des Textes, Paris.

*Verzeichnis der in den Stuttgarter Bibliotheken vorhandenen mittelalterlichen Rechtshandschriften, by Emil Seckel (1899). 266 single sheets plus 4 sheets introd. and index. Ms. hist. 4º 522. (Communication from S. Kuttner, based on information received from Dr. Thomas Miller; cf. Genzmer, *Zeitschrift der Savigny-Stiftung, Rom. Abt.* XLVII [1927] p. 381).

*Subiaco, Italy. See *Archiv* XII; Mazzatinti I.
I Monasteri di Subiaco. 2 vols. Rome 1904.
II: V. Federici, *La Biblioteca e l'Archivio.*
lxxxi, 467 pp. p. 1-16; 357-59: 380 mss.
Index (p. 411-12). (DLC)
*Sucha, Poland. The mss. are now in War-
saw (Archive) and Wroclaw (Ossolineum).
J. C., 'Rękopisy biblioteki hr. Branickich w
Suchej,' *Przewodnik bibliograficzny* XXXI
(1908) 146-48; 170-71; 194-96; 232-33;
294-95; XXXII (1909) 26-28; 48-50; 72-
73; 94-95; 121-22; 145-46; 169-71; 196-97;
228-29; 253-55; 282-83; XXXIII (1910)
23-24; 44-45; 70-71; 96-97; 119-21; 142-
143. 546 mss. Mostly modern. No index.
(NN) Also published separately. Cracow
1910. 86 pp. (Cracow, Biblioteka Jagel-
lonska)
*Sulmona, Italy. See Mazzatinti VI.
*Suzzara, Italy. Biblioteca Capilupi. See
Andres.
G. Capilupi, *Catalogo dei manoscritti della
Biblioteca Capilupi.* Typed thesis, University of Padua, 1950. 79 mss.
*Świdnica, Poland.
Aug. Friede, *Verzeichniss der in der Gymna-
sial-Bibliothek befindlichen Handschriften
und älteren Druckschriften.* progr. Schweid-
nitz 1877. 40 pp. p. 20-25: 7 Latin mss.
No index. (MH)
*Szczecin (Stettin), Poland. See *Archiv* XI.
—Wojewódzka i Miejska Biblioteka Publicz-
na.
The library has some mss. of the former
Marienstiftgymnasium. List kindly sup-
plied by the librarian. The other mss.
are scattered or lost.
H. Lemcke, *Die Handschriften und alten
Drucke der Bibliothek des Marienstift-Gym-
nasiums.* progr. Stettin 1879. 54 pp. p. 1-
44: 42 mss. from Cammin. No index. (NIC)
*Szombathely, Hungary. See Radó.
—*Egyaházmegyei Könyvtár.
**G. Palinkas, 'A szombathelyi székesegy-
házi Könyvtár régi Kéziratainak és ös-
nyomtatványainak jegyzéke,' *A vasme-
gyei régészeti egylet évkönyve* XIX-XX

(1891-92) 10-44.
—*Ferencs-Rendház Könyvtára (Francis-
can Library). It received in 1919 the mss.
formerly preserved at the Franciscan Li-
brary in Bratislava.
J. Csontosi, 'A Pozsonyi Sz. Ferencziek
Tartományi Könyvtáránák Codexei,'
Magyar Könyvszemle III (1878) 45-54.
22 mss. No index. (MiU)
*Tallinn (Reval), Estonia.
**G. von Hansen, *Die Codices manuscripti
und gedruckten Bücher der Revaler Stadt-
bibliothek.* Tallinn 1893.
*Tambach, West Germany. See *Serapeum*
V and *Intelligenzblatt 1864.*
*Taranto, Italy.
**C. Drago, 'Su alcuni manoscritti esistenti
nella Civica Biblioteca "P. Acclavio",'
Taras VI (1931) 1-4.
*Tarascon, France. See France, *Cata-
logue Général, Départements* XIV.
Tarazona, Spain. Biblioteca de la Catedral.
See Fransen; Leclercq.
Typed catalogue, by Canon Julian Ruiz.
Mss. no. 1-172 (with some gaps). Not
complete (1955). (Seen at the Instituto
Flores, Madrid)
*Tarragona, Spain. See *Anuario* II; Cor-
doliani; Villanueva; Volger.
J. Serra Vilaró, 'Archivo y Libreria capi-
tulares de la Santa Metropolitana Iglesia
de Tarragona, Primada de las Españas,'
Boletín Arqueológico, Ser. IV, vol. XLIV
(1944) 105-135. Not a catalogue. (DLC)
—Biblioteca Provincial.
J. López de Toro, *Contribución al conoci-
miento de la Biblioteca Provincial de Tarra-
gona.* Tarragona 1936. 222 pp. p. 148-91:
245 mss (NN)
*Libro Registro de Codices, cartularios y
demas manuscriptos.* Pt. 1 lists 171 mss.
(Communication of D. P. Lockwood.)
*Tartu, USSR. Tartu Riikliku Ülikooli
Pearaamatukogu. See Clossius.
List of 17 Latin mss. kindly supplied by the
librarian.
*Taunton, England.
N. R. Ker, 'Four medieval Manuscripts

in the Taunton Castle Museum,' *Proceedings of the Somersetshire Archaeological and Natural History Society* XCVI (1951, published 1952) 224-228. (NN)

*Tenbury, England.
Edmund H. Fellowes, *The Catalogue of Manuscripts in the Library of St. Michael's College, Tenbury.* Paris 1934. 319 pp. 1386 mss., all musical compositions. (DLC)

*Teplá Klášter (Tepl), Czechoslovakia. Krajská vědecká a studijní Knihovna.
Beiträge zur Geschichte des Stiftes Tepl. I. Zum 700 jährigen Todestage des seligen Hroznata, des Gründers der Klöster Tepl und Chotieschau (Marienbad 1917), pt. II, p. 83-114: M. Nentwich, 'Verzeichnis der Handschriften in der Bibliothek des Stiftes Tepl, Erster Teil.' 192 mss. p. 118-29: W. Vacek, 'Die Choralhandschriften des Stiftes Tepl.' *II. Festschrift zur 25 jährigen Abtfeier Sr. Gnaden des hochwürdigsten Herrn Prälaten Dr. Gilbert Helmer* (Marienbad 1925), p. 205-58: Nentwich, 'Verzeichnis..., Zweiter Teil.' Mss. no. 193-660. No index. (British Museum; reprints at NNC)

*Terlizzi, Italy. See Mazzatinti VI.
Terni, Italy. Biblioteca Comunale. See Mazzatinti (1887).
Inventario dei manoscritti. 252 nos. (Communication of the librarian; cf. AB V 425).

*Tetschen, see **Děčín**.
*Thiers, France. See France, *Catalogue Général, Départements* XIII.
Thorn, see **Toruń**.
*Tilsit, see Sovetsk.
*Titusville, Pennsylvania, U.S.A. See De Ricci. See also under Princeton.
*Todi, Italy.
L. Leonij, *Inventario dei codici della Comunale di Todi.* (Todi 1878). xx, 103 pp. 229 mss. (MH)
List of 4 additional Latin mss. kindly supplied by the librarian.

*Tokyo, Japan. See Weiss.
*Toledo, Ohio, U.S.A. See De Ricci.
Toledo, Spain. See *Archiv* VIII; Carini; Haenel; Institut de Recherches; Millares

Carlo; Millás Vallicrosa; *Revista*; Octavio de Toledo.
—Biblioteca del Cabildo.
A. López and L. M. Núñez, 'Descriptio Codicum Franciscalium Bibliothecae Ecclesiae Primatialis Toletanae,' *Archivo Ibero-Americano* I (1914) 369-90; 542-63; III (1915) 88-103; VII (1917) 255-81; XI (1919) 72-91; XII (1919) 390-409; XIII (1920) 81-96. 143 mss. No index. (NN)
A. Cordoliani, 'Les manuscrits de comput ecclésiastique de la Bibliothèque Capitulaire de Tolède,' *Revista de Archivos, Museos y Bibliotecas* LVIII (1952) 323-52.
MMSS. Biblioteca de la Santa Iglesia de Toledo primada de las Españas (1808). 2 vols. I: Alphabetical catalogue of authors, arranged by first names, and in a second part, by family names. Titles mostly in Spanish. Mss. transferred to Madrid are marked. Printed catalogue by Octavio de Toledo lists only a part of both remaining and transferred mss. II: Catalogue by subjects.
—Biblioteca Provincial.
Cuerpo Facultativo de Archiveros, Bibliotecarios y Arqueólogos. Biblioteca Pública de Toledo. Catálogo de la Colección de Manuscritos Borbon-Lorenzana, by Franc. Esteve Barba. Madrid 1942. 493 pp. 534 mss., mostly late.
A. López, 'Descripción de los manuscritos franciscanos existentes en la Biblioteca Provincial de Toledo,' *Archivo Ibero-Americano* XXV (1926) 49-105; 173-244; 334-82. 78 mss. No index. (NN)
*Tonnerre, France. See France, *Catalogue Général, Départements* VI
Torino, Italy. See *Analecta Bollandiana* XXVIII; *Archiv* V; IX; *Giornale*; Leclercq; Mazzatinti XXVIII; *Neues Archiv*; Reifferscheid; *Serapeum* XXI and *Intelligenzblatt* 1865; Zaccaria, *Iter*.
—Accademia delle Scienze.
F. Patetta, 'Una raccolta manoscritta di versi e prose in morte d'Albiera degli Albizzi,' *Atti della R. Accademia delle*

Scienze di Torino LIII (1917-18) 290-294; 310-328.

The same, 'Di alcuni manoscritti posseduti dalla Reale Accademia delle Scienze di Torino,' *Ibid.* 543-559; 631-653; 903-932.

The same, 'Di un manoscritto dei Trionfi e dei Sonetti del Petrarca posseduto dalla R. Accademia delle Scienze di Torino,' *Ibid.* LXX (1934-35) 283-297.

Card index in 2 boxes, arranged alphabetically by authors and subjects.

New list of mss., with changed shelf marks. 398 mss.

—Archivio di Stato.

Catalogo del Museo storico dell' Archivio di Stato in Torino. Preface signed by P. Vayra. Turin 1881. 62 pp. p. 55-62: 31 mss. No shelf marks. No index. (Vatican Library; microfilm at NNC)

C. Cipolla, 'Notizia di alcuni Codici dell' antica Biblioteca Novaliciense,' *Memorie della Reale Accademia delle Scienze di Torino,* Ser. II vol. XLIV (1894), *Classe di Scienze Morali, Storiche e Filologiche,* 193-242.

The same, 'Codici sconosciuti della Biblioteca Novaliciense,' *Ibid.* L (1901) 137-52. 3 mss.

Indice dei Manoscritti cartacei e membranacei, delle stampe in pergamena e del secolo XV esistenti nella Biblioteca dei Regii Archivi di Corte (1840). Arranged alphabetically. Centuries not given.

Inventario della Raccolta Mongardino. Card index, arranged by subjects.

—Biblioteca Civica.

Inventario manoscritti. Mss. 1-163; 301-447. Centuries not given (Cf. AB IV 175).

The Fondo Bosio (*ca.* 150 mss.) has no inventory.

—Biblioteca del Duca di Genova. Most of the mss. are now deposited in the Biblioteca Del Re.

Biblioteca del Duca di Genova, Catalogo dei Manoscritti. Alphabetical. 2 vols. I: A-M. II: M-Z (seen at the Biblioteca del Re through the kindness of Dottoressa Marina Bersano).

Elenco dei Manoscritti della Biblioteca Du-

cale. 2 typed sheets (seen at the Biblioteca del Re).

—Biblioteca del Re.

Militari. 1 box of ms. sheets (by Promis). 428 mss.

Miscellanea Patria Manoscritti. 3 ms. vols. Arranged by subjects.

(Miscellanea Vernazza). *Manoscritti e Stampati Vernazza.* 1 box of ms. sheets. Arranged alphabetically. Mostly late.

Storia d'Italia. 1 box of ms. sheets (by Promis). 180 mss.

Catalogo dei Manoscritti di Storia Patria della Biblioteca di Sua Maestà (by Promis, 1859). 4 vols. 1169 mss.

Varia. Inventory of ms. sheets in 1 box, (by Promis): 732 mss.

—Biblioteca Nazionale.

A. Avetta, 'Primo contributo di notizie bibliografiche per una bibliografia dei codici manoscritti della Biblioteca Nazionale (già Universitaria) di Torino,' *Centralblatt für Bibliothekswesen* XVI (1899) 168-75; 480-89. For Latin mss. see p. 171-75 and 481-83.

The same, 'Secondo contibuto . . . *Ibid.* XX (1903) 209-21. For Latin mss. see p. 211-16.

J. Pasinus, *Codices manuscripti Bibliothecae Regii Taurinensis Athenaei.* 2 vols. Turin 1749. II, 1-402: 1184 Latin mss. Index (501-30). (NNUT)

Scip. Maffei, *Storia teologica delle dottrine e opinioni corse nei primi cinque secoli della chiesa in proposito della divina grazia, del libero arbitrio e della predestinazione . . .,* in his *Opere* (Venice 1790) XIV-XVII. Vol. XVII p. 325-45: 'Succinta notizia de' manoscritti che si conservano nella libreria di Torino.' (NN)

Amad. Peyron, *Notitia librorum manu typisve descriptorum qui donante Ab. Thoma Valperga-Calusio ; . . illati sunt in R. Taurinensis Athenaei Bibliothecam.* Leipzig 1820. 89 pp. Few Latin mss. (p. 23-24).

*The same, *M. Tullii Ciceronis orationum... fragmenta inedita . . . Idem praefatur de Bibliotheca Bobiensi.* Stuttgart and Tübingen 1824. xxxvii, 228 pp. Lists mss. extant at Turin and in other libraries. No index. (NIC)

G. Ottino, *Codici Bobbiesi nella Biblioteca Nazionale di Torino.* Turin and Palermo 1890. viii, 72 pp. 71 mss. (DLC)

E. Stampini, G. De Sanctis, C. Cipolla and C. Frati, 'Inventario dei codici superstiti greci e latini antichi della Biblioteca Nazionale di Torino,' *Rivista di Filologia* XXXII (1904) 385-588. p. 430-581: Latin mss. No index.

B. Peyron, *Codices Italici manu exarati qui in Bibliotheca Taurinensis Athenaei ante diem XXVI Januarii MCMIV asservabantur* (ed. C. Frati). Turin 1904. XXXII, 690 pp. Mss. N I 1 - P II 23. 976 nos. Most of the mss. were burned in 1904.

C. Cipolla, *Codici Bobbiesi della Biblioteca Nazionale Universitaria di Torino.* Milan 1907. 2 vols. (NN)

G. Vinay, 'Contributo alla identificazione di alcuni manoscritti frammentari della Nazionale di Torino,' *Aevum* XXI (1947) 209-32. Lists 132 mss. Bibliography of catalogues (p. 212).

Appendice al Pasini. 1 ms. vol. arranged by languages and alphabetically. Does not give the new shelf marks, but indicates the extant mss.

—*Museo Civico.

A. Venturi, 'Museo Civico di Torino, Alcune miniature,' *Le Gallerie Nazionali Italiane* III (1897) 160-70. (NN)

—*Seminario Metropolitano. Cf. Leclercq. 'La biblioteca del seminario metropolitano di Torino,' *Accademie e Biblioteche* V (1931) 390-93.

*Handwritten inventory (Communication of Dom J. Leclercq).

Toronto, Ontario, Canada. See De Ricci.

Tortosa, Spain. See Grubbs (Section A, under Richardson); Villanueva.

H. Denifle and E. Chatelain, 'Inventarium codicum manuscriptorum capituli Dertusensis,' *Revue des Bibliothèques* VI (1896) 1-61. 147 mss.

*R. O'Callahan, *Los códices de la Catedral de Tortosa.* Tortosa 1897. 136 pp. (Paris, Bibliothèque Nationale)

The same, *El Archivo y los códices de la Catedral de Tortosa.* Tortosa 1911. 47 pp. Not a catalogue. (MH)

(J. Rubió y Balaguer), 'La Biblioteca del Capítol Catedral de Tortosa,' *Institut d'Estudis Catalans, Anuari* V, 2 (1913-14) 745-57. Mss. no. 148-246. No index.

J. Rubió, 'La Biblioteca Capitular de Tortosa,' *Butlletí de la Biblioteca de Catalunya* V (1918-19) 199-31. Mss. no. 247-59 (p. 128-30). No index.

Toruń (Thorn), Poland. See Aland (Section A); *Archiv* XI.

—Biblioteka Uniwersytecka.

Inwentarz Rękopisów. 1 ms. folder. 861 mss.

Card file. Arranged by subjects.

—Książnica Miejska im. Mikołaja Kopernika.

P. Jaenichius, *Notitia Bibliothecae Thorunensis qua de eius origine et incrementis codicibusque msstis aliisque notatu dignis nonnulla ... exponuntur ...* Jena 1723. 56 pp. 148 mss. (p. 17-35). No index. (NN)

Katalog der Gymnasial-Bibliothek zu Thorn. Torun 1871. 267 pp. p. 261-265: Mss., arranged by subjects. (Torun, City Library)

Katalog der Bibliothek des Königl. Gymnasiums zu Thorn. I. Nachtrag: 1871-1882. Torun 1883. 48 pp. Nothing on mss. — *II. Nachtrag: 1883-1891.* Torun 1892. 38 pp. p. 38: 2 late mss. (Torun, City Library; verified by the librarian)

M. Curtze, *Die Handschriften und seltenen alten Drucke der Gymnasialbibliotheke zu Thorn.* 3 pts. progr. Torun 1875-78. pt. 1, 1875. 40 pp. *Die Handschriften und Incunabeln.* 162 mss. (p. 3-27). Index (p. 34-37). (NIC, microfilm at NNC). pt. 2, 1877. IV, 20 pp. *Das XVI. Jahrhundert und Nachträge.* p. 1-3: Mss. no. 163-183. pt. 3, 1878. 46 pp. Has index for parts 2 and 3 (p. 46). (Erlangen, University Library)

*Toul, France. See France, *Catalogue Général, Départements* XXI.

*Toulon, France. See France, *Catalogue Général, Départements* XIV; XLIII.

*Toulouse, France. See France, *Catalogue Général, Départements* VII (Quarto Series); XLIII; *Universités*.

*Tournai, Belgium. See *Archiv* VIII; *Catalogue général* VI; Haenel.

(A. Wilbaux, *Catalogue de la bibliothèque de la Ville de Tournai*. 4 vols. Tournai 1860-76. I p. 1-138: 245 mss. No index. (I-III: DLC. IV: Vatican Library)

*Tournus, France. See France. *Catalogue Général, Départements* VI; XLIII.

*Tours, France. See France, *Catalogue Général, Départements* XXXVII; *Giornale*; *Notices et Extraits*.

A. Dorange, *Catalogue descriptif et raisonné des Manuscrits de la Bibliothèque de Tours*. Tours 1875. viii, 582 pp. 1503 mss. No index.

The library lost many mss. during the last war.

*Trani, Italy. See Mazzatinti VI; LX.

Trapani, Italy. Biblioteca Fardelliana. See *Studi Italiani* XIII.

F. Mondello, *Bibliografia Trapanese*. Palermo 1876. 491 pp. p. 176-184: 8 mss. No index. (Palermo, Bibl. Naz.)

The same, 'La Biblioteca e la Pinacoteca in Trapani,' *Nuove Effemeridi Siciliane*, Ser. III vol. XII (1881) 223-68. Lists some mss. (234-38). No index. (MH)

The same, *La Biblioteca e la Pinacoteca Fardelliana in Trapani*. Palermo 1882. 53 pp. Lists some mss. (p. 18-22). No index. (Palermo, Biblioteca Comunale)

The same, *Resoconto bibliografico ed artistico...* Trapani 1904. 43 pp. Discusses 5 liturgical mss.

Catalogo ragionato dei Manoscritti della Biblioteca Fardelliana, by Fortunato Mondello (1898), 191 mss. (Cf. AB VI 552).

*Trappist, Kentucky, U.S.A. See De Ricci.

*Traú, see Trogir.

*Třeboň (Wittingau), Czechoslovakia. See Burdach; *Soupis*.

Trento, Italy. See Italy, *Publicazioni degli Archivi di Stato*; Mazzatinti LXVII; LXXI; LXXIV; Tietze; Wickhoff.

G. Gerola, 'Elenco dei cataloghi, inventari e registri a stampa degli archivi, biblioteche, musei e raccolte varie del Trentino,' *Alba Trentina* I (Rovigo 1917) 220-224; 262-264; 291-294; 328-332. (Trent, Biblioteca Comunale)

Jo. Ben. Gentilottus, 'Catalogus Mss. Codicum Tridenti in Bibliotheca, Secretiorique Tabulario Episcopali, necnon in Bibliotheca Capitulari asservatorum, in *Monumenta Ecclesiae Tridentinae*, vol. III, pt. ii. (by B. Bonelli), Trent 1765, 383-403. 280 mss. Some of the mss. are now in the Bibl. Comunale or the Museo Nazionale. Others are scattered or lost. Vols. I-II of Bonelli's work (1760-61) are entitled: *Notizie istorico-critiche intorno al B. M. Adelpreto...* whereas vol. III, pt. I (1762) has the title: *Notizie istorico-critiche della Chiesa di Trento*. (Trent, Bibl. Com.)

E. Gottardi, *Ricerca e illustrazione di codici latini nelle Biblioteche di Trento*. Thesis, Università Cattolica, Milan, 1949.

—Archivio di Stato.

A. Galante, *La corrispondenza del Card. Cristoforo Madruzzo nell' Archivio di Stato di Innsbruck*. Innsbruck 1911. XII, 35 pp.

Corrispondenza Clesiana. 1 ms. vol.

—Biblioteca Comunale.

I. Lunelli, *La Biblioteca Comunale di Trento*. Trent 1937. 151 pp. Lists a few mss. (p. 146). (Trent, Comunale)

A. Cetto, *La Biblioteca Comunale di Trento nel Centenario della sua apertura*. Florence 1956. X, 237 pp. p. 219-233: 139 mss. before 1500.

Catalogo dei Manoscritti. 5 vols. I: mss. 1-1548 (superseded by Mazzatinti LXVII, LXXI, and LXXIV). II: 1549-2888 (superseded to no. 2145 by Mazzatinti LXXIV). III: 2889-4098. IV: 4099-5308. V: 5309-5431. (Cf. AB III 362).

—*Biblioteca Francescana.

F. G(uardia) and L. R(osat), 'I manoscritti del P. Giangrisostomo Tovazzi,' *Studi*

Trentini III (1922) 142-144; 187-194; 271-277; IV (1923) 68-70; 166-168; 255-261. 133 late mss.

T. Asson, 'I manoscritti della Biblioteca Francescana di Trento,' *Ibid.* VIII (Classe I: Storico-Letteraria, 1927) 174-190. Mss. no. 134-326. Also late.

—Museo Diocesano and Biblioteca capitolare.

V. Casagrande, 'Catalogo del Museo Diocesano di Trento,' *Rivista Tridentina* VIII (1908) 3-80; IX (1909) 95-98; 129-165; XI (1911) 222-237; XII (1912) 22-37; 249-256. Lists a few mss. (Trent, Biblioteca Comunale). Also printed separately, 2 vols., Trent 1908-13. 160 pp. numbered continuously.

—Museo Nazionale.

For the group of mss. returned from Vienna after the first World War, there is no inventory. Yet see Tietze; see also Bitterer (under Vienna). See also G. Tarugi Secchi, *La Biblioteca Vescovile Trentina* (Trent 1930, 107 pp.), p. 80-87, for a list of the mss., with their former shelf marks, but without an indication of their content. The latter can then be ascertained from the catalogues of the Vienna archive and library.

Trèves, see **Trier.**

Treviso, Italy. See *Archiv* XII.

—Biblioteca Capitolare.

Alphabetical card file was lost, along with several mss., during the last war.

—Biblioteca Comunale.

Catalogo numerico di Manoscritti. 2 vols. I: mss. 1-800. II: 801-1004.

Accession list in 3 vols. I: 1005-1145. II: 1146-1312. III: 1354-1534.

*Trévoux, France. See France, *Catalogue Général, Départements* VI.

*Trie-sur-Baise, France. See *ibid.* XXXI.

Trier, West Germany. See *Analecta Bollandiana* XLIX; LII; LX; *Archiv* VII; VIII; XI; Diekamp; Gercken; Leclercq; *Neues Archiv* XVII.

—Dombibliothek.

P. Weber, *Der Domschatz zu Trier.* Augsburg 1928. 31 pp. and plates. p. 18-23:

15 mss. (Morgan Library)

F. Jansen, 'Der Paderborner Domdechant Graf Christoph von Kesselstatt und seine Handschriftensammlung,' in: *Sankt Liborius, sein Dom und sein Bistum,* ed. P. Simon (Paderborn 1936, 423 pp.) p. 355-368. Identifies some mss. in Trier, but says nothing about their content. (NjP)

Catalogus descriptivus Codicum Manuscriptorum Ecclesiae Cathedralis Treverensis (by H. V. Sauerland, 1890-91). Mss. no. 1-218 and 250-345. The list is complete.

Manuscripta Liturgica Ecclesiae Cathedralis Treverensis in Archivio Episcopali. Mss. 400-586 (renumbered). Supersedes the other catalogue for the liturgical mss.

Verzeichnis der Handschriften des historischen Archivs der Stadt Trier. Trierisches Archiv II-X (1899-1907) and XIX-XXIII (1912-14), *Anhang.* 351 pp. 749 mss. and index. (NN)

J. Marx, *Handschriftenverzeichnis der Seminar-Bibliothek zu Trier* (Trierisches Archiv, Ergänzungsheft XIII). Trier 1912. 136 pp. 184 mss. (NN)

M. Keuffer, G. Kentenich and others, *Beschreibendes Verzeichniss der Handschriften der Stadtbibliothek zu Trier.* 10 pts. Trier 1888-1931. I (1888): *Bibelhandschriften,* nos. 1-112. II (1891): *Kirchenväter,* nos. 113-214. III (1894): *Predigten,* nos. 215-353. IV (1897): *Liturgische Handschriften,* nos. 354-522. V (1900): *Ascetische Schriften, I. Abteilung.* Nos. 523-653. VI (1910): ... *Zweite Abteilung.* Nos. 654-804. VII (1911): *Die deutschen Handschriften,* by A. Becker. Nos. 805-36. VIII (1914): *Handschriften des historischen Archivs.* 749 mss. IX (1919): *Die juristischen Handschriften.* Nos. 836-1003. X (1931): *Die philologischen Handschriften.* Nos. 1079-1110. Vols. I-VI have no index.

Trieste, Italy. Biblioteca Civica. See Wickhoff VII.

Documenti raccolti e pubblicati in occasione di collocazione di busti enei sulla facciata del Duomo di Trieste in onore di Enea Silvio

Piccolomini vescovo di Trieste poi papa Pio II, di Andrea Rapicio vescovo di Trieste, consigliere imperiale e di Rinaldo Scarlichio vescovo di Trieste, luogo tenente dell' Austria Inferiore. (Cover title: *In onore e memoria dei tre vescovi di Trieste Enea Silvio dei Piccolomini poi papa Pio II…, Andrea dei Rapicii…, Rinaldo Scarlichio… per occasione di dedicazione di tre busti enei al Duomo di Trieste*). Trieste 1862. II, 28, and many unnumbered pp. p. 19-28: F. De Fiori, 'Dalle Raccolte Rossettiane di cose del Papa Pio II.' Lists 23 mss. (p. 19-25). (Vatican Library; microfilm at NNC)

A. Hortis, *Catalogo delle opere di Francesco Petrarca esistenti nella Petrarchesca Rossettiana di Trieste.* Trieste 1874. XIII, 215 pp. p. 189-195: 10 mss.

Mostra Petrarchesca della Raccolta Rossettiana della Biblioteca civica. (By A. Tassini). Trieste 1953. 19 pp. p. 6-10: 10 mss.

Biblioteca Civica 'Attilio Hortis' Trieste. Mostra Petrarchesca della Raccolta Rossettiana. (By A. Tassini). Trieste 1956. 24 pp. p. 11-12: 11 mss.

*Card index (AB III 363).

Trogir (Trau), Yugoslavia. See Wickhoff.

Troppau, see **Opava**.

Troyes, France. See France, *Catalogue Général, Départements* II (Quarto Series); XLIII.

L. Morel-Payen, *Les plus beaux manuscrits et les plus belles reliures de la Bibliothèque de Troyes.* Troyes 1935. XIII, 194 pp. and plates. p. 49-160: Description of the mss.

Truro, England. See Frere.

Tübingen, West Germany. Universitätsbibliothek. See Lehmann, *Mitteilungen* I; *Serapeum* IV; Stälin. See also under Berlin.

Verzeichnis der Handschriften der königlichen Universitätsbibliothek in Tübingen, by Adelb. Keller (1839-41). 3 vols. Vol. I contains mss. Mc 1-365 (Codices latini). Index in vol. III.

Typed notes taken by Mme Vernet in 1951 are available at the Institut de Recherches et d'Histoire des Textes, Paris.

—*Wilhelmsstift. 52 mss. No further information.

Tulle, France. See France, *Catalogue Général, Départements* XIII; XLIII.

Tuy, Spain. See Fransen.

Überlingen, West Germany. Leopold-Sophien-Bibliothek.

A. Semler, 'Die historischen Handschriften der Leopold-Sophien-Bibliothek in Überlingen,' *Zeitschrift für die Geschichte des Oberrheins*, N. F. XLI (LXXX, 1928) 117-31. Lists a few mss. No index. (NN)

*Handgeschriebener Katalog (ca. 1894, by O. Kunzer). Lists some Latin mss. not mentioned by Semler. (Communication of the librarian).

Udine, Italy. See Mazzatinti III; XLVI; XLIX; LXXVIII.

—Biblioteca Arcivescovile.

Fondo Arcivescovile or Principale. Catalogue in 3 vols. by Coleti. (II). *Catalogus codicum mss. latinorum Bibliothecae Archiepiscopalis Utinensis* (by J. D. Coletus, 1784). (III). *Catalogo de' Mss. Italiani della Biblioteca Arcivescovile di Udine* (by G. D. Coleti, 1787).

Fondo Principale. 6 notebooks, by Mons. Vale. I: Mss. 1-83. II: 84-163. III: 164-270. IV: 271-357. V: 358-447. VI: 448-506; 235-265.

I codici della Biblioteca Arcivescovile di Udine. 3 notebooks. 12 mss.

(Fondo Bartoliniano). *Indice dei Manoscritti del Fondo Bartolini, Biblioteca Arcivescovile,* Udine. 3 notebooks, by Mons. Vale, I: mss. 1-69. II: 70-149. III: 150-177.

Indice dei Manoscritti della Bartoliniana. 2 notebooks. 17 mss.

*Card file for both collections.

—Biblioteca Capitolare.

Index codicum manuscriptorum Archivi Capituli Utinensis.

3 notebooks (by Mons. G. Vale). I: 1-55. II: 56-98, and Raccolta Bini. III: Documents. Mazzatinti III is incomplete.

—Biblioteca Comunale.

Catalogo-inventario dei manoscritti, Fondo Principale. 3 vols. I: mss. 1-890. II: 891-3510. III: 3511-3936. Superseded until no. 479 by Mazzatinti.

(Fondo Joppi). G. Bragato, 'Catalogo analitico descrittivo della collezione dei manoscritti dei fratelli Joppi,' *Pagine Friulane* XVII (1905-06) 6-10; 21-24; 39-42; 56-60; 66-69; 88-91; 104-07; 122-26; 139-42. Describes mss. 1-148. (MH). A separate edition has 44 pp. and goes to no. 185, middle. (NNC)

G. Bragato, 'Catalogo analitico descrittivo...' *Bollettino della Civica Biblioteca e del Museo* (Udine) II (1908) p. 8-22 (describes nos. 1-36, identical with nos. 151-86 of the other numbering); 89-94 (mss. 187-208). (DSI-M; reprint at NNC)

Catalogo-inventario dei manoscritti della Collezione dei Fratelli A. e V. Joppi, vol. II (in ms., continuing Bragato's printed list). mss. 209-711. Cf. Apolloni II 87; AB III 477-78.

(Fondo Manin, recently acquired). *Manoscritti Manin.* 1 typed vol. 1575 mss. Centuries not given.

—*Biblioteca Florio. See Mazzatinti III; Mano scritti e Libri rari.

*—Bibliot eca del Seminario. No inventory. (Communication of the librarian of the Comunale.)

*Ulm, West Germany. Stadtbibliothek. See Gercken; *Serapeum, Intelligenzblatt* 1861. Catalogue of Latin mss. lost in the war (Communication of the librarian).

Uppsala, Sweden. Universitetsbiblioteket (Carolina). See *Archives* V; Barwinski; Collijn; Dudik, *Forschungen*; Högberg; Hipler; Institut de Recherches; Lampen; Leclercq; Lehmann; Malin.

O. Celsius, *Bibliothecae Upsaliensis historia.* Uppsala 1745. 154 pp. Lists the 65 mss. given by De la Gardie (p. 86-113) and some other mss. (p. 116ff.). No index. (NN)

(E. Benzelius and O. Celsius) *Catalogus centuriae librorum rarissimorum manuscriptorum et partim impressorum arabicorum persicorum turcicorum graecorum latinorum etc. qua anno 1705 bibliothecam publicam Academiae Upsalensis auxit et exornavit . . . Jo. Gabr. Sparvenfeldius . . .* Uppsala 1706. 74 pp. Latin mss. (p. 62-64, nos. 50-61). (NN)

Notitia codicum manuscriptorum latinorum Biblioth. Acad. Upsaliensis, quam . . . praeside Petro Fabiano Aurivillio . . . publico examini subjicit Petrus Södermark. pt. 1 (Uppsala 1806). 8 pp. 2 mss. pt. 2, . . . subjicit Gabriel Marklin (1807). p. 9-14. No. 3-5. pt. 3, ... subjicit Carolus Ludovicus Lalin (1813). p. 15-22, no. 6-8. (NN)

O. J. A. Almquist, *Codices manuscripti latini bibliothecae Regiae Academiae Upsaliensis.* Praeside Jo. Henr. Schröder. Uppsala 1836. 8 pp. 21 mss. No index.

C. Annerstedt, *Upsala Universitetsbibliotekets Historia intill år* 1702 (K. Vitterhets Historie och Antiquitets Akademiens Handlingar N.F. 12,2). Stockholm 1894. 119 pp. p. 79-80: Shelf marks for mss. from Vadstena, Franciscans in Stockholm, Sigtuna, and other collections.

I. Collijn, *Katalog der Inkunabeln der Kgl. Universitäts-Bibliothek zu Uppsala* (Arbeten utgifna med Understöd af Vilhelm Ekmans Universitetsfond, Uppsala, no. 5). Uppsala and Leipzig 1907. XXXVIII, 507 pp. Has an index of provenances (p. 471-491), and occasional mention of manuscript additions.

The same, 'Die in der Universitätsbibliothek zu Uppsala aufbewahrten Bücher aus dem Besitze des Leipziger Professors und Ermländer Domherrn Thomas Werner,' in: *Universitati Lipsiensi saecularia quinta... a. D. MCMIX celebranti gratulantur Universitatis Upsaliensis Rector et Senatus* (Uppsala 1909, 73 pp.), p. 9-62. p. 33-58: List of mss. and books from Thomas Werner at Uppsala.

E. Rooth, 'Die mittelalterlichen deutschen Handschriften einschliesslich der lateinischen mit deutschen Bestandteilen der Universitätsbibliothek zu Uppsala,' *Upp-*

sala Universitets Biblioteks Minnesskrift 1621-1921 (Acta Bibliothecae R. Universitatis Upsaliensis I, 1921) 40-96. No index.

F. Stegmüller, *Analecta Upsaliensia theologiam Medii Aevi illustrantia.* Tomus I. *Opera systematica* (Upsala Universitets Årsskrift II, no. 7). Uppsala 1953. 451 pp. Covers also 1 ms. at the Domkyrkobibliothek, and 1 in Stockholm. Index of mss. (p. 446-447).

Handskriftskatalog. 25 mss. or typed vols., arranged by subjects. The following ones are of special interest: (III). Erici Benzelii Fil. *Catalogus codd. Mss. Bibliothecae Upsaliensis.* 13 Greek mss. and Latin mss. C I-V and C 1-93 (superseded by vol. VI below). (IV): C 94-257 (superseded by vols. VI-VII below). (V): C 258-933 (superseded to no. 871 by vols. VII-VIII below). (VI): *Codices Medii Aevi Latini etc.* Reviderad af C. Annerstedt (1904). C I-IV; 1-155. (VII): C 156-529. (VIII): C 530-871. (XII): G. Brefväxlingar. (XIII): H. Allmän och Utländsk Historia. (XIV): K. Kyrkohistoria. (XVII): P. Filosofi. (XVIII): R. Språkvetenskap. (XX): T. Teologi. (XXI): U. Undervisning. (XXII): V. Vitterhet.

Card index, alphabetical.

Register öfver Palmkiöldiske Samlingen af Handskrefne och Tryckte Handlingar... (1935). 1 typed vol.

Katalog öfver Westins Handskriftsamling. 1 typed vol.

Typed catalogue of medieval mss. of the Bible and of systematic theology, by F. Stegmüller.

Schematisk Översikt över Uppsala Universitetsbiblioteks Allmänna Handskriftssamling. 1 typed vol.

*Urbana, Illinois, U.S.A. See De Ricci.
*Urbania, Italy. See Mazzatinti XXXIV.
Urbino, Italy. Biblioteca Universitaria. See Mazzatinti LXXX.

Inventario dei Manoscritti (1887). Describes the Fondo Comunale, according to its old shelf marks. Superseded to Busta 148 (new number) by Mazzatinti. (Communication of the librarian).

Registro dei manoscritti.
*Card index.
*Urgel, Spain. See Seo de Urgel.
*Ushaw, England. See Great Britain, *Historical Manuscripts Commission.*
*Utrecht, Holland. Bibliotheek der Universiteit. See Lehmann, *Holländische Reisefrüchte*; *Société française.*

Catalogus codicum manu scriptorum Bibliothecae Universitatis Rheno-Traiectinae, by P. A. Tiele and A. Hulshof. 2 vols. Utrecht 1887-1909. I: 1582 mss. of which no. 29-1005 (p. 7-242) are Latin. II: Mss. no. 1583-1907 of which no. 1583-1687 (p. 71-128) are Latin. Each vol. indexed.

Supplement op de handschriftencatalogus. Card file of acquisitions after 1909. (Communication of the librarian).

Typed list of 10 Latin mss. kindly supplied by the librarian.

*Uzès, France. See France, *Catalogue Général, Départements* XIII.
*Valence, France. See France, *Catalogue Général, Départements* XIII; XLIII.

Valencia, Spain. See Grubbs (Section A, under Richardson); *Anuario; Archiv* VIII; Haenel; De Marinis; Villanueva.

—Archivo y Biblioteca del Ayuntamiento.

Biblioteca del Excmo. Sr. D. José E. Serrano y Morales, Inventario general de los libros y manuscritos que la componen (1908). Alphabetical, mostly printed editions.

—Biblioteca de la Catedral.

E. Olmos Canalda, *Catálogo descriptivo de los Códices de la Catedral de Valencia.* Madrid 1928. 201 pp. 300 mss. Index in Grubbs. (Pierpont Morgan Library). Also in *Boletín de la Real Academia de la Historia* XCI (1927) 390-469; XCII (1928) 218-333. (NN)

The same, *Catálogo descriptivo: Códices de la Catedral de Valencia.* 2nd ed. Valencia 1943. 248 pp. 310 mss. Index (p. 15-16). (NN)

A. López, 'Descriptio codicum franciscalium Bibliothecae Cathedralis Valentinae,' *Ar-*

chivo Ibero-Americano XXXVI (1933) 172-222. 51 mss. No index. (NN)

—Biblioteca Universitaria.

(M. Repullés), 'Catálogo de los códices procedentes del Monasterio de S. Miguel de los Reyes,' *Revista de Archivos, Bibliotecas y Museos* V (1875) 9-13; 52-55; 68-72; 87-91; 103-105. Alphabetical list of 233 mss. (NjP)

M. Gutiérrez del Caño, *Catálogo de los manuscritos existentes en la Biblioteca Universitaria de Valencia.* 3 vols. n. d. (ca. 1913-14). Arranged alphabetically. I: No. 1-889. II: no. 890-1716. III: No. 1717-2422. Index in Grubbs. Shelf marks added in library copy.

*Valenciennes, France. See France, *Catalogue Général, Départements* XXV; XLIII.

(J. Mangeart, *Catalogue descriptif et raisonné des Manuscrits de la Bibliothèque de Valenciennes.* Paris 1860. xv, 764 pp. 642 mss.)

*Valladolid, Spain. See Carini; *Serapeum* VIII.

M. Gutiérrez del Caño, *Códices y manuscritos que se convervan en la Universidad de Valladolid.* Valladolid 1888. 210 pp. Arranged alphabetically. Mostly modern. No shelf marks.

S. Rivera Manescau, 'Catálogo de Manuscritos de la Biblioteca Universitaria y de Santa Cruz, de Valladolid,' *Anales de la Universidad de Valladolid* II (1929) 288-305; 321-52; 385-416; III (1930) 1-32; 81-96. 192 mss. No index. (DLC)

The same and P. Ortega Lamadrid, 'Catalogo de los manuscritos de las Bibliotecas Universitaria y de Santa Cruz de Valladolid.' *Ibid.* VIII (1935) no. 22-23, p. 75-144; no. 24-25, p. 30-172. Mss. no. 192-390.

*Vallbona de las Monjas, Spain. See Cordoliani.

*Valletta, Malta. See *Archiv* IX.

Catalogo dei codici e dei manoscritti inediti che si conservano nella Pubblica Biblioteca di Malta. (By C. Vassallo). Valletta 1856. 80 pp. 21 and 324 mss. No index. (NN)

C. Vassallo, 'Catalogo dei codici e dei ma-noscritti inediti che si conservano nella pubblica biblioteca di Malta,' *Archivio storico di Malta,* N.S. X (1939) 283-380; XI (1940) 112-176; 271-309. 23 and 1214 mss. No index. (MH)

*Valls, Spain.

F. de Moragas i Rodes, *Càtaleg dels llibres, pergamins i documents antics de l'Arxiu Municipal de. la ciutat de Valls.* Valls 1916. vii, 216 pp. (Hispanic Society)

*Valognes, France. See France, *Catalogue Général, Départements* X.

*Vannes, France. See France, *Catalogue Général, Départements* XX; XLIII.

*Västerås, Stifts- och Landsbiblioteket.

Förteckning på Handskrifter i Westerås Allm. Läroverks Bibliotek. Preface signed by W. M(olér). (Västerås 1882). II, 19 pp. Mostly late mss. No shelf marks. Not complete.

Vaticano, Città del. Biblioteca Apostolica Vaticana. See also under Roma (esp. Guide-Manuel; Pastor; Poncelet). See *Analecta Bollandiana* LIV; *Archiv* III; IV; V; XII; *Archives* XXII; XXVIII; XXIX; Bernards; Blume; *Giornale*; Caselli; Lampen; Mittarelli; Montfaucon; *Neues Archiv*; Palacky; Pellegrin; Reifferscheid; *Rivista delle Biblioteche*; Ruysschaert; Saxl; *Serapeum* XV; XVII; XVIII; *Intelligenzblatt*, 1869; *Société française*; Thorndike; Wickhoff.

G. B. De Rossi, 'La Biblioteca della Sede Apostolica ed i cataloghi dei suoi manoscritti,' *Studi e Documenti di Storia e Diritto* V (1884) 317-368.

F. Ehrle, 'Zur Geschichte der Katalogisierung der Vatikana,' *Historisches Jahrbuch* XI (1890) 718-727.

J. Bignami-Odier, 'Guide au Département des Manuscrits de la Bibliothèque du Vatican,' *Mélanges d'archéologie et d'histoire* LI (1934) 205-239.

E. Tisserant, 'Bibliothèques Pontificales,' *Dictionnaire de Sociologie . . .* III (1936) coll. 766-81.

G. Borghezio, 'La Biblioteca Vaticana,' *Enciclopedia Italiana* XXXIV (1937) 1045-47.

C. J. Ermatinger, 'A Partial List of Catalogues, Inventories and Indices, both Printed and Handwritten, on file in the Vatican Manuscript Depository of the Knights of Columbus Foundation,' *Manuscripta* (preliminary, offset printed series) I, no. 2 (1954) 8-23.

The same, 'Catalogues in the Knights of Columbus Vatican Film Library at Saint Louis University,' *Manuscripta* (definitive series) I (1957) 5-21; 89-101.

Recensio manuscriptorum codicum qui ex universa bibliotheca Vaticana selecti ... a. 1797 procuratoribus Gallorum ... traditi fuere. Leipzig 1803. 151 pp. (NN)

Carl Greith, *Spicilegium Vaticanum: Beiträge zur nähern Kenntniss der Vatikanischen Bibliothek für deutsche Poesie des Mittelalters.* Frauenfeld 1838. x, 303 pp. p. 30-134: 'Verzeichniss und Beschreibung altdeutscher, lateinischer und französischer Handschriften der Vatikana und anderer römischer Bibliotheken, die sich auf die deutsche Litteratur des Mittelalters beziehen.' Discusses some Latin mss. (p. 75ff.). (MH)

L. Delisle, 'Notice sur vingt manuscrits du Vatican,' *Bibliothèque de l'École des Chartes* XXXVII (1876) 471-527.

V. Forcella, *Catalogo dei manoscritti riguardanti la storia di Roma che si conservano nella Biblioteca Vaticana.* 4 vols. Rome 1879-85. Arranged by shelf marks. Each volume indexed. (DLC)

St. Beissel, *Vaticanische Miniaturen.* Freiburg i.Br. 1893. 59 pp. and plates.

H. Ehrensberger, *Libri Liturgici Bibliothecae Apostolicae Vaticanae manu scripti.* Freiburg i.Br. 1897. 519 pp. (PU)

A. Fayen, 'Notices sur les manuscrits de la Bibliothèque Vaticane concernant la Belgique,' *Revue des Bibliothèques et Archives de Belgique* III (1905) 1-9; 137-43; 234-43.

A. Poncelet, *Catalogus Codicum hagiographicorum latinorum Bibliothecae Vaticanae.* Brussels 1910. 595 pp. (NNUT)

G. Mercati, 'Codici del Convento di S. Francesco in Assisi nella Biblioteca Vaticana,' *Miscellanea Francesco Ehrle* V (Studi e Testi XLI, Rome 1924) 83-127.

F. Ehrle, *Los manuscritos Vaticanos de los teólogos Salmantinos del siglo XVI* (Biblioteca de 'Estudios Eclesiásticos,' Serie de Opúsculos I). Madrid 1930. xvi, 136 pp. Arranged by authors. (DLC) Also in: *Estudios Eclésiasticos* VIII (1929) 145-72; 289-331; 433-55; IX (1930) 145-87. (DCU). Originally published in German: 'Die Vaticanischen Handschriften der Salmanticenser Theologen des 16. Jahrhunderts,' *Der Katholik*, year LXIV (1884), pt. II (vol. LII) 495-522; 632-54. (MH)

G. Mercati, 'Altri codici del sacro convento di Assisi nella Vaticana,' *Aus der Geisteswelt des Mittelalters* (Beiträge zur Geschichte der Philosophie und Theologie des Mittelalters, Supplementband III, pt. 1, Münster 1935) 52-68. No index. Reprinted in G. Card. Mercati, *Scritti Minori* IV (Studi e Testi LXXIX, Vatican City 1937) 487-505.

The same, *Codici Latini Pico Grimani Pio e di altra biblioteca ignota del secolo XVI esistenti nell' Ottoboniana e i codici greci Pio di Modena con una digressione per la storia dei codici S. Pietro in Vaticano.* (Studi e Texti LXXV, Vatican City 1938). XII, 321 pp. and plates. Index of mss. (p. 293-96).

L. Thorndike, 'Some Medieval Medical Manuscripts at the Vatican,' *Journal of the History of Medicine and Allied Sciences* VIII (1953) 263-283.

The same, 'Notes upon Some Medieval Latin Astronomical, Astrological and Mathematical Manuscripts at the Vatican,' *Isis* XLVII (1956) 391-404; XLIX (1958) 34-49.

P. O. Kristeller, 'Renaissance Research in Vatican Manuscripts,' *Manuscripta* I (1957) 67-80.

J. Leclercq, 'Textes et manuscrits cisterciens à la Bibliothèque Vaticane,' *Analecta Sacri Ordinis Cisterciensis* XV (1959) 79-103. (NNF)

Loren C. MacKinney, 'Medical Illustrations in Medieval Manuscripts of the Vatican Library,' *Manuscripta* III (1959) 3-18; 76-88.

Fondo Vaticano Latino.

Miscellaneorum ex Mss. Libris Bibliothecae Collegii Romani Societatis Jesu tomus primus (secundus). Preface signed by Petrus Lazeri. 2 vols. Rome 1754-57. Most of the mss. discussed are now in the Fondo Vaticano Latino.

E. Narducci, 'Intorno alla vita del Conte Giammaria Mazzuchelli ed alla collezione de' suoi manoscritti ora posseduti dalla Biblioteca Vaticana,' *Giornale Arcadico* CXCVIII (N. S. LIII, Nov.-Dec. 1865, publ. 1867) 1-79. Covers Vat. lat. 9260-94. Index. (CtY, reprint at NN)

V. Beltrani, *I libri di Fulvio Orsini nella Biblioteca Vaticana.* Rome 1886. xv, 56 pp. 428 Latin mss. (p. 25-53). No index. (DLC)

P. De Nolhac, *La bibliothèque de Fulvio Orsini.* (Bibliothèque de l'École des Hautes Études, Sciences Philologiques et Historiques, LXXIV). Paris 1887. 489 pp.

Codices Vaticani Latini. Vol. I (1902), by M. Vattasso and P. Franchi de' Cavalieri. 586 pp. Vat. lat. 1-678. Vol. II, 1-2 (1931-33), by A. Pelzer. 775 and 356 pp. Vat. lat. 679-1134. Vol. III (1912), by B. Nogara. 498 pp. Vat. lat. 1461-2059. [Vol. IV] (1914), by M. Vattasso and E. Carusi. 800 pp. Vat. lat. 9852-10300. [Vol. V] (1920), by M. Vattasso and E. Carusi. 778 pp. Vat. lat. 10301-10700. [Vol. VI] (1947), by J. B. Borino. 588 and 308 pp. Vat. lat. 10701-10875. [Vol. VII] (1955), by the same. 451 pp. Vat. lat. 10876-11000. [Vol. VIII] (1959), by E. Carusi and J. Ruysschaert. XXVI, 716 pp. Vat. lat. 11414-11709. Each vol. indexed. Not complete.

Th. J. Scherg, 'Die Rulandsche Handschriftensammlung in der Vatikanischen Bibliothek zu Rom,' *Archiv des Historischen Vereins von Unterfranken und Aschaffenburg* XLIX (1907) 159-99. Vat. Lat. 10069-11150 (p. 175-84).

L. Thorndike, 'Vatican Latin manuscripts in the History of Science and Medicine,' *Isis* XIII (1929) 53-102. 91 mss. Index (94ff.).

S. Lattès, 'Recherches sur la bibliothèque d'Angelo Colocci,' *Mélanges d'archéologie et d'histoire* XLVIII (1931) 308-344.

H. Kämpf, 'Die Codices Latini 4008-4010 der Vatikanischen Bibliothek,' *Quellen und Forschungen aus Italienischen Archiven und Bibliotheken* XXVI (1935-36) 143-71.

P. Micheloni, *La medicina nei primi tremila codici del Fondo Vaticano Latino* (Pubblicazioni dell' Istituto di Storia della Medicina dell' Università di Roma, Collezione C: Studi e Ricerche storico-mediche). Rome 1950. 116 pp. 181 mss. described in serial order. Gives only the medical parts of miscellaneous mss. Indices.

Inventarium librorum latinorum Mss. Bib. Vat. 13 vols. in 14. I: Vat. Lat. 1-607 (superseded by the printed catalogue of Vattasso and Franchi de' Cavalieri). II: 608-1318 (superseded to no. 1134 by the same catalogue and that of Pelzer). III: 1319-2141 (superseded for mss. 1461-2059 by the catalogue of Nogara). IV: 2142-3915. V: 3916-4888. VI: 4889-6025. VII: 6026-6477. (Vols. I-VII by the Rainaldi brothers and others, s. xvii.) VIII (by E. Ceccucci, 1882): 6459-7058. IX: 7059-7244. X pt. 1 (by G. B. De Rossi, 1876-78): 7245-8066. pt. 2: 8067-8471. XI (by G. B. De Rossi and others, 1852-55): 8472-9019. XII (by G. B. De Rossi, 1856-71): 9020-9445. XIII (by the same, 1872-75): 9446-9851. Centuries not given in vols. I-VII. Each vol. indexed. Separate indices for I-VI and XI-XIII (Cf. De Rossi 320; Bignami 208; Tisserant 778). (Micr. at MoSU)

Vat. lat. 9852-11000 are described in printed catalogues.

Codices ex Archivo in Bybliothecam Vaticanam translati an. 1920 aliique codices manu exarati qui in dies accedebant. Covers

Vat. lat. 11710-12847 (Cf. Bignami 208). (micr. at MoSU)

Inventario dei còdici Vat. lat. 12848-13331, 13357-13756, 14014-14062, by Ada Alessandrini and others. 1 typed vol.

Inventario dei codici Vaticani latini musicali 14501-14768, by G. Baronci. (Micr. at MoSU)

Inventario dei codici musicali già Rospigliosi ora Vaticani 14769-14788, by the same (1934). (Micr. at MoSU)

Inventario dei codici ... 14789-14850, by the same (1936). (Micr. at MoSU)

Inventario dei codici ... 14851-14912, by the same (1938). (Micr. at MoSU)

For the remaining sections of the Vaticani latini, the notes and files of the catologuers of the library are the only source of information.

Fondo Vaticano Greco.

Inventarium Graecorum codicum, 4 vols. Vol. II is still needed for Vat. gr. 867-992. Vol. III (Vat. gr. 993-2160) is still needed for mss. 993-1484 and 1684-2160. IV: mss. 1501-2402. (Micr. at MoSU) Alphabetical index in 3 vols. by Leone Allacci (De Rossi 320; Bignami 209; Tisserant 778). (Micr. at MoSU)

Fondo Urbinate Latino.

C. Stornaiolo, *Codices Urbinates Latini.* 3 vols. Rome 1902-21. I: Urb. lat. 1-500. II (1912): Urb. lat. 501-1000. III: Urb. lat. 1001-1779. Each volume indexed.

Fondo Palatino Latino. See also Wilken, under Heidelberg.

E. Stevenson and I. B. De Rossi, *Codices Palatini Latini Bibliothecae Vaticanae.* I, Rome 1886. 327 pp. Mss. no. 1-921. No index. Not complete.

L. Thorndike, 'Little known names of medical men in Vatican Palatine Manuscripts,' *Annals of Medical History,* N.S. VIII (1936) 145-159.

The same, 'Unfamiliar medical works by known and anonymous authors in Vatican Palatine Latin Mss., *Ibid.,* 297-305.

Inventarium Manuscriptorum Latinorum Bibliothecae Palatinae. 2022 mss. Super-

seded to no. 921 by the printed catalogue of Stevenson and De Rossi. (Bignami 214). (micr. at MoSU)

Codicum mmss. latinorum vatic. palatinae Bibliothecae Index, by J. V. Marchesius (1678). (Bignami 214). (micr. at MoSU)

Fondo Reginense Latino.

A. Wilmart, *Codices Reginenses Latini.* I (Vatican City 1937). 846 pp. Regin. lat. 1-250. II (1945). 991 pp. Regin. lat. 251-500. Each volume indexed. Not complete.

Inventario dei Mss. Regin. 2120 mss. Centuries not given. Superseded to no. 500 by the printed catalogue of Wilmart. (Cf. Bignami 218). (micr. at MoSU)

Index codicum manuscriptorum latinorum reginae Suecorum (Bignami 218). (micr. at MoSU)

Fondo Ottoboniano Latino.

Bibliotheca Stoschiana sive Catalogus Librorum Bibliothecae Philippi Baron de Stosch... 2 parts. Lucca 1758. Part II (96 pp.): Index codicum manuscriptorum. Arranged by subjects. No index. The mss. are now among the Ottoboniani. (ICN)

G. de Manteyer, 'Les manuscrits de la reine, Christine aux Archives du Vatican,' *Mélanges d'Archéologie et d'Histoire* XVII (1897) 285-322; XXIV (1904) 371-423. Discusses a few Ottoboniani. No Index.

H. M. Bannister, 'A Short Notice of some manuscripts of the Cambridge Friars, now in the Vatican Library,' *Collectanea Franciscana* I (British Society of Franciscan Studies V), Aberdeen 1914, p. 124-40. Describes some Ottoboniani.

Inventarii Codicum Manuscriptorum Latinorum Bibliothecae Vaticanae Ottobonianae Pars I: Ottob. lat. 1-1676. Pars II: mss. 1677-3394. No centuries given in pt. I. (Cf. Bignami 221). (micr. at MoSU)

Index alphabeticus codicum manuscriptorum Ottobonianae (Bignami 221). (micr. at MoSU).

Fondo Capponi.

(*Catalogo della Libreria Capponi o sia de' libri italiani del fu Marchese Alessandro*

Gregorio Capponi... Rome 1747. XII, 476 pp. p. 433-454: Alphabetical list of mss.)

G. Salvo Cozzo, *I codici Capponiani della Biblioteca Vaticana.* Rome 1897. 486 pp. 286 mss.

Fondo Borghese.

F. Ehrle, 'Die historischen Handschriften der Borghesiana,' *Archiv für Litteratur-und Kirchengeschichte des Mittelalters* I (1885) 151-53. 4 mss. No index.

The same, *Historia Bibliothecae romanorum pontificum tum Bonifatianae tum Avenionensis.* I (Rome 1890). xvi, 786 pp. Identifies some mss. of the Borthese collection in the Vatican. No general index.

A. Pelzer, *Addenda et Emendanda ad Francisci Ehrle Historiae Bibliothecae Romanorum Pontificum tum Bonifatianae tum Avenionensis Tomum I.* Vatican City 1947. viii, 184 pp. No general index.

G. Calenzio, 'Dei manoscritti Borghesiani ora Vaticani,' 20 pp. In: *Nel giubileo episcopale di Leone XIII, Omaggio della Biblioteca Vaticana.* (Rome) 1893. Irregular pagination. (NN)

Anneliese Maier, *Codices Burghesiani Bibliothecae Vaticanae* (Studi e Testi CLXX). Vatican City 1952. 496 pp. 390 mss.

Fondo Borgia.

Inventario provvisorio dei mss. del Museo Borgiano. Begins with a list of the 800 Latin mss. Summary. Centuries not given to no. 320 (Cf. Bignami 222). (micro. at MoSU) This collection formerly belonged to the Collegium de Propaganda Fide.

Fondo Barberini Latino.

Th. Silverstein, *Medieval Latin Scientific Writings in the Barberini Collection: A Provisional Catalogue.* Chicago 1957. VII, 147 pp. Arranged in serial order. Indices.

Inventarium Codicum mmss. Bibliothecae Barberinae, by S. Pieralisi. 24 vols. of which I-II describe Greek mss. III: Barb. lat. 1-357. IV: 358-627. V: 628-897. VI: 898-1228. VII: 1229-1656. VIII: 1657-1927. IX: 1928-2115. X: 2116-2480. XI: 2481-2683. XII: 2684-2984. XIII: 2985-

3251. XIV: 3252-3639. XV: 3640-3906. XVI: 3907-4129. XVII: 4130-4451. XVIII: 4452-4724. XIX: 4725-5086. XX: 5087-5321. XXI: 5322-5624. XXII: 5625-5911. XXIII: 5912-6337. XXIV (Appendice, by A. Pieralisi): 6338-6558. (Cf. Bignami 224). (micr. at MoSU)

Inventario dei Carteggi Diplomatici, by S. and A. Pieralisi. 13 vols. Barb. lat. 6559-9807. (Cf. Bignami 224). (micr. at MoSU)

Card index of the Barberini mss. in 59 bound volumes. (Bignami 224). (micr. at MoSU)

A. Solerti, 'Notizie dei libri postillati da Torquato Tasso che si conservano nella Barberiniana di Roma,' *Rivista delle Biblioteche* VI (1895) 115-17.

Fondo Rossiano. See Caselli; Wickhoff.

E. Gollob, 'Die Bibliothek des Jesuitenkollegiums in Wien XIII (Lainz) und ihre Handschriften,' *Sitzungsberichte der Kaiserlichen Akademie der Wissenschaften* [Vienna], *Philosophisch-Historische Classe* CLXI (1909) no. 7, 31 pp. Lists 120 mss. (p. 10-21). No index.

'La Biblioteca Rossiana,' unsigned article (reportedly by C. Silva Tarouca), *Civiltà Cattolica,* Anno LXXIII (1922), vol. I, quaderno 1720, p. 320-335.

The same article, *Rivista delle Biblioteche* N.S. I (1923) 19-32.

Bybl. Ross. Invent. 6 vols. I: 1-58. II: 59-310. III: 311-619. IV: 620-847. V: 848-1004. VI: 1005-1195. (Cf. Bignami 226). (micr. at MoSU).

(No title). A typed volume which describes mss. no. 1196-1203.

Codicum Rossianae Bybliothecae index, by A. Dichtl (Bignami 226). (micr. at MoSU)

Fondo Chigi.

A. Muñoz, 'I codici miniati della Biblioteca Chigi in Roma,' *Revue des Bibliothèques* XV (1905) 359-76. No index.

Ms. Chigiani, Inventario. 6 vols. I: A I 1 - D VII 108 (739 mss.). II: D VII 109 - H III 68 (804 mss.). III: H III 69 - L VIII 299 (800 mss.). IV: L VIII 300 - R I 6 (382 mss.). V: R I 7 - VIII

61; a 1-67; M IV I-M VIII LXXXVII;
O IV 43 - VII 158; R V a-d (409 mss.).
VI: R V e - R VIII q; S I 1 - S V 20;
T I 1 - IV 13; Q IV 1 - VIII 212 (414
mss.). (micr. at MoSU).

(No title). Card index in 54 vols. (micr. at
MoSU)

Fondo Ferraioli.

F. A. Berra, *Codices Ferraioli.* I (Vatican
City 1939). 898 pp. Mss. Ferraioli 1-425.
II (1948). 904 pp. Nos. 426-736.

Schedario Ferraioli. Alphabetical card index in 3 boxes. I: A-E. II: F-O. III:
P-Z. Largely superseded by the printed
catalogue of Berra, which goes to no. 736.

Archivio di S. Pietro, deposited in the Vatican Library.

F. Cancellieri, *De secretariis Basilicae Vaticanae Veteris ac Novae.* 4 vols. Rome
1786. II 906-24: Mss. of Cardinal Giorda-
no Orsini, and of the Archivio di S. Pietro.
No index.

O. Rossbach, 'Zu Ammian und den codices
Petrini,' *Philologus* LI (N. F. V, 1892)
512-18. Lists classical mss. of S. Pietro
(p. 516-18). No index.

Inventory in 2 vols. I: A 1-79; B 1-141;
C 1-154; D 1-217. II: E 1-42; F 1-45;
G 1-72; H 1-98.

Archivio di S. Maria Maggiore, deposited
in the Vatican Library.

Paulus de Angelis, *Basilicae S. Mariae Maioris de Urbe... Descriptio et Delineatio.*
Rome 1621. p. 148-150: mss.

*Växjö, Sweden. Stifts- och Gymnasie-
biblioteket. See Institut de Recherches;
Lehmann.

*Catalogue på Kongl. gymnasii bibliotequets
i Wexiö manuscripter,* by A. H. Collin
(1805). Mss. Fol. 1-215; Qu. 1-615; Oct.
1-113. (photographic reproduction seen
at the University Library in Lund).

*Vegla, see Verbenico.

*Vendôme, France. See France, *Catalogue
Général, Départements* III; XLIII.

*Venegono Inferiore (Varese), Italy. Se-
minario Arcivescovile di Milano.

See *Le biblioteche Milanesi* (Milan 1914)

145-154 (see above under Milano).

Venezia (Venice), Italy. See *Archiv* IV;
V; XII; *Archives* I; Blume; Gerbert;
Manoscritti e stampe; Mazzatinti LXVIII;
LXXVII; LXXXI; Mittarelli; *Neues Ar-
chiv*; Palacky; Reifferscheid.

—Archivio di Stato.

Miscellanea Codici (shelf mark 228). 941
mss.

*Miscellanea di atti diversi manoscritti, In-
ventario* (shelf mark 225).

—Biblioteca Nazionale Marciana.

La Biblioteca Marciana nella sua nuova sede.
Venice 1906. 117 pp. p. 89-116: Gino
Levi, 'Bibliografia Marciana.' Covers
printed catalogues and handwritten inventories.

C. Frati, 'Bollettino bibliografico Marciano:
Pubblicazioni recenti relative a codici o
stampe della Biblioteca Marciana di Venezia,' *Bibliofilia* X (1908-09) 168-87;
XI (1909-10) 140-48; 213-28; 255-62;
307-24; XII (1910-11) 102-12; 211-26;
400-19; XIII (1911-12) 78-91; 253-78;
XIV (1912) 94-100; 131-57; 397-412; 452-
61; XV (1913-14) 90-104; 134-41; 393-410.
Index.

P. La Cute, 'Le vicende delle biblioteche
monastiche veneziane dopo la soppressione
Napoleonica,' *Rivista mensile della Città
di Venezia* VIII (1929) 597-646. Covers
the printed and handwritten catalogues
of the former monastic collections absorbed by the Marciana (633-642). (NN)

Maria Luxoro, *La biblioteca di San Marco
nella sua storia.* Florence 1954. VII,
187 pp.

Jac. Phil. Tomasinus, *Bibliothecae Venetae
manuscriptae publicae et privatae.* Udine
1650. 111 pp. Index in the beginning.
Covers many collections later absorbed by
the Marciana. (MH)

The same, *Bibliothecae patavinae manuscriptae publicae et privatae.* Udine 1639.
142 pp. (Listed also under Padova). Describes several collections partly or entirely absorbed by the Biblioteca Marciana, such as S. Giovanni in Verdara, and

the old collection of the University of Padua.

A. M. Zanetti, *Latina et Italica D. Marci Bibliotheca codicum manuscriptorum per titulos digesta.* Venice 1741. 268 pp. 550 Latin mss.

J. Morelli, *Biblioteca manoscritta di T. G. Farsetti.* Venice 1771. xxii, 404 pp. 78 Latin mss. (p. 1-132). 165 Italian mss. (133-381). Shelf marks added in library copy.

Della Biblioteca manoscritta di Tommaso Giuseppe Farsetti . . . Parte seconda. Venice 1780. (Preface by J. Morelli). xix, 270 pp. Latin mss. no 79-114 (p. 1-68). Italian mss. no 166-236 (p. 69-262). Index (p. 263-70). (ICU)

Catalogo di libri latini (of the Farsetti library, by G. Morelli). Venice 1788. XV, 220 pp. p. 147-149: Latin mss. no. 115-122. p. 150-182: Italian mss. no 237-264 No index. (Venice, Biblioteca Marciana)

J. Morelli, *Codices manuscripti latini Bibliothecae Nanianae.* Venice 1776. 202 pp. 127 mss. Shelf marks added in library copy.

The same, *I codici manoscritti volgari della Libreria Naniana.* Venice 1776. 204 pp. 166 mss. Shelf marks added in library copy.

Fr. Dominicus Maria Berardelli O P., 'Codicum omnium latinorum, et italicorum, qui manuscripti in Bibliotheca SS. Johannis, et Pauli Venetiarum apud PP. Praedicatores asservantur, catalogus,' *Nuova Raccolta d'Opuscoli Scientifici e Filologici* (ed. Calogerà) XXXII (1778) no. 6, 132 pp. 103 mss.—XXXIII (1779) no. 3, 164 pp. No. 104-263.—XXXV (1780) no. 3, 158 pp. No. 264-392.— XXXVII (1782) no. 4, 96 pp. No. 393-492.—XXXVIII (1783) no. 2, p. 97-170. No. 493-548.—XXXIX (1784) no 6, 144 pp. No. 549-607.—XL (1784) no. 5, 78 pp. No. 608-48. Each part indexed. (PPAP)

J. Morelli, *Bibliotheca manuscripta graeca et latina.* Vol. I (all published), Bassano 1802. XI, 499 pp. 17 Latin mss. (p. 321-477), marked as V (Marciana), M (Morelli),

C (Canonici). The last group is now at the Bodleian, at least for the most part, the others at the Marciana. (ICU)

Isis 1822, *Beylage* no. 13 coll. 1-4: 'Auf der Marcus-Bibliothek zu Venedig befinden sich unter vielen andern folgende Codices.' Lists a few. (NNM)

Bibliografia Dalmata tratta da' codici della Marciana di Venezia (by G. Valentinelli). Venice 1845. II, 45 pp. (DLC)

J. Valentinelli, 'Catalogus codicum manuscriptorum de rebus foroiuliensibus ex bibliotheca palatina ad d. Marci Venetiarum,' *Archiv für Kunde österreichischer Geschichts-Quellen* XVIII (1857) 331-473. Index (451ff.).

The same, *Bibliotheca Manuscripta ad S. Marci Venetiarum.* 6 vols. in 2, Venice 1868-73. Arranged by subjects. Arrangement does not correspond to library shelfmarks (which are given in parentheses). Each vol. indexed. Not complete.

L. G. Pélissier, 'Catalogue des Documents de la collection Podocataro à la Bibliothèque Marciane à Venise,' *Centralblatt für Bibliothekswesen* XVIII (1901) 473-93; 521-41; 576-98. Covers Marc. lat. X 174-178.

A. Segarizzi, 'Reliquie d'una biblioteca monastica veneziana,' *Il libro e la Stampa* N.S. III (1909) 1-5. 14 mss. of Marciana. (NN)

C. Frati and A. Segarizzi, *Catalogo dei codici Marciani Italiani.* 2 vols. Modena 1909-11. I: Fondo Antico; classes I-III. II: Classes IV-V.

Biblioteca Manoscritta Farsetti, Parte Terza. 1 ms. vol. Begins with Latin mss. no. 117 and Italian ms. no. 237. Largely superseded by the printed lists.

Appendice. Codici Orientali. 2 ms. vols. (AB III 255).

Appendice. Codici Greci. 1 ms. vol. and 1 index vol. (AB III 256). 11 classes.

Appendice. Codici Latini. 4 ms. vols. and 2 index vols. Vol. I: Class I (Biblia Sacra et Interpretes), 103 mss. Class II (Patres et Scriptores Ecclesiastici), 145 mss. Class

III (Theologi), 245 mss. Class IV (Concilia et Ius Canonicum), 122 mss.—Vol. II: Class V (Ius civile), 142 mss. Class VI (Philosophi), 318 mss. Class VII (Medicina et Historia Naturalis), 68 mss. Class VIII (Mathematici et Astronomi), 158 mss. Class IX (Historia ecclesiastica), 200 mss. —Vol. III: Class X (Historia profana), 413 mss. Class XI (Rhetores), 162 mss. Class XII (Poetae), 253 mss.—Vol. IV: Class XIII (Philologi et grammatici), 157 mss. Class XIV (Miscellanea et epistolae), 339 mss. Actual shelf marks added in the margins. This appendix lists the mss. acquired after the publication of Zanetti's printed catalogue of 1741. It is superseded for about two thirds by the printed catalogue of Valentinelli who follows a different arrangement of his own not corresponding to the actual shelf marks of the library, and who omits Classes XI-XIV and scattered mss. of the other classes (Cf. AB III 256).

Appendice. Codici Italiani. 6 ms. vols. and 3 index vols. Vol. I: Class I (Biblia Sacra e scrittori ecclesiastici), 110 mss. Class II: (Giurisprudenza e filosofia), 180 mss. Class III (Medicina, Istoria naturale), 80 mss.—Vol. II: Class IV (Matematici, ed arti del disegno e musica), 2041 mss. Class V (Istoria ecclesiastica), 133 mss.— Vol. III: Class VI (Istoria civile, e Geografia), 502 mss.—Vol. IV: Class VII (Istoria ecclesiastica e civile Veneziana), 2522 mss.—Vol. V: Class VIII (Oratori), 34 mss. Class IX (Poeti), 697 mss.— Vol. VI: Class X (Grammatici, Filologi, ed Epistolari), 485 mss. Class XI (Miscellanea), 435 mss. Actual shelf marks added in the margins. This section is superseded by printed catalogues through Class VII, cod. 500 (vol. IV middle) (Cf. AB III 258) (micr. of vols. IV-VI at DLC)

Appendice. Codici francesi e stranieri (AB III 256). (micr. at DLC)

Concordanze Segnature Manoscritti. N(uova) Collocazione-Classi. 1 ms. vol. Goes to

no. 12286.

Concordanze Segnature Manoscritti. Classi-N(uova) Collocazione. 1 ms. vol.

Elenco dei Codici Manoscritti Latini Italiani Riservati in Appendice ai descritti negli altri elenchi. 1 ms. vol. 179 mss. Some of them have been transferred to the main sections. (micr. at DLC)

Catalogo Zorzanello. A large set of ms. sheets in many boxes, prepared by the late Prof. Pietro Zorzanello, as a supplement to the printed catalogues. It covers the Fondo antico (Zanetti), classes I-XIV of the Latin mss., and classes VI-XIV of the Italian mss. The sections covering class VI, and class VII no. 1-500, have now been published in Mazzatinti LXXVII and LXXXI. This catalogue largely supersedes the inventories of the *Appendice*, and offers much better descriptions.

—Biblioteca Querini-Stampalia.

L. Perosa, 'Dei codici manoscritti della Biblioteca Querini-Stampalia recentemente ordinati e registrati, Relazione,' *Archivio Veneto* XXVIII (1884) 244-61. Not a catalogue.

Catalogo dei codici manoscritti della Biblioteca Querini-Stampalia (1883). Arranged by subjects. Mss. I 1-30; II 1-23; III 1-61; IV 1-640; V 1-41; VI 1-153; VII 1-104; VIII 1-35; IX 1-66. (micr. at DLC)

* *Repertorio alfabetico dei codd. mss.* (1884). (Communication of D. Schullian).

—Frati Francescani di S. Michele in Isola. A few mss. No inventory.

—Museo Civico Correr.

Fondo Cicogna.

** *Descrizione di alquanti codici e libri già posseduti da E. A. Cicogna ed ora passati in proprietà del Museo Civico.* Venice 1868. (Not located in Italy or the United States)

Catalogo dei codici mss. posseduti da Emmanuele Cicogna. (Inside:) *Catalogo della Biblioteca di Emmanuele Cicogna di Venezia. Codici Manoscritti...* (1841-64). 7 vols. I: mss. 1-1000. II: 1001-2000. III: 2001-2500. IV: 2501-3000. V: 3001-

3500. VI: 3501-4100. VII: 4101-4439.
The serial numbers of the catalogue are
different from the actual shelf marks which
are entered in red ink (Cf. AB III 369).
(micr. at DLC)

*Concordance for the old and new nos. of
the Fondo Cicogna. (Communication of
D. Schullian). (micr. at DLC)

Fondo Correr. Card index in 4 boxes
(AB III 369).

Fondo Miscellanea Correr. *Correr Miscellanea Mss.* 85 ms. vols. and 2752 items.

Fondo Donà dalle Rose. *Catalogo dei
Codici che componevano l'Archivio dei Nobili Conti Donà dalle Rose, ora presso il
Museo Civico e Raccolta Correr.* 500 mss.
(Cf. AB III 369). (micr. at DLC)

Fondo Gradenigo. *Codici Gradenigo, Catalogo ed Indice.* 230 mss. (Cf. AB III
369). (micr. at DLC)

Fondo Malvezzi. *Indice dei manoscritti di
storia Veneta e d'altre materie posseduti
dall' Avvocato Giuseppe M. Malvezzi.* Venice 1861. 15 pp. Preface signed by V.
Lazari. 200 nos. Shelf marks in parentheses. No index. (MH)

Provvenienze diverse. Card index (AB
III 369). Covers also the Fondo Wcovich-Lazzari. (micr. at DLC)

Fondo Morosini-Grimani. *Card index (AB
III 369). See now Mazzatinti LXVIII.

Fondo Wcovich-Lazzari.

*Elenco manoscritti lasciati al Museo Civico
e Correr dal Can. Michiele Wcovich Lazzari* (communication of D. Schullian).
(micr. at DLC)

—Padri Redentoristi. A few mss. No inventory.

—Seminario Patriarcale.

(No title). Handwritten list for mss. 1-518.
Centuries not given. (micr. at DLC)

(No title). Alphabetical list of mss. to no.
959. Several mss. missing.

Card index. Covers all mss. (*ca.* 1000).

Ventimiglia, Italy. Biblioteca Aprosiana.

*Catalogo dei Libri e Manoscritti della Biblioteca Aprosiana (ora Civica) riordinata
nel 1901 a cura del munifico Commenda-*

tore *Sir Tommaso Hanbury.* Alphabetical
list of mss. and edd. Most mss. were
lost during the last war.

*Verbenico (Veglia), Italy. See Wickhoff.

Vercelli, Italy. See Andres; *Archiv* XII;
Blume; Mazzatinti XXXI; Reifferscheid;
Serapeum XVIII.

—Biblioteca Agnesiana.

(No title). 1 ms. folder. Lists 14 parchment
mss. and 28 paper mss. Not complete.

—Biblioteca Capitolare.

(G. De-Gregory, *Istoria della Vercellese letteratura ed Arti.* 4 pts. in 3 vols. Turin
1819-24. pt. 4 p. 562-66: 'Bianchini elencus Manuscriptorum bibliothecae seu archivii Eusebiani Cathedralis Vercellensis.'
61 mss. p. 567-69: 'Anno MDCII index
librorum et codicum manuscriptorum
membranaceorum archivii cathedralis Vercellensis per Joannem Franc. Leonem
canonicum...' 177 mss.)

Appendice. Aggiunti al Catalogo dei Manoscritti dell' Archivio Capitolare di Vercelli, by P. Marinone. 2 pp., privately
printed and dated 1955. Supplementing
Mazzatinti XXXI, the list covers mss.
no. 219-225.

—Biblioteca Civica.

*Card index (AB IV 179).

*Verden, West Germany. See Cooper (Section A).

*Verdun, France. See France, *Catalogue
Général, Départements* V (Quarto Series);
XLIII.

*Verneuil, France. See France, *Catalogue
Général, Départements* II; Martin.

*Veroli, Italy. See Mazzatinti XXXIV.

Verona, Italy. See *Archiv* V; XII; *Archives*
I; Blume; *Giornale;* Montfaucon; Reifferscheid.

—Biblioteca Capitolare.

(Sc. Maffei), *Istoria teologica delle dottrine e
delle opinioni corse ne' cinque primi secoli
della Chiesa in proposito della divina Grazia, del libero arbitrio, e della Predestinazione . . .* Trent 1742. 508, 272 pp. Appendix p. 56-61: 'Notizia generale de
gl'insigni manuscritti, che si conservano

nel Capitolo Canonicale di Verona . . .'
p. 62-95: 'Bibliothecae Veronensis Manuscriptae pars prima Capitularium codicum notitiam complectens.' Mostly without shelf marks. (NNG)

(Jac. Dionisi), 'Notizia d'alcuni codici manoscritti,' *Storia letteraria d'Italia* XIV (Modena 1759) 108-29.

Sc. Maffei, *Verona Illustrata*, 4 pts. in 5 vols. Milan 1825-26. pt. 3 vol. IV (1826) p. 351-401: Mss. Saibante, Capitolare, Maffei. No index.

G. B. Carlo Giuliari, 'La Capitolare Biblioteca di Verona,' *Archivio Veneto* X (1875) 239-71; XI (1876) 51-74; XII (1876) 56-79; 274-93; XIV (1877) 39-48; XVI (1878) 219-38; XVII (1879) 233-50; XVIII (1879) 5-22; XIX (1880) 72-89; XX (1880) 5-41; 203-34; XXI (1881) 203-31; XXII (1881) 271-88; XXIII (1882) 5-27; XXVII (1884) 453-71; XXVIII (1884) 223-43; 427-39; XXX (1885) 477-514; XXXIII (1887) 203-17; 511-27; XXXV (1888) 191-205. A history of the library, with occasional mention of some mss.

The same, 'Spicilegium Capitularis Bibliothecae Veronensis,' *Archivio Storico Italiano*, Ser. III, vol. XXV (1877) 135-39. Describes mss. no. 1-6. No index.

A. Spagnolo, 'Storia letteraria della biblioteca capitolare di Verona,' *Nuovo Archivio Veneto* XII (1896) 259-71; XIII (1897) 375-84. Recent chronicle of the library only. (NN)

V. Lazzerini, 'Scuola Calligrafica Veronese del secolo IX,' *Memorie del Reale Veneto Istituto di Scienze, Lettere ed Arti* XXVII (1902-07), no. 3 (1904), 14 pp. Describes c. 14 mss. No index.

A. Spagnolo, 'La scrittura minuscola e le scuole calligrafiche veronesi del VI e IX secolo,' *Atti e Memorie dell' Accademia d'agricoltura scienze lettere arti e commercio di Verona*, Ser. IV, vol. XII (LXXXVII, 1912) 31-50. Describes 32 early mss. (p. 46-50). (NN)

E. Carusi and W. M. Lindsay, *Monumenti paleografici Veronesi*. (Codices ex ecclesiasticis Italiae Bybliothecis delecti phototypice expressi). 2 pts. Rome 1929-34. (Pierpont Morgan Library)

Maria Venturini, *Vita ed attività dello 'Scriptorium' Veronese nel secolo XI*. Verona 1930. 132 pp. Discusses a few mss. (p. 66ff.). No index. (MH)

Maria Luisa Giuliano, *Coltura ed attività calligrafica nel secolo XII a Verona*. (R. Università di Padova. Pubblicazioni della Facoltà di Lettere e Filosofia V). Padua 1933. 127 pp. Lists some mss. (p. 44ff.). (NN)

Catalogo dei Manoscritti Capitolari, by A. Spagnolo. 3 vols. Vol. I: mss. I-CCVII. II: CCVIII-DCCXLIX. III: DCCL-MCXIV.

*Alphabetical index, by Mons. G. Turrini. (Communication of D. Schullian).

—Biblioteca Comunale.

G. Biadego, *Catalogo descrittivo dei manoscritti della Biblioteca Comunale di Verona*. Verona 1892. 664 pp. 1366 mss. Not complete. Valid shelf marks in parentheses.

(No title) Handwritten inventory for mss. 1-3032. The printed catalogue by Biadego (*Traditio* VI 314) follows a different arrangement and arrives with many omissions only at no. 2224 of the inventory. (micr. at DLC)

*Versailles, France. See France, *Catalogue Général, Départements* IX; XLIII.

*Vervins, France. See France, *Catalogue Général, Départements* XLIII.

*Veselí, Czechoslovakia. See under **Brno**.

*Vesoul, France. See France, *Catalogue Général, Départements* VI; XLIII.

*Vibo Valentia (Catanzaro), Italy. Biblioteca dei Conti Capialbi. See Mazzatinti VII 195-205 under Monteleone.

Vicenza, Italy. See *Archives* I; Blume; *Giornale*; Mazzatinti II.

—Biblioteca Comunale Bertoliana.

D. Bortolan and S. Rumor, *La Biblioteca Bertoliana di Vicenza*. Vicenza 1892. 223 pp. Surveys some mss. (p. 137-148). No shelf marks. (MH)

(Fondo principale). *Inventario della Camera G. Manoscritti e qualche stampato prezioso.* This inventory contains more than the printed list in Mazzatinti II which is based on it and does not always give give the actual shelf marks (Cf. AB III 368).

Carteggio collocato nella Camera G. Contains section on autographs of the sixteenth century.

*Card index. In 1 box (AB III 367-68).

(Fondo Gonzati). *Inventario dei Man. della lib. Gonzati.* (Inside:) *Biblioteca Bertoliana. Manoscritti che si trovano nella Libreria di M.r Lodovico Gonzati da aggiungersi a quelli della Bertoliana. Catalogo fatto nel 1878.* Most of these mss. are not listed in Mazzatinti II (Cf. AB III 368).

*Card index of Fondo Gonzati, in 3 boxes (AB III 367-68).

*Vich**, Spain. Museo Episcopal. See Beer (Section A); Grubbs (Section A, under Richardson); *Serapeum* VIII; Villanueva; Volger.

Josep Gudiol, 'Catàleg dels llibres manuscrits anteriors al segle XVIII del Museu episcopal de Vich,' *Butlletí de la Biblioteca de Catalunya* VI (1920-22) 50-97; VII (1923-27) 59-154; VIII (1928-32) 46-120. 231 mss. Also published separately, with added index. Barcelona 1934. 230 pp. Index also in Grubbs. (Hispanic Society of America, New York).

Vienna, see **Wien**.

*Vienne**, France. See France, *Catalogue Général, Départements* XXI; XLIII.

*Vigevano**, Italy. See Mazzatinti V.

A. Tornielli, *I corali miniati di Vigevano* (Fontes Ambrosiani 23). Milan 1946. 111 pp. and plates. Lists 27 liturgical mss. at the Cattedrale and S. Ignazio. (NN)

*Villanueva y Geltrú**, Spain. Biblioteca Balaguer. See Cordoliani.

Ca. 1000 mss.

*Villefranche** (Rhône), France. See France, *Catalogue Général, Départements* XX; XLIII.

*Villefranche-de-Rouergue**, France. See *ibid.* XXXI.

*Villeneuve-sur-Lot**, France. See *ibid.* XXXI; XLIII.

*Villeneuve-sur-Yonne**, France. See *ibid.* IX.

*Vipiteno-Sterzing**, Italy.

I. V. Zingerle, 'Bericht über die Sterzinger Miscellaneen-Handschrift,' *Sitzungsberichte der Philosophisch-Historischen Classe der Kaiserlichen Akademie der Wissenschaften* LIV (Vienna 1867) 293-340.

No information concerning the present location of the ms.

*Vire**, France. See France, *Catalogue Général, Départements* X; XLIII.

Viterbo, Italy. Biblioteca Capitolare.

L. Dorez, 'Latino Latini et la bibliothèque capitulaire de Viterbe,' *Revue des Bibliothèques* II (1892) 377-91; V (1895) 237-60. 82 mss. (V, 241-55). Index (256-60). Not complete. Does not give the present shelf marks.

Catalogo di bolle, brevi pont., codici e documenti. 3 vols. I: mss. 1-58. II: mss. 59-259. III: Charters.

—Biblioteca Comunale.

**Catalogo Inventario dei Manoscritti*, by Avv. Signorelli (1915, with additions to 1939). 1932 mss. (Communication of the librarian, cf. AB V 517).

*Vitré**, France. See France, *Catalogue Général, Départements* XXIV.

*Vitry-Le-François**, France. See France, *Catalogue Général, Départements* XIII; XLIII.

*(G. Hérelle, *Catalogue des manuscrits de la Bibliothèque de Vitry-le-François*. Paris 1877. xv, 88 pp.) (ICU)

*Viviers**, France. See Martin.

Volterra, Italy. Bibliotheca Guarnacciana. See Mazzatinti II; *Studi Italiani* XVIII. The library copy of Mazzatinti has ms. notes and a ms. appendix listing 96 mss. acquired after 1896.

Archivio Maffei, Inventario. 49 mss. Copy kindly supplied by Dott. Tito Cangini.

*Vorau**, Austria. See *Archiv* X; Wickhoff.

P. Fank, *Catalogus Voraviensis seu codices manuscripti Bibliothecae Canoniae in Vorau.* Graz 1936. 276 pp. 416 mss. (NN)

(M. Pangerl, 'Die Handschriftensammlung des Chorherrenstiftes Vorau,' *Beiträge zur Kunde steiermärkischer Geschichtsquellen* IV [1867] 85-137. Describes some mss.) (NN)

*Vyšší Brod (Hohenfurt), Czechoslovakia. See *Archiv* X; *Xenia Bernardina.*

Warszawa, Poland. See Aland (Section A); *Société française.* See also under Sucha.

(Naczelna Dyrekcja Archiwów Państwowych). *Straty Bibliotek i Archiwów Warszawskich w Zakresie Rękopiśmiennych Źródeł Historycznych.* 3 vols. Warsaw 1955-57. I (1957) and II (1956): Archives. III (1955): Libraries. Covers the war losses of the Warsaw collections. (MH)

—Biblioteka Narodowa.

Before the war, the nucleus of this collection consisted of a large group of Zaluski mss. returned from Leningrad after 1918. See also under Leningrad. Most of these mss. were destroyed during the last war.

J. D. A. Janozki, *Specimen catalogi codicum manuscriptorum Bibliothecae Zaluscianae.* (Dresden) 1752. II, 175 pp. 500 mss. (NN; micr. at NNC)

J. Korzeniowski, *Zapiski z Rękopisów Cesarskiej Biblioteki Publicznej w Petersburgu i innych Bibliotek Petersburgich* (Archiwum do Dziejow Literatury i Oswiaty w Polsce XI). Cracow 1910. XLI, 408 pp. 491 mss. of which over 260 in Latin (p. 1-196 and 351ff.). (NN)

Sigla codicum manuscriptorum qui olim in Bibliotheca publica Leninopolitana exstantes nunc in Bibliotheca universitatis Varsoviensis asservantur. (By W. Suchodolski). (Prace Bibljoteczne Krakowskiego Koła Związku Bibljotekarzy Polskich IV). Cracow 1928. 75 pp. Lists shelf marks. No content given.

Supplementum ad sigla codicum manuscriptorum qui olim in Bibliotheca Publica Leninopolitana exstantes nunc in Bibliotheca Universitatis Varsaviensis asservantur. Edita cura Delegationis Polonicae in Mixta Polono-Sovietica Commissione Peculiari Moscoviae (Prace Bibljoteczne Krakowskiego Koła Związku Bibljotekarzy Polskich IV). Cracow 1928. 7 pp. (Warsaw, Biblioteka Narodowa)

P. Bánkowski, *Rękopisy Rewindykowane Przez Polskę z Z.S.R.R. na Podstawie Traktatu Ryskiego i ich Dotychczasowe Opracowania* Cracow 1937. 51 pp. (NN)

B. Horodysky, 'Spuścizna Działu Rękopiśmiennego Biblioteki Załuskich,' *Przegląd Biblioteczny* XVI (1948) 40-63. Gives a list of shelf marks of the mss. kept in Ottawa during the last war and hence preserved. (NN)

Mme. Z. Ameisenowa, 'De quelques précieux manuscrits français à peintures, provenant de la Bibliothèque de Wilanów actuellement à la Bibliothèque Nationale de Varsovie,' *Bulletin International de l'Académie Polonaise des Sciences et des Lettres, Classe de Philologie, Classe d'Histoire et de Philosophie* 1933 (published 1934) 5-10. 3 mss.

Katalog rękopisów Bibljoteki Narodowej. 4 vols. in 5, 1929-55. I (Warsaw 1929), by A. Lewak. Mss. no. 1-1314. II, pts. 1-2 (1938), by A. Lewak and H. Więckowska. Mss. no. 1315-2299. III (1933), by H. Więckowska. Mss. no. 2300-2666. IV (Wroclaw 1955), by B. Horodyski. Mss. no. 2667-3000; 7001-7200. The mss. listed in vols. I-III were all lost during the last war. The mss. listed in vol. IV are extant. All mss. listed in this catalogue are late. (NN)

For the mss. between 3000 and 7000, not yet described in the printed catalogue, there is a card file in 3 boxes, arranged by temporary numbers. I: 1-2200. II: 2201-4110. III: 4111-6460.

Card file of recent accessions, in 4 boxes. Mostly late.

Accession list, arranged by temporary numbers. Covers mss. 6001 (1950)-7410 (1958). Above 6000, it repeats the items in box 3 of the first card file.

(Krasiński collection). Most of the mss. were lost during the last war. Those which are preserved now form a section of the Biblioteka Narodowa.

F. Pulaski, *Opis 815 rękopisów Biblioteki Ord. Krasińskich*, (Biblioteka Ordinacyi Krasińskich Muzeum Konstantego Swidżińskiego XXIII-XXIX). Warsaw 1915. 937 and 70 pp. 815 mss. of which some are Latin. (NN)

Marja Hornowska, *Rękopisy Bibljoteki Ord. Krasińskich, dotyczące dziejów Szkolnictwa Polskiego*. Warsaw 1930. 320 pp. Covers a few Latin mss. (NN)

Spis Rękopisów Biblioteki Ord. Krasińskich. Typed list of 23 extant Krasinski mss.

(Zamoyski collection). Also this collection now forms a part of the Biblioteka Narodowa, but most of its mss. have been preserved.

R. Förster, 'Zur Handschriftenkunde und Geschichte der Philologie, VI: Handschriften der Zamoyski'schen Bibliothek,' *Rheinisches Museum* N. F. LV (1900) 435-59. Lists Latin mss. (p. 450).

V. Hahn, 'Griechische und lateinische Handschriften der Gräflich Zamoyskischen Bibliothek in Warschau,' *Wochenschrift für klassische Philologie* XVII (1900) 1323-27. 8 Latin mss. (1326-27).

Typed list of preserved Zamoyski mss. Covers over 200 mss.

Spis Rękopisów Biblioteki Ordynacji Zamojskiej. Typed continuation of the preceding list. Covers mss. 801-1970. Mostly late.

(Bawerowski collection). *Wykaz rękopisów ze zbiorów W. Bawerowskiego.* Typed list of 1329 mss.

(Morstin collection).

J. Czubek, *Rękopisy Hr. Morstinów w Krakowie*. Cracow 1911. VII, 21 pp. 100 mss. (NN)

*Warwick, England. See Bernardus.

Washington, D.C., U.S.A. See De Ricci.

*Weilburg, West Germany. See under Wiesbaden.

*Weert, Holland. See *Archivum Francisca-*

num Historicum XLIX.

Weimar, East Germany. Landesbibliothek. See *Archiv* VIII.

H. L. Schurzfleischi *Notitia Bibliothecae Vinariensis* . . . Wittenberg 1712. 295 pp. Historical survey, not a catalogue. Index. 'Beschreibung seltener Bücher und merkwürdiger Handschriften, die sich auf der Gross-Herzoglichen Bibliothek zu Weimar befinden,' *Curiositäten der physisch-literarisch-artistischen Vor- und Mitwelt* VII (1818) 255-68; VIII (1820) 171-81. Lists only printed editions and 3 German mss. *Hss.-Kat.* (by Preller). 3 ms. vols. Arranged by subjects.

*Wellesley, Massachusetts, U.S.A. See De Ricci.

Margaret Hastings Jackson, *Catalogue of the Frances Taylor Pearsons Plimpton Collection of Italian Books and Manuscripts in the Library of Wellesley College*. Cambridge Mass. 1929. 434 pp. p. 393-433: Mss., some in Latin. Arranged alphabetically.

*Wellington, New Zealand. See Taylor.

Wells, England. See Bernardus; Schenkl; Williams.

*Werden, West Germany. Pfarrarchiv. See Schmidt.

*Wernigerode, East Germany. See under Halle.

*Wertheim, West Germany. Evangelische Kirchenbibliothek. 56 mss. Card catalogue. (Communication of Dr. Alfred Friese)

—Fürstl. Löwenstein-Wertheim-Rosenbergsches Archiv. See Lehmann.

*Wesel, West Germany.

Braun, *Die Handschriften und alten Drucke der Gymnasial-Bibliothek*. progr. Wesel 1876. 88 pp. p. 50-51; 5 mss. No index. (Erlangen, Univ. Library)

*Wesseli, see **Veseli**.

*Westeras, see **Västeras**.

Wien (Vienna), Austria. See *Analecta Bollandiana* XIV; *Archiv* I; III; VI; VIII; X; Diekamp; Durrieu; Lampen; Saxl; *Société française*; Wickhoff; Wolkan.

For the mss. returned to Italy after 1918, see Coggiola; Modigliani; Tietze. See also under Napoli; Trento.

—*Dominikanerkonvent. See Gottlieb; Scheeben.

Verzeichnis der Handschriften des Dominikanerkonventes in Wien bis zum Ende des 16. Jahrhunderts, by Dr. Felix Czeike (1952). 1 typed vol. 240 ms.. (micr. at DLC).

Handschriften-Katalog, by R. Henz. 240 nos. Largely superseded by the preceding catalogue.

Some mss. were taken during the last war to Munich. See under Munich.

—*Minoritenkonvent. See *Archivum Franciscanum Historicum* XLIX.

*Handwritten inventory, by P. Barnabas Strasser (1768). Lists 82 mss.

H. Vollmer, 'Notizen zu österreichischen Bibliotheken,' *Zentralblatt für Bibliothekswesen* XXVII (1910) 165-166. Lists 5 mss. (p. 166). The library suffered some losses, and has not yet been rearranged after the last war. (Communication of the librarian).

—*Kunsthistorisches Museum.

Most of the mss. have been turned over to the Nationalbibliothek.

—Österreichische Nationalbibliothek.

P. Lambecius, *Commentariorum de augustissima Bibliotheca Caesarea Vindobonensi*. 2 vols. in 4, Vienna 1665-69. (NN)

The same work, 2nd ed. by A. F. Kollarius, 8 vols. Vienna 1766-82. Vol. II coll. 521ff.: Mss. transferred from Ambras. (NNUT)

Bibliotheca Antiqua Vindobonensis Civica seu Catalogus librorum antiquorum, cum manuscriptorum tum ab inventa typographia ad annum 1560 typis excusorum, qui in Bibliotheca Vindobonensi Civica asservantur... (By Ph. J. Lambacher). Vienna 1750. pt. I, *Libros theologicos complectens.* 286 and 42 pp. Arranged by subjects, mostly printed editions. (MH)

M. Denis, *Codices manuscripti theologici bibliothecae palatinae Vindobonensis Latini aliarumque Occidentis linguarum.* 2 vols. in 6 pts. Vienna 1793-1802. I: 975 mss. II: 945 mss. Each volume indexed. (NN)

S. Endlicher, *Catalogus codicum philologicorum latinorum Bibliothecae Palatinae Vindobonensis.* Vienna 1836. 401 pp. 432 mss.

J. Chmel, *Die Handschriften der k.k. Hofbibliothek in Wien, im Interesse der Geschichte, besonders der österreichischen, verzeichnet und excerpirt.* 2 vols. Vienna 1840-41. 404 mss. Each volume indexed.

E. von Sackur, *Die K. K. Ambraser Sammlung.* 2 vols. in 1, Vienna 1855. II, 197-260: 112 mss. No index.

Tabulae codicum manuscriptorum praeter graecos et orientales in Bibliotheca Palatina Vindobonensi asservatorum. 11 vols. Vienna 1864-1912. I (1864): No. 1-2000. II (1868): No. 2001-3500. III (1869): No. 3501-5000. IV (1870): No. 5001-6500. V (1871): No. 6501-9000. VI (1873): No. 9001-11500. VII (1875): No. 11501-14000. VIII (1893): No. 14001-15500. IX (1897): No. 15501-17500. X (1899): No. 17501-19500. XI (1912): Series Nova 1-1600. Each volume indexed. (I-X: NNC; XI: PU)

T. Gottlieb, *Die Ambraser Handschriften.* Vol. I (all published): *Büchersammlung Kaiser Maximilians* I. Leipzig 1900. VI, 172 pp. List of mss. (p. 169). (NN)

H. Gerstinger, 'Johannes Sambucus als Handschriftensammler,' *Festschrift der Nationalbibliothek in Wien*, Vienna 1926, 251-400. Lists his mss. (p. 349ff.). Index (397-400).

Nationalbibliothek in Wien, Katalog der Ausstellung von Neuerwerbungen aus den Jahren 1930-1935. Vienna 1936. 89 pp. and plates. 475 nos. No index.

F. Unterkircher, *Inventar der illuminierten Handschriften, Inkunabeln und Frühdruczke der Österreichischen Notionalbibliothek.* Part I: *Die abendländischen Handschriften.* (Museion, N.F. II, part 1). Vienna 1957. XIV, 322 pp. Indices.

Die Sammlungen der Vereinten Familien- und Privat-Bibliothek Sr. M. des Kaisers.

(By M. A. Becker) 3 vols. in 4, Vienna 1873-82. I (1873) i-xxii: Mss. (DLC)
Card index for the main collection.
Inventory on cards, in 4 boxes, continuing the printed catalogue. I: Series Nova 1601-2599. II: 2600-3149. III: 3150-3999. IV: 4000-4123.
Card index for the Series Nova.
Concordia von Ser. nova, Mss. autogr., Einbänden. A summary list.
Series Nova 4850-12000 are uncatalogued and mostly modern.
Series Nova 12001-13262 are from the private library of the emperor. See the printed catalogue by Becker.
Bibliotheca domestica Francisci I. imperatoris Austriaci. Pars I. Sectio secunda. Quae Catalogum Codicum manuscriptorum ordine alphabetico digestum complectitur (1811, shelf mark S.N. 12696). More detailed than the printed catalogue by Becker.
Konkordanz von den Signaturen (Inventarnummern) der Handschriften aus der ehemaligen Fideikommissbibliothek auf die nunmehr gültigen Series nova-Nummern (1952).
—*Österreichisches Staatsarchiv.
C. Edler von Böhm, *Die Handschriften des k. und k. Haus-, Hof- und Staats-Archivs.* Vienna 1873. VI, 418 pp. 1108 mss. *Supplement.* Vienna 1874. IV, 136 pp. 431 mss. (ICU)
Supplementissimum zu Böhm. 1 typed vol., covering mss. to no. 1334, and 1 vol. of indices. (Communication of the archivist)
Inventare Oesterreichischer Staatlicher Archive. V. *Inventare des Wiener Haus-, Hof- und Staatsarchives.* VI. *Gesamtinventar des Wiener Haus-, Hof- und Staatsarchivs,* by L. Bitterer. Vol. III (Vienna 1938), p. 167-169, cf. 215-217. Lists the mss. turned over to Italy and other countries after 1918, giving their Böhm numbers, but not their content.
—*Schottenkloster.
A. Hübl, *Catalogus codicum manuscriptorum qui in Bibliotheca Monasterii B. M. V. ad*

Scotos Vindobonae servantur. Vienna and Leipzig 1899. 609 pp. 750 mss.
—*Stadtbibliothek. The mss. listed in the catalogue of 1750 (see above) are now in the Nationalbibliothek.
Katalog der Bibliothek der K.K. Reichshaupt- und Residenzstadt Wien. Vienna 1865. 216 pp. Includes some late local mss. (DLC)
—Universitätsbibliothek.
Inventory, in 3 boxes. Arranged by languages.
*Wiener-Neustadt, Austria. See *Xenia Bernardina.*
*Wiesbaden, West Germany. See *Archiv* XI; *Neues Archiv* IX; XI.
A. v. d. Linde, *Die Handschriften der Kgl. Landesbibliothek in Wiesbaden.* Wiesbaden 1877. 146 pp. 78 mss. (DLC)
G. Zedler, *Die Handschriften der Nassauischen Landesbibliothek zu Wiesbaden.* (Zentralblatt für Bibliothekswesen, Beiheft LXIII). Leipzig 1931. 135 pp. 238 mss.
*Handwritten supplement to Zedler's catalogue, describes mss. no. 239-360. Partial microfilm supplied by the librarian. These mss. are mostly late, but they include the 5 mss. formerly owned by the Gymnasialbibliothek in Weilburg. These 5 mss., along with a few others, were lost during the last war. (Communication of the librarian)
R. Gropius, *Die älteren Handschriften der Gymnasialbibliothek zu Weilburg.* progr. Weilburg 1885. 38 pp. p. 3-15: 5 mss. No index. (Erlangen, University Library)
Hans-Georg Böhme, *Geschichte der Bibliothek des Gymnasiums zu Weilburg.* (Sonderdruck aus dem Nachrichtenblatt für die Mitglieder der Wilinaburgia, Verein ehemaliger Angehöriger des Gymnasiums zu Weilburg E. V.). Weilburg 1949. 139 pp. p. 49-50: 5 mss. (MH)
*Wilhering, Austria. See *Xenia Bernardina.*
*Williamstown, Massachusetts. Williams College. See De Ricci.
The Chapin Library, Williams College. A Short-Title List, by Lucy E. Osborne.

Portland, Maine, 1939. VIII, 595 pp.
p. 3-5: 17 early mss.

*Wilten, Austria. See Wickhoff.

Winchester, England. See Holtzmann
(Section A); Bernardus; *Neues Archiv*
XXII; Schenkl.

—Cathedral Library.

Description of Manuscripts, by Dr. G. F.
Warner. (Inside:) *Catalogue of Manuscripts in the Cathedral Library Winchester.*
1 folder of typed sheets. 19 mss.

—Winchester College. The Warden and
Fellows' Library.

Catalogue of Mss. A topographical list (by
W. F. Oakeshott). 1 folder of ms. sheets
Ca. 76 mss.

*Windberg, West Germany. See Cooper
(Section A); Gercken.

*Windsheim, West Germany. Stadtbibliothek.

*Handwritten inventory. Lists 100 mss.
Selective list of 21 mss. kindly supplied by
the librarian.

Windsor, England.

—Royal Library.

R. R. Holmes, *Specimens of Royal Fine,
and Historical Bookbinding, selected from
the Royal Library, Windsor Castle.* London 1893. V, 16 pp. and plates. 152 nos.
(mss. and edd.). This catalogue is nearly
complete for the mss., and its numbers
serve as shelf marks.

—*St. George's Chapel.

M. R. James, 'The Manuscripts of St.
George's Chapel, Windsor,' *The Library,*
Fourth Series XIII (Transactions of the
Bibliographical Society, Second Series,
XIII, Oxford 1933) 55-76. 6 mss. (p.
72-76). No index.

John N. Dalton, *The Manuscripts of St.
George's Chapel, Windsor Castle.* (Windsor
1957). XXXVI, 629 pp. Hardly relevant.

*Winnocsberg, see Bergues.

*Winterthur, Switzerland. Stadtbibliothek.

*Katalog der Bürgerbibliothek in Winterthur
(by U. Hegner). Winterthur 1836. 252 pp.
p. 247-52: 135 mss. (Winterthur)

*Katalog der Bürgerbibliothek in Winterthur.
Winterthur 1855. 184 pp. p. 124-27:
137 mss. (Winterthur)

**Catalogus der Handschriften der Stadt-
Bibliothek Winterthur*, by A. Hafner
(1877). 758 mss.

Typed list of Latin mss. before 1600 kindly
supplied by the librarian.

*Wisbech, England. See M. R. James;
Schenkl.

*Wittem, Holland. See *Archivum Franciscanum Historicum* XLIX.

*Wittenberg, East Germany. Bibliothek
des Evangelischen Predigerseminars.

*Verzeichnis der Manuskripte, 1 ms. notebook
(Nr. 11), dated 1910. 100 mss.

*Verzeichnis der Raritäten. 1 ms. notebook
(Nr. 12) dated 1910. Ca. 100 mss., and
some editions. (Communication of the
librarian)

—*Lutherhalle.

*Handwritten catalogue lists ca. 4000 mss.
and letters. (Communication of the librarian)

*Wittingau, see **Třeboň**.

*Wittstock, East Germany.

*R. Grosser, *Beobachtungen auf dem Ge-
biete des altsprachlichen Unterrichtes;
Schulnachrichten.* progr. Wittstock 1876.
40 pp. p. 29: Note on 3 mss. (by A. Detto).
— The same, *Schulnachrichten... nebst
einem Nachtrag.... über alte Handschriften
und Drucke — vom Gymnasiallehrer
Albert Detto.* progr. 1877. 22 pp. The
note on p. 10 has nothing on mss. (Heidelberg, University Library; data and partial micr. supplied by Dr. Haas)

*Włocławek, Poland. Biblioteka Kapitulna.

Biblioteka Kapituły Włocławskiej, by S. Cho-
dyński and S. Librowski (Monumenta historica dioecesis Vladislaviensis XXVI,
Supplement of *Kronika Diecezji Włocławskiej* XLIII). Włocławek 1949. 131 pp.
(also numbered 169-216; 233-280; 33-67).
p. 74-130: 412 mss. No index. (Poznań,
Biblioteka Głowna; micr. at NNC).

*Schloss Wolfegg, West Germany. Fürstlich Waldburg-Wolfegg'sche Bibliothek.

The collection is being rearranged. (Communication of the librarian)

Wolfenbüttel, West Germany. See *Serapeum* XVIII.

(*Catalogus insignium ac praestantissimorum codicum MStorum Graecorum, Arabicorum, Latinorum ut et Librorum cum MStis collatorum... quos dum viveret colligere licuit... Marquardo Gudio..* Kiel 1709. 68 pp. p. 27-55: 352 Latin mss. p. 56-57: Appendix of 42 mss. in different languages. p. 57-68: 107 books with ms. notes.) (PU)

(F. A. Ebert, *Bibliothecae Guelferbytanae codices Graeci et Latini classici.* Leipzig 1827. 179 pp. Arranged alphabetically. 942 mss. Also in his: *Die Bildung des Bibliothekars,* 2nd ed. II, 2, 1827). (NN)

(Carl Ph. C. Schönemann, *Merkwürdigkeiten der Herzogl. Bibliothek zu Wolfenbüttel.* 2 pts. in 1 vol. Hanover 1849-52. 71 and 65 pp. 232 mss. Index in pt. 2). (DLC)

O. von Heinemann and others, *Die Handschriften der Herzoglichen Bibliothek zu Wolfenbüttel.* Sections I-IV and VIII in 11 vols. Wolfenbüttel 1884-1913. *Erste Abtheilung: Die Helmstedter Handschriften.* Vol. I (1884). 380 pp. Mss. no. 1-540. Vol. II (1886) 340 pp. No. 541-1102. Vol. III (1888). 280 pp. No. 1103-1562, and index for vols. I-III. *Zweite Abtheilung: Die Augusteischen Handschriften.* Vol. I (1890). 320 pp. No. 1563-2131. Vol. II (1895). 364 pp. No. 2132-2326. Vol. III (1898). 411 pp. No. 2327-2759. Vol. IV (1900). 381 pp. No. 2760-3400. Vol. V (1903). 263 pp. No. 3401-4083. *Dritte Abtheilung: Die Weissenburger Handschriften.* p. 265-322. No. 4084-4187, then index for section II and III (p. 323-443). *Vierte Abteilung: Die Gudischen Handschriften,* by F. Koehler and G. Milchsack (1913). 292 pp. No 4188-4662 and index. *Abtheilung VIII: Die Handschriften nebst den älteren Druckwerken der Musikabtheilung,* by E. Vogel (1890). 280 pp.

Extravagantes. 3 ms. vols. I: 1-84,2. II: 84,3-221,16. III: 221,17-317; Supplementa.

Novi. 1 ms. vol. 1166 mss.

Katalog der Novissimi. 1 ms. vol. Fol. 1-49; Qu. 1-24; Oct. 1-206; 12° 1-14.

Manuscripta Blancoburgensia. 1 ms. vol. 315 mss.

*Woodchester, England. See Great Britain, *Historical Manuscripts Commission.*

*Woodstock, Maryland, U.S.A. See De Ricci.

*Worcester, England. See Bernardus; Schenkl.

J. K. Floyer, *Catalogue of Manuscripts Preserved in the Chapter Library of Worcester Cathedral,* ed. Sidney G. Hamilton. Oxford 1906. 196 pp. 277 mss.

Catalogus librorum manuscriptorum Bibliothecae Wigorniensis, made in 1622-1623 by Patrick Young, ed. I. Atkins and N. R. Ker. Cambridge 1944. 84 pp. Concordance of modern shelf marks (p. 75-76).

R. Woof, *Catalogue of Manuscript Records and Printed Books in the Library of the Corporation of Worcester.* Worcester 1874. 51 pp. p. 9-24: Manuscript Books. Charters only. (British Museum; micr. at NNC)

*Worcester, Massachusetts, U.S.A. See De Ricci.

Wrocław (Breslau), Poland. See Aland (Section A).

—*Archiwum Państwowe.

The mss. formerly belonging to the Milich'sche Bibliothek in Görlitz are now divided between the Archive and the University Library in Wroclaw.

Wykaz zaakcesjonowanych rękopisów ze zbioru Milicha. Typed list of 649 mss. in which the mss. kept at the Archive are indicated (Seen at the University Library).

However, a few mss. of the former collection are now missing. For older descriptions, see the following catalogues. See also *Archiv* XI.

J. G. Geislerus, *Historia Bibliothecae Milichianae.* 5 parts progr. Görlitz 1764-68. parts I-IV, 34 pp. Part V, 24 pp. Part III (1766) p. 19 - V, p. 24: Mss. no. 1-120 from Milich; no. 121-135, Oriental mss.;

no. 136-186, not from Milich; 181 mss. from a monastic collection annexed to the Milich library; 14 mss. in the city archive; 7 mss. in the church of St. Peter and Paul; 1 ms. in a private library. (Berlin, Staatsbibliothek; micr. at NNC)

(J. G. Neumann) *Die Bibliothek der Oberlausitzischen Gesellschaft der Wissenschaften.* 2 vols. Görlitz 1819. II, 545-58: 28 mss. 561-80: 282 late ms. (DLC)

C. Th. Anton, *Codicis Luciani qui in bibliotheca Milichiana nostra asservatur descriptio.* 2 pts. progr. Görlitz 1835-36. 16 and 12 pp. (NjP)

E. E. Struve, *Die italiaenischen und lateinischen Handschriften der Bibliothek des Gymnasium [sic] zu Görlitz.* progr. Görlitz 1836. 21 pp. Describes a few mss. No index. Not complete. (NjP)

The same, *Verzeichniss und Beschreibung einiger Handschriften aus der Bibliothek des Gymnasiums zu Görlitz, Erste Fortsetzung.* progr. Görlitz 1837. 16 pp. 2 mss.—*Zweite Fortsetzung.* progr. 1839. 12 pp. 5 mss.—*Beschreibung einiger Handschriften der Milichschen Gymnasialbibliothek.* progr. 1841. 20 pp. 6 mss.—*Nachricht über eine ältere Handschriften-Bibliothek in Görlitz.* progr. 1846. 14 pp. 40 mss. from the Klosterbibliothek, also belonging to the Gymnasialbibliothek. (Görlitz, Oberlausitzische Bibliothek der Wissenschaften; micr. at NNC)

Th. Neumann, 'Die Handschriften der Milich'schen Bibliothek in Görlitz,' *Neues Lausitzisches Magazin* XXIII (1846) 147-99; XXVI (1849) 230-67. Describes 2 mss. (NN)

Verzeichniss der Handschriften und geschichtlichen Urkunden der Milich'schen (oder Stadt- oder Gymnasial-)Bibliothek in Görlitz. Als Anhang zum Neuen Lausitzischen Magazin, Band 44 u. folgg. herausgegeben vom Sekretär. [Görlitz 1868-69]. 154 pp. An alphabetical index of authors and titles. (DLC)

R. Joachim, *Geschichte der Milich'schen Bibliothek und ihrer Sammlungen.* 2 pts. progr. Görlitz 1876-77. 32 and 20 pp. pt. I p. 30-31: Summary list of Latin mss. No shelf marks. No index.

—Biblioteka Kapitulna.

W. Urban, *Rękopisy Biblioteki Kapitulnej w Wrocławiu* (1956). 1 typed vol. Arranged by shelf marks. Lists 603 mss. of the main collection, and 85 mss. from Nysa (Neisse).

Zachowane Rękopisy i Inkunabuly Biblioteki Kapitulnej we Wrocławiu, by W. Urban (1954). 1 typed vol. Arranged by subjects, and chronologically. (Cracow, Biblioteka Jagiellonska; micr. at NN). The library now has the mss. formerly belonging to the parish library in Nysa (Neisse). For the latter, see the following catalogue:

F. Schuppe, *Katalog der Bibliothek der katholischen Stadtpfarrei zu Neisse.* Neisse (1865). VII, 303 pp. Arranged by subjects. Mss. listed with edd. (Wrocław, Biblioteka Kapitulna)

—Biblioteka Uniwersytecka. The library has all the mss. preserved from the former Universitatsbibliothek, from the former Stadtbibliothek (Rehdigeriana), as well as from other collections in Wrocław and in other towns of Silesia. For a list of the preserved mss., see Aland (Section A), p. 37-39; 42-44. There is a photostatic copy of a typed list for the additional mss. recently returned from Russia.

The following catalogues refer to several collections now in the University library. Cooper (Section A); Archiv III; IV; VI; XI.

Viro perillustri Ernesto Horn . . . gratulatur Ordo Medicorum Universitatis Litterarum Vratislaviensis interprete A. G. E. Th. Henschel. *Insunt de coaicibus medii aevi medicis et physicis bibliothecarum Vratislaviensium manuscriptis notitiae quaedam generales adjecta eorundem Catalogi particula prima.* Breslau 1847. 56 pp. 18 mss. No index. (DSG; micr. at NNC)

Viro illustrissimo gravissimo Gulielmo *Hermanno Georgio Remer* . . . *pie gratulatur Ordo Medicorum Universitatis Litterariae Vratislaviensis* interprete A. G. E. Th. Henschel. *Inest synopsis chronologica scriptorum medii aevi medicorum ac physicorum quae codicibus Bibliothecarum Vratislaviensium continentur.* Breslau 1847. 60 coll. 937 items. No index. (DSG, photostat at NNC)

(Former Universitätsbibliothek). For mss. I F 1-155, see *Verzeichnis der Handschriften im Deutschen Reich.*

A typed continuation of this catalogue, prepared by Prof. W. Göber, was returned from Russia to Wrocław where I saw it in 1958, and is now presumably in the possession of the author in East Berlin.

Catalogus codicum scriptorum qui in Bibliotheca Regia ac Academica Wratislaviensi servantur (by Friedrich). 1 ms. vol., arranged by subjects. Still the only complete list of the collection.

M. Jezienicki, 'O Rękopisie Biblioteki krolewskiej i uniwersyteckiej w Wrocławiu z roku 1515 . . .,' *Archivum do Dziejów Literatury i Oświaty w Polsce* IX (1897) 268-94. (NN)

Staender, 'Die Handschriften der Königlichen und Universitäts-Bibliothek zu Breslau,' *Zeitschrift des Vereins für Geschichte und Alterthum Schlesiens* XXXIII (1899) 1-66. Not a catalogue.

A. Stara, 'Praemonstratenserhandschriften in der Universitätsbücherei Breslau,' *Analecta Praemonstratensia* XVIII (1942) 143-144.

H. Szwejkowska, *Biblioteka Klasztoru Cystersek w Trzebnicy.* Wrocław 1955. 104 pp. and plates. p. 27-57: 62 mss. from Trzebnica (Trebnitz), most of them now at the University Library in Wrocław. (Former Stadtbibliothek or Rehdigeriana)

A. W. J. Wachler, *Thomas Rehdiger und seine Büchersammlung in Breslau.* Breslau 1828. 80 pp. Lists many mss. No index. (ICU)

K. Ziegler, *Catalogus codicum latinorum classicorum qui in Bibliotheca Urbica Wratislaviensi adservantur.* Breslau 1915. 289 pp. 177 selected mss.

Catalogus codd. Rehd. (Inside:) *Katalog der Handschriften der Rehdigeriana.* 3 ms. vols. I (by M. A. Guttmann): Mss. no. 1-502. II (by H. Markgraf): 503-1000; 2001-3100. III: 3100-3526.

Briefe des XVI. Jahrhunderts. 4 ms. vols. Arranged alphabetically. Covers mainly Rehd. 241-249 and 252.

Verzeichnis der Handschriften der Kirchenbibliothek zu St. Maria Magdalena (by G. W. Keller, 1729, revised by K. Schönhorn, 1847). 1 ms. vol. Mss. no. 1001-1581.

Card file for the entire Rehdigeriana, in 3 boxes, arranged by shelf marks. It covers the Codices Bernardiniani (no. 1582-2000) omitted in the other inventories.

(New acquisitions). There is a list of accessions, in 1 ms. folder. It has no title, and begins in 1948. It includes the mss. from Legnica (Liegnitz). For this latter group, see also:

W. Gemoll, *Die Handschriften der Petro-Paulinischen Kirchenbibliothek zu Liegnitz.* progr. Liegnitz 1900. 68 pp. 67 mss. No index.

For the Milich mss. from Görlitz, see above under Archiwum Państwowe.

Biblioteka Uniwersytecka w Wrocławiu, Związ Kulturalne Śląska z Polską w Epoce Odrodzenia. Wrocław 1953. 105 pp. and plates. Exhibition catalogue.

—Biblioteka Zakładu Narodowego im. Ossolińskich (Ossolineum).

This collection, formerly in Lwow, was transferred to Wrocław after the last war. For its older nucleus, see the following catalogues. See also Dudik, *Archive.*

W. Kętrzyński, *Catalogus codicum manuscriptorum Bibliothecae Ossolinianae Leopoliensis. Katalog Rękopisów Biblioteki Zakładu Nar. Im. Ossolińskich.* 3 vols. Lwów 1881-98. I: 226 mss. II (1886): Mss. no. 227-561. III: Mss. no. 562-1504. Each volume indexed. (NN)

Inwentarz rękopisów Bibljoteki Zakładu Narodowego imienia Ossolińskich we Lwowie (*Nr. 1505 do 5500*). Lwów 1926. 518 mimeographed pages. Mostly late material. No index.—The same (*Nr. 5501 do 6000*). Lwów 1934. 91 pp. (NN)

Katalog Rękopisów Bibljoteki im. Gwalberta Pawlikowskiego, by M. Gębarowicz. (Lwow) 1929. 159 pp. 290 mss. (Cracow, Biblioteka Jagiellonska; microfilm at NN).

Inwentarz rękopisów Biblioteki Zakładu Narodowego im. Ossolińskich we Wrocławiu. 2 vols. Wroclaw 1948-49. Vol. I, by J. Tarski. Mss. 1-7325. No index. Vol. II, by the same. Mss. 7326-11923. Vol. II, pt. 2 is a reprint of the 1929 catalogue of the Pawlikowski collection. (NN)

Ze Skarbca Kultury, Biuletyn informacyjny Biblioteki Zakładu im. Ossolińskich 2 (3) 1952: Mss. no. 11981-12213; 1 (6) 1954, p. 9-113; Mss. no. 12214-12437; 2 (8) 1955: Mss. no. 12438-12667. Mostly modern material. (MH)

There are also handwritten lists of recent accessions. They include some mss. from the Branicki collection in Sucha. See under Sucha.

*Wunsidel, West Germany.

P. Willmann, 'Handschriften und Frühdrucke im Besitze der Kgl. bayerischen Stadt Wunsiedel,' *Korrespondenzblatt des Gesammtvereins der deutschen Geschichts- und Alterthumsvereine* XLIII (1895) 143-44. 6 mss. No index. (DLC)

*Würzburg, West Germany. See Bischoff and Hofmann; Cooper (Section A); *Analecta Bollandiana* XXXII; *Archiv* VII; Gercken; Hirsching; Lampen; Leclercq; Lehmann, *Mitteilungen* I; Nürnberger; *Serapeum* III.

J. A. Oegg, *Versuch einer Korographie der Erz w. grossherzogl. Haupt- u. Residenzstadt Würzburg...* Vol. I (no more published) Würzburg 1808. 829 pp. p. 293-571: Mss. Index (807-818). (Prof. E. A. Lowe, Princeton)

—***Minoritenkloster.** See *Archivum Franciscanum Historicum* XLIV.

F. Falk, 'Bibliographische Reisefrüchte,' *Centralblatt für Bibliothekswesen* XIX (1897) 361-65. Describes some mss. of Franciscans at Würzburg. No index.

Contzen, *Die Sammlungen des Historischen Vereins für Unterfranken und Aschaffenburg.* 3 vols. Würzburg 1856-64. I, p. 233-300: 1187 mss. No index.

—***Priesterseminar.**

Before the war, the library owned about 50 mss. They were all destroyed during the war, along with the inventory in which they were described. Cf. Reuss, 'Kurze Beschreibung merkwürdiger altdeutscher Handschriften in unterfränkischen Bibliotheken, *Archiv des historischen Vereines für Unterfranken und Aschaffenburg* VIII (1845) 148-154. 1 ms. (p. 153-154). — O. Handwerker, 'Die Psalterhandschrift des Würzburger Klerikalseminars,' *Archiv des historischen Vereins von Unterfranken und Aschaffenburg* LXVIII (1929) 510-12. — *T. Freudenberger, *Quellen zur Geschichte der Wallfahrt und des Augustinerchorherrenstiftes Birklingen bei Iphofen (Mfr.) 1457-1546.* (Würzburger Diozesangeschichtsblätter V). Würzburg 1937. XII, 208 pp. See esp. 193-195. (Würzburg, University Library; data supplied by Dr. A. Wendehorst).

After the war, the library acquired some mss. from regional parish libraries. See A. Wendehorst, 'Verlorene und gewonnene Schätze. Aus der Bibliothek des Würzburger Priesterseminars,' *Die Mainlande* (Beilage zur Main-Post) III (1952) 64. Describes 4 mss.

—**Universitätsbibliothek.**

Reuss, 'Manuscriptenkatalog der vormaligen Dombibliothek zu Würzburg, *Archiv des historischen Vereins von Unterfranken und Aschaffenburg VII*, 2 (1843) 166-176. 183 mss., most of which are now at the University Library. No index.

(D. Kerler), *Die Pergament-Handschriften der K. Universitäts-Bibliothek Würzburg.* Würzburg 1886. 21 pp. Alphabetical. (Würzburg; micr. at NNC)

*G. Schepss, *Die ältesten Evangelienhand-schriften der Würzbuger Universitäts-bibliothek.* Würzburg 1887. 38 pp. 12 mss. (MH)

Ign. Schwarz, *Die medizinischen Handschriften der Kgl. Universitätsbibliothek in Würzburg.* Diss. Würzburg 1907. 96 pp. 64 old mss. and 70 later mss. (DLC)

O. Handwerker, 'Zur Geschichte der Handschriftensammlung der Würzburger Universitätsbibliothek,' *Zentralblatt für Bibliothekswesen* XXVI (1909) 485-516. Mentions several mss.

The same, 'Überschau über die Fränkischen Handschriften der Würzburger Universitätsbibliothek,' *Archiv des Historischen Vereins für Unterfranken und Aschaffenburg* LXI (1919) 1-92.

Handschr. Katalog. Abschrift. (Inside:) *Die Pergamenthandschriften der Würzburger Universitäts-Bibliothek. Abschrift des Ruland-Stamminger'schen Handschriften-Zettelkatalogs* (1931-32). 4 typed vols. I: M(anuscr.) p(erg). th(eol). f(ol). m(ax). 1-24, f(ol). 1-70a. II: f. 71-174. III: M.p.th.q. 1-74, o(ct). 1-24, d(uod). 1-7. M.p. h(ist). f. 1-5, q. 1-2; j(ur). f.m. 1-14, q. 1-2; med.f.m. 1, f. 1-3, q. 1-2; misc. f. 1-20, q. 1-4; gr(aec). f. 1.

(Inside:) *Die Papierhandschriften der Würzburger Universitätsbibliothek. Abschrift des Ruland-Stamminger'schen Handschriften-Zettelkatalogs.* 10 typed vols. I: M(anuscr.) ch(art). f.m. 1, f. 1-80. II-VIII: M.ch. f. 81-651 (II: 81-160; III: 161-240; IV: 241-310b; V: 311-400; VI: 401-500; VII: 501-585; VIII: 586-651). IX: M.ch.q. 1-70. X: M.ch.q. 71-100. The continuation is given in the old card file in open folders: M.ch.q. 101-380; M.ch.o. 1-103; M.ch.d.1-7.

Typed information on the collection is available at the Institut de Recherches et d'Histoire des Textes, Paris.

York, England. Minster Library.

See Holtzmann (Section A); Bernardus; Frere; Schenkl.

1 folder with typed sheets (by the Rev.

F. Harrison), *ca.* 60 ms. books.

***Ypres**, Belgium. See Van de Putte.

***Zadar** [(Zara), Yugoslavia. See Wickhoff.

—*Naučna Biblioteka.

**Catalogo dei mss. e dei documenti membranacei.* 4 vols. (Apolloni II 114).

Inventario dei manoscritti, incunaboli e rari della Biblioteca Comunale Paravia di Zara. A pack of typed sheets. 867 mss.

*—School Library (destroyed during the last war).

J. Danilo and J. Boglič, *Catalogus librorum qui in Bibliotheca Patria Archigymnasii Iadrensis asservantur.* progr. Zara 1860, pt. II, p. 13-170. p. 157-169: Alphabetical list of mss. No shelf marks. (Venice, Biblioteca Marciana)

Catalogo sistematico dell' i.r. biblioteca ginnasiale-provinciale di Zara (by V. Brunelli). progr. Zara 1899-1900 and following vols. progr. 1901-02, p. 31-63: Alphabetical list of mss. (Venice, Biblioteca Marciana)

Zagreb (Agram), Yugoslavia. See *Archiv* VI.

D. Kniewald, 'Zagrebački liturgijski kodeksi XI.-XV. stoljeća,' *Croatia Sacra* X (1940) 1-128. Describes liturgical mss. in Zagreb collections. (DDO)

—Knjižnica Jugoslavenske Akademije Znanosti i Umjetnosti.

Inventar Kodeksa Jugosl. akademije (by V. Mošin and others, 1947). Mss. I a 1 - IV d 105. Centuries not always given.

—Sveučilišna (or Universitetska) i Narodna Knjižnica.

Inventarni katalog rukopisa Sveučilišne i narodne knjižnice. 2 ms. folders. I: R 3001-6376. II: 6377-6632.

Alphabetical card index in 5 boxes. (Metropolitanska knjižnica, annexed to the University Library).

G. Morin, 'Manuscrits liturgiques hongrois des XIᵉ et XIIᵉ siècles,' *Jahrbuch für Liturgiewissenschaft* VI (1926) 54-67. 12 mss. (NNUT)

A. Markov, 'Katalog Metropolitanskih Riedkosti,' in: *Dissertationes et monumenta historiam culturae gentis Croaticae illus-*

trantia, Tomus I, pars 1 (Zagreb 1945), p. 505-550. p. 505-510: Summary list of mss. MR 1-197, in serial order. p. 511-549: A more detailed description of the same mss., arranged by subjects. No index. (Zagreb; micr. at NNC)

C. Balić, 'Les anciens manuscrits de la Bibliothèque Métropolitaine de Zagreb,' *Studia medievalia in honorem R. J. Martin* (Bruges 1948) 437-474. 18 mss. The index is contained in that of the volume.

Catalogus Manuscriptorum Bibliothecae Cathedralis Ecclesiae Zagrebiensis, by S. E. Ledinzky (1830). 1 ms. vol. Arranged alphabetically. Does not give the actual shelf marks.

Inventar Metropolitanske crkve zagrebačke, by F. Suk and L. Ivančan (1915). (Communication of Prof. J. Badalić).

Alphabetical card file, in 5 boxes.

M. P. Noviji Rukopisi. A pack of ms. sheets. It describes the recent acquisitions, mostly late.

*Zara, see Zadar.

Zaragoza (Saragossa), Spain. See Beer (Section A); Borao (Section A); Grubbs (Section A, under Richardson); *Anuario* I and II; Cordoliani; Fransen.

M. S. y S. (Serrano y Sanz), 'Catálogo de los manuscritos de la Biblioteca del Seminario de San Carlos de Zaragoza,' *Revista de Archivos, Bibliotecas y Museos*, Ser. III vol. XIX, año XII (1908) 417-31; vol. XX año XIII (1909) 117-35. 25 mss. No index.

Consejo Superior de Investigaciones Científicas. Real Seminario Sacerdotal de San Carlos de Zaragoza. Manuscritos e Incunables de la Biblioteca del Real Seminario Sacerdotal de San Carlos de Zaragoza. (By Luis Latre). Zaragoza 1943. 167 pp. p. 7-104: 225 mss. No index.

M. Sancho Izquierdo and J. Sinnés, 'Catálogo de los manuscritos de la Biblioteca Universitaria de Zaragoza,' *Revista de Archivos, Bibliotecas y Museos*, Ser. III vol. XXXIV, año XX (1916) 114-41. 28 mss. No index. Not complete.

—Biblioteca Capitular (de la Seo).

J. M. March, 'Codexs Catalans i altres llibres manuscrits d'especial interès de la Biblioteca Capitular de Saragossa,' *Butlleti de la Biblioteca de Catalunya* VI (1920-22) 357-65.

Codices. A tray of index cards, arranged alphabetically.

*Schloss Zeil, West Germany. Fürstl. Waldburg-Zeil'sche Bibliothek.

No inventory. List of older mss. kindly supplied by the librarian.

Zeitz, East Germany. See *Archiv* VIII; XI.

—Domherren-Bibliothek.

F. Bech, *Verzeichnis der alten Handschriften und Drucke in der Domherren-Bibliothek zu Zeitz.* Berlin 1881. xi, 58 pp. p. 1-26: 86 mss. No index. (DLC)

—Stiftsbibliothek.

P. Wegener, *Verzeichnis der auf der Zeitzer Stiftsbibliothek befindlichen Handschriften.* progr. Zeitz 1876. 22 pp. 78 mss. No index. Not complete. New shelf marks in library copy.

Verzeichnis der Handschriften der Zeitzer Stiftsbibliothek. 1 ms. vol. Describes mss. 1-86; mss. of Julius Pflugk; Appendix 1-31. More complete than the printed catalogue by Wegener.

*Zerbst, East Germany.

H. Zurborg, *Mittheilungen aus der Gymnasialbibliothek.* progr. Zerbst 1879. 20, XXV pp. p. 15-19: 14 Latin mss. No index. (Erlangen, University Library)

*Zirc, Hungary. Ciszterci Apátság Könyvtára. 701 mss. No information.

*Zittau, East Germany. Stadtbibliothek. See Bruck.

Jo. Gottfr. Kneschke, *Geschichte und Merkwürdigkeiten der Rathsbibliothek in Zittau.* Zittau and Leipzig 1811. 164 pp. p. 135-39: 20 mss. No index. (MH)

*Handwritten inventory. (Communication of Dr. Emilie Boer)

*Znojmo (Znaim), Czechoslovakia. See Feifalik.

F. M. Bartoš, 'Dantova Monarchie, Cola di Rienzo, Petrarka a počátky reformace a humanismu u nás,' *Věstník Královské*

České Společnosti Nauk, Třída Filosoficko-Historicko-Filologická 1951, no. 5 (1952), 23 pp.

A. Fialová, 'Znojemský rukopis Dantovy Monarchie,' *Listy Filologické* III (LXXVIII, 1955) 52-56.

*Zofingen, Switzerland. See *Beiträge*.

'Merkwürdige Sammlung handschriftlicher Briefe von schweizerischen und deutschen Reformatoren und Gelehrten auf der Bibliothek der Stadt Zofingen,' *Helvetia* (ed. Joseph Anton Balthasar) I (Zurich 1823) 665-71. (NN)

**Katalog der grösseren Stadtbibliothek in Zofingen.* Zofingen 1874. 528 pp. p. 16-24: mss. (Zofingen)

**Katalog der Stadtbibliothek Zofingen.* 2 vols. Zofingen 1932-35. Vol. II, p. 607-21: ca. 200 general and local mss., each listed in alphabetical order. 4 supplements (1937-55) also list a few mss. (Communication of the librarian)

Zürich, Switzerland. See *Archiv* VII; Bruckner; Buchon; Esposito; Gercken; Haenel; Halm; Stelling-Michaud; *Traditio* XIV; Zapf.

—*Staatsarchiv. See *Inventare*.

For some manuscript fragments, see Mohlberg (under Zentralbibliothek), p. 301-336.

*For the collection of letters of the sixteenth century contained in class E II, there is a large alphabetical card file of senders and addressees. (Communication of the archivist).

—Zentralbibliothek.

O. F. Fritzschius, *Catalogi librorum msscr. qui in Bibliotheca Reipublicae Turicensis adservantur, particula I.* progr. Zurich 1848. 20 pp. 17 mss. No index. (PU)

Katalog der Handschriften der Zentralbibliothek Zürich. I. Mittelalterliche Handschriften, by C. Mohlberg. 5 parts. Zurich 1932-1952. *Einführung* (1952), XXVIII pp. fasc. 1-2 (1932). 156 pp. 367 mss. fasc. 3 (1936), p. 159-342. Mss. from Rheinau; acquisitions; mss. of Landesmuseum (295-300), Staatsarchiv (301-336), Kunstgewerbemuseum (337-342). mss. no. 368-

648. fasc. 4 (1952), p. 343-637. Addenda and indices.

—II. *Neuere Handschriften seit 1500*, by E. Gagliardi and L. Forrer. fasc. 1-3 (1931-1949). 1602 coll. Index to follow.

G. Goldschmidt, 'Katalogisierung der mittelalterlichen medizinischen und alchimistischen Handschriften der Zentralbibliothek Zürich, *Gesnerus* II (1945) 151-162. Selective catalogue. No index.

***Zutphen**, Holland. Librije der St. Walburgskerk.

K. O. Meinsma, *Catalogus van De Librye der St. Walburgskerk te Zutphen.* Zutphen 1903. 48, 51 pp. pt. 2, p. 1-2: 8 mss.

***Zweibrücken**, West Germany. Herzog Wolfgang-Gymnasium.

Katalog der Bibliothek d. K. B. Studien-Anstalt zu Zweibrücken. Zweibrücken 1871. 310 pp. p. 5-6: 47 mss.

***Zwettl**, Austria. Zisterzienserstift. See *Archiv* VIII; X; Haenel, *Supplement*; *Xenia Bernardina*.

Besides the mss. listed in *Xenia Bernardina*. there are 482 mss. later than the middle of the 16th century, for which several card files are available. (Communication of the librarian).

**(J. v. Frast, 'Handschriften welche in der Bibliothek des Stiftes Zwettl befindlich sind,' *Österreichische Blätter für Literatur* 1846 and 1847).

Zwickau, East Germany. Ratsschulbibliothek. Annexed to the Städtisches Museum. See *Archiv* VIII; Bruck; *Serapeum* IX.

De codicibus (pt. 4: *et editionibus vetustis*) *bibliothecae Zwiccaviensis.* 4 pts. progr. Zwickau 1825-36. pt. 1 (1825), 44 pp. *De tribus Juvenalis codicibus brevis disputatio*, by Frid. God. Guil. Hertel. (NjP). pt. 2 (1826). 32 pp. *De duobus codicibus librorum Ciceronis de officiis*, by the same (p. 3-16). (Bodleian Library). *pt. 3 (1827). *De tribus codicibus Boethii de consolatione philosophiae*, by H. Lindemann. pt. 4 (1836). 23 pp. *De Petri Marsi librorum Ciceronis de finibus editione.* (NNC)

O. Clemen, 'Handschriften und Bücher aus dem Besitze Kaspar v. Barths in der Zwickauer Ratsschulbibliothek,' *Zentralblatt für Bibliothekswesen* XXXVIII (1921) 267-89. No index.

Manuscripta et chartae palantes Bibliothecae Cygneae in fasciculos collectae et a dispersu vindicatae (by J. J. Crudelius). 1 ms. vol. Alphabetical inventory of the mss.

Zwolle, Holland. See *Société française*.

SUPPLEMENTARY MATERIAL

SECTION A

Bibliography and Statistics of Libraries and Their Collections of Manuscripts

P. 1.

Annuario delle Biblioteche italiane, 2nd. ed., vol. 3. Rome 1959.

Archive, Bibliotheken und Dokumentationstellen der Schweiz. . . 3rd. ed. Bern 1958. xvi, 144 pp. Arranged alphabetically by cities. The previous editions appeared in 1942 and 1946 under the title: *Führer durch die schweizerische Dokumentation.*

Bibliographie Nationale Suisse. Fasc. 1 a. *Travaux bibliographiques préliminaires. Catalogue des Bibliothèques de la Suisse.* Bern 1894. 67 pp. Arranged alphabetically by cantons.

Biblioteche e Istituti di Cultura delle Marche. Bologna 1959. 173 pp. Libraries arranged by provinces and cities. With statistics of the mss. and a few data.

P. 2.

P. Bohigas, *El libro español.* Barcelona (1962). iii, 342 pp.

Curt F. Bühler, *The Fifteenth-Century Book.* Philadelphia (1960). 195 pp.

P. 3.

*G. Comelli, 'Le biblioteche del Friuli,' in *Il Friuli.* Udine 1951, 201-228. Also in *Bolletino ufficiale della Camera di Commercio, industria e agricultura di Udine* IV 11 (1950) 5-23 (micr. NNC)

C. Dionisotti, *Indici del Giornale storico della letteratura italiana, Volumi 1-100 e*

Supplementi (1883-1932). Turin 1948. 438 pp. p. 415-438 : index of mss.

D. Diringer, *The Hand-Produced Book.* New York 1953. 603 pp.

The same, *The Illuminated Book.* London 1958. 524 pp. and plates.

The English Library before 1700, ed. F. Wormald and C. E. Wright. London 1958. 273 pp.

P. 4

Führer durch die schweizerische Dokumentation. See above under *Archive.*

P. 6

R. Lievens, *Middelnederlandse Handschriften in Oost-Europa.* Gent 1963. 244 pp. and plates.

M. A. E. Nickson, 'Provisional List of Austrian Libraries containing Medieval Manuscripts,' *Bulletin of the Institute of Historical Research* XXXI (1958) 195-202.

P. 7.

S. Prete, 'The Bibliography of Latin Manuscripts,' *Scriptorium* XV (1961) 93-97.

(under Richardson, vol. II:) Whitewill. Read: Whitehill.

P. 8.

S. Samek Ludovici, *Le Biblioteche dell'Emilia.* Modena 1959. 135 pp. and plates. Arranged by provinces.

Scriptorium XIV (1960) 111-153. M.-Th.

Vernet, 'Les publications françaises re-latives aux manuscrits 1951-1955.'

P. 9.

Studie o rukopisech 1963, Prague 1963, 185-208: J. Pražák, 'Novější zahraniční soupisy rukopisů (Les catalogues étran-gers de manuscrits, récemment publiés).' 209-228: The same, 'Československá lite-ratura kodikologická I (Les travaux tchecoslovaques de codicologie I).'
— 1964, 191-220: (The same), 'Českoloven-ská literatura kodilologická II.'
Bayerns Kirche im Mittelalter. Munich

(1960). Exhibition catalogue. 63 pp. and plates. 293 mss. in Munich and other Bavarian libraries.

M. Tallon, *Church of Ireland Diocesan Libraries.* Dublin 1959. 30 pp. Ar-ranged alphabetically by cities.

Zeitschrift für Bibliothekswesen und Biblio-graphie, Sonderheft: Zur Katalogisierung mittelalterlicher und neuerer Handschriften. Frankfurt (1963). x, 191 pp. 74-85: J. Autenrieth, 'Literaturbericht, Neuere Handschriftenkataloge und Hilfsmittel für die Katalogisierung.'

SECTION B

Works Describing Manuscripts of More than One City

P. 13.

Analecta Bollandiana LX (1942) 213-215: M. Coens, 'Appendice au Catalogue des manuscrits hagiographiques de Trèves' (13 frs. in Koblenz and Trier). (NNUT) —LXXVII (1959) 108-134: The same, 'Les mss. de Corneille Duyn donnés jadis à Héribert Rosweyde et conservés actuellement à Bruxelles (14 mss.) (NNUT) (*Annuario.*) Read: *Anuario.*

P. 17.

(Under *Archiv* X):) Milulov. Read: Mikulov.

P. 19.

Ars Sacra. Munich 1950. 155 pp. Lists many mss. Exhibition catalogue.

Arte Lombarda dai Visconti agli Sforza. Milan 1958. 181 pp. and plates. Lists many illuminated mss. in Milan and elsewhere. Exhibition catalogue.

El Arte Románico. Barcelona and Santiago de Compostela 1961. lxxv, 650 pp. and plates. Lists many mss. and cites bibliography on them. Exhibition catalogue.

P. 20.

M. Bateson, *Catalogue of the Library of Syon Monastery, Isleworth.* Cambridge 1898. xxx, 262 pp. Identifies 6 mss. in Cambridge, London and elsewhere (p. xvii-xviii).

B. Bauerreiss, 'Bayrische Handschriften der Jahrtausendwende in Italien,' *Studien und Mitteilungen zur Geschichte des Benediktinerordens und seiner Zweige* LXX (1960) 182-188. 6 mss. in Bologna, Brescia, the Vatican and Verona. (NN)

P. 21.

Morton W. Bloomfield, *The Seven Deadly Sins.* Lansing 1952. xiv, 482 pp. Lists of mss. (257-258, 479-481).

P. Bohigas, *La ilustración y la decoración del libro manuscrito en Cataluña . . . Período Románico.* Barcelona 1960. xiv, 140 pp. and plates. Indices of authors (127-129) and mss. (129-131). (NN)

W. H. Bond (and C. U. Faye), *Supplement to the Census of Medieval and Renaissance Manuscripts in the United States and Canada.* New York 1962. xix, 626 pp. Arranged alphabetically by states, cities and libraries. Includes many small libraries not mentioned here. p. l: Birmingham, *Alabama*, University of Alabama. 5 mss. 1-9: Berkeley, *California*, University of California. Mss. no. 29-72, and other collections. 9-15: Camarillo, *California*, St. John's Seminary, Edward Laurence Doheny Memorial Library. 68 mss. 15: Claremont, *California*, Honnold Library, Bodman Collection. 9 letters. 16: Los Angeles, *California*, Elmer Belt Library. 16-18: Ibid., University of Southern California. 17 mss. 19-22: San Juan Capistrano, *California*, Robert B. Honeyman Jr. 25 mss. 23-24: San Marino, *California*, Henry E. Huntington Library. 25-64: New Haven, *Connecticut*, Yale University. Mss. no. 38-291 and other collections. 64-96: Ibid., Thomas E. Marston. 276 mss. 96-103: Ibid., James M. Osborn. 61 mss. 103-106: Washington, *District of Columbia*, Catholic University. Mss. no. 179-191. 106-109: Ibid., Folger Shakespeare Library. 109-110: Ibid., Georgetown University. 110-126: Ibid., Library of Congress. Several collections. 126-130. Ibid., National Gallery of Art, Rosenwald Collection. 47 mss. 130-146: Ibid., National Library of

Medicine. Mss. no.5-76. 146-162: Chicago, *Illinois*, Newberry Library. Several collections. 162-164: Ibid., University of Chicago. 165-166: Evanston, *Illinois*, Northwestern University. 167-175: Urbana, *Illinois*, University of Illinois. 176-177: Wilmette, *Illinois*, Louis H. Silver (now in the Newberry Library, Chicago). 177-186: Bloomington, *Indiana*, Indiana University. Mss. no. 3-132. 186-187: Notre Dame, *Indiana*, University of Notre Dame. Mss. no. 4-8. 187-188: Iowa City, *Iowa*, State University of Iowa. Mss. no. 2-33. 189-192: Lawrence, *Kansas*, University of Kansas. 24 mss. 193-194: Baltimore, *Maryland*, Johns Hopkins University. Mss. no. 4-23 and other collections. 194-200: Ibid., Walters Art Gallery. Mss. no. 558-578. 201: Queenstown, *Maryland*, Arthur A. Houghton Jr. 9 mss. 201-204: Amherst, *Massachusetts*, Amherst College. 24 mss. 204-206: Boston, *Massachusetts*, Boston Medical Library. Mss. no. 26-41. 206-222: Ibid., Boston Public Library. Mss. no. 73-197. 222-283: Cambridge, *Massachusetts*, Harvard University. Many collections. The Manuscripts in the Department of Printing and Graphic Arts (p. 250-281, 489 mss.) include the personal collection of Mr. Philip Hofer, now deposited in the Harvard University Library. 283-284: Ibid., Giles Constable. 5 mss. 285: Wellesley, *Massachusetts*, Wellesley College. Mss. no. 19-26. 285-287: Williamstown, *Massachusetts*, Williams College. 27 mss. and other collections. 287-297: Ann Arbor, *Michigan*, University of Michigan. Mss. no. 209-238 and other collections. 297: Detroit, *Michigan*, Detroit Public Library. 5 mss. 298-300: Minneapolis, *Minnesota*, University of Minnesota. 14 mss. 300: Rochester, *Minnesota*, Mayo Clinic. 5 mss. 303-313: Princeton, *New Jersey*, Princeton University. Several collections. 314: Ibid., Scheide Library (formerly in Titusville, Pennsylvania).

Mss. no. 66-74. 316-317: Corning, *New York*, Corning Museum. 10 mss. 318-319: Ithaca, *New York*, Cornell University. 8 mss. 320-327: New York, *New York*, Columbia University. Several collections. 327-328: Ibid., Metropolitan Museum. 328-334: Ibid., New York Public Library. Mss. no. 120-160 and other collections. 334-386: Ibid., Pierpont Morgan Library. Mss. no. 851-881 and other collections. 386-387: Ibid., Union Theological Seminary. Mss. no. 69-73. 388-391: Ibid., Curt F. Bühler. 25 mss. 391-397: Ibid., William S. Glazier. 41 mss. 398-404: Ibid., Mrs. Phyllis Goodhart Gordan and Mr. John D. Gordan. Mss. no. 50-151. 405-407: Ibid., Robert S. Pierie (now in Hamilton, Massachusetts). 13 mss. 408-409: Rochester, *New York*, University of Rochester. 409-412: St. Bonaventure, *New York*, St. Bonaventure University. Several collections. 412-414: Sands Point, *New York*, Mrs. Louis Rabinowitz. 13 mss. 414-415: Yonkers, *New York*, St. Joseph's Seminary. 4 mss. 415-420: Chapel Hill, *North Carolina*, University of North Carolina. Mss. no. 10-91. 421-425: Ibid., Berthold Louis Ullman (formerly in Chicago, Illinois). Mss. no. 5-54. 425-429: Cleveland, *Ohio*, Cleveland Museum of Art. 431-433: Eugene, *Oregon*, University of Oregon. 22 mss. 433-436: Bryn Mawr, *Pennsylvania*, Bryn Mawr College. 19 mss. 436-441: Devon, *Pennsylvania*, Boies Penrose. 31 mss. 441-449: King of Prussia, *Pennsylvania*, John F. Reed. 85 mss. 449-468: Philadelphia, *Pennsylvania*, Free Library. Several collections. 468-469: Ibid., Library Company. Mss. no. 12-13. 470-472: Ibid., Philadelphia Museum of Art. 27 mss. 472-474: Ibid., Temple University. 24 mss. 474-494: Ibid., University of Pennsylvania. Several collections. 495-497: Providence, *Rhode Island*, Brown University. Mss. no. 34-54. 497-511: Austin, *Texas*, University of Texas. Several collections. 511-513: Dallas, *Texas*, Lyle M. Sellers. 13 mss. 513-516: Charlottesville, *Virginia*, University of Virginia. 15 mss. 516-517: Ibid., Marvin L. Colker. 14 mss. 517-524: Covington, *Virginia*, Harry A. Walton, Jr. 524-525: Hollins College, *Virginia*, Hollins College. 13 mss. 525-530: Upperville, *Virginia*, Paul Mellon. 41 mss. 531-532: San Juan, *Puerto Rico*, Casa del Libro. 9 mss. 533: Toronto, *Canada*, Pontifical Institute of Mediaeval Studies. 3 mss. 533-534: Ibid., Royal Ontario Museum of Archaeology. 20 mss. 535-538: Ibid., University of Toronto. Several collections. 539: Los Angeles, *California*, University of California. 9 mss. 543-626: Indices.

Cf. G. Szabó, 'Museum Hungaricum II,' *Hungarian Quarterly* 4 (1963) 45-51.

The Book Collector. VI (1957) 343-349: H. Chadwick, 'Stonyhurst College.' Surveys 78 medieval mss. (348-349).

—VII (1958) 381-395: A. Rau, 'Bibliotheca Bodmeriana I.' Surveys the mss. of the Bodmer collection in Genève-Cologny. 128-138: G. H. Bushnell, 'St. Andrews University Library.' 253-264: R. J. Hayes, 'The Chester Beatty Library' (Dublin).

—X (1961) 40-48: A. R. A. Hobson and A. N. L. Munby, 'J. R. Abbey' (Redlynch House). 147-155: L. F. Casson, 'The Manuscripts of the Grey Collection in Cape Town.'

—XI (1962), 332-337: K. V. Sinclair, 'Phillipps Manuscripts in Australia.' Decribes 16 mss. in Ballarat, Boxhill, Melbourne, Sydney.

—XIII (1964) 305-326. Francis R. Walton 'Joannes Gennadius.' Describes the collection now in Athens.

A. Boutemy, 'Les enlumineurs de l'Abbaye de Saint Amand,' *Revue Belge d'archéologie et d'histoire de l'art* XII (1942) 131-167; 'Quelques manuscrits à miniatures peu connus de l'Abbaye de Saint-Amand,' *ibid.*, 215-228. Discusses

mss. now in Paris and Valenciennes. Bruckner, *Scriptoria.* ** IX (1964): Constance. Covers mss. in Beromünster, Eschenbach, Luzern, Neuenkirch.

H. Buchthal, *Miniature Painting in the Latin Kingdom of Jerusalem.* Oxford 1957. xxxiv, 163 pp. and plates. p. 139-153: Catalogue of mss.

P. 22.

F. Carmody, *Arabic Astronomical and Astrological Sciences in Latin Translation.* Berkeley 1955. vi, 193 pp.

Catálogo de la exposición de códices miniados españoles. Barcelona 1962. 75 pp. 158 mss. (Pierpont Morgan Library).

Catalogo delle Opere Musicali teoriche e pratiche di autori vissuti sino ai primi decenni del secolo XIX, esistenti nelle Biblioteche e negli Archivi pubblici e privati d'Italia (Pubblicazioni dell'Associazione dei Musicologi Italiani). Published irregularly in several series and volumes. Rome 1914-1939. Mentions mss. in Milan, Parma, Pisa and Venice.

P. 23.

Catalogus librorum italicorum, latinorum et manuscriptorum magno sumptu et labore per triginta annorum spatium Liburni collectorum. Livorno 1756. 663, 20 pp. pp. 625-663: 215 mss. owned by the English consul Jackson, later acquired by the Duc de la Vallière.

Catalogus Translationum et Commentariorum, vol. I, ed. P. O. Kristeller. Washington 1960. xxiii, 149 pp. Lists many mss.

A. Cordoliani, 'Les manuscrits de comput ecclésiastique conservés dans les bibliothèques d'Aragon,' *Universidad* (Zaragoza) XXVII (1950) 592-616. Covers Huesca and Zaragoza. (NN)

P. 24.

Corvinen, Bilderhandschriften aus der Bibliothek des Königs Matthias Corvinus (by I. Berkovits). Berlin (1963). 145

pp. and plates. p. 119-132: List of Corvinus mss. in Budapest and other Hungarian libraries. 141-145: index of names.

**Illuminated Manuscripts from the Library of Matthias Corvinus*, by I. Berkovits. Budapest 1964. 147 pp. and plates.

K. Csapodi-Gárdonyi, *Mátyás Király Könyvtárának Scriptorai, Petrus Cenninius* (Az Országos Széchényi Könyvtár Kiadványai 45). Budapest 1958. 18 pp.

The same, 'Les scripteurs de la Bibliothèque du Roi Mathias,' *Scriptorium* XVII (1963) 25-49.

P. 25.

A. Dold, 'Beachtenswerte Fragmente alter Sakramentare und Missalien,' *Miscellanea liturgica in honorem L. Cuniberti Mohlberg* (2 vols., Rome 1948-49) II, 267-293. Describes frs. in Munich, Paris, Stuttgart.

J. Dominguez Bordona, *El escritorio y la primitiva biblioteca de Santes Creus.* Tarragona 1952. 153 pp. and plates. 173 mss. in Barcelona, Madrid, Poblet, and mostly in Tarragona. (Hispanic Society of America).

The same, 'La biblioteca del Virrey Don Pedro Antonio de Aragón (1611-1690)', *Boletín Arqueológico* (Tarragona), Ser. 4, vol. 48 (1948) 37-54; 71-106; 50 (1950) 66-86. Lists 20 mss. in Tarragona (48, 71-76) and 22 mss. in Poblet (50, 71-76). No index. (Hispanic Society of America)

P. Duhem, *Études sur Léonard de Vinci.* 3 vols., Paris 1906-1913 (and 1955). vol. III, p. 601: List of mss.

Europäische Kunst um 1400. Vienna 1962. 536 pp. and plates. pp. 163-220, nos. 102-214: Mss. in Paris, Vienna and other collections. Exhibition catalogue.

A. Fairbank and B. Wolpe, *Renaissance Handwriting.* Cleveland and New York (1960). 104 pp. and plates. 96 mss., mostly in London.

G. Fink-Errera, 'A propos des Bibliothèques d'Espagne, Tables de concordances,' *Scriptorium* XIII (1959) 89-118. Gives

concordances for shelf marks of manuscripts in Madrid, Salamanca, Sevilla and Toledo.

K. Foltz, *Geschichte der Salzburger Bibliotheken.* Vienna 1877. 119 pp. Mentions mss. now in Munich, Salzburg and Vienna. Index of Mss. (113-115) and of names (116-117). (PP)

P. 29.

(France, *Catalogue général, Départements,* vol. XXXI:) Baguères-de-Bigorre. Read: Bagnères-de-Bigorre.

P. 30.

(The same, vol. XL:) The same change.

P. 32.

(The same:) - LII (1960). xx, 270 pp. Chantilly, Bibliothèque Lovenjoul, by G. Vicaire. 1367 modern mss.

—LIII (1962). xvi, 52 pp. Manuscrits des Bibliothèques sinistrées de 1940 à 1944, by A. Masson. Lists lost mss. (and their extant reproductions) in Beauvais, Brest, Caen, Chartres, Douai, Falaise, Lisieux, Metz, Neufchatel-en-Bray, Pont-à-Mousson, Saint-Malo, Strasbourg, Tours, Vire, Vitry-le-François.

—LIV (1962). xix, 321 pp. Paris, Bibliothèque de l'Institut de France (Supplément), by J. Tremblot de la Croix. Nos. 3800-6200, mostly late.

(*Catalogue général*, Paris:) Read: *Paris.*

P. 33.

Franconia Sacra. Würzburg 1952. 72 pp. and plates. pp. 38-39, 47-58: 54 mss. Exhibition catalogue.

P. 34.

K. Gamber, *Codices Liturgici Latini Antiquiores* (Spicilegii Friburgensis Subsidia I). Fribourg 1963. xvi, 334 pp. Indices of mss. and authors.

E. B. Garrison, *Studies in the History of Mediaeval Italian Painting.* 4 vols. (Florence) 1953-1961. Discusses illuminated mss. in Calci, Turin and elsewhere. *Gelehrten- und Schriftstellernachlässe in den Bibliotheken der Deutschen Demokratischen Republik.* Part I. Berlin 1959. 103 pp. Alphabetical.

P. 35.

(T. Gottlieb, *Mittelalterliche Bibliothekskataloge Österreichs*). vol. III: Steiermark, by G. Möser-Mersky. Graz, Vienna and Cologne 1961. viii, 129 pp.

P. 36.

C. R. Gregory (ed.) *Novum Testamentum Graece* (ed. C. Tischendorf), Editio Octava critica maior, 3 vols. Leipzig 1869-1894. III, pt. II (1894), p. 948-1108. List of Latin bibical mss., arranged by countries and libraries.

A. Güntherová and J. Mišianik, *Illuminierte Handschriften aus der Slovakei.* Prague 1962. 175 pp. 45-46: 60 mss. in Bratislava, Budapest, Alba Julia, Eger, Vienna, Kremnica, Bardejov, Banská Bystrica, Esztergom, Zips.

C. H. Haskins, *Studies in Mediaeval Culture.* Oxford 1929 (and New York 1958). viii, 295 pp. pp. 271-275: Index of mss. The same, *Studies in the History of Mediaeval Science.* 2nd. ed. Cambridge Mass. 1927 (and New York 1960). 411 pp. pp. 379-385: Index of mss.

P. 37.

P. Hinschius, 'Nachrichten über juristische (insbesondere kanonistische) Handschriften in italienischen Bibliotheken,' *Zeitschrift für Rechtsgeschichte* I (1862) 467-480; II (1863) 455-473. Covers Naples (I 468-480), Rome (II 455-463) and Modena (II 463-473).

V. Ilardi, 'Fifteenth-Century Diplomatic Documents in Western European Archives and Libraries,' *Studies in the Renaissance* IX (1962) 64-112. Survey with bibliography.

Illuminated Books of the Middle Ages and Renaissance. Baltimore 1949. 85 pp.

and plates. 233 nos. Lists mss. in American collections. Exhibition catalogue.

P. 38.

(Institut de Recherche et d'Histoire des Textes, *Bulletin d'Information*)

—III (1954) 71-86: E. Brayer, 'Jubinal et les manuscrits de la Bibliothèque royale de la Haye.'

—IV (1955) 107-176: M. Pecqueur, 'Répertoire des manuscrits de la Bibliothèque de l'Arsénal peints aux armes de leur premier possesseur (xiie-xvie siècles).'

—VII (1958, published 1959) 7-22: E. Pellegrin, 'Notes sur divers manuscrits latins des bibliothèques de Milan. 23-31: E. Brayer, 'Manuscrits français du moyen âge conservés à Léningrad.'

—VIII (1959, published 1960) 7-46: M.-Th. Vernet, 'Notes de Dom André Wilmart sur quelques manuscrits latins anciens de la Bibliothèque nationale de Paris.'

—IX (1960, published 1961) 7-37: E. Pellegrin, 'Essai d'identification de fragments dispersés dans des manuscrits des bibliothèques de Berne et de Paris.' 71-100: M. Pecqueur, 'Répertoire des manuscrits de la Bibliothèque Mazarine peints aux armes de leur premier possesseur.'

—X (1961, published 1962) 7-72: E. Pellegrin, 'Notes sur quelques mss. de sermons provenant de Fleury-sur-Loire.' Discusses mss. in Orléans and Paris. 73-96: M. Pecqueur, 'Répertoire des manuscrits de la Bibliothèque Sainte-Geneviève peints aux armes de leur premier possesseur.'

The International Style. Baltimore 1962. 153 pp. and plates. pp. 41-77, nos. 38-76: illuminated mss. from American collections. Exhibition catalogue.

(Italy, Ministero dell'Interno, *Publicazioni degli Archivi di Stato*) XXIII: Archivio di Stato di Siena, *Le sale della mostra e il museo delle tavolette dipinte, Catalogo.* Rome 1956. Preface signed by

G. Cecchini. xviii, 163 pp. and plates. Lists some letters and literary documents. (Italy, Ministero dell'Istruzione Pubblica, *Indici e Cataloghi*)—V: G. Mazzatinti, *Inventario dei manoscritti italiani delle biblioteche di Francia.* 3 vols., Rome 1886-88. No index.

—VII: *I manoscritti Panciatichiani della Biblioteca Nazionale Centrale di Firenze,* vol. I, Prefazione e Indici, by B. Maracchi Biagiarelli. Rome 1962. xxiii, 351-433.

(The same, Nuova Serie II: *Catalogo dei manoscritti della Biblioteca Casanatense*) Vol. IV (1961), by M. Ceresi. 118 pp. Mss. no. 301-400. No index.

—V: *La Collezione Galileiana della Biblioteca Nazionale di Firenze.* Vol. I (1959), by A. Procissi. xxiv, 331 pp. Covers Div I 1—II 99. Indices.

—VII: *Catalogo dei manoscritti della Biblioteca Vallicelliana.* Vol. I (1961), by A. M. Giorgetti Vichi and S. Mottironi. xii, 473 pp. Mss. I-XXVI. Indices.

P. 39.

**T. Kaeppeli, *Inventari di libri di San Domenico di Perugia (1430-80).* Rome 1962. 386 pp. 43 mss. located in Perugia and elsewhere. Cf. W. A. Hinnebusch, *Speculum* 39 (1964) 707-709.

N. R. Ker, *English Manuscripts in the Century after the Norman Conquest.* Oxford 1960. 67 pp. and plates. pp. 63-66: index of mss.

The same, *Medieval Libraries in Great Britain.* 2nd ed. London 1964. xxxii and 424 pp.

P. 40.

P. O. Kristeller, *Iter Italicum.* Vol. I, London and Leiden 1963. xxviii, 533 pp. 1: Agrigento, Biblioteca Lucchesiana. Aquila, Archivio Provinciale di Stato. 1-2: Ibid., Biblioteca Provinciale. 2-4: Arezzo, Biblioteca della Fraternita dei Laici. 4-5: Assisi, Biblioteca Comunale. 5-6: Avellino, Biblioteca Provinciale. 6: Benevento, Biblioteca Capitolare. 6-16: Bergamo, Biblioteca Civica. 16: Ibid., S. Alessandro in Colonna. 16-18: Bologna, Biblioteca Comunale dell'Archiginnasio. 18-26: Ibid., Biblioteca Universitaria. 27: Ibid., Cassa di Risparmio. 27-28: Ibid., Collegio di Spagna. 28-30: Ibid., Biblioteca Comunale annessa al Conservatorio di Musica G. B. Martini. 30-36: Brescia, Biblioteca Civica Queriniana. 37: Bressanone-Brixen, Archivio del Seminario (Seminararchiv). 38: Brindisi, Biblioteca Arcivescovile. 38-39: Camerino, Biblioteca Valentiniana. 39: Capestrano, Biblioteca dei Minori Francescani. 40-41: Casale Monferrato, Seminario Vescovile. 41-42: Catania, Biblioteche Riunite Civica e A. Ursino-Recupero. 42-43: Cava dei Tirreni, Biblioteca della Badia. 43: Cento, Biblioteca Comunale. 43-46: Cesena, Biblioteca Malatestiana. 46-48: Como, Biblioteca Comunale. 48: Ibid., Seminario Maggiore. Correggio, Biblioteca Comunale. 48-49: Cortona, Biblioteca Comunale e dell'Accademia Etrusca. 49-52: Cremona, Biblioteca Governativa. 52: Faenza, Biblioteca Comunale. 53: Fermo, Biblioteca Comunale. 53-62: Ferrara, Biblioteca Comunale Ariostea. 63: Firenze, Accademia della Crusca. 63-72: Ibid., Archivio di Stato. 72-106: Ibid., Biblioteca Medicea Laurenziana. 106-110: Ibid., Biblioteca Marucelliana. 110-112: Ibid., Biblioteca Moreniana. 112-177: Ibid., Biblioteca Nazionale Centrale. 177-226: Ibid., Biblioteca Riccardiana. 226: Ibid., Conservatorio di Musica L. Cherubini. Ibid., Galleria degli Uffizi. 227: Ibid., Società Colombaria. 228: Ibid., Principe Ginori Conti. 229: Ibid., Conte Guicciardini Corsi Salviati. Ibid., Avv. Piero Marrucchi. Ibid., Libreria Olschki. Ibid., Conte Bernardo Rucellai. 229-230: Ibid., Marchese Filippo Serlupi. 230: Ibid., Marchese Roberto Venturi Ginori. Foligno, Biblioteca Comunale. 231: Ibid., Biblioteca del Seminario.

231-235: Forlì, Biblioteca Comunale. 235-237: Frascati, Archivio della Congregazione Camaldolese di Monte Corona. 237: Genova, Archivio di Stato. 237-238: Ibid., Archivio Storico Comunale. 238: Ibid., Biblioteca Brignole Sale. 238-240: Ibid. Biblioteca Civica Berio. 240: Ibid., Biblioteca Franzoniana. 241-242: Ibid: Biblioteca della Congregazione de' RR. Missionari Urbani. 242-246: Ibid., Biblioteca Universitaria. 246-248: Ibid., Biblioteca Durazzo (Marchesa Matilde Negrotto Cambiaso Giustiniani). 248: Grottaferrata, Biblioteca della Badia Greca. Iesi, Archivio Storico Comunale. 248-249: Ibid., Biblioteca Comunale. 250: Livorno, Biblioteca Labronica. 250-252: Lodi, Biblioteca Comunale. 252-253: Lonato, Fondazione Ugo da Como. 253: Lucca, Archivio di Stato. 253-256: Ibid., Biblioteca Capitolare. 257-262: Ibid., Biblioteca Governativa. 262-263: Lugo, Biblioteca Comunale F. Trisi. 263-264: Macerata, Biblioteca Comunale. 264-269: Mantova, Archivio di Stato. 269-275: Ibid., Biblioteca Comunale. 275-276: Messina, Biblioteca Universitaria. 276: Milano, Archivio Capitolare della Basilica Ambrosiana. Ibid., Archivio della Curia Arcivescovile. 276-277: Ibid., Archivio di Stato. 277-350: Ibid., Biblioteca Ambrosiana. 351: Ibid., Biblioteca Capitolare del Capitolo Metropolitano. 351-359: Ibid., Biblioteca Nazionale Braidense. 359-364: Ibid., Biblioteca Trivulziana. 365: Ibid., Società Storica Lombarda. 366-367: Modena, Archivio di Stato. 367-368: Ibid., Archivio Storico Comunale. 368-392: Ibid., Biblioteca Estense. 393: Ibid., Collegio S. Carlo. Monreale, Biblioteca Comunale. 393-395: Montecassino, Biblioteca della Badia. 396: Napoli, Archivio di Stato. 396-397: Ibid., Biblioteca Governativa dei Girolamini (Oratoriana). 398-437: Ibid., Biblioteca Nazionale. 438: Ibid., Biblioteca Universitaria. 438-439: Ibid.,

Società Napoletana di storia patria. 439-440: Novacella-Neustift, Convento dei Canonici Regolari (Augustiner-Chorherrenstift). 440: Novara, Biblioteca Capitolare. Ibid., Biblioteca Negroni e Civica. Ibid., Biblioteca di S. Gaudenzio. 441-533: index.

*J. Leclercq, 'Les manuscrits de l'abbaye de Liessies,' *Mémoires de la Société archéologique et historique de l'arrondissement d'Avesnes (Nord)* XIX (1948-53) 21-31. 19 mss. in Avesnes and elsewhere. (MiU)

P. 41.

The same, 'Textes et manuscrits cisterciens dans diverses bibliothèques, ' *Analecta Sacri Ordinis Cisterciensis* XVIII (1962) 121-134. Lists mss in Brussels, Chicago, Covington, Solesmes, Strasbourg, Rome, Fribourg. (NN).

P. 42.

P. Lehmann *Erforschung des Mittelalters.* 5 vols. Leipzig 1941 - Stuttgart 1962. Vol. III (1960) 110-120: 'Verschollene und wiedergefundene Reste der Klosterbibliothek von Weissenau.' Describes mss. in Leningrad. IV (1961) 40-82: 'Handschriften aus Kloster Weissenau in Prag und Berlin.' 83-89: 'Handschriften und Handschriftenbruchstücke des 8.-15. Jhr. in Esztergom.'

The same, *Eine Geschichte der alten Fuggerbibliotheken.* 2 vols. Tübingen 1956-60. I 306-308; II 454-600: mss. in Harburg, Heidelberg, Munich, the Vatican, Vienna and elsewhere.

**G. I. Lieftinck, *Manuscrits datés conservés dans les Pays-Bas.* 2 vols, 1964. 142 pp. and plates.

K. Löffler, *Kölnische Bibliotheksgeschichte im Umriss.* Cologne 1923. 86 pp. p. 66-82: lists mss. in Cologne, Darmstadt and elsewhere. (MH)

(E. A. Lowe, *Codices Latini Antiquiores*). Vol. IX, 1959: Germany—Maria Laach —Würzburg. xii, 70 pp. Mss. no. 1230-

1442. Vol. X, 1963: Austria, Belgium, Czechoslovakia, Denmark, Egypt, and Holland. xx, 54 pp. Mss. no. 1443-1588.
The same, *Codices Lugdunenses antiquissimi.* Lyons 1924. 52 pp. p. 51-52: lists mss. in Lyons and elsewhere.
The same, 'A new List of Beneventan Manuscripts,' *Collectanea Vaticana in honorem Anselmi M. Card. Albaredae,* vol. II (Studi e Testi 220, Vatican City 1962) 211-244. Arranged alphabetically by cities.
The same, 'Codices rescripti: A list of the Oldest Palimpsests with Stray Observations on their Origin,' *Mélanges Eugène Tisserant* V (Studi e Testi 235, Vatican City 1964) 67-113. CXXX (234) nos. Indices (77-81).

P. 43.

L. MacKinney, 'Medieval Medical Miniatures in Central and Eastern European Collections,' *Manuscripta* V (1961) 131-150. List of mss. (142-150).
The same and T. Herndon, 'American Manuscript Collections of Medieval Medical Miniatures and Texts,' *Journal of the History of Medicine and Allied Sciences* XVII (1962) 284-307.
Anneliese Maier, *Studien zur Naturphilosophie der Spätscholastik.* 5 vols., Rome 1949-1958. Each volume has an index of mss.
K. Manitius, 'Eine Gruppe von Handschriften des 12. Jahrhunderts aus dem Trierer Kloster St. Eucharius-Matthias,' *Forschungen und Fortschritte* XXIX (1955) 317-319. Discusses mss. in Brussels, Darmstadt, Kues and London.
T. De Marinis, *La legatura artistica in Italia nel secolo XV e XVI.* 3 vols. Florence 1960. Each section has a list of mss. (and edd.) with shelf marks and short titles. vol. III, p. 135-161: General authors' index for all volumes.
The same, 'Di alcuni calligrafi napoletani del sec. *XV,*' *Italia Medioevale e Umanistica* V (1962) 179-182. Discusses mss. in Oxford, Siena, Turin and the Vatican.

The same, 'Nota per Bartolomeo Sanvito calligrafo del Quattrocento,' *Mélanges Eugène Tisserant* IV (Studi e Testi 234, Vatican City 1964) 185-188.

P. 48.

(Mazzatinti and Sorbelli, *Inventari dei Manoscritti delle Biblioteche d'Italia*).
—LXXXIII (1959) 1-192: Foligno, Biblioteca Comunale, by A. Messini. Mss. C 1-176, F 1-365, M 1-171.
—LXXXIV (1962) 1-175: Lugo, Biblioteca Comunale 'Trisi,' by A. Servolini. Several collections.
—LXXXV (1963) 1-165. Venezia, Biblioteca Marciana, by P. Zorzanello. Mss. Ital. VII 501-1001.
See also under Pistoia.
Mediaeval and Renaissance Illuminated Manuscripts. Los Angeles 1953-54. 37 pp. and plates. 137 mss. in American collections. Exhibition catalogue.
M. Meertens, *De Godsvrucht in de Nederlanden.* 6 vols., Malines 1930-34 (4 and 5 not published). Vol. VI (1934). xi, 317 pp. Description of mss. in Antwerp, Averbode, Brussels, Gent, 's Gravenhage, Leuven and Park.
M. Meiss, *Andrea Mantegna as Illuminator.* New York 1957. ix, 114 pp. and plates.
G. Mercati, *De fatis bibliothecae monasterii S. Columbani Bobiensis et de codice ipso Vat. lat. 5757.* Vatican City 1934. xii, 260 pp. With *M. Tulli Ciceronis De Re Publica libri e codice rescripto Vaticano Latino 5757 phototypice expressi* (volume of plates). Lists mss. of Parrasius in Naples (p. 112-113), and Bobbio mss. in Milan, Turin, the Vatican and elsewhere (255-259). p. 260: index of mss.
The same, *Note per la storia di alcune biblioteche romane nei secoli XVI-XIX* (Studi e Testi 164). Vatican City 1952. iv, 190 pp. and plates. Discusses mostly Greek mss.
A. Millares Carlo, 'Manuscritos Visigóticos' *Hispania Sacra* XIV (1961) 337-444. 241 mss., index.

La miniature flamande. Brussels 1959. 204 pp. and plates. 274 mss. from Brussels and other collections.

Catalogo di Mss. della Biblioteca di Camillo Minieri Riccio. 3 vols. in 7 parts. Naples 1868-69. (Napoli, Biblioteca Nazionale; micr. NNC)

Mittelalterliche Buchmalerei aus Westfalen. Hamm 1954. 40 pp. and plates. 123 mss. from Münster, Detmold, Hamm and other collections. Exhibition catalogue.

P. 50.

Neues Archiv V 457-65. Read: Lists 6 mss. Now Kynžvart.

P. 51.

*G. Nortier, 'Les bibliothèques médiévales des abbayes bénédictines de Normandie,' *Revue Mabillon* XLVII (1957) 1-33; 57-83; 135-71; 219-44; XLVIII (1958) 1-19; 99-127; 165-175; L (1960) 229-243; LI (1961) 332-346 ; LII (1962) 118-133. Old inventories of eight monasteries, giving for each extant ms. its shelf mark. Covers Alençon, Avranches, Évreux, Le Havre, Paris, Rouen and the Vatican. No index. (CtY, incomplete)

P. 52.

E. Pellegrin, 'Bibliothèques d'humanistes lombards de la cour des Visconti Sforza,' *Bibliothèque d'Humanisme et Renaissance* XVII (1955) 218-245. Indices (243-245).

P. 53

A. N. L. Munby, *The Formation of the Phillipps Library to the Year 1840.* Cambridge, 1954. xii, 177 pp.

The same, *The Formation of the Phillipps Library from 1841 to 1872.* Cambridge 1956. xvi, 227 pp.

P. G. Ricci, 'Notizie di Manoscritti, Codici riguardanti l'Italia in alcune biblioteche della Spagna,' *Lettere Italiane* XVI (1964) 322-323. Covers Barcelona, Granada, Huesca, Tarragona, Zaragoza.

P. 55.

(De Ricci, *Census*) Add: 1204-1205: Ibid., Adrian Van Sinderen. 12 mss.

P. 57.

*I. da Rosa Pereira, 'Manuscritos de Direito Canónico existentes em Portugal,' *Arquivo histórico da Madeira* XI (1959, published 1960) 196-242; XIII (1962-63, published 1964) 28-41. Describes 45 mss. in Evora, Lisbon, Porto. No index. (Prof. S. Kuttner)

W. H. Rubsamen, 'Music Research in Italian Libraries,' *Music Library Association Notes,* Second Series, vol. VI, no. 2 (1949) 220-233; 543-569. Lists mss. in Rome, the Vatican and other Italian collections.

P. Ruf, 'Eine altbayrische Gelehrtenbibliothek des 15. Jahrhunderts und ihr Stifter Bernhard von Kraiburg,' *Festschrift Eugen Stollreither . . . gewidmet* (Erlangen 1950) 219-239. Lists mss. in Munich, Salzburg, Vienna. Index (234-239). (NN)

J. Ruysschaert, 'Dix-huit manuscrits copiés par le florentin Pietro Cennini, '*La Bibliofilia* 59 (1957) 108-112.

The same, 'Recherches des deux bibliothèques romaines Maffei des xve et xvie siècles,' *La Bibliofilia* LX (1958, and *Studi e ricerche nella Biblioteca e negli Archivi Vaticani in memoria del Cardinale Giovanni Mercati,* Florence 1958, published 1959) 306-355. 120 mss. No index.

R. Sabbadini, *Le scoperte dei codici latini e greci ne' secoli XIV-XV.* 2 vols. Florence 1905-14. Cites many mss.

The same, 'La biblioteca di Zomino da Pistoia,' *Rivista di filologia e di istruzione classica* XLV (1917) 197-207. Lists mss. in Pistoia and elsewhere.

Ch. Samaran and R. Marichal, *Catalogue des manuscrits en écriture latine portant des indications de date, de lieu ou de copiste.* Vol. I: Musée Condé et Bibliothèques Parisiennes. Paris 1959. xix,

505 pp. and 193 plates. II: Bibliothèque Nationale, Fonds Latin (Nos. 1 à 8000), éd. M. Th. d'Alverny. Paris 1962. xix, 597 pp. and 210 plates.

P. 58.

H. Schiel, 'Handschriften aus Trier und aus Klöstern und Stiften des Trierer Raumes in Brüssel und Gent,' in *Armaria Trevirensia, Beiträge zur Trierer Bibliotheksgeschichte* (Trier 1960) 83-92. Lists 57 mss. Covers mss. from Kues. No index (NN)

P. 59.

(*Serapeum* XXV:) XXVII (twice). Read: XXVI.

P. 60.

Keith V. Sinclair, 'Mediaeval Manuscripts in Australia,' *The Australian Library Journal* X (1961) 62-64. Surveys mss. in Canberra, Melbourne and Sydney.

The same, 'Some Late Manuscripts of the Works of Classical Authors,' *Phoenix* XVI (1962) 276-280. Discusses mss. in Hobart, Melbourne and Sydney.

*Dorothy Waley Singer, *Hand-List of Western Scientific Manuscripts in Great Britain and Ireland dating from before the sixteenth century.* Cards in 101 boxes, deposited in the British Museum. Cf. T. C. Skeat, *The Catalogues of the Manuscript Collections*, Revised Edition (London 1962) 41-43. (micr. at DLC)

The same and Annie Anderson, *Catalogue of Latin and Vernacular Plague Texts in Great Britain and Eire in Manuscripts written before the sixteenth century* (Collection de Travaux de l'Académie Internationale d'Histoire des Sciences 5, Paris and London 1950). xi, 269, 5 pp. Offset printed. 74 nos. and several appendices.

P. 62.

(after Doucet) ** M. Gołaszewska and others, 'Commentaires sur les Sentences,

Supplément au répertoire de F. Stegmüller,' *Mediaevalia philosophica Polonorum* II (1958) 19-21.

(F. Stegmüller, *Repertorium Biblicum*). Vol. VII. Madrid 1961.

The same, *Filosofia e Teologia nas Universidades de Coimbra e Evora no seculo XVI.* Coimbra 1959. viii, 472 pp. pp. 101-290: Mss. in Lisbon, Coimbra, Evora, Braga, Porto. Indices.

P. 64.

L. Thorndike, 'Notes upon some medieval, astronomical, astrological and mathematical manuscripts at Florence, Milan, Bologna and Venice,' *Isis* L (1959) 33-50. 21 mss.

The same, 'Notes on Medical Texts in Manuscripts at London and Oxford,' *Janus* XLVIII (1959) 141-202.

The same, 'Some Medieval and Renaissance Manuscripts in Physics,' *Proceedings of the American Philosophical Society* CIV (1960) 188-201. Discusses mss. in Paris, Bologna, Florence, the Vatican, and Naples.

The same and P. Kibre, *A Catalogue of Incipits of Mediaeval Scientific Writings in Latin.* Revised and Augmented Edition. Cambridge Mass. 1963. xxii pp., 1938 coll.

(*Traditio*) XV (1959) 449-505: (S. Kuttner), Institute of Research and Study in Medieval Canon Law, 'Bulletin for 1959.'

—XVI (1960) 531-571. (S. Kuttner), 'Bulletin for 1960.' Includes: R. Weigand, 'Mitteilungen aus Handschriften' (556-564).

—XVII (1961) 163-183: J. Leclercq, 'Textes et manuscrits cisterciens dans des bibliothèques des États-Unis.' Covers New Haven, Camarillo, Berkeley, Cambridge, Covington. 503-553: (S. Kuttner), 'Bulletin for 1961.' Includes 'Notes on mss.' (533-544).

—XVIII (1962) 447-490: The same, 'Bulletin for 1962.'

—XIX (1963) 487-507: A. Strittmatter,

'Liturgical Manuscripts Preserved in Hungarian Libraries.' Index of mss. (506-507). 509-556: (S. Kuttner), 'Bulletin for 1963.'

(L. Traube, *Vorlesungen und Abhandlungen*). 3 vols., Munich 1909-20. III 343-344: Index of mss. cited in all vols.

Trésors des bibliothèques d'Écosse. Brussels 1963. xii, 127 pp. pp. 1-28, nos. 1-48: Mss. from Glasgow, Edinburgh, Fort Augustus, Aberdeen, St. Andrews, Paisley. (Frick Art Reference Library).

E. Troeger, 'Handschriften aus der Bibliotheca Corvina in den Bibliotheken der Deutschen Demokratischen Republik,' *Zentralblatt für Bibliothekswesen* LXXVIII (1964) 152-161. Covers Berlin, Dresden, Jena, Leipzig.

B. L. Ullman, *The Origin and Development of Humanistic Script. Rome* 1960. 146 pp. and plates. Index of mss. (142-144).

P. 65.

(*Aristoteles Latinus*) *Codices, Supplementa Altera*, ed. L, Minio-Paluello. Bruges and Paris 1961. 229 pp. Nos. 2013-2195 and addenda. Indices.

**L. Vernier, 'La bibliothèque de l'abbaye de Moyenmoûtier,' *Bulletin de la Société philomatique vosgienne* LXXXVII (1961) 5-30. Mss. in Epinal, Saint-Dié, and Nancy (Grand Séminaire).

(*Verzeichnis der Handschriften*). Remove the paragraph after Krüss, and add Leipzig as place of publication.

H. Walther, *Initia carminum ac versuum Medii aevi posterioris Latinorum (Carmina Medii Aevi Posterioris Latina* I). Göttingen 1959. xiv, 1186 pp. Cites many mss.

J. Wardrop, *The Script of Humanism.* Oxford 1963. xix, 57 pp. and plates. Index of mss. (p. 56).

Westfalia Sacra. Münster 1952. 56 pp. and plates. pp. 46-48: 10 mss. from Minden, Münster, Paderborn and elsewhere. Exhibition catalogue.

P. 67.

A. Zumkeller, 'Manuskripte von Werken der Autoren des Augustiner-Eremiten-ordens in mitteleuropäischen Bibliotheken,' *Augustiniana* XI (1961) 27-86; 261-319; 478-532 ; XII (1962) 27-92; 299-357; XIII (1963) 418-473; XIV (1964) 105-162. Arranged alphabetically by authors. No index.

SECTION C

Printed Catalogues and Handwritten Inventories of Individual Libraries, by Cities

P. 69.

(Aachen) Gutzweiler. Read: Gatzweiler.

(Aarau, catalogue of 1806) Add: Hardly relevant. Partial micr. at NNC

*Abbéville. Read: *Abbeville

*Aberdeen, Scotland. See *Trésors des Bibliothèques d'Écosse.*

*Aberystwyth, Wales
Handlist of Manuscripts int he National Library of Wales. (The National Library of Wales Journal. Supplement Series II). vols. I-IV (pts. I-XXIV, 1940-64). 12325 mss. Index for vols. I-II in vol. II, pt. XII (1951). Index of vol. III in pt. XXI (1961).

(Admont, *Catalogus codicum*, by Wichner) The mss. which were sold are clearly indicated.

P. 70.

Agrigento, Italy. See Kristeller.

*Alba Julia, Rumania. See Günterova.

Catalogus concinnus librorum manuscriptorum Bibliothecae Batthyanyanae Albae in Transsilvania, by R. Szentiványi. Szeged 1947. 104 pp. 651 nos. 766 mss. (Budapest, Szechenyi Library)

*Alençon, France. See Nortier.

*Altenburg, East Germany. See also under Jena.

*Altenfurt, West Germany. See under Fischbach.

P. 71.

*Amalfi, Italy. Archivio Arcivescovile.

R. Brentano, 'The Archiepiscopal Archives at Amalfi,' *Manuscripta* IV (1960) 98-105. Surveys 34 mss. (104-105).

*Amherst, Mass. USA. Amherst College Library. See Bond.

Amsterdam, Holland. Read: Bibliotheek der Universiteit.

(*Catalogus Bibliothecae Publicae Amstelaedamensis* (by H. C. Cras). Amsterdam 1796. 290 pp. 221-231: 73 mss. (ICN)

Gids voor de Bibliotheek der Universiteit van Amsterdam. Amsterdam 1919. xxxii pp. and several separately paged appendices (total about 230 pp.). Handschriften, 18 pp. : 68 mss.

(Ancona)
M. Natalucci, *Il Tesoro e l'Archivio della Cattedrale di Ancona.* Ancona 1938. 119 pp. p. 116: 8 mss. No index. (Vatican Library)

P. 72.

*Annaberg, East Germany. Bibliothek der erweiterten Oberschule Annaberg-Buchholz. The mss. listed by Wilisch (1724) are apparently lost. Communication of the librarian through Dr. Emilie Boer. —St. Annenkirchgemeinde.

Bücherliste, by Dr. Harms von Spreckel (1931). 1 ms. vol. f. 116-117ᵛ: mss. no. 2234-2284. This library also has the Jenisius collection of letters mentioned by Wilisch. Reported by Dr. Emilie Boer.

*Ann Arbor, Mich., USA. See Bond.

*Antwerp (Anvers).

Aquila, Italy. See Kristeller.

Arezzo, Italy. See Kristeller.

P. 73.

*Armagh, Northern Ireland.

F. Blatt, 'Studia Hibernica,' *Classica et Mediaevalia* XIV (1953) 226-232. Describes the older mss. of the Public Library.

*Arundel Castle, England. Duke of Norfolk. Has some old mss. Communication of Prof. R. Harrier.

Aschaffenburg, West Germany. Hofbibliothek.

(Merkel). 32 mss. Read: 36 mss. Typed catalogue, by Dr. J. Hofmann. 51 nos. (some skipped). (Würzburg, Universitätsbibliothek).

—Stiftsarchivbibliothek. Typed list, by Dr. J. Hofmann. 37 parchment and 40 paper mss. Copy kindly supplied by the author. (Würzburg, Universitätsbibliothek).

Assisi, Italy. See Kristeller.

Athenai, Greece. Ἐθνικὴ βιβλιοθήκη τῆς Ἑλλάδος.

Supplement to Sakkelion on ms. sheets in 6 bound vols. Title: Συμπληρωματικὸς κατάλογος Χειρογράφων Ἐθνικῆς βιβλιοθήκης. I: no. 1857-2000. II: 2001-2159. III: 2160-2259. IV: 2260-2395. V: 2396-2570. VI: 2571-2730.

—American School of Classical Studies, Gennadeion Library. See The Book Collector.

Catalogue of Manuscripts in the Gennadius Library (London 1922). 1 typed vol. 231 mss.

P. 74.

Augsburg, West Germany. Stadtarchiv. Namens-Register zur Litteraliensammlung von 1290-1538. I. Band. 1 ms. vol. Autographen-Sammlung. 1 ms. vol. Arranged chronologically.

*Austin, Texas, USA. See Bond.
*Avellino, Italy. See Kristeller.
*Avesnes, France. See Leclercq.
*Avranches, France. See Nortier.
*Baguères. Read: Bagnères.
*Ballarat, Australia. See The Book Collector.

Baltimore, Maryland, USA. See Bond.
*Bangor, Wales. Cathedral Library.
*Catalogue of the Bangor Cathedral Library, now deposited in the University College of North Wales, by E. G. Jones and J. R.

V. Johnston. Bangor 1961. xxiv, 172 pp. Section on mss.

*Banská Bystrica, Czechoslovakia. See Günterova.

P. 75.

Barcelona, Spain. See Ricci.
—*Biblioteca del Cabildo.
*J. Oliveras Caminal, El problema de la divisibilidad del continuo. Barcelona 1949. 101 pp. p. 87-101: 'Codicum in Sanctae Barcinonensis Ecclesiae segregatis asservatorum tabulae.' Lists 166 mss. by subjects (90-97). Index of names (98-99). (Barcelona, Biblioteca Central; partial micr. NNC)

*The same, 'Codicum in Sanctae Barcinonensis Ecclesiae segregatis asservatorum tabulae,' Scrinium VII (1952) 6-16. Lists mss. by subjects (7-13). Index of names (14-15). (Barcelona, Biblioteca Central; partial micr. NNC)

Read: J. Massó i Torrents and J. Rubió i Balaguer, 'Catàleg dels manuscrits de la Biblioteca de Catalunya,' Buttletí de la Biblioteca de Catalunya.

Guía de la Biblioteca Central de la Diputación Provincial de Barcelona. Barcelona 1959. 281 pp. p. 41: list of catalogues. 53-120: Short list of 1805 mss. 121-213: list of mss. by subjects. 227-246: Index of authors.

*Inventario de la coleccion de libros donada por D. Santiago Espona y Brunet. Barcelona 1960.

P. Bohigas, 'Les manuscrits à miniatures de la "Biblioteca Central" de Barcelone,' Librarium VII (1964) 39-58.

P. 76.

—Biblioteca Universitaria.

F. Miquel Rosell, Inventario General de Manuscritos de la Biblioteca Universitaria de Barcelona. Vols. I-III. Madrid 1958-1961. I: Mss. no. 1-500. II (1958): 501-1000. III: 1001-1500. Not complete. No index.

*Bardejow, Czechoslovakia. See Günterova.

P. 77.

Basel, Switzerland. Öffentliche Bibliothek der Universität.

Gustav Meyer and Max Burckhardt, *Die mittelalterlichen Handschriften der Universitätsbibliothek Basel. Abteilung B. Theologische Pergamenthandschriften.* vol. I: B I 1-B VIII 10. Basel 1960. xlvii, 882 pp. No index.

*Autographen-Sammlung von Geigy-Hagenbach. Basel 1929. 299 pp. Includes *Nachtrag* I and II. *Nachtrag III zur Autographen-Sammlung . . .* 1933. pp. 301-376. *Nachtrag IV . . .*1939. pp. 377-415. For the pieces now in the Basel Library, the shelf marks are entered in the library copy. (Basel, University Library; partial micr. NNC)

**Beauvais, France. See France, *Catalogue Général* LIII.

P. 77.

Belluno, Italy. Biblioteca Civica.

Registro, in 2 ms. vols. 1096 nos. Mazzatinti II gives only a selection from this inventory, adds his own serial numbers, and fails to give the original shelf marks.

—Seminario Gregoriano. Biblioteca Gregoriana. Late mss., no list.

—Seminario Gregoriano. Biblioteca Lolliniana. Property of the Capitolo del Duomo, but deposited in the Seminario. *Biblioteca Lolliniana Belluno. Inventario dei Manoscritti.* 1 typed vol. 59 mss. Cf. Mazzatinti II. The collection has 38 more uncatalogued mss.

P. 78.

Benevento, Italy. See Kristeller.

Bergamo. Italy. See Kristeller.

G. Cremaschi, 'Testi umanistici in codici della Biblioteca Civica di Bergamo,' *Aevum* XXXIII (1959) 266-273.

Berlin, Germany. Staatsbibliothek (East Berlin). See Lehmann.

Deutsche Staatsbibliothek 1661-1961. 2 vols. Leipzig (1961). I 319-380: H. Luelfing, 'Die Handschriftenabteilung.' II 107-113:

bibliography of the mss.

Deutsche Staatsbibliothek Berlin, Handschriften- und Inkunabelabteilung. *Signaturenliste der Handschriften und kurzes Verzeichnis der Nachlässe.* Compiled by H. Luelfing, U. Winter and U. Bruckner. Berlin 1963. 12 pp. p. 4-8: 'Signaturenliste der Hss.'

P. Gehring and W. Gebhardt, 'Signaturenverzeichnis abendländischer und Musikhandschriften der ehem. Preussischen Staatsbibliothek, die jetzt in der Westdeutschen Bibliothek (WDB) in Marburg und der Universitäts-Bibliothek (UB) Tübingen aufbewahrt werden,' *Scriptorium* XIII (1959) 127-130. Arranged by shelf marks.

P. 79.

Savigny mss. They constitute a separate group and are now in Tübingen.

The library received in 1958 many mss. from Russia that were formerly in the libraries of Bremen, Hamburg, Lübeck and Magdeburg. To my knowledge, there are no lists.

P. 80.

—Kunstbibliothek (West Berlin).

Graphische Sammlungen Band 6. Meisterwerke des Buchdrucks. Vormals Bibliothek Hans Grisebach. 1 ms. vol. Part 1: mss. Gris 1-24.

Lipperheide'sche Kostümbibliothek. *Katalog der Freiherrlich von Lipperheide'schen Kostümbibliothek.* 2 vols. Berlin 1896-1905. A few mss. are listed among the printed books. See the subject index, vol. II, p. 835 and 837.

—*Marienbibliothek (East Berlin). A few theological mss. Communication of Dr. Wilhelm Risse.

*Bern, Switzerland. Bürgerbibliothek. See Institut de Recherche.

O. Homburger, *Die illustrierten Handschriften der Bürgerbibliothek Bern. Die vorkarolingischen Handschriften.* Bern 1962. 182 pp. and plates.

*Beuron, West Germany. Erzabtei. Card file. 230 mss.

*Birmingham, England. Selby Oak College. Has a few mss. Communication of Bernard M. Peebles.

*Bloomington, Indiana, USA. Indiana University Library. See Bond.

J. W. Halporn, 'Two Manuscripts in the Lilly Library, Bloomington,' *Transactions and Proceedings of the American Philological Association* XCII (1961) 220-227.

*Bogota, Colombia. Biblioteca Nacional. Typed list of selected mss. supplied by the librarian.

Bologna, Italy. See Kristeller; Thorndike.

P. 82.

—Biblioteca Universitaria.

G. Manfré, 'La Biblioteca dell'umanista Bolognese Giovanni Garzoni (1419-1505).' *Accademie e Biblioteche d'Italia* XXVII (N.S. X, 1959) 249-278; XXVIII (N.S. XI, 1960) 17-72. List of mss. (XXVIII 17-64). Index (65-69).

—*Cassa di Risparmio. Acquired in 1948 most of the Biblioteca Raimondo Ambrosini. See Mazzatinti XIV (1909) 9-58 for a list of 355 mss. The numbers given in parentheses are those of the original catalogues. Of the mss. listed by Mazzatinti, 26 are missing, as well as some not listed by him. The library now has 493 mss.

(*Raccolta di opere riguardanti Bologna, Nella Biblioteca di Raimondo Ambrosini.* Bologna 1906. vii, 388 pp. 4767 nos. Mss. listed with printed books. See index under Autografi (p. 331) and 'Manoscritti' (p. 335). ICN).

(The same, *Appendice I.* Bologna 1908. 122 pp. Nos. 4768-6913. See index under Manoscritti, p. 121. ICN).

*Appendice II a. 1 ms. vol. Nos. 6449-8587.

*Appendice III a. 1 ms. vol.

*Catalogo dei Manoscritti. 1 ms. vol. The information on this library was reported by Herbert Matsen.

—*S. Domenico.

V. Alce and A. D'Amato, *La Biblioteca di S. Domenico in Bologna.* Florence 1961. 174 pp. p. 141-151: 35 liturgical mss.

—*S. Francesco.

M. Fanti, 'Inventario dei manoscritti della Biblioteca di S. Francesco in Bologna,' *L'Archiginnasio* LIII-LIV (1958-59, published 1961) 285-321. Lists 45 mss., mostly late (294-321). No index. (NN)

P. 83.

Bonn, West Germany. Universitätsbibliothek.

Chirographorum in Bibliotheca Academica Bonnensi servatorum catalogus. Volumen II quo libri descripti sunt praeter Orientales relicui, by A. Klette and J. Staender. Bonn 1858-76. 250 pp. 856 mss. Index. (Bonn, Universitätsbibliothek; micr. NNC)

Rheinische Handschriften der Universitätsbibliothek Bonn. (Bonn 1941). 35 pp. *ca.* 30 mss., arranged by provenance. (Bonn, Universitätsbibliothek).

Katalog der Handschriften der Universitätsbibliothek Bonn, 2, 1876-1943. *Libri manu scripti praeter orientales relicui.* 1 bound vol. of photostats taken from a handwritten inventory lost during the last war. Mss. no. 876-2586.

Boston, Mass., USA. See Bond.

*Boxhill, Australia. See *The Book Collector*.

*Braga, Portugal. See Stegmüller.

*Braniewo, Poland. Hosianum. Mss. lost during the last war. Communication of Dr. Peter L. Schmidt.

*Bratislava, Czechoslovakia. See Günterova.

P. 84.

*Bregenz, Austria. Kapuzinerkloster. Alphabetical and subject catalogue. Cf. Nickson.

*Bremen, West Germany. See also under **Berlin, St. Gallen.**

Namens- und Ortsregister der Brief- Samm-lungen des 16. und 17. Jahrhunderts der Staatsbibliothek Bremen. Typed indices. (micr. DLC)

Brescia, Italy. See Kristeller.

Bressanone-Brixen, Italy. See Kristeller.

*Brest, France. See France, *Catalogue Général* LIII.

*Brighton, England. Brighton Public Library.

*Brighton Public Library, Catalogue of Manuscripts and Printed Books before 1500. Brighton 1962. 22 pp. (British Museum)

P. 85.

*Brindisi, Italy. Biblioteca Arcivescovile. See Kristeller.

G. Moscardino, 'Ritorna alla luce un prezioso tesoro per la Cultura universale,' *Il Meridionale* V (1959), no. 22, p. 7-11. Note on the library, with a mention of its mss.

Brno, Czechoslovakia, Universitni knihovna. *Soupis Rukopisů knihovny frantiskanů r Dacicich* (by V. Dokoupil). Mimeographed list (1957). 48 pp. D 1-111. Index.

P. 86.

Bruxelles, Belgium. See *Analecta Bollandiana* ; Schiel.

P. 87.

(P. Thomas) 110 pp. Read: 111 pp.

H. Silvestre, 'Incipits des traités médiévaux de sciences expérimentales dans les manuscrits latins de Bruxelles,' *Scriptorium* V (1951) 145-160.

L. M. J. Delaissé, *Miniatures médiévales, De la Librarie de Bourgogne au Cabinet des Manuscrits de la Bibliothèque royale de Belgique.* Geneva (1959). 221 pp. and plates. List of mss. (p. 221). (Pierpont Morgan Library).

The same, *Mittelalterliche Miniaturen, Von der Burgundischen Bibliothek zum Handschriftenkabinett der koeniglich Belgischen Bibliothek.* Cologne (1959). 221 pp. and plates. List of mss. (p. 221). (NN)

P. 88.

Bryn Mawr, Pennsylvania, USA. See Bond.

Budapest, Hungary. See *Corvinen*; Günterova.

—Egyetemi Könyvtár (University Library).

Catalogus manuscriptorum . . . Tomus II, Pars III. *Catalogus collectionis Kaprinayanae et supplementa* (by Z. Ferenczi). 1907. vi, 848 pp. (PU). Pars IV. *Index alphabeticus et chronologicus cum tabula,* 1910. 280 pp. (PU)

Codices Latini Medii Aevi Bibliothecae Universitatis Budapestinensis, by L. Mezey and A. Bolgar. Budapest 1961. 391 pp. 132 mss. Index.

—Magyar Tudományos Akadémia Könyvtára.

Kódexek. 1 ms. notebook. 89 nos. Alphabetical card index.

—Országos Széchényi Könyvtár.

Codices medii aevi (ab anno 1945). 1 box. Contains handwritten list for mss. Clmae 450-526.

Fragmenta Katalógus. 1 box of cards. mss. A1-E94.

Inventarium Codicum Manuscriptorum Latinorum in folio Bibliothecae Széchényiano-Regnicolaris in Museo Nationali Hungarico. 1 ms. vol. 4627 nos. The mss. transferred to the medieval group (Clmae) are marked in red.

Inventarium Codicum Manuscriptorum Latinorum in quarto Bibliothecae Széchényiano-Regnicolaris . . . 1 ms. vol. 3894 nos. Likewise.

Inventarium Codicum Manuscriptorum Latinorum Bibliothecae Széchényiano-Regnicolaris in octavo (1174 nos.) and *in duodecimo* (154 nos.). 1 ms. vol. Likewise.

Inventarium Codicum Manuscriptorum Medii Aevi Bibliothecae Musei Nat. Hungarici. Variae Linguae. 1 ms. vol. Covers the Greek and Italian mss.

P. 89.

*Burgos, Spain.

*N. López Martínez, 'Un grupo de manuscritos escolásticos en la Catedral de Burgos,' *Revista Española de Teologia* XVIII (1958) 317-330. 23 mss. No index. (PU)

*Busto Arsizio, Italy.

P. Mancarella, 'I codici della Biblioteca Capitolare di S. Giovanni Battista in Busto Arsizio,' *Aevum* XXIX (1955) 237-254. Mss. M I 1-20, M II 1-8. Some nos. skipped. No index.

*Caen, France, See *Catalogue Général* LIII.

*Cagliari, Italy. Biblioteca Universitaria. *Ca.* 200 mss. Described in a ms. list. Communication of Prof. E. Cortese.

*Calci, Italy. See Garrison.

*Camaldoli, Italy. Archivio del Sacro Eremo.

Has a few mss. from S. Michele di Murano. Communication of P. Vittorino Meneghin.

*Camarillo, California, USA. See Bond.

P. 90.

Cambridge, England.

A. N. L. Munby, *Cambridge College Libraries*. Cambridge (1960). 55 pp. 2nd. ed. 1962. xv, 56 pp. Gives data on mss. and their catalogues.

M. R. James. *The Sources of Archbishop Parker's Collection of Mss. at Corpus Christi College, Cambridge*. (Cambridge Antiquarian Society, Octavo Publications, no. 32). Cambridge 1899. 84 pp. p. 15-75: mss. no. 1-482. No index.

Bibliotheca Pepysiana. Add: 51 mss.

P. 91.

Cambridge, Mass., USA. See Bond.

Camerino, Italy. See Kristeller.

*Canberra, Australia. See Sinclair.

*Cape Town, South Africa. South African Public Library. Grey Collection. See *The Book Collector*.

The Library of His Excellency Sir George Grey, K.C.B., presented by him to the South African Public Library. Manuscripts and Incunables. Vol. III, part I. Preface signed by W. H. I. Bleek. London

1862. viii, 24 pp. p. 1-13: 5 Western mss. (NN).

An Index of the Grey Collection in The South African Public Library, by Th. Hahn. Cape Town 1884. 404 pp. p.1-39: Part I. Manuscripts and Incunables. No shelf marks. Index (p. 371-374).

E. Bizzarri, 'Inediti italiani della "Grey Collection,"' *La Rinascita* IV (1941) 860-870. Mentions several mss.

A. M. L(ewin) R(obinson), 'The Illuminated Manuscripts in the Grey Collection, A General Survey,' *Quarterly Bulletin of the South African Library* III (1948-49) 45-56. Mentions 115 mss., describes 19 mss.

L. F. Casson, 'The Medieval Manuscripts of the Grey Collection in Saleroom and Bookshop', *ibid.* XIV (1959-60) 3-33. Lists the mss.

*Capestrano, Italy. See Kristeller.·

*Capua, Italy. Museo Provinciale Campano. Has 22 packs of mss. from Camillo Minieri Riccio (not including the old mss. owned by him). Communication of the librarian.

P. 92.

*Carpi, Italy. Biblioteca Comunale.

A. G. Spinelli, 'Catalogo sommario dell'Archivio Guàitoli per la storia Carpense,' *Memorie storiche e documenti sulla città e sull'antico principato di Carpi* VII. Carpi 1897. xix, viii, 426 pp. 1022 nos. p. 89-138: 'Manoscritti,' nos. 143-252. p. 351-352: 'Appendice, Manoscritti.' Nos. 1021 and 251.

Casale Monferrato, Italy. See Kristeller.

Catania, Italy. See Kristeller.

P. 93.

Cava, Italy. See Kristeller.

*Cento, Italy. See Kristeller.

Cesena, Italy. See Kristeller.

*Châlons-sur-Marne, France.

***R. Gandilhon and J. Houslier, 'Inventaire sommaire des fragments de manuscrits et d'imprimés conservés aux Ar-

chives de la Marne, sous-série 3 J,'
*Mémoires de la Société d'agriculture,
commerce, sciences et arts de la Marne,*
Ser. II, vol. XXX (1956) 57-130. (MH)
*Chambéry, France.
*Bibliothèque Municipale de Chambéry, Cata-
logue Méthodique et Alphabétique des
Imprimés et des Manuscrits,* by F. Per-
pechon. Chambéry 1901. vii, 943 pp.
p. 706-728: 154 mss. Covered by the
general index of the volume. (NN)
Musée de Chambéry, Catalogue raisonné,
by J. Carotti. Chambéry 1911. iv, 178 pp.
p. 135-138: 3 mss. of the Bibliothèque
de la Ville. p. 100: 1 ms. fragment of
the museum. (NNMM)
Chantilly, France. Musée Condé. See
France, *Catalogue Général* LII; Samaran.
Le Cabinet des Livres, Manuscrits, 3 vols.
The serial numbers of this catalogue
constitute the valid shelf marks of the
manuscripts.
Chapel Hill, North Carolina, USA. See
Bond.
*Charlottesville, Virginia, USA. See Bond.
*Chartres, France. *Speculum* 24. Read:
29. See also France, *Catalogue Général*
LIII.

P. 94.
*Chatellerault and **Chatillon-sur-Seine**.
Read: **Châtellerault** and **Châtillon-
sur-Seine**.
*Chester, England. Cathedral Library.
List of 3 mss. kindly supplied by the
librarian.
Chicago, Illinois, USA. See Bond.
*Chipiona, Spain. Biblioteca del Semi-
nario Mayor Franciscano.
Has 2 biblical mss. See J. Dominguez
Bordona, *Manuscritos con pinturas* I
(1933) 107, no. 210.
*Chur, Switzerland. Bischoefliche Biblio-
thek.
Has some ms. frs. Communication of
Peter L. Schmidt.
—Kantons-Bibliothek.
The mss. have been deposited in the Bünd-

nerisches Staatsarchiv. Communication
of the same.

P. 95.
*Ciudad Real, Spain. Biblioteca Pro-
vincial.
Some mss. No catalogue. Communication
of Father García.
*Civitanova, Italy.
G. Pagnani, *Catalogo dell'Archivio Storico
Comunale di Civitanova Marche con
sede a Civitanova Alta e dell'annessa
Biblioteca.* Preface dated Falconara 1959.
1959. Offset printed. 30 pp. p. 29:
4 late mss.
Claremont, California, USA. Honnold
Library. See Bond.
W. H. J. Kennedy, 'Some Unpublished
Letters of the Italian Renaissance (from
the Collection of Harold C. Bodman),'
Studies in the Renaissance VII (1960)
67-75.
Cleveland, Ohio, USA. See Bond. The
National Library of Medicine is now again
in Washington.
*Cluj (Klausenburg), Rumania. Biblioteca
Academiei Republicii Populare Romîne.
A. Pirnát, *Die Ideologie der Siebenbürger
Antitrinitarier in den* 1570er *Jahren.*
Budapest 1961. 217 pp.
—*Biblioteca Universitară.* List of older
mss. kindly supplied by the librarian.
Coburg, West Germany. Landesbibliothek.
I. Hubay, *Die Handschriften der Landes-
bibliothek Coburg.* Coburg 1962. 183 pp.
236 nos.
F. G. Kaltwasser, *Die Handschriften der
Bibliothek des Gymnasium Casimirianum
und der Scheres-Zieritz-Bibliothek.* Co-
burg 1960. 240 pp. and plates. Mss.
Cas. 1-110. Sche. 1-19. Some nos. skipped.
Coimbra, Portugal. See Stegmüller.
'Catalogo..' in *Boletim* III (1916). *236-
240. Read: 234-240.

P. 96.
*Colchester, England. Colchester and
Essex Museum.

Typed list of 25 mss. kindly supplied by the librarian. Cf. B. Corrigan, 'An Unrecorded Manuscript of Machiavelli's "La Clizia,"' *La Bibliofilia* LXIII (1961) 73-87.

Como, Italy. See Kristeller.

P. 97.

Cordoba, Spain. *Biblioteca Episcopal. Has at least one old ms. No inventory. Communication of Father García.

*Corning, New York, USA. See Bond.

*Correggio, Italy. Biblioteca Comunale. See Kristeller. Has 120 mss. Communication of the librarian.

Cortona, Italy. See Kristeller.

*Covington, Virginia, USA. See Bond.

Cracow, see **Kraków**.

Cremona, Italy. See *Arte Lombarda;* Kristeller.

Biblioteca Governativa.*Fondo Albertoni. 247 mss., mostly late. Card files by authors and shelf marks. Communication of the librarian.

P. 98.

*Cuneo, Italy. Biblioteca Civica. The mss. not listed by Mazzatinti are described in a card index. Information supplied by the librarian and by Prof. Ludwig Bieler.

*Dallas, Texas, USA. See Bond.

Darmstadt, West Germany. Hessische Landes- und Hochschulbibliothek. See Löffler.

Walther, *Beiträge.* Add: No shelf marks. Walther, *Neue Beiträge.* Add: No index. No shelf marks. (NN)

Standortsverzeichnis. Add: Mss. 2003-2192 were returned in 1867 to the Dombibliothek, Köln.

H. Knaus, 'Darmstädter Handschriften mittelrheinischer Herkunft (Blankenheim, Koblenz, Steinfeld, Trier),' *Archiv für hessische Geschichte und Altertumskunde* N. F. XXVI (1958) 43-70. A survey. Mentions some mss.

The same, 'Die Handschriften des **Leander** van Ess,' *Archiv für Geschichte des Buchwesens* I (1958) 331-336. Survey.

The same, 'Sieben Gladbacher Handschriften in Darmstadt,' *ibid.* I (1958) 374-380.

The same, 'Handschriften der Grafen von Nassau-Breda,' *ibid.* III (1960) col. 567-580.

The same, 'Maugérard, Hüpsch und die Darmstädter Prachthandschriften,' *ibid.* V (1963) col. 1227-1240.

Deutsche und niederländische Gebethandschriften der Hessischen Landes- und Hochschulbibliothek, by G. Achten and H. Knaus. Darmstadt 1959. 405 pp. 125 nos.

*Dendermonde, Belgium.

E. Dhanens, *Dendermonde* (Inventaris van het kunstpatrimonium van Oostvlaanderen IV). Gent 1961. xii, 255 pp. and plates. p. 158-159: 2 mss. (nos. 439-440). (NNFr)

Dessau, East Germany. Landesbibliothek. Now: Universitäts- und Landesbibliothek Sachsen-Anhalt, Zweigstelle Dessau.

Georghandschriften. 199 nos. Typed list. (micr. NNC)

Detmold, West Germany. Lippische Landesbibliothek. See *Mittelalterliche Buchmalerei.*

—*Staatsarchiv. Has 7 mss. from St. Marien, Lemgo. Communication of the archivist.

*Detroit, Michigan, USA. See Bond.

P. 99.

Devon, Pennsylvania, USA. See Bond.

Donaueschingen, West Germany. Fürstlich Fürstenbergische Hofbibliothek.

Nachtrag des Hss-Katalogs. 1 typed vol. Mss. A I 1-G II 10.

*Dortmund, West Germany. Stadt- und Landesbibliothek.

Read: *Aus 1000 Jahren (900-1900): Kostbarkeiten in Handschrift und Buchdruck* (Dortmund 1929). Compiled by E. Schulz and A. Schill. vii, 38 pp. pp. p. 1-5: 31 mss. (Dortmund; micr. NNC)

*Douai, France. See France, *Catalogue Général* LIII.

*Dresden, East Germany. See *Archiv* I; VI; VIII.

Sächsische Landesbibliothek Dresden, 1556-1956, Festschrift zum 400-jährigen Bestehen. Leipzig 1956. vi, 298 pp. and plates. p. 139-146: M. Kremer, 'Die Handschriftenabteilung.' Mentions mss., their catalogues and losses. p. 175-205: H. Deckert and others, 'Das neue Buchmuseum der Sächsischen Landesbibliothek.' Mentions several mss. p. 209-279: C. Alschner and M. Bundesmann, 'Bibliographie zur Geschichte der Sächsischen Landesbibliothek' (p. 258-261 on mss.).

List of some lost mss. kindly supplied by the librarian.

Handwritten continuation of the printed catalogue. Covers Appendix 184-1110.

The library acquired a part of the mss. from Meissen and Schneeberg, and the surviving mss. from Moritzburg.

For Moritzburg, see: J. Petzholdt, *Catalogi Bibliothecae Secundi Generis Principalis Dresdensis Specimen primum (—duodecimum).* Leipzig 1839-65. (Dresden; micr. NNC)

Typed list of Moritzburg mss. (Dresden, ms. App. 560-562). Fol. 1-61, Qu. 1-134, Oct. 1-82, with some gaps. Most of them are lost. (micr. NNC)

P. 100.

Dublin, Ireland. *Chester Beatty Library. See *The Book Collector.*

The Library of A. Chester Beatty, A Descriptive Catalogue of the Western Manuscripts, by Eric George Millar. Vol. I; London 1927. xii, 148 pp. Mss. 1-43. II: 1930. xv, 264 pp. Mss. 44-81. 2 vols. of plates (1927-30). (NN).

Chester Beatty Library, *Catalogue of Western Manuscripts,* by L. Bieler. Typed list. Mss. W.1-196. Omits the mss. that were sold. Microfilm kindly supplied by Dr. R. Hayes.

*Durham, England. University Library.

F. J. W. Harding, 'Mickleton & Spearman Mss.' *The Durham Philobiblon,* vol. I, no. 6 (1951) 40-44. Surveys 100 local mss.

D. Ramage, 'University Library Mss.,' *ibid.,* no. 7 (1952) 48-49. Surveys the additional mss.

D. Ramage, *Summary List of the Additional Manuscripts Accessioned and listed between September 1945 and September 1961.* (Durham University Library Publication, no. 5). Newcastle 1963. 30 pp. Alphabetical List. Mostly late.

P. 101.

Düsseldorf, West Germany. *Dominikanerkloster. Now Walberg near Bonn, Bibliothek St. Albert.

Verzeichnis der alten Handschriften und Drucke in der Bibliothek des Dominikanerklosters zu Düsseldorf. (By P. v. Löe). Cologne (1904). 48 pp. 270 nos. Mss. listed with edd. Indices. (MH ; micr. NNC)

Edinburgh, Scotland. See *Trésors des Bibliothèques d'Écosse.*

C. P. Finlayson, 'Notes on C. R. Borland's "A Descriptive Catalogue of the Western Mediaeval Manuscripts in Edinburgh University Library, 1916,"' *The Bibliotheck* III 2 (1961) 44-52.

*Eger (Erlau), Hungary. See Günterova.

P. 102.

**Az Egri érseki könyvtár szakszerü czimjegyzéke* (by M. Michalek). 2 vols. Eger 1893. Vol. I, part 2, p. 1289-1308: chronological list of mss. Supplement I (1894) p. 152-158: late mss. Supplement II (1900) p. 111-112: late mss. Communication of Helga Hajdu Juhasz. (partial micr. NNC)

Varjum. Read: Varjú.

Einsiedeln, Switzerland.

Gabriel Meier, *Catalogus.* Add: New shelf marks added in library copy.

*Eisleben, East Germany. Turmbibliothek.

Katalog der Turmbibliothek der Sanct Andreaskirche zu Eisleben, by Pastor Kawerau (1881, copied 1883). 1 ms. vol.

At the end, a list of mss. Micr. sent on loan by the Deutsche Akademie der Wissenschaften.

*Elton Hall (near Peterborough), England. Sir Richard Proby.

List of 6 mss. kindly supplied by the owner.

*Engelberg, Switzerland.

W. Hafner, 'Unsere aufgefundenen Bücher,' Titlisgrüsse XLIX (1962-63) 109-120; 'Die Mariensequenz aus Muri in der Engelberger Überlieferung,' ibid. L (1963-64) 15-21. Describes 9 mss. recently rediscovered. No index.

*Epinal, France. See Vernier.

P. 103.

*Erlau, Hungary. See Eger.

*Essen, West Germany. Domkirche.

A few mss. No catalogue. Communication of Ludwig Bieler.

—*Stiftskirche.

Some mss. No catalogue. Communication of Ludwig Bieler.

*Esztergom, Hungary. See Günterova; Lehmann.

P. 104

—*Föegyházmagyei Könyvtár (Erzdiözesanbibliothek).

*Magyarország Müemléki Topográfiája, ed. T. Gerevich. I. Kötet. Esztergom. I. rész. Budapest 1948. p. 287-371: 34 illuminated mss. (partial micr. NNC)

—*Simor könyvtár.

*Catalogus Bibliothecae Joannis Cardinalis Simor . . . Strigonii 1887. coll. 177-184: 20 mss. No index. (partial micr. NNC)

*Catalogus operum Bibliothecae Joannis Cardinalis Simor . . quae ab anno 1869 usque praesens tempus comparata fuere. Strigonii 1904. coll. 9-16: alphabetical list of mss. (partial micr. NNC)

Eugene, Oregon, USA. See Bond.

*Evanston, Illinois, USA. See Bond.

*Evora, Portugal. See Rosa Pereira; Stegmüller.

*Évreux, France. See Nortier.

Faenza, Italy. See Kristeller.

*Falaise, France. See France, Catalogue général LIII.

*Fano, Italy. Mabellini. Add: p. 124: Mss. Several collections. (NNC)

Fermo, Italy. See Kristeller.

Serafino Prete, Studia Picena. Read: XXIII (1955) 21-51. Add: XXV (1957) 25-65 (nos. 71-94)

The same, 'Un antologia umanistico-religiosa del sec. XV (Ms. 31 della Biblioteca di Fermo),' ibid. XXVI (1958) 1-51.

The same, I codici della Biblioteca Comunale di Fermo (Biblioteca Bibliografia italiana XXXV). Florence 1960. xvi, 194 pp. and plates. 122 mss. Indices.

P. 105.

Ferrara, Italy. See Kristeller.

Le figure principali della Medicina Ferrarese del Quattro e Cinquecento. Ferrara 1962. Unpaged. 165 nos. No index. (Revised edition). Ferrara 1962. Unpaged. 183 nos. Index. Exhibition catalogue. Lists some mss.

*Typed list of mss. II 1-485.

*Typed list of Nuove Accessioni 1-11.

Fiesole, Italy. Biblioteca del Seminario.

D. Brunoro, Il Seminario di Fiesole. Fiesole 1925. 333 pp. p. 301-306: La Biblioteca. Mentions several mss. All of them were lost during the last war.

Firenze, Italy. See Italy, Indici e Cataloghi; Kristeller; Thorndike.

—Archivio di Stato.

Inventario sommario del R. Archivio di Stato di Firenze. Florence 1903.

Carte Cerviniane. 1 typed folder. Lists 54 filze.

Manoscritti Cerviniani. 1 ms. vol. (shelf mark 340). Lists 3 series of 75, 21 and 42 nos.

P. 106.

Miscellanea di Acquisti e Doni, inventario I (the only one). 1 ms. vol. (shelf mark 351). 325 nos. Index. (micr. DLC)

—Biblioteca Medicea Laurenziana.

*F. Mattesini, 'La biblioteca francescana di S. Croce e Fra Tedaldo Della Casa,' *Studi Francescani* LVII (1960) 254-316. Discusses 64 mss. No index. (Ct Y)

Charles T. Davis, 'The Early Collection of Books of S. Croce in Florence,' *Proceedings of the American Philosophical Society* CVII (1963) 399-414. Lists 46 mss. in Laurenziana and Nazionale (400-409).

P. 107.

Fondo Acquisti e Doni.

Summary list of mss. 447-633 kindly supplied by Dott. Irma Merolle Tondi.

Fondo Martelli.

Elenco mss. Martelli. 1 typed folder. 77 mss.

Archivio Buonarroti (deposited in the Laurenziana).

K. Tolnai, 'Die Handzeichnungen Michelangelos im Archivio Buonarroti,' *Münchner Jahrbuch der Bildenden Kunst* N.F. V. (1928) 377-476. p. 458-476: 'Anhang II. Verzeichnis der Handzeichnungen des Archivio Buonarroti'. Lists 29 mss.

Inventario dell'Archivio Buonarroti. 1 ms. vol. 156 mss.

P. 108.

—Biblioteca Moreniana.

I manoscritti della Biblioteca Moreniana. Add: Vol. II, fasc. 15-16 (1960). 120 pp. Preface by B. Maracchi Biagiarelli. Contains indices of vol. II.

—Biblioteca Nazionale Centrale. See Davis (above under Biblioteca Laurenziana).

Bartoli. Read: IV, fasc. 1 (1885). 64 pp. (Biblioteca Nazionale, Florence; micr. NNC)

B. Becherini, *Catalogo dei manoscritti musicali della Biblioteca Nazionale di Firenze.* Kassel, Basel, London and New York 1959. xii, 178 pp. 144 mss. Arranged by collections. Indices.

Fondo Principale.

P. G. Ricci, 'Aneddoti di letteratura fiorentina,' *Rinascimento*, Ser. II, vol. III (1963) 115-144. p. 134-144: 'Alcuni manoscritti non catalogati della Biblioteca Nazionale di Firenze.' Describes mss. II I 512-535 and II III 509-516 that had been omitted by Mazzatinti. Some nos. skipped. No index.

P. 109.

Fondo Magliabechiano.

List of mss. VII 1239-1406 kindly supplied by Dott. Eugenia Levi.

Autografi Palatini. One large envelope containing a list by shelf marks (partly handwritten and partly typed).

P. 110.

Fondo Postillati.

Card file appended to that of the Banco Rari. 100 mss.

Fondo Passerini.

Catalogo Passerini. 1 ms. vol. At the end, a section describing 182 mss.

Fondo Cappugi-Passerini.

Schedario Cappugi. Card file arranged by shelf marks. 623 mss.

Fondo Ginori Conti.

Atto di Donazione. 1 typed vol.

—Biblioteca Riccardiana.

Nota di alcuni manoscritti per la Riccardiana di Firenze. 2 typed sheets listing 22 mss. acquired in 1953.

P. 111.

—Museo di S. Marco.

Ministero della Pubblica Istruzione, Inventario del Museo di S. Marco e Cenacoli (1915). 1 ms. vol. The mss. are nos. 515-635.

—Comm. Tammaro De Marinis.

Many mss. No inventory.

—Marchese Venturi Ginori.

Catalogo dei Manoscritti della Nobile Famiglia Venturi Ginori. 1 ms. vol. 260 mss.

Fischbach bei Nürnberg, West Germany. Freiherren von Scheurl.

Familien-Archiv von Scheurl. Large card file.

Bandkatalog. 1 ms. vol. Lists the mss.

at the end of the section on the printed books in small folio (Kleinfolio).

Scheurlsches Archiv. 1 ms. folder. (Nürnberg, Germanisches Nationalmuseum, Archiv)

Foligno, Italy. See Kristeller; Mazzatinti.

Forlì, Italy. See Kristeller.
Read: *Biblioteca del Seminario.

***Fort Augustus,** Scotland. See *Trésors des Bibliothèques d'Écosse.*

***Fossombrone,** Italy.

E. Sgreccia, 'Il Fondo "Card. Passionei" della Biblioteca Civica di Fossombrone,' *Studia Picena* XXXI (1963) 122-166. p. 128-147: 20 mss. No index.

Frankfurt a. M., West Germany. See Roth under **Darmstadt.**

P. 112.

Frascati, Italy. See Kristeller.

***Freiberg,** East Germany. Bibliothek der Oberschule.

Samuel Moller, *Manuscripta ad rem sacram, ad iura, ad philosophiam atque ad historiam pertinentia.* progr. Freiberg 1727. 7 unnumbered pp. (p. 4-6): Some mss. listed without shelf marks (Dresden; micr. NNC)

**Handschriften-Catalog.* (partial micr. NNC)

Freiburg i. Br., West Germany. Augustiner-Museum. Card file of 16 mss.

—Stadtarchiv. *Handschriften.* Card file in one box, arranged by subjects.

P. 113.

***Fréjus,** France. See under **Toulon.**

Fribourg, Switzerland. See Leclercq.

—Bibliothèque Cantonale et Universitaire.

J. Matt, *Die Miniaturen in den Handschriften der ehemaligen Bibliothek von Altenryf.* diss. Fribourg 1939 (Freiburger Geschichtsblätter 34). 61 pp. and plates. 5 mss. (Pierpont Morgan Library)

A. Bruckner, 'Scriptorum Altaripense,' *Medievalia et Humanistica* XIV (1962) 86-94. Survey.

—Couvent des Cordeliers.

General catalogue of the library (no title).

1 ms. vol. Section on mss. lists 147 nos.

O. Perler, *Sebastian Werro (1555-1614), Beitrag zur Geschichte der katholischen Restauration zu Freiburg in der Schweiz.* Fribourg 1942. 169 pp. Cites many mss., including some that have no shelf marks and are not included in the inventory.

Fritzlar, West Germany. Stiftskirche (Dombibliothek).

More than 100 mss. No inventory. Cf. *Fritzlarer Handschriften.* Typed inventory of 123 mss. some of which are now in Fulda. (Fulda, Priesterseminar).

Fulda, West Germany. Landesbibliothek. *Catalogi. continns.* Read: *continens.*

—Priesterseminar. A group of mss., some of which were acquired from Fritzlar. Only the latter group is described in the typed inventory entitled *Fritzlarer Handschriften.* The majority of the Fritzlar mss., once deposited in Fulda, are again in Fritzlar. See above. For one mss. which is now in Fulda, see: A. Landgraf, 'Werke aus dem Bereich der Summa Sententiarum und Anselms von Laon,' *Divus Thomas* (Freiburg) XIV (1936, 209-216) 215, no. 11. Weisweiler, *Scholastik* XXXI (1956) 474-475.

P. 114.

Genève, Switzerland. Bibliothèque Publique et Universitaire.

Aubert. Add: Printed also separately (Paris 1911, 207 pp.) with additions, corrections (p. 185-199) and an index (p. 200-207).

Inventaire des Manuscrits grecs . . . 141-332. Read: 126-332.

Typed description of the correspondence of the Reformers (by L. Micheli). Covers mss. lat. 106-121, franç. 194-197b, 401-441.

Catalogue des Manuscrits de la Bibliothèque Publique et Universitaire de Genève. Tome III. Manuscrits français 201-600.

L. Micheli, 'Inventaire de la Collection Edouard Favre,' *Bulletin Hispanique* XI (1909) 295-322; XII (1910) 49-70; 140-

162; 317-326; XIII (1911) 61-74; 195-204; 337-347; XIV (1912) 77-95. 82 nos. No index.

—*Musée historique de la Réformation.

Catalogue de la partie des Archives Tronchin acquise par la Société du Musée historique de la Réformation, by F. Gardy. Geneva 1946. xvii, 193 pp. 135 nos. Index. (NN)

Genève-Cologny. See *The Book Collector.*

Genova, Italy. See Kristeller.

—Biblioteca Civica Berio.

Manoscritti. Alphabetical card file in 6 (another copy in 14) bound vols. New shelf marks.

P. 115.

Gent, Belgium. See Schiel.

*H. Knaus, 'Die Trierer Handschriften in Gent,' *Handelingen van de Maatschappij van Geschiedenis en Oudheidkunde te Gent* N. S. XVI (1962) 1-17. (NjP)

The Crypt of St. Bavon's Cathedral, Ghent, A Guide-Book. No date (1960?). 24 pp. p. 17-20 (nos. 329-342): mss.

Gerona, Spain.

J. Janini and J. M. Marqués, 'Manuscritos de la Colegiata de San Félix de Gerona,' *Hispania Sacra XV* (1962) 401-437. Lists 46 mss. now kept in the Seminario and the Museo Diocesano. Indices (434-437). Also gives a Summary list of other mss. in the Seminario (403-404).

—* Biblioteca del Seminario. Card index of mss. Communication of Father García.

P. 116.

Glarus, Switzerland.

Read: *Katalog der Landesbibliothek in Glarus.* Glarus 1879 (172 pp.). Supplement of 1886 (56 pp.). p. 141-147 and suppl. p. 47: mss. No shelf marks.

Katalog der Landesbibliothek. Read: Arranged alphabetically. No shelf marks.

Katalog der Landesbibliothek in Glarus. Glarus 1924. 427 pp. p. 344-353: Mss. listed in alphabetical order, mostly modern. No shelf marks, but the collections

are indicated. p. 354-415: Index.

I. Nachtrag zum Katalog von 1924. Glarus 1937. 100 pp. p. 81: 2 late mss. p. 82-97: index.

Glasgow, Scotland. See *Trésors des Bibliothèques d'Écosse.*

*Gloucester,** England. Cathedral Library. Information on 34 mss. received from Neil Ker.

*Gorsley,** England. See **Ross-on Wye.**

*Göteborg,** Röhsska Konstlöjdmuseet.

G. Axel-Nilsson, 'Medeltida Miniatyrer och schriftprov i Röhsska Konstlöjdmuscet,' *Röhsska Konstlöjdmuseet Göteborg, Årstryck* 1954, 47-79. p. 70-79: 38 nos. (NN)

P. 117.

*Göttweig,** Austria. *Manuscripten-Catalog.* V. Moelt. Read: V. Werl.

P. 118.

Granada, Spain. See Ricci.

—*Biblioteca del Sacro Monte. Some mss. No inventory. Communication of Father García.

*Grand-Saint-Bernard,** Switzerland. Hospice. 6 liturgical mss. Communication of Ludwig Bieler.

's Gravenhage, Holland. See Institut de Recherche.

—Koninklijke Bibliotheek.

**P. J. F. Vermeeren, 'Handschriften van het Kapittel van Sint Servaas in de Koninklijke Bibliotheek te 's Gravenhage,' in *Miscellanea Traiectensia* (Maastricht 1962) 179-193.

(*Catalogus van de Boekerij der Koninklijke Academie van Wetenschappen gevestigd te Amsterdam.* 3 vols. Amsterdam 1858-81. Vol. I, part 1 (new ed., Amsterdam 1874) p. I-XXXIII: 197 mss. of which nos. 1-14 (p. I-IV) are in Latin. Vol. III (1876-81), p. XXXV-XXXVI: mss. 198-209.

—Museum Meermanno-Westreenianum.

P. J. H. Vermeeren and A. F. Dekker, *Inventaris van de Handschriften van het Museum Meermanno-Westreenianum.* Hague 1960. xv, 121 pp. 332 mss. Arranged by subjects. Shelf marks in parentheses. Concordance (p. 105-108). Indices.

*Graz, Austria. *Franziskanerbibliothek. Has the mss. of the Vienna Franciscans and of other Austrian Franciscan monasteries. No inventory. Communication of the librarian.

P. 119.

*Gries (near Bolzano-Bozen), Italy. See under **Sarnen**.

*Grottaferrata, Italy. See Kristeller.

P. 120.

*Güssing, Austria. Bibliothek des Franziskanerklosters. Typed list of older mss. kindly supplied by P. Theodor Tabernigg in Graz.

Haarlem, Holland. *Teylers Stichting. See Byvanck.
Fondation Teyler, Catalogue de la Bibliothèque. 4 vols. Haarlem 1885-1915. Vol. IV (1915, by J. J. Verwijnen), p. 951: 3 mss. (NN)

Halle, East Germany. Universitäts- und Landesbibliothek. Alphabetical card index, in 5 boxes.

P. 121.

Hamburg, West Germany. Staats- und Universitätsbibliothek. See also under Berlin.
Bibliothek der St. Katharinenkirche, Handschriften. Typed list of 78 mss. (micr. NNC)
H. Luedtke, 'Joachimi Jungii Lubecensis . . . Handschriftlicher Nachlass in der Bibliothek der Freien und Hansestadt Hamburg, Ein Katalogisierungs-Versuch,' *Archiv für Geschichte der Medizin* XXIX (1937) 366-405. 4 sections of 78, 40 and 27 nos.

P. 122.

*Hameln, West Germany. Stadtbücherei. Has the mss. of the Schiller-Gymnasium described by Bachof. 3 of them are lost. Communication of Ludwig Bieler.

*Hamilton, Mass., USA. See Bond.

*Hamm, West Germany. Gustav Luebcke-Museum. See *Mittelalterliche Buchmalerei.*

Hannover, West Germany. Kestner-Museum.
Card file of mss. Arranged by shelf marks.
Autographen. Alphabetical card file in 12 boxes.
Reformation. 1 box. Describes the autographs of the Reformation period.

Harburg, West Germany. See Lehmann. Read: *Standortkatalog.*

*'s Heerenberg, Holland. Mr. J. H. van Heek. Has ca. 70 mss. and some frs. Communication of the owner.

Heidelberg, West Germany. See Lehmann.

P. 123.

*Helmingham Hall, England. At least a part of the collection was sold in 1961.

*Helsinki, Finland. Haapanen covers only about one third of the frs. in the collection. Communication of Ludwig Bieler.

*Hereford, England.
M. Tallon, *Hereford Cathedral Library.* (Athlone 1963). 79 pp. Survey of mss. (p. 18-38) and bibliography (p. 59 and 79).

P. 124.

*Hobart, Tasmania, Australia. See Sinclair.
'Important Mss. in the University Library' (by K. Sinclair), *The University of Tasmania Gazette* XI (1961) 47. 3 mss.

*Hof, West Germany. Jean-Paul-Gymnasium.
*Bandkatalog. Lists 12 mss. along with the printed books. Communication of the librarian.

Holkham Hall, England. Hassell. Read: Hassall.
Add: See also under London and Oxford.

*Hollins College, Virginia, USA. See Bond.

Hradec Králové (Königgrätz), Czechoslovakia. Krajské vlastivědné museum. Typed list of 35 Latin mss. Communication of Dr. J. Šůla.

*Huesca, Spain. See Cordoliani; Ricci.

A. Durán, 'Los manuscritos de la Catedral de Huesca,' *Argensola* IV (1953) 293-322. 85 mss. No index. (DLC; photostat NNC)

Iesi, Italy. See Kristeller.

P. 125.

Innsbruck, Australia. *Universitätsbibliothek.

Read: *Handschriften, Zettelkatalog.*

—Servitenkloster.

Catalogus codicum manu scriptorum qui in bibliotheca conventus Ord. Serv. B. M. V. ad S. Joseph Oeniponte asservantur. (Outside:) *Servitenkloster Innsbruck, Handschriften Katalog.* Card file in 1 bound vol. 129 mss. Some mss. were lost during the war, and the library was not yet rearranged in 1962.

—Bibliothek des Tiroler Landesmuseums Ferdinandeum.

The inventory was lost during the war.

Acquisitions are reported in the *Zeitschrift des Ferdinandeums* (for example, Ser. 3, no. 31, 1887, p. xliv-xlvi).

14. und 15. Jhr. Handschriften religiösen Inhalts. A small file.

Nominal-Register (Authoren-Catalog) der Bibliotheca Tirolensis Dipauliana. 1 ms. vol.

Ferdinandeum-Bibliothek. Has 32891 nos. Mss. are shelved with the printed books. No list.

Werner Winkler Legat. No list.

Autographensammlung. Arranged in alphabetical order. No list.

—Stift Wilten. Ca. 20 mss. No inventory.

*Iowa City, Iowa, USA. See Bond.

Isny, West Germany. Bibliothek der Nikolaikirche.

Die Handschriften der Nikolauskirche in Isny, by Dr. Karl Müller (1936). Typed list of 80 mss.

*Issoudin. Read: *Issoudun.

Istanbul, Turkey. Topkapi Sarayi Müzesi, Kütüphane.

The Western mss. are in the Fonds Ahmet III, Manuscrits occidentaux. They are completely described by Deissmann.

Ithaca, New York, USA. See Bond.

P. 126.

Jerusalem, Israel. Beth Hasefarim Haleumi Whauniversitai (The Jewish National and University Library).

List of the Friedenwald collection. 1 ms. notebook. Covers mss. and printed books.

List of Varia. 1 ms. notebook. Describes 296 mss. in Western languages.

*Kalocsa, Hungary. Typed list of 511 mss. (Budapest, Szechenyi Library)

P. 127.

*Karl-Marx Stadt (Chemnitz), East Germany. Most mss. were lost during the war, but the one described by Lehnerdt is extant.

P. 128.

*Kew, England. Sir Sydney Cockerell's mss. have been sold. Some of them are now in the Victoria and Albert Museum, London.

P. 129.

Killiney, Ireland. Dun Mhuire, Franciscan Library.

Canice Mooney, 'The Franciscan Library, Merchants' Quay, Dublin,' *An Leabharlaan* VIII 2 (1942) 29-37. Mentions some mss.

The same, 'Franciscan Library, Killiney: A short Guide for the Student of Irish Church History,' *Archivum Hibernicum* XVIII (1955) 150-56. (NN)

*King of Prussia, Pennsylvania, USA. See Bond.

*Klausenburg, see Cluj.

*Kłodzko, Poland. The mss. are now in Wrocław.

Klosterneuburg, Austria.

H. J. Zeibig, 'Die Bibliothek des Stiftes Klosterneuburg,' *Archiv für Kunde Österreichischer Geschichtsquellen* V (vol. III, pt. 2, 1850) 261-316. Mentions many mss. No index.

København, Denmark. Kongelige Bibliotek.
N. C. L. Abrahams, *Description des manuscrits français du moyen âge de la Bibliothèque Royale de Copenhague, précédée
d'une notice historique sur cette bibliothèque.* Copenhagen 1844. xvi, 152 pp.
58 mss. Index.

P. 130.
Read: *Katalog over det store Kongelige Bibliotheks Haandskriftsamling.* 13 ms. vols.
Petri Johannis Resenii Bibliotheca. This
collection was destroyed by fire in 1728.
*Bibliotheca J. A. Fabricii. 4 vols. Hamburg 1738-41. Vol. IV (1741). 218, 80,
30 pp. p. 173-218: 'Designatio auctorum
veterum cum codd. mss. collatorum,
item codicum manu exaratorum vett.
et recentiorum qui haeredibus Fabricianis servabuntur. (Copenhagen; partial
micr. NNC). Verified by Mr. Kåre Olsen.
**Catalogus bibliothecae Beati Herm. Sam.
Reimari prof. Hamburg.* 2 vols. Hamburg 1769. *Pars II. sistens libros philologicos, geographicos et historicos. Ven-
ditio fiet A.S.R. MDCCLXX d. 5. Fe-
bruarii. Accedit Designatio auctorum veterum cum codd. ms. collatorum item
codicum exaratorum veterum et recentiorum maximam partem ex bibliotheca
Jo. Alb. Fabricii superstitum iunctim
vendendorum.* 240, 24 pp. p. 195-240:
'Designatio auctorum veterum cum codd.
mss. collatorum, item codicum manu
exaratorum vett. et recentiorum ex bibliotheca J. A. Fabricii superstitum.
Accedunt quaedam mss. H. S. Reimari,
Jo. Adolphi Hofmanni, et Henr. Walth.
Gerdes, quae iunctim vendenda eruditis
offeruntur. ' Actual shelf marks added
in library copy of the reprint. (Copen-
hagen; partial micr. NNC). Verified by
Mr. Kåre Olsen.
—*Rigsarkivet. Many frs. Card index.
Communication of Ludwig Bieler.
Koblenz, West Germany. See *Analecta
Bollandiana*; Roth under **Darmstadt**.
—*Goerres-Gymnasium.

15 mss. No catalogue. Communication of
Ludwig Bieler.
—*Stadtbibliothek.
**Bücherverzeichnis der Stadtbibliothek Ko-
blenz,* by A. Marhoffer. Koblenz 1896.
456 pp. Mss. listed among the printed
books, but indicated in the library copy.
Communication of the librarian. (Ko-
blenz)
*Königgrätz. See **Hradec Králové.**

P. 131.
Konstanz, West Germany. Heinrich-Suso-
Gymnasium.
Weisgerber. Add: 6 mss. (Freiburg, Uni-
versitätsbibliothek; photostat supplied by
Dr. Beckmann).
*Handschriften der Bibliothek des Suso-
Gymnasiums.* Typed list. 82 mss. Copy
supplied by Oberstudienrat Oskar Fried-
lein.
No title. 1 ms. notebook. Gives additional
data.

P. 132.
Kórnik, Poland. Biblioteka Kórnicka Pol-
skiej Akademii Nauk.
*Katalog Rękopisów Średiowiecznych Bi-
blioteki Kórnickiej (Catalogus codicum
manuscriptorum Medii Aevi Bibliothecae
Cornicensis),* by J. Zathey. Wrocław,
Warsaw and Cracow 1963. lii 736 pp.
Nos. 1-1725 (some nos. skipped). Ample
indices.
Kraków (Cracow), Poland.
Read: *Archivum Kapituły Metropolitalnej.
Read: *Bibljoteka Jagiellońska. Katalog
Wystawy . . . Węgierskich*
—*Biblioteka Polskiej Akademii Nauk.
*Biblioteka Polskiej Akademii Nauk w
Krakowie. Katalog rękopisów (Sygnatury
1811-3248),* by Z. Jabłoński and A. Preiss-
ner. Wrocław, Warsaw and Cracow 1962.
xii, 317 pp. Largely modern. (NN)

P. 133.
*Kremnica, Czechoslovakia. See **Günterova.**

Kues, West Germany. Read: *Serapeum* XXV; XXVI.

*Kynžvart (Königswart), Czechoslovakia. Zámecka Knihovna. See *Neues Archiv* V. Typed descriptions of selected mss. kindly supplied by Prof. F. Čáda. Cf. G. Billanovich and F. Čáda, 'Testi Bucolici della Biblioteca del Boccaccio,' *Italia Medioevale e Umanistica* IV (1961) 201-221.

Lambach, Austria. Bibliothek des Benediktinerstiftes.

Handschriften-Katalog Lambach. The mss. which have been sold are clearly marked.

Oesterreichische Kunsttopographie, vol. XXXIV. *Die Kunstdenkmäler des politischen Bezirkes Wels*. Part II. *Die Kunstdenkmäler des Gerichtsbezirkes Lambach*. By E. Hainisch. Vienna (1959). 532 pp. p. 213-265: List of selected mss. (by K. Holter). Index of the volume not quite adequate for the mss.

P. 134.

Lausanne, Switzerland. Bibliothèque Cantonale et Universitaire.

Catalogue des Manuscrits (A 3112). Typed list. Describes mss. acquired until 1900.

Manuscrits, Catalogue des manuscrits . . . des nouveaux fonds. 3 ms. vols. I: (Octavo) 1-403. II: (Quarto) 5001-38. III: (Folio) 7001-7002.

Inventaire sommaire des manuscrits non catalogués. 4 ms. notebooks.

*Lawrence, Kansas, USA. See Bond.

*Lecce, Italy. Biblioteca Provinciale.

The library now has 348 mss. Communication of the librarian and of Dr. Maria Teresa Liaci.

*Leeuwarden, Holland.

Catalogus van de boeken en handschriften van de Jezuïetenstatie te Leeuwarden. Preface signed by M. P. van Buijtenen. Leeuwarden 1941. vii, 167 pp. p. 149-154: survey of *ca.* 30 mss. (Leiden, University Library)

*Le Havre, France. See Nortier.

P. 135.

Leiden, Holland. Bibliotheek der Rijksuniversiteit.

Bibliotheca Universitatis Leidensis. Codices manuscripti. Add: Each volume indexed.

P. 136.

Leipzig, East Germany. Stadtbibliothek. Naumann. Read: 937 mss., many of which are in Latin.

The mss. are now deposited in the University Library. See J. Müller, 'Die Überführung der Handschriftenbestände der Leipziger Stadtbibliothek in die Universitätsbibliothek,' *Scriptorium* XVII (1963) 122. D. Debes, 'Bibliotheca Senatoria Civitatis Lipsiensis, Zur Übergabe ihrer Handschriften an die Universitätsbibliothek,' *Libri* XIII (1964) 175-180.

—Universitätsbibliothek. The 68 mss. (nos. 6-66 in Latin) once owned by Gustav Hänel (*Serapeum* VII 1846, 234-237) are now in the Universitätsbibliothek as a separate group and have received new shelf marks.

*Lemgo, West Germany. See also under **Detmold**.

Gerlach. Lists 1 ms. (A 1-17) of the Gymnasialbibliothek, which is now in the Archiv der Alten Hansestadt, along with two other mss. listed by E. Weissbrodt, 'Die ältesten Bestände der Lemgoer Gymnasialbibliothek,' *Zeitschrift für Bücherfreunde* XII (1908-1909) 489-499, at 490-491.

Gerlach also lists 6 mss. (B 1-6) of St. Marien in Lemgo, which are now in Detmold, Staatsarchiv. Communication of the archivists.

Leningrad, USSR. See Institut de Recherche; Lehmann.

—Gosudarstvennyj Ermitazh. Biblioteka. Typed list of 11 mss. supplied by Prof. M. A. Goukovsky.

—Publichnaja Biblioteka im. M. E. Saltykova-Shchedrina.

Katalog pisem i drugikh materialov zapadno-jevropejckikh uchenykh i pisatelej XVI-XVIII vv. iz sobranja P. P. Dubrovskogo (Catalogue of Letters and other papers of European Scientists and Writers of XVI-XVIII Centuries Deposited in P. Dubrovsky's Collection). By M. P. Aleksjeva. Leningrad 1963. 110 pp. Indices.

P. 138.

*****Le Puy**, France. Read: Rouchon.
*****Lérida**, Spain. See *Arte Romanico*.
Leuven (Louvain), Belgium.

P. 139.

Ligugé, France.

H. Rochais, 'Liste sommaire des manuscrits de l'Abbaye de Ligugé,' *Revue Mabillon* XLIII (1953) 138-146. 158 mss., mostly late. (NN)

P. 140.

Lisboa, Portugal. See Rosa Pereira; Stegmüller.

P. 141.

*****Lisieux**, France. See France, *Catalogue général* LIII.
Liverpool, England.

A Guide to the Manuscript Collections in the Liverpool University Library. (By D. F. Cook; preface signed by D. A. Clarke). Liverpool 1962. 32 pp. p. 9-25: 147 Western mss. 29-32: index.
Livorno, Italy. See Kristeller.
Lodi, Italy. See Kristeller.
Cremascoli. Read: Pallavicino.
Archivio Storico Lodigiano 1955, 64-69 (note by L. Cremascoli, without title). Describes 3 liturgical mss. deposited in the Biblioteca Civica.
L. Cremascoli, 'I corali miniati di Lodi,' *Archivio Storico Lodigiano* 1957, 53-64. Describes 14 more liturgical mss.
Lonato, Italy. See Kristeller.
London, England. See Thorndike.

P. 142.

—British Museum.
The Catalogues of the Manuscript Collections, by T. C. Skeat. Revised edition. London 1962. 45 pp.
Fanchiotti. Read: *Il Museo Britannico*.
H. L. D. Ward, *Catalogue of Romances in the Department of Manuscripts in the British Museum.* 3 vols. London 1883-1910. Includes Latin texts. No index.

P. 143.

*****List of Additions*, 1831-35. (DLC)
Catalogue of Additions to the Manuscripts, 1926-1930. London 1959. xiv, 644 pp. Add. mss. 41296-42181 and Egerton 3039-3048.

P. 144.

The British Museum Quarterly XXIII (1960-61) 27-38: 'Manuscripts from the Dyson Perrins Collection,' by T. J. Brown and others. Lists 8 mss. (p. 27-28).

P. 145.

—Guildhall Library.
A Guide to the Records in the Corporation of London Records Office and The Guildhall Library Muniment Room. London (1951). vii, 203 pp. p. 22-24: 'Custumals (sic) and ancient books.' p. 182-184: 'Miscellaneous Manuscripts and Documents.' Index.
Catalogue of Mss. (*Accessions Register*). 13 ms. vols.
—Inner Temple.
The library copy of *Historical Manuscripts Commission, Eleventh Report, Appendix,* Part VII (London 1888) 227-308, by W. D. Macray, is used as a catalogue.
Mss. shelf list. 1 ms. vol.
A Catalogue, 1833. Delete: Charters only.
—Lincoln's Inn.
Hunter's catalogue, in a separate edition of 1838, is used as a catalogue. The library copy has typed additions and an index.

—Robinson Trust. It has the remainder of the Phillipps collection.

—Royal Institute of British Architects. Has a few mss. No inventory.

—Sir John Soane's Museum.
For mss. 1-9 and 11, see Millar, *Société française de reproductions de manuscrits à peintures, Bulletin* IV (1914-20), p. 83-128. Typed list of additional mss. kindly supplied by the curator.

P. 146.

—Wellcome Historical Medical Library.
Catalogue of Western Manuscripts on Medicine and Science in Wellcome Historical Medical Library. By S. A. J. Moorat. I. Mss. written before A. D. 1650. London 1962. vii, 679 pp. 801 mss. Arranged alphabetically. Ample indices. Former shelf marks not given.

—Dr. Brian Lawn.
Checklist of Medieval and Renaissance Manuscripts. Typed list of 30 mss. Copy kindly supplied by the owner.

Los Angeles, California, USA. See Bond.

Louvain (Leuven), Belgium, Bibliothèque de l'Université.
Université Catholique de Louvain, Bibliothèque. Katholieke Universiteit te Leuven, Bibliotheek. *Catalogue des manuscrits 1940-1954. Katalogus der Handschriften.* 1 typed vol. A 1-31, B 1-243, C 1-38, DA 1-47, M 1-15, UA 1-7.

Lübeck, West Germany. See also under **Berlin**.

P. 147

Lucca, Italy. See Kristeller.

Lugano, Switzerland. Biblioteca Cantonale.
Catalogo generale della Biblioteca Cantonale. Bellinzona 1915. xxiii, 1474 pp. p. 37-47: Mss. (Lugano ; partial micr. NNC)

Lugo, Italy. See Kristeller; Mazzatinti.

P. 148.

*****Lugo**, Spain. Museo Provincial.

Several ms. frs. Communication of Father García.

Luzern, Switzerland. *Pfarrer F. J. Zinniker.
Ca. 25 ms. frs. No catalogue. Communication of Ludwig Bieler.

*****Lyon**, France. See Lowe.

P. 149.

Macerata, Italy. See Kristeller.

Madrid, Spain. See Fink-Errera.

P. 150.

—Biblioteca Nacional.
Inventario General. V (1959): 1599-2099. VI (1962): 2100-2374. VII (1963): 2375-2474.

J. Gómez Pérez, 'Siete palinsestos en la Biblioteca Nacional de Madrid,' *Revista de Archivos, Bibliotecas y Museos* LXV (1958) 439-450.

Exposición de la biblioteca de los Mendoza del Infantado en el siglo XV. Madrid 1958. 65 pp. and plates. 191 mss. (Hispanic Society of America)

*List of mss. from Toledo. Photocopy at Paris, Institut de Recherche.

—*Museo Arqueologico Nacional.

J. Janini, 'Manuscritos latinos del Museo Arqueologico Nacional de Madrid,' *Hispania Sacra* XV (1962) 221-231. 9 mss. Indices.

P. 151.

—*Duque de Alba.
Has a collection of mss. No detailed information.

—*Biblioteca de la Fundacion Lazaro Galdiano.
Several mss. Card index. Communication of Father García.

*****Magdeburg**, East Germany. See also under **Berlin**.

Mainz, West Germany. See Roth under **Darmstadt**.

*****Malvern**, England. The collection was sold in 1958-60.

P. 152.

Mantova, Italy. See Kristeller.

—Archivio di Stato.

Registri Davari, F II 8. 5 ms. vols.

Registri Davari, Serie E. 32 ms. vols.

—Biblioteca Comunale.

B. Benedini, 'I manoscritti Polironiani della Biblioteca Comunale di Mantova,' *Accademia Virgiliana di Mantova, Atti e Memorie* N. S. XXX (1958). 119 pp. Also published separately. 89 mss. No index.

Biblioteca Comunale di Mantova, Catalogo dei Manoscritti 1962. Monastero Benedettino di S. Benedetto Po (detto Polirone), Codici dei secoli XI-XIII. By Ubaldo Meroni. Typed volume. Covers mss. A II 1-D III 20. Index.

P. 153.

Marburg, West Germany, Westdeutsche Bibliothek. Now called: Stiftung Preussischer Kulturbesitz, Staatsbibliothek.

Mariemont, Belgium. Musée Warocqué.

Catalogue de la Collection des Autographes, Manuscrits et documents se trouvant à Mariemont. 1 ms. vol. Arranged alphabetically.

Autographes (Accroissements), Répertoire. (Inside:) *Inventaire des accroissements et acquisitions de la collection d'autographes depuis 1935.* 1 ms. vol.

Read: ***Mechelen** (Malines)

*Meissen, East Germany. See also under **Dresden**.

*Meissen und seine Fürstenschule (Afranisches Merkbuch). 2nd. ed. Dresden 1929. viii, 232 pp. p. 147: mss. (Dresden; partial micr. NNC). The mss. are partly in Meissen, Stadtarchiv, and partly in Dresden, Landesbibliothek.

*Melbourne, Australia. See *The Book Collector*; Sinclair.

*Melk, Austria. *Catalogus codicum.* Read: II: 235-707.

P. 154.

Merseburg, East Germany. *Katalog der*

Kapitelsbibliothek. Read: 208 mss.

Messina, Italy. See Kristeller.

*Metz, France. See France, *Catalogue général* LIII.

Michaelbeuern, Austria. See also under **Salzburg**.

*Middelburg, Holland. Provinciale Bibliotheek van Zeeland. See Byvanck, *Société française, Bulletin* XV (1931).

J. P. van Visvliet, *Inventaris der Handschriften van het Zeeuwsch Genootschap der Wetenschapen te Middelburg.* Middelburg 1861. 87 pp. (NN)

Many of the mss. were lost during the last war.

Milano, Italy. See *Catalogo*; *Institut de Recherche*; Kristeller; Thorndike.

P. 155.

—Archivio dell' Ospedale Maggiore.

(Inventario). Codici, Diplomi, Archivi Ereditarii, Atti Mercantili, Varie. (Inside:) *Archivi speciali, Codici, Registri, Manoscritti e Carte varie, Inventario.* 1 ms. vol. Lists 124 codices, and many autographs, letters and miscellaneous mss.

—Archivio della Congregazione di Carità (now Ente Comunale di Assistenza).

A. Noto, *Gli amici dei poveri di Milano: Sei secoli di lasciti e donativi cronologicamente esposti.* Milan 1953. 609 pp.

Congregazione di Carità di Milano, Archivio Storico, Famiglie. 1 ms. vol. Alphabetical.

Congregazione di Carità di Milano, Archivio Storico, Elenco di Diplomi Bolle Brevi papali. 1 ms. vol. Covers also cardinals and princes.

Congregazione di Carità, Inventario dell' Archivio. 1 ms. vol.

Many documents were lost during the last war.

—Archivio di Stato.

It acquired many mss. from the Papadopoli collection. Cf. *Notizie degli Archivi di Stato* III (1943) 39-40. No inventory.

—Biblioteca Ambrosiana.

G. Galbiati, *Itinerario per il visitatore della*

Biblioteca Ambrosiana, della Pinacoteca e dei monumenti annessi. Milan 1951. 358 pp. and plates. p. 66-84: bibliography.
Biblioteca Ambrosiana 1609-1959. (Milan) 1959. 95 pp. p. 71-75: catalogues.
A. Paredi, *La biblioteca del Pizolpasso.* Milan (1961). viii, 243 pp. p. 89-168: 59 mss.
Card. Federico Borromeo Arciv. di Milano, Indice delle lettere a lui dirette conservate all'Ambrosiana. Appendice: Opere manoscritte e a stampa del Card. Federico esistenti all' Ambrosiana. (*Fontes Ambrosiani* XXXIV). Preface signed C. Castiglioni. Milan 1960. xvi, 391 pp. Arranged alphabetically by senders. Covers mss. G 138-257 inf. p. 377-382: 233 mss. containing works of Card. Federico Borromeo.

P. 156.

Indice-Inventario compilato dal Sac. Dr. Adolfo Rivolta dell' Epistolario di San Carlo Borromeo in ordine di codice e di foglio per ciascun codice . . . (Cons. F VII 2). 1 ms. vol. Covers F 36-175 inf. and a few other mss. (micr. DLC)
—Biblioteca Nazionale Braidense.
C. Pecorella, 'Inventario ragionato dei manoscritti giuridici della Biblioteca Nazionale Braidense di Milano,' *Studi Parmensi* VIII (1958) 71-156. Index (p. 155-56).
Fondo Gerli.
Livres de liturgie imprimés aux XVᵉ et XVIᵉ siècles faisant partie de la Bibliothèque de son Altesse Royale Le Duc Robert de Parme. Paris and Milan (Hoepli) 1932. xi, 162 pp. p. ix: index of 19 mss. (NN)
La Biblioteca liturgica dei Duchi di Parma. Milan and Rome (Hoepli) 1934. 231 pp. p. 1-13: 76 mss.
*Minden, West Germany. See *Westfalia Sacra.*
*Minneapolis, Minnesota, USA. See Bond.
Mirandola, Italy. Biblioteca Comunale.
Opuscoli-Manoscritti e Pergamene. 1 ms. vol. Alphabetical.

Lascito Molinari. No inventory.

P. 157.
Modena, Italy. See Hinschius; Kristeller.
—Accademia Nazionale di Scienze Lettere ed Arti.
Has a few mss. No inventory.
—Archivio di Stato.
Documenti storici spettanti alla medicina, chirurgia, farmaceutica conservati nell' Archivio di Stato in Modena. Preface signed by C. Foucard. Modena 1885. 115 pp. (National Library of Medicine; micr. NNC)
Archivi per materia. 1 typed vol. Arranged by subjects.
Archivio di Stato Modena, Manoscritti della Biblioteca. 1 folder. Part 1: *Manoscritti della Biblioteca del R. Archivio di Stato di Modena* (typed list of 204 mss.). Part 2: *Elenco di Manoscritti esistenti in diverse serie d'atti d'Archivio* (ms. list).
—Biblioteca Estense.
Catalogus Estensium Manuscriptorum veteri eorum ordinatione servata. 3 ms. vols. (1768). (Modena, Archivio di Stato, Amministrazione della Casa Estense, Biblioteca, 209, vols. 10-12). Communication of Bernard M. Peebles.
—Raccolta Molza-Viti (Principessa Beatrice Rospigliosi). Typed list of 32 mss.

P. 158.
*Mondovì, Italy. Biblioteca del Seminario Vescovile.
List of 3 mss. supplied by the librarian.
*Monnickendam, Holland. Gemeentearchief.
Typed list of 3 mss. supplied by the archivist.
Monreale, Italy. See Kristeller.
—*Biblioteca del Seminario Arcivescovile.
Has some mss. Cf. A. Daneu Lattanzi, 'Di un manoscritto miniato eseguito a Palermo nel terzo quarto del sec. XII e d'alcuni altri manoscritti . . .' *Accademie e Biblioteche d'Italia* XXXII (1964) 225-236; 309-320.

*Monselice, Italy. Collegiata di S. Giustina.
S. de Kunert, 'Due codici miniati da Girolamo Campagnola?,' *Rivista d'Arte* XII (Ser. II, no. 2, 1930), 51-80. 2 liturgical mss.

Montecassino, Italy. See Kristeller.

*Montefalco, Italy.
The catalogue by Pambuffetti was never published. Communication of the librarian.

S. Nessi, 'Inventario dei codici e delle pergamene esistenti nel Ven. Monastero di S. Chiara a Montefalco,' *Archivi*, Ser. II, vol. XXVIII (1961) 232-251. 8 mss. (p. 235). No index.

*Montefano, Italy.
G. Pagnani, 'I Codici dell' Archivio del PP. Benedettini-Silvestrini di Montefano presso Fabriano e un elogio di S. Francesco d'Assisi della fine del 1200,' *Studia Picena* XXVI (1958) 119-134. p. 121-129: 20 mss. No index.

*Monte Oliveto Maggiore, Italy. Archivio dell' Abbazia.
Has a few literary mss. Communication of the Abbot.

F. Gualdi, 'I corali di Monte Morcino,' *Rivista d'Arte*, XXXIII (Ser. III, vol. VIII, 1960) 1-26. 22 liturgical mss. now in Monte Oliveto.

*Montevergine, Italy. Biblioteca dell'Abbazia.
G. Mongeli, 'I codici dell' Abbazia di Montevergine,' *Archivi*, Ser. II, vol. XXVI (1959) 151-199. 18 mss. No index.

P. 159.

*Montreal, Canada. McGill University.
Bibliotheca Osleriana: A Catalogue of Books Illustrating the History of Medicine and Science collected, arranged, and annotated by Sir William Osler. Oxford 1929. xxxv, 786 pp. p. 663-688: mss. no. 7506-7638. Alphabetical. Index.

Monza, Italy. Biblioteca Capitolare.
Catalogo de 'Manoscritti membranacei esistenti nella Biblioteca dell'Insigne Coll. ta Basilica di Monza l'anno 1851. (In-

side:) *Codici manoscritti esistenti nella Biblioteca dell'Insigne Collegiata Basilica di Monza nel 1851.* 1 ms. vol. Arrangement as in Frisi. New shelf marks added.

*Morella, Spain. Arxiu de l'Arxiprestal.
M. Betí, 'Noticies de dos manuscrits de l'Arxiu de l'Arxiprestal de Morella,' *Butlletí de la Biblioteca de Catalunya* IV (1917) 47-67. 4 mss. No index.

Moskva, USSR. Biblioteka Lenina.
Sistematičeskij Katalog Biblioteki Glavnago Štaba. 2 vols. St. Petersburg 1879-80. Vol. II, p. 915-927: Mss. no. 37418-37843. The mss. are now Fond 68 of the Biblioteka Lenina. (Leningrad, Publichnaja Biblioteka; partial micr. NNC) List of foreign autographs. 1 ms. vol.

München, West Germany. See Foltz; Lehmann; Ruf.

—Bayerische Staatsbibliothek.
J. B. Schneyer, 'Beobachtungen zu lateinischen Sermoneshandschriften der Staatsbibliothek München,' *Bayerische Akademie der Wissenschaften, Philosophisch-Historische Klasse, Sitzungsberichte,* Jahrgang 1958, Heft 8. 148 pp. Describes many mss. Index (144-148).

J. Brummer, 'Drei Weihenstephaner Handschriften,' *Zehntes Sammelblatt des Historischen Vereins Freising* (1913-15, published 1916) 1-21.

P. Ruf, *Säkularisation und die Bayerische Staatsbibliothek*, vol. I. Wiesbaden 1962. IX, 628 pp.

P. 160.

Codices Latini Monacenses. Nos. 27269-28801 (continues the printed catalogue). *Libri impressi cum notis manuscriptis.* 1 ms. vol. Arranged alphabetically according to the authors of the printed editions.

(No title). Another such list arranged by shelfs marks. 1104 nos. (some skipped).

Codd. Germ. Mon. 5155-7385. (Inside:) *Neue Reihe, d. h. nach Erscheinen des gedruckten Catalogs (1866) erworbene oder nachträglich zur Aufstellung gebrachte deutsche Handschriften N. 5155-7385.* (Another volume). Describes 7386-8035.

Codices iconographici monacenses. Ms. List of over 400 mss.

Autographen. Alphabetical card file in 63 boxes.

—Bayerisches Nationalmuseum.

Lehmann. Add: Not complete.

Bayerisches Nationalmuseum in München. Katalog der Büchersammlung. By Joseph Aloys Mayer. (Munich 1887). ix, 153 pp. p. 119-124: mss. Shelf marks added in libarry copy. Index (p. 152-153) inadequate. (NNMM)

Card file. 2 boxes. Arranged by shelf marks. Many nos. skipped.

Some of the mss. were recently turned over to the Bayerische Staatsbibliothek.

—*Geheimes Hausarchiv.

Old inventory (which listed 325 mss.) and many mss. lost during the last war.

*New inventory lists 135 preserved mss. and 41 recently acquired ones. Communication of the archivist.

—*Stadtarchiv. Has as a deposit the mss. of the Historischer Verein von Oberbayern.

*Card file describing the mss.

*Card file describing the Nachlass Stark (Hs. 2° Nr. 18).

*Münster, West Germany. See *Mittelalterliche Buchmalerei*; *Westfalia Sacra*.

P. 161.

Staender. Read: 801 mss., 761 nos. Shelf marks in parentheses. Concordance (p. 195-197).

The library recently acquired the mss. of the Familienarchiv der Grafen Plettenberg und Fuerstenberg in Schloss Nordkirchen. For 33 mss. formerly in that library see *Archiv* VI.

Schloss Nordkirchen, Familienarchiv der Grafen Plettenberg und Fuerstenberg. Typed list of 211 mss., mostly late. (Muenster; micr. NNC).

*Nancy, France. See Vernier.

Napoli, Italy. See Hinschius; Kristeller; Thorndike. See also Hermann under **Wien.**

P. 163.

Padiglione. Add: Shelf marks added in library copy.

*G. Guerrieri, 'Manoscritti in scrittura beventana nella Biblioteca Nazionale di Napoli,' *Samnium* XXIX (1956) 115-123. 31 mss. No index. (NjP)

—Biblioteca Governativa dei Girolamini (Oratoriana).

The shelf marks given by Mandarini have been changed. Concordance available. Partial typed copy supplied by the librarian.

*Neufchâtel-en-Bray, France. See France, *Catalogue général* LIII.

New Haven, Conn., USA. See Bond.

Read: *Yale University Library Gazette.*

The Harvey Cushing Collection of Books and Manuscripts. New York 1943. xvi, 207 pp. p. 3-5: 60 mss. Arranged alphabetically.

New York, USA. See Bond; De Ricci.

— Columbia University Library.

Columbia Library Columns I (1951)ff. Mentions important accessions.

P. 164.

—Hispanic Society of America.

A. García y García, 'Los manuscritos juridicos medievales de la Hispanic Society of America'' *Revista de Derecho Canónico* XVIII (1963) 501-560. Index. (Hispanic Society of America)

Card file. Arranged by subjects.

—*William S. Glazier.

Manuscripts from the William S. Glazier Collection. By J. Plummer. New York 1959. 34 pp. and plates. 51 mss.

P. 165.

*Notre Dame, Indiana, USA. See Bond.

Novacella-Neustift, Italy. See Kristeller.

Novara, Italy. See Kristeller.

**G. De Ferrari, 'I più antichi codici

della biblioteca capitolare di Santa Maria di Novara,' *Bollettino storico per la provincia di Novara* XLVI (1956) 158-203.

P. 166.

Nürnberg, West Germany. Germanisches National-Museum. Bibliothek.

Handschriften. Alphabetical card file, in 21 bound vols., plus 3 more for Stammbücher.

Sammlung Merkel. Old inventory which lists the mss. along with the printed books.

Deposita. Merkel'sche Bibliothek, Handschriften. Alphabetical card file in 9 boxes.

—Germanisches National-Museum. Archiv.

Autographen. Alphabetical card file of senders and one of addressees.

—Stadtbibliothek.

Autographen. Alphabetical card file in 4 boxes (1950).

—Freiherren von Scheurl. See under **Fischbach**.

*Oeiras, Portugal. Fundação Calouste Gulbenkian. Has illuminated mss. No catalogue. Communication of the director.

*Oelenberg, France. Bibliothèque de l'Abbaye.

Of its 59 mss., it now retains only 4 mss. Communication of the librarian through Ludwig Bieler.

*Old Windsor, England. Beaumont College.

Has some old mss. Communication of Prof. R. Raymo.

P. 167.

Olomouc, Czechoslovakia. Statni Archiv.

M. Boháček, *Literatura středověkých právních škol v rukopisech kapitulní knihovny olomoucké* (Rozpravy Československé akademie věd, Řada společenských věd, Ročník 70, Sešit 7). Prague 1960. 87 pp. p. 74-80: Liste alphabétique des œuvres juridiques dans les manuscrits de la Bibliothèque du Chapître d'Olomouc'.

247 nos. in various mss. 81-87 (summary): 'La littérature des écoles médiévales de droit dans les manuscrits de la bibliothèque du chapître d'Olomouc.'

J. Bistřický, M. Boháček and F. Čáda, 'Seznam Rukopisů Metropolitní Kapituly v Olomouci,' in *Státní Archiv v Opavě, Průvodce po archivních fondech* III, *Pobočka v Olomouci (Průvodce po státních archivech* XIV), Prague 1961, 103-185. p. 105-154: Summary list of 635 mss. Index (p. 156-177).

—Universitni Knihovna..

E. Petrů, *Z rukopisných sbírek Universitní Knihovny v Olomouci.* Prague 1959. 103 pp. and plates. A survey of the mss.

M. Boháček, 'Rukopisná sbirka učeného právníka a bishupa Bohuše ze Zvole v Universitní knihovně olomoucké,' *Sborník historický* VII (1960) 79-122. p. 117-118: alphabetical list of mss.

*Opladen, West Germany. Archiv des Grafen von Fürstenberg-Stammheim.

Has several mss. from the Fürstenberg collection. Communication of Prof. Josef Koch.

*Oporto, Portugal. See Rosa Pereira; Stegmüller.

*Orense, Spain.

E. Duro Peña, 'Los códices de la Catedral de Orense,' *Hispania Sacra* XIV (1961) 185-212. 47 mss.

*Orléans, France. See *Institut de Recherche*.

P. 168.

*Oslo, Norway. Riksarkivet.

*Registratur over membran-fragment med noteskrift, by E. Eggen. Typed card file in 3 boxes. *Ca.* 100 frs. Communication of Ludwig Bieler.

*Osnabrück, West Germany. Niedersächsisches Staatsarchiv.

Has the remaining mss. of the Ratsgymnasium and of the Gymnasium Carolinum. The others were lost during the war, and are marked in the archive copies of Thyen and Kuhlenbeck.

Thyen, 2 parts. No index. (Osnabrück; micr. NNC)

Kuhlenbeck, 3 parts. pt. 2 also lists 16 other mss., and pt. 3, 21 other mss. No index. Typed additions in the copy of the archives. (Osnabrück; micr. NNC)

Ottobeuren, West Germany. Archiv des Benediktinerstiftes.

Catalog der Manuscripte der Bibliothek des Klosters Ottobeuren 1879. 1 ms. vol. Does not include some mss. returned in 1918 from St. Stephan in Augsburg. 655 mss., and 159 late mss. (micr. DLC)

Oxford, England. See Thorndike.

P. 170.

—*Balliol College.

R. A. B. Mynors, *Catalogue of the Manuscripts of Balliol College, Oxford.* Oxford 1963. lvii, 401 pp. 450 mss.

—*Brasenose College.

Accessions, Collections A-L. 1 typed vol. Describes mss. 58-78. (Bodleian Library)

—Pembroke College.

Pembroke College Mss. Typed list of 21 mss.

—*St. John's College.

Summary Catalogue of Manuscripts 213-311, being a Supplement to Coxe's Catalogue of 1852, by H. M. Colvin. Oxford 1956. Mimeographed.

P. 171.

Paderborn, West Germany. See *Westfalia Sacra*.

P. 172.

Padova, Italy.

A. Moschetti, 'Il tesoro della cattedrale di Padova,' *Dedalo* VI (1925-26) 79-109; 277-310. 3 mss. (p. 84-91; 302-304).

—Università, Archivio Antico.

G. Giomo, 'L'Archivio Antico della Università di Padova,' *Nuovo Archivio Veneto* VI (1893), pt. II, pp. 377-460. Lists 774 mss. (NN).

*Paisley, Scotland. See *Trésors des Bibliothèques d'Écosse*.

**W. M. Metcalfe, *The Arbuthnot Manuscripts: A Description.* Paisley, s. a.

*Palencia, Spain.

M. Andrés, 'Manuscritos teológicos de la Biblioteca Capitular de Palencia,' *Anthologica Annua* I (1953) 477-550. 57 mss. Index (p. 547-48). (NN).

P. 173.

*Pamplona, Spain.

*J. Goñi Gaztambide, 'Catálogo de los manuscritos teológicos de la Catedral de Pamplona,' *Revista Española de Teologia* XVII (1957) 231-258; 383-418; 557-594; XVIII (1958) 61-85. 96 mss. Each vol. indexed. (PU)

Paris, France. See France, *Catalogue général* LIV; Institut de Recherche; Nortier; Samaran.

P. 174.

—Bibliothèque Nationale.

Les Catalogues imprimés de la Bibliothèque Nationale. Liste établie en 1943, suivie d'un supplément (1944-1952). Paris 1953. 204, xxviii pp. p. i-xxviii: Supplément (1944-52). p. iii-v: Manuscrits.

H. Omont, *Anciens inventaires et catalogues de la Bibliothèque Nationale.* 5 vols. Paris 1908-21. (NN)

Bibliothèque Nationale. Catalogue général des manuscrits latins. Vol. III. Edited by J. Porcher. IV (1958): Mss. no. 3014-3277. No indices.

P. 176.

S. Solente, 'Nouvelles acquisitions latines et françaises du Département des Manuscrits de la Bibliothèque Nationale pendant les années 1951-1957,' *Bibliothèque de l'École des Chartes* CXVII (1959, published 1960) 135-273: Nos. 2617-2674; 3086-3093 (p. 155-164). Index (p. 141-154).

P. 177.

P. Arnauldet, 'Inventaire de la librairie du Château de Blois en 1518,' *Le Bibliogra-*

phe *Moderne* VI (1902) 145-174; 305-338;
VII (1903) 215-233; VIII (1904) 121-
156; IX (1905) 373-393; X (1906) 339-
366; XI (1907) 192-222; XII (1908) 295-
323; XIV (1910) 280-340; XVIII (1916-
17) 193-232. Describes 1324 mss. No
index.

Fonds Espagnol.

*Catalogue des Manuscrits Espagnols et des
Manuscrits Portugais,* by A. Morel-Fatio.
Paris 1892. xxvii, 423 pp. 685 Spanish
and 106 Portuguese mss. Contain many
Latin texts. Actual shelf marks added
in library copy.

P. 178.

Fonds italien.

*Table alphabétique des Manuscrits du Fonds
Italien de la Bibliothèque Nationale,* by
P. Flament (1901). 1 ms. vol. Covers
ms. 1-2136. Later additions cover mss.
2137-2333.

*Manuscrits à Peintures offerts à la Biblio-
thèque Nationale par le Comte Guy de Bois-
rouvray.* (Paris) 1961. 147 pp. and plates.
30 mss. (Paris, Bibliothèque Nationale)
—*Petit Palais.

La Collection Dutuit, Livres et Manuscrits.
(Paris 1899). Preface signed by E.
Rahir. viii, 328 pp. 12 mss. listed among
the printed books (cf. p. vii).

—*Mme. Raphael Salem. List of annotated editions of the fifteenth and sixteenth
centuries supplied by the owner.

Parma, Italy. See *Catalogo.*

—Archivio di Stato.

*Archivio di Stato in Parma, Guida gene-
rale.* 1 typed vol.

Biblioteca Mss. Alphabetical card file.

*Indice alfabetico dei documenti ed auto-
grafi contenuti nell'Epistolario scelto.*
1 ms. vol. Alphabetical.

Indice degli autografi. 1 ms. vol.

Indice Raccolta Storica. 1 ms. vol.

—Biblioteca Palatina.

*Mostra del Libro Raro, Biblioteca Pala-
tina* (by A. Ciavarella). Parma 1954.
xxi, 89 pp. and plates. p. 1-13: 33 mss.

*Monumenti di varia letturatura tratti dai
manoscritti di Monsignor Lodovico Beccadelli arcivescovo di Ragusa* (By Giam-
battista Morandi). 2 vols. in 3 parts.
Bologna 1797-1804. (British Museum).

G. Tommasino, *I carmi latini inediti di
Mons. Ludovico Beccadelli.* S. Maria
Capua Vetere 1923. 59 pp. p. 47-48:
ms. Pal. 971-1031 (some nos. skipped).
(Florence, Biblioteca Nazionale)

**Inventario dei Manoscritti Geografici della
R. Biblioteca Palatina di Parma.* Preface signed P. Gribaudi. Parma 1907. 24
pp. 47 mss. No index. (micr. NNC)

P. 179.

Lettere autografe. 282 boxes (not including the Carteggio di Lucca). No
inventory. For boxes 236-264, see: C.
Frati, 'Parma, Archivi privati e raccolte bibliografiche parmensi II 4. Raccolta Sanvitale-Simonetta,' *La Bibliofilia* XIX (1917-18) 348-355.

Pavia, Italy

**F. Pietra, 'Codici membranacei gregoriani
dell' Archivio Notarile di Pavia,' *Ticinum*
X (1940), no. 8. 6 unnumbered pages.

Perugia, Italy. See Kaeppeli.

P. 180.

Pesaro, Italy.

Studia Oliveriana IV-V (1956-57) 203-
204: no. 2027-28.

Philadelphia, Pennsylvania, USA. See
Bond.

—Free Library.

*Catalog of the Hampton L. Carson Col-
lection, Illustrative of the Growth of the
Common Law, in the Free Library of
Philadelphia* (by Ellen Shaffer). 2 vols.
Boston 1962. v, 1842 pp. Vol. II, pp.
1285-1293: 111 mss. No index.

—University of Pennsylvania Library.

Lyman W. Riley, *Aristotle Texts and Commentaries to 1700 in the University
of Pennsylvania Library, A Catalogue.*
Philadelphia (1960). 109 pp. p. 85-
89 and 102-103: Mss. (by N. P. Zacour).

N. P. Zacour, 'A Catalogue of Manuscripts in the Libraries of the University of Pennsylvania to 1800,' *The Library Chronicle* XXVII (1961) 16-54; 128-162; XXVIII (1962) 29-71; 115-125; XXIX (1963) 43-75; 124-157. Several collections.

John F. Benton, 'University of Pennsylvania Manuscript Catalogue: Notes for a New Edition,' *Ibid.* XXX (1964) 23-35.

Piacenza, Italy.

G. Manfredi, 'I codici e gli antifonari della Basilica di S. Antonino in Piacenza,' *Bollettino Storico Piacentino* L (1955) 123. Lists codici 1-9 and Antifonari A-U. No index.

E. Nasalli-Rocca, 'La biblioteca-archivio della Cattedrale di Piacenza in una nuova sede,' *Accademie e Biblioteche* XXVIII (N. S. XI, 1960) 247-259. Gives summary list of 69 mss. (p. 258-259).

A. C. Quintavalle, *Miniatura a Piacenza, I codici dell'archivio capitolare.* Venice 1963. 200 pp. and plates. p. 95-199: Catalogo dei codici.

P. 181.

Pienza, Italy. Museo dei Duomo. Has a group of liturgical mss. No list.

Pisa, Italy. See *Catalogo*.

Pistoia, Italy. Biblioteca Forteguerriana. *Biblioteca Forteguerriana, Pistoia*, by Giancarlo Savino (*Aggiunte e correzioni agli Inventari dei manoscritti delle Biblioteche d'Italia I*). Florence 1962. 22 pp. 30 mss.

P. 182.

*Poblet, Spain. See Dominguez Bordona.

*Pont-à-Mousson, France. See France, *Catalogue général* LIII.

Poznań, Poland. *Archiwum Archidiecezjalne (Biblioteka Seminaryjna). Lisiecki's catalogue is not complete. Many mss. have been acquired since 1905. Communication of the librarian.

P. 183.

Praha, Czechoslovakia. See Lehmann.

—Narodni Museum. Delete the mention of Osek and *Xenia Bernardina*.

—Universitni knihovna.

Truhlář, *Catalogus codicum.* Complete for the main collection. Valid shelf marks in parentheses.

P. 184.

Lobkowitz collection from **Roudnice**.

E. Gollob, 'Verzeichnis der griechischen Handschriften in Oesterreich ausserhalb Wiens,' *Sitzungsberichte der Kais. Akademie der Wissenschaften in Wien, Philosophisch-Historische Klasse*, vol. CXLVI (1903), no. 7. 173 pp. p. 136-143: Selective list of Latin mss. in Roudnice. Add: The library also has the mss. from Osek (Ossegg). See *Xenia Bernardina.*

V. Černý, 'Les manuscrits en langues néolatines de la Bibliothèque du Grand Prieuré de l'Ordre des Chevaliers de Malte à Prague,' *Sborník Narodního muzeu* (*Acta Musaei Nationalis Pragae*) C.VIII (1963), no. 3, p. 109-169. Lists 77 mss. in French, Italian and Spanish, mostly late. Index (164-169). (NN)

Prato, Italy. Biblioteca Roncioniana. The library recently lost some mss. through theft.

Princeton, New Jersey, USA. See Bond.

*Providence, Rhode Island, USA. See Bond.

*Quedlinburg, East Germany. The mss. of the Gymnasialbibliothek described by Eckhard were taken to Halle in 1938. The shelf marks have been changed.

*Queenstown, Maryland, USA. See Bond.

P. 185.

*Redlynch House, England. See *The Book Collector*.

Reggio Emilia, Italy. *Archivio Capitolare della Cattedrale. Has a few mss. Communication of the archivist.

—*Biblioteca del Seminario.
Has a few mss. Communication of the same.
Reichersberg, Austria. Bibliothek des Augustiner-Chorherrenstiftes.
Has 10 old mss.

P. 186.
Rochester, Minnesota, USA. See Bond.
Rochester, New York, USA. See Bond.
Roma, Italy. See Hinschius; Italy, *Indici e Cataloghi*.

P. 187.
—*Abbazia delle Tre Fontane.
17 liturgical mss. Communication of Ludwig Bieler.
—Abbazia di S. Girolamo. Handwritten list. 4 mss.
—Archivio di Stato.
A. Lodolini, *L'Archivio di Stato di Roma*. Rome 1960. 230 pp.
—Biblioteca Alessandrina. See Ruysschaert under **Vaticano**.

P. 188.
—Biblioteca Corsiniana.
O. Pinto, *Storia della Biblioteca Corsiniana e della Biblioteca dell'Accademia dei Lincei*. Florence 1956. 69 pp. Bibliography and catalogues (p. 44-45; 61).
A. Petrucci, 'Alcuni codici corsiniani di mano di Tommaso e Antonio Baldinotti,' *Atti della Academia Nazionale dei Lincei, Anno 353, 1956, Ser. VIII, Rendiconti, Classe di Scienze morali, storiche e filologiche XI* (1956) 252-263.
—*Biblioteca Nazionale Centrale Vittorio Emanuele* II.
*G. Brugnoli, 'Catalogus codicum Farfensium,' *Benedictina* VI (1952) 287-303; VII (1953) 85-120; 287-294. 33 mss. Index (p. 287-294). (University of Notre Dame).
Archivio Maffei. Delete: No inventory.
R. *Biblioteca Nazionale Centrale Vittorio Emanuele II, Roma. Indice degli autografi e documenti staccati (dalla Busta I alla Busta 67)*. 1 ms. vol.

Same title (*dalla Busta 68 alla Busta 87*) 1 ms. vol.
Same title (*Busta A 86-162*). 1 ms. vol.
Indice degli autografi e documenti staccati 1-29. More detailed.
Il quattrocento negli autografi e negli incunabuli della Biblioteca Nazionale di Roma. Catalogo della mostra. (Rome) 1950. 128 pp. and plates. No shelf marks. Index.

P. 189.
—English College.
List of Documents in Scritture. 1 typed vol.
Inventario dei libri che si conservano nell'Archivio del Collegio Inglese di Roma. Typed list of printed books and mss.
—*S. Clemente.
L. Boyle, 'Manuscripts and Incunabula in the Library of San Clemente, Roma,' *Archivum Fratrum Praedicatorum* XXIX (1959) 206-227. 15 mss. (p. 210-218).
—*S. Giovanni in Laterano, Archivio.
A few medieval mss. and documents. Communication of the archivist.
—S. Maria sopra Minerva.
No inventory. Some notes placed at my disposal by the Rev. T. Kaeppeli O. P. Mss. seen on the shelves.
—S. Sabina, Archivio dei PP. Domenicani.
Inventarium Archivi Ordinis Praedicatorum, by A. Walz (1930). 2 typed vols. Arranged by subjects in 21 series.
Ross-on-Wye, Herefordshire, England. Clough Renaissance Institute, Gorsley.
List of 7 mss. supplied by Dr. Cecil Clough.
Rottenburg, West Germany. Priesterseminar.
Die Handschriften der Stiftsbibliothek St. Moriz zu Ehingen in der Seminarbibliothek Rottenburg, by H. Hummel (1963). 1 typed vol. 41 mss. Copy supplied by Subregens Dr. Laupheimer.

P. 190.
Rouen, France. See Nortier.
*Catalogue des manuscrits de la Bibliothè-

que Municipale de Rouen, relatifs à la Normandie, by E. Frère. Rouen 1874. xvi, 208 pp. (Bibliothèque Nationale). *Jumièges, Congrès scientifique du XIIIe centénaire.* 2 vols. Rouen 1955. II 681-690: L. Guizard, 'Manuscrits canoniques du Fonds de Jumièges: Recueils de Décrétales.' 721-736: R.-J. Hesbert, 'Les manuscrits enluminés de l'ancien Fonds de Jumièges.' 855-872: The same, 'Les manuscrits liturgiques de Jumièges.' 901-912: The same, 'Les manuscrits musicaux de Jumièges.' (NN)

Saint Andrews, Scotland. See *The Book Collector ; Trésors des Bibliothèques d'Écosse.*

*****Saint Bonaventure**, New York, USA. See Bond.

*****Saint-Dié**, France. See Vernier.

*****Sainte-Menchould**,France. Read: *****Sainte-Menehould.**

P. 191.

*****Saint-Malo**, France. See France, *Catalogue général* LIII.

*****Saint-Maudé**, France. Read: **Saint-Mandé.**

*****Saint-Omer**, France.

(*Catalogue sommaire des manuscrits de la Bibliothèque de la Ville de Saint-Omer.* [By Michelant and Duchet]. s. l. a. (Préface dated 1845). 465, 39, 90 pp.) (Paris, Bibliothèque Nationale).

Salamanca, Spain. See Fink-Errera.

A. M. Olivar, 'Los manuscritos patristicos y liturgicos latinos de la Universidad de Salamanca, '*Analecta Sacra Tarraconensia* XXII (1949) 75-82. 7 mss.

G. Beaujouan, *Manuscrits scientifiques médiévaux de l' Université de Salamanque et de ses 'colegios mayores.'* (Bibliothèque de l'École des Hautes Études Hispaniques XXXII). Bordeaux 1962. viii, 232 pp. Indices.

*****Salisbury**, England.

N. Ker, 'Salisbury Cathedral Manuscripts and Patrick Young's Catalogue,' *The Wiltshire Archaeological and Natural History Magazine* LIII (1949-50) 153-183. Concordances. (NN)

P. 192.

Salzburg, Austria. See Foltz; Ruf.

K. Forstner, 'Schriftfragmente des 8. und frueheren 9. Jahrhunderts in Salzburger Bibliotheken, *Scriptorium* XIV (1960) 235-256. 18 mss.

The same, *Die karolingischen Handschriften und Fragmente in den Salzburger Bibliotheken* (Mitteilungen der Gesellschaft für Salzburger Landeskunde, Ergänzungsband III). Salzburg 1962. 70 pp. and plates. 56 mss. Covers also Michaelbeuern.

San Daniele, Italy. Biblioteca Guarneriana.

The stolen mss. were all recovered.

La Guarneriana I (1958)-IV (1961). Contains articles on individual mss. by E. Patriarca. Shelf marks not always given. (San Daniele).

—*Biblioteca Concina. See Mazzatinti III. Still extant, but inaccessible.

*****Sandomierz**, Poland.

*****W. Wójcik, 'Celniejsze rękopisy Biblioteki Seminarium Duchownego w Sandomierzu,' *Archiwa, Biblioteki i Muzea Kóscielne* IV (1962) 259-330. (MH)

*****San Ginesio**, Italy. Biblioteca Comunale.

E. Gazzera, *San. to Ginesio et lo suo Antiquo Archivio, sec. XII-sec. XVIII.* Tolentino 1915. 131 pp. Surveys the mss. (p. 33-60). No index. (NIC) Typed list of 6 mss. kindly supplied by the librarian.

*****San Juan**, Puerto Rico, USA. See Bond.

*****San Juan Capistrano**, California, USA. See Bond.

Sankt Gallen, Switzerland. Stiftsarchiv. *Gewölbe C Kasten IV.* (Inside:) *Verzeichniss der Bücher-Handschriften des Stifts Pfävers,* 1881 (by Scherrer). 30 mss., and a few additional vols.

—Stiftsbibliothek.

Nachtrag zum Handschriftenverzeichniss der Stiftsbibliothek in St. Gallen, Abschrift nach dem Manuskript. Typed list. Mss. no. 1726-1981.

—Vadianische Bibliothek (Stadtbibliothek).

P. 193.

Verzeichnis der aus Bremen zurückerhaltenen Briefe. Typed list. 402 nos. (some skipped).

San Marino, California, USA. See Bond.

The Huntington Library Quarterly I (1937) ff. Mentions acquisitions.

*Santander, Spain.

M. Artigas and E. Sánchez Reyes, *Catálogos de la Biblioteca de Menéndez Pelayo. I. Manuscritos (Primera Parte).* Santander 1957. xii, 69*, 521 pp. 377 mss. Arranged by subject. Index. (NN)

*Sands Point, New York, USA. See Bond.

Sarnen, Switzerland. Benediktinerkollegium.

Muri-Archiv Gries u. Sarnen, by P. Bruno Wilhelm (1938). 1 ms. vol. 86 parchment and 508 paper mss.

Older inventory by P. Martin Kiem. Has the same content, but indicates specifically which mss. are now in Sarnen. Some mss. are in Gries near Bolzano-Bozen.

*Saróspatak, Hungary. A Tiszáninneni Ref. Egyházkerület Nagykönyvtára.

Card index. Communication of Dr. H. Hajdu Juhasz.

P. 194.

*Schneeberg, East Germany.

Daniel Traugott Müller, *De Bibliotheca Schneebergensi,* no. 16 and 17. progr. Schneeberg 1764. 7 unnumbered pages each. 7 mss. (Dresden; micr. NNC)

The handwritten catalogue by Weicker (1883) was lost during the last war. Most mss. have been preserved, but some of them have gone to Dresden.

**Handschriftenverzeichnis.* 38 mss. Copy kindly supplied by Dr. Emilie Boer.

Schwaz, Austria. Franziskanerkloster.

Card file of mss., arranged by shelf marks.

Ca. 200 mss., of which the first 27 are old.

Sélestat, France. Bibliothèque Municipale.

P. Adam, *L'Humanisme à Sélestat.* Sélestat 1962. 159 pp. p. 95-145: 'Catalogue sommaire des manuscrits de la Bibliothèque de Sélestat.' Arranged by subjects. *Ca.* 450 nos. Index (p. 147-153).

P. 195.

*Senigallia, Italy.

A. Menchetti, *Alcuni codici del Vescovado di Sinigaglia dei secoli XIV e XV.* Iesi 1910. 27 pp. p. 6-7: 14 mss. No index. (Vatican Library)

Sevilla, Spain. See Fink-Errera.

*G. Beaujouan, 'Manuscrits scientifiques médievaux de la Bibliothèque Columbine de Seville,' *Actes du dixième Congrès International d'Histoire des Sciences (Proceedings of the Tenth International Congress of the History of Science),* Ithaca 1962 (published Paris 1964), I 631-634.

*Typed list of mss., by Mlle. Galland. (Paris, Institut de Recherche).

Siena, Italy. Archivio di Stato. See Italy, *Pubblicazioni degli Archivi di Stato.*

P. 196.

*Silos, Spain. Read: Whitehill.

Sion, Switzerland. Archives du Vénérable Chapître de Sion.

Card file: *Manuscrits.* By shelf marks. 130 mss.

P. 197.

*Solesmes, France. See Leclercq.

Solothurn, Switzerland. Zentralbibliothek.

A. Schönherr, *Die mittelalterlichen Handschriften der Zentralbibliothek Solothurn.* Solothurn 1964. xxxv, 365 pp. mss. S 160 to U 4/2 (many nos. skipped). Indices.

*Stargard, Poland.

The mss. are partly lost, partly in Szczecin.

P. 198.

Stockholm, Sweden. Kungl. Biblioteket.

Illuminated Manuscripts and other remarkable documents from the Collection of the Royal Library, Stockholm. Stockholm 1963. 32 pp. and plates. Exhibition catalogue.

R. Erikson, 'Notes on Medical Manuscripts of the Royal Library, Stockholm, especially Ms. Holm. X. 93,' *Libri* XI (1961) 355-363.

Huseby Collection. *Handskrifter.* Typed list of 85 recently acquired mss. Copy kindly supplied by the Librarian.

—Riksarkivet.

Card file for *ca.* 2500 frs. Catalogue in preparation. Communication of Ludwig Bieler.

Schröder. Read: XII-XV (1825-30) and XVII (1832). 72 and 116 pp.

—*Mr. Frank Allan Thomson. Typed list of 4 mss. supplied by the owner.

*Stonyhurst College, England. See *The Book Collector.*

*Strasbourg, France. See France, *Catalogue général* LIII: Leclercq.

—*Archives et Bibliothèque de la ville. The old collection was destroyed in 1870, and no inventories have been preserved. A summary list, without shelf marks, is given by Haenel, *Catalogi librorum manuscriptorum* (Leipzig 1830) col. 445-475. Rathgeber's book refers to this same collection.

For the new collection begun in 1872, see Ristelhuber.

R. Reuss, 'Les manuscrits alsatiques de la Bibliothèque de la ville de Strasbourg,' *Revue d'Alsace* XLVIII (N.S. XI, 1897) 5-31; 185-214. 1029 nos. No index. (OCI; micr. NNC)

Catalogue des manuscrits de la Bibliothèque municipale de Strasbourg. Typed vol. 1148 nos. Communication of the librarian.

Inventaire des Archives du Chapître de St-Thomas de Strasbourg. Preface by J. Adam. Strasbourg 1937. coll. 1-476, pp. 477-501, I-IV, I-XLVI. 2204 nos. Indices.

—*Bibliothèque du Grand Séminaire.

J. Gass, *Die Bibliothek des Priesterseminars in Strassburg.* Strasbourg 1902. 35 pp. (Strasbourg, Bibliothèque de la Ville; micr. NNC)

Typed list of 36 mss. kindly supplied by the librarian.

*Strathfield Saye (near Silchester), England. Duke of Wellington.

List of 5 mss. kindly supplied by the librarian.

P. 199.

*Stresa, Italy. Biblioteca Rosminiana.

G. Soranzo, 'Preziosi codici già del Convento di Santa Giustina di Padova nella Rosminiana di Stresa,' *Atti e Memorie dell'Accademia Patavina di Scienze, Lettere ed Arti* LXXIII (1960-61), pt. 3, 43-54. 28 mss. (p. 50-54). No index. (NN)

Stuttgart, West Germany. Württembergische Landesbibliothek.

J. Autenrieth, *Die Handschriften der ehemaligen königlichen Hofbibliothek Stuttgart.* Vol. III: *Codices iuridici et politici, Patres.* Wiesbaden 1963. xix, 270 pp. Describes mss. HB VI 1-139 and VII 1-71. Indices.

**Die Handschriften der Württembergischen Landesbibliothek, Stuttgart.* 2. Reihe. Vol. 6: *Codices musici,* by C. Gottwald. Wiesbaden 1963, 208 pp.

P. 200.

*Sydney, Australia. See *The Book Collector*; Sinclair.

*K. Sinclair, 'Mediaeval Manuscripts in the Fisher Library,' *University of Sydney Gazette* II (1961) 22-24.

Typed list of 9 mss. supplied by Dr. Keith Sinclair.

*Syracuse, New York, USA. Syracuse University Library.

H. O. Brogan, A. Pace and A. Weinberger, *The Leopold von Ranke Manuscripts of Syracuse University.* Syracuse (ca. 1950). 150 pp. Describes mss. 1-100.

Index. Many more mss. are uncatalogued. Most of them seem to be late Italian mss. Communication of the librarian.

Cecil H. Clough, 'A Forgotten Library: The Leopold von Ranke Collection of Books and Manuscripts,' *Librarium* VII (1964) 73-76. Survey.

*Szombathely, Hungary. Püsköpi Könyvtár (Episcopal Library).
Typed list of 19 mss. (Budapest, Szechenyi Library)

*Taranto, Italy.
C. Drago, 'Su alcuni manoscritti esistenti nella Civica Biblioteca P. Acclavio,' *Taras* VI (1931) 77-84. 11 late mss., hardly relevant. (Vatican Library; micr. NNC)

Tarazona, Spain. Biblioteca de la Catedral. Copy of the typed catalogue available in Paris (Institut de Recherche).

*Tarragona, Spain. See Dominguez Bordona; Ricci.
J. Domínguez Bordona, 'Manuscritos de la Biblioteca Publica de Tarragona, Inventario general,' *Boletin Arqueologico* (Tarragona), Ser. IV, Vol. LIII-LIV (1953-54) 50-75. 294 mss. Index (72-75). (Hispanic Society)

P. 201.
*Teramo, Biblioteca Provinciale.
Has 2 older mss. Communication of the librarian.

*Tîrgu-Mures (Marasvásárhely), Rumania. Biblioteca Documentară Teleki.
Has at least one old ms. Communication of Mlle. Jeanne Vielliard.

Toledo, Spain. See Fink-Errera.
Torino, Italy. See Garrison.

P. 202.
—Biblioteca del Re. Read: Biblioteca ex Reale.
M. Bersano Begey. 'Les manuscrits de la Bibliothèque Royale de Turin,' *Libri* V (1954-55) 29-34. Survey.

P. 203.
—*Seminario Metropolitano.

Most of its mss. were recently sold. Communication of Dom J. Leclercq.
Toronto, Ontario, Canada. See Bond.
*Tortosa, Spain.
E. Bayerri Bertolomeu, *Los Códices Medievales de la Catedral de Tortosa. Novísimo inventario descriptivo.* Barcelona 1962. 698 pp. 353 mss. Indices.

P. 204.
*Toulon, France.
V. Saxer, 'Les manuscrits de l'Évêché de Fréjus,' *Scriptorium* XVII (1963) 1-24. 9 mss., deposited in the Evêché of Toulon.
*Tours, France. See France, *Catalogue général* LIII.

P. 205.
Trento, Museo Nazionale. Bitterer. Read: Bittner. Add: Most of them are now in the Biblioteca Comunale.
A. Cetto, 'I codici viennesi della Biblioteca Vescovile di Trento,' *Studi Trentini di scienze storiche* XXXVII (1958) 483-97. List 48 mss. from Vienna, which were until 1957 in the Museo Nazionale and are now deposited in the Biblioteca Comunale.
Trier, West Germany. See *Analecta Bollandiana*.
—*Historisches Archiv der Stadt. *Verzeichnis der Handschriften . . .*
—*Seminar-Bibliothek. J. Marx, *Handschriftenverzeichnis*.
—Stadtbibliothek. Keuffer, Kentenich and others.
**H. Schiel, 'Erwerb von zwei Mattheiser Handschriften des 11. und 12. Jahrhunderts für die Stadtbibliothek Trier,' *Vierteljahrblätter der Trierer Gesellschaft für nützliche Forschungen* I (1955) 6-9.

P. 206.
Tübingen, West Germany. Universitätsbibliothek.
Stiftung Preussischer Kulturbesitz. Tübinger Depot der Staatsbibliothek. See under **Berlin**.

—Wilhelmsstift.

Handschriften und Inkunabeln. Card file in one tray, arranged by shelf marks. 36 mss.

*Überlingen, West Germany. Leopold-Sophien-Bibliothek.

**D. H. Stolz, 'Handschriften der Überlinger Leopold-Sophien-Bibliothek,' *Bodenseehefte* XI (1960) 213-217.

P. 207.

*Upperville, Virginia, USA. See Bond.

Uppsala, Sweden.

**E. Rooth, *Die mittelalterlichen deutschen Handschriften.* Uppsala 1921. 64 pp. Offprint which adds corrections and indices. Communication of Bernard Rosenthal.

Urbana, Illinois, USA. See Bond.

P. 208.

*Utrecht, Holland.

A. Cordoliani, 'Les manuscrits de comput des bibliothèques d'Utrecht,' *Scriptorium* XV (1961) 76-85.

—*Aartsbisschoppelijk Museum.

W. de Vreese, 'Verluchte handschriften in het Aartsbisschoppelijk Museum te Utrecht,' *Het Gildeboek* V (1923) 201-221 (micr. NNC)

*Handwritten inventory. 109 mss. and frs. Communications of Ludwig Bieler and of the librarian.

P. 209.

Valencia, Spain. *R. Colegio de Corpus Christi ('El Patriarca').

Typed list of 18 mss. supplied by Prof. F. de A. Carreras.

*Valladolid, Spain. Biblioteca Universitaria.

Gutierrez del Caño describes the University collection proper, whereas Rivera Manescau describes the collection of the Colegio de Santa Cruz.

Universidad de Valladolid, Fiesta del Libro, XIV Exposicion. Obras de Filosofos griegos, romanos y comentaristas. (Val-

ladolid) 1958. 58 pp. p. 5-11: **12 mss.**

*Vallbona, Spain.

J. Janini, 'Los Manuscritos del **Monasterio** de Vallbona (Lérida),' *Hispania Sacra* XV (1962) 439-452. 28 mss. Index (451-452).

P. 211.

Vaticano, Città del. Biblioteca Apostolica Vaticana. See Lehmann; Nortier; Thorndike.

J. Ruysschaert, 'Nouvelles recherches au sujet de la bibliothèque de Pierre Leoni, médecin de Laurent le Magnifique,' *Académie Royale de Belgique, Bulletin de la Classe des Lettres et Sciences Morales et Politiques,* Ser. V, vol. XLVI (1960) 37-65. 29 mss., mostly at the Vatican.

W. L. Grant, 'Neo-Latin Materials at Saint Louis,' *Manuscripta* IV (1960) 3-18.

Mélanges Eugène Tisserant (Studi e Testi 231-237), 7 vols., Vatican City 1964. VI (236) 1-87: R. Avesani, 'Per la biblioteca di Agostino Patrizi Piccolomini, vescovo di Pienza.' 45 mss. Index. VII (237) 29-95: A. Marucchi, 'Stemmi di possessori di manoscritti conservati nella Biblioteca Vaticana. 139 mss. Index. 261-326: J. Ruysschaert, 'Costantino Gaetano, O.S.B., Chasseur de Manuscrits.' Describes many mss. in the Fondo Chigi and in the Biblioteca Alessandrina, Rome. Indices. 441-450: J. Vielliard, 'Manuscrits de la Chartreuse de Villeneuve-lès-Avignon conservés à la Bibliothèque Vaticane.'

Fondo Vaticano Latino.

Codices Vaticani Latini, Codices 1135-1266, by M.-H. Laurent. Vatican City 1958. 555 pp. No index.

Codices Vaticani Latini, Codices 2188-2192, by Anneliese Maier. Vatican City 1961. x, 250 pp. Index.

***Codices Vaticani Latini, Codices 11001-11241,* by J. B. Borino. In the press.

Inventarium librorum latinorum Mss. Bib. Vat. 13 vols. in 14. Vols. 1-7 have each its index. No index for vols. 8-13.

P. 212.

Inventario dei codici Vat. Lat. 12848-13331, 13357-13756, 14014-14062 by Ada Alessandrini and others. This inventory has been withdrawn.

*Vaticani latini 12898-13725. Typed inventory.

The musical mss. 14501-14932 have been reclassified as Vat. Mus. 55-473 and 1-10. These numbers have been reoccupied up to Vat. lat. 14666.

Fondo Palatino.

G. M. Cagni, 'I codici Vaticani Palatino-Latini appartenuti alla biblioteca di Giannozzo Manetti,' *La Bibliofilia* LXII (1960) 1-43. 171 mss. No index.

I. Schunke, *Die Einbände der Palatina in der Vatikanischen Bibliothek* (*Studi e Testi* 216-218). 2 vols. in 3. Vatican City 1962. Vol. II, pt. II (*Studi e Testi* 218) pp. 809-913: Manuscripts. Gives the content of some. No index.

Fondo Reginense.

J. Bignami Odier, 'Le Fonds de la Reine à la Bibliothèque Vaticane,' *Collectanea Vaticana in honorem Anselmi M. Card. Albareda a Bibliotheca Apostolica edita* I (*Studi e Testi* 219, Vatican City 1962) 159-189.

Les manuscrits de la Reine de Suède au Vatican, Réédition du Catalogue de Montfaucon et côtes actuelles (*Studi e Testi* 238). Vatican City 1964. 135 pp. Concordances. Preface signed by A. Raes. Compiled by J. Bignami Odier and F. De Marco.

Fondo Ottoboniano.

John F. Daly, 'Mathematics in the Codices Ottoboniani Latini,' *Manuscripta* VIII (1964) 3-17.

P. 213.

Fondo Barberini.

L. J. Daly, 'Some Political Theory Tracts in the Vatican Barberini Collection,' *Manuscripta* V (1961) 28-34; 88-95.

A. M. Carini, 'I postillati "Barberiniani" del Tasso,' *Studi Tassiani* XII (1962) 97-110 and plates. 51 nos.

P. 214.

Fondo Ferraioli.

F. A. Berra, *Codices Ferraioli.* III (1960). viii, 822 pp. Mss. 737-977. Indices.

Autografi Ferraioli. 14 bound vols. No inventory.

Cappella Sistina.

Capellae Sixtinae Codices musicis notis instructi sive manu scripti sive praelo excussi, by J. M. Llorens (*Studi e Testi* 202). Vatican City 1960. xxii, 555 pp. and plates. 660 nos.

Fondo Patetta. No inventory. Catalogue in preparation.

*Lascito De Marinis. No inventory.

Alphabetical catalogue of all Vatican mss. Card file in 252 trays. Not complete.

Venezia, Italy. See *Catalogo*; Mazzatinti; Thorndike.

P. 216.

—Biblioteca Marciana.

Archivio Morelliano.

Catalogo degli Studj e Carteggi del fu Bibliotecario della Marciana Ab. Jacopo Cav. Morelli esistenti presso l'illmo. e r. mo Monsignor Fr. Pietro Dott. Pianton, Abate di S. M. della Misericordia ecc. dei quali i proprietari vogliono fare la vendita. Venice 1847. 16 pp. 109 mss. and 226 groups of letters. New numbers added in pencil. No index. (Marciana, Cons. mss. 20 b)

P. 217.

—Museo Civico Correr.

R. F(ulin), 'Saggio del Catalogo dei codici di Emmanuele A. Cicogna, 'Archivio Veneto* IV (1872) 59-132; 337-398. Describes selected mss. in serial order.

Codici Malvezzi. Typed list of 160 mss. By shelf marks. (micr. DLC)

—Fondazione Giorgio Cini.

Typed list of 8 mss. kindly supplied by Prof. V. Branca.

P. Toesca, *Miniature di una collezione veneziana.* Venice 1958. 95 pp. and plates.

6 mss. and 220 fragments. (Pierpont Morgan Library).

—Conte Alessandro Marcello.

Inventario dell'Archivio della Nob. Famiglia Marcello Patrizia Veneta (by Dalla Santa). 1 ms. vol.

Verona, Italy.

M. Carrara, 'Scritture veronesi del secolo XV,' *Atti dell'Accademia di Agricoltura, Scienze e Lettere di Verona*, Ser. VI, vol. VIII (1956-57, published 1958), 77-103. Not a catalogue. No index. (WU; micr. NNC)

P. 218.

V. Lazzarini. *Reprinted in his *Scritti di paleografia e diplomatica*, Venice 1938, 11-31. Communication of G. Billanovich.

G. Turrini, 'La Biblioteca Capitolare di Verona,' *Italia Medioevale e Umanistica* V (1962) 401-423. p. 419-23: 30 mss.

—*Sezione di Archivio di Stato.

Has a few old manuscripts scattered in its collections. Communication of the archivist.

—*Accademia Filarmonica.

Has mss. which are deposited in the Biblioteca Capitolare.

**G. Turrini, *L'Accademia Filarmonica di Verona dalla Fondazione (Maggio 1543) al 1600 e il suo patrimonio musicale antico*. Verona 1941.

P. 219.

Vigevano, Italy. Istituto Roncalli.

Inventario. 1 ms. vol. Lists 14 mss. Cf. Mazzatinti V.

Vire, France. See France, *Catalogue général* LIII.

***Vitry-le François**, France. See France, *Catalogue général* LIII.

P. 220.

***Walberg**, West Germany. See under Düsseldorf.

Warszawa, Poland. Biblioteka Narodowa.

**H. Kozerska, *Straty w Zbiorze Rękopisow Biblioteki Uniwersyteckeij w Warzawie w czasie I i II Wojny Światowej (Acta Bibliothecae Universitatis Varsoviensis II)* Warsaw 1960. 135 pp. Describes 693 mss. lost in Warsaw during the two world wars.

B. S. Kupść, 'Powrót skarbów kultury narodowej z Kanady,' *Przęglad Biblioteczny* XXVII (1959) 136-139. Lists the mss. recently returned from Canada to Poland.

P. 221.

Washington, District of Columbia, USA. See Bond.

—The Library of Congress.

The Rosenwald Collection. A Catalogue of Illustrated Books and Manuscripts, of Books from Celebrated Presses, and of Bindings and Maps, 1150-1950. The Gift of Lessing J. Rosenwald to the Library of Congress. Preface signed by Frederick R. Goff. Washington 1954. vi, 292 pp. p. 1-4: 13 mss.

The Library of Congress, Quarterly Journal of Current Acquisitions I (1943)ff. Reports on ms. acquisitions. See e.g. 'Rare Books,' by F. R. Goff, XVI (1958-59) 152-162.

***Wellesley**, Massachusetts, USA. See Bond.

***Westmalle**, Belgium. Abdij O. L. Vr. 2 liturgical mss. Communication of Ludwig Bieler.

Wien, Austria. See Foltz; Lehmann; Ruf.

P. 222.

—Dominikanerkonvent.

The mss. sent to Munich during the last war have all been returned.

—*Minoritenkonvent.

The mss. have all been transferred to Graz, Franziskanerbibliothek.

—Österreichische Nationalbibliothek.

A. Primisser, *Die Kaiserlich-Königliche Ambraser-Sammlung*. Wien 1819. x, 402 pp. p. 256-300: Mss.

T. Gar, 'I codici storici della collezione Foscarini conservate nella Imperiale Biblioteca di Vienna,' *Archivio storico italiano* V (1843) 281-505. Index.

E. von Sackur. Read: E. von Sacken.

T. Frimmel, 'Urkunden, Regesten und artistisches Quellenmaterial aus der Bibliothek der Kunsthistorischen Sammlungen des Allerhöchsten Kaiserhauses,' *Jahrbuch der Kunsthistorischen Sammlungen des Allerhöchsten Kaiserhauses* V (1887), pt. 2, p. i-xxiv.

H. J. Hermann, 'Miniaturhandschriften aus der Bibliothek des Herzogs Andrea Matteo III. Acquaviva,' *ibid.* XIX (1898) 147-216. Discusses also mss. in Naples.

H. Modern, 'Die Zimmern'schen Handschriften der k.k. Hofbibliothek,' *ibid.* XX (1899) 113-180.

F. Unterkircher, *Inventar der illuminierten Handschriften.* Read: Frühdrucke.

The same, part II. Vienna 1959. 269 pp. Mostly oriental and Greek mss.

P. 223.

Maximilian I. Vienna 1959. x, 251 pp. and plates. p. 4-65: 215 mss. Exhibition catalogue.

Katalog der Abendländischen Handschriften der Österreichischen Nationalbibliothek. "Series Nova" (Neuerwerbungen). *Teil 2/1. Cod. Ser. N. 1601-3200. Katalogtext.* By O. Mazal and F. Unterkircher. Vienna 1963. xv, 510 pp. *Teil 2/2. Cod. Ser. N. 1601-3200. Register.* By O. Mazal. 293 pp.

Autographensammlung.

*Repertorium über die Autographensammlung der Hofbibliothek. 1 ms. vol. Arranged by countries and professions, and chronological for each section. Covers the holdings up to 1852.

**Alphabetical catalogue for the entire collection. Communication of Dr. O. Mazal.

—Österreichisches Staatsarchiv.

Böhm. The archive copy adds the new shelf marks.

Supplementissimum zu Böhm. 1 typed vol. Mss. no. 432-1340 (some nos. skipped).

Bitterer. Read: Bittner.

*Wiesbaden, West Germany.

*F. W. E. Roth, 'Die Handschriften der ehemaligen Benediktiner- und Cisterzienserklöster in der K. Landesbibliothek zu Wiesbaden,' *Studien und Mittheilungen aus dem Benedictiner- und dem Cisterzienser Orden* VII (1886) 172-180. 67 mss. No index. (Ct Y)

*Wigan, England. Free Public Library. *Wigan, Free Public Library, Catalogue of Books*, by Henry T. Folkard. 13 parts. Wigan 1886-1918. 5256 pp. (continuously paged). Alphabetical catalogue of the library. A few mss. are listed among the printed books. (NN: parts 1-7, 9-11, 13)

*Wilanów, Poland.

*W. Semkowica, *Przewodnik po zbiorze rękopisów Wilanowskich.* Warsaw 1961. viii, 367 pp.

*Williamstown, Massachusetts, USA. See Bond.

P. 224.

Wilten, Austria. See under Innsbruck.

*Windsheim, West Germany. Stadtbibliothek.

*Handschriften-Verzeichnis, by C. W. Schirmer, 1832-1848. 1 ms. notebook. 152 mss. (Würzburg, Historischer Verein für Unterfranken und Aschaffenburg, ms. q. 266).

E. Stahleder, *Die Handschriften der Augustiner-Eremiten und Weltgeistlichen in der ehemaligen Reichsstadt Windesheim.* Typed thesis, Würzburg 1960. 418 pp. 117 mss. (Würzburg, Universitätsbibliothek) Published Würzburg 1963. xvi, 284 pp.

*Winterthur, Switzerland.

*Katalog der Bürger-Bibliothek in Winterthur (by U. Hegner). (Winterthur) 1836. 252 pp. p. 247-252: 135 mss. No shelf marks. (Winterthur; partial micr. NNC)

*Katalog der Bürger-Bibliothek in Winterthur. (Winterthur 1855). 184 pp. p. 124-127: Alphabetical list of mss. No shelf marks. (Winterthur; partial micr. NNC)

*Catalogus der Handschriften der Stadtbibliothek Winterthur, by A. Hafner (1877-79). 1 ms. vol.

*Katalog der Manuscripte. Card file.

A. Hafner, Die Handschriften der alten Chronisten von Winterthur, Mit besonderer Berücksichtigung der Manuscriptensammlung hiesiger Bürgerbibliothek. Neujahrs-Blatt von der Stadtbibliothek in Winterthur auf das Jahr 1880 (and 1881). 217tes (and 218tes) Stück. Winterthur 1879 (and 1880). 22 (and 33) pp. 30 mss.

300 Jahre Stadtbibliothek Winterthur 1660-1960, by E. Dejung, P. Sulzer and P. Brunner. 291. Neujahrsblatt der Stadtbibliothek Winterthur. Winterthur 1960. 139 pp. p. 87-96: P. Sulzer, 'Handschriften.' Survey. p. 129-130: list of printed and unpublished catalogues.

P. 225.
Wolfenbüttel, Herzog-August-Bibliothek.
**Die Handschriften der Bibliothek zu Wolfenbüttel. Neue Reihe, Bd. X. Die Weissenburger Handschriften. Neu bearbeitet von H. Butzmann. Frankfurt (1964?). xvi, 361 pp. Perhaps not yet published.

P. 227.
Wrocław, Poland. Biblioteka Uniwersytecka.
The list of new acquisitions begins in 1945 (not in 1948).
A. Schmidtová, 'Z bohemik vratislavské universitni knihovny,' Listy filologické VIII (LXXXIII, 1960) 98-105. Survey, (NN)
*W. Schenk, 'Rękopisy liturgiczne od XIII do XV wieku w Bibliotece Uniwersyteckiej w Wrocławiu,' Archiwa, Biblioteki i Muzea Kóscielne II (1961) 185-206. 50 mss. (MH)
Selectio epistolarum virorum illustrium in humanitatis disciplinis XVI saec. ex Bibliothecae Universitatis Wratislaviensis manuscriptis, by M. Walter. Typed list. Copy kindly supplied by the librarian. 1159 nos.

P. 229.
Würzburg, West Germany. Universitätsbibliothek.
Handschr. Katalog. Read: IV: M. p. h(ist.). f. 1-5.
The older inventory, in 7 boxes, is clearer and more complete than the typed copy.
*Yonkers, New York, USA. See Bond.

P. 230.
Zaragoza, Spain. See Cordoliani; Ricci.
—Biblioteca Capitular (de la Seo).
A number of mss. were recently sold. They are reportedly listed in the following rare publication: Manuscritos, Incunables, Raros (1501-1753). (Zaragoza 1961). 77 pp. p. 5-17: 107 mss., arranged by subjects. No shelf marks. (Seen in a private library)
Ždár nad Sázavon, Czechoslovakia.
M. Boháček, Rukopisy Mladovožické Zámecké Knihovny. Les manuscrits de la Bibliothèque du Château de Mladá Vožice (Sborník Národního Muzea v Praze. Acta Musei Nationalis, Ser. C, vol. VI, nos. 1-2). (Prague) 1961. 74 pp. 77 mss. Index.
Zeitz, East Germany.
Bech and Wegener. Add: Valid shelf marks in parentheses.
*Zips, Czechoslovakia. See Günterova.
*Zittau, East Germany. Stadtbibliothek, now called Christian-Weise-Bibliothek.
*Handwritten catalogue, by C. A. Tobias (1862). Arranged by shelf marks. Communication of Dr. Emilie Boer.

P. 231.
Zürich, Staatsarchiv des Kantons Zürich.
Verzeichnis des Antistitialarchivs, neu bearbeitet 1961 von U. Helfenstein. 1 typed vol. 502 nos. Subject index. Covers the important section E II.
Antistitialarchiv (Abt. E II). Zettelregister. Alphabetical card file for senders (27 boxes) and addressees (20 boxes).
—Zentralbibliothek.

Index chronologicus alphabeticus Collectionis Simlerianae Mscr. in Bibliotheca Civica Tigurina asservatae . . . 4 ms. vols. Covers the important Simler collection which is not analyzed in the printed catalogue. Arranged chronologically. I: 1501-31. II: 1532-1550. III: 1551-75. IV: 1576-1620. Gives no shelf marks, but cross references to another inventory in which the shelf marks may be ascertained.

*Zweibrücken, West Germany.

*Katalog der Bibliothek. Add: Preface signed by F. Butters. (Zweibrücken; partial photostat NNC)

The following pages are provided for additional notes as may be desired.